IN 1979, A SELECT COMMITTEE OF CONGRESS NAMED THE MAFIA AS A PRIME SUSPECT IN A PROBABLE CONSPIRACY TO KILL PRESIDENT JOHN F. KENNEDY . . .

NEW EVIDENCE PROVES IT!

—In the mid 70's, West Coast mobster Jimmy Roselli began telling associates, journalists, and Senate investigators that Dallas nightclub owner Jack Ruby was "one of our boys" who had been delegated to silence accused presidential assassin Lee Harvey Oswald. Several months later, Roselli's lifeless body was found floating in Miami's Biscayne Bay.

—The one man who could link Oswald to Ruby before the assassination was found dead in 1964, his throat cut amid the shattered glass of a Pensacola department store window. Police called his death a "suicide."

—All references to Jack Ruby's connections with the underworld were mysteriously deleted from the Warren Commission's final report.

—After the death of his natural father, Lee Harvey Oswald lived with an uncle who soon took on the role of surrogate parent for the remainder of Oswald's life. That man was Charles "Dutz" Murret, an New Orleans bookmaker and underworld figure with ties to Mafia kingpin Carlos Marcello.

NOW, AT LAST, THE TRUTH CAN BE TOLD ABOUT THE MOST SHOCKING CONSPIRACY IN HISTORY!

CONTRACT ON AMERICA
THE MAFIA MURDER OF
PRESIDENT JOHN F. KENNEDY

David E. Scheim

CONTRACT ON AMERICA

THE MAFIA MURDER OF PRESIDENT JOHN F. KENNEDY

BY
DAVID E. SCHEIM

ZEBRA BOOKS
KENSINGTON PUBLISHING CORP.

ZEBRA BOOKS

are published by

Kensington Publishing Corp.
475 Park Avenue South
New York, NY 10016

First Zebra Books printing: April, 1989

Printed in the United States of America

The author is indebted to the following sources for the photographs reproduced in the insert:

Library of Congress: photos of Jimmy Hoffa and J. Edgar
Hoover.

Bob Jackson: photo of Jack Ruby shooting Lee Harvey Oswald,
copyright 1963.

National Archives: photos of Jack Ruby with strippers and Lee
Harvey Oswald in custody.

Theodore Charach collection in Assassination Archives and Research Center: photos of Thane Eugene Cesar and the bill of sale
for his gun.

AP/Wide World: photos of Ronald Reagan and Paul Laxalt;
Raymond Donovan and Jackie Presser

All other photographs from the Assassination Archives and Research Center, Washington, D.C.

To John and Robert Kennedy, that we might better appreciate their heroism and carry on their legacy

Contents

Introduction 9
Acknowledgments 15
Prologue 17

1. Precedents 23

Part I: Assassins at Large

2. Crossfire in Dealey Plaza 39
3. A Telltale Trail of Murder 50
4. Intrigue in New Orleans 60
5. The Why and the Wherewithal 75

Part II: Mob Fixer in Dallas

6. Molding of a Mobster 99
7. The Move to Dallas 109
8. Jack Ruby's Criminal Activities 115
9. Jack Ruby's Underworld Contacts 121
10. Jack Ruby and the Dallas Police 139
11. Jack Ruby, Mobster 148

Part III: Murder on Cue

12. Perjury and Premeditation 158
13. Conspiracy 171
14. Jack Ruby's Startling Testimony 185

Part IV: Pilgrims and Pirates

15. The Anti-Castro Coalition   207
16. Jack Ruby's Cuban Connection   219
17. The Warren Commission Cover-Up   230

Part V: A Mafia Contract

18. Nationwide Mob Contacts   257
19. The AGVA Alibi: Mob Perjury   270
20. The Mafia Killed President Kennedy   284

Part VI: Echoes of November 22

21. More Assassinations   309
22. Richard Nixon and the Mob   333
23. The Reagan Administration   345

Epilogue   371

Recommendations   379

Appendix 1. Additional Information on Jack Ruby 381
Appendix 2. Sources on the Mafia   385
Notes   487
Principal Sources   601
Index   611

Introduction
by John H. Davis

Hundreds of books have been written on the assassination of President John F. Kennedy and the various investigations of the crime. Spanning a broad spectrum of competence and integrity, some have been wildly speculative, others painstakingly scientific; some barefacedly amateurish, others eminently professional. So diverse, in fact, have been the approaches, motives, abilities and conclusions of those who have had the courage, or the foolishness, to write about what has been aptly called The Crime of The Century, that the terrain has become as pathless and bewildering as the Louisiana Bayou country that spawned the suspected mastermind of the crime. It was no wonder that Arthur M. Schlesinger, Jr. termed the Kennedy assassination "a quagmire for historians."

It has also been a quagmire for investigators. The FBI's initial probe of the crime, which became the basis for the Warren Commission's subsequent investigation, was, on the whole, professional and thorough in the field. It eventually foundered, however, in Director J. Edgar Hoover's psyche, where considerations of political expediency, personal ambition and bureaucratic self-preservation overcame what was left of an already sclerotic sense of justice. Although Hoover's agents soon presented him with ample circumstantial evidence suggesting conspiracy, the director chose the politically expedient course of blaming the assassination on a "lone gunman" who could not defend himself or implicate others because he, too, had been murdered shortly after the assassination.

Subsequently, the Warren Commission, almost wholly dependent upon FBI information and thus vulnerable to Hoover's ma-

9

nipulation, also foundered in a quagmire—this time a collective one of cowardice, ignorance, self-deception and naive acceptance of the gospel according to Hoover.

It wasn't long before several books challenged the Warren Commission's conclusions so effectively that it became apparent those conclusions never could have withstood the adversarial proceedings of a court of law. Unfortunately, those revisionary books were overshadowed by less professional, more sensationalistic works that claimed wider public attention and so kept the Kennedy assassination waters as muddied as ever.

Around the time these books began appearing, roughly four years after the Warren Commission report, the district attorney of New Orleans launched a new investigation of the Kennedy assassination. It was to meet the same fate as its predecessor. The New Orleans probe initially succeeded in casting new light on certain mysterious circumstances surrounding the crime. It illuminated, for the first time, such previously neglected areas as the botched and manipulated autopsy of the president and the FBI's suppressed investigation of a suspect associated with the Mafia boss of Louisiana. Arrested three days after the assassination, the suspect was subjected to a scandalously superficial interrogation, then quickly released. But, as time wore on and the New Orleans district attorney began making one irresponsible accusation after another, his probe also became hopelessly mired, this time in a morass of vanity, personal ambition and external pressure. Representative of these pernicious influences was a Mob attempt to coerce the district attorney into implicating in the assassination the government's chief prosecution witness against the Teamsters' ex-boss, Jimmy Hoffa. The inevitable collapse of the D.A.'s case compromised the entire field of Kennedy assassination research and relegated several credible investigatory efforts to oblivion.

It took almost eight years for reexamination of the Kennedy case to recover from the New Orleans debacle. The turning point in the official attitude toward the assassination came with the findings of the Senate Intelligence Committee of 1975 and 1976, otherwise known as the Church Committee. The Committee established conclusively that both the FBI and the CIA had repeatedly lied to the Warren Commission and withheld vital information from it. As a result of these findings and various private investigative efforts, Congress voted overwhelmingly in 1976 to hold another official investigation of the crime. This one was to be conducted by a select committee of the House of Representatives.

To its enduring credit, the House Select Committee on Assassinations succeeded in uncovering much new circumstantial evidence suggesting Mafia complicity in the JFK killing, a possibility that the previous investigations had largely overlooked, or deliberately avoided. The Committee failed, however, to follow through on the many promising leads it developed suggesting the complicity of organized crime in both the assassination of the president and the murder of his accused assassin—primarily, it has been claimed, because it ran out of time, money and Congressional support. It also failed to persuade the Justice Department to pursue all the new leads the Committee had developed and to persuade the press to bring the issue of those new leads to the public's attention.

Meanwhile, the House, Senate and Warren Commission investigations had developed a great deal of significant information and evidence on the assassination that lay deposited in various archives, collections and published reports, waiting for a mind capable of sifting through the massive documentation and making some sense of it all.

It is the special merit of David Scheim that he chose to construct *Contract on America* almost wholly out of evidence that already had been gathered by the official investigators of the crime, who, for various reasons, had either ignored, suppressed or failed to evaluate properly the evidence before them. In confining his research to documented records, Mr. Scheim rides above the pitfalls of hearsay, rumor and speculation. His evidence had already been accumulated by the official investigators who preceded him, but they did not possess Mr. Scheim's analytical skills, intelligence and moral courage to make the case the evidence demanded.

In *Contract on America* David Scheim lifts the Kennedy assassination case out of its quagmire of twenty-five years and exposes it to the clear, dry light of an exceptionally keen intellect and a refreshingly unbiased spirit.

11

On the basis of the enormous amount of evidence now available to us, Mr. Scheim concludes that the Mafia played a preponderant role in both the assassination of President Kennedy and the murder of his accused assassin. These conclusions were not drawn from speculative hunches, but rather from the patient, intelligent analysis of the available evidence in the case. David Scheim has pieced together bits of evidence that have been sitting all along in the Warren Commission's twenty-six volumes of hearings and exhibits, its documents in the National Archives, and the House Assassinations Committee's twelve volumes of hearings and appendices. In several instances, particularly in his treatment of Jack Ruby's role in the assassination and in the murder of the president's alleged assassin, Mr. Scheim has unearthed previously ignored documents and made connections that had not occurred to investigators before him.

Not only has Mr. Scheim convincingly identified the Mafia as the core of the assassination conspiracy, but his research has also reinforced the suspicion of the House Committee on Assassinations that the one Mafia family in the United States most likely to have participated in a unilateral plan to assassinate the president was the Marcello criminal organization of Louisiana and Texas. Mr. Scheim's evaluation of the available evidence in the case is an impressive achievement. It was accomplished not by a mercenary sensationalist, an "assassination buff" or a career criminologist, but rather by a computer systems analyst with a Ph.D. in mathematics from MIT. Mr. Scheim's sole motivation for devoting more than ten years of his life and much of his personal financial resources to research on the Kennedy assassination has been a passion for historical truth. In the vast and uneven field of writings on the case, *Contract on America* stands out as a monument of good sense, effective logic and judicial passion.

But Mr. Scheim's search for truth and justice was not limited to his investigation of the John F. Kennedy assassination. He has also applied his analytical powers and moral courage to the murder case of Robert F. Kennedy, as well as those of Malcolm X and Martin Luther King, Jr. As in the John F. Kennedy case, Mr. Scheim has detected the fingerprints of the underworld on these crimes. While nowhere near as exhaustive as his ten-year inquiry into the JFK assassination, the author's thoughtful appraisal of the available evidence in these three cases likewise raises the possibility of Mafia involvement.

Robert F. Kennedy, in his 1960 book, *The Enemy Within*, identified organized crime as an "invisible government" and wrote that "if we do not attack organized criminals with methods and techniques as effective as their own, they will destroy us." History has borne out Kennedy's prophetic convictions. If it is true that the assassination of President John Kennedy was planned and executed by organized criminals, then the United States government, either through cowardice, incompetence or connivance, has let them get away with murder. We should then legitimately ask ourselves whether, during the last twenty-five years, the nation has been ultimately governed by our visible elected representatives in Washington or by an invisible network of schemers and murderers powerful enough to change the course of American political history at will.

What David Scheim has done in *Contract on America* has been to make an appalling scenario so believable that we may finally take Robert Kennedy's admonition seriously. We may yet find the courage to "attack organized criminals with methods and techniques as effective as their own" — before they destroy us.

JOHN H. DAVIS
New York

John H. Davis is the author of several books, including *THE GUGGENHEIMS*, *THE BOUVIERS*, and *THE KENNEDYS: Dynasty and Disaster*, a national best-seller. A *cum laude* graduate of Princeton, he studied in Italy on a Fulbright Scholarship and served as a naval officer with the sixth fleet.

Acknowledgments

This book could not have been written without the help of seven student interns—Susan Brown, Myrna Goldman, Kristin Goss, Richard Kreindler, Kenneth Ryan, Frank Schwartz, and Ilana White—who checked every reference and contributed research, writing and editing assistance, primarily during the summers of 1979, 1981 and 1987. For assistance in arranging five of these internships, I am indebted to the staff of the Phillips Brooks House and the Office of Career Services at Harvard University. I am especially grateful to Clark Mollenhoff and Dan Moldea, whose distinguished reporting on organized crime is cited frequently in this book, for background briefings to this talented crew and for invaluable further assistance and advice.

Back in 1973, Peter Dale Scott pointed me toward documents in the National Archives indicating Jack Ruby's connection to organized crime. Paul Hoch's conscientious stewardship of information on the JFK case has provided an important resource for this book, as it has for many other works on this subject. Greg Stone furnished many pages of materials on the RFK assassination and cogent, meticulous criticism of the section of this book on that case. Bernard Fensterwald, Jr., founder of the Assassination Archives and Research Center, and Marion Johnson, staff archivist for the Warren Commission materials at the National Archives, both helped greatly in locating documents and photographs. G. Robert Blakey offered kind consultation on the JFK assassination case and organized crime. John Davis gave me invaluable encouragement, criticism and suggestions in the final stage of the book's development.

Alvin Rottman and Laurette Tuckerman helped me with typing in an early, difficult stage. Another friend and mentor, Jeff Hatschek, offered several cogent suggestions. David Epstein, Terry

Gillen, Gus Goldberger, Bob Lande, Mark Levine and Dov Weitman read drafts of the book and offered much helpful criticism. Earl Goldberger, Art Levine, Sarna Marcus and Larisa Wanserski contributed important help in different facets of getting out a preliminary, privately published version of my work. I gleaned many ideas for more effective presentation from hours of stimulating conversations with Jerry Drake and William Scott Malone in preparation for a television documentary on the JFK assassination. Finally, weekly newspaper clippings, unfailing support and dogged idealism came from my mother, Sonia Scheim.

In our sleep, pain which cannot forget
falls drop by drop upon the heart until,
in our own despair, against our will,
comes wisdom through the awful grace of God.

Aeschylus, quoted by Robert Kennedy
on the death of Martin Luther King

The committee believes, on the basis of the evidence available to it, that President John F. Kennedy was probably assassinated as a result of a conspiracy.[1]

The House Select Committee on Assassinations, in its 1979 report

Prologue

A clearly presented, flawlessly documented exposé of who performed the murder is all that can justify yet another book on the much-confounded Kennedy assassination riddle. But the reader probably requires even more: that the bitter facts offer some glimmer of wisdom to sweeten the unforgotten pain, some historical insight to help us finally overcome this tragedy. Only for this do we dare reopen the memory of John F. Kennedy's presidency, when it seemed that America could right any wrong, realize any vision. Only for this can we bear to hear again the shattering sound that still rings in our nightmares—echoing in subsequent assassinations, ghetto riots, the Vietnam War, Watergate crimes: the fatal gunshot of November 22, 1963 in Dallas. The horror was not so much that President Kennedy was killed, but that he was cut down by the meaningless act of a deranged individual, or so it appeared. The lesson was clear: moral purpose was for heaven, hell and Sunday school; history was gray and godless.

To some observers across the Atlantic, however, it was the official explanations, not the moral repercussions of Kennedy's slaying that were hollow. Reporting for *Paris-Match* in December 1963, Raymond Cartier observed that Europe "almost in its totality" refused to dismiss the assassination, together with the subsequent slaying of accused killer Lee Harvey Oswald by Jack Ruby, as "the chance encounter of an anarchist and an exhibitionist."[2] More likely, certain European journalists deduced, was that "Kennedy was murdered by the Mafia."[3] Particularly forthright was Serge Groussard, the distinguished French journalist and author, who wrote in *l'Aurore*:

17

> The Chicago gangsters of 1963. . . . are the men whom
> President Kennedy was relentlessly tracking down. . . .
> Feeling themselves to be driven back, little by little, from
> the labor unions they controlled and other screens for their
> activities, and drunk with rage, they must have decided for
> many months to strike at the very top—to kill the head of
> the Kennedy family.[4]

Groussard also reported that Oswald's killer, Jack Ruby, was a
"front man" for the Mob, sent to Dallas in 1946 to run a night
club "for the underworld, or for the Mafia, as you prefer."[5]

The above-quoted observations from Europe were featured in
the worldwide best seller *Who Killed Kennedy?* by Thomas Buchanan. The British edition, that is. The American edition, published by Putnam later in 1964, was conspicuously different in
one respect: virtually all of the many original references to organized crime were deleted or watered down. Among the items
excised were Groussard's striking accusations of Mafia culpability.[6] Also cut from the Putnam edition was Buchanan's own conclusion that "gangsters were involved in this case."[7] Further
comments along these lines were retained with key words sani-
tized: "the Mafia" became "gangsters";[8] "a gangster murdered
Oswald" became "a man named Ruby murdered Oswald."[9] From
"Ruby was one of the most notorious of Dallas gangsters," this
banality emerged: "Ruby was one of the best-known figures in
that border world which lives under continual police surveillance."[10]

The censorship of *Who Killed Kennedy?* was, unfortunately,
not an isolated occurrence. A larger pattern of cover-up in the
Kennedy murder case was discernible to Raymond Cartier as
early as December 1963. Buchanan again quotes Cartier's article:

> The professional gangster killing the President's assassin
> out of patriotic indignation, Europe does not believe it for
> a moment. . . . It justifies suspicion of a deliberate and
> desperate concealment, carried out by all the organs of
> authority in the American nation, from the White House
> to Murder, Incorporated.[11]

Adding ironic emphasis to Cartier's assertion, the concluding seven words—"from the White House to Murder, Incorporated"—were deleted in the American edition of Buchanan's book.[12]

In the spring of 1973, sharing Groussard's and Cartier's suspicions, I joined other researchers at the National Archives to pore over the government's massive files on the Kennedy assassination case. One point became immediately clear: despite official denials, Jack Ruby had indeed been a "professional gangster." Furthermore, telephone records and other documents showed extensive contacts between Ruby and underworld figures from across the country in the months before the assassination.

It also emerged, disturbingly, that evidence establishing these criminal ties had been repeatedly suppressed or distorted by the Warren Commission, the government body initially charged to investigate Kennedy's murder. For example, the Commission reported that "virtually all of Ruby's Chicago friends stated he had no close connection with organized crime."[13] But a trace of the Commission's cited references revealed that one of these "friends" was a notorious Mob hit man credited with planning some of its more important executions. More than half of these cited friends, in fact, had some racketeering associations.[14]

Even more blatant methods were used to conceal Ruby's close Mafia ties in Dallas. Consider, for example, the fate of an FBI report that described Ruby's frequent contacts with Joseph Civello, the Mafia boss of Dallas in the 1950s and early 1960s. The Commission published the first page of this report—with the paragraphs describing the contacts between Ruby and Civello blanked out of an otherwise perfect photoreproduction (see photo section).

With his underworld background exposed, Ruby's story of killing Oswald in a fit of patriotic vengeance became hard to swallow. Indeed, buried in National Archives files I found a record of criminal associations, incriminating activities and contradictory alibis demonstrating that the November 24 shooting was a cold-blooded, carefully coordinated conspiracy. In startling testimony before the Warren Commission, Ruby himself hinted at complicity in this slaying by the underworld, corrupt policemen and a night club stripper who was the key prop in his alibi. An excerpt:

19

"Who else could have timed it so perfectly by seconds. If it were timed that way, then someone in the police department is guilty of giving the information as to when Lee Harvey Oswald was coming down."[15]

The sinister circumstances of Oswald's slaying compelled a closer look at Jack Ruby's activities in the months before the Kennedy murder. Especially illuminating were his telephone records from this period, which revealed dramatically intensifying contacts with underworld figures nationwide. Other activities of his, including a November 21 visit to Houston in the vicinity of the presidential party, compounded suspicion that Ruby and organized crime may have been involved in the assassination, as well. Given the Mafia's clear motive to murder the president, it was not a rash assumption.

The case strengthened in 1979, with the publication of the report, hearings and exhibits of the House Select Committee on Assassinations. After reexamining the JFK killing for two years—twice as long as the Warren Commission's term—the House Assassinations Committee concluded that two gunmen fired at President Kennedy, that critical evidence had been suppressed, and that the Mob had the "motive, means and opportunity" to kill him.[16] Although the Committee reached no clear dertermination of culpability, it released wiretap transcripts and testimony showing Mobsters discussing and planning President Kennedy's death. Among these plotters was New Orleans Mafia boss Carlos Marcello, who, according to a reliable federal witness, discussed having Kennedy killed by an outsider who would not be traced to the Mob. The committee also uncovered a portentous lead: that Oswald's uncle, "surrogate father" and close 1963 contact was a bookmaker associated with Marcello's criminal organization.

The pieces of the JFK assassination puzzle began to fit. The House spotlighted key Mob suspects; government documents and transcripts buried in Warren Commission files detailed the progression of the plot. Integrating all of this evidence, with the help of other investigators' findings and additional government sources, I finally assembled a compelling case for Mob culpability. The Oswald killing, the alibis for Ruby's timely Mob contacts, and Ruby's pre-assassination activities were three areas in which I broke significant new ground through synthesis of previously overlooked evidence.

Yet the satisfaction of seeing the Dealey Plaza murder solved is overshadowed by the dark realization of its ramifications. The record demonstrates that the Mafia accomplished its objective: the Kennedy anti-crime crusade died with the president. Shielded by cover-up, the Mob extended its contract on America, terrorizing and plundering with impunity. Furthermore, as will be shown, other major Kennedy initiatives were reversed following November 22, with similarly debilitating consequences for the nation. The assassinations of two other visionary leaders, Robert Kennedy and Martin Luther King, in which organized crime may have had a role,[17] pushed America further along this murderously misdirected course.

With this anguishing insight, however, comes the redemptive opportunity to realize the Kennedy legacy. That President John Kennedy and very possibly his brother Robert were martyred in a valiant struggle against organized crime underscores their heroism — a heroism that cover-up denied us. It is left for us to carry on their crusade against the "enemy within" and return to other enlightened Kennedy policies that were aborted by assassination. The past beckons us to revive the ideals that the brothers lived and died for.

Organized crime, gentlemen, has its own scale of justice. If . . . they have more to gain by someone's death than they have to lose, then he's a dead man, whether he's a cop, the President of the United States, or whoever.[1]

Ralph Salerno, New York City Police organized crime expert

1
Precedents

In 1963, the Kennedy Administration was becoming increasingly successful in its crusade to eradicate organized crime. Incensed and obstructed, some Mob figures spouted venomous oaths against brothers John and Robert Kennedy. Others discussed specific plots to kill them.[2]

Before tracing the outcome of these assassination plots, however, it is important to put them in perspective. Other prominent Americans have led crusades against the Mob—Chicago Mayor Anton Cermak was one, labor leader Walter Reuther another. Their fates provide interesting precedents to the Kennedy murders.

THE ASSASSINATION OF CHICAGO
MAYOR ANTON CERMAK

After being elected mayor of Chicago in 1931, Anton J. Cermak "made it his mission to drive the mob from Chicago," reported Judge John Lyle, a political contemporary.[3] Cermak organized special police squads to go after Al Capone's gang[4] and according to racketeer Roger Touhy, offered the services of "the entire police department."[5] Although Cermak's motives can be questioned (he was apparently aligned with a rival group of racketeers, which included Touhy and Ted Newberry[6]), his determination "to wipe out the Mafia" was clear.[7] The mayor's resolve became increasingly evident as the 1933 Chicago World's Fair

23

approached;[8] by its opening, he pledged, there would be "no hoodlums left."[9] Success seemed within Cermak's grasp when, on December 19, 1932, a special mayoral police squad illegally raided Mob headquarters and sprayed chieftain Frank Nitti with bullets.[10]

But Nitti recovered, and Cermak supporter Ted Newberry was murdered in apparent retaliation three weeks later.[11] Now terrified of assassination, Cermak bought a bullet-proof vest and moved into a penthouse apartment with a private elevator.[12] Believing that Nitti had imported Louis "Little New York" Campagna into Chicago to kill him, Cermak also increased his bodyguard force from two to five and placed guards at the homes of his two daughters.[13] Nitti was in fact gambling that "the crime crusade would blow up if they got rid of Mayor Cermak," two police officers later maintained.[14]

On February 15, 1933, one month after the Newberry slaying, Mayor Cermak was on hand while President-elect Franklin Roosevelt greeted dignitaries at a political rally in Miami's Bayfront Park.[15] Suddenly, Giuseppe Zangara stepped forward and fired a series of shots with a revolver, wounding five people in the crowd.[16] One of those hit was Cermak, who died three weeks later.[17]

On the surface, the case was clear-cut. Zangara claimed that he had been trying to kill President Roosevelt.[18] His grudge: chronic stomach pains, which he blamed on capitalists.[19] He was tried, convicted and executed within two weeks of Cermak's death, no questions asked.[20] He was a model lone assassin, the Warren Commission concluded many years later: "a failure" and "a victim of delusions."[21] Indeed, he was a natural prototype for the Commission's characterization of Lee Harvey Oswald.[22]

But Zangara's tale of senseless vengeance was dubious. For one thing, an autopsy revealed that Zangara was a "healthy, well-nourished individual" who had nothing wrong with his stomach.[23] Also, it is difficult to explain how, firing from close range and ostensibly aiming at Roosevelt, he managed to hit a cluster of people near Cermak, several feet from Roosevelt.[24] For Zangara was an experienced marksman,[25] and he told his lawyer that no one grabbed his arm or deflected his aim before he had finished firing.[26]

24

Other factors discredit the "lone nut" explanation and indicate Mob culpability. Zangara was a drifter who had lived in Philadelphia, Los Angeles and New Jersey[27] and whose chief activity during his last two years in Florida had been betting on horses and dogs.[28] According to *Lightnin'*, a Chicago magazine that exposed several instances of Capone-era corruption,[29] Zangara had also worked in a Mob narcotics-processing plant in Florida.[30] The magazine's editor, the Reverend Elmer Williams, conjectured that Zangara had run into trouble with the Syndicate and been given a choice: shoot Cermak, or be killed or tortured himself.[31]

Frank Loesch, president of the Chicago Crime Commission during the 1930s, also believed that "Mayor Cermak was deliberately murdered in a Capone gang plot."[32] Loesch stated he had information that Philadelphia Mafia members had assisted the Chicago branch by recruiting Zangara.[33] Judge John Lyle, a well-known Chicago political figure and friend of Cermak,[34] concluded succinctly that Cermak "was killed by the blackhanders," i.e., "the Mafia."[35]

Several historians agreed.[36] So did Cermak himself. On his hospital bed, the mayor told a reporter friend that he had been threatened before his trip to Miami for trying to break up Syndicate control.[37] And when his secretary first visited him at the hospital, Cermak told her, "So you arrived all right. I thought maybe they'd shot up the office in Chicago too."[38] Before he died, Cermak said he thought the Mob was behind his shooting.[39]

Years later, sociologist Saul D. Alinsky corroborated Cermak's suspicions. Alinsky was a member of the prison board supervising Roger Touhy,[40] a Chicago racketeer of the Prohibition era, who was imprisoned from 1934 to 1959 on a kidnapping conviction.[41] After Touhy's death in 1959, Alinsky made public a story of Touhy's that had been "commonly known for many years in many circles in Chicago."[42] As reported by Kenneth Allsop in *The Bootleggers,*

In the crowd near Zangara was another armed man—a Capone killer. In the flurry of shots six people were hit—but the bullet that struck Cermak was a .45, and not from the .32-calibre pistol used by Zangara, and was fired by the unknown Capone man who took advantage of the confusion to accomplish his mission.[43]

THE SHOOTING OF UAW PRESIDENT
WALTER REUTHER

The Cermak slaying thus established a precedent for Mob murder in the political arena and for the Mob's use of a "lone nut" to divert suspicion from itself. A second precedent was the shooting of another prominent individual—this time in the labor movement—in which the Mob again went to some length to mask its culpability. This second shooting highlights the Mob's long history of labor union infiltration, which is discussed briefly by way of introduction.

The Mafia's brutal assault on the labor movement was described in the bristling, heart-rending book, *The Enemy Within*, by Robert Kennedy. Published in 1960, the book was based upon Kennedy's experiences as counsel to a U.S. Senate committee that investigated labor racketeering in the 1950s.[44]

The characters in this sordid story, whom RFK grilled during the Senate probe, included Joey and Larry Gallo, who had 30 arrests and eight convictions between them.[45] Joey was the "chief suspect in a murder where the victim was shot so many times in the head that facial recognition was impossible."[46] The brothers, along with another hoodlum named Joseph DeGrandis, gained control of Teamster Local 266 and used it to muscle into the New York juke-box industry.[47]

Kennedy recounted what happened when Milton Green, a juke-box distributor, tried to protest gangster domination of the Gallo-DeGrandis local:

> He went to a meeting and voiced his opposition, even though he had been warned to keep quiet. His objections were overruled. On his way home, he said: "They came out with steel bars and they split my skull open for me and I was taken to the hospital."

Kennedy noted that seven months later, "Milton Green was a thin, wan, pathetic figure, still without full use of his faculties."[48]

Another whom RFK questioned during the Senate labor hearings was Johnny Dioguardi, a Mafia gangster and convicted extortionist[49] who was the director of the United Auto Workers Union, AFL, in New York during the 1950s.[50] Kennedy noted that Dioguardi was a close associate of Jimmy Hoffa, then Teamster president, and "had brought into the union movement about forty hoodlums with 178 arrests and 77 convictions between them."[51] Dioguardi escaped conviction for conspiracy in the 1956 acid blinding of labor columnist Victor Riesel after a prosecution witness refused to testify.[52] (The blinding was performed by Abraham Telvi, a Mob outsider who was murdered four months later.[53] This attack plus two others were cited by the House Assassinations Committee as instances in which Mobsters recruited "dupes or tools" for high-profile crimes "to place the blame on generally nondescript individuals."[54])

Robert Kennedy's close observation of this brutal underworld assault against unions, which continues today,* propelled him as attorney general to make the eradication of organized crime a top priority. It also drew another idealist and friend of his, Walter Reuther, into a confrontation with the Mob.

Walter Reuther was a self-made man who worked his way through college as an expert die-maker in an auto plant.[56] His determination extended into social concerns, delivering messages from the German underground to European contacts at the peril of the Gestapo.[57] He later fought for civil rights well before that cause became popular.[58] And he was a visionary who strove to infuse the highest ideals into the labor movement.[59]

---

*The extent of such control was noted by Commissioner Eugene Methvin in an Appendix to the 1986 report of the President's Commission on Organized Crime. "Today we still find the 'Bad Four' major unions . . . dominated by the La Cosa Nostra crime syndicate [the Mafia] and its auxiliaries and allies. The Longshoremen's Union embraces 200,000 members; the Laborers about 625,000; the Hotel and Restaurant Employees about 400,000; and the Teamsters has about 1.9 million. . . . Thus, altogether, nearly three million workers, their families and dependents, depend for their livelihoods, job safety, pension and welfare funds upon international unions controlled by gangsters whose power relies upon secrecy enforced by terror and murder. This is a screaming national scandal."[55]

Reuther's principled behavior drew him wide acclaim; he was ranked in a widely published poll of the late 1940s as one of the world's ten most influential men.[60] And it was evidenced in an uncompromising stand on one important issue:

American labor had better roll up its sleeves, it had better get the stiffest broom and brush it can find, and the strongest disinfectant, and it had better take on the job of cleaning its own house from top to bottom and drive out every crook and gangster and racketeer we find.[61]

The job would not be easy.

Reuther's first run-in with gangsters occurred on May 26, 1937, when he was viciously beaten during a union leafletting drive at the Ford Motor Company's River Rouge plant in Detroit.[62] His assailants: the Ford "Service Department," an antiunion goon squad of 3,000 "ex-convicts, thugs and musclemen."[63] The head of this Service Department was Harry Bennett, a top assistant to Henry Ford who courted Mob muscle with cozy Ford contracts.[64] A U.S. Senate committee chaired by Senator Estes Kefauver reported one case in which Detroit Mafioso Anthony D'Anna became a 50-percent owner of a Ford dealership a few weeks after meeting with Bennett.[65] The committee was also concerned that Ford had awarded a regional distributorship to a New Jersey firm whose controlling stockholder was Brooklyn Mafioso[66] Joe "Adonis" Doto.[67]

Reuther and his co-workers succeeded in organizing the United Auto Workers despite such efforts by Bennett's men and a thwarted attack against him by two armed thugs in April 1938.[68] But in 1947, when Reuther won the UAW presidency and control of its executive board,[69] he again found himself at odds with the Mob. The issue this time was illegal gambling in factories, which, according to a 1948 *Business Week* survey, was a widespread activity dominated by national syndicates.[70] The Kefauver Committee concurred that in-plant gambling was "very widespread" and "very highly organized,"[71] reporting that

on some occasions organized gamblers would throw very large funds into union elections in major locals in the Detroit area in the hopes of securing the election of officials who would tolerate in-plant gambling.[72]

The Mob thus had much at stake when Reuther, after winning the 1947 UAW election, promptly launched a crusade against racketeer-controlled gambling in the auto factories.[73]

On the evening of April 20, 1948, Walter Reuther was seriously wounded by a 12-gauge shotgun blast fired through his kitchen window.[74] The gunman's careful planning and deadly aim, foiled only by Reuther's last-second turn to speak to his wife,[75] convinced police that a professional killer had been responsible.[76] A year later, on May 22, 1949, it was Reuther's brother's turn.[77] Also a high UAW official, Victor Reuther was hit in the face, throat and shoulder and blinded in one eye by another shotgun blast.[78]

A prime suspect in these incidents was cited in the *Business Week* article on in-plant gambling:

In their search for a murder motive, Detroit police questioned gambling syndicate personnel whose in-plant operations were being impeded at Reuther's direction. It was an entirely logical field for the police investigation.[79]

Two other logical suspects in the shootings were Communists, whom Reuther had purged from the union after the 1947 election,[80] and antiunion employers.[81] Interestingly enough, investigations of each of these groups led right back to the Mob.

About the Communists, Reuther biographers Cormier and Eaton wrote:

The UAW's left wing, the Reuther opposition, had mutually profitable links with underworld figures who dominated illegal gambling in the auto factories, an operation grossing perhaps $20 million a year. Because of the freedom of movement accorded local union stewards and shop committeemen, they made ideal collectors and runners for the crime syndicate. The Reuthers realized this and were trying to stop betting in the plants.[82]

Particularly unscrupulous was Melvin Bishop, one of the leaders of the Communist faction that Reuther had purged in December 1947[83] (after which Jimmy Hoffa made Bishop a Teamster official[84]). Curiously, Bishop was discovered to be friendly with Santo Perrone, who was identified in a 1965 U.S. Senate report as one of the top ten Mafiosi in Detroit.[85] Bishop kept Perrone's private number in his telephone pad,[86] and the two were once arrested together for illegal deer hunting.[87]

When UAW investigators of the Reuther shootings focused on employers who had given the union the most trouble, Santo Perrone's name came up again. In 1934, a local of the Congress of Industrial Organizations (CIO) struck the Detroit, Michigan Stove Works, one of the largest nonautomotive manufacturing plants in the Detroit area.[88] Soon afterward, John A. Fry, the stove works president and deputy commissioner of the Detroit Police, enlisted the Perrones to recruit strikebreakers.[89] The strike was broken and the union driven out.[90] Santo Perrone was then given a contract to haul scrap from the plant, and Perrone's brother Gaspar got a high-paying, do-nothing position.[91]

The same strategy was later used by the Briggs Manufacturing Company of Detroit, then the largest independent auto-body manufacturer in the world, whose president was a close friend of Fry.[92] On April 7, 1945, Briggs awarded a scrap handling contract to Santo Perrone's 28-year-old son-in-law, Carl Renda.[93] Renda, who had "no equipment, know-how or capital whatsoever,"[94] promptly assigned the job to companies that for many years had been removing the scrap.[95] A week later, the first of six vicious beatings was inflicted by unknown assailants on leading labor officials at the Briggs plant.[96] The Kefauver Committee concluded, "The inference is inescapable that what Renda, the entirely unequipped college student, was being paid for, was the service of his father-in-law, the 'muscle' man, Sam Perrone."[97]

Such sleazy incidents of collusion grounded Walter Reuther's own suspicions that his shooting was traceable to a coalition of the Mob, Communists and a "small group of diehard employers . . . who also were willing to work for the underworld."[98] The underworld, Reuther later explained, figured that I was the kind of person who would do everything that I could to try to keep them from taking control of this union and using it for the rackets and everything else that they use unions for.[99]

In 1949 the UAW received two important leads that supported Reuther's suspicions. Obtained through a *Detroit News* secret witness plan, the first suggested an investigation of one Clarence Jacobs, an ex-con once bailed out by Mafioso Santo Perrone.[100] The second called attention to a Detroit service station owned by Perrone,[101] which proved intriguing when the police later disclosed reports that the Reuther shootings had been plotted in a bar two doors away.[102]

As the long inquiry into the shootings of Walter and Victor Reuther continued, wrote biographers Gould and Hickok, "it became more obvious than ever that thugs and underworld characters were gunning for them, or had been hired to do the job."[103] The biggest break came in 1953, however, when UAW investigators located Donald Joseph Ritchie, a nephew of Clarence Jacobs, in a Canadian jail.[104] Ritchie agreed to cooperate, but fearing murder, asked for a $25,000 payment to his wife; the UAW paid.[105] Brought to Detroit on December 31, 1953, he was interviewed by Wayne County Prosecutor Gerald O'Brien.[106] Six days later O'Brien issued warrants for the arrests of Mafia members[107] Santo Perrone and Peter Lombardo, Perrone's son-in-law Carl Renda, and Ritchie's uncle Clarence Jacobs.[108] Prosecutor O'Brien also released Ritchie's statement to the public:

I was in the car the night Walter Reuther was shot. For about four or five years I had been working for Santo [Sam] Perrone. I made about $400 or $500 a week.

In the occupation, I was — well, it just wasn't what people would call work.

Clarence Jacobs approached me for this particular job. He told me I would get five grand.

I was approached about five days before it happened and asked if I wanted to go. This conversation took place in Perrone's gas station. Perrone asked me several days before the shooting if I was going on the job. I said I was.

I didn't ask a lot of questions. These people don't talk things over very much.

All I knew was that Perrone had once said: "We'll have to get that guy out of the way." Did he mean Reuther? Yeah. . . .

Jacobs did the shooting. He was the only one who got out of the car. I don't know how long he was gone. It's hard to remember time.

I heard the report of the gun. Then Jacobs got back in the car and said: "Well, I knocked the bastard down." We took off in a hurry.

After the job they dropped me back at the Helen Bar, about 200 feet from the gas station. I don't know what they did with the car. I heard later it was demolished and junked. I haven't any idea what happened to the gun.[109]

Predictably, Ritchie never took this testimony to trial. Held as a material witness at a Detroit hotel, Ritchie supposedly slipped out by fooling his two police guards into thinking he was taking a shower.[110] Ritchie then fled to Canada and reportedly disclaimed his story as a hoax to collect the $25,000 from the union.[111] Yet given the Mob's demonstrated ability to strike out at heavily guarded witnesses[112] and precedents of extensive Mob-police corruption in Detroit,[113] the purported retraction is hardly credible; there are better ways to con a buck than to finger the Mafia. Indeed, the circumstances of the case justify the UAW's belief[114] that Ritchie's confession is accurate—that the Mob tried to kill labor paragon Walter Reuther.

THE MURDER OF UAW-AFL
PRESIDENT JOHN KILPATRICK

Like Reuther's CIO-affiliated United Auto Workers, its counterpart in the American Federation of Labor, the UAW-AFL, came under gangland attack. A member described the situation in a letter to George Meany, which was examined during a Senate investigation:

32

While living in New York, I was employed in a plant where the union is the AFL Auto Workers. . . . The union is run by an ex-convict John Dio and his henchmen. I tried to protest a contract sellout at a meeting and was called at home by these thugs and told if I loved my children to shut up. . . . I'm no hero, so I did. We moved to Chicago and I got a job . . . where the UAW-AFL is the union. This was worse than before. A local hoodlum, Angelo Inciso, runs this union. . . . I was told to keep my mouth shut or I would be thrown down the steps.[115]

Angelo Inciso, boss of UAW-AFL Local 286 in Chicago, was indeed a hoodlum—a close associate of Chicago Mafia boss Tony Accardo[116] with many arrests and convictions.[117] But when Inciso began to plunder the local,[118] John Kilpatrick, international president of the UAW-AFL,[119] stepped in and had him ousted.[120] Kilpatrick also assisted the federal effort to prosecute Inciso,[121] leading to a ten-year prison sentence for him in June 1960.[122]

Although convicted, Inciso still had almost $500,000 in defrauded union funds,[123] so Kilpatrick filed civil suit against him to recover this sum.[124] Detroit Police Commissioner George Edwards described what happened when the case came to trial:

About 10 a.m. on April 28, 1961, John A. Kilpatrick was standing outside of [the] superior court room on the eighth floor of the County Building in Chicago and Inciso approached him and snarled, "I am going to kill you." When Kilpatrick was taken aback at the threat, Inciso said, "I am not going to do it personally but I'll have it done."[125]

Five months later, on October 20, Kilpatrick was found dead in his car, a single bullet hole behind his left ear.[126] Two men were arrested and convicted for the murder;[127] one fingered Inciso's right-hand man, Ralph Pope, as the one who ordered it.[128] But no other witness would implicate Pope, and neither Pope nor Inciso was prosecuted. "Again the insulation at some point worked," Commissioner Edwards commented.[129]

Although the Mafia's top brass was thus untouched, the successful prosecution of two of Kilpatrick's killers was an unusual triumph. For not since 1934 had a conviction been obtained for any of Chicago's thousand gangland slayings.[130] But this success was not accidental. When news of Kilpatrick's murder reached the new U.S. attorney general, Robert Kennedy, he ordered the Justice Department to "find out who's behind this killing, and get him."[131] Fifty FBI agents were then detailed to Chicago,[132] marking the first time the Bureau ever investigated a gangland murder in that city.[133]

Indeed, the Kennedy Administration was combating the Mob on a national scale[134] as Mayor Cermak had done in Chicago, as the Reuthers had done in the UAW-CIO and as Kilpatrick had done in the UAW-AFL. Harry Anslinger, the Federal Commissioner of Narcotics, observed in 1963 that this

determination to wipe out organized crime has had a significant impact all over the United States. The gangsters are running for their lives.[135]

PART I

Assassins at Large

On Friday, November 22, 1963, shortly after 11:50 a.m., President John F. Kennedy left Love Field, the Dallas airport, for a motorcade procession through the city.[1] He rode in the second car of the motorcade with his wife, Jacqueline, Texas Governor John Connally and his wife, Nelly, and two Secret Service agents.[2] At 12:30 p.m., as the presidential limousine turned left onto Elm Street from Houston Street, a series of shots rang out.[3] President Kennedy was hit in the shoulder, and Governor Connally was struck in the back; several seconds later, a bullet tore into President Kennedy's head.[4] The mortally wounded president was then rushed to Parkland Hospital, where he was pronounced dead at 1 p.m.[5]

Fifteen minutes later, Dallas Police Officer J.D. Tippit was shot to death as he stopped his patrol car beside a pedestrian in the Oak Cliff section of Dallas.[6] Shortly before 2 p.m., police arrested Lee Harvey Oswald, who worked in the Texas School Book Depository Building, as a suspect in both slayings.[7] The next day, a Dallas Police official announced that the case was "cinched": Oswald, unassisted, had shot President Kennedy from the sixth floor, southeast corner window of that building, beside which a rifle and three cartridges had been found.[8] Oswald maintained that he was innocent, exclaiming, "I'm just a patsy."[9]

On Sunday, November 24, Oswald was escorted to the basement exit ramp of the heavily guarded Dallas Police building for transfer to the county jail.[10] And at 11:21 a.m., as millions of television viewers watched Oswald approach the ramp, Dallas night club owner Jack Ruby lurched forward and fatally shot him in the stomach with a .38-caliber revolver.[11] Ruby told police that he had killed Oswald in a temporary fit of depression and rage over the president's death.[12]

With Oswald's protestations of innocence silenced by Ruby's revolver, the newly sworn-in president, Lyndon B. Johnson, hastened to wrap up the case. "Almost immediately after the assassination," reported the Senate Intelligence Committee in 1976, the Administration pressured the FBI to "issue a factual report supporting the conclusion that Oswald was the lone assassin."[13] Indeed, on the day of Oswald's death, both FBI Director J. Edgar Hoover and Deputy Attorney General Nicholas Katzenbach expressed the need to "convince the public that Oswald is the real assassin."[14] Katzenbach also mandated, "Speculation about Oswald's motivation ought to be cut off."[15]

On November 29, as noted in an FBI memo, President Johnson told Hoover that the only way to stop the "rash of investigations" was to appoint a high-level committee.[16] The same day, Johnson issued an executive order creating a commission to probe the assassination case,[17] which would be chaired by Chief Justice Earl Warren.[18] As the presidential commission was being assembled, Hoover orchestrated press leaks proclaiming that Oswald had killed President Kennedy "in his own lunatic loneliness."[19] Ten months later, the Warren Commission issued its final report, with an obliging verdict: Oswald was the lone, demented assassin, and Ruby the president's unassisted avenger.[20]

But the Commission's tranquilizing findings wore thin as its massive files of primary evidence were publicly released and examined. In books, leading journals, and legal and medical forums, critics exposed the Commission's serious distortions of its own cited evidence.[21] By 1966, joining the call for a new investigation were William F. Buckley, Richard Cardinal Cushing, Walter Lippmann, Arthur Schlesinger, Jr., Life magazine, the London Times and the American Academy of Forensic Sciences.[22] And by 1976, according to a Gallup poll, four out of five Americans believed that the assassination of President Kennedy was a conspiracy.[23]

In September 1976, more than a decade after the first Congressional call for a new probe,[24] Congress chartered the House Select committee on Assassinations to reexamine the murders of President Kennedy and the Reverend Martin Luther King, Jr.[25] Two years later, the Committee terminated its hearings with the dramatic presentation of new evidence leading it to conclude that the Kennedy assassination was probably a conspiracy.[26] These new findings confirmed longstanding public doubts about the official version of what happened on November 22, 1963. And they underscored ominous questions as to what forces have shaped America's course from that day onward.

In contrast to the testimony of the witnesses who heard and observed shots fired from the Texas School Book Depository, the Commission's investigations disclosed no credible evidence that any shots were fired from anywhere else.[1]

The Warren Commission, in its 1964 report

Scientific acoustical evidence establishes a high probability that two gunmen fired at President John F. Kennedy.[2]

The House Select Committee on Assassinations, in its 1979 report

2
Crossfire
in Dealey Plaza

You can't say Dallas doesn't love you," Nelly Connally told President Kennedy, as the presidential limousine rode north on Houston Street that sunny Friday, November 22, 1963.[3] At 12:30 p.m., the limousine turned left onto Elm Street, passing the Texas School Book Depository Building at the corner of Houston and Elm.[4] Sloping upward on Elm Street, ahead and to the right of the limousine, was a stretch of grass that came to be called the "grassy knoll" (see map in photo section[5]). Farther ahead, Elm Street ducked beneath a railroad overpass and turned into Stemmons Freeway. Nelly Connally looked past the overpass toward the freeway, remarking to Jacqueline Kennedy, "We're almost through, it's just beyond that."[6]

Standing on the overpass, enjoying his commanding view of the motorcade, railroad signal supervisor S. M. Holland heard a series of shots.[7] Holland glanced left toward a five-foot picket fence atop the grassy knoll, which bordered a railroad parking lot to the north.[8] His eyes immediately fixed on a cluster of trees 60 yards away, near the corner of the fence.[9] And at that moment, as Holland reported in a sheriff's affidavit later that day, he saw "a puff of smoke come from the trees."[10] He subsequently told the Warren Commission, "There was a shot. . . . And a puff of smoke came out about 6 or 8 feet above the ground right out from under those trees."[11] Holland was not alone in this observation. Six other railroad workers situated atop the railroad overpass—Richard C. Dodd,[12] Clemon E. Johnson,[13] Austin L. Miller,[14] Thomas J. Murphy,[15] James L. Simmons,[16] and Walter L. Winborn[17]—reported seeing smoke in the same area just after they heard the shots. The smoke could not be explained as exhaust fumes or steam or otherwise dismissed.* Moreover, several witnesses sniffed gunpowder in that vicinity.[23] Senator Ralph Yarborough, who rode past the picket fence, downwind from it, seconds after the shooting,[24] reported, "you could smell powder on our car" nearly all the way to Parkland Hospital.[25] Dallas Patrolman Joe M. Smith also caught the smell of gunpowder behind the picket fence, in the railroad parking lot.[26] Smith had headed for the fence when a bystander exclaimed to him, "They are shooting the President from the bushes."[27]

Just after the shooting, railroad workers Holland, Simmons and Dodd jumped over a steam pipe, scrambled over a "sea of cars" in the railroad parking lot and dashed to the picket fence, where they had spotted the smoke.[28] There, between the fence and a station wagon parked just west of the fence corner,[29] they found "about a hundred foottracks in that little spot," going in every direction.[30] Holland later told the Warren Commission he had the impression that "someone had been standing there for a long period."[31] Holland also noted two spots of mud on the bumper, "as if someone had cleaned their foot, or stood up on the bumper to see over the fence."[32] Simmons reported the same thing,[33] and Dodd added, "There were tracks and cigarette butts

---

*Johnson suggested that the smoke they observed may have come from a motorcycle abandoned by a policeman.[18] Holland reported, however, that he saw the smoke before the policeman abandoned the motorcycle.[19] Some have alternatively proposed that the smoke was actually steam. But the only nearby steam line ran along the railroad overpass—practically underfoot of the witnesses there—and nowhere near the corner of the picket fence.[20] Others have argued that the "smokeless powder" used in modern weapons leaves no smoke.[21] But in actuality, the term "smokeless powder" has the same exaggerated connotation as "seedless grapefruit." As reported by a panel of firearms experts commissioned by the House Assassinations Committee, the propellant in modern cartridges "is not completely consumed or burned. Due to this, residue and smoke are emitted."[22]

laying where someone had been standing on the bumper looking over the fence."[34]

Many other witnesses also indicated that a shot had come from that same area.[35] One was William Newman, Jr., who was watching the motorcade with his wife and two children from the curb of Elm Street at the bottom of the grassy knoll.[36] In a Dallas County Sheriff's affidavit of November 22, Newman reported:

> the President's car turned left off Houston onto Elm Street . . . all of a sudden there was a noise, apparently gunshot. . . . then we fell down on the grass as it seemed that we were in the direct path of fire. . . . I thought the shot had come from the garden directly behind me.[37]

Newman and his wife fell to the ground, each covering a child.[38]

Mary Elizabeth Woodward was standing on the Elm Street curb near the Newmans watching the motorcade.[39] When the president's car approached, Woodward told a reporter on November 22, "there was a horrible, ear-shattering noise coming from behind us and a little to the right."[40] Behind and to her right was the picket fence.[41] Woodward then fell to the ground, along with the Newmans and three other men in the vicinity.[42]

Gordon Arnold, home from basic training in the army, was standing about three feet in front of the stockade fence in the grassy knoll as the motorcade approached. He felt a bullet whiz by his left ear, and then heard a crack, as if he were "standing there under the muzzle." Arnold hit the ground, as he had been trained to do, and then heard another shot go over him.[43]

Dallas law enforcement officers immediately focused attention on the railroad parking lot north of the fence and on the surrounding railroad property. Just after the shooting, Dallas Police Chief Jesse E. Curry broadcast on his police microphone, "Get a man on top of that triple underpass [the railroad overpass] and see what happened up there."[44] Riding in the lead car of the motorcade with Curry, Dallas County Sheriff Bill Decker radioed the order to "move all available men out of my office into the railroad yard to try to determine what happened in there."[45] His deputies proceeded into the railroad parking lot behind the picket fence.[46]

But these official directives were unnecessary. Right after the shots were fired, as reported by witnesses and shown in photographs, dozens of police officers and bystanders charged up the grassy knoll.[47] Among them were two motorcycle policemen in the motorcade: one who rode over the curb and up the grass, and another who dropped his motorcycle on Elm Street and ran up with his pistol drawn.[48] A large crowd also swarmed toward the knoll from the corner of Houston and Elm Streets, near the Texas School Book Depository Building.[49] That building, in contrast, attracted no immediate attention from bystanders.[50] Within minutes after the shooting, at least 50 policemen were searching the railroad parking lot and surrounding railroad yard.[51]

Four of this police contingent — Dallas County Deputy Sheriffs L. C. Smith, A. D. McCurley, J. L. Oxford and Seymour Weitzman — reported that bystanders mentioned smoke or shots coming from the vicinity of the picket fence.[52] Weitzman, for one, was running up the grassy knoll when someone said that a "firecracker or shot had come from the other side of the fence."[53] Weitzman vaulted over the fence into the parking lot,[54] where a railroad yardman told him that the source of gunfire was "the wall section where there was a bunch of shrubbery."[55] The yardman also related that "he thought he saw somebody throw something through a bush."[56] Weitzman eventually joined Holland, Simmons and Dodd near the corner of the picket fence, where he saw "numerous kinds of footprints that did not make sense because they were going different directions."[57]

Reports from three additional witnesses reinforced suspicions that a gunman had fired from behind the picket fence. Lee Bowers, stationed atop a 14-foot railroad tower, observed three cars cruising around the railroad lot less than half an hour before the assassination,[58] although police had sealed off the area.[59] Two of the cars had out-of-state license plates, one of which, a 1961 or 1962 Chevrolet Impala, was muddy up to the windows.[60] Lone male drivers rode in the Chevrolet and the third car;[61] one held something to his mouth that appeared to be a microphone or a telephone.[62] As the motorcade came within his commanding view, Bowers noticed two men standing behind the picket fence.[63] They were the only people in the vicinity unfamiliar to the 15-year Dallas railroad veteran.[64] When the shots were fired, "a flash of light or smoke" or "some unusual occurrence" near the two strangers attracted Bowers' eye.[65]

J. C. Price watched the motorcade from the roof of the Terminal Annex Building, near the Depository Building.[66] After the volley of shots, Price saw a man running full-speed from the picket fence to the railroad yard.[67] Price noted that the man held something in his right hand, which "could have been a gun."[68]

After the shooting, Dallas Police officer Joe M. Smith encountered another suspicious man in the lot behind the picket fence.[69] Smith told the Warren Commission that when he drew his pistol and approached the man, the man "showed [Smith] that he was a Secret Service agent."[70] Another witness also reported encountering a man who displayed a badge and identified himself as a Secret Service agent.[71] But according to Secret Service Chief James Rowley and agents at the scene, all Secret Service personnel stayed with the motorcade, as required by regulations, and none was stationed in the railroad parking lot.[72] It thus appeared that someone was carrying fraudulent Secret Service credentials—of no perceptible use to anyone but an escaping assassin.

In 1966, Haverford College professor Josiah Thompson began a meticulous study of reports, photographs, medical documents and other evidence bearing on the Dealey Plaza shooting.[73] Thompson focused on indications that a shot had come from behind the picket fence: the accounts and immediate reactions of bystanders, the sight and smell of gunpowder, the rapid convergence of police, and the reports of unusual activity in the vicinity, including encounters with a phantom Secret Service agent.[74] He was particularly interested in the smoke, footprints and cigarette butts observed behind the picket fence by railroad workers at the scene.[75] To pinpoint the details of these observations, Thompson interviewed signal supervisor S. M. Holland on November 30, 1966, at Holland's home in Irving, Texas.[76]

Holland told Thompson that he heard four shots, the last two closely spaced.[77] He saw a puff of white smoke come out from the trees after the third or fourth shot.[78] The smoke was positioned over the picket fence, "about ten or fifteen feet" west of the corner.[79]

Holland then described to Thompson what he found behind the fence minutes later:

And I got over to the spot where I saw the smoke come from and heard the shot. . . . Well, you know it'd been raining that morning and behind the station wagon from one end of the bumper to the other, I expect you could've counted four or five-hundred footprints down there.[80]

He continued, "And on the bumper, oh about twelve or eighteen inches apart, it looked like someone had raked their shoes off; there were muddy spots up there, like someone had been standing up there."[81] Holland summarized his impression of the footprints with the comment, "It looked like a lion pacing a cage."[82]

Holland's remarks to Thompson were featured in the latter's highly regarded treatise, *Six Seconds in Dallas*, published in 1967. In that book, Thompson noted that many questions remained unanswered about the shots fired in Dealey Plaza.[83] But "with regard to the shot from behind the stockade fence," he concluded, "the evidence indicates unambiguously that a shot came from that location."[84] The details "may yet fill in," Thompson added, through "a future investigation, a sudden revelation or the patient labors of other researchers and historians."[85]

Eleven years later, in March 1978, the House Select Committee on Assassinations located a trunkful of 1963-vintage Dallas Police records in the custody of a former intelligence director of the department.[86] Among them was a dictabelt recording of "channel one" transmissions by police on the day of the JFK assassination.[87] And on the dictabelt was a ten-second series of loud clicks and pops, transmitted from a police motorcycle whose microphone control button had stuck in the "on" position.[88] Transcripts and testimony covering the assassination-day police transmissions, dating back to 1963 and 1964, established that the dictabelt was authentic.[89] Moreover, recorded time annotations fixed the time of the sounds at seconds after 12:30 p.m. — just when the shooting occurred.[90]

Seeking possible clues concerning the shots fired at President Kennedy, the House Assassinations Committee commissioned two prominent acoustical experts to study the dictabelt sounds. One was Dr. James Barger, chief scientist of the Cambridge, Massachusetts firm of Bolt, Beranek and Newman, Inc., who supervised the initial phase of this study.[91] His acoustical expertise had been relied upon in applications ranging from tracking submarines for the Navy to determining the source of gunfire from sound tapes for a federal grand jury investigating the 1970 Kent State shootings.[92] The second expert was Professor Mark Weiss of Queens College, the City University of New York, who reviewed Dr. Barger's work and then spearheaded a refinement of it.[93] Recommended to the Committee by the Acoustical Society of America, Professor Weiss had served with Dr. Barger on the panel of technical experts appointed in 1973 by Judge John Sirica to examine the Watergate tapes.[94]

On September 11, 1978, after comparing the dictabelt sounds with recorded test firings in Dealey Plaza, Dr. Barger presented his initial findings to the Committee.[95] He concluded that four of the sounds (the last three occurring 1.65, 7.56 and 8.31 seconds, respectively, after the first) were probably sounds of gunshots from Dealey Plaza.[96] The indicated firing positions: lots one, two and four from the Texas School Book Depository, the third shot from the grassy knoll.[97] Each of these four recorded impulses passed several screening tests designed to rule out sounds that were not gunshots fired in Dealey Plaza at the time of the assassination.[98] Nevertheless, given the available data, Dr. Barger could ascertain the origin of the third firing position with only an indeterminate 50–50 probability.[99]

A frustrated House Assassinations Committee then asked Professor Mark Weiss and his research associate, Ernest Aschkenasy, whether an extension of Dr. Barger's work could move that probability off center—one way or another.[100] The refinement Weiss and Aschkenasy proposed was an ingenious application of basic physical principles to pinpoint Dr. Barger's estimates of the firing and microphone positions of the third shot.[101] This refinement would reduce the margin of error six-fold, and make the results far more conclusive.[102] After more than two months of calculations using this refinement, Weiss and Aschkenasy determined the pair of firing and microphone positions whose computed echo pattern precisely matched the third dictabelt impulse.[103] They had identified the "acoustical fingerprint"[104] of a gunshot fired from the grassy knoll toward the presidential limousine in Dealey Plaza.

On December 29, 1978, in dramatic public testimony, Weiss

and Aschkenasy presented their findings to the House Assassinations Committee.[105] Their conclusion, Professor Weiss testified, was that "with a probability of 95 percent or better," the third shot was fired from the grassy knoll.[106] Aschkenasy added,

> The numbers could not be refuted. . . . The numbers just came back again and again the same way, pointing only in one direction, as to what these findings were.[107]

After reviewing the new acoustical work, Dr. Barger was recalled to testify. He concurred that "the probability of this being a shot from the grassy knoll was 95 percent or better."[108]

This acoustical determination by Aschkenasy and Barger of a grassy knoll shot was disputed by three subsequent critiques. The first was presented unsolicited to the House Assassinations Committee by Anthony Pellicano,[109] a private investigator from Chicago who subsequently handled a controversial tape for the defense of auto maker John DeLorean that was leaked to the press by *Hustler* magazine publisher Larry Flynt.[110] Pellicano's criticisms were disposed of by Dr. Barger in subsequent testimony before the House Committee.[111]

The next two critiques were commissioned by the Department of Justice, in a narrowly circumscribed response to a recommendation from the House Assassinations Committee to pursue further the leads that it had uncovered.[112] The first of these, an FBI study completed in November 1980, concluded that the acoustical findings on which the Committee relied "must be considered invalid."[113] The FBI study was quickly forgotten, however, after stinging rebuttals from the Committee's chairman, counsel and scientists who performed the work pointed out that the FBI "fundamentally misunderstood" the Committee's scientific analysis.[114]

After the FBI critique fell flat, the Department of Justice commissioned another review of the acoustical evidence by a panel of the National Academy of Sciences. The chairmanship of the panel was initially offered to Luis Alvarez, a scientist who had been outspoken in his skepticism of conspiracy theories in the JFK assassination case.[115] Alvarez had the good sense to turn it down but became a panel member.[116]

In a report released on May 14, 1982, the panel concluded that "the acoustic analyses do not demonstrate that there was a grassy knoll shot."[117] The new study called attention to a point raised in the Pellicano critique, that sirens could not be heard for almost two minutes after the time that the House experts had delineated as that of the shooting.[118] It made no mention, however, of the explanation offered by Dr. Barger in prior testimony that the officer with the stuck microphone, as shown in a UPI photo, had lagged behind the motorcade after the shooting, and that the placement of his microphone was such that the sirens would not have been heard over the noise of his motorcycle's motor.[119] While the panel offered some valid criticisms of the methodology used in the House acoustical studies, it introduced complex and controversial assumptions and made several errors of its own.[120] In a letter of February 18, 1983, Dr. Barger noted enigmatic features in a recording upon which the National Academy of Sciences panel relied and pointed out that it "did not examine the several items of evidence that corroborated our original findings." Barger stood by the acoustical determination of a grassy knoll shot as accepted by the House Select Committee on Assassinations.[121]

Indeed, there were important additional elements that corroborated the conclusion of Barger, Weiss and Aschkenasy. The positions they determined for the motorcycle at the time of the four shots traced out a path on Houston Street that fit the actual course and speed of the motorcade.[122] The testimony of a Dallas Police officer established that his motorcycle had been in that vicinity when the shots were fired, and that his microphone had been mounted in the configuration indicated by the acoustical study.[123] Moreover an "N-wave," characteristic of supersonic gunfire, appeared in each dictabelt impulse for which the police microphone was in an appropriate position to detect it, including the recorded sound of the third shot.[124]

The most striking finding, however, was the exact location of the grassy knoll gunman. According to the acoustical calculations, this firing position was behind the picket fence, eight feet west of the corner.[125] That was just *two to seven feet* from where S. M. Holland, a dozen years earlier, had placed the signs observed by himself and fellow railroad workers: the puff of smoke, muddy station wagon bumper, cigarette butts, and cluster of footprints.[126] But it was more than 300 feet from Oswald's alleged firing position.[127] And it was in front and to the right of the presidential limousine during the shooting,[128] although at least one bullet struck from behind.[129] The acoustical evidence thus established "a high probability," as the House Assassinations Committee concluded, "that two gunmen fired at President John F. Kennedy."[130] The "logical and probable inference," the Committee observed, was that President Kennedy was killed "as a result of a conspiracy."[131]

A third gunman may have been caught by the camera of Phillip Willis, a retired U.S. Air Force major, in a photograph he took from Elm Street immediately after the first shot was fired.[132] This photograph shows the picket fence in the grassy knoll, a nearby concrete wall and what appears to be the upper part of a person behind the wall.[133] After performing computer analysis of this figure, a panel of photographic experts concluded that it was, indeed, "most probably an adult person standing behind the wall."[134] The panel noted that the figure was no longer visible in a subsequent photograph of the same area, and that its shape, height and distribution of flesh tones were consistent with those of an adult person.[135]

The person in the Willis photo could have been an innocent bystander trying to see President Kennedy. Yet why would such a person have chosen a concealed position behind the concrete wall, when the grassy knoll just yards away provided an open view of the motorcade?[136] A more ominous alternative is suggested by something else near the figure in the photo.[137] "Visible near the region of the hands," the House photographic panel noted, "is a very distinct straight-line feature."[138]*

---

*There are conflicting indications as to which firing position was the source of the fatal shot to President Kennedy's head.[139] But common sense dictates the grassy knoll, given the distinct snap of his head to the left and rear shown in the well-known motion picture film made by Abraham Zapruder.[140] Furthermore, a profuse amount of blood and brain matter flew out in the same direction.[141] Dallas Police Officer Bobby W. Hargis, for example, who was riding a motorcycle to the left and rear of the presidential limousine, was splattered so forcefully with blood and brain tissue that he "thought at first [he] might have been hit."[142] And Dallas Police Chief Jesse Curry noted, "by the direction of the blood and brains from the president from one of the shots it would just seem that it would have to be fired from the front rather than behind."[143]

To faithful adherents of Warren Commission doctrine, however, the demonstrated existence of two or more assassins simply required casting more demented gunmen in its meaningless melodrama. As one such believer put it in 1967, the evidence of multiple assassins "is not sensational: it simply means that Oswald must have had an accomplice."[144] In 1971, one of Sirhan Sirhan's lawyers would use a similar argument to dismiss indications that a second gunman fired at Robert Kennedy. Such an attacker would have been someone with no connection to his client, the attorney would claim, "who seized on the impulse of the moment" to fire a bullet into the senator's brain.[145]

Yet to most Americans, the Congressional determination of conspiracy raised more penetrating questions. Was Lee Harvey Oswald merely an expendable participant in a much larger conspiracy, pegged as the lone culprit by officials under pressure to wrap up the case? Was an assassination contract in fact executed by some group with a demonstrated murder capability, a known hatred of President Kennedy, and a rational motive for killing him? An initial clue suggesting this possibility is a sinister series of incidents that followed the assassination.

You can not exist in a society where the ultimate solution to everything is to kill somebody, which is the answer of organized crime to any problem.[1]

> Mob defector Michael Raymond, testifying in 1971
> before a U.S. Senate committee

What the committee witnessed here yesterday is . . . that fear that is all too often characteristic of people called to testify in matters touching on organized crime. A fear that, frankly must be recognized as justified. Indeed, I would note that . . . between 1961 and 1965 . . . more than 25 informants were lost in organized crime cases, killed by those who would prevent their testimony from being made public.[2]

> G. Robert Blakey, chief counsel to the House Assassinations
> Committee, speaking of one frightened Committee witness

3
A Telltale Trail of Murder

On December 17, 1969, a federal grand jury indicted Newark Mayor Hugh Addonizio, Mafia boss Anthony Boiardo and 13 others on charges of splitting $1.5 million in payoffs extorted from city contractors.[3] Following the indictment, Michael Dorman reported in *Payoff*, it was feared that Mob violence might subvert the case.[4] A critical prosecution witness was placed under guard after receiving threats from Boiardo.[5] A defendant was "killed in a mysterious automobile crash" after meeting with the prosecutor and offering to cooperate.[6] A cooperative government witness died in another auto crash.[7] One of those indicted "died of what was officially described as a heart attack."[8]

The same pattern of violence, so characteristic of organized crime cases,[9] was brutally enacted following the Kennedy assassination.

THREE JOURNALISTS

Like their European counterparts,[10] some American newsmen quickly came to suspect Mafia ties to the Kennedy murder. Witness the official synopsis of a December 12, 1963 FBI interview of *Chicago Daily News* reporter Morton William Newman.[11] Newman had covered the Dallas assassination and discussed with colleagues a story suggesting that Jack Ruby had underworld ties:[12]

> Newman informed that as a result of this story, which apparently has been rumored around some, some of the people of the news media think that possibly the "Syndicate" hired Oswald to assassinate President Kennedy.
>
> He further stated that it is his understanding that when [Ruby's sister] Eva Grant was at the police station after Jack Ruby's arrest, as she was leaving the police station, she made a remark to the effect that Jack didn't see why "Kennedy was killed when a man like Mafia defector Joseph Valachi was permitted to live."[13]

But Ruby's suspected ties to the Mob, eventually confirmed,[14] received virtually no coverage in the American press for more than a decade. The following series of events may partially explain why.

On Sunday night, November 24, 1963, award-winning journalist Bill Hunter of the *Long Beach* (Calif.) *Press Telegram* and reporter Jim Koethe of the *Dallas Times Herald* went to Jack Ruby's apartment.[15] There they met with Ruby's roommate, George Senator, and attorneys Jim Martin and Tom Howard,[16] all of whom had visited Ruby in jail that day.[17]

Five months later, Hunter was shot dead in the heart by a policeman in the press room of the Public Safety Building in Long Beach, California.[18] The policeman initially claimed that his gun fired when he dropped it and tried to pick it up.[19] But he later changed his story after the determined trajectory of the bullet proved this impossible.[20]

Jim Koethe was killed on September 21, 1964 by a karate chop to the throat in his Dallas apartment, inflicted by an unknown assailant.[21] His apartment was found ransacked.[22] Koethe had been working on a book about the Kennedy assassination, in conjunction with two other reporters.[23]

Attorney Tom Howard, age 48, died in March 1965 of what

was called a heart attack;[24] no autopsy was performed.[25]

Ruby's roommate, George Senator, told the Warren Commission that after November 24, he feared he would be hurt or killed.[26] Senator testified he was so terrified for ten days afterward that he "was afraid to sleep in the same place twice," and in fact slept at a different friend's house each night.[27]

Dorothy Kilgallen, a well-known crime reporter, went to Dallas after the assassination to investigate the case.[28] In March 1964, she was granted an exclusive private interview with Jack Ruby in a judge's chambers in the Dallas Police Building.[29] Author Joachim Joesten noted her continuing interest:

> [To find *New York Journal American*] columnists Bob Considine and Dorothy Kilgallen muckraking the Oswald case and casting doubts on the official theory has been both refreshing and hopeful. . . . On April 14, 1964, the *Journal American* ran a column by Miss Kilgallen which opens up many embarrassing questions for the Dallas Police. . . . [30]

Kilgallen's interest may well have disturbed more sinister circles; in another column, she reported that Ruby was a gangster.[31]

On November 8, 1965, Dorothy Kilgallen, age 52, died in her New York home, the cause of death reported eight days later as ingestion of barbiturates and alcohol.[32] Two days later, her close friend Mrs. Earl Smith died; the autopsy conclusion: cause of death unknown.[33] Texas newspaper editor Penn Jones reported that "shortly before her death, Miss Kilgallen told a friend in New York that she was going to New Orleans in 5 days and break the case wide open."[34]

HANK KILLAM

The Warren Commission speculated that "one conceivable association" between Ruby and Oswald

> was through John Carter, a boarder at 1026 North Beckley Avenue while Oswald lived there. Carter was friendly with Wanda Joyce Killam, who had known Jack Ruby since

shortly after he moved to Dallas in 1947 and worked for him from July 1963 to early November 1963.[35]

In the middle of this possible Ruby-Oswald link was Hank Killam, Wanda's husband, who had worked as a house painter with John Carter.[36]

On March 17, 1964, Hank Killam was found dead, his throat cut, amid the shattered glass of a department store window in Pensacola, Florida.[37] His death became the subject of a nationally publicized investigation in 1967 by County Solicitor Carl Harper,[38] during which members of Killam's family were questioned. According to his brother Earl, Hank said he had left Dallas because he was "constantly questioned by 'agents' or 'plotters.' "[39] He had "moved to Pensacola, then Tampa, then back to Pensacola to escape these 'agents.' "[40] Earl Killam told reporters that two days before Hank's death, Hank had told him, "I'm a dead man. I've run as far as I'm going to run."[41] And Hank's mother related that at 4 a.m. on the day of his death, Hank received a call at her home.[42] He dressed and left the house, after which she "heard a car drive off . . . although [he] did not own a car."[43]

The police ruled the death a suicide,[44] the local coroner an accident.[45] But Hank's wife felt that suicide was unlikely,[46] and his brother Earl remarked, "Did you ever hear of a man committing suicide by jumping through a plate glass window?"[47]

ROSE CHERAMIE

On November 20, 1963, a bruised and battered woman was found lying on a road near Eunice, Louisiana.[48] She was Rose Cheramie, a heroin addict and prostitute with a long history of arrests.[49] Taken to Louisiana State Hospital near Jackson, Louisiana, Cheramie spoke of the assassination of President Kennedy, to occur two days later.[50]

Over the years, Cheramie's remarks were reported by various sources,[51] including a policeman who became associated with the assassination probe of New Orleans District Attorney Jim Garrison.[52] Perhaps most credible is the account of Dr. Victor Weiss, a resident physician at Louisiana State Hospital in 1963.[53] In 1978,

53

Dr. Weiss told an interviewer from the House Assassinations Committee, as the Committee summarized, that

> on Monday, November 25, 1963, he was asked by another physician, Dr. Bowers, to see a patient who had been committed November 20 or 21. Dr. Bowers allegedly told Weiss that the patient, Rose Cheramie, had stated before the assassination that President Kennedy was going to be killed. Weiss questioned Cheramie about her statements. She told him she had worked for Jack Ruby. She did not have any specific details of a particular assassination plot against Kennedy, but had stated the "word in the underworld" was that Kennedy would be assassinated.[54]

On September 4, 1965, Cheramie was struck by an auto and killed on a highway near Big Sandy, Texas.[55] The driver said that he saw Cheramie lying on the road and tried to avoid hitting her, but ran over the top of her skull.[56]

LEE BOWERS

Stationed atop a 14-foot tower near Dealey Plaza,[57] as previously related, railroad worker Lee Bowers noticed several unusual incidents on the morning of November 22. Bowers described them to the FBI, the Warren Commission,[58] and later, in a filmed and tape-recorded interview on March 31, 1966, to a private assassination researcher.[59]

As reported in the *Midlothian* (Texas) *Mirror*, Bowers had received death threats and purchased a large life insurance policy before he was killed in an unusual automobile accident in Midlothian, Texas.[60] On the morning of August 9, 1966, according to two eyewitnesses, his car swerved off the road into a concrete bridge abutment.[61] "The doctor from Midlothian who attended Bowers stated that he did not have a heart attack and that he thought Bowers was in some sort of 'strange shock.' "[62]

WARREN REYNOLDS AND ACQUILLA CLEMONS

Situated at a car lot a block west of the place where Dallas police officer J.D. Tippit was shot, Warren Reynolds observed

Tippit's assailant run by.[63] The Warren Commission asserted in its report that

> Reynolds did not make a positive identification when interviewed by the FBI, but he subsequently testified before a Commission staff member and, when shown two photographs of Oswald, stated that they were photographs of the man he saw.[64]

Amazingly, however, the Commission failed to mention[65] a sinister series of events leading up to Reynolds' new-found certainty.

On January 23, 1964, two days after his initial interview with the FBI,[66] at approximately 9:15 p.m., Reynolds walked down to the basement of the auto dealership at which he was employed.[67] He flipped on the light switch, but the basement remained dark; the bulb had been removed.[68] As the FBI reported, "Thinking the light bulb was burned out, he proceeded downstairs to the basement fuse box and, as he reached for the fuse box, was shot in the head with a .22-caliber weapon";[69] fortunately, he survived.[70] Police investigators determined that "Reynolds was not robbed of anything."[71] Yet the assailant had been waiting in the basement for more than three hours before he shot Reynolds.[72]

On February 3, 1964, Darrell Garner was arrested as a suspect in the shooting.[73] Garner was released, however, after Nancy Jane Mooney gave an affidavit two days later stating that she was with Garner at the time of the shooting.[74] But then, as reported by the FBI, "on February 13, 1964, at 2:45 a.m., Nancy Jane Mooney was arrested and charged with disturbing the peace. . . . After being placed in a cell at the Dallas City Jail, Nancy Jane Mooney hung herself with her toreador trousers."[75]

When interviewed by the FBI[76] and questioned by Warren Commission counsel in July,[77] Reynolds stated that he believed he was shot because he had witnessed the flight of Tippit's assailant.[78] Reynolds said that he "had been scared as a result of having been shot through the head after the assassination of President Kennedy."[79] He also related that about three weeks after he got out of the hospital, someone tried to abduct his ten-year-old daughter.[80] About the same time, someone unscrewed the light bulb from his front porch.[81] Reynolds admitted that these incidents made him apprehensive, and felt that they were related to the events of November 22.[82]

By July 1964, as the Commission so neatly recorded, Reynolds was willing to identify Tippit's assailant as Lee Harvey Oswald.[83]

Another eyewitness to the Tippit slaying, Acquilla Clemons, was questioned by independent investigators.[84] She reported that the gunman was "kind of a short guy" and "kind of heavy,"[85] a description incompatible with Oswald's appearance.[86] Clemons also related that just two days after the Kennedy and Tippit killings, a man who appeared to be a policeman came to her house.[87] His message: "He just told me it'd be best if I didn't say anything because I might get hurt."[88]

ALBERT BOGARD

Albert G. Bogard was a salesman at the Downtown Lincoln-Mercury dealership in Dallas.[89] Bogard testified that on the afternoon of November 9, 1963, a man came into his showroom and asked for a demonstration ride in a Mercury Comet, which he drove somewhat recklessly.[90] The man said his name was Lee Oswald,[91] which Bogard wrote down on a business card.[92] But when Bogard heard on November 22 that Oswald "had shot a policeman,"[93] he tore up the card in the presence of other salesmen.[94] Bogard told his colleagues, "He won't be a prospect any more because he is going to jail."[95]

Bogard passed an FBI-administered lie detector test on his account,[96] and his testimony was corroborated in its essentials by three other employees of the auto agency.[97] One of these employees told the FBI that he also remembered the name "Oswald," and had written it down before the assassination.[98] Bogard and the other employees related that this customer had told them that he had a new job and no cash or credit but expected some money in the next two or three weeks, and had sarcastically remarked that he might have to go back to Russia to get a car.[99]

The perplexing features of this account were that Oswald did not know how to drive,[100] and that the testimony of two other witnesses precluded a visit by Oswald to the auto showroom on November 9.[101] In fact, several incidents were reported in which a man positively identified as Oswald appeared where he could not have been,[102] indicating that he may have been impersonated and framed.

In an interview with a private researcher on April 4, 1966 in Dallas, fellow salesman Oran Brown described what happened to Bogard:

> You know, I am afraid to talk. . . . Bogard was beaten by some men so badly that he was in the hospital for some time, and this was after he testified. Then he left town suddenly and I haven't heard from him or about him since. . . . I think we may have seen something important, and I think there are some who don't want us to talk. Look at that taxi driver who was just killed [William Whaley, who gave Oswald a ride shortly after the assassination[103]], and the reporters.[104]

Brown might have been even more reluctant to speak had he known Bogard's ultimate fate. On February 14, 1966, Bogard was found dead in his car in Hallsville, Louisiana, with a hose running from the exhaust pipe into the passenger compartment.[105] Suicide, it was ruled.[106]

ROGER CRAIG

Roger D. Craig, a Dallas deputy sheriff who was in Dealey Plaza during the assassination,[107] gave testimony on Oswald's movements that suggested conspiracy and contradicted the official reconstruction.[108] Shortly afterward, Deputy Craig, who had been voted "Man of the Year" in 1960 by the Dallas County Sheriff's department,[109] became *persona non grata* in Dallas and was eventually fired.[110] In 1967, Craig went to New Orleans and furnished information to District Attorney Jim Garrison.[111] After his return to Dallas, Craig was shot walking to a parking lot; a bullet grazed his head.[112] In 1973, his car was forced off the road in West Texas, and he seriously injured his back.[113] And in 1974, Craig was shot in the shoulder by a stranger with a shotgun when he answered the door at a house in Waxahachie, Texas.[114]

A possible basis for these incidents was related by California CBS-TV producer Peter Noyes:

> For a time Craig went into hiding, after receiving information from one of his few remaining friends in law enforcement that the Mafia had put a price on his head.[115]

On May 15, 1975, Craig was found shot to death in his father's home in Dallas.[116] The police homicide investigator found an apparent suicide note and termed the fatal wound self-inflicted.[117] Craig had appeared on radio talk shows expressing his views on the JFK assassination shortly before his death.[118]

JOHNNY ROSELLI AND GEORGE DeMOHRENSCHILT

Two men who may have had important information about the assassination of President Kennedy were killed around the times they were sought for questioning by Congressional probers. Johnny Roselli was a West Coast Mafia figure closely involved in Mob-CIA plots to assassinate Cuban Premier Fidel Castro in the early sixties.[119] In the mid-1970s, the aging Mobster, who was linked to Oswald's killer, Jack Ruby,[120] began to describe Ruby as "one of our boys" and speak of Ruby's having been ordered to eliminate Oswald to silence him.[121] Roselli provided this information, discussed in more detail later, to associates, Senate investigators, columnist Jack Anderson and a newspaper publisher.[122] A few months after he testified in secret session before the Senate Intelligence Committee in 1976, Roselli's dismembered body was found in an oil drum in Miami's Biscayne Bay.[123]

George DeMohrenschilt was a friend of Oswald[124] mentioned frequently in both government and private sources on the assassination.[125] On March 29, 1977, he was found shot to death, just after the House Assassinations Committee had tried to reach him for questioning.[126] Another apparent suicide.[127]

The deaths of more than a dozen additional witnesses, many of them violent or unnatural, have also been reported.[128]

The incidents described above are singularly characteristic of one organization that routinely kills and intimidates witnesses to cover its crimes. And the fingerprints of this organization became apparent following the death of an additional key witness in New Orleans.

> One must wonder about Jim Garrison's motives . . . in light of the D.A.'s extremely questionable background. . . . Garrison was being courted by the Mafia, taking their payoffs and proclaiming himself as the man who had solved the crime of the century.[1]

Peter Noyes, producer for CBS-TV affiliate KNXT in Los Angeles

4
Intrigue
in New Orleans

In February 1967, the Kennedy assassination case took a dramatic turn following a sensational development in New Orleans. Jim Garrison, the city's district attorney, announced that he had uncovered an assassination conspiracy and would prosecute the culprits.[2] The press quickly identified and descended upon one of Garrison's key suspects, David Ferrie, a pilot with a bizarre personality who had worked for Carlos Marcello, the Mafia boss of New Orleans.[3] Among the reporters who pursued Ferrie was George Lardner, Jr. of the *Washington Post*, who spoke with him between midnight and 4:00 a.m. on February 22.[4] The drama intensified when Ferrie was found dead in his apartment with a cerebral hemorrhage later that day.[5]

As the Garrison probe continued, as will be discussed shortly, its thrust became increasingly questionable. Yet the New Orleans leads to which Garrison called attention put critics on an intriguing trail—a trail that led to Mafia boss Carlos Marcello.

DAVID FERRIE

In the case of David Ferrie, the link to Marcello was, as *Look* magazine summarized, "strong" and "well-known."[6] Ferrie knew Marcello well,[7] telephoned him several times,[8] and was reported by several sources to have flown Marcello back to the United States after Marcello's deportation to Guatemala.[9] Ferrie's ties with the

Mafia boss were particularly intensive in the fall of 1963, when Ferrie was employed by attorney G. Wray Gill on Marcello's deportation case.[10] And Marcello was listed as a sponsor for a service station Ferrie operated in 1964.[11]

Ferrie was also a rabid anti-communist, demonstrating a dual affiliation that was common in the wake of Castro's appropriation of the Mob's lucrative gambling casinos in Cuba. He provided flight instruction, armaments and money to the Cuban Revolutionary Council (CRC), an anti-Castro organization.[12] And he associated with men like Guy Banister, a private detective and a reputed bigwig in the ultraright Minutemen.[13] Even in his anti-Castro activities, Ferrie may have served as a financial conduit for Marcello, as suggested by an FBI report of April 1961.[14]

Like his associates in organized crime and anti-Castro circles, Ferrie loathed President Kennedy. Questioned by the FBI after Kennedy's death, Ferrie admitted that following the Bay of Pigs invasion, he had "severely criticized" Kennedy both in public and private.[15] Ferrie claimed he had no real murderous intent but "might have used an offhand or colloquial expression, 'He ought to be shot.' "[16] Ferrie also admitted that he had said anyone could hide in the bushes and shoot the president.[17]

Ferrie's questionable alibi for November 22 and the few days following hardly precludes the possibility that he followed through on his "offhand" remark.[18] Carlos Marcello, attorney G. Wray Gill, Gill's secretary, and FBI agent Regis Kennedy all asserted that Ferrie was in New Orleans attending to Marcello's deportation case at the time of the assassination.[19] But the only one of the four not actually involved in Marcello's case was FBI agent Kennedy—who had been strangely derelict in his assigned surveillance of Marcello,[20] and who had passed on Marcello's preposterous claim that he earned his living as a tomato salesman and real estate investor.[21] Kennedy and Marcello both said that Ferrie was in the courtroom at Marcello's trial at 12:15 p.m. on November 22.[22] But Gill and his secretary said that Ferrie was at Gill's office at that time.[23]

Ferrie told FBI investigators that later in the day, in "celebration" of Marcello's acquittal, Ferrie and two friends decided on the spur of the moment to go "hunting, drinking or driving."[24] "Merely to relax," his story continued, Ferrie, Alvin Beauboeuf and Melvin Coffey then drove several hundred miles all night in a heavy rainstorm to Houston and Galveston, Texas, hoping to go ice-skating and goose-hunting.[25] But Ferrie's alibi was seriously flawed. According to one witness in Texas, the three men did no ice-skating whatsoever.[26] And they would have had a hard time goose-hunting since, according to Ferrie, they brought no guns.[27] Also, a conflict in the records of two hotels placed Ferrie and his friends in both Houston and Galveston during a 12-hour period between November 23 and 24.[28]

Two aspects of Ferrie's assassination weekend whereabouts, however, were incontrovertible and significant. First, Ferrie was in Texas within hours after, if not during, the assassination of President Kennedy. Second, in the same period, Ferrie made several contacts with Marcello and Marcello's attorney, G. Wray Gill. Among these contacts were telephone calls Ferrie placed to Gill from various points in Texas.[29] Ferrie also called the Town and Country Motel, Marcello's headquarters in New Orleans,[30] from one of his stops: the Alamotel in Houston, another Marcello property.[31] Perhaps most interesting, however, were meetings on November 9 and 16 between Ferrie and Marcello at the Mobster's Churchill Farms estate;[32] Ferrie claimed they were there "mapping strategy in connection with Marcello's trial."[33]

The connecting thread to the presentation of Ferrie's alibi was again Carlos Marcello. Alvin Beauboeuf, for one, freely discussed Ferrie with the FBI on November 25, 1963, until asked about their post-assassination travels in Texas.[34] Beauboeuf suddenly refused to say anything more without Gill's counsel.[35] The same day, Beauboeuf was arrested in New Orleans along with Layton Martens,[36] who had been in contact with Ferrie during the Texas trip.[37] When questioned about Ferrie, they refused to talk without the help of another Marcello attorney, Jack Wasserman.[38] Also on November 25, when Ferrie presented himself to New Orleans authorities for questioning about the assassination, he showed up with none other than Gill as his counsel.[39]

Initial police suspicions of Ferrie thus proved to be solidly founded. He had made overtly threatening statements against the president. His alibi for November 22 through November 25 was incongruous, contradictory, and curiously reliant on counsel by attorneys of Carlos Marcello. And Ferrie was closely involved with the Mafia boss during and before this period, meeting him personally on the two Saturdays before the assassination. These contacts were especially significant in light of Ferrie's contacts with another prime assassination suspect.

LEE HARVEY OSWALD

Lee Harvey Oswald, age 24, had moved to Dallas from New Orleans in October 1963 with his wife, Marina, and two daughters.[40] His marksmanship was marginal, and he had no apparent motive to kill President Kennedy.[41] Yet after the Dallas shooting, with remarkable dispatch, Oswald was arrested, proclaimed the lone assassin and then permanently silenced by Jack Ruby's revolver.

This rapid apprehension and judgment fixed Oswald in the public mind as President Kennedy's assassin. But serious problems in the police case against him[42] and evidence of a grassy knoll gunman raise questions as to his role in the events of November 22. Was Oswald set up as a fall guy, as he maintained,[43] possibly recruited to perform some compromising action to link him to the assassination? If he was assigned to fire some shots at the motorcade, did he follow through, or did he back out at the last minute, perceiving the trap that had been laid? Was Oswald a Marxist, as some of his actions suggest,[44] or were his many contacts with anti-Castro elements[45] a better reflection of his political orientation?

These questions are provocative, yet thousands of official documents and scores of independent investigations have failed to yield definitive answers. And a further plunge into the Oswald quagmire is rendered unproductive by hard evidence, in contrast, that definitively reveals the background and assassination involvement of another key player—Jack Ruby. There is one line of evidence concerning Oswald, however, as developed by the House Assassinations Committee, that may shed light on his sponsor in whatever assassination role he played.

The circumstances surrounding an arrest for disturbing the peace provide a hint of the helping hand behind Oswald. On August 9, 1963, Oswald was handing out pro-Castro leaflets in New Orleans for the Fair Play for Cuba Committee.[46] He got into a scuffle with three Cuban exiles, and police intervened, arresting all four men.[47] On the surface, the incident appeared to illustrate Oswald's commitment to Communist causes and his propensity to commit erratic actions to further his beliefs.[48]

Yet two features of Oswald's arrest indicate far different involvements. First, the building at 544 Camp Street, the address on Oswald's pro-Castro leaflets, housed only Cuban activists of the anti-Castro bent — including the Cuban Revolutionary Council, Guy Banister and David Ferrie.[49] Moreover, as the House Assassinations Committee reported, Oswald was associated with quite a few anti-Castro activists in 1963,[50] despite his professed pro-Castro leanings.[51]

The second interesting feature of this arrest was the source of Oswald's assistance in dealing with it. Oswald was bailed out of jail by Emile Bruneau,[52] a liquor store owner, state boxing commissioner and associate of Nofia Pecora,[53] one of Marcello's three most trusted aides.[54] (Pecora was called by Jack Ruby a month before President Kennedy was assassinated, as will be discussed later.) Bruneau was also an associate of another Syndicate deputy of Marcello.[55] And Oswald was visited the night after his arrest by his uncle Charles F. "Dutz" Murret, who questioned him at length and advised him how to resolve it.[56] Murret, a criminal operative in the empire of New Orleans Mafia boss Marcello, had in fact had a lifelong influence on his nephew.[57]

Since his earliest childhood, his natural father having died two months before his birth, Oswald looked upon uncle "Dutz" Murret as a surrogate father.[58] Oswald lived with Murret and Murret's wife, Lillian, until age three and at other periods during his childhood and adolescence.[59] When Oswald and his mother got their own apartment, Oswald visited the Murrets weekly.[60] And Oswald kept in touch with the Murrets during his years in the Marines and the Soviet Union.[61]

When questioned by the Warren Commission in 1964, Murret testified that he kept his distance from his nephew after Lee's return from the Soviet Union.[62] But the record shows that their close contact continued. In April 1963, when Oswald returned to New Orleans, he stayed with the Murrets while scouting out a job and a home for his family.[63] Oswald and his wife Marina saw the Murrets frequently during 1963, during which period Murret loaned money to Oswald, gave him rides and provided him with other assistance.[64] One of these many contacts occurred in July 1963, when Oswald traveled with Charles and Lillian Murret to Mobile, Alabama to visit their son.[65] While in Mobile, Oswald gave a talk about his experiences in Russia.[66] Dutz Murret paid for the trip.[67]

Murret's close contact with Oswald is noteworthy given his status as a long-time and lucrative bookmaker who subscribed to the Marcello-controlled racing wire service.[68] Implicated in FBI files as having operated illegal gambling clubs in New Orleans since the 1940s,[69] Murret worked closely with Sam Saia, a top underworld gambling figure in New Orleans who was close to Carlos Marcello.[70] Several witnesses told the House Assassinations Committee that Murret was probably associated with other New Orleans Mob figures, including Marcello himself.[71] Oswald was familiar with his uncle's criminal activities, discussing them with his wife, Marina, in 1963.[72]

Murret was not Oswald's only point of contact with organized crime. Oswald had grown up on Exchange Alley in New Orleans, a center of notorious underworld joints and Mafia-affiliated gambling operations.[73] His high school was regarded by some "as the alma mater, so to speak, of kids who frequently graduated to various criminal and underworld careers."[74] Furthermore, Marguerite Oswald, Lee's mother, was for many years a close friend of Mobster Sam Termine,[75] who in turn was close to Carlos Marcello.[76] Termine had in fact "spoken of serving as a Marcello chauffeur and bodyguard," the House Assassinations Committee reported, "while he was actually on the State payroll, in the Louisiana State Police"[77] (similar Mob-police affiliations have surfaced frequently in both New Orleans[78] and Chicago[79]). Marguerite Oswald twice refused to provide any specific information about Termine when questioned by the House Assassinations Committee.[80]

These underworld family connections of Oswald, which surfaced in the assistance he received following his August 9 arrest, suggest a different picture than that of the erratic, pro-Marxist loner portrayed in the Warren Report. Also jarring to the latter was the testimony of Sylvia Odio, a wealthy Cuban exile, the most significant of several reports linking Oswald to anti-Castro activity.[81]

Odio told the Warren Commission that two months before President Kennedy was assassinated, three men—two Latins and an American—came to her Dallas home requesting her help in an anti-Castro fundraising campaign. The American was introduced to her as "Leon Oswald." The next day, one of the Latins telephoned Odio to tell her that he was bringing the American into the exile underground. The man told Odio that the American was an ex-Marine and kind of crazy. He also related to her that the American had said that "President Kennedy should have been assassinated after the Bay of Pigs."* Following the assassination, after seeing television footage of Oswald, Odio confirmed that the "Leon Oswald" she had met was in fact the suspected assassin.[83]

The Warren Commission discounted Odio's testimony based on the conflicting and later impeached account of another witness plus inconclusive evidence that Oswald was elsewhere around the date of the meeting she reported.[84] After reinterviewing Odio and conducting an extensive background check on her testimony, however, the House Assassinations Committee concluded that Odio was telling the truth.[85] The Committee noted that Odio's sister, Annie, who was present at the meeting, supported her story and found other circumstances that supported Odio's credibility.[86]

Oswald's accessibility to both organized crime and the anti-Castro movement was represented in his association with assassination suspect David Ferrie. Their acquaintance probably began in the mid-1950s, when Oswald was a cadet in a Louisiana Civil Air Patrol squadron commanded by Captain David Ferrie.[87] Several witnesses confirmed to the House Assassinations Committee that Oswald and Ferrie were in the squadron at the same time;

---

*Anti-Castro activists and Mobsters both became bitter toward President Kennedy after he failed to provide the air support for the invasion that the CIA had promised, as will be discussed in chapter 15. One source recounted for the author the reaction of her old-line Mafia housemate to a television report on the abortive Cuban invasion. On hearing the news, the Mafioso sadly commented to her about President Kennedy: "Girl, he just signed his own death warrant."[82]

one reported that "it is a certainty."[88] Six other witnesses, whom the Committee found "credible and significant,"[89] testified that Ferrie and Oswald were definitely together in Clinton, Louisiana, in early September 1963, less than three months before the assassination.[90]

This early September meeting thus brought together two assassination suspects, David Ferrie and Lee Oswald, who had spoken of a need to assassinate President Kennedy and were accessible to those with the motive to kill him. A third suspect, whose path also crossed New Orleans, was Eugene Hale Brading.

EUGENE HALE BRADING

Both ballistic evidence[91] and witnesses' reports[92] suggest that one bullet fired on November 22 came from a group of three structures facing Dealey Plaza: the Records, Criminal Courts and Dal-Tex buildings. The latter, in particular, was the scene of a Dallas Police search immediately after the fateful shooting on November 22.[93] And the possibility that a gunman had been situated there was suggested by the prompt arrests of two suspects.

One man, wearing a black leather jacket and black gloves, was led out of the building by two policemen.[94] He was then driven off in a police car to the catcalls of the crowd.[95] The police report states only that this man had been in the building "without a good excuse" and had been taken to the Dallas County Sheriff's Office.[96] Incredibly enough, police records contain no further reference to this suspect.[97]

The other man arrested in the Dal-Tex Building shortly after the assassination, in contrast, presented an affluent appearance and a polished alibi.[98] He identified himself as Jim Braden, a 48-year-old Californian in Dallas on oil business.[99] Braden explained his presence in the Dal-Tex Building by relating in some detail how he had gone in to find a public telephone right after President Kennedy was assassinated.[100] Yet according to the Dallas County Sheriff's Office, he was in the building when the president was shot.[101] Braden's identity and address were confirmed by a California driver's license and credit card,[102] and he too was released without fingerprinting or further police investigation.[103]

Braden's assassination-day arrest drew more attention in 1969, however, when the license number he had furnished to police[104] was checked through the California Department of Motor Vehicles.[105] It turned out that "Jim Braden" was a changed name that appeared on a new driver's license requested on September 10, 1963 by a Eugene Hale Brading.[106] In the past, Eugene Brading had in fact used four other aliases.[107] And the need for Brading's many aliases was revealed through an investigation spearheaded by Peter Noyes, the producer of CBS-TV affiliate KNXT in Los Angeles.[108] Among Noyes' sources were federal and local law enforcement agencies,[109] including the Los Angeles Police Department,[110] which had questioned Brading about his presence in Los Angeles — 100 miles from his home — on the night of the Robert Kennedy assassination.[111] Concerned about his possible involvement in both Kennedy assassinations, the Los Angeles Police compiled an extensive report on Brading.[112]

It turned out that Brading's associations ranged from "Mafia and oil contacts" to friendships "with 'far-right' industrialists and political leaders" in the Dallas area, noted Robert Houghton, chief of detectives of the Los Angeles Police.[113] Most conspicuous were Brading's Syndicate ties, such as his close contacts with Mafia bosses Eugene and Clyde Smaldone of Denver.[114] Brading was also an associate of California Mafia executioner James Fratianno, Mobster Harold "Happy" Meltzer, California Mafioso Joe Sica and other underworld figures.[115] And Brading's rap sheet showed 35 arrests,[116] with convictions for burglary, bookmaking and embezzlement.[117] He was on parole for the last offense at the time President Kennedy was shot.[118] As California television producer Noyes summarized, Brading was "a man linked over the years to the Mafia."[119]

Under critical reexamination, the alibi provided by "Jim Braden" for his November 22 arrest proved flimsy. When questioned by the Los Angeles Police Homicide Division in connection with the Robert Kennedy assassination,[120] Brading said he had viewed President Kennedy's motorcade from outside the Federal Parole Building.[121] Adding a touch of specificity, Brading claimed to have noticed a parole officer there, a "Mr. Flowers."[122] Yet Roger Carroll, chief probation officer in Dallas, reported that all employees of the Parole Building had walked over to Harwood

Street to watch the motorcade, since the view from the Parole Building was almost completely obstructed.[123] And Carroll stated that he had no "Mr. Flowers" employed at his office in November 1963 or at any time since then.[124] Also contradicted was Brading's claim that he left Dallas for Houston on the night of November 22: federal parole records do not place him in Houston until four days later.[125]

Interesting, too, were Brading's whereabouts the day before the assassination. When Brading checked in on November 21 with Officer Carroll, as reported in federal parole records,[126] he stated that he "planned to see Lamar Hunt and other oil speculators" while in Dallas.[127] Brading claimed that he never actually saw Lamar Hunt,[128] but confirmed that three business associates did visit Hunt on November 21, 1963.[129] The three were Roger Bauman, Morgan Brown and Duane Nowlin[130]—all with strong underworld ties.[131]

Further information was furnished by Paul Rothermal, a former FBI agent who was chief of security for Hunt Oil in Dallas.[132] Rothermal reported that the company log for November 21 showed a visit to Lamar and Nelson Hunt by Bauman, Brown, Nowlin "and friend."[133] Rothermal said he believed this "friend" was Eugene Brading.[134] This contact was noteworthy given sponsorship by Nelson Hunt and others of a black-bordered ad harshly critical of President Kennedy's policies that appeared in the *Dallas Morning News* on November 22. And Nelson's father, H. L. Hunt, the Dallas oil magnate and extreme right-wing propagandist, was reported to have said at a party before the president's fatal visit, referring to him, that there was "no way left to get these traitors out of our government except by shooting them out."[135]

Brading's travels also brought him into New Orleans and revealed another interesting proximity. During his several trips to that city in the fall of 1963,[136] he used the office of an oil geologist in room 1701 of the Marquette Building, where he received mail.[137] On one occasion, Brading informed parole authorities that he could be contacted at room 1706 of that building.[138] The office of G. Wray Gill, Marcello's attorney, which David Ferrie frequented in the fall of 1963, was room 1707.[139] Yet the activities of Brading, Ferrie and Ferrie's contact Oswald would become obscured by the subsequent machinations of another New Orleans resident.

JIM GARRISON

By the year 1967, the lone-nut theory of the Warren Commission had been trampled to a new low of credibility by an onslaught of independent critical research. A Congressional resolution calling for a reexamination of the Warren Commission findings had been introduced[140] with the support of several prominent Americans.[141] And the American public, which had accepted the lone-assassin hypothesis almost universally in 1963,[142] rejected it by a three-to-two margin in a 1966 Louis Harris poll.[143]

But critical review of the Kennedy case was put on hold in February 1967,[144] following the dramatic announcement of New Orleans District Attorney Jim Garrison that he had uncovered an assassination conspiracy. In the wake of Garrison's sensational allegations, Congressional calls for a new investigation were soon forgotten.[145] And thinking the D.A. had a genuine lead, many leading assassination probers rushed down to New Orleans to jump on his bandwagon.[146]

Through the efforts of these researchers, a good deal of legitimate information was exchanged and disseminated from Garrison's office. Yet as Garrison's case unfolded, his specific accusations became increasingly outlandish and the thrust of his efforts increasingly questionable. Especially bizarre was Garrison's prosecution of Clay Shaw, who became his prime culprit.[147] A retired director of the New Orleans International Trade Mart, Shaw was a soft-spoken liberal who devoted most of his time to restoring homes in the Old French Quarter and writing plays.[148] It took the jury less than an hour to find Shaw innocent of Garrison's extravagant accusations.[149]

As summarized by Walter Sheridan, a former aide to Robert Kennedy who investigated the New Orleans probe for NBC, Garrison's effort was "an enormous fraud," involving "bribery and intimidation of witnesses."[150] The particulars were reported by *Newsweek*,[151] the *New York Times*,[152] *Look* magazine,[153] the *Saturday Evening Post*,[154] an NBC News special,[155] and the book

Counterplot by Edward J. Epstein.[156] The methods, as documented in these sources, included promised or transacted bribes of cash, gifts, an airline job, financing for a private club, heroin and a paid vacation in Florida.[157] Garrison and his aides also resorted to threats of imprisonment and death,[158] a plot to plant evidence in Clay Shaw's home[159] and indoctrination of witnesses to parrot invented charges under the influence of hypnosis and drugs.[160]

Although Garrison made extravagant charges against an assortment of Cuban exiles, CIA agents, Minutemen, White Russians and Nazis,[161] he conspicuously avoided any reference[162] to one prime assassination suspect: the Mafia. For example, in discussing testimony concerning Ruby's anti-Castro activities, which he quoted at length, Garrison described Ruby as a "CIA bagman" and an "employee of the CIA."[163] But Garrison said nothing about Ruby's organized crime involvement.[164] The cited testimony, in contrast, contains not one allusion to the CIA.[165] Yet it is replete with references to the "Mafia" and the "syndicate" in connection with both Ruby's Cuban activities and his night club operations.[166] Amazingly, Garrison also refrained from mentioning[167] the close and portentous ties of his key suspect, David Ferrie, to Mafia boss Carlos Marcello.

But such ties were of little concern to Garrison, who declared on national television that Marcello was a "respectable businessman"[168] and who stated that there was no organized crime in New Orleans.[169] According to Garrison, "people worry about the crime 'syndicate,' but the real danger is the political establishment, power massing against the individual."[170] Skeptical of Garrison's professed ignorance about organized crime, a team of *Life* magazine reporters once asked him about Frank Timphony, a notorious Syndicate figure in Garrison's own district.[171] Garrison claimed never to have heard of him and, carrying the act further, placed a call to an aide in the reporters' presence.[172] The Garrison aide "promptly assured" his boss that Timphony was "one of the biggest bookies in New Orleans."[173]

It became apparent, however, that the district attorney's knowledge of organized crime was quite direct and intimate. Garrison's hand-picked chief investigator during his first years as district attorney was Pershing Gervais,[174] an admitted associate of Carlos

Marcello.[175] Gervais was formerly a New Orleans policeman but was fired after twice stealing the payoff money awaiting distribution to his fellow officers.[176] In 1967, *Life* magazine reported that Garrison had been given free lodging and a $5,000 line of credit on three trips to the Mob-controlled Sands Hotel in Las Vegas.[177] One of Garrison's tabs was personally signed by Marcello lieutenant Mario Marino,[178] who took the Fifth Amendment when questioned about the matter.[179] And in June 1969, as *Life* subsequently reported, Marcello bagman Vic Carona died after suffering a heart attack in Garrison's home during a political meeting.[180]

Throughout his career, Garrison demonstrated his fidelity to his reported friend,[181] Carlos Marcello. This loyalty was exhibited in the early 1960s, when Garrison conducted a cleanup of the Bourbon Street night club district after being elected district attorney as a reform candidate;[182] his raids selectively avoided the clubs controlled by Marcello.[183] From 1965 through 1969, Garrison won just seven cases against Marcello gangsters.[184] Yet he dismissed 84 such cases,[185] including one charge of attempted murder, three of kidnapping and one of manslaughter.[186]

In 1971, Garrison was on the receiving end of an indictment — on the federal charge of accepting $50,000 a year in payoffs to protect illegal gambling.[187] The tax evasion case against Garrison became "airtight," as evaluated by U.S. Attorney G. Gallinghouse,[188] when six of Garrison's codefendants turned state's evidence against him.[189] The jury was presented with first-hand testimony corroborated by IRS agents describing four $1,000 bribes to Garrison and with actual tape recordings of the bribe transactions.[190] But Garrison was acquitted,[191] possibly with the help of reported bribes of $50,000 and $10,000 offered to rig his trial and swipe evidence.[192] The outcome was reminiscent of Marcello's acquittal on a fraud charge on November 22, 1963, after a juror had been offered a $1,000 bribe and the key witness against him set up to be murdered.[193]

Although Garrison, now a judge, vigorously denies any corrupt links to organized crime, his congenial relationship with the Marcello fiefdom has been repeatedly demonstrated in both his conduct and contacts, as reported in several sources.[194] Indeed, as recently as 1987, Garrison was seen dining at La Louisiane restaurant in New Orleans with two of Carlos Marcello's brothers, Sammy and Joe Jr.[195] The latter is allegedly the acting Mafia boss of Louisiana now that Carlos is in jail.

Given Garrison's coziness with the Marcello organization and his strange blindness toward Mob leads in his Kennedy assassination probe, it is reasonable to question his motive in pursuing it. Indeed, the possibility that Garrison deliberately tried to obscure Mafia ties to the case is indicated by his false charges against an Edgar Eugene Bradley of California,[196] described in Los Angeles Police files as "the man Garrison mistook for Eugene Hale Brading."[197] There were enough similarities between Bradley and Brading for Garrison's accusations to confound reports about Brading.[198] But to a professional investigator, the distinction between Bradley, an uninvolved Californian, and Dal-Tex felon Brading was apparent.[199]

A further incident raised the possibility of Mob input into Garrison's Kennedy probe even more sharply. On March 3, 1967, during a campaign by the Mob and Teamsters to spring the latter's former boss, Jimmy Hoffa, from prison,[200] James "Buddy" Gill tried to bribe government witness Edward Partin to invalidate his testimony against Hoffa.[201] Gill, the intermediary in this Mob ploy, had been an administrative assistant and close associate of former Senator Russell Long.[202] Long, in turn, was an old political ally of Garrison[203] who assisted the Marcello-coordinated effort to spring Hoffa.[204]

During Gill's approach to Partin, apparently to apply additional pressure, Gill informed him that Garrison was going to subpoena Partin in his assassination probe.[205] And on June 23, 1967, Baton Rouge Radio Station WJBO broadcast that Partin had been "under investigation by the New Orleans District Attorney's Office in connection with the Kennedy Assassination investigation."[206] The station quoted a Garrison assistant as saying that a man drove Oswald and Ruby during alleged encounters in New Orleans, and that Garrison's office was "checking the possibility it was Partin."[207]

Garrison thus exhibited the same underworld affinity as assassination suspects David Ferrie, Lee Oswald and Eugene Brading. This pattern, combined with precedents for Mob assassination of prominent public figures, ballistic indications of conspiracy and murders of witnesses in the JFK case, raises a natural question: did organized crime have a hand in the Kennedy assassination? An affirmative answer is suggested by specific assassination designs against the Kennedys expressed by three top Mob figures in the summer months of 1962.

Cuba was gone. As long as Kennedy was in the White House there was no chance of getting it back. . . . [Hoffa] was under indictment. Nevada was threatened. From coast to coast their activities were under investigation and harassment as never before. And now even the Indochina [narcotics] connection was coming undone. . . . The question was whether organized crime could survive another five years of the brothers Kennedy.[1]

Robert Sam Anson, television producer and political correspondent

5
The Why and
the Wherewithal

Fundamental to the solution of any crime are two considerations. Who benefited from it? And who had the capability to commit it? In the case of the murder of President Kennedy, as this chapter will show, the Mob fit the bill on both counts. For it was obstructed and incensed by the Kennedy Administration's intensive anticrime crusade. Its thirst for revenge was expressed in invectives against John and Robert Kennedy, recorded by FBI electronic surveillance during 1962 and 1963. It was also evidenced, more ominously, in specific assassination plans and predictions by Mob bosses Carlos Marcello and Santos Trafficante and by their Teamster ally, Jimmy Hoffa. Furthermore, the Mafia had both the traditional proclivity and expertise to resolve its desperate dilemma by murder.

AN ATTORNEY GENERAL FIGHTS CRIME

Early in his political career, as counsel to a Senate committee investigating military procurement, Robert Kennedy learned of the machinations of America's directorate of crime.[2] As Kennedy noted in 1956, the committee discovered that military uniforms were being supplied by "some of the leading East Coast gangsters. . . . We found corruption, violence, extortions permeated all their activities."[3] Later that year, journalist Clark Mollenhoff

75

gave Kennedy a tip on underworld infiltration of the Teamsters — a union of which Kennedy at the outset "had only a vague impression" as "big and tough."[4] This led to the formation of a special Senate committee to investigate such infiltration of labor, chaired by Senator John McClellan, with Robert Kennedy as general counsel.[5] The ensuing series of hearings exposed the Mob's brutalization and plunder of labor unions,[6] sickening an American public that had not yet come to accept such subjugation as normal. Kennedy himself was profoundly affected by his ringside view of these atrocities.[7]

While Robert Kennedy conducted a sustained drive against labor racketeering in the late 1950s,[8] the Mob drew little fire from a fragmented, ineffectual Justice Department[9] and an FBI chief who opposed measures against it.[10] But in 1961, when Kennedy assumed the post of attorney general in his brother's administration, bureaucratic lethargy was shattered. As Victor Navasky noted in *Kennedy Justice*, Robert Kennedy channeled his boundless energy and expertise into a "total commitment to the destruction of the crime syndicates":[11]

> Operating with a direct line to the top, the Organized Crime "whiz kids" [the Justice Department's anti-racketeering section] fanned out across the country and began raiding gambling establishments, closing down bookies' wire services, indicting corrupt mayors and judges, and generally picking off, one by one, the names on the "hit list."[12]

Attorney General Kennedy was personally involved on all fronts. According to former Justice Department official William Geoghegan, Kennedy "got five anti-crime bills moved through the Judiciary Committee so quickly that nobody had a chance to read them."[13] Harry Anslinger, federal commissioner of narcotics in the Kennedy Administration, described the attorney general's performance in the field:

> He traveled over the country, calling special meetings with our agents, exhorting them to nail the big traffickers. . . . He knew the identity of all the big racketeers in any given

district, and in private conference with enforcement officials throughout the country he would go down the line,
name by name, and ask what progress had been made. . . .
He demanded action and got it.[14]

Under Robert Kennedy's leadership, by the year 1963 the size of
the Justice Department's antiracketeering section had quadrupled,[15] the list of Mob targets for prosecution had grown from 40
to more than 2,300,[16] and the rate of convictions against racketeering figures had more than quadrupled.[17]

But Attorney General Kennedy was not satisfied. As he wrote
in the *New York Times Magazine* in October 1963:

> It would be a serious mistake, however, to overestimate the
> progress Federal and local law enforcement has made. . . .
> The job ahead is very large and very difficult. We have yet
> to exploit properly our most powerful asset in the battle
> against the rackets: an aroused, informed, and insistent
> public.[18]

Yet even as Kennedy's words appeared in print, the public outrage required for a final crushing onslaught was being effectively
mobilized. For during the RFK-coordinated Senate rackets hearings that October, a defector from New York's Genovese Mafia
Family, Joseph Valachi, dramatically exposed the Mafia to
Americans on nationwide television:

> Then they called us [new recruits] in one at a time. . . .
> there was a gun and a knife on the table. . . . I repeated
> some words they told me. . . . He [Salvatore Maranzano]
> went on to explain that they lived by the gun and by the
> knife and you die by the gun and by the knife. . . . That is
> what the rules were, of Cosa Nostra. . . . Then he gave me
> a piece of paper, and I was to burn it. . . . This is the way I
> burn if I expose this organization.[19]

There were, in fact, more than a dozen other Mafia members
and associates before and after Valachi who described the organization's inner workings.[20] But Valachi's bold defiance of the Ma-

fia code of silence severely demoralized the Mob.[21] Laced with hundreds of names and corroborated descriptions of dozens of slayings, his week-long, televised testimony stunned the American public.[22] And to pyramid its impact, Attorney General Kennedy pledged during the fall hearings to expand his war on organized crime.[23] According to journalist Robert Anson, Kennedy also "had begun laying plans for a massive, frontal assault" on the Mob's Las Vegas base, involving "all the investigative resources of the federal government, from FBI to IRS."[24]

While the Mafia chafed under the aggressive anticrime program of Robert Kennedy, the root of its problem was his brother, the president. As a senator on the McClellan Committee in the late 1950s,[25] John Kennedy had acquired the same orientation as Robert toward what he called a "nationwide, highly organized, and highly effective internal enemy."[26] And the president gave the drive against organized crime his personal backing,[27] placing it at the top of his domestic priorities.[28] If Attorney General Kennedy were killed, President Kennedy would spare no effort to track down the culprits and continue his brother's work. But if presidential support were severed, Robert Kennedy would effectively become "just another lawyer"—as Jimmy Hoffa gleefully described him on November 24, 1963.[29]

The Mob's exasperation with the Kennedys was bared in FBI wiretaps of 1962 and 1963, which were made public by the House Assassinations Committee in 1978. Buffalo Mafia boss Stefano Magaddino complained, "They know everything under the sun. They know who's back of it, they know Amici [members], they know Capodecina [captains], they know there is a Commission [the Mafia's national governing body]."[30] In a subsequent conversation, he exclaimed, "they should kill the whole [Kennedy] family."[31] Chicago Mafiosi and political front men complained that local operations were virtually shut down, and made inflammatory remarks about the Kennedys.[32] Philadelphia Mafia associate Willie Weisberg raged, "With Kennedy, a guy should take a knife. . . . Somebody should kill the [obscenity]. . . .Somebody's got to get rid of this [obscenity]."[33] And New York Mafioso Michelino Clemente observed, "Bob Kennedy won't stop until he puts us all in jail all over the country."[34] Clemente declared that the situation would not change "until the Commission meets and puts its foot down."[35]

AN ASSASSINATION PLAN BY CARLOS MARCELLO

One particular member of the Mafia National Commission[36] had the power, the jurisdiction and the rabid hatred of the Kennedys to coordinate an assassination contract against the president in Dallas.

As head of the Mafia's "first 'family,'" established in New Orleans in the 1880s,[37] Carlos Marcello is today among the most powerful of the Mafia bosses in the United States.[38] One manifestation of Marcello's stature is the exceptional financial and political success of his three-decade reign[39] in Louisiana. The *Saturday Evening Post* reported in 1964 that the Mafia's annual income in New Orleans "runs to $1,114,000,000, making it by far the State's largest industry."[40] And as reviewed for Congress in 1970 by Aaron Kohn, director of the New Orleans Metropolitan Crime Commission, Marcello's criminal enterprise

> required, and had, corrupt collusion of public officials at every critical level including police, sheriffs, justices of peace, prosecutors, mayors, governors, judges, councilmen, licensing authorities, state legislators and at least one member of Congress.[41]

In short, Marcello "controlled the state of Louisiana," as summarized by *Life* magazine in 1970.[42] Although currently serving a ten-year prison sentence on bribery charges,[43] Carlos still gives orders from jail while his brothers manage the family's criminal empire.

Yet Marcello's influence extends far beyond his home state, earning him the *Wall Street Journal*'s appellation as the "undisputed patriarch of the Cosa Nostra in Louisiana and the nearby Gulf Coast area."[44] Indeed, he has sponsored operations over the years in such diverse locations as California,[45] Las Vegas,[46] Indiana[47] and Cuba.[48] Of particular interest to the assassination case are his close and longstanding ties with underworld figures in Dallas and other areas of Texas.[49] For example, Marcello has had frequent telephone contact with two top-ranking Mafiosi from Dallas: Joseph Civello and Joseph Campisi[50] (both associates of Jack Ruby, as later shown[51]). If an important Mob contract were to be performed in Dallas, the strings would be pulled by regional boss Carlos Marcello.

Before Kennedy became president, Marcello enjoyed the dearth of official interference characteristic of his profession. His only major judicial setback prior to his recent imprisonment occurred in 1930 at age 20, when he was convicted of assault and robbery and sentenced to 9 to 14 years in prison.[52] But in 1935, after serving less than five years of his sentence, he was freed on a pardon by Louisiana Governor O. K. Allen.[53] Over the next several years, Marcello's underworld career was marked by several further offenses for which he was charged but never prosecuted, including sale of narcotics and assault of a policeman with intent to murder.[54] Finally convicted for drug sales in 1938, he settled a $76,830 fine with a $400 payment and served just ten months of a lengthy prison sentence.[55] Although federal deportation proceedings were initiated against him in 1953,[56] and his deportation was later urged by senators Kefauver, Mundt, Curtis and Ervin,[57] Marcello thwarted authorities with endless delaying maneuvers.[58] In the process, he spent a record amount on legal fees for such a case.[59]

But Marcello's free ride came to a halt in 1960, with the election of President Kennedy. Even before the president's inauguration, Attorney General-designate Robert Kennedy targeted the Mafia overlord of Louisiana for special attention by the Justice Department.[60] And just three months after President Kennedy assumed office, under Robert's instructions, Marcello was arrested, handcuffed, and summarily flown to Guatemala, pursuant to a longstanding order to deport him.[61] When the enraged Mafia boss[62] illegally reentered the United States and had his lawyers challenge the order, the Kennedy Justice Department greeted him with federal indictments on charges of fraud, perjury and illegal reentry.[63] In addition, following Robert Kennedy's guidelines, the FBI intensified its scrutiny of Marcello.[64]

In November 1963, Marcello was cleared of the fraud charge,[65] after a trial marred by alleged jury tampering and a plot to murder a key prosecution witness.[66] His acquittal was announced just three hours after the event that spelled his ultimate freedom from the law: the assassination of President Kennedy.[67] And the following report provides an initial clue that this, too, was within the sphere of Marcello's murderous machinations. The information was first disclosed in *The Grim Reapers*, published in 1969, by Ed Reid, a Pulitzer Prize-winning author and former newspaper editor.[68] The source was Edward Becker, a businessman and sometime private investigator. Becker confirmed Reid's report and provided additional information in a 1978 interview with the House Assassinations Committee.[69]

In September of 1962, Becker and an associate, Carl Roppolo, met with Marcello to seek financing for an oil additive product they were planning to market.[70] The meeting was arranged without difficulty because of Roppolo's close relationship with Marcello.[71] The site of the gathering was an elegantly furnished office in a farmhouse on Churchill Farms, Marcello's 3,000-acre plantation outside New Orleans.[72] As author Reid recounted, the conversation began with underworld pleasantries, the talk becoming relaxed and familiar as the Scotch flowed. But Carlos' mood changed when the government's drive against organized crime was brought up and Robert Kennedy's name mentioned:

> "*Livarsi na petra di la scarpa*" Carlos shrilled the Mafia cry of revenge: "Take the stone out of my shoe!"
>
> "Don't worry about that little Bobby son of a bitch," he shouted. "He's going to be taken care of!"[73]

Becker told the House Assassinations Committee that Marcello had been very angry and had "clearly stated that he was going to arrange to have President Kennedy murdered in some way."[74] Marcello explained his intentions with an analogy comparing President Kennedy to a dog and Attorney General Kennedy to its tail.[75] "The dog will keep biting you if you only cut off its tail," Marcello observed, but the dog would die if its head were cut off.[76] Marcello also offered a less allegorical rationale for the choice of victim, as reported in an FBI synopsis of a 1967 interview with Reid:

They could not kill Bobby because the President would use the Army and the Marines to get them. The result of killing the President would cause Bobby to lose his power as Attorney General because of the new President.[77]

Becker told the House Assassinations Committee that Marcello's plan to murder President Kennedy appeared serious and deliberate.[78] Marcello had even alluded to the manner in which he intended to carry out the contract.[79] According to Becker, Marcello indicated that an outsider would be used or manipulated to do the job, so that his own lieutenants would not be linked to the crime.[80]

Although Becker was disturbed by Marcello's words, he did not believe Marcello would be able to follow through on his plan, and had grown accustomed to underworld figures making such vituperative remarks about their adversaries.[81] But after the assassination, as the House Assassinations Committee paraphrased, Becker

quickly came to believe that Carlos Marcello had in fact probably been behind it. He reached this opinion because of factors such as Lee Oswald having been from New Orleans, as well as Jack Ruby's alleged underworld associations. Becker stated that "it was generally thought in mob circles that Ruby was a tool of some mob group." Becker further stated that he had learned after the assassination that "Oswald's uncle, who used to run some bar, had been a part of the gambling network overseen by Marcello. He worked for the mob in New Orleans."[82]

When questioned by the House Assassinations Committee on January 11, 1978, Marcello denied that the meeting or discussion reported by Becker had ever occurred.[83] But two points Marcello advanced in support of his denial were particularly unconvincing. First, in conflict with his own expressed feelings[84] and information from other sources,[85] Marcello claimed he had not been terribly concerned about Robert Kennedy's anticrime stance until his April 1961 deportation and that he did not hold a grudge against Robert Kennedy.[86] Second, Marcello testified that he used his Churchill Farms estate only for hunting and not for meetings.[87] This second assertion was directly contradicted by Marcello associate David Ferrie, who told the FBI that he had met there with Marcello on November 9 and 16, 1963 to map "strategy in connection with Marcello's trial."[88]

Notwithstanding the Mobster's denial, Becker's account of Marcello's intention to murder President Kennedy rang true. Becker reiterated to the House Assassinations Committee: "It was [truthful] then and it is now. I was there."[89] Author Ed Reid told the Committee that he believed that Becker was credible and trustworthy and that he had previously furnished "unusually reliable" information about organized crime.[90] Independent sources confirmed that Becker went to New Orleans in September 1962[91] and that Becker's associate Carl Roppolo was close to Carlos Marcello.[92] Also significant were the statements of Julian Blodgett, a former FBI agent and chief investigator for the district attorney of Los Angeles County, for whom Becker did investigative work in the early 1960s.[93] Blodgett told the House Assassinations Committee that Becker was honest and one of "the most knowledgeable detail men" in the private investigative business.[94] Blodgett said he would believe Becker's account of the Marcello meeting.[95]

AN ASSASSINATION PREDICTION BY SANTOS TRAFFICANTE

If Carlos Marcello had exhorted the Mafia National Commission to arrange the murder of President Kennedy, an eager second might well have come from Tampa Mafia boss Santos Trafficante, Jr.

Like his very close associate[96] Marcello, Trafficante was, until his death in 1987, a longstanding Mafia power[97] with influence extending into the Bahamas and the Caribbean.[98] Trafficante's Mob stature was highlighted by his presence at two Mafia meetings in New York State: the 1957 convention at Apalachin[99] and the 1966 mini-conclave at La Stella Restaurant in Queens.[100] Indicative of their close relationship, Trafficante sat at Marcello's left at the latter gathering of 13 top Mafia figures.[101]

Trafficante had been the leading figure in the Mob's Cuban

gambling empire during the 1950s.[102] Following Castro's shut-down of Mob rackets, as will be discussed, Trafficante became a principal in Mafia-CIA assassination attempts on the Cuban premier.[103] Trafficante was also a key figure in worldwide narcotics operations[104]—a preoccupation that may explain his visit in 1968 to Singapore, Hong Kong and South Vietnam.[105] The Florida Mafia boss could thus hardly have favored two foreign policy initiatives of President Kennedy in the fall of 1963: moves toward accommodation with Castro and the ordered withdrawal of one thousand American troops from South Vietnam, an underworld narcotics stronghold.[106] But Trafficante was hurt closer to home by the Kennedy Administration's anticrime crusade, as he expressed in an obscene diatribe recorded by an FBI bug in 1963.[107]

In its 1979 report, the House Assassinations Committee noted Mafia boss Trafficante's predisposition to participate in a murder contract against President Kennedy:

> Santos Trafficante's stature in the national syndicate of organized crime, notably the violent narcotics trade, and his role as the mob's chief liaison to criminal figures within the Cuban exile community, provided him with the capability of formulating an assassination conspiracy against President Kennedy. . . . In testimony before the committee, Trafficante admitted participating in the unsuccessful CIA conspiracy to assassinate Castro, an admission indicating his willingness to participate in political murder.[108]

One incident carried these suspicions beyond the realm of conjecture.

In September 1962, while an inebriated Carlos Marcello outlined a presidential assassination contract at Churchill Farms, Trafficante spouted injudicious remarks of his own at the Scott Byron Motel in Miami Beach.[109] Trafficante expressed them during a meeting with José Aleman, Jr., a wealthy Cuban exile, about a $1.5 million Teamster loan.[110] According to Aleman, as reported by the *Washington Post* in 1976, the subject turned to John and his brother Robert Kennedy, at which point Trafficante became quite bitter:

Have you seen how his brother is hitting Hoffa, a man who is a worker, who is not a millionaire, a friend of the blue collars? He doesn't know that this kind of encounter is very delicate. Mark my words, this man Kennedy is in trouble, and he will get what is coming to him.[111]

When Aleman suggested that Kennedy would probably get reelected, Trafficante replied, "No, José, he is going to be hit."[112]

Aleman said that he reported this and subsequent conversations with Trafficante to FBI agents[113] and was questioned closely by the FBI about this threat shortly after the assassination.[114] According to the *Washington Post*, two of the agents named by Aleman, George Davis and Paul Scranton, "acknowledge their frequent contacts with Aleman but both declined to comment on Aleman's conversation with Trafficante."[115] Scranton explained he required clearance to furnish such comment and "wouldn't want to do anything to embarrass the Bureau."[116]

Trafficante was summoned before the House Assassinations Committee on March 16, 1977 and asked if he had known or discussed information that President Kennedy would be assassinated.[117] The Mafia boss declined to answer, citing his Constitutional right to avoid self-incrimination.[118] He likewise remained silent when asked if he had visited Jack Ruby in Cuba.[119] "There was considerable evidence," the Committee reported, that such an encounter "did take place" in 1959.[120] When Trafficante was subsequently granted immunity and recalled to testify, he admitted meeting with Aleman to discuss a Teamster loan but denied ever predicting President Kennedy's murder.[121]

Aleman was questioned under oath by the Committee on September 27, 1978, and he described his conversation with Trafficante exactly as the *Washington Post* had reported.[122] In particular, Aleman repeated Trafficante's menacing words about President Kennedy, including the phrase "he is going to be hit."[123] Expressing pronounced fear of reprisal from Trafficante,[124] however, Aleman professed he had interpreted this remark to mean Kennedy would be hit "with a lot of votes from the Republican Party or something like that."[125]

Yet in two previous interviews with Committee staff members, Aleman said that he had clearly understood this phrase and additional statements by Trafficante to indicate that the president would be murdered before the 1964 election.[126] As one staff interviewer paraphrased, Aleman reported that Trafficante "was not guessing about the killing; rather he was giving the impression that he knew Kennedy was going to be killed."[127] Aleman also told a staff interviewer that he gathered "that Hoffa was to be principally involved in the elimination of Kennedy."[128]

ASSASSINATION PLOTS BY JIMMY HOFFA

To be sure, if any Mafia associate had been inclined to assist an assassination contract against President Kennedy, it would have been the late Teamster boss James Riddle Hoffa.

Hoffa had been a close ally of the Mob since he courted it to gain control of the Teamsters[129]—turning the union into a "mob subsidiary"[130] and its Central States Pension Fund into a Mob grab bag.[131] In particular, Hoffa was exceptionally close to both Carlos Marcello and Santos Trafficante,[132] each instrumental in a massive Mob campaign attempting to keep the Teamster boss out of jail.[133] Along with Marcello, Trafficante and Chicago Mafia boss Sam Giancana, Hoffa was a principal target of Robert Kennedy's campaign against organized crime.[134] And Hoffa made no effort to conceal his loathing of both John and Robert Kennedy.[135] For example, on November 22, 1963, Hoffa flew into a rage and became abusive when notified that Teamster headquarters had been closed in President Kennedy's memory.[136]

Hoffa had expressed similar vitriolic sentiments about the Kennedys to a trusted lieutenant, Edward Partin.[137] A tough Teamster official from Louisiana, Partin had been a Hoffa confidant since 1957.[138] The Teamster boss had believed Partin to be a man of proper loyalties, as Partin later explained: "Hoffa always just assumed that since I was from Louisiana I was in Marcello's hip pocket."[139] But in the summer of 1962, when Hoffa's remarks about Robert Kennedy escalated from diatribes to proposed murder plots, Partin was shocked into becoming a government informant.[140] He became a highly productive source, furnishing details of conversations with Hoffa and aides that were repeatedly corroborated.[141] Partin also demonstrated his credibility by passing an FBI polygraph test on his account of the Kennedy murder plot "with flying colors."[142]

Partin told federal officials that Hoffa first spoke to him of killing Robert Kennedy in July or August 1962, when Partin was in Hoffa's Washington office.[143] Hoffa asked Partin if he knew anything about plastic explosives and mentioned throwing a bomb in Kennedy's car or home.[144] Hoffa explained to Partin, "I've got to do something about that son of a bitch Bobby Kennedy. He's got to go."[145] Hoffa also mentioned that he knew where to get a silencer for a gun.[146] In a subsequent telephone conversation between Hoffa and Partin, which was taped by federal officials, Hoffa asked Partin to bring plastic explosives to Nashville;[147] Hoffa was on trial there for allegedly receiving hundreds of thousands of dollars in payoffs from a trucking firm.[148]

A second murder plan that Hoffa discussed with Partin was strikingly similar to the one carried out against President Kennedy. As the House Assassinations Committee summarized, Hoffa proposed "the possible use of a lone gunman equipped with a rifle with a telescopic sight. . . . an assassin without any identifiable connection to the Teamster organization or Hoffa himself."[149] He spoke of "the advisability of having the assassination committed somewhere in the South," where extreme segregationists could be blamed.[150] And Hoffa noted "the potential desirability of having Robert Kennedy shot while riding in a convertible."[151]

Partin told the House Assassinations Committee, as it paraphrased, that "Hoffa had believed that having the Attorney General murdered would be the most effective way of ending the Federal Government's intensive investigation of the Teamsters and organized crime."[152] Yet as Hoffa's close friend[153] Carlos Marcello noted soon afterward in September 1962,[154] the assassination of the president was a more logical step. And Partin found it possible that one Kennedy assassination plan by Hoffa could have developed into another.[155] Partin noted that Hoffa "hated Jack as much as Bobby. . . . After all, he was the man who'd always been in charge of Bobby."[156] Hoffa would "fly off" when the name of President Kennedy "was even mentioned."[157]

Both the FBI and the House Assassinations Committee concluded that Partin had been truthful in reporting Hoffa's assassination plots against Robert Kennedy.[158] Indeed, as the

Committee reported, "the Justice Department developed further evidence supporting Partin's disclosures, indicating that Hoffa had spoken about the possibility of assassinating the president's brother on more than one occasion."[159] And author Steven Brill reported that Hoffa's top aide, Harold Gibbons, had overheard Hoffa discuss the possibility of having Robert Kennedy murdered.[160]

AN ACHILLES HEEL

While sparked by the Kennedys' anti-crime crusade, the assassination designs of Marcello, Trafficante and Hoffa were also partially grounded in a tragic personal vulnerability of the president. Whether out of fear of government retribution or an underlying moral dynamic, the Mob characteristically reserves lethal revenge for those whom it has first compromised in some way. As noted by G. Robert Blakey and Richard Billings in *The Plot to Kill the President*, "You are all right, it is said, just as long as you do not 'sleep with them,' that is, you do not take favors, either money or sex."[161]

One crack in this moral line for JFK was the widely rumored involvement of family patriarch Joseph Kennedy in bootlegging during the Prohibition era.[162] Another was Mob help for John Kennedy in the 1960 presidential contest. On election night, the presidential aspirant called Chicago Mayor Richard J. Daley, who told him that "with a bit of luck and the help of a few close friends, you're going to carry Illinois," a state crucial to victory. Sure enough, Kennedy did carry Illinois, after eleventh-hour vote stealing in Cook County wards by the Mob-dominated "West Side Bloc."[163] Said Mobster Mickey Cohen: "Certain people in the Chicago organization knew that they had to get John Kennedy in. . . . John Kennedy was the best of the selection. But nobody in my line of work had an idea that he was going to name Bobby Kennedy attorney general."[164]

These two underworld interactions involved neither wrongdoing nor a personal Mob connection on President Kennedy's part. But a third association, an affair with the concurrent mistress of a Mobster, was far more serious. It was this dalliance that removed Kennedy from his presidential pedestal in the Mob's perception, as Blakey and Billings postulate, enabling them to deal with him as one of their own.

Young and divorced, a coiffed glamor girl with silver screen aspirations, Judith Campbell met Kennedy in February 1960, while he was still a senator and she was romantically involved with Frank Sinatra.[165] Sinatra, an associate of several Mobsters, introduced Campbell to Kennedy, beginning a two-year affair between them that would include multiple meetings across the country.[166] Evidence of their liaison included a $2,000 check from Kennedy to Campbell and White House phone records of some seventy calls to or from Campbell between 1960 and 1962.[167] At the same time, Campbell was in close contact with at least three prominent underworld figures: John Roselli, Sam Giancana and Giancana business partner Paul "Skinny" D'Amato.[168] By her own admission, she carried on a simultaneous affair with Giancana for the last six months of her involvement with Kennedy.[169]

The end of the Kennedy-Campbell tryst came in March 1962, following a four-month FBI investigation of phone records showing Campbell's calls to Kennedy's secretary at the White House.[170] In March 1962, FBI Director J. Edgar Hoover and Kennedy had lunch; two hours after that, Kennedy placed his last call to Campbell.[171] The following summer, Kennedy cooled his associations with Sinatra. This dashed the singer's hopes that Kennedy would use the helicopter pad and extra wing Sinatra had built at his Palm Springs home for the president's use.[172] "I can't stay there . . . while Bobby's handling [the Giancana] investigation," Kennedy told brother-in-law Peter Lawford.[173]

Although Kennedy terminated the Campbell affair, Blakey and Billings note, "From the mob's point of view, Kennedy had been compromised. He had crossed the line. In the Greek sense, the liaison with Judith Campbell was, we came to believe, Kennedy's fatal flaw."[174]

MASTERS OF MURDER

After President Kennedy dropped his friendships with Judith Campbell and Frank Sinatra, the Mob realized that any hopes of accommodation were doomed. Pushed to desperation and fury by the Kennedys' anticrime crusade, the Mob saw even more drastic federal action against it portended by the televised Valachi hearings of October 1963. On November 22, 1963, however, its problem was suddenly solved—solved by an assassination that had been outlined or predicted within three months in 1962 by Marcello, Trafficante and Hoffa, all intimate associates. The Mob's abundant capability to have performed the murder is demonstrated by its century-long record of slaughter, which continues to this day.

While it is generally believed that every Mafia member is required at some time to kill,[175] the height of the art is cultivated by salaried hit squads maintained by each of the families.[176] Whether the victim is to be strangled and left in the city dump as an example,[177] punctured through the ear with an ice pick to mimic a natural cerebral hemorrhage,[178] smashed in the face with a baseball bat for effect,[179] shot and robbed at home to appear as "street crime"[180] or gunned down at a public rally,[181] the Mafia has hundreds of professionals with the expertise to carry it off smoothly.[182] Whether the victim is a cooperative witness,[183] a Mobster out of line,[184] a radio announcer,[185] a reporter,[186] a policeman,[187] a labor leader[188] or an exiled South American democrat,[189] the Mafia can devise a plan to eliminate the victim with the finest killers and weapons available.[190]

Although local talent is usually abundant, Mafia bosses often handle important contracts with the best of the national field.[191] As New England Mafia defector Vincent Teresa reported,

> The idea of importing gunmen from other mobs isn't new. Anastasia used to send out assassins all over the country [from the infamous "Murder, Inc."] to handle hits for other mobs. Today, every mob has its own assassination squads who are available for lend-lease assignments. Whether you go to Chicago, New York, Montreal, Newark or Boston, they have assassination squads made up of men who get a regular weekly salary just to be ready for the day a hit is needed.[192]

Teresa named both killers and victims in three slayings in which hit men from other families were used, exemplifying this nationwide murder network.[193] He also mentioned one instance in which assassins from his Mafia family were sent to New Orleans to handle a contract for Carlos Marcello; Teresa did not know who the targeted victim was.[194]

As *Look*'s Washington bureau chief, Warren Rogers, wrote in 1969,

> If it was a conspiracy that killed President Kennedy . . . the Cosa Nostra should have been a prime suspect. The Mafia *is* a conspiracy, and it had the organization, the assassination know-how, the skilled manpower and a motive.[195] [Emphasis in original.]

As the House Assassinations Committee phrased it, Marcello, Trafficante, Hoffa and the Mob as a whole "had the motive, opportunity and means" to carry out the November 22 assassination.[196] A televised execution two days later brought this possibility beyond the realm of conjecture.

PART II

Mob
Fixer
in
Dallas

The compelling suspicion that the Mafia killed President Kennedy is borne out through an extraordinary source: a detailed record of the background and activities of a Mobster involved in the crime. The Mobster is Jack Ruby; the record is the National Archives file generated by an extensive FBI investigation into Oswald's murder. This file contains thousands of documents, which include a bewildering mass of details. Yet when significant information is extracted, accounts of witnesses cross-checked and names cross-referenced with organized crime sources, this voluminous file documents Mob culpability in the assassination.

The Ruby material will be unraveled in three steps. This part, focusing on his activities before 1963, establishes that he was a long-time Mafia functionary. The next part examines the period between November 22 and 24; it proves that Ruby shot Oswald not on impulse, but as part of a carefully coordinated conspiracy. After a three-chapter interlude to provide further background, Part V then goes back to April 23, 1963, when President Kennedy's visit to Dallas was first announced. It considers a dramatically intensifying series of telephone calls and meetings between Ruby and many Mobsters from across the country—including several associates of Marcello, Trafficante and Hoffa. It unmasks a concertedly fabricated alibi with which these Mobsters covered these contacts, conspiracy in its own right. And it links this timely series of Mob contacts to the assassination of President Kennedy.

It is important to understand, however, that Ruby was by no means a dominant figure in the assassination conspiracy. Rather, his role emerges like that of a plant foreman or a stage manager. His qualification for the final act of this role, the spectacular execution of Oswald, was his special position in the Syndicate. For Ruby was not so notoriously linked to the Mafia to have made its assassination involvement obvious. Yet he was close enough to have been expected to have kept its code of silence—without the help of yet another execution.

But in the last analysis, this balance of proximity collapsed on both counts. For under post-assassination scrutiny, Ruby's Mob ties were exposed. And by the time of his final official hearings, Ruby had neither the criminal loyalty nor the callousness to maintain his silence about the horrible act in which he had conspired.

To put Ruby's ties to the Mafia in perspective, a brief characterization of this criminal organization is provided here from testimony before the House Assassinations Committee. It was presented by Ralph Salerno, retired organized crime expert of the New York City Police Department, whom the *New York Times* credited with "the reputation of knowing more about the Mafia than any other nonmember."[1]

There is a national conspiratorial criminal organization within the United States whose members refer to as La Cosa Nostra. The organization is made up of groups known to the members as families. The families are headed by a leader who is referred to as a boss or the Italian word capo is used. The families have a second in command, executive officer to the leader, who is referred to as the underboss, and they use the Italian word sottocapo.

The families have a position known as counselor, or they use the Italian word consigliere, who is considered to be an adviser and who is available to all of the members of the family.

The family has within it subunits, known originally as Decina. . . . The subunits are headed by a person with a title of caporegime, or the head of the regime. This position is often referred to in the anglicized word captain. The individual members of the family are referred to as members, soldiers, or as a made man or as a button man.

The families are governed in matters of import of policy and in matters arising between families by the national commission whose numbers can vary, which is made up of the leaders of the major families. Those families whose leaders do not serve on the commission may have their interests represented by a commission member.

Other terms for the organization or its individual families, often used by outsiders, are the Mafia, the organization, the clique, the boys, the office, the arm.

There are rules which are known to members, though not written anywhere. They use relatives and friends as couriers. . . . They have elaborate systems of prearranged times and telephone numbers in order to communicate with each other and to thus avoid electronic surveillance.

They engage in political activity to an inordinate degree. They make direct political contributions. They engage in fundraising in obtaining contributions from others for political purposes. . . .

They will hold elective and appointive positions at all levels of government. They will help relatives achieve elected and/or appointed positions at all levels of government. They will try to influence the outcome of government decisions. They will lobby in favor of legislation they consider in their best interests. . . .

They will campaign against candidates considered to be inimical to their best interests. They will assassinate other family leaders in order to replace them. They will employ public relations efforts, such as protesting Italian defamation, when the term Mafia or La Cosa Nostra are ever used.

They will make illegal deals with high and lower level labor leaders. They will get finders fees for arranging union loans. They will get percentages for helping someone obtain Government loans.

They will operate an intelligence-gathering capability. . . . They will intimidate or kill informants and witnesses. They will fake illnesses, and once even a kidnapping, in order to avoid legal process. They will utilize bribery as a tactic. They will utilize other forms of corruption. They will engage in blackmail. They will try to influence media stories.[2]

The Mafia's incursion into America was reported by a New Orleans grand jury in 1890: "the existence of a secret organization known as the Mafia has been established beyond doubt."[3] Since then, its "existence, structure, activities, personnel," to quote a government report of 1972, "have been confirmed and reconfirmed beyond rational dispute."[4] As detailed in numerous government hearings and court proceedings, its structure and workings have been penetrated by these sources: 1) the testimony of dozens of Mafia defectors; 2) tape-recorded conversations of Mafiosi in operation, obtained through electronic surveillance; 3) a pattern of thousands of convictions, indictments and arrests involving associated individuals and related crimes; and 4) police busts of national Mafia conclaves.[5] When provided the opportunity to refute the findings so derived, Mafia members have repeatedly declined by invoking their Fifth Amendment right to avoid self-incrimination.[6]

To clarify the terminology used in this volume, the word "Mafia" denotes the specific criminal organization characterized above by Salerno. The words "Mob" and "Syndicate" refer to a larger conglomeration composed of the Mafia plus thousands of underlings and other criminals from assorted ethnic groups who function as semi-autonomous satellites. Since the Mafia works closely with these underlings and satellites, however, the distinction between "Mafia" and "Mob" applies mainly to the underworld status of individuals, not to criminal operations. For variety, or to describe criminal activity without clear Mafia affiliation, looser terms such as "organized crime," "underworld" and "gangster" are used with their usual connotations.

A final comment is in order concerning the Italian origins of the Mafia — as noted above by Ralph Salerno, himself of Italian descent. The Mafia is an aberration that victimized those of its own extraction before migrating to other domains. The preposterous notion that its frank discussion slights Italians has been promoted almost exclusively by Mafia members themselves.[7]

Jack Ruby . . . would be important in history even without the events in Dallas because of his relation to the history of organized crime in Chicago.[1]

Peter Dale Scott, University of California, Berkeley

6
Molding
of a Mobster

Jack Ruby's involvement with the Mob dates back to his earliest years in Chicago. The story of how it was forged provides both background for the assassination case and insight into the workings of organized crime in America. Moreover, it is an engrossing personal drama, which builds to a poignant climax in Ruby's final testimony before the Warren Commission.

JUVENILE DELINQUENCY AND
UNDERWORLD INTRODUCTIONS

Jack Rubenstein was born to Joseph and Fanny Rubenstein in 1911 in a poor Jewish neighborhood in Chicago.[2] During his youth, he lived with his family in several apartments in similar areas, generally near Italian neighborhoods.[3] Then, in 1923, because of his "bad behavior" and family problems, he was placed in a foster home by a Chicago juvenile court and spent the next four or five years in foster homes.[4] Without the influence of a stable family, young Ruby was predictably attracted to the glamorous Prohibition riches of the gangsters rather than to hypocritical canons of law enforcement in the corrupt Capone era.

Ruby's induction into Mob circles began under a prominent mentor. Boxer Barney Ross, a friend of Ruby,[5] told the FBI that in 1926 he associated with a group of about twelve youths, among whom was Jack Ruby."[6] Ross said that members of this group became acquainted with Al Capone, who would give them a dollar "to run innocuous errands."[7] Ross told the FBI that

99

Ruby "might have run innocuous errands for Capone."[8]

Ruby's association with this young band of Capone minions continued for several years,[9] leading to further criminal associations. Three sources reported that around 1940, Ruby belonged to the South Side "Dave Miller Gang," headed by Chicago boxing referee Dave Miller.[10] The Warren Commission touched on this early affiliation of Ruby, reporting his disruption of pro-Nazi Bund meetings with other Miller gang members.[11] But it failed to point out that Miller was a notorious gambling boss[12] with a long police record.[13]

Dave Miller's gym, where Ruby hung out and boxer Barney Ross trained,[14] was a place to observe and associate with still more important racketeers. Indeed, fans of Ross included Ralph Capone, Matty Capone, Murray Humphreys, Frank Nitti, Sam Hunt and Tony Capezio[15] — all notorious Capone gang members. Another Ross follower was Al Capone himself,[16] who would buy up all the tickets to some early Ross fights, allowing other fans free admission.[17]

Ruby also hung out at the Sherman Hotel Lobby and the Gym Club.[18] A friend of his told the FBI that Ruby would "accept or make bets amongst the group of individuals who used to frequent both locations."[19] The old Gym Club crowd, according to the same friend, "currently hangs around the H&H Restaurant located on North La Salle Street";[20] the H&H was described in a contemporaneous FBI report as "a known hangout for Chicago bookmakers, gamblers, juice men, and petty hoodlums."[21] The manager of the H&H Restaurant, Maish Baer,[22] who knew Ruby,[23] was identified by a U.S. Senate committee as a nonmember associate of the Chicago branch of the Mafia.[24] (Baer was murdered in 1977 after he "allegedly failed to heed a suggestion that he stop competing with the mob in the loan shark business."[25])

Ruby rapidly acquired the precepts of his peers, as indicated by his arrest at age 19 for selling pirated music sheets.[26] He was sentenced to 30 days in jail because, according to Ruby, he "wouldn't tell the judge who was behind the business."[27] And his budding criminal character was unblemished by any steady employment.[28] An old friend related that "Ruby seemed to be always well off financially, and former friends often wondered where he obtained his income."[29]

In 1933, a lean year for the Chicago Mob with the repeal of Prohibition, Ruby and some neighborhood buddies headed to the Santa Anita Race Track in Los Angeles.[30] This race track was described in testimony before the Kefauver Committee as a meeting place for Mobsters.[31] After a few months at Santa Anita, Ruby moved on to San Francisco.[32] There he worked for "gambler"[33] Frank Goldstein[34] and spent time with a racketeer associate from Chicago,[35] Solly Schulman.[36]

UNION OFFICIAL

Ruby returned to Chicago in 1937, and until 1940 he was active in Local 20467 of the Scrap Iron and Junk Handlers Union.[37] Initially, Ruby organized and collected dues;[38] eventually, he became a top union official.[39] A fellow boss of Local 20467, Paul Dorfman, told the FBI he believed "Ruby was never a salaried employee of the union but probably drew some expense money from collected dues."[40] Dorfman also reported that there was approximately six cents left in the treasury when he took charge in 1940.[41]

Ruby maintained that he worked for the union because he "always wanted to be a humanitarian."[42] Yet he was as qualified to have been a labor leader as his brother Hyman — once declared an "incorrigible" delinquent by a Chicago juvenile court[43] — was to have worked for Governor Horner and obtained a political patronage job.[44] A more credible explanation for Ruby's labor involvement was furnished by Paul Roland Jones, a Mobster[45] and long-time acquaintance of his.[46] Jones told the FBI he "knew that the syndicate had an interest in this union and presumed this was Ruby's connection."[47] Indeed, during Ruby's tenure in the local, the State of Illinois seized its books on the grounds that it was a "front for organized crime."[48] The AFL-CIO arrived at the same assessment, deeming it "largely a shakedown operation,"[49] and the *Chicago Tribune* cited its criminal ties.[50] Jones also told the FBI that Ruby "was accepted and to a certain extent his business operations [were] controlled by the syndicate."[51]

On December 8, 1939, the founder of Local 20467,[52] Leon

Cooke, was fatally shot, under circumstances described in conflicting accounts.[53] According to a friend of Ruby, Cooke was the son of a scrap iron dealer who wanted to help the workers, and was "a very high type of individual."[54] Ruby's sister Eva Grant testified that Cooke "was a highly reputable lawyer. That's why they killed him."[55]

Immediately after the shooting, the local was taken over by Paul Dorfman, the Chicago Mob's notorious trade-union liaison,[56] who brought the local into the Teamsters.[57] A subsequent Senate investigation termed the Local 20467 leadership a "link between Mr. Hoffa and the underworld," and attributed to it incidents of graft, beatings and killings.[58] Dorfman invoked the Fifth Amendment when questioned by Senator McClellan about his position and function in the local.[59]

Ruby's role in the Mob takeover of Local 20467 was illuminated in union minutes two months after Dorfman became its head: his name appeared right after Dorfman's on an apparently hierarchical list of local officials.[60] And Ruby retained his leadership position until the AFL temporarily took control.[61] Furthermore, the possibility that Ruby was involved in the killing itself is raised by a Chicago Police homicide report. The report states that Ruby was arrested on the day of the Cooke shooting, and "was held at the Police Station in the investigation."[62] The assumption that Ruby was held as a suspect is supported by a remark of Ruby's acquaintance Lenny Patrick, that "Rubenstein had been involved in the investigation into the murder of Leon Cooke but had been cleared."[63] Yet the Chicago homicide report strangely failed to record either the disposition of Ruby's arrest or the outcome of the murder investigation,[64]* casting doubt on the assertion that Ruby was cleared.

Nor was Ruby convincingly absolved by a story, related by both himself[68] and Paul Dorfman,[69] that union official John Martin shot Cooke in an argument. Although the Warren Com-

---

*The disappearance of criminal records and reports on Mobsters from Chicago Police files has been a common occurrence. Chicago journalist Ovid Demaris cited several such instances[65] and related that at one time Chicago policemen did not even bother to make a written report on a racketeer "because if they did it would be stolen from the files and sold to the hood within an hour."[66] Similar flagrant gaps and misinformation on Mobsters in the police files of several other cities have been reported.[67]

mission reported this story as fact,[70] it cited in support only the account of a *Chicago Tribune* employee describing an article that allegedly pegged Martin as the killer.[71] This article, however, was apparently neither produced nor excerpted by the Commission.[72] And the report of the *Tribune* employee reveals that the source of the article was Ruby![73]

Thus with no credible exculpation of Ruby, the one person whose arrest was reported in connection with the Cooke homicide,[74] the following account must be given serious consideration. It was related by David Byron, an industrial manager and a neighborhood acquaintance of Ruby in Chicago.[75] Byron told the FBI he remembered reading in a Chicago newspaper that Ruby had been

> president of some "Junk Dealers' Union" in Chicago. . . . A shooting occurred and Rubenstein was charged with killing a man. He was arrested, convicted and sentenced in Chicago on this charge and served in prison . . . for "a little over a year."[76]

RACKETEERING IN THE CHICAGO NIGHT CLUB DISTRICT

After leaving Local 20467, Ruby became involved in several sales ventures, interspersed with long stretches of unemployment.[77] Between 1941 and 1943, Ruby and relatives reported, he sold everything from punchboards to novelties to miscellaneous items such as salt and pepper shakers.[78] The true nature of these ventures, however, was illuminated by Ruby's acquaintance Paul Roland Jones. Jones told the FBI that he had once given the name of a large bootlegging customer in Oklahoma to Hyman Rubenstein, Jack's brother.[79] Jones said that Hyman then shipped whiskey to the customer from Chicago, "in cases labeled to indicate they were *salt and pepper shakers*."[80]* And representative of Ruby's associates in such operations was Ben Epstein, a

---

*An italicized phrase denotes author's emphasis, unless a specific note to the contrary follows the phrase in question.

bookmaker until his retirement in 1951,[81] who was involved in a "business venture" with Ruby in the 1930s.[82]

But these ventures were merely supplemental to Ruby's operations in Chicago strip joints, which have been Mob-controlled for decades.* One report of Ruby's operations there came from John Cairns, who operated a jukebox route in Chicago from 1942 to 1947.[85] His route included McGovern's bar, described by the FBI as a "bar and bookmaking establishment that was frequented by gamblers and hoodlums"[86] and characterized by the Illinois Crime Commission as a notorious criminal establishment.[87] Cairns told the FBI that he often saw a Jack Rubenstein at that bar and later recognized him from news photos as Oswald's killer.[88] Cairns stated that Rubenstein "was well known to others frequenting McGovern's and it was rumored that he was also a connection for narcotics traffic in the area."[89] Cairns said he had learned in addition that Ruby "had an interest" or was "employed in some managerial capacity" in a strip joint on North Clark Street.[90]

Edward Morris, Jr., another Chicago resident, told the FBI that Ruby ran the Torch Club on Walton and Clark Streets in Chicago in the early 1950s.[91] Morris identified Ruby by photograph and recollected that his name was Rubenstein "or similar."[92] Jack Kelly, who had sporadic contacts with Ruby through the 1940s and 1950s, reported that Ruby sold combination gambling tickets for horse racing in 1945 or 1946 at the Gaity Club.[93] Robert Lee Shorman, who knew Ruby in Dallas, said that Ruby told him he had worked floating crap games in the Chicago area,[94] confirming Ruby's illegal gambling involvement. Also interesting was the report of Maish Baer, a Chicago Mafia nonmember associate,[95] that he and Ruby had been "hustlers" in the Maxwell Street Market area during the late 1940s.[96]

Because Ruby was identified in these reports through acquaintances or from photographs, as well as by name, quite perplexing

---

*A federal report issued shortly before 1969 stated, "The criminal element is in complete control of many establishments serving liquor to patrons and all the cabarets featuring strip tease entertainment in the [six] main Chicago night life areas."[83] In fact, the *Chicago Daily News*, which ran a series of Mob exposés in 1964, called special attention to one Chicago night club that it discovered was *not* outfit-sponsored.[84]

were claims that he was being confused with another man: "Harry Rubenstein."[97] This "Harry Rubenstein," not Jack, was active in the Chicago night club district in the 1940s, according to Club 19 manager Leo Denet.[98] The same was reported by Nate Zuckerman,[99] an employee of James Allegretti,[100] whom the FBI described as a "top local organized crime figure."[101] This story was also presented, with great conviction, by Frank Loverde, described by federal sources as a Chicago Mafia member "active in the management of strip shows in Chicago's north side."[102] Loverde insisted that Ruby was not connected with organized crime in Chicago.[103] He further "indicated that he believed the [FBI] agents were questioning him in the mistaken belief that the Oswald killing had some organized crime overtones."[104] He advised that many people in Chicago confused Ruby with Harry Rubenstein, whom Loverde claimed had killed a man in 1946, was run out of Chicago and was believed to have gone to Texas.[105] Loverde declined to furnish any particulars about Harry Rubenstein to the FBI.[106]

But it appeared that Loverde was confused, for the only Harry Rubenstein who turned up for the FBI said that he resided continuously in Chicago from 1925 to 1963, and had never been to Texas.[107] This Harry Rubenstein listed several night clubs he had run or owned, but mentioned neither the Torch Club, the Gaity Club nor McGovern's[108] — three bars where Ruby was reported to have operated.[109] And any possibility of mistaken identity was precluded by further reports of Ruby's activity in the Chicago night club district by three additional persons who knew him.[110] Thus the man described by several witnesses as a gambler, night club operator and rumored narcotics connection in this Mob-controlled domain was unmistakably Jack Ruby.

Although Ruby's military service between 1943 and 1946[111] provided a respite from Chicago night club operations, it did not entirely disrupt his life style. The corporal of Ruby's training unit was Hershey Colvin, who "considered himself Ruby's closest associate during the training period" and who often traveled with Ruby to New Orleans on weekends.[112] Colvin was described by Ruby's brother Hyman as a "professional gambler" who dealt cards or ran a crap table and "maybe booked horses."[113] Consistent with this assessment, Colvin was employed at the hoodlum-owned[114] Vertigo Key Club in Chicago when interviewed by the FBI on November 26, 1963.[115] A further indication of Ruby's interests was provided by his fellow soldier Urban Roschek. Roschek told the FBI that Ruby informed him that "after the war, he could get Roschek a job picking up numbers in Chicago, and Roschek could make about $200 a week."[116]

THE FINE REPORTS OF "RUBY'S CHICAGO FRIENDS"

The details of Ruby's early underworld involvements take on special significance in light of an utterly fantastic conclusion advanced by the Warren Commission. In its review of Ruby's Chicago background, the Commission reported, "There is no evidence that he ever participated in organized criminal activity."[117] And not to put the lie to its own assertion, the Commission omitted mention of almost all of the evidence in its own files presented in this chapter.[118]

But Ruby's Chicago underworld ties could not be concealed by mere omission, since they had been too well reported (e.g., an article of November 26, 1963 in the *New York Times*, entitled "Ruby Linked to Chicago Gangs; Boasted of Knowing Hoodlums"). So the Commission fashioned a specific denial of such ties, based solely on the following observations:

> Virtually all of Ruby's Chicago friends stated he had no close connection with organized crime. In addition, unreliable as their reports may be, several known Chicago criminals have denied any such liaison.[119]

Of course, it is ludicrous to expect that such men as Chicago Mafiosi John Capone,[120] James Allegretti[121] and Frank Loverde[122] would reveal any of Ruby's Mob connections if they knew of them, and predictably they did not.[123] But the Commission's first sentence, concerning "Ruby's Chicago friends," seems persuasive—until the 11 documents cited in the supporting footnote are examined and cross-checked against other sources.

For one of these "Chicago friends" turns out to be Lenny Patrick, who absolved Ruby of sinister involvements by telling the FBI, "No matter how much you investigate, you'll never learn nothing, as he [Ruby] had nothing to do with nothing."[124] It so happens that Lenny Patrick is a notorious Syndicate killer,[125] identified in a U.S. Senate report as a Chieago Mafia nonmember associate.[126] He was described in a source on organized crime as a reputed "expert on gangland executions," credited by police with "masterminding some of the Syndicate's more important liquidations."[127] A second cited friend "admits knowing Lenny Patrick."[128] A third was a bookmaker;[129] a fourth, a gambler and employee of a hoodlum-owned bar;[130] a fifth, a Chicago bar owner from the gang that ran errands for Al Capone;[131] a sixth, a partner with Ruby in the sale of gambling devices.[132] Needless to say, the unmentioned backgrounds of Mob killer Patrick and others of "Ruby's Chicago friends" puts the Commission's denial of Ruby's underworld connections in drastically different light.

The Commission exhibited an equally grotesque disregard for the evidence in a similar claim it advanced about Ruby's underworld ties in Dallas: "Numerous persons have reported that Ruby was not connected with [organized criminal] activity."[133] One of this group of "numerous persons" turns out to be Joseph Campisi,[134] a leading Dallas Mafia figure.[135] Another is Roy Pike,[136] alias Mickey Ryan,[137] a close contact of Ruby during the fall of 1963,[138] whose alibi for November 22 was suspicious.[139] A third such person is union official Irwin Mazzei.[140] That Mazzei is used as a reference is incredible, for the only portion of his cited FBI interview relevant to Ruby's underworld connections was his comment that he

knew nothing of his [Ruby's] background, hoodlum or gambling connections or Police Department connections, other than those mentioned by Ruby. Ruby had mentioned that he had connections with the "Syndicate" and labor in Chicago and used to work for the "Syndicate" in Chicago.[141]

It is indeed bizarre that the Warren Commission represented Mazzei as absolving Ruby of underworld ties, when Mazzei merely confirmed the extensive evidence of Ruby's such ties as a young man in Chicago. Yet Chicago racketeering was but a training arena for Ruby's Syndicate career, which was launched in earnest with the Mob's plunge to plunder the rich frontiers of the American West.

The rats had become bloated and all-powerful rodents, rulers of an invisible empire whose boundless billions surpassed those of Detroit's motor industry. This enormous wealth . . . gave the rodents in charcoal suits the resources to buy New York skyscrapers; to gain control of brokerage houses and banks; to muscle into competition in major industries, hotels and motels, steel and oil, vending machines and race tracks, dress factories and meat-packing plants.

Wherever they went, the rulers of this nether world carried with them the taint of their money and the contamination of their tactics. A proprietor didn't want their vending machines? Wreck his joint and teach him a lesson. A union was causing trouble? Buy off its business agent or murder him. A bank wasn't returning a Shylock's profit? Substitute phony paper for its good securities—loot the till and bankrupt it. Meat prices were high? Well horses come cheap; so do dead and diseased cows. . . .

These things have happened, do happen, are happening.[1]

Fred Cook, journalist

7
The Move to Dallas

While Texas has long been a haven for racketeering,[2] Dallas boasts particular notoriety.[3] From the 1930s to the mid-1940s, according to expert testimony before the Kefauver Committee, "all forms of gambling, including policy [numbers racketeering], flourished in Dallas."[4] And in 1946, when Steve Guthrie was elected sheriff of Dallas County, the city "was 'wide open' with prostitution and gambling and other vices running full steam."[5] These activities were punctuated by "an average of 2 or 3 murders a month which looked like murders by gangs."[6]

The Chicago branch of the Mafia decided that it was time to bring these lucrative rackets within its more disciplined clutches, as the Mob had already done in its westward expansion to such cities as St. Louis,[7] Detroit[8] and Kansas City.[9] An unusually detailed account of this invasion of Dallas was given to the Kefauver[10] and McClellan[11] committees by Dallas Police Lieutenant George Butler.

According to Butler, in 1946 the "boys from Chicago came in, looked the situation over, and decided that they wanted to take over not only Dallas but the whole State of Texas and the Southwest."[12] About 20 Chicago Mobsters came down, including hoodlums Danny Lardino, Paul Labriola, James Weinberg, Martin Ochs, Marcus Lipsky and Paul Roland Jones, bankrolled by top-ranking Chicago Mafioso Pat Manno.[13] While Lipsky wanted to "kill the four top gamblers in the Dallas area . . . and let everybody know how tough he was,"[14] Jones deemed it wiser to make a deal with the officials.[15] Jones' approach prevailed, and he entered into negotiations with newly elected Sheriff Guthrie and Lt. Butler, who were secretly reporting to the Dallas police chief and taping the conversations.[16]

Jones offered Sheriff Guthrie a substantial cut of the profits in exchange for completely protected gambling operations, including bookmaking, slot machines and card and dice games.[17] As Jones later told the FBI, "the substance of the arrangements made was simply that the syndicate group would run the County and the Sheriff was to take their orders and that the syndicate group would provide sufficient people to handle the operations."[18] The Mob was also eager to gain a foothold in its drive to take over the unions.[19] In particular, Butler testified, it aimed to "unionize every truck driver in the Nation," so it could *bring industry to its knees, and even the Government.*"[20]

During the bribery negotiations, Jones told Guthrie that his cut could add up to $150,000 a year or more.[21] And when the next election came around, Jones promised, the Mob would "buy off all competition and pay all of his campaign expenses."[22] In addition, they would furnish letters praising Guthrie from important people throughout the nation.[23]* Jones indicated that the Syndicate, which operated "from coast to coast and in Canada and Spain,"[25] already had this arrangement in St. Louis, Kansas City, New Orleans, Little Rock and several other cities.[26] When

---

*By the 1950s, Michael Dorman wrote in *Payoff*, "the racketeers dominated the election machinery in many parts of Texas. Even more than the oilmen and the giant construction companies looking for public works contracts, the racketeers served as financiers of political campaigns. They decided long in advance of elections whom they would run for office. Their money, influence, and other assets determined who would win various positions from the top to the bottom of the ticket."[24]

Guthrie and Butler asked Jones if they could "meet some of these people that he had been bragging about,"[27] Jones brought down Pat Manno—reputed fifth-ranking Chicago Mafioso at the time[28]—whose conversation with Jones, Butler and Guthrie was recorded.[29]

A "SMALL TIME PEANUT" WITH THE CHICAGO MOB

Jack Ruby, too, went from Chicago to Dallas in 1947, after an earlier visit.[30] If Ruby had been "run out of Chicago by the Mob," as several associates reported,[31] he certainly found himself in good company in Dallas. Sheriff Guthrie told the FBI, as it summarized, that at the time of the bribery negotiations,

> there were approximately 25 "thugs" and hoodlums from Chicago in Dallas from time to time. . . . Jack Ruby at that time was a "small time peanut" with this group who were going to bribe Guthrie. Ruby's name came up on numerous occasions . . . as being the person who would take over a very fabulous restaurant at Industrial and Commerce Streets in Dallas. . . . the upper floor would be used for gambling. . . . Ruby's name constantly came up as being the person who would run the restaurant.[32]

Guthrie stated, "if the records can still be heard, Ruby's name will be heard on numerous occasions."[33]

The Warren Commission dismissed Guthrie's report of Ruby's involvement, claiming that "22 recordings of the conversations between Guthrie, Butler, and Jones fail to mention Ruby."[34] But the Commission's claim was based merely on "incomplete transcriptions of the recordings," and the recordings were "almost completely inaudible," the House Assassinations Committee later clarified.[35] The Commission also neglected to note that the FBI agent who reviewed these incomplete transcriptions found one of the recordings inexplicably missing.[36]

Sheriff Guthrie's description of Ruby's association with the Chicago Mob group was in fact corroborated by others, including *Chicago Daily News* reporter Jack Wilner. Wilner stated his

" 'syndicate sources' reflect that Ruby was reportedly involved in 1947 with Nick St. John [Nick DeJohn] Paul Labriola, Marcus Lipsky and Paul Roland Jones in [an] effort to take over gambling in the Dallas, Texas area."[37] All of these cited associates of Ruby were linked to the Dallas Mob incursion in Butler's Senate testimony.[38] Confirmation from another Chicago source was reported by Milton Viorst in *The Washingtonian*:

> Louis Kutner, a Chicago attorney who had worked for the Kefauver Crime Committee, said Ruby had appeared before Kefauver's staff in 1950, and in the course of subsequent investigation it was learned that Ruby was a syndicate lieutenant who had been sent to Dallas to serve as a liaison for Chicago mobsters.[39]

Giles Miller, a Dallas businessman who knew Ruby well, provided further insight into Ruby's move to Dallas:

> Jack Ruby would sit at the table where I was seated and discuss how he was sent down here by "them"—he always referred to "them"—meaning the syndicate in Chicago. He always complained that if he had to be exiled, why couldn't he have been exiled to California or Florida?[40]

Although the Mob's attempt to bribe Sheriff Guthrie backfired, its conquest of Dallas proceeded as planned. According to Lt. Butler's testimony before the McClellan Committee, the Chicago gang "took over coin machine and amusement companies in Texas, Louisiana and Arkansas,"[41] including slot machine, pinball machine and jukebox routes.[42] By 1957, as a U.S. Senate committee reported, Dallas was graced with its own Mafia boss, Joseph F. Civello,[43] who represented the city at the famous Mafia convention in Apalachin, New York.[44] And by 1967, Dallas rated inclusion in a federal report as one of 25 centers of Mafia activity in the United States.[45]

SETTLING IN DALLAS

Ruby established permanent residence in Dallas in the latter part of 1947[46] and officially changed his name from Jack Rubenstein to Jack Leon Ruby on December 30 of that year.[47] His first business venture there was the Silver Spur Club at 1717 South Ervay, of which he was manager and part owner for several years.[48] Lt. Butler described this club as a hangout during the late 1940s of Paul Roland Jones and other Chicago Mobsters involved in the Dallas bribe attempt.[49] In a medical interview after his arrest, Ruby himself said of the Silver Spur,

> You had to know this place to know what went on. You could get exonerated for murder easier than you could for burglary.[50]

In 1952, Ruby and two associates purchased the Bob Wills Ranch House on Corinth and Industrial Streets.[51] After a short stay in Chicago later that year, Ruby returned to Dallas and secured an interest in the Vegas Club at 3508 Oaklawn.[52] He also managed the Ervay Theater and Hernando's Hideaway, and became a distributor for pizza crusts and medicine within the next few years.[53]

One element of Ruby's "magic touch" in his business acquisitions was manifested in his takeover of the Vegas Club. Irving Alkana, the club's previous owner, told the FBI that Ruby purchased a one-third interest in it from him in the early 1950s.[54] Then, in April or May 1954, Alkana related, Ruby attacked and beat him during an argument over finances.[55] Describing this or a similar altercation with Alkana, Ruby remarked: "They had me for assault to murder."[56] Alkana related that two months after this beating, he sold his remaining two-thirds interest to Ruby and later left Dallas.[57] Assisting Ruby in the takeover and operation of the Vegas Club was Joseph Locurto, alias Joe Bonds,[58] a thug with six arrests in three states.[59]

Although Ruby's other ventures were temporary, he retained ownership of the Vegas Club through November 1963.[60] But in 1959, its management was assumed by his sister Eva Grant[61] when Ruby and business partner Joe Slatin established the Sovereign Club, a plush private club at 1312½ Commerce Street.[62] In 1960, the Sovereign was converted into the Carousel Club, a public club serving beer, champagne, setups for drinks and pizza, and featuring striptease shows.[63] Jack Ruby and his associate

Ralph Paul assumed ownership of the Carousel Club,[64] and Ruby operated it from its opening until the assassination.[65]

While these and similar ventures[66] provided Ruby a front and base of operations, the focus of his life, as in Chicago, lay in a different realm.

For at least the past half-century, organized crime was permitted to establish octopus-like tentacles throughout this nation and its communities. It is now identified as our biggest industry in dollar volume. Through violence, corruption and deception the underworld established itself as a conglomerate industry and grew to proportions which now influence every aspect of American life: our mores, our economy, our political system, government processes and competitive free enterprise.[1]

Aaron Kohn, director of the New Orleans Metropolitan Crime Commission

8
Jack Ruby's Criminal Activities

Jack Ruby's occupational pursuits in Dallas encompassed three standard underworld arenas: illegal gambling, narcotics and prostitution. In conjunction with his close Mafia ties and corrupt police encroachments, as discussed in subsequent chapters, these endeavors solidly establish his Mob credentials. Most significant is Ruby's participation in the first, illegal gambling, the Mob's leading money maker since the repeal of Prohibition, which it has come to control in most major cities in the United States.[2]

GAMBLING

In April 1959, the Dallas Police received a list of 15 names, including Ruby's, found on the person of Dallas gambler Sidney Seidband.[3] The police described 12 as known gamblers and two as known associates of gamblers;[4] Ruby's was the only name not so identified.[5] His mention there was not anomalous given the following three accounts of his illegal gambling operations.

William Abadie was sought out by FBI agents and questioned in Los Angeles on December 6, 1963.[6] The agents told him that they "wanted to interview him concerning his knowledge and

115

associations with Jack Leon Ruby, of Dallas, Texas."[7] Relieved to learn he was not being nabbed for jumping bail on a drunken driving charge, Abadie advised them that "he hardly knew Ruby and was entirely willing to discuss anything concerning Ruby."[8]

Abadie told the FBI that beginning in March 1963, he "was hired by Ruby's shop foreman as a slot machine and juke box mechanic" for a period of about seven weeks.[9] He stated that while performing his duties as a mechanic, he "did see Ruby in the warehouse shop,"[10] adding that "on one occasion for a few days he 'wrote tickets' as a bookie in one of Ruby's establishments."[11] When asked about Ruby's political affiliations, Abadie volunteered that Ruby and his gambling employees were all "anti-integrationists" who "would not allow Negroes to place bets,"[12] hardly unusual for that region and period.

Abadie said that while working in Ruby's warehouse, he gathered "it was obvious that to operate gambling in the manner that he did, that he must have racketeering connections with other individuals in the City of Dallas, as well as Fort Worth, Texas."[13] This opinion "applied also to police connections with the two cities."[14] And Abadie reported that "while he was making book for Ruby's establishment, he did observe police officers in and out of the gambling establishment on occasion."[15]

The FBI report of Abadie's interview spans five consecutive pages of Commission Document 86 in the National Archives.[16] Yet the version published in the Warren Commission Hearings and Exhibits, Commission Exhibit 1750, contains only four pages. The first page of this report, which describes Abadie's employment in Ruby's slot machine warehouse and bookmaking establishment, is missing.[17] This omission is most curious, particularly since the unpublished first page lists Abadie's full name, his address and other important matters of record[18] routinely included in published exhibits.

Jack Hardee, an inmate at the Mobile County Jail in Alabama, provided further information on Ruby's gambling operations. Interviewed by the FBI on December 26, 1963,[19] Hardee told agents that "approximately one year ago, while in Dallas, Texas, he attempted to set up a numbers game, and he was advised . . . that in order to operate in Dallas it was necessary to have the clearance of Jack Ruby."[20] He was also told that "Ruby had the 'fix' with the county authorities."[21] Hardee is a credible witness, since other particulars he furnished concerning Ruby were corroborated.[22]

Harry Hall, whom the Secret Service judged a reliable witness,[23] told Secret Service and FBI agents that in the early 1950s he was involved in a scheme to bilk rich Texans through high-stake bets.[24] The report of his interview states that

> Ruby on occasion provided Hall with a bankroll and introduced him to likely victims, with Ruby taking 40% of any deal. . . . because he was supposed to have influence with the police, so that [Hall] would have no worry about any gambling arrest.[25]

Hall related that one of these victims, from whom they won a large sum of money on football bets, was Texas billionaire H. L. Hunt.[26] Hunt had in fact patronized an illegal gambling casino and had been swindled in gambling deals, other sources reported,[27] lending credibility to this assertion. Hall also reported that while on a trip with Ruby, they passed through Tulsa, Oklahoma, and Shreveport, Louisiana, and he observed that "Ruby seemed to have good connections in gambling circles" in these cities.[28]

NARCOTICS

Another important facet of Ruby's underworld career was his narcotics dealings. According to an atypically informative Warren Commission memo, in 1947, Jack Ruby "became the subject of a narcotics investigation along with his brother, Hyman, and Paul Roland Jones."[29] Ruby was in fact interrogated by federal narcotics agents that year in connection with this case, as summarized in an official report which lists "Mafia" as a related file.[30] Ruby was not prosecuted,[31] however, although Jones was convicted of flying 60 pounds of opium over the Mexican border.[32] But when Ruby again came to the attention of federal authorities a decade later, there was little doubt that he was participating in a major narcotics operation.

On March 20, 1956, the FBI filed a report of an interview with Eileen Curry, an informant for the FBI and the Los Angeles

Police.[33] Curry told the FBI that about the first of the year she moved to Dallas with her boyfriend, James Breen, after they had jumped bond on narcotics charges.[34] While in Dallas, she related, Breen told Curry that he had "made connection with a large narcotics setup operating between Mexico, Texas, and the East."[35] Curry reported in that FBI interview, filed seven years before the assassination, that "in some fashion James got the okay to operate through Jack Ruby of Dallas."[36]

In an FBI interview after Ruby killed Oswald, Eileen Curry confirmed her 1956 account and elaborated on Ruby's operation.[37] She related to the FBI that early in 1956 she saw Ruby drive up to her apartment on Gaston Boulevard in Dallas, pick up her boyfriend, James Breen, and depart.[38] Later that day, when Breen returned, he told her that "he had accompanied Ruby to an unnamed location, where he had been shown moving pictures of various border guards" plus narcotics agents and contacts on the Mexican side.[39] She said that "Breen was enthused over what he considered an extremely efficient operation in connection with narcotics traffic."[40] Curry had seen Ruby several times at her apartment and at Ruby's club and recognized him as Oswald's killer from news photos;[41] there was no question of identification.

Eileen Curry's two detailed and consistent accounts to the FBI describing Ruby's narcotics involvement are difficult to discount. Moreover, they square with the earlier indications of such involvement by Ruby[42] and with close contacts between Ruby and narcotics trafficker Joseph Civello, soon to be discussed.[43] Yet, as in Ruby's gambling operations, the important feature of his narcotics dealings is his level of function—a controlling role in a "large narcotics setup operating between Mexico, Texas and the East."[44] Just as Ruby was described by Abadie, Hardee and Hall as supervising or granting clearance for bookmaking, numbers and other gambling ventures, so he was cited by Curry as the person who approved James Breen's narcotics dealings in Dallas.

PROSTITUTION AND OTHER CRIMINAL ACTIVITIES

Also fitting the underworld mold were prostitution and other criminal activities run by Ruby. Former Dallas County Sheriff

Steve Guthrie told the FBI that he believed "Ruby [had] operated some prostitution activities and other vices in his club since Ruby had been in Dallas."[45] Jack Hardee, who knew Ruby in 1962, reported that "Ruby hustled the strippers and other girls who worked in his club," setting up dates for them and taking half the earnings.[46] This arrangement explained a transaction involving Chicago businessman Larry Meyers and Carousel stripper Joy Dale; Meyers got to know Dale and then made out a check for $200 to Jack Ruby, half of which Ruby paid to Dale.[47]

Restaurant operator Carl Maynard informed the FBI that one of his waitresses, who had once worked at the Carousel, told him "all girls employed did fill $100 a night dates after work."[48] Maynard believed that Ruby "got a percentage of prostitution dates."[49] Joe Bonds, a close associate and business partner of Ruby in the early 1950s, told the FBI that Ruby would "make women available" to Dallas police officers.[50] And Kenneth Dowe, a Dallas disc jockey, testified that Ruby "was known around the station for procuring women for different people who came to town."[51]

Ruby used his time at the Carousel Club, his base of operations, to pursue other criminal sidelines. Jack Marcus, a Chicago attorney, spoke with Ruby at the Tropicana Night Club in Havana in 1959.[52] Marcus told the FBI that Ruby "indicated he had 'everything' at the night club [the Carousel] including gambling."[53] Other witnesses reported that Ruby operated a number of criminal activities out of the Carousel Club, including the distribution of stolen razor blades[54] and pornography,[55] both of which are lucrative Mob rackets.[56]*

---

*One curious feature of the relatively few specific reports of Ruby's criminal activities is the location of their sources. William Abadie was interviewed in Los Angeles,[57] Jack Hardee in Mobile, Alabama,[58] Harry Hall in Los Angeles,[59] Eileen Curry in Los Angeles[60] and Chicago,[61] and Carl Maynard in Burbank, California.[62] Virtually all other witnesses who provided such specifics also lived far from Dallas when they were interviewed.[63] This strange lack of information from Dallas is comparable to the consistent denial of Ruby's underworld involvement by Chicago Mobsters.[64] It suggests that an edict of silence may have been issued throughout the Dallas underworld and underworld fringe circles—the most likely source of information on Ruby's criminal activity. The frightened behavior and perjury of Ruby's Dallas associates, as examined later,[65] supports this possibility.

Of course, Ruby's most infamous criminal exploit was murder. And as will be shown later, the killing of Oswald, like Ruby's other activities, was Mafia-directed.

So much is being written and filmed and spoken today that glamorizes the Mob. This is a gross misrepresentation of what these people are really like. They are the scum of the earth.[1]

Mob defector Patsy Lepera, testifying in 1973
before a U.S. Senate committee

9
Jack Ruby's
Underworld Contacts

Complementing Jack Ruby's criminal activities was an extraordinary collection of associations with notorious underworld figures from across the nation. Some, such as Paul Roland Jones, Dallas Mafia boss Joseph Civello and versatile Mob "gambler and murderer" Lewis McWillie, maintained longstanding ties with Ruby. But others, including several associates of Marcello, Trafficante and Hoffa, were in touch with Ruby only during a brief period: the seven months between the first report of President Kennedy's visit to Dallas and his assassination.

Discussed below are the backgrounds and links with Ruby of 16 of his most significant underworld and Teamster contacts (seven more are covered in Appendix 1). These associations of Ruby are considered here to demonstrate his overall involvement with organized crime; contacts in the pre-assassination period, to be covered in depth later, are only summarized at this point. In the course of establishing Ruby's Mob affiliation, however, this chapter also profiles the Mob's infiltration into various spheres of American enterprise—from unions to gambling casinos, from Medicare clinics to the U.S. Senate. Many of the Mobsters listed are still active.

A close associate of Jimmy Hoffa,[2] **Barney Baker** worked as a Teamster "organizer" under Hoffa's direct orders[3] until jailed on a federal racketeering conviction in 1961.[4]

Baker started out in the late 1930s and early 1940s as a strong-arm man for a racketeering outfit on the New York City water-front.[5] During this period he was wounded in one gangland-style execution,[6] was questioned about another,[7] and at one point was on the lam himself for a dock murder.[8] After a stretch in the mid-1940s as doorman for Mobsters Jake Lansky and Mert Wertheimer at the Colonial Inn in Florida,[9] and a stint with Bugsy Siegel in Las Vegas,[10] Baker had the necessary background for a leadership role in the Teamsters. In 1952 he was "elected" president of Teamsters Local 730[11] and soon became organizer for the Central States Conference.[12]

Baker functioned in the Teamsters as "a versatile labor goon,"[13] or as Robert Kennedy phrased it, one of Hoffa's "roving emissaries of violence."[14] The FBI identified him as "a reported muscle and bagman for Teamster President James Riddle Hoffa."[15] And the House Assassinations Committee described him as a "hoodlum with organized crime and Teamsters connections."[16] Baker maintained close and frequent contacts with notorious Mobsters throughout the country.[17]

Contacts with Ruby. On November 7, 1963, Baker called Ruby from Chicago;[18] Ruby called Baker the next day.[19] The name "Barney," with three of Baker's phone numbers, was found in one of Ruby's notebooks.[20]

Joseph Campisi is identified in Drug Enforcement Administration files as a member of organized crime,[21] and is linked to organized crime in several other sources.[22] He is by all indications a top-ranking Dallas Mafia member. Illustrating his standing in the Mafia hierarchy is his close friendship with Joseph Civello,[23] the former Mafia boss of Dallas, who represented the city at the 1957 Mafia convention at Apalachin, New York.[24] According to one FBI informant, Campisi was slated to take over Civello's position.[25] Complementing Campisi's associations with Civello and other Dallas crime figures[26] are his reported close contacts with state judges and Dallas law enforcement officials.[27]

Although Campisi has been connected with illegal gambling for years, he was arrested only once, in 1944, for murder;[28] Campisi pleaded self-defense, and no indictment was pressed.[29] His business operations have included promotion of Las Vegas gambling junkets and partnership in an insurance firm.[30] He has also run the Egyptian Lounge, a Dallas restaurant and bar, since the late 1950s; his brother Sam was a partner until Sam's death in 1970.[31] That establishment was so notorious as a Dallas underworld hangout, according to one Dallas intelligence officer, that you could not go in "without getting your picture taken by the FBI."[32]

Yet Campisi has attracted most attention from law enforcement officials through his very close friendship with the Marcellos of Louisiana. Campisi often visited Carlos Marcello and four brothers of Carlos who are reportedly also Mafia-involved.[33] In addition, telephone records show calls between Marcello-tied enterprises in New Orleans and Campisi's Egyptian Lounge in Dallas[34] and between Campisi and Carlos Marcello himself.[35] The Campisi-Marcello relationship was reported by intelligence agencies in Texas and Louisiana,[36] and was confirmed by Campisi.[37]

Contacts with Ruby. Joseph Campisi was described by Ruby's sister Eva Grant as a close friend of Ruby.[38] Ruby's roommate, George Senator, named "a Mr. Campisi, who operates the Egyptian Lounge" as one of Ruby's three closest friends.[39] But Campisi had difficulty presenting a consistent account of his relationship with Ruby. On December 6, 1963, Campisi told the FBI he had known Ruby casually since 1948, but "never associated with him. . . . never socialized with him" and knew "nothing of Ruby's background or associates."[40] But in 1978, Campisi provided the House Assassinations Committee with a rather detailed description of Ruby's background and associates,[41] and reported that he had once invited Ruby home for a barbecue.[42] Campisi also gave conflicting accounts concerning a large sum of cash found on Ruby when Ruby shot Oswald.[43]

In December 1963, Campisi told the FBI that he had visited Ruby on November 30, 1963 in the Dallas County Jail,[44] as confirmed by police records.[45] During the same FBI interview, Campisi reported that his "last contact with Ruby" prior to then occurred on the night before the assassination, "when Ruby came to the Egyptian Restaurant for a steak."[46] In 1978, however, Campisi once again reversed himself and denied this assassination-eve contact.[47]

Frank Caracci was identified in a 1970 Judiciary Committee hearing as a "Cosa Nostra involved" gambler and strip joint operator.[48] *Life* magazine described him as a "Marcello Mobster,"[49] and the *Wall Street Journal* reported that he was "closely affiliated" with Carlos Marcello.[50]

In 1969 Caracci was involved in an incident that once again demonstrated how Marcello, as *Life* magazine put it, "controlled the State of Louisiana."[51] In September of that year, Caracci was arrested when police raided a Syndicate gambling operation at the Royal Coach Inn in Houston, Texas.[52] Nabbed with Caracci were three men who all showed up later, along with the Marcello clan, for the Dallas wedding of a son of Joseph Campisi.[53] The arrest proved particularly embarrassing for one of them, Frank "Tickie" Saia—a prominent political, business and sports figure in Louisiana,[54] who was caught with a bunch of gambling slips on his person.[55]

When police examined the phone records of the raided gambling operation, they found calls to Mobsters across the country.[56] Juxtaposed with these were calls to top Louisiana politicians, including Saia's close friend[57] Senator Russell Long.[58] Long had in fact sponsored Saia for a job as regional adviser to the U.S. Small Business Administration.[59] By 1974, as the *New York Times* reported, "millions of dollars" in Louisiana SBA money had gone to "persons with known Mafia backgrounds" as a result of Mob subversion of the regional office.[60]

Given Saia's gambling arrest and his ties to Caracci,[61] Campisi[62] and Marcello himself,[63] his sponsorship for a federal post by Senator Long was disturbing. A similar situation was noted in a staff report of the House Assassinations Committee:

> On June 16, 1961, the FBI received a report that a U.S. Senator from Louisiana might have sought to intervene on Marcello's behalf [in his fight to avoid deportation]. This Senator had reportedly received "financial aid from Marcello" in the past and was sponsoring a Louisiana official for a key INS [Immigration and Naturalization Service] position from which assistance might be rendered.[64]

"Financial aid from Marcello" was apparently a reference to substantial campaign contributions which Senator Russell Long received from Carlos Marcello, as documented, according to *Life*, in a 1951 internal staff report of the Kefauver Crime Committee.[65]*

Additional information on Caracci was presented by Aaron Kohn, director of the New Orleans Metropolitan Crime Commission, during a Congressional hearing in 1972:

> There were close connections between the Cosa Nostra organizations of Zerelli in Detroit and of Carlos Marcello in Louisiana. . . . A major figure in the Marcello organization, Frank Caracci, recently convicted and imprisoned on three counts of conspiracy to bribe a Federal tax agent, was in the Detroit area in 1969 in company of Zerelli Mob members. With him was his brother-in-law, Nicholas J. Graffagnini of Jefferson Parish, Louisiana.[74]

Contacts with Ruby. Caracci was one of those Mob figures whose contacts with Ruby were apparently confined to the pre-assassination period. Between June and October of 1963, as detailed later, Ruby visited one of Caracci's New Orleans night clubs, telephoned another several times, and met with Caracci on at least one occasion.[75]

Frank Chavez was a thug with arrests for obstruction of justice and for attempted murder by hurling a firebomb.[76] This background made him an ideal choice to head Teamster Local 901 in Puerto Rico,[77] and to lead Hoffa's drive to take control of the AFL-CIO-affiliated Union Gastronomica.[78] The drive succeeded

---

*"Two generations of the Long family," *Life* magazine summarized, "have coexisted with the Mafia."[66] The alliance began in 1934, when Huey Long, Russell's father, "invited New York Mob boss Frank Costello to come into Louisiana and organize gambling for a percentage of the take."[67] For his personal bodyguard, Huey hired James Brocato,[68] also known as "Diamond Jim" Moran, a convicted racketeer close to Carlos Marcello.[69] The continuity of political traditions was later demonstrated when Robert Brocato, a nephew of James and friend of the Marcellos,[70] became chairman of the New Orleans Board of Health.[71] Not to be inhibited by his official position, Brocato tried to run down a police officer during a traffic altercation in 1971;[72] no charges were pressed by the district attorney's office.[73]

after the union's headquarters was blown up by five Molotov cocktails in February 1962.[79]

After President Kennedy was killed, Chavez sent Robert Kennedy a letter stating that he was soliciting money to supply Lee Harvey Oswald's grave with flowers.[80] In 1964 and again in 1967, Chavez set out from Puerto Rico with the reported intention of killing Robert Kennedy.[81] But Chavez's designs were squelched a year after the latter trip, when he was killed by one of his own bodyguards.[82*]

Contacts with Ruby. Between 1960 and 1962, Leopoldo Ramos Ducos was Chavez's organizer for Teamster Local 901.[88] Ramos Ducos told the FBI on November 27, 1963 that he had heard Chavez "mention the name of one Jack Ruby as someone connected with the Teamsters union."[89] Ramos Ducos also stated that in the fall of 1961, Chavez had told him he "had an appointment to meet Richard Kavner, International Vice President of [the] Teamsters Union, and Jack Ruby as well as a third Teamster official."[90] Kavner, described by author Dan Moldea as "another key member of the Hoffa circle" who "carried a gun," was linked to several dynamite bombings and had been to Puerto Rico on Teamster business.[91]

A link between Ruby and Chavez was further documented by a Justice Department memorandum of November 26, 1963, indicating "a connection between Rubenstein [Jack Ruby] and Frank Chavez and Tony Provenzano."[92] The third man, Provenzano, was a Teamster international vice president and a captain in the Genovese Mafia Family.[93] He was convicted of extortion in 1963[94] and of murder in 1978.[95] The connections are credible in view of Ruby's one-time involvement with Paul Dorfman in a Chicago Teamster local[96] and other Teamster links of Ruby to be discussed.

Joseph Francis Civello was the Mafia boss of Dallas during the

---

*Following in Chavez's footsteps, a member of Teamster Local 901, Hector Aponte, was later arrested and charged with murder and arson[83] in connection with a fire at the Dupont Plaza Hotel in San Juan on December 31, 1986, on the eve of a Teamster strike against the hotel.[84] The fire, which Aponte admitted setting "in agreement with others,"[85] killed 96 people; one survivor was later found bludgeoned to death.[86] Another member of the local was charged with conspiracy.[87]

1950s and 1960s[97] and was one of the 59 delegates apprehended at the 1957 Mafia convention in Apalachin, New York.[98] (Civello was temporarily put out of commission by his arrest, and intelligence officers believe that New York Genovese Family representative Peter Pelligrino was sent to Dallas to watch Mob interests during that period.)[99] Civello's criminal record dates back to 1928 and includes an arrest for murder and a conviction for a federal narcotics violation.[100] Born in Louisiana, Civello was friendly with Carlos Marcello,[101] to whom he was connected by toll call records.[102]

Contacts with Ruby. In an FBI interview on January 14, 1964, Civello stated that he had known Ruby casually "for about ten years."[103] Like fellow Mafioso Joseph Campisi,[104] however, Civello was being modest about the extent of his association with Ruby.

The Ruby-Civello relationship was illuminated by Bobby Gene Moore, who grew up in Dallas and worked for Ruby at various times between 1952 and 1956 as a pianist in the Vegas Club.[105] After the assassination, Moore was prompted to contact the FBI by a statement on television that his former employer had no gangster connections.[106] He was interviewed by agents on November 26, 1963 in Oakland, California.[107]

Moore told the FBI of deals involving Ruby, two Dallas policemen, and local underworld figures; several of his allegations were verified years later by arrests for the activities he described.[108] But most interesting was Moore's report about an Italian importing company at 3400 Ross Avenue in Dallas, where Moore was employed during the early 1950s.[109] Moore was characteristically accurate when he told the FBI he suspected that his employers, Joseph "Cirello" and Frank LaMonte, might have been importing narcotics.[110] For the Dallas directory listed the store at 3400 Ross Avenue to a brother of Mafia boss Joseph Civello.[111] The Joseph "Cirello" transcribed by the FBI was thus Joseph Civello, whose business fronts included import-export, olive oil and cheese,[112] and whose criminal activities did in fact include narcotics dealings.[113]

Given Civello's top Mob status, an additional statement of Moore is quite significant. Moore told the FBI in his November 1963 interview that Ruby was "a *frequent visitor and associate of*

Cirello and LaMonte."[114] Interviewed in 1964 by the FBI, La-Monte admitted having known Ruby since the early 1950s,[115] further corroborating Moore's assertions. Additional confirmation was provided by author Ovid Demaris, who reported that Civello told him, "Yeah, I knew Jack—we were friends and I used to go to his club."[116]

Bobby Gene Moore's FBI interview, spanning two pages in National Archives files,[117] was published by the Warren Commission as Exhibit 1536 (both are reproduced in the photo section). But the Commission's published version gave no inkling of Ruby's frequent visits with Dallas Mafia boss Joseph Civello. Also excluded was Moore's expressed belief that Ruby "was connected with the underworld in Dallas."[118]

In fact, the entire second page of the original National Archives report was omitted in Commission Exhibit 1536. And three paragraphs of the original's first page, mentioning Joseph "Cirello," were *blanked out from an otherwise perfect photocopy of that page.* In this fashion, with seven of the original nine paragraphs omitted or excised, Moore's account became almost compatible with the Warren Commission's denial of a "significant link between Ruby and organized crime."[119]

Ruby's sister Eva Grant testified that **Joseph Glaser** was one of New York City's wealthiest booking agents, who "probably could have been in rackets."[120] This last phrase was characteristic of Grant's mild or euphemistic descriptions of such individuals as Lewis McWillie,[121] Lenny Patrick[122] and Dave Yaras[123]—all of whom were described by independent sources as Mobsters and killers.[124]

Glaser's Syndicate connection was recently confirmed in a *New York Times* series on Los Angeles attorney and Mobster Sidney Korshak.[125] Describing Korshak as "the most important link between organized crime and big business,"[126] the *Times* related that senior Justice Department officials ranked him among "the most powerful members of the underworld."[127] His underworld clout was suggested by one incident in 1961, in which Jimmy Hoffa was displaced from the best suite in the Las Vegas Riviera Hotel to accommodate him.[128]

The *Times* reported that one of the companies over which

Korshak "has virtually absolute control," an investment "he has sought to keep secret," is the Associated Booking Corporation.[129] "In 1962, according to court documents," as the *Times* further noted,

> Joseph Glaser, the head of Associated Booking Company, the nation's third-largest theatrical agency, assigned all of the "voting rights, dominion and control" of his majority stock in the concern to Mr. Korshak and himself. The agreement meant that Mr. Korshak, who through the 1960's had seemed merely to be the agency's legal counsel, was able to assume complete control over the company upon Mr. Glaser's death in 1969.[130]

Contacts with Ruby. On August 5, 1963, Jack Ruby visited Joseph Glaser in New York City.[131] Ruby placed two calls to Glaser ten days later.[132]

Alexander Gruber described himself to the FBI as an all-American guy who was a member of no organization "other than the Democratic Party or the Boy Scouts of America."[133] While the Warren Commission published the four-page FBI interview of Gruber containing this self-appraisal,[134] it omitted an accompanying two-page FBI report[135] that was withheld even from National Archives files until 1970. This FBI report summarizes Gruber's police record of six arrests under two aliases in Illinois, Indiana and California, with a conviction for grand larceny.[136] According to Seth Kantor, a White House press corps reporter, Gruber was "running with Frank Matula, whom Hoffa had installed as a Teamsters official shortly after Matula got out of jail on perjury charges. Gruber also maintained known connections with hoodlums who worked with racketeer Mickey Cohen."[137]

Contacts with Ruby. Al Gruber was a friend of Ruby from Chicago, where they had roomed together for a year.[138] In mid-November 1963, after a ten-year separation, Gruber paid an extended visit to Ruby in Dallas.[139] Ruby then called Gruber in Los Angeles three hours after President Kennedy was shot.[140] The two described these contacts in grossly conflicting accounts.[141]

Paul Roland Jones is best known for leading the Chicago Mob delegation in the Dallas bribe attempt,[142] but his criminal record is quite well-rounded. His first major infraction was the murder of a state witness in Kansas,[143] for which he was sentenced to life imprisonment in 1931.[144] But in 1940, with typical Mob political aplomb, Jones secured a pardon from Governor Husman.[145] In 1946, after extricating himself from a felony warrant issued in Cleveland,[146] Jones arrived in Dallas to represent the Chicago Mob in its abortive bribe attempt.[147] While appealing his 1947 conviction in that affair,[148] Jones was convicted of flying 60 pounds of opium over the Mexican border.[149] In 1960, Jones was indicted for perjury in connection with the Texas Adams Oil Company swindle.[150]

Contacts with Ruby. Jones told the FBI that he got to know Ruby quite well in the late 1940s in Dallas and visited him occasionally thereafter.[151] Jones claimed the relationship was just a friendly one,[152] but Ruby's interrogation by the Federal Bureau of Narcotics in connection with Jones' opium smuggling arrest[153] may indicate otherwise. Jones dropped in from out of state to see Ruby at the Carousel Club a week before the assassination of President Kennedy.[154]

Russell D. Matthews was described in one FBI report as a burglar, armed robber, narcotics pusher and murderer.[155] He worked for Mob-controlled Cuban casinos in the late 1950s[156] and turned to Dallas underworld pursuits in the 1960s.[157] The *Dallas Morning News* reported that "Matthews was arrested more than 50 times by Dallas area law authorities but served time in prison only once—two years on a federal narcotics violation."[158] In January 1974, Matthews was subpoenaed by a federal grand jury in Houston concerning a reported contract to kill informants of corruption in the Houston Police Narcotics Division.[159] He is now employed at the Horseshoe Club in Las Vegas.[160]

Matthews is an associate of Mafia figures Santos Trafficante[161] and Joseph Campisi.[162] Matthews and Campisi were seen together in both Dallas and Las Vegas in 1978.[163]

Contacts with Ruby. Four witnesses described Matthews as an associate or friend of Ruby.[164] On October 3, 1963, a call was placed from the Carousel Club to a number in Shreveport, Louisiana listed to Elizabeth Matthews, Russell's former wife.[165]

Lewis J. McWillie, described by Dallas Police as a "gambler and murderer,"[166] served the Syndicate in several domains. After moving to Dallas as a young man, he became a "prominent figure in illegal gambling" in the 1940s, according to an FBI report.[167] Social Security records establish McWillie's employment in 1942 and 1943 by local rackets bosses[168] Lester "Benny" Binion and Benny Bickers at the Southland Hotel in Dallas,[169] owned by New Orleans Mafioso[170] Sam Maceo.[171] Throughout the 1940s and 1950s, McWillie was involved in the operation of several gambling spots in the Dallas area,[172] including the Top of the Hill Club,[173] Cipango's[174] and a gambling house at 2222 Jacksboro Highway in Fort Worth.[175]

From September 1958 until May 1960, McWillie was manager of the Mob-owned Tropicana Hotel in Havana;[176] the hotel's other top men included Mobsters Giuseppe Cotrini, John Gueglielmo, Norman Rothman, Willie Bischoff and Meyer and Jake Lansky.[177] After being expelled from the Tropicana by the Castro regime, McWillie managed to stay on as the pit boss of the Capri Hotel Casino,[178] in which Santos Trafficante held a major interest.[179] While in Havana, according to an FBI report in the National Archives, McWillie associated with Meyer and Jake Lansky, Santos Trafficante, Willie Bischoff, Dino Cellini and other top Mobsters.[180] He was finally forced out of Cuba in January 1961, along with the rest of the Mob,[181] with most of his assets confiscated.

After his departure from Cuba, McWillie spent several months working on the Caribbean islands of Aruba and Curaçao.[182] He then became pit boss at the Cal Neva Lodge in Lake Tahoe, Nevada,[183] the same hotel in which Frank Sinatra was forced to relinquish his 50-percent ownership because of contacts with Sam Giancana, then Chicago Mafia boss.[184] Shortly afterward, McWillie became pit boss at the casino of the Riverside Hotel in Reno,[185] which was owned by Mobsters from Detroit.[186] In 1962, following the receipt of a $2.75 million Teamsters Pension Fund loan, the Riverside declared bankruptcy,[187] and McWillie landed a job at the Thunderbird Hotel in Las Vegas.[188] In all instances,

131

McWillie testified, he was in a supervisory role, "overseeing the gambling."[189] McWillie was still at the Thunderbird, in which Meyer and Jake Lansky held interests,[190] at the time of the assassination.[191] When McWillie testified before the House Assassinations Committee in 1978, he was employed at the Holiday Inn casino in Las Vegas.[192]

Contacts with Ruby. Ruby, McWillie and others reported that the two were close friends.[193] Their close association was exhibited during a week-long trip to Havana by Ruby in 1959, during which he saw McWillie frequently.[194] Moreover, Ruby reported, he once had four guns shipped to McWillie in Cuba.[195] And on May 10, 1963, according to sales records confirmed by McWillie, Ruby had a .38 Smith and Wesson revolver shipped from Ray's Hardware Store in Dallas to McWillie in Las Vegas.[196] Over the following four months, Ruby called McWillie eight times at the Thunderbird in Las Vegas.[197]

Murray W. "Dusty" Miller was the head of the Southern Conference of Teamsters in 1963[198] and later became secretary-treasurer of the Teamsters International.[199] The House Assassinations Committee reported that Miller "was associated with numerous underworld figures."[200]

Contacts with Ruby. On November 8, 1963, Ruby called Miller person-to-person at the Eden Roc Hotel in Miami.[201]

Lenny Patrick was identified in a 1965 U.S. Senate report as a high-ranking nonmember associate of the Chicago branch of the Mafia.[202] His activities included "extortion, mayhem and murders," plus gambling, loan sharking and narcotics dealing, which he reportedly controlled on Chicago's West Side.[203] He is profiled in *Captive City* as the "Syndicate overlord of the 24th and 50th wards" in Chicago,[204] with business interests including hotels, restaurants, supermarkets, liquor stores, aluminum products, a disposal service, vending machines, insurance and industrial uniforms.[205] His police record includes 28 arrests on charges including murder,[206] a 1933 conviction for bank robbery[207] and a 1975 conviction for contempt of court.[208]

According to one FBI informant, Patrick was a close contact of Sam Giancana,[209] the former Mafia boss of Chicago.[210] Like several of Ruby's other Mob contacts, Patrick reportedly once held an interest in a Cuban gambling casino.[211] But Patrick was best known as one of the Mob's leading killers.[212]

Contacts with Ruby. Patrick told the FBI that he and Ruby were casual friends in Chicago,[213] but had not been in touch since the early 1950s.[214] According to Ruby's sister, however, Ruby called Patrick in 1963.[215]

Aaron Kohn, director of the New Orleans Metropolitan Crime Commission, described **Nofio J. Pecora** of New Orleans as an "exconvict with extensive past history in the heroin traffic" and a partner of Carlos Marcello.[216] G. Robert Blakey, chief counsel of the House Assassinations Committee, testified that "the FBI, Justice Department, and Metropolitan Crime Commission of New Orleans have identified Pecora as one of Marcello's three most trusted aides."[217] The *New York Times* also identified Pecora as an associate of Marcello and the recipient of a $210,000 loan granted by the New Orleans office of the Small Business Administration.[218]

Contacts with Ruby. On August 4 and October 30, 1963, calls were exchanged between a Dallas phone listed to Ruby and a New Orleans phone of Pecora.[219] Each had virtually exclusive use of his respective telephone.[220]

Johnny Roselli was a prominent Mafia figure active in Las Vegas and Los Angeles.[221] A former associate of Al Capone,[222] Roselli was convicted in 1944 with other top Mobsters for conspiring to extort $1 million from Hollywood's major motion picture studios.[223] The group perpetrated the extortion scheme by gaining control over the International Alliance of Theatre Stage Employees, then demanding massive payoffs with the threat of a nationwide strike.[224] During the early 1960s, Roselli was a principal in joint plots by the Mob and CIA to assassinate Fidel Castro.[225] In August 1976, Roselli's body was found floating in an oil drum in Florida's Biscayne Bay shortly after testifying in secret session to the Senate Intelligence Committee.[226]

Contacts with Ruby. Roselli told columnist Jack Anderson that he knew Ruby,[227] and described Ruby as "one of our boys."[228] The two may have first met in 1933, when both became involved with the newly opened Santa Anita Race Track in Los Angeles.[229] Ruby and Roselli reportedly met twice in Miami during the fall of 1963.[230]

A Chicago bail bondsman with no felony record, **Irwin S. Weiner** maintains his office a few doors away from Chicago Police headquarters.[231] He is also one of the Mob's leading front men in Chicago,[232] "thought to be the underworld's major financial figure in the Midwest."[233] "A comprehensive list of his associates," the House Assassinations Committee noted, "would include a significant number of the major organized crime figures in the United States."[234] Among them have been Jimmy Hoffa, Santos Trafficante, Sam Giancana, Paul and Allen Dorfman, Sam Battaglia, Marshall Califano and "lord high executioner"[235] Felix ("Milwaukee Phil") Alderisio.[236]

Weiner's activities illustrate how the Mob operates in America. One of them, as reported by the House Assassinations Committee, "defrauding the national welfare and medicare systems located in Chicago,"[237] was typical. He did this "through the manipulation of funds" and "the deliberate burning of Medicare clinics for insurance claims."[238] He has also "been linked to the arson of restaurants and nightclubs, resulting in insurance fraud."[239] Weiner's business interests have included partnerships with Felix Alderisio in three meat processing firms and a real estate company.[240] One shortening firm was closed by a Chicago judge in 1961 after allegations of strong-arm sales techniques;[241] Weiner was charged as an accessory when Alderisio was later indicted for extortion.[242] A 1973 FBI report "states that Weiner was handling all the skimmed money from Las Vegas for Chicago's organized crime community."[243] And a 1974 FBI transcript of electronic surveillance, again summarized by the House Assassinations Committee, "reports an alleged bribe by Weiner to an assistant U.S. Attorney in Chicago to have organized crime figure Sam Battaglia released from prison."[244]

Like many of Ruby's other Mob contacts, and like Ruby himself,[245] Weiner had been involved in the Mob's Cuban operations. For example, a 1962 FBI memo reported that "Weiner has boasted, and those who were in the know in Cuba have confirmed, that for his services to Phil Alderisio[,] Santos Trafficante, etc., he was given a substantial interest in the Deauville Gambling Casino and the Capri Gambling Casino in Havana. When Weiner last talked about this he was crying about the loss of a vast fortune occasioned by Castro."[246]

Weiner was also active in the Teamsters, as demonstrated by his frequent mention in FBI files with Jimmy Hoffa and union big-wig Allen Dorfman.[247] (Weiner was with Dorfman when Dorfman was shot to death in a 1983 gangland-style execution in Chicago.[248]) In one 1959 transaction, a company headed by Weiner was promoted by the Teamster International leadership to handle the multimillion-dollar bonding requirements of the locals.[249] But the letter of endorsement came the day before Weiner's company was even incorporated.[250]

In 1974, Weiner, Allen Dorfman, two trustees of the Teamsters Central States Pension Fund and other Mobsters were indicted by a Chicago federal grand jury on charges of defrauding the fund of more than $1.4 million.[251] The case involved a Teamster pension fund loan to a New Mexico firm that was then drained bankrupt by the Mob;[252] federal officials have estimated that similar transactions have defrauded the Teamsters of at least $385 million.[253] As the House Assassinations Committee summarized, "the prosecution's seemingly strong case" against Weiner and his codefendants "crumbled when its key witness, David Siefert, was brutally murdered on September 27, 1974, just before the trial was scheduled to begin."[254]

Contacts with Ruby. Ruby and Weiner knew each other, at least casually, as youths in Chicago.[255] On October 26, 1963, Ruby placed a 12-minute call from the Carousel Club, person-to-person, to Weiner in Chicago.[256] When questioned by the FBI three days after Ruby shot Oswald, Weiner refused to provide any information about this call.[257] He subsequently furnished a series of contradictory explanations.[258]

Like his close associate[259] Lenny Patrick, **David Yaras** was included in a U.S. Senate list of Chicago Mafia nonmember associates, characterized by an activity code indicating "extortion, mayhem and murder."[260] Arrested 14 times,[261] Yaras is described in *Captive City* as "a prime suspect in several gangland slayings"—one of "more than a score of top-rated exterminators who work strictly on contracts for the board of directors."[262] Yaras was one of a group of Mobsters monitored by an FBI bug in 1962 while planning a murder contract in Miami and discussing previous killings.[263] The bug provided grisly transcripts detailing Mob executions, later published by *Life* magazine,[264] and saved the life of the intended victim.[265]

Yaras served as a go-between for Carlos Marcello and Santos Trafficante,[266] the Mafia bosses who had spoken of President Kennedy's murder in the summer months of 1962. Yaras was also a crony of Jimmy Hoffa,[267] who had outlined plans to kill Robert Kennedy within the same brief period. Along with Trafficante, Yaras was instrumental in founding Teamster Local 320 in Miami.[268] As author Dan Moldea reported, that local "served as a front for many of the Mob's gambling and narcotics activities."[269]

Like Marcello, Trafficante, Hoffa, Ruby, Matthews, McWillie, Patrick, Roselli and Weiner,[270] Yaras had engaged in Mob operations in Cuba.[271] According to Charles Siragusa, a federal narcotics officer, Yaras "ran a number of gambling operations on the island and was also the Chicago mob's liaison to the Cuban exile community after the fall of Batista."[272] And the House Assassinations Committee reported that "Yaras has served, it is alleged, as a key lieutenant of Chicago Mafia leader Sam Giancana."[273]

Yaras also played a part in a conquest which brought the Mob nationwide control over bookmaking operations—the takeover of Continental Press, the leading racing wire service of the 1940s.[274] In 1946, while Mafiosi Carlos Marcello and Jack Dragna muscled into regional distributorships of Continental,[275] national manager James Ragen tried to hold out against the Mob.[276] At the same time, Paul Roland Jones bragged to Sheriff Guthrie and Lt. Butler in Dallas about how his backers were going to take over the wire service, and how Ragen was going to be killed.[277] Thus it came as no surprise when, soon afterward, Ragen was ambushed and shot.[278] Six weeks later, he was fatally poisoned by mercury slipped into his soft drinks despite a 24-hour guard at his hospital bed.[279]

Lt. Butler testified he learned that the Chicago Mob group, specifically Dave Yaras, was behind the Ragen slaying.[280] Indeed, in 1947, Dave Yaras, Lenny Patrick and William Block were indicted for Ragen's murder.[281] Charges were dropped, however, after one witness was murdered, one fled, and two changed their testimony.[282]*

Contacts with Ruby. Yaras told the FBI that he knew Ruby for about 15 years in Chicago,[288] and related enough details about Ruby's habits and personality to indicate more than a remote acquaintance.[289] Yaras also confirmed that Ruby knew Lenny Patrick.[290]

Although Yaras had no recorded contacts with Ruby in 1963, a curious indirect link brings us full circle alphabetically among Ruby's associates. Recall that on November 7 and 8, 1963, Jack Ruby exchanged calls with Teamster thug Barney Baker.[291] Two weeks later on November 21, 1963, at 6:17 p.m., the night before the assassination, a 3-minute call was placed from the home phone of Baker in Chicago to a "Dave" in Miami, Florida.[292] The "Dave" called person-to-person by Baker,[293] as identified by telephone records,[294] was Ruby's old friend, Syndicate killer Dave Yaras.

Further indications of Ruby's Mob affiliation were furnished by two witnesses. Louisville tavern operator Carlos Malone told the FBI that in the summers of 1957 and 1958, he visited the Ellis Park Race Track in Kentucky with Jack Ruby;[295] Malone identified Ruby by name and photograph.[296] Accompanying the two was Ellis Joseph, a former Louisville policeman who had resigned from the force in 1952 after being charged with theft.[297] Malone reported that Joseph, who appeared well-acquainted with Ruby, had described Ruby as a "syndicate man out of Chi-

---

*In contrast to the fate of the three Mobsters was that of Chicago Police Captain Thomas E. Connell and Lieutenant William Drury, who secured the indictment against them.[283] When the two policemen brought in Chicago Mobster Jake Guzik for questioning about the case, Guzik was ordered freed within two hours.[284] Connell and Drury, on the other hand, were indicted for depriving Guzik of his civil rights and thrown off the force.[285] Drury fought for reinstatement in the courts until September 25, 1950, the night before he was scheduled to give information to a Kefauver Committee investigator—he was then shotgunned to death in his garage.[286] Attorney Marvin Bas, another scheduled witness, was also murdered, a few days before the Kefauver Committee opened hearings in Chicago.[287]

cago."[298] Joseph also mentioned to Malone that Ruby had some tips on horses from the Syndicate,[299] and Malone observed that Ruby had several winners that day.[300]

Nancy Perrin Rich, a former bartender and waitress at the Carousel Club,[301] told the FBI that "she saw syndicate men from Chicago and St. Louis in Ruby's night club."[302] Rich "entertained them as hostess and observed money payments made to Ruby."[303] In subsequent sworn testimony, she related:

> Ruby had had various characters visit him, both from New York, Chicago, and even from up in Minneapolis. . . . I was introduced to some of them. I was asked to go out with some of them. . . . I saw them come and go.[304]

It is explicitly clear from context[305] that she was referring to the Syndicate. And Rich was among dozens of witnesses[306] who described Ruby's remarkable association with the flip side of the Dallas criminal establishment: the Dallas Police Department.

You and I know what the problem is. They buy off the judge, they buy off the prosecutor, they buy off the sheriff, and they buy off the law enforcement officers locally, directly or indirectly.[1]

> Senator Henry Jackson, referring
> to Syndicate gambling operatives

The oilmen, the politicians, the construction firms and organized crime—call it the Mafia, the Cosa Nostra, the Syndicate, the Mob, whatever you will—have all grown up in Texas together in an orgy of mutual back-scratching.[2]

> *Ramparts* magazine

10
Jack Ruby and
the Dallas Police

All levels of American government are subverted by the Mafia, as reflected by its estimated annual corruption expenditure of more than $15 billion.[3] But the most deeply penetrated segment is local law enforcement.[4] As the Massachusetts Crime Commission concluded in 1957, the Mafia mainstay of illegal gambling "could not exist within a community without the knowledge and protection of the local police."[5] And as organized crime expert Rufus King wrote, whoever controlled a community's illicit gambling operations more often than not "also controlled—the word is responsibly chosen, controlled—the community's local law enforcement agencies."[6]

A textbook model of Mob-police corruption is provided by the city of Dallas. Even before the Mafia takeover of Dallas rackets in the late 1940s, according to two sources quoted in *Green Felt Jungle*, "The police force was rotten from top to bottom"; gangsters controlled "the sheriff, the police, the judges . . . everything in the state."[7] The standard pattern of gambling nonenforcement was reflected in the criminal record of Isadore Max Miller, a major Dallas bookmaker active for decades.[8] He was finally convicted on federal gambling charges in 1965[9] but had not been arrested by Dallas authorities since 1949.[10] Mob associate Russell D. Matthews, on the other hand, was arrested 59 times by Dallas police but convicted only once on a federal narcotics violation.[11] It appeared that Matthews was accurate when he told an associate that he had Dallas all wrapped up ("It is my town").[12]

By all indications, the corruption in Dallas approached the venal level of Ruby's native Chicago, where the Mafia still helps to determine police promotions[13] and where policemen are regularly convicted of various Syndicate-tied crimes, including murder.[14]* During the 1950s, several Dallas-area gambling houses continued to operate[17] — well after most such establishments had been closed in the heat of the Kefauver hearings. In 1967, in fact, one Dallas Police lieutenant was arrested by federal authorities for running his own bookmaking business.[18] And 30 days of telephone conversations of a local gambling boss, taped by the FBI prior to gambling raids in 1972, reportedly included the voices of at least a dozen Dallas Police officers.[19]

Bill Decker, the Dallas County sheriff, was reportedly a key figure in underworld corruption. During the November 7, 1946 session of the Dallas bribery negotiations, tape-recorded by police, Mobster Paul Roland Jones described Decker, then undersheriff, as an "oldtime bootlegger here."[20] Sheriff Steve Guthrie added, "We all know Bill Decker is a payoff man with [rackets boss[21]] Bennie Binion."[22] Dallas Police Lt. George Butler concurred with Guthrie.[23] Consistent with this assessment was Decker's admitted long-time acquaintance with hoodlum Russell D. Matthews[24] and his friendship with Mobster Joseph Campisi.[25]

It is hardly comforting to note that the same Sheriff Decker rode in the "rolling command car" in front of President Kennedy's limousine on November 22, 1963.[26] And Decker was also involved in the abortive arrangements to transfer Oswald from

---

*In a December 6, 1968 article entitled "Corruption Behind the Swinging Clubs," *Life* magazine concluded that a major cause of the wholesale misconduct by Chicago Police at the 1968 Democratic convention was rampant Mob corruption in the department.[15] The article detailed several shocking cases of payoffs, favors and Mob-police ties, and summarized: "There is a climate around Chicago police in which organized crime thrives like jungle shrubbery."[16]

the Dallas Police jail.[27] Yet it was Oswald's killer and Decker's prisoner,[28] Jack Ruby, who perhaps provided the most penetrating glimpse into Mob-police corruption in Dallas. Although some of Ruby's police contacts appear typical for a night club operator, their exceptional scope and nature demonstrate a connection of far greater consequence.

POLICE CONTACTS AND FAVORS

Ruby was "well acquainted with virtually every officer of the Dallas Police force," noted his friend Lewis McWillie.[29] Amazing as it seems, given the roughly 1,200 officers on the force,[30] this claim was confirmed by many other acquaintances of Ruby.

"Ruby knew every police officer in Dallas," reported Robert Craven.[31] "He knew most of the policemen on the police force," said Breck Wall;[32] "all the policemen in town," related Joseph Cavagnaro.[33] Reagan Turnman told the FBI that Ruby "was acquainted with at least 75 percent and probably 80 percent" of the police force.[34] Another acquaintance of Ruby commented that he "seemed to know every policeman in Dallas and every important official and newspaper man."[35]

"Ruby was well known among members of the Dallas Police Department," noted a police lieutenant who said he knew Ruby well.[36] "Many Dallas Police officers" were on a "first name basis" with Ruby, according to a former Dallas policeman.[37] Ruby was "on speaking terms with about 700 out of the 1200 men on the police force";[38] he was "very friendly with members of the Dallas Police Department";[39] he "knew everyone on the Police force," three other witnesses reported.[40]

But Dallas Police Chief Jesse Curry, under fire for permitting Oswald's killing in his own headquarters, held a different opinion. According to Chief Curry, "no more than 25 to 50 of Dallas' almost 1200 policemen were acquainted with Ruby."[41] Complementing Ruby's extensive Dallas Police ties were other official contacts, as indicated by documents he kept. Among the items found in his possession were the business cards of the chief of the Narcotics Division in Austin, Texas[42] and of the captain of the Traffic Division in El Paso;[43] a card of the Chicago Police Department;[44] permanent passes to the Carousel Club, issued to and signed by the recipients, Dallas Assistant District Attorney W. F. Alexander, Garland Deputy J. T. Ivey and city hall officials Ray Hawkins and John D. Bailey;[45] five bail bond cards;[46] and various lists with the notations "Rosemary Allen . . . Deputy Sheriff Decker's secretary,"[47] "Buddy Walthers . . . Deputy Sheriff,"[48] "Travis Hall . . . County Clerk Deputy"[49] and "Clint Lewis . . . Deputy Sheriff."[50] Also found was a card bearing Ruby's name and the Dallas County official seal, signed by Justice of the Peace Glen W. Byrd.[51] Similar to a card once furnished to Capone Mobster Jack Zuta,[52] it read:

> To all public officials: kindly extend to the individual whose signature appears above any and all assistance which may be properly given in keeping with your official duties and obligations.[53]

One place of contact between Ruby and the Dallas Police was his Carousel Club. The Carousel "was frequented by most of the officers of the Dallas Police Department," most of whom Ruby knew "on a first-name basis," according to a hostess at the club.[54] "Law enforcement officers, both plainclothes and uniformed police and deputy sheriffs, frequently came to the Sovereign Club to converse with Ruby," according to the food service manager at Ruby's Sovereign Club, precursor of the Carousel.[55] Others reported that "many officers of the Dallas Police Department came in and out of the Carousel";[56] "Ruby's club was frequented by Dallas Police officials";[57] "numerous officers came into the club."[58] These statements were corroborated by the accounts of three former Dallas Police officers.[59]

A former Carousel bartender, James Rhodes, told the FBI that Ruby "gave orders to the bartender and waitresses that the officers should never be charged for anything they received at the club."[60] Nancy Perrin Rich, a former bartender and waitress at the Carousel, testified that Ruby had given a standing order to serve hard liquor free to any Dallas policeman who wanted it,[61] even though it was illegal for Ruby to serve hard liquor in the club.[62] Robert Shorman, a musician at the Carousel Club, said that he saw "between 150 to 200 police officers at the Carousel at one time or another," including Captain Will Fritz, chief of the Police Homicide Detail, but he "never saw a police officer pay for a drink."[63] Five others, including two Dallas Police officers, also reported that Ruby routinely gave free drinks and food to Dallas policemen.[64]

Other witnesses reported more substantial favors. Herbert Kelly, food service manager of Ruby's Sovereign Club, told the FBI that each Sunday night Ruby would "entertain as many as eight law enforcement officers, furnishing them gratis expensive dinners and drinks."[65] James Rhodes reported that he once bartended for Ruby at a Carousel Club party for "thirty or forty police officers."[66] Ruby told Rhodes that the group included the chief,[67] and Rhodes gathered that Ruby paid for the party.[68] Rhodes also described an after-hours party held at the Carousel by Ruby for 14 members of the Dallas Police vice squad.[69]

Janice Jones, once a waitress at the Carousel, told the FBI that Ruby gave a fifth of whiskey to each Dallas policeman who came by around Christmas[70] — a rather expensive proposition considering the number of Ruby's police acquaintances. Dallas Policeman Hugh Smith confirmed that Ruby gave bottles of liquor to numerous policemen.[71] He also related that a bachelor on the Dallas Police Force had "used Ruby's apartment on several occasions."[72] Ruby's acquaintance Joe Bonds advised the FBI that Ruby "made women available to officers."[73] And Dallas hardware store owner Ray Singleton told the FBI that Ruby once came into his store to purchase a revolver — accompanied by a police officer.[74]

Also significant were many reports that Ruby employed off-duty policemen as bouncers in his night clubs.[75] This arrangement violated Dallas Police regulations,[76] which is perhaps why E. E. Carlson, a detective on the force, refused to discuss it when questioned by the FBI.[77] And it was incongruous given Ruby's proficiency as a fighter,[78] which he often demonstrated by abusive ejections of unruly patrons at his clubs.[79] In fact, six witnesses specifically reported that Ruby served as his own bouncer.[80] It thus appears likely that this reported employment arrangement was a fiction to cover payoffs by Ruby to policemen who frequented his clubs.

Ruby's police favors certainly bought him personal immunity from law enforcement, beginning with his night club operations. James Barrigan, a Dallas night club owner, told the FBI that Ruby illegally served drinks after midnight in the Carousel Club, even when Dallas policemen were present.[81] Ruby's friend Paul Roland Jones stated that Ruby "could not have operated his businesses [or] been permitted to put on the 'raw shows' that he did" without payoffs to the police.[82] Carousel employee Joan Leavell said that the Dallas Police permitted Ruby to run shows rougher than those of other Dallas clubs.[83] And Carousel stripper Janet Conforto ("Jada") told the FBI that Ruby boasted that the police let him "get away with things at his club" because of his friendship with them.[84]

Ruby was "known to have brutally beaten at least 25 different persons," as reported in a February 24, 1964 memo by two Warren Commission staff members.[85] But the police seemed as reluctant to arrest Ruby for assault as for liquor violations. Dallas attorney John Wilson, Jr. told the FBI that he saw Ruby assault a man in a local bar without apparent provocation, probably using brass knuckles, causing a large amount of bleeding.[86] Wilson related that when policemen arrived, they intended to arrest the man Ruby had beaten, but not Ruby.[87] They took no action against Ruby, even after Wilson told them what happened.[88] Wilson observed that the officers "were extremely reluctant to do anything about Ruby."[89]

Mrs. Paul Calgrove, who had worked for Ruby, reported that she had complained to the Dallas Police of physical abuse by him.[90] The police told her that she was crazy to press charges against him and laughed at her desire to do so.[91] Similarly, when Carousel employee Nancy Rich complained that Ruby had pushed and injured her, the police warned her that by filing suit against him, she would only get herself "in more trouble than [she] bargained for."[92] Rich testified that when she tried to prosecute Ruby, she was arrested twice on phony charges,[93] and told by the police that she might find the climate outside Dallas more to her liking.[94] One witness told the FBI that in reference to this or a similar incident, Ruby once boasted that "he had just squashed [sic] a complaint against him for beating one of his dancers."[95]

Ruby's own police record provides another example of his favored treatment by Dallas law enforcement officials. Ruby was arrested nine times between 1949 and 1963 on charges including assault, carrying a concealed weapon and liquor infractions.[96] But he was convicted only once, in 1949, for which he paid a $10 fine.[97] The dispositions of the other arrests were recorded as "complaint dismissed," "no charges filed," "no further disposition shown" and acquittal in one case.[98] Likewise, Ruby's traffic record shows no payments on nine violations committed after 1956, including negligent collision, speeding and running a red light.[99] As concluded in an atypical Warren Commission staff memo of February 24, 1964, Ruby avoided prosecution "through the maintenance of friendship with police officers, public officials, and other influential persons in the Dallas community."[100]

The handling of one of Ruby's infractions is probably representative. On December 5, 1954, at 1:30 a.m., Ruby was arrested by Dallas policemen E. E. Carlson and D. L. Blankenship for permitting the consumption of alcoholic beverages in his night club during forbidden hours.[101] The arresting officers' report states that the officers saw beer on the table, and observed that a customer attempted "to hold the bottle and said that it was her beer."[102] In an interview with a physician, Ruby described his arrest that night by Officers Carlson and Blankenship, adding "but then they found out I had good friends and they came out the next night sort of apologetic."[103] Not surprisingly, the charge against Ruby was dropped two months later.[104] Signed by Dallas District Attorney Henry Wade, the motion dismissing the charge asserted:

The police report states that they [Blankenship and Carlson] observed customers consuming beer after hours. Both officers stated that this is incorrect and they did not observe the customers consuming beer. It is recommended that this case be dismissed because of insufficient evidence.[105]

145

Yet both Carlson and Blankenship later told the FBI that their police report was accurate.[106] Blankenship stated that he did not know why the charge was dismissed.[107]

MOB-POLICE LIAISON

Perhaps the most important indication, however, of unusual ties between Ruby and the Dallas Police was his frequent presence at police headquarters. "It was common knowledge that Ruby spent time almost every day at the Dallas Police Department," Benny Bickers told the FBI on November 24, 1963.[108] "On numerous occasions after receiving a telephone call Ruby would go to the police station," according to Herbert Kelly, food service manager of Ruby's Sovereign Club.[109] Indeed, Ruby was in the Dallas Police building several times between Thursday, November 21, and Sunday, November 24,[110] although perhaps not for his usual business. The many accounts of Ruby's contact with the police were well summarized by Carousel employee Nancy Rich, who testified,

> I don't think there is a cop in Dallas that doesn't know Jack Ruby. He practically lived at that station. They lived in his place.[111]

Ruby's extensive and often irregular ties with the Dallas Police thus indicate a connection beyond the realm of corrupt night club politics. Given these extraordinary police ties, in fact, it was quite credible that Ruby was "the pay off man for the Dallas Police," as reportedly stated,[112] and then denied,[113] by Mickey Ryan, an associate of Ruby.* Regardless of Ruby's precise role in

---

*Ryan, alias Roy Pike, a close contact of Ruby during the fall of 1963,[114] had a suspicious alibi for the time of the assassination. The only thing Ryan could recall about his activities on November 22–24 was that he was watching television with his wife when "he heard a news flash that President Kennedy had been shot."[115] Yet Carousel stripper Nancy Powell testified that she was with Ryan and a friend Pete—no mention of Ryan's wife[116]—when Ryan was informed of the assassination in a telephone conversation.[117] Powell related, "Then [Ryan] came out of the bedroom and he said, the President has just been shot, he walked right to the TV and turned it on."[118] Ryan left Dallas for California at the end of November 1963,[119] having arrived in the city only two months earlier.[120]

146

the underworld's corruption network, however, it is clear that he was an important intermediary in arranging the gambling fix. To review three previously cited observations, Harry Hall told the FBI that Ruby received 40 percent of Hall's gambling profits because Ruby "was supposed to have influence with the police, so that he [Hall] would have no worry about any gambling arrest."[121] William Abadie saw Dallas officers frequenting Ruby's gambling establishment and concluded, "It was obvious that to operate gambling in the manner that he did," Ruby must have had both "racketeering connections" and "police connection[s]" in Dallas and Fort Worth.[122] And Jack Hardee reported being told that "Ruby had the 'fix' with the County authorities, and that any other fix being placed would have to be done through Ruby."[123]

Although "Mob-police liaison" has a sinister ring, the reality of Ruby's police connection can be comprehended in human terms. Ruby enjoyed playing the glad-hander, speeding around town with impunity, delivering bribes to police and officials and doling out the favors of his Carousel Club strippers. Jack Ruby, the slum hustler, had become the generous benefactor — buying popularity among a high-placed constituency as an intermediary for the gangster elite he had idolized since childhood. And for the Mob, Ruby filled a critical role, spreading the fix with the happy-go-lucky aura that its corruption specialists would ordinarily take great pains to cultivate.[124]

Yet for all its free-wheeling banality, the corrupt function that Ruby performed had the sinister stamp of the organization he served. And there would come an undertaking in Dallas that would require police collusion — that would demand the final payment of the Mafia's lien on the glad-handing of Jack Ruby.

The [FBI] files make clear that the Warren Commission failed abysmally to pursue FBI leads linking Oswald's own assassin, Jack Ruby, to the Mob. Ruby had ties to mobsters in Chicago, New York, Los Angeles and Dallas, and even, as a boy, to the infamous Al Capone.[1]

Time magazine

Wasn't it pretty well known to the FBI that Jack Ruby, No. 1, was a member of organized crime, No. 2, he ran a strip joint and has been somewhat commonly referred to as a supplier of both women and booze to political and police figures in the city of Dallas[?][2]

Congressman Stewart McKinney, addressing an FBI representative in the House assassinations hearings

11
Jack Ruby, Mobster

Notwithstanding the fine recommendations of his "Chicago friends,"[3] Ruby's Mob connection is apparent from the activities, contacts and background considered in the previous chapters. It is further demonstrated by personality traits compatible with his underworld station.

Ruby played the part of a gangster in classic Chicago style. He dressed extravagantly; his outfit the day of the Oswald shooting included a silk necktie with gold-plated tie clasp, an imported leather belt, a ring with three diamonds, a 14-carat gold Le Coultre diamond-studded wristwatch and his "Chicago hoodlum hat."[4] Sometimes he also wore brass or aluminum knuckles[5] to complement his natural proficiency with his fists;[6] two sets of them were found in his car.[7] One acquaintance described Ruby as an "intense racketeer and hustler" who was "interested solely and entirely in his businesses and gambling."[8] A close friend testified, "He always reminded me of a gangster. . . . he just reminds me of a real hood."[9] And another friend of Ruby testified that "because of his character automatically people would take him as a thug."[10]

Ruby's "one outstanding characteristic . . . was his own personal intense interest in gambling of any kind," former employee William Abadie told the FBI.[11] A one-time acquaintance reported that Ruby "bet heavily, made frequent telephone bets on horse races and basketball games."[12] And according to Harry Hall, Ruby once won $5,000 on a telephone bet with a Montreal bookie and sent Hall there to collect the winnings.[13] Ruby's affinity for betting was also demonstrated in the summer of 1957, when he went to the races in Hot Springs, Arkansas with Mobster Lewis McWillie.[14]

Ruby's relationships with women were characteristic of his occupation. Carousel employee Larry Crafard testified that Ruby told him he had a sexual relationship with every one of the women who worked for him;[15] Carousel stripper Karen Carlin named some of her fellow entertainers with whom Ruby went to bed.[16] Another Carousel employee said that Ruby "was always on the make" and would frequently date female employees and other women.[17] One woman told the FBI that Ruby had tried to rape her when she was a waitress at his Silver Spur Club at age 14.[18]

Ruby's reading material included articles pertaining to his business. A "partially complete" copy of the November 18,1963 *Wall Street Journal*, including the first page, was found in Ruby's car.[19] That issue featured a front-page article entitled "Mafia and Business," which mentioned Ruby's associate Joseph Civello.[20] A "partial copy" of the September 8, 1963 *New York Daily Mirror* was also found in Ruby's car.[21] Page 11 of that day's *Mirror* contained an article about Mafia defector Joseph Valachi.[22] That article also described how one Mafia figure went about "setting up a patsy and luring him into a narcotics conspiracy."[23]

Ruby observed the Mob custom of carrying and stashing away large sums of cash. The *Dallas Morning News* reported that police detectives found two large wads of bills of undisclosed amounts when they searched Ruby's apartment on November 24.[24] Police inventories reported that Ruby was carrying more than $2,000 in cash when he shot Oswald.[25] Bank bags containing an additional $1,015.78 in small bills and change, probably night club receipts, were found among his possessions.[26] And a printer who did some work for Ruby noticed about five to twenty

$100 bills in Ruby's wallet, a considerable sum in those days, when he took it out on one occasion.[27]

Ruby's spending habits also typified success in his affiliation. When out of town, he stayed at such luxury hotels as the Sheraton Lincoln in Houston (on May 9, 1963[28]) and the New York Hilton (from August 4 to 6, 1963[29]). Johnny Branch, manager of the Empire Room in Dallas, said that Ruby would come in there from time to time and hand out $5 bills to random customers.[30] Even during his last year in Chicago, while he was still a relatively small-time operator, Ruby lived at the Congress Hotel[31] — also the home of Mayor Anton Cermak in the 1930s.[32] Yet Ruby reported no earnings to the Social Security Office between 1940 and 1956.[33]

Indeed, Ruby was consistently modest about his finances in his official accounts, declaring a median income of $6,000 on his tax returns for the years 1956 through 1962.[34] But the Internal Revenue Service did not find his appraisals too reliable, holding a claim against him for $44,400 in delinquent excise and income taxes in 1963.[35] And this IRS scrutiny, which had put so many of Ruby's predecessors in prison,[36]* explains his thrift in documentable transactions. Thus it makes sense that Ruby resided in a small apartment in Dallas[44] but lodged at the Sheraton in Houston[45] and the Hilton in New York;[46] that he owned a 1960 Oldsmobile[47] yet was seen by two witnesses driving a Cadillac.[48]

Ruby's frequent travels across the country provided a further indication of his apparent affluence. The assassination material contains reports of Ruby's visits to the following cities after he moved to Dallas in 1947: New York,[49] Chicago,[50] Los Angeles,[51] San Francisco,[52] Wichita,[53] Tulsa,[54] Hot Springs (Arkansas),[55] Henderson (Kentucky),[56] Las Vegas,[57] New Orleans,[58] Miami[59] and Havana (Cuba).[60]

---

*Ever since such notables as Al Capone, Frank Costello, Johnny Torrio, Waxey Gordon and Moe Annenberg were convicted on tax evasion charges,[37] Syndicate figures have been careful to maintain a low financial profile. Top boss Vito Genovese, for example, owned a modest home and auto.[38] So did Meyer Lansky,[39] who was investigated for income-tax evasion from 1950 to 1953.[40] "Don Peppino," a former top New England Mafioso,[41] would drive around in an old Chrysler for fear of the IRS.[42] And Louisiana Mafia boss Carlos Marcello once carried the act a bit further by successfully pleading poverty to settle a $76,830 fine for a rare conviction with a $400 payment.[43]

With this personal glimpse into Ruby's criminal side, his underworld activities and associations begin to fall into place. The following highlights deserve special attention.

Ruby served an elite criminal apprenticeship in Chicago, starting out in a group that ran errands for Al Capone, appropriating a union with notorious Mobster Paul Dorfman and learning the basic rackets in the Chicago night club district. In the late 1940s, Ruby earned his stripes as part of the Chicago delegation that muscled in on the Dallas area rackets. Within 15 years, several members of this group died,[61] were murdered[62] or left Dallas.[63] Thus, although Ruby came to Dallas as a "small time peanut"[64] with the Chicago gang, by 1963 he had become one of a select group of Syndicate pioneers there.

During his years in Dallas, Ruby made contact with dozens of underworld figures in the area and across the country. These included Marcello associates Joseph Campisi, Frank Caracci and Nofio Pecora; Teamster goons Barney Baker and Frank Chavez; notorious Mobsters Paul Roland Jones, Lewis McWillie, Lenny Patrick and Irwin Weiner; and Dallas Mafia boss Joseph Civello. A common interest probably led to Ruby's visits with Civello, since Civello was convicted on federal narcotics charges[65] and Ruby's name came up twice before 1963 in federal narcotics investigations.[66] Indeed, it is unlikely that Ruby could have given "the okay to operate" in a major narcotics network "between Mexico, Texas and the East"[67] without an okay, in turn, from Civello.

But of all the criminal arenas in which Ruby operated, the most important was undoubtedly the Mob's top-dollar monopoly,[68] illegal gambling. As reported by three credible witnesses and corroborated by other sources, Ruby operated his own slot machine warehouse and bookmaking establishments and was instrumental in coordinating the "fix" with police and local authorities. It is this key niche in illicit gambling operations, in conjunction with his Mob ties, that establishes Ruby's position in the upper echelons of the Dallas Mob organization.

But there is probably a dichotomy between his functional importance and his clout. As a Jew, Ruby found opportunities in the Dallas underworld that were closed to him in the more established East and Midwest, where the Mafia had beaten competing ethnic gangs into subservience or oblivion.[69] It was indeed such areas as California, Nevada, Florida, the Caribbean and the Bahamas that nurtured the rise of Meyer Lansky, Moe Dalitz, Mickey Cohen, Bugsy Siegel and other ethnic counterparts of Ruby prominent in the Syndicate.[70] Yet in any region, a sharp distinction is always drawn between associates of the Mafia, however valuable, and the core group of members.[71] For example, the late Syndicate financier[72] Meyer Lansky could take no action without the approval of Mafia superiors, who, during one period, kept him under the constant escort of Vincent Alo ("Jimmy Blue Eyes"),[73] a Genovese Family caporegime.[74] It is thus likely that despite Ruby's importance in Dallas Mob operations, he had virtually no governing power.

Whatever Ruby's exact position in the underworld pecking order, however, it is clear from his background, activities, lifestyle and associations that he was intimate with the Mob. Ruby himself hinted to the Warren Commission that some thought he was "put here as a front of the underworld and sooner or later they will get something out of me that they want done to their advantage."[75] That particular service of Ruby—and more of his remarkable testimony—will be covered in the following part.

PART III

Murder
on
Cue

It was Sunday morning, November 24, 1963, two days after the assassination of President Kennedy. Police were making final preparations for the transfer of suspect Lee Harvey Oswald from Dallas Police headquarters to the county jail.[1] At the same time, Jack Ruby was in the downtown Dallas Western Union office wiring $25 to his Carousel entertainer, Karen Carlin, in nearby Fort Worth.[2] According to Bruce Carlin (her husband), Ruby, and herself, Karen had requested the money for rent and groceries in a 10:19 call to Ruby that morning.[3] Ruby received a receipt for the $25, time stamped 11:17 a.m., and headed for the Dallas Police building one block away.[4]

Three minutes later, at 11:20 a.m. — an hour and 20 minutes after the scheduled transfer time — Oswald was moved from his cell in the Dallas Police building.[5] Police escorts guided him down through the basement, which was swarming with reporters, to the ramp of the garage.[6] The transfer had been elaborately planned,[7] and word had been given that everything was ready.[8] Yet when Oswald reached the ramp, as described by police escort L. D. Montgomery, he

> had to stop, because [the transfer] car wasn't in position. . . .
> It was supposed to have been in position when we got there, but
> it wasn't there, so, we had to pause, or slow down for the car to
> come on back.[9]

And at 11:21 a.m. as Oswald paused at the garage ramp, standing in place of the out-of-position transfer car was Jack Ruby.[10] Ruby pulled out a .38-caliber revolver, and fired one fatal shot into Oswald's abdomen.[11]

The murder of Lee Oswald simplified the Kennedy assassination case in several respects. The long and cumbersome trial necessitated by Oswald's protests of innocence was circumvented by Ruby's professedly impetuous act.[12] And the perplexing questions about November 22 were overshadowed by a straightforward series of events on November 24. The 10:19 a.m. call from the Carlin residence in Fort Worth to Ruby's apartment in Dallas.[13] The 11:17 a.m. telegram from Ruby to Karen Carlin.[14] And then the 11:21 a.m. televised shooting in the police basement.[15] On first examination, they all seemed just the series of fateful coincidences that Ruby described.

Yet the Oswald murder provided another, more disquieting simplification. For Lee Oswald, a man of assorted involvements, was upstaged by Jack Ruby—a man whose singular identification could not, despite the best of efforts, be concealed. Jack Ruby was a professional gangster, who would hardly commit a crime aimlessly or explain it truthfully. And Jack Ruby was intimately tied to the Mob—an organization with the motive, means and declared intention to kill President Kennedy.

Indeed, knowing Ruby's background, the natural presumption concerning the November 24 shooting was that immediately believed by Europeans: "The professional gangster killing the President's assassin out of patriotic indignation . . . . justifies suspicion of a deliberate and desperate concealment."[16] This suspicion was more specifically and authoritatively expressed in the 1970s by the aging Mobster Johnny Roselli, who knew Ruby. Roselli described Ruby as "one of our boys" and said that Ruby was ordered to kill Oswald to silence him.[17] (Roselli, whose body was found floating in an oil drum in 1976 after talking to Senate probers, evidently received the same treatment.[18])

As a point of penetration into the Kennedy assassination case, this part will dissect the evidence concerning the Oswald murder. It will show that Ruby's alibi for his assassination weekend activities was totally fraudulent. His story of shooting Oswald out of sympathy for the Kennedy family was fabricated. The Carlin call and telegram were staged. And the shooting of Oswald was a meticulously coordinated murder contract. These are underscored in the amazing final hearings of Jack Ruby himself—in which, on record, Ruby indicated his alibi was prepared with others, mocked his recitation of it and stated he could not tell the truth because his life was in danger. A preview:

> Who else could have timed it [the Oswald shooting] so perfectly by seconds. If it were timed that way, then someone in the police department is guilty of giving the information as to when Lee Harvey Oswald was coming down.[19]

Clearly, neither the timing of the shooting nor the existence of a conspiracy could have been hypothetical issues to Jack Ruby. And the cited conspiracy will assume grippingly real dimensions in the coordinated perjury of some terrified witnesses.

In the underworld that Ruby had frequented since his childhood, when a witness who is soon to testify in court is murdered, it is for a single purpose: to prevent him from confessing, and from implicating his associates in some crime that has been committed.[1]

Thomas Buchanan, a journalist who covered
the trial of Jack Ruby for
the French weekly *l'Express*

12
Perjury and Premeditation

In official interviews following the fatal shooting of Oswald, Ruby and several associates presented detailed accounts covering Ruby's activities prior to that event.[2] The contradictions are virtually endless. Their implications for conspiracy, as laid out in the following two chapters, become progressively more serious. A good starting point to examine these stories and the events leading up to the Oswald murder is the afternoon of President Kennedy's assassination.

AT PARKLAND HOSPITAL

Jack Ruby told the FBI and the Warren Commission that on Friday afternoon, November 22, 1963, he placed a night club ad at the Dallas Morning News building and then went to the Carousel Club.[3] At no time that day, claimed Ruby, did he visit Parkland Hospital,[4] where President Kennedy and Governor Connally were treated.

But journalist Seth Kantor reported in the Scripps-Howard newspapers,[5] told the FBI[6] and testified before Warren Commission counsel[7] that he saw Ruby there on Friday afternoon. A member of the White House press corps, Kantor related that at 1:30 p.m., he met, shook hands with and spoke to Ruby in a corridor at Parkland Hospital.[8] Kantor was quite sure it was Ruby, as they had become well-acquainted when Kantor was a reporter in Dallas.[9]

Kantor stated that he would testify to the Parkland encounter in a court of law,[10] reiterating that he was "indelibly sure"[11] it took place. He was clear about the time and place the meeting occurred, reporting that "Ruby shook hands numbly, having minutes earlier witnessed the tragic events of the President's assassination," and was anxious "for news about the President's condition."[12] And Kantor's account was corroborated by another witness, Wilma Tice. Tice testified that she saw a man at Parkland Hospital Friday afternoon whom she heard addressed as "Jack"; she identified him as Ruby from news photos.[13]

Indeed, as the House Assassinations Committee recently asserted,[14] Kantor's corroborated account of Ruby's visit to Parkland Hospital was in all likelihood accurate.

AT THE DALLAS POLICE BUILDING

Later that day, around midnight, Ruby attended a news conference in the Dallas Police building.[15] As can be heard on videotape, Ruby interjected the correction "Fair Play Cuba" when District Attorney Henry Wade stated to reporters that Oswald belonged to the "Free Cuba Committee."[16]

But the midnight press conference was not the only time that Ruby visited the Dallas Police building during the assassination weekend. Detective August Eberhardt, who had known Ruby five years,[17] testified that he spoke with Ruby in the third-floor hallway of the police building between 6 and 7 p.m. Friday.[18] Detective Roy Standifer, also well-acquainted with Ruby,[19] testified that they exchanged greetings in the same place at about 7:30 p.m.[20] The encounter occurred shortly after Standifer's supper break, which he routinely began at 6:30 p.m.[21]

Dallas television reporter Vic Robertson, Jr., another acquaintance of Ruby,[22] was positive that early Friday evening he saw Ruby try to open the door to Captain Will Fritz's office, where Oswald was being questioned.[23] Robertson then heard a voice say, "You can't go in there, Jack."[24] John Rutledge, a *Dallas Morning News* reporter, also saw Ruby directly across from Captain Fritz's office before 6 p.m. that night.[25] And other witnesses reported Ruby's presence in the Dallas Police building Friday between 4 and 7 p.m.[26]

About noon on Saturday, November 23, Ruby visited the police building again. His presence was noted in a rather amusing account to the FBI by *France-Soir* reporter Phillippe Labro:

> Ruby encountered Mr. Labro and asked him who he was and what he did for a living. Mr. Labro advised Ruby that he was a French newspaper reporter. Ruby's response was "ooh la la Folies Bergere," which, according to Labro, were probably the only French words known to Ruby. Ruby then presented Mr. Labro with a card advertising his night club "The Carousel" containing the picture of a nude woman and invited him to stop and have a drink with him. . . . There is no question in his mind as to the identity of the person whom he talked with on November 23, 1963, as Ruby.[27]

Possibly in reference to this encounter, Ruby told a medical interviewer, "I even passed out some of my cards to those newspaper men from all over the world."[28]

Thayer Waldo, a Fort Worth reporter, ran into Ruby in the police building at 4 p.m. Saturday.[29] Waldo testified that Ruby introduced himself, gave Waldo a Carousel card and invited him and other newsmen over to the club for free drinks.[30] NBC News Producer-Director Fred Rheinstein testified that Saturday afternoon before 5 p.m., he saw a man in the police building who he was "reasonably certain was Ruby."[31] This man entered a police building office in which District Attorney Henry Wade was reportedly working and from which newsmen had been excluded.[32] UPI photographer Frank Johnston,[33] French journalist François Pelou[34] and others[35] also saw Ruby at police headquarters Saturday afternoon and evening.

In Ruby's version of his assassination weekend activities, however, his only visit to the Dallas Police building before Sunday morning occurred on Friday, at the time of the midnight press conference.[36]

"NOT GRIEVING"

Ruby's exuberant behavior Saturday afternoon at the police station — handing out Carousel cards and inviting reporters for drinks — typified his mood during much of the assassination weekend. Friday night at police headquarters, "Ruby appeared to be anything but under stress or strain," noted television newsman Vic Robertson, Jr. "He seemed happy, jovial, was joking and laughing."[37] At radio station KLIF early Saturday, Ruby "was not grieving," and, "if anything," was "happy that the evidence was piling up against Oswald," announcer Glen Duncan said.[38] Ruby even commented that Oswald was a good-looking guy who resembled Paul Newman and expressed "no bitterness against the man," according to Russ Knight, a disc jockey.[39] Johnny Branch, manager of the Empire Room, testified that Ruby came into his club Saturday night at about 10 p.m., mentioned nothing about the assassination and handed out some $5 bills to customers as he had on other occasions.[40]

But Ruby told the FBI he was "in mourning" Friday and Saturday.[41] He said he cried when he heard the president was shot,[42] "cried a great deal" Saturday afternoon[43] and was depressed Saturday night.[44] He explained that this grief, so little in evidence, was caused by his great love for the martyred president and his sympathy for the Kennedy family.[45] This anguish over the assassination, Ruby stated, finally "reached the point of insanity,"[46] suddenly compelling him to shoot when Oswald walked to the police ramp that Sunday morning.[47]

But a handwritten note from Ruby to one of his lawyers exposed this story, in the words of the House Assassinations Committee, as "a fabricated legal ploy."[48] Disclosed by *Newsweek* in 1967, the note from Ruby to attorney Joe Tonahill read:

> Joe, you should know this. Tom Howard told me to say that I shot Oswald so that Caroline and Mrs. Kennedy wouldn't have to come to Dallas to testify. OK?[49]

Indeed, the patriotic sentiments Ruby professed were quite out of character. Harry Hall, his partner in a gambling operation, told the FBI that "Ruby was the type who was interested in any way to make money."[50] Hall "could not conceive of Ruby doing anything out of patriotism."[51] Jack Kelly, who had known Ruby casually since 1943, "scoffed at the idea of a patriotic motive being involved by Ruby in the slaying of Oswald."[52] And Ruby's friend Paul Roland Jones was paraphrased by his FBI interviewers as affirming that

> from his acquaintance with Ruby he doubted that [Ruby] would have become emotionally upset and killed Oswald on the spur of the moment. He felt Ruby would have done it for money. . . .[53]

Perhaps Ruby himself shed the most light on his "tremendous emotional feeling"[54] in testimony before the Warren Commission on June 7, 1964, following his conviction for first-degree murder. Referring to a Saturday morning eulogy for President Kennedy, Ruby recalled that the rabbi

> eulogized that here is a man that fought in every battle, went to every country, and had to come back to his own country to be shot in the back [starts crying].[55]

Following his tearful recital, however, Ruby interjected a candid appraisal of his sincerity: "I must be a great actor, I tell you that."[56]

In a polygraph hearing a month later, Ruby offered even bolder indications of his true feelings. At one point he remarked, "They didn't ask me another question. 'If I loved the President so much, why wasn't I at the parade?' " (referring to the president's motorcade).[57] Ruby added, "It's strange that perhaps I didn't vote for President Kennedy, or didn't vote at all, that I should build up such a great affection for him."[58] Although Ruby volunteered this remark under the pretext of defending himself against unspecified detractors,[59] his reference to the private matter of his vote could only have been a candid confession. And Ruby dropped the hypothetical guise when he later interjected, speaking of himself, "Here's a fellow that didn't vote for the President, closes his clubs for 3 days, made a trip to Cuba. . . ."[60]

A possible indication of Ruby's actual feelings for the Kennedys was expressed in a November 24 ABC-TV interview with "Jada," a Carousel Club stripper.

> Jada: I have heard Jack talk about the Kennedys and I've been trying to think and it's so confusing today, but I believe he disliked Bobby Kennedy.
>
> Q: Got no recollection of what he had ever said about the President?
>
> Jada: Yes. He followed that statement up about Bobby with something about Jack Kennedy. . . .[61]

For Ruby to have harbored the typical Mob hostility toward the crime-busting attorney general and president while professing love of the brothers would have been hardly surprising. Yet Ruby's lies about his motive for shooting Oswald and about his assassination weekend whereabouts highlight the questionable nature of his actual activities, especially the November 22 visit to Parkland Hospital. Even more suspicious, however, were fabrications he presented that were supported by others, several of whom exhibited fear, and incidents that demonstrated premeditation in the murder of November 24.

AN ENCOUNTER WITH DALLAS
POLICEMAN HARRY OLSEN

Ruby told the FBI that after he left the Friday midnight press conference in the police building, he went directly to the newsroom of Dallas radio station KLIF.[62] He said that he arrived there at about 2 a.m. and stayed for an hour.[63]

But there are serious discrepancies between the accounts of Ruby, KLIF personnel and Ike Pappas, then a visiting New York radio announcer, concerning Ruby's purported sojourn there.[64] Most problematical were the assertions of two KLIF employees that Ruby was in the KLIF newsroom speaking with Pappas early Saturday morning; Pappas, who had met Ruby briefly the previous night, emphatically denied that Ruby was in the KLIF newsroom while he was there.[65] These conflicts are curious in light of Ruby's close relationship with the owner, Gordon McLendon, and other staff of KLIF.[66]

When questioned by the FBI in December 1963, Ruby reported that he "left Radio Station KLIF at about 3:00 A.M. on November 23, 1963, and drove to the Dallas Times Herald newspaper building."[67] But in his subsequent Warren Commission hearing, Ruby revised this story to acknowledge an encounter with Dallas Police Officer Harry Olsen and Olsen's girlfriend, Kathy Kay, a Carousel Club stripper:

> Mr. Ruby: . . . I left the KLIF at 2 a.m., and I spent an hour with the officer and his girlfriend, so it must have been about 3:15 approximately. No, it wasn't. When you are not concerned with time, it could have been 4 o'clock.
> Chief Justice Warren: It doesn't make any difference.
> Mr. Ruby: Forty-five minutes difference.[68]

Ruby's emphasis on this minor time discrepancy in the Olsen encounter was perhaps a hint of its once-again improvised character. For Olsen and Kay both testified that they left together from a Dallas bar around midnight November 22 and went directly to the nearby Simon's Garage to chat with garage attendant Johnny Simpson.[69] Kay testified that she, Olsen and Simpson were sitting in a parked car talking when Ruby drove by.[70] They waved, and Ruby pulled in between 12:30 and 1:00 a.m., she related.[71] Olsen testified that Simpson took part in the subsequent conversation, and he related a specific response of Simpson to a statement by Ruby.[72]

But garage attendant Johnny Simpson presented a totally different story. He told the FBI that around 1 a.m., November 23, Olsen "came to Simon's garage exit to wait for his girl friend."[73] Next, "the girl friend came and got into Olsen's car, they started to drive off, but the girl apparently saw Jack Ruby walking down the street and she yelled a greeting to him."[74] Simpson told the FBI he "did not take part in any of the conversation."[75] Except for one overheard remark, Simpson said, he did "not know what the three talked about."[76]

Ruby, on the other hand, testified that he drove past Simon's Garage after leaving KLIF at 2:00 a.m., heard a loud honk and saw Olsen and Kay in a car "very much carried away."[77] He did not mention Simpson at all in his description of this encounter.[78]

Compounding these blatant discrepancies in accounts of the basic circumstances of this incident was significant variation in its reported duration. Ruby testified that he stayed with Olsen and Kay for an hour.[79] But Olsen told the FBI in December 1963 that the early Saturday morning conversation between himself, Ruby, Simpson and Kay lasted "about ten minutes."[80] In subsequent testimony before Warren Commission counsel, however, Olsen stated this conversation lasted "two or three hours."[81]

Olsen's latter account of timing is perhaps most credible; a meeting with Ruby between about 1:00 and 4:00 a.m. would explain discrepancies in the story that Ruby was at KLIF past its 2:00 a.m. newscast. The contradictory accounts of the roles of Kay and Simpson, whose presence adds an innocent flavor to the encounter, also suggests that Kay was not there and that Simpson, as he told the FBI,[82] just observed from a distance.

This early Saturday morning encounter with Ruby, however, was but one of several suspicious points in the assassination weekend alibi of Dallas Policeman Harry Olsen. Olsen testified that he spent all day Friday, November 22 guarding an estate whose name and address he could not recall.[83] The job was arranged through a fellow police officer whose name he could not recall,[84] and Olsen stated twice that he finished his shift around 8 p.m.[85] Yet Kathy Kay testified first that Olsen left his guard duty at 4 p.m.,[86] then changed the time to 6 p.m.[87]

As for their activities between Friday and Saturday night, Olsen and Kay were vague and inconsistent.[88] Both mentioned persons they reportedly encountered but whose names they could not furnish.[89] Both did recall, however, running into Jack Ruby again on Saturday night, in front of the Carousel Club,[90] which was closed for the weekend.[91]

Olsen and Kay were more specific about their activities on Sunday, November 24. Olsen testified he spent all day Sunday with Kay at her Dallas home.[92] Then, at 9 or 10 p.m. that evening, they visited Dealey Plaza.[93] But Kay testified that on Sunday, November 24, she and Olsen visited Olsen's parents in Henrietta, Texas, 160 miles from Dallas.[94] Kay said that they left Dallas at about 4 p.m., spent three hours in Henrietta, headed back at about 10 p.m., and went directly to bed after returning to Dallas.[95] Also conflicting were Olsen's and Kay's reports about how they learned of an event that morning memorable to both: the uncannily timed shooting of Oswald by their friend Jack Ruby.[96] And given these striking disparities, one can only wonder whether the whereabouts of police officer Olsen were related to the slaying.

After the assassination, Olsen and Kay seemed anxious to leave Dallas. Kay did not go back to work at the Carousel Club after Ruby was arrested[97] and about a week later began an engagement in Oklahoma City.[98] Tom Palmer, a Dallas union official, testified that Kay did not return to work because she "said she was afraid to and wanted to get out of town."[99] Palmer said that when he saw Kay on Tuesday, November 26, and told her that her contract was still valid, she replied, "I don't care, I just want to get out of town. I don't like it."[100]

On December 7, 1963, Olsen was driving his car when it veered off the road and crashed into a telephone pole, injuring him seriously enough to require two weeks of hospitalization.[101] After he was released from the hospital, Olsen left the Dallas Police,[102] and he and Kay moved to California on February 1, 1964.[103]

A PHOTOGRAPHY EXCURSION

Filling out Ruby's Saturday morning activities, after the meeting with Olsen and a trip to the Times Herald building,[104] was a strange alleged sojourn.

Jack Ruby, Carousel employee Larry Crafard and Ruby's roommate, George Senator, testified that at about 4 a.m. Saturday, they all went to photograph an "Impeach Earl Warren" billboard near the expressway.[105] Ruby claimed it had aroused his curiosity because of its similarity to an anti-Kennedy ad in the newspaper on Friday.[106] Afterward, the three testified, they proceeded to a post office to check the box number that had appeared in that ad, and then to the Southland Hotel Coffee Shop.[107] This strange excursion was described with some degree of consistency, despite discrepancies concerning the presence of Crafard during different parts of the trip[108] and the order of events.[109]

But there was one major problem. George Senator was interviewed by the FBI on Sunday, November 24,[110] the day Ruby shot Oswald—just one day after the events in question. And in that interview, Senator mentioned nothing about this outing, relating only that he and Ruby talked awhile in their apartment and then went together to the Southland Hotel about 4:30 or 5:00 a.m.[111] When Senator described his Saturday morning activities in a subsequent interview that Sunday, he again omitted any reference to the purported photography excursion.[112]

During his hearing before Warren Commission counsel, Senator was questioned intensively about the discrepancy between his testimony concerning the photography excursion and his original accounts.[113] He was cross-examined skeptically when he claimed it initially had just slipped his mind.[114] Indeed, more likely, the story of this excursion—explaining three photos of the "Impeach Earl Warren" sign found on Ruby's person after he shot Oswald[115]—was communicated to Senator only after November 24. And it is interesting that the part of the story originally reported by Senator,[116] which was corroborated by independent witnesses,[117] was Ruby's visit to the Southland Hotel. That hotel was a long-time Mafia hangout,[118] owned by Mafioso Sam Maceo.[119]

In fact, Senator's testimony concerning the entire assassination weekend was suspect. Even the Warren Commission was compelled to observe that Senator "was unable to account specifically for large segments of time when he was not with Ruby" and that the information he did provide could not be verified.[120] The House Assassinations Committee also noted that Senator's testimony was "extremely vague" and "not consistent."[121]

Senator's behavior after Ruby shot Oswald was unusual. For ten days, Senator so feared being hurt or killed that he "was afraid to sleep in the same place twice"—and didn't.[122] Senator claimed he had no particular reason for this fear and that it was just "a natural instinct in a situation such as this";[123] his interrogator replied, "I am saying it is not natural."[124]

Attorney Jim Martin told the FBI that Senator was practically "overwhelmed with fear,"[125] and this fear was "one of the primary reasons he left the Dallas area."[126] Martin was one of those present, along with Senator, attorney Tom Howard and newsmen Bill Hunter and Jim Koethe, at a meeting in Ruby's apartment on the night of November 24.[127] Perhaps Senator had cause, however, to be so afraid of some person or group as to refuse to specify even whom he feared.[128] For within 16 months after the meeting in Ruby's apartment, as related in chapter 3, Howard died of a reported heart attack, and Hunter and Koethe were brutally murdered.

Carousel employee Larry Crafard also behaved strangely after the assassination. Around noon on Saturday, November 23, Crafard left Dallas without telling anyone and hitchhiked to Michigan with $7 in his pocket.[129] He was located by the FBI several days later in a remote part of that state.[130]

PLANNING THE OSWALD KILLING

The following three incidents and circumstances concern the matter of premeditation, so pivotal to this case. For if Ruby shot Oswald on the spur of the moment, just after wiring $25 to Karen Carlin and more than an hour after the scheduled transfer time, it could only have been a solitary action expedited by freak coincidence. But if the shooting had been planned in advance, Ruby's movements were then timed "perfectly, by seconds"—as he testified[131]—to place him where the transfer car should have been when Oswald appeared.[132] In this case, the Carlin telegram, the shooting and the fabrication of Ruby's alibi could only have been the workings of a well-coordinated conspiracy.

At about 1:30 p.m. on Saturday, November 23, Ruby placed a phone call from Nichols Garage.[133] Tom Brown, a garage attendant, told the FBI that during this call, he "overheard Ruby inform the other party to the conversation as to the whereabouts of Chief of Police Curry."[134] Around 3 p.m., Ruby made another call from the garage to someone he called "Ken."[135] Garrett Hallmark, general manager of the garage, overheard Ruby discuss the transfer of Oswald.[136] Ruby seemed to be seeking confirmation of its scheduled time and said in that context: "You know I'll be there."[137]

KLIF announcer Ken Dowe testified that he was the party Ruby called on Saturday afternoon to inquire about Oswald's transfer[138] and that Ruby merely offered to cover the event for the radio station.[139] But his story is suspect, considering Ruby's questionable involvement with KLIF personnel[140] and conflicts in Dowe's account.[141] In particular, Dowe told the FBI that when Ruby identified himself on the telephone Saturday afternoon, the name Jack Ruby "meant nothing to him."[142] But Dowe subsequently testified that he had been introduced to Ruby at KLIF before the assassination and had learned that Ruby ran a night club and procured women for record promoters.[143] Indeed, Ruby indicated familiarity with the person to whom he spoke by his statement, "You know I'll be there"—referring to the Oswald transfer[144] with apparent specific intent.

Ruby further exposed his plans for the Oswald transfer during a later telephone conversation, which was overheard by Wanda Helmick, a carhop at the Bull-Pen Drive-In Restaurant in Arlington, Texas.[145] The Bull-Pen was operated by Ralph Paul, a financial partner in the Carousel Club.[146]

Helmick testified that on Saturday evening, November 23, she was sitting in the Bull-Pen three to six feet from a pay telephone when it rang at about 8 or 9 p.m.[147] She said that it was answered by another waitress, who handed it to Ralph Paul after calling out, "It is for you. It is Jack."[148] Helmick testified that during the course of the conversation, Ralph Paul "either said 'are you crazy? a gun?' or something like that, or he said something about a gun."[149] Helmick was sure Paul "did say something about a gun, and he asked him if he was crazy."[150] She reported that after the Oswald shooting, "these people that I worked for, they was trying to keep everything so much of a secret . . . they was trying to keep Ralph Paul hid, sort of."[151]

It is difficult to interpret Paul's remarks to Ruby as anything but a response to Ruby's decision to murder Oswald with a gun—the plan he carried out the next day. And indeed, when Ruby ostensibly felt a sudden urge to kill Oswald, just as Oswald reached the police basement ramp,[152] he conveniently had a loaded gun in his trouser pocket.[153] When first questioned by the FBI on Monday, November 25, Ruby "declined to say why he brought his revolver with him when he came downtown."[154] A month later, however, Ruby explained to the FBI that "he had his revolver in his right front trouser pocket" the entire assassination weekend, "because he had a lot of money on his person and always carried his gun when he carried money."[155]

During his June hearing before the Warren Commission, Ruby was again asked if he carried a gun prior to the Oswald killing, specifically during the Friday midnight press conference. This time Ruby testified, "I lied about it. It isn't so. I didn't have a gun."[156] Ruby now explained that during the assassination weekend, he kept his gun in its customary place, in a money bag.[157] Five of his associates testified, in fact, that Ruby rarely kept the gun anywhere but in such a bag.[158]

Therefore, when Ruby carried his gun without a bank bag into the police basement that fateful Sunday morning, it was but a final step in a well-conceived plan—a murder plan he had discussed with Ralph Paul the preceding night. Some of the details were illuminated in the final hours before he carried it out.

If there was a conspiracy, then this little girl that called me on the phone in Fort Worth then is a part of the conspiracy.[1]

Jack Ruby, referring to Carousel stripper Karen Carlin, from the official transcript of his July 18, 1964 polygraph examination at the Dallas County Jail

Mrs. Carlin was highly agitated and was reluctant to make any statement to me. She stated to me that she was under the impression that Lee Harvey Oswald, Jack Ruby and other individuals unknown to her, were involved in a plot to assassinate President Kennedy and that she would be killed if she gave any information to the authorities.[2]

Secret Service agent Roger C. Warner, reporting a November 24, 1963 interview with Karen Carlin

13
Conspiracy

The telegram of $25 from Ruby to Carousel stripper Karen Carlin at 11:17 Sunday morning is the key to the shooting in the police headquarters four minutes later. If the telegram was sent for the reason that Ruby and Carlin described, as noted earlier, the Oswald shooting could only have been impetuous. But if the telegram was staged, the killing could only have been part of a carefully coordinated conspiracy — a conspiracy involving both Carlin and "someone in the police department," as Ruby intimated in his startling testimony, to be covered in depth shortly.

In light of Ruby's background, his fabricated alibi and evidence of premeditation, the story of his wiring money to someone in nearby Fort Worth whom he saw almost daily was not, in fact, especially credible. Supporting it, however, were accounts related by several of his associates of two prior transactions between Ruby and Carlin. The first was a loan of five dollars that Ruby purportedly made to Carlin the night before.[3] The second was a call one hour prior to the telegram, in which Carlin claimed to have requested the additional $25 from Ruby.[4] Presentations of both incidents relied heavily on Karen and Bruce Carlin.

THE CARLINS

Karen Carlin ("Little Lynn") was a Carousel Club stripper during October and November of 1963.[5] Like her co-workers,[6] Carlin reportedly doubled as a prostitute for Ruby.[7] And it appears that the 20-year-old[8] Carlin was at most a pawn—a very reluctant pawn—in a more important underworld activity.

In her first official interview on November 24, 1963, Carlin "was reluctant to make any statement."[9] She explained that she suspected an assassination conspiracy and that she "would be killed if she gave any information to the authorities."[10] As Secret Service agent Roger C. Warner described, she "twisted in her chair, stammered in her speech, and seemed on the point of hysteria."[11] She would give information only "through the aid of her husband"[12] and then asked "that all information she had related be kept confidential to prevent retaliation against her in case there was a plot afoot."[13]

Carlin's fears persisted, as indicated by her arrest for carrying a gun at Ruby's bond hearing.[14] And when questioned by Warren Commission counsel, she related a further incident of interest:

> Q: Do you recall that during the course of the Ruby trial when you were waiting to testify that there was a jail break there and some people got out of the jail, and I think they passed right near by you, I believe?
>
> Mrs. Carlin: Yes.
>
> Q: Do you remember what you screamed or said?
>
> Mrs. Carlin: "Oh, my God, they're after me."
>
> Q: Yes—what made you believe that "they" were after you?
>
> Mrs. Carlin: Because I was scared I was going to get killed before I ever got to court.[15]

According to one report, shortly after the trial, Karen Carlin "was found shot to death in her Houston hotel."[16]

Karen's common-law husband,[17] Bruce, age 23,[18] was described by Ruby as a "pimp" whom Karen "was supposed to be married to."[19] This characterization was supported by a reliable[20] Dallas Police informant, who observed several suspected prostitutes and pimps going in and out of the Carlins' Fort Worth residence.[21] And Nancy Powell, a stripper at the Carousel Club, testified that Bruce didn't work, "and Lynn was pregnant, and he beat her up all the time."[22]

The testimony of Tom Palmer, Dallas branch manager of the American Guild of Variety Artists, further illuminated Bruce Carlin's character:

Q: What was Little Lynn's boyfriend or husband or whatever he is attempting to do for her?
[testimony apparently deleted]
Mr. Palmer: I had that feeling. I had no proof of that.
Q: Anything else that you think he was attempting to do?
Mr. Palmer: Not that I am aware of, no. I thought that was what it was, plus having her in a club where he could call as her manager and probably circulate and pander for her.[23]

The only clue to Palmer's missing response to the first question was the preceding topic of discussion: diet pills and narcotics.[24] Also suggestive of criminal involvement was Carlin's habit of calling assorted public pay phones, including one at "Cy's Wee Wash It" in Hialeah, Florida.[25]

Most suspicious, however, was Bruce Carlin's assassination alibi. He testified that on November 20 or 21 he and his partner Jerry Bunker embarked on a sales trip for the "Motel Drug Service" to supply various motels with drugs and sundries.[26] The firm had no office or telephone number.[27] Carlin testified that they left Dallas together in a station wagon,[28] spent November 21 in Houston[29] and were in a motel in New Orleans when they heard about the assassination.[30] Yet under extensive questioning, Carlin could provide no further details concerning this trip,[31] nor could he recall his activities on November 23.[32] Carlin could not even remember that President Kennedy had visited Houston on November 21,[33] although he claimed that he was there that same day and had picked up some Houston newspapers.[34]

One of the few things Carlin was sure of, that he made the 250-mile trip from Dallas to Houston by car with Jerry Bunker on

173

November 20 or 21,[35] was contradicted by telephone records. For on November 20 at 9:42 p.m., Bunker, in Houston, placed a person-to-person call to Carlin in Dallas,[36] followed four hours later by a call *from* Carlin in Houston to Dallas.[37] Bunker clearly would not have called Carlin in Dallas from Houston if they had arrived in Houston together.

Another conflict concerning Bruce's whereabouts around the time of the assassination was introduced by the testimony of his wife:

> Q: Do you remember whether he had been on a trip that weekend?
>
> Mrs. Carlin: No, I don't even remember that.
>
> Q: Was he in town when the President was killed, do you remember that?
>
> Mrs. Carlin: Yes—well, I don't know. I don't know whether he was or not, I believe he was, though.[38]

Karen's inability to account for Bruce's assassination whereabouts is particularly dubious in light of a point noted in 1978 by former Texas Governor John Connally:

> Ask any adult person, over the age of 30, in this country, or over the age of 35 we will say, where they were when they first heard the news of the assassination. They can tell you where they were, what they were doing, and who they were with. I have not asked one human being in the world, not anywhere in the world, that hasn't been able to tell me. . . .[39]

Thus Bruce Carlin, a pimp, and Karen Carlin, a terrified Carousel Club stripper, do not appear to be especially credible witnesses. Their accounts of the evening prior to the Oswald shooting confirm this impression.

A $5 LOAN TO KAREN CARLIN

The story of a loan of $5 from Ruby to Karen Carlin on Saturday night, November 23, established a reasonable precedent for the $25 telegram on Sunday. Perhaps for this reason, it was re-cited by so many people: Carousel stripper Nancy Powell, Nich-ols Garage attendant Huey Reeves, Ruby's sister Eva Grant, plus the Carlins and Ruby.[40] Yet the presentations of this group suf-fered from conspicuously flawed direction. For not one facet of the purported incident was described consistently—not the date, the participants, the reason for the loan, nor the payment. In-deed, only through a few common elements is it possible to de-termine that any two witnesses are attempting to narrate the same events.

The basic story. Karen Carlin's version of events was that on Saturday evening, November 23, she, Bruce and Carousel Club stripper Nancy Powell took Powell's car from Fort Worth to Dal-las.[41] They arrived at Nichols Garage, next door to the Carousel Club, at about 8:30 p.m., and Karen walked up to the club to perform in the evening's show.[42] Finding it closed, however, they decided to go home.[43] But first they called Ruby to request a small loan, since all three were broke,[44] and Ruby asked to speak to garage attendant Huey Reeves.[45] The outcome was that Ruby told Reeves to give $5 to Karen and keep a receipt; Reeves did so.[46]

Below are some of the most flagrant of a virtually continuous succession of contradictions in the accounts of the various wit-nesses.

The reason for the trip. Karen Carlin testified that the three drove to Dallas Saturday night believing the Carousel Club would be open.[47] She related being called the preceding afternoon by Carousel handyman Andrew Armstrong, who had told her the club would not open Friday night but "would open the next night."[48]

In his first version of events, however, Armstrong told the FBI that on Friday afternoon he had notified Karen and other Carou-sel employees that "the club would be closed Friday night, Satur-day night and Sunday night."[49] Carousel employee Larry Crafard confirmed that Armstrong had learned of the Saturday closing before he called any employees.[50] When questioned by Warren Commission counsel in April 1964, however, Armstrong categori-cally denied that he called Karen Carlin at all that Friday after-noon.[51] Later in his testimony, Armstrong reversed himself and presented yet a third version of events.[52] But his multiple revisions only underscored the absence of any legitimate reason for the Saturday night trip to the Carousel Club.

Means of transportation to Dallas. Karen Carlin had some difficulty getting her story straight as to how she got from Fort Worth to Dallas that Saturday night:

> Q: How did you come?
> Mrs. Carlin: Bus.
> Q: Did you come alone?
> Mrs. Carlin: No, I didn't. I didn't come by bus. I came with Tammi True [Nancy Powell], another stripper.[53]

Carlin's initial response reverted to the story she told the FBI on November 26. At that time she had mentioned no companions on her Saturday night trip to Dallas[54] and had asserted that she "called Ruby as she did not have enough money for transportation back to her home in Fort Worth."[55]

The payment. Karen, Bruce and garage attendant Huey Reeves testified that Karen received $5 from Reeves that night.[56] And in June 1964, Reeves was shown a receipt for $5 from Ruby to Karen, time-stamped "1963 Nov 23 PM 10 33."[57] Reeves then stated that he believed he stamped the receipt, but was unsure when he did so.[58] But earlier, Reeves had reported that he had given Karen $5 at about 7:30 p.m. and did not believe he had time-stamped the receipt.[59] Also curious was Reeves' initial response when asked whether Karen was accompanied by anyone when she came to the garage that night:

> I don't remember whether her husband was with her or not. Let's see, I didn't think about having to go through this. . . .[60]

But the story about the payment was most seriously fumbled by Nancy Powell. Powell testified that she was with Karen at Nichols Garage when Karen called Ruby.[61] And both Nancy and Bruce testified that they were with Karen essentially the whole time during the Saturday night trip to Dallas.[62] Yet when asked by the Warren Commission about the purported payment to Karen, Nancy adamantly denied that Karen received any money:

> Q: Did she get any money there in the parking lot?
> Mrs. Powell: No.
> Q: Were you at the parking lot?
> Mrs. Powell: Yes.
>
> . . .
>
> Q: You don't remember getting any money on Saturday night?
> Mrs. Powell: Her getting any money?
> Q: Yes.
> Mrs. Powell: I don't know where she would get it from, because she was with me, and we didn't go any place to get any money.[63]

Powell testified instead that she believed Karen had asked for $25 in her conversation with Ruby,[64] and that Ruby could not comply that night but promised to send the money the next day.[65] Thus it appears that Nancy Powell confused the script for the Saturday night $5 loan with that of the Sunday morning $25 telegram.

The date of the incident. Ruby told the FBI that "on Friday night, November 22, 1963, he had to give her [Karen] $5.00 so she could get home."[66] Yet Karen testified that she stayed in Fort Worth all evening on Friday, November 22,[67] so Ruby evidently cited the wrong date for the same Saturday night incident. Although a lapse in memory could account for one such error, it is harder to overlook that same confusion about the date by three others: Andrew Armstrong,[68] Eva Grant[69] and Nancy Powell.[70] Particularly dubious was Nancy Powell's insistence that the incident occurred the same night that Ruby went to synagogue,[71] Friday night.[72] She explained, "Maybe somebody told me, but I know he went to the synagogue that day [of Karen's trip]. . . . I'm saying this is a fact, you understand?"[73] Perhaps Powell's eagerness to support Ruby's alibi was inspired by her boyfriend,[74] Ralph Paul, Ruby's night club partner[75] — the one overheard that night telling Ruby, "Are you crazy? a gun?"[76]

The person who received the loan. Ruby's sister Eva Grant was one of the witnesses who confused the date of the loan at Nichols Garage.[77] Yet it is clear that she could have referred only to the Saturday night loan of $5 to Karen Carlin. For that $5, Huey Reeves testified, was the only money he had ever lent on Ruby's behalf to any of Ruby's employees.[78] Reeves worked the 7 p.m. to 7 a.m. shift at Nichols' Garage from November 22 through November 24, as he had for more than a year before the assassination.[79]

Grant also muddled a more critical point in her version of the story, which she eagerly volunteered during her testimony:

Q: Well, Mrs. Grant, just let —
Mrs. Grant: And [Vegas Club pianist] Leonard Wood wanted some money, and I think it was Friday night.
Q: I don't want the details.
Mrs. Grant: Wait a minute, this is very important.
Q: All right.
Mrs. Grant: He wanted some money, so I think, it seems to me, I said — Jack was in the house — "You will tell the guys at the garage next door to the Carousel Club, you give him your name, and he will put $10 in an envelope." Now, Jack made this call from the house. . . .[80]

Grant later stated that the conversation may have occurred on Saturday, November 23,[81] rather than on Friday. Yet she insisted that it was Leonard Wood, pianist at the Vegas Club, which she managed,[82] who telephoned her and requested a loan.[83] And she testified that Ruby then telephoned the garage and gave instructions to leave money for Leonard Wood.[84]

With the testimony of Eva Grant, the variety in renditions of the $5 loan from Ruby to Carlin reaches ludicrous proportions. The lack of even a core of consistency in the accounts demonstrates that the entire incident was manufactured, apparently to support Ruby's Sunday morning alibi — which proves equally spurious.

A CALL FROM KAREN CARLIN

Telephone company records show a call at 10:19 a.m., Sunday, November 24, 1963, from the Fort Worth residence of the Carlins to the Dallas residence of Jack Ruby.[85] Ruby and the Carlins testified that in this call, Karen asked Ruby for money for rent and groceries.[86] This would have accounted for Ruby's $25 wire to Karen Carlin at 11:17 a.m., four minutes before the Oswald shooting—if the witnesses had not all been lying, once again, about the call.

One indication of fakery concerning this call was the testimony of George Senator, Ruby's roommate. In April 1964, Senator testified that Ruby left his apartment Sunday morning November 24 about a half hour after receiving a call from Karen Carlin,[87] supporting Ruby's story of events.[88] Senator mentioned no other activities that morning before Ruby's trip downtown.[89] But when Senator had been questioned later that same Sunday by the FBI, he related only that Ruby had left his apartment at 10:30 a.m. to take one of his dogs to the Carousel Club.[90] Senator mentioned nothing about a call from Karen Carlin.[91] As the FBI paraphrased, *"The only thing*, therefore, Senator knew Ruby was going to do when he left the apartment was take the dog back down to the club."[92]

In fact, neither of Senator's conflicting accounts was truthful. For Ruby spent Sunday morning not in his apartment, but in the vicinity of the Dallas Police building; he could not possibly have received the call from Karen Carlin. This was established through the testimony of three television crewmen who were stationed in front of police headquarters that morning, preparing to cover the Oswald transfer.

WBAP crewman Ira Walker testified that shortly after 10:30 a.m., a man came up to Walker's TV truck and asked, "Has he [Oswald] been brought down?"[93] Soon after Oswald was killed, a mug shot of Ruby was telecast on a monitor in the truck.[94] At that time, Walker testified, he recognized the man as Ruby:

Well, about four of us pointed at him at the same time in the truck, I mean, we all recognized him at the same time.[95]

Walker testified that because of the close conjunction in time between talking with the man and seeing Ruby's mug shot, he was positive that the man was Ruby.[96] And Walker reaffirmed this positive identification in testimony at Ruby's trial.[97]

Warren Richey reported that while on top of the TV truck with his camera, he took note of a man in front of the police building at approximately 8 a.m. and again about 10 a.m.[98] Richey testified that he was "positive, pretty sure in [his] own mind" that this man was Jack Ruby.[99] He explained that he recognized Ruby from videotapes and news photos without knowing of the on-the-spot identification made by the men inside the truck.[100]

John Smith, stationed inside the TV truck, testified that he saw a man twice between about 8 and 10 a.m. Sunday.[101] The second time, the man came up to the window of the truck, within three feet of him, and inquired about the transfer of Oswald.[102] When the mug shot of Ruby was telecast, Smith immediately associated the face with the man he had seen; "I was convinced to myself that that was the same man."[103] Smith testified that he would positively identify the man as Ruby except for "this thing of the hat. . . . I couldn't see his hairline and I couldn't see the complete face."[104] When asked if "with that reservation" he "would have no doubt it is the same person," Smith responded affirmatively.[105] In prior FBI interviews of December 4, 1963, both Richey and Smith had identified the man as Ruby with no reported qualification.[106]

The testimony of Walker, Richey and Smith was corroborated by Donald C. Roberts, then West Coast editor of NBC's Huntley-Brinkley report, who was monitoring NBC transmissions from Dallas affiliate WBAP-TV that morning.[107] Roberts told the FBI that three WBAP-TV technicians

> instantly recognized Ruby on TV transmission immediately after Oswald was shot and so advised Roberts by telephone before Ruby's name was announced over the air. Technicians told Roberts that Ruby had been present at the WBAP mobile remote unit at Dallas City Hall [in the same building as police headquarters], about two hours before Oswald was shot. . . .[108]

The observations of Ruby by WBAP-TV crewmen Walker, Richey and Smith demonstrate that Ruby was at the police building awaiting Oswald's transfer—not at his apartment talking to Karen Carlin—in the hours before the shooting. This was corroborated by the reports of two additional witnesses.

Ray Rushing was a preacher from Plano, Texas, who attempted to visit Oswald at police headquarters on the morning of November 24.[109] In an interview with Dallas Police Lt. Jack Revill, Rushing reported that he had a short conversation with Ruby during a ride in a police elevator at about 9:30 a.m.[110] Lt. Revill evaluated Rushing as "truthful" and treated his information as fact.[111] Revill noted, however, that the district attorney "didn't need [Rushing's] testimony, because he had placed Ruby there the morning of the shooting."[112]

The second corroborating witness was Elnora Pitts, who testified that she had done housecleaning for Ruby every Sunday for several weeks before the assassination.[113] Pitts explained that she would call each Sunday morning to make sure Ruby wanted her to come that day.[114] On November 24, however, when she called Ruby's home sometime after 8 a.m., a male voice answered the phone and their conversation proceeded as follows (arranged into responsive form, for clarity, from the transcript of her testimony):

> Voice: What do you want?
> Mrs. Pitts: What do I want? This is Elnora.
> Voice: Yes, well, what—you need some money?
> Mrs. Pitts: No, I was coming to clean today.
> Voice: Coming to clean?
> Mrs. Pitts: This is Elnora.
> Voice: Well, what do you want? . . .
> Mrs. Pitts: Do you want me to come today?
> Voice: Well, yes, you can come, but you call me.
> Mrs. Pitts: That's what I'm doing now. . . .[115]

Pitts testified, "He sounded so strange to me," and she asked "Who am I talking to? Is this Mr. Jack Ruby?" The party responded "Yes. Why?"[116] She said that she was scared by "the way he talked. He didn't talk like—he never did sound like hisself."[117] Indeed, the man did not sound like Ruby, did not recognize Pitts and had no knowledge of their weekly cleaning arrangement because Ruby was outside the Dallas Police building when she called.

A METICULOUSLY COORDINATED CONSPIRACY

Thus the 11:17 a.m. Sunday telegram to Karen Carlin was just an act, staged to support Ruby's performance as the demented avenger—the crowning element of a totally fraudulent assassination weekend alibi. The production was elaborate, requiring coordination and coercion to elicit the somewhat synchronized recitations of the cast. Yet most critical was the cue for Ruby to stroll to the Western Union office, and to arrive in the police basement just as Oswald reached the ramp. Possible clues to how it was transmitted so quickly from police headquarters to Ruby are provided by three incidents that occurred just before the shooting.

Shortly before 11:21 a.m., Ruby's attorney Tom Howard entered the Dallas Police building, Detective H. L. McGee reported later that day.[118] McGee related that Howard

> came in through the Harwood Street entrance and walked up to the jail office window. At this time, Oswald was brought off the jail elevator and Tom Howard turned away from the window and went back toward the Harwood Street door. He waved at me as he went by and said, "That's all I wanted to see." Shortly after that I heard a shot.[119]

When questioned by the FBI on December 11, Howard confirmed almost every detail of the movements described by McGee.[120] But Howard claimed his remark to the detective had been the innocent question, "Are they fixing to take him out of here?"[121] And Howard reported that he "said nothing to anyone except the detective" about Oswald's movements before the shooting.[122]

Just as Oswald became visible to the spectators in the police basement, a car horn let out a blast, as heard on both television and radio soundtracks.[123] A further event that occurred just then was noted by Tom Pettit, an NBC News correspondent who was broadcasting live from the police basement.[124] Pettit told the FBI that "almost simultaneously with the shooting, a blue car, which had been parked on the ramp immediately behind the armored car, backed rapidly down the ramp and came to a stop with a screeching of brakes at the bottom of the ramp."[125] This was one of the circumstances that caused Pettit to conjecture that "a conspiracy existed to kill Oswald."[126]

Pettit was also disturbed by the seemingly purposeless loitering of Captain Will Fritz, chief of the Police Homicide Detail, who was at the scene of the Oswald shooting, but not in uniform.[127] Similar misgivings about Fritz were reported by Travis Kirk, an established Dallas attorney who was well-acquainted with local law enforcement officials.[128] Kirk told the FBI he suspected that "Fritz had deliberately arranged to have Oswald shot in order to close the case."[129] Kirk "based this on the fact that Fritz and Jack Ruby were very close friends, and that Jack Ruby, in spite of his reputation of being a 'hood,' was allowed a complete run of the Police station."[130] In fact, as noted previously, two reporters saw Ruby near Fritz's office on the evening of the assassination, and one saw Ruby try to go in.[131]

Kirk also furnished background on Tom Howard, the lawyer who popped in to observe Oswald's transfer with such uncanny timing. Kirk told the FBI, as the interviewing agent paraphrased, that

> at one time Howard had several prostitutes working for him and, as far as he, Kirk, was concerned, Howard is still a hoodlum himself. He stated Howard had been prosecuted in Federal Court for the Mann Act several years ago, but that the matter had been hushed up and attempted action against him by the Texas Bar Association had been dismissed.[132]

Another potential police-underworld liaison for Oswald's murder was Dallas County Sheriff Bill Decker. Decker played an important role in the assassination case, riding ahead of the presidential limousine,[133] helping to plan Oswald's transfer,[134] then supervising the custody of Jack Ruby.[135] At the same time, Decker was well-connected in the underworld, having been characterized in the Dallas bribe tapes as an "old-time bootlegger" and an underworld "payoff man."[136] Decker maintained friendships with two notorious local hoodlums[137] and served as a character reference for Joseph Civello when the Dallas Mafia boss applied for parole on a narcotics conviction.[138] Equally suspicious was another of Ruby's friends on the force, Harry Olsen, who met with Ruby in Simon's Garage during the early morning of November 23.[139] Olsen's alibi for the entire assassination weekend was questionable.[140]

Especially pivotal in the events of November 24 was Dallas Police Sergeant Patrick T. Dean, who was responsible for security in the police basement that morning. Dean supported Ruby's belatedly reported account that he entered the police basement through the main ramp,[141] but flunked a police polygraph test on this story.[142] Dean was another good friend of Ruby.[143] He also, as G. Robert Blakey noted, "had been on good terms with prominent organized crime figures," including Dallas Mafia boss Joseph Civello.[144]

In any event, it was clear that "someone in the police department," as Ruby intimated in his testimony, was "guilty of giving the information as to when Lee Harvey Oswald was coming down."[145] Also assisting the plot was Karen Carlin, so instrumental in establishing Ruby's alibi, whom Ruby again described with his thin hypothetical facade as "part of the conspiracy."[146] Another who lent a hand was the man in Ruby's apartment who impersonated him in the telephone conversation with Elnora Pitts. And the conspirators included whoever secured the perjured testimony of the terrified Karen Carlin, murdered soon after; of the equally terrified George Senator; of the frightened Kathy Kay, who left Dallas with Harry Olsen after his auto accident; and of the fleeing Larry Crafard, who hitchhiked to Michigan on November 23 with $7 in his pocket.

Finally, of course, the star of Oswald's murder contract was the long-time Dallas Mobster and police fixer, Jack Ruby. His performance was masterful; the shot was fired with deadly accuracy and right on cue. But when the Warren Commission came to Dallas the following June, Ruby proved much too outspoken for his part.

I would like to request that I go to Washington. . . .[1]

I want to tell the truth, and I can't tell it here.[2]

Gentlemen, my life is in danger here.[3]

> Jack Ruby, from the official transcript of his June 7, 1964
> hearing before the Warren Commission

Representative Ford: Is there anything more you can tell us if you went back to Washington?
Mr. Ruby: Yes; are you sincere in wanting to take me back?[4]

> From the same transcript

14
Jack Ruby's Startling Testimony

On November 25, 1963, the day after he shot Oswald, Jack Ruby's prospects did not seem particularly bleak. For Ruby had every reason to expect that through his Mob connections, some way could be found to evade a serious sentence—just as he had escaped all but a $10 fine on his previous nine arrests,[5] as his friend Paul Roland Jones had been pardoned for killing a state witness in Kansas,[6] as his friends Patrick and Yaras had gone free for the murder of James Ragen.[7] Moreover, Ruby's portrayal of an enraged patriotic avenger had been accepted readily, even sympathetically.[8] A reduced sentence was thus a distinct possibility.

It was thus understandable that in his first FBI interview of November 25, 1963, Ruby recited the chronicle of an aggrieved loner who desired only to spare the Kennedy family the anguish of a trial.[9] He briefly described his activities during the assassination weekend but refused to tell the FBI why he was carrying a gun when he shot Oswald.[10] He also refused to say how he got into Dallas Police headquarters that morning[11] or to detail his activities and contacts.[12] Ruby filled in these specifics on December 21, when the FBI interviewed him again.[13]

But Oswald's murder was an exceptional case; a fix yielding Ruby a light sentence would have aroused too much public suspicion. And on March 14, 1964, Ruby was convicted of first-degree murder and sentenced to death.[14] Within a month, through letters from his sister Eileen Kaminsky and his lawyers, he petitioned the Warren Commission for a hearing.[15] His request was finally granted, and on June 7, 1964, he testified in Dallas before Commission chairman Earl Warren, member Gerald Ford, Texas special counsel Leon Jaworski and other officials.[16]

The transcript of Ruby's testimony is startling both as history and as drama. During part of the hearing, Ruby recounted the same pat alibi that he had recited to the FBI.[17] Yet Ruby repeatedly interrupted his narrative with statements of a completely different character. The significance of both these statements and the official response to them is particularly clear in light of the background presented in the preceding chapters. For, as shown, Ruby's pat alibi was a complete sham, and the accumulated evidence blared this to the Commission by the time Ruby's testimony was taken. Let us now go back to this June 1964 hearing in the Dallas County Jail, as recorded by the government stenographer, for a first-hand sampling of this amazing testimony.

A CANNED ALIBI

After some preliminary dialogue, Chairman Warren instructs Ruby, "tell us your story";[18] Ruby complies.[19] But it soon becomes quite clear that this "story" is not Ruby's alone. At one point, after denying his Friday afternoon visit to Parkland Hospital, Ruby interjects, "Does this conflict with my story and yours in great length?"[20] Secret Service agent Elmer Moore replies, "Substantially the same, Jack, as well as I remember."[21] At another point, while describing his activities after the assassination, Ruby remarks, "I may have left out a few things. Mr. Moore remembers probably more. . . ."[22]

One remark by Ruby's attorney, Joe Tonahill, indicates just how carefully Ruby's alibi has been rehearsed. When Ruby digresses from this alibi at one point during the hearing, Tonahill instructs him, "You go on and keep telling it to *Caroline* and *the truth*."[23] Sure enough, later in his narrative, Ruby describes "a most heartbreaking letter" to "*Caroline*" Kennedy.[24] Fifteen transcribed lines later he interjects, "I am going to tell *the truth* word for word."[25]

"I WOULD LIKE TO REQUEST THAT I GO TO WASHINGTON"

Ruby first departs from his prepared narrative after an interruption caused by the entrance of a Commission staff member:[26]

Mr. Ruby: Is there any way to get me to Washington?

Chief Justice Warren: I beg your pardon?

Mr. Ruby: Is there any way of you getting me to Washington?

Chief Justice Warren: I don't know of any. I will be glad to talk to your counsel about what the situation is, Mr. Ruby, when we get an opportunity to talk.

Mr. Ruby: I don't think I will get a fair representation with my counsel, Joe Tonahill, I don't think so. I would like to request that I go to Washington and you take all the tests that I have to take. It is very important.[27]

After more dialogue concerning Ruby's plea, Chief Justice Warren directs Ruby to resume his story.[28] But a page later in the transcript, Ruby interrupts and repeats his request:

Gentlemen, unless you get me to Washington, you can't get a fair shake out of me.

If you understand my way of talking, you have to bring me to Washington to get the tests.[29]

Ruby is again directed to continue his narrative, this time by his lawyer, Joe Tonahill.[30]

187

"I WANT TO TELL THE TRUTH, AND I CAN'T TELL IT HERE"

Later in his hearing, after receiving no response to his requests to be taken to Washington, Ruby once more departs from his prepared alibi. He begins by asking Sheriff Decker and other policemen to leave the room.[31] The conversation continues:

Mr. Decker: You want all of us outside?

Mr. Ruby: Yes.

Mr. Decker: I will leave Tonahill and Moore. I am not going to have Joe leave.

Mr. Ruby: If you are not going to have Joe leave—

Mr. Decker: Moore, his body is responsible to you. His body is responsible to you.

Mr. Ruby: Bill, I am not accomplishing anything if they are here, and Joe Tonahill is here. You asked me anybody I wanted out.

Mr. Decker: Jack, this is your attorney. That is your lawyer.

Mr. Ruby: He is not my lawyer.

(Sheriff Decker and law enforcement officers left room.[32])

Ruby then requests once again to be taken to Washington, this time explicitly stating the reason, thereby indicating that everything he has already recited is a sham:

I want to tell the truth, and I can't tell it here. I can't tell it here. Does that make sense to you?[33]

At this point, Ruby questions two of the people in the room. He first asks Commission staff member Joe Ball, an attorney from Los Angeles, whether he has any connection with another California lawyer, Melvin Belli.[34] Ruby has reason to be wary of a connection with Belli, a member of his defense team.[35] For Belli went out socially many times with notorious California Mobster Mickey Cohen and provided favors, including a $3,000 loan, to the hoodlum.[36] Moreover, Belli was brought into Ruby's case by Michael Shore[37]—a Los Angeles record executive[38] who was a business partner and very close associate of Chicago Mobster Irwin Weiner.[39]

Ruby next asks Secret Service agent Elmer Moore, "Where do you stand, Moore?"[40] Then Ruby remarks, "Boys, I'm in a tough spot, I tell you that."[41] He soon afterward returns to his original request:

> Mr. Ruby: When are you going back to Washington?
> Chief Justice Warren: I am going back very shortly after we finish this hearing—I am going to have some lunch.
> Mr. Ruby: Can I make a statement?
> Chief Justice Warren: Yes.
> Mr. Ruby: If you request me to go back to Washington with you right now, that couldn't be done, could it?
> Chief Justice Warren: No; it could not be done. It could not be done. There are a good many things involved in that, Mr. Ruby.
> Mr. Ruby: What are they?[42]

Ruby continues with an extended but futile argument to persuade Warren to take him to Washington;[43] Warren's incredible responses will be considered shortly. Although Ruby fails to sway Warren, he does put on the record exactly why he cannot tell the truth in Dallas:

> Mr. Ruby: Gentlemen, my life is in danger here. Not with my guilty plea of execution.
> Do I sound sober enough to you as I say this?
> Chief Justice Warren: You do. You sound entirely sober.
> Mr. Ruby: I tell you, gentlemen, my whole family is in jeopardy. My sisters, as to their lives.[44]

"WOULD YOU RATHER I JUST DELETE WHAT I SAID AND JUST PRETEND THAT NOTHING IS GOING ON?"

When Ruby finally sees there is no hope of going to Washington, he briefly drops all pretense. He plunges in by naming an organization to whom he had no direct allegiance, and from whom he had least to fear.

> Mr. Ruby: All right, there is a certain organization here—
>
> Chief Justice Warren: That I can assure you.
>
> Mr. Ruby: There is a certain organization here, Chief Justice Warren, if it takes my life at this moment to say it, and Bill Decker said be a man and say it, there is a John Birch Society right now in activity, and Edwin Walker is one of the top men of this organization—take it for what it is worth, Chief Justice Warren.
>
> Unfortunately for me, for me giving the people the opportunity to get in power, because of the act I committed, has put a lot of people in jeopardy with their lives.
>
> Don't register with you, does it?
>
> Chief Justice Warren: No; I don't understand that.
>
> Mr. Ruby: *Would you rather I just delete what I said and just pretend that nothing is going on?*
>
> Chief Justice Warren: I would not indeed. I am only interested in what you want to tell this Commission. That is all I am interested in.
>
> Mr. Ruby: Well, I said my life, I won't be living long now. I know that my family's lives will be gone. When I left my apartment that morning—
>
> Chief Justice Warren: What morning?
>
> Mr. Ruby: Sunday morning.
>
> Chief Justice Warren: Sunday morning.[45]

By his blank response to Ruby's indication of conspiracy and his sudden curiosity about Ruby's resumed alibi, Warren cuts off further meaningful discussion about the assassination. During the remainder of the hearing, however, Ruby slips in some significant disclosures in other digressions. Then, toward the end of the session, Ruby engages in extraneous and at times disjointed discourse and otherwise attempts to prolong the hearing.[46] For example:

> Chief Justice Warren [addressing Commissioner Ford]: Congressman, do you have anything further?

Mr. Ruby: You can get more out of me. Let's not break up too soon.[47]

This behavior is clearly understandable, given Ruby's several explicit statements expressing fear of being killed shortly after the interview.[48] One example is this remark:

Mr. Bill Decker said be a man and speak up. I am making a statement now that I may not live the next hour when I walk out of this room.[49]

In fact, Ruby does not let the hearing end before securing repeated assurances from Warren that he will be given a lie detector examination, which would allow him further contact with federal officials.[50]

Ruby's explicit fears of death may appear fanciful, but only to someone unfamiliar with the assassination evidence. Recall the case of Rose Cheramie, a criminally involved drug addict, who told doctors in a Louisiana hospital that the "word in the underworld" was that Kennedy would be assassinated.[51] Less than two years later, in September 1965, she was run over by an automobile in Texas.[52] Two days after Ruby shot Oswald, Teamster official Leopoldo Ramos Ducos informed FBI agents of contacts between Ruby and two top Teamster officials.[53] His decision to talk was evidently known, for earlier that day he had received the message, "We killed Kennedy and the next will be Ramos Ducos."[54]

Dallas Sheriff Roger Craig, who reported incidents indicating conspiracy, went into hiding after learning "the Mafia had put a price on his head."[55] Craig was shot in the shoulder by an unknown assailant in 1974 and then found dead of a rifle wound in 1975, which the police reported as self-inflicted, after discussing the case on a radio talk show.[56]

Ruby's intimations of death threats are indeed credible given the aftermath of a November 24, 1963 meeting at his apartment between his roommate, George Senator, two journalists and two attorneys. Within 16 months, both journalists were brutally murdered,[57] and one attorney died of what was called a heart attack.[58] Senator was terrified for days after the meeting.[59] Others who backed Ruby's alibi exhibited similar fears or unusual behavior—including Kathy Kay, Larry Crafard, and Karen Carlin.[60] Carlin, in the words of an interviewing Secret Service agent, "seemed on the point of hysteria," believing there was "a plot to assassinate President Kennedy" and that she "would be killed if she gave any information to the authorities."[61] She was shot to death several months later.[62] Other cases of murders, assaults and intimidation of witnesses have been described in chapter 3.

And Ruby's Dallas jail cell was hardly a sanctuary from Mob retribution. As he knew well from personal dealings, the Mafia can kill a witness in a maximum security cell as easily as a loan shark defaulter in a dilapidated tenement.* Indeed, Ruby could hardly have felt secure in the custody of Sheriff Bill Decker[68]—a reputed underworld payoff man.[69] Nor could Ruby have been reassured by the Mob murder of another witness in Dallas Police custody, of which he knew well: the murder of Lee Harvey Oswald. The message was perhaps reiterated to Ruby by Mafioso Joseph Campisi, an associate of the Marcellos,[70] who visited Ruby in jail on November 30, 1963.[71]

THE COMMISSION'S CONDUCT OF RUBY'S HEARING

Potential Mob retribution and police corruption were not the only factors, however, that inhibited Ruby from speaking freely at his Dallas hearing. As will be discussed in a subsequent chapter, the federal government's handling of the assassination probe was also compromised.[72] And it is inescapably clear that one member of the Warren Commission took extraordinary steps to

---

*In 1941, for example, Mob informant Abe Reles plunged to his death from a hotel window while under guard by six New York City policemen.[63] In 1945, Peter LaTempa was poisoned in a maximum security cell in a Brooklyn jail while waiting to testify against Mafia boss Vito Genovese.[64] In 1954, Gaspare Pisciotta, a witness against the Sicilian Mafia, was poisoned in his isolated cell in Palermo with enough strychnine to kill 40 dogs.[65] And during the 1970s, four Mob defectors were murdered and six others died unnatural deaths under a federal alias program that was allegedly compromised by corrupt officials.[66] Almost 20 of the FBI's Mob informants were killed in 1976 and 1977.[67] Fortunately for Ruby, however, killing him would have aroused too much suspicion following his own murder of Oswald.

encourage Ruby's silence at the hearing—steps that defy any legitimate explanation.

Jack Ruby, the most important source of information on the Kennedy assassination then alive, was not called to testify until June 1964, and then only because of his repeated requests.[73] Three times during the hearing, in fact, Ruby expressed regret that the Commission had not interviewed him earlier.[74] Chairman Warren explained, "I wish we had gotten here a little sooner after your trial was over, but I know you had other things on your mind, and we had other work, and it got to this late date."[75] Later on, Warren added, "Unless you had indicated not only through your lawyers but also through your sister . . . that you wanted to testify before the Commission, unless she had told us that, I wouldn't have bothered you."[76]

By waiting until June to question Ruby, however, the Commission gained one advantage. For the evidence amassed by then had demonstrated that Ruby's alibi and his actual activities prior to Oswald's murder were extremely suspicious. And sufficient time had elapsed to prepare questions on dozens of critical points. Several important areas of interrogation were listed in just one memorandum of February 24, 1964, by Commission staff members Leon Hubert and Burt Griffin.[77] This memo stated that Ruby "became the subject of a narcotics investigation," and was "peripherally, if not directly connected with members of the underworld" in Dallas.[78] It noted that Ruby "very carefully cultivated friendships with police officers and other public officials," and "became interested . . . in the possibility of opening a gambling casino in Havana."[79] The memo also listed groups, persons and locations to investigate in connection with the assassination.[80] These included the Teamsters Union, the "Las Vegas gambling community," the Dallas Police Department, radio station KLIF, H. L. Hunt and the City of New Orleans.[81] It was also apparent that Ruby's pre-assassination telephone conversations and visits with Mobsters from across the country,[82] including top lieutenants of Carlos Marcello,[83] merited close scrutiny.

Yet the Commission grilled Ruby on none of these matters and rarely even questioned him about his transparently perjured alibi.[84] The Commission's complete lack of interest was illustrated by one flagrant gap in his ten-page narrative of his assassination weekend activities, in which he skipped over a 28-hour period with only brief references to watching television and visiting a night club.[85] It was clear that much was omitted; several witnesses described more than a dozen activities of Ruby during this period.[86] But the Commission was forced to report conjectures of what "Ruby apparently did" in that interval,[87] because it had allowed Ruby to skip over this gap without even one question.[88]

Indeed, most of the interventions by Warren, who took almost complete charge of the hearing, were efforts to steer Ruby back to his canned story whenever he digressed.[89] Warren did this when Ruby asked to be taken to Washington,[90] reported that his life was in danger,[91] stated he could not tell the truth in Dallas[92] and finally made one attempt to do so.[93] Warren's exclusive interest in Ruby's canned story was illustrated when he responded "I don't understand that" to Ruby's disclosure about the Birch Society.[94] Later on, however, Ruby resumed the recital of his alibi, and stated, "I realize it is a terrible thing I have done, and it was a stupid thing, but I just was carried away emotionally. Do you follow that?"[95] This time Warren replied, "Yes; I do indeed, every word."[96]

Indeed, when Ruby, the Warren Commission's most important witness, asked to be taken to Washington to provide information he felt endangered to disclose in Dallas, there was only one proper official response. Even if these requests had not been so persistent, Ruby's pat alibi so obviously fraudulent or his background and pre-assassination contacts so markedly suspicious, Warren had only one legitimate option—to assure Ruby that the government would protect him and enable him to tell the full truth. The following excerpt from Ruby's hearing can therefore be read only with amazement.

Mr. Ruby: . . . Chairman Warren, if you felt your life was in danger at the moment, how would you feel? Wouldn't you be reluctant to go on speaking, even though you request me to do so?

Chief Justice Warren: I think *I might have some reluctance* if I was in your position, yes; I think I would. I think *I would figure it out very carefully* as to *whether it would endanger me or not.*

If you think anything that I am doing or anything that I am asking you is endangering you in any way, shape, or form, I want you to feel absolutely free to say that the interview is over.[97]

The subsequent dialogue reveals that the silence Warren advised for Ruby was to be permanent, although the opportunity to talk freely that Ruby requested could have been easily arranged.

Mr. Ruby: What happens then? I didn't accomplish anything.

Chief Justice Warren: No; nothing has been accomplished.

Mr. Ruby: Well, then you won't follow up with anything further?

Chief Justice Warren: There wouldn't be anything to follow up if you hadn't completed your statement.

Mr. Ruby: You said you have the power to do what you want to do, is that correct?

Chief Justice Warren: Exactly.

Mr. Ruby: Without any limitations?

Chief Justice Warren: Within the purview of the Executive order which established the Commission. We have the right to take testimony of anyone we want in this whole situation, and we have the right, if we so choose to do it, to verify that statement in any way that we wish to do it.

Mr. Ruby: But you don't have the right to take a prisoner back with you when you want to?

Chief Justice Warren: *No; we have the power to subpoena witnesses to Washington* if we want to do it, but we have taken the testimony of 200 or 300 people, I would imagine, here in Dallas without going to Washington.

Mr. Ruby: Yes; but those people aren't Jack Ruby.

Chief Justice Warren: No; they weren't.

Mr. Ruby: They weren't.[98]

Warren later repeated his advice to Ruby: "I want you to feel that you are free to refrain from testifying any time you wish."[99]

Warren's inexplicable behavior* had tragic personal as well as historical consequences. For Jack Ruby had nothing to gain by implicating himself in premeditated murder and conspiracy while his appeals were pending; evidently he had much to fear in doing so. Nevertheless Ruby, a lifelong criminal, briefly rose to a level of nobility by attempting to put the truth on the record. And it must have been a stunning blow to him to discover, as he phrased it toward the end of his hearing, "Maybe certain people don't want to know the truth that may come out of me."[110]

THE POLYGRAPH EXAMINATION

Several times in his testimony, Ruby expressed a desire to take a polygraph test.[111] As his hearing drew to a close, and the moment approached when he would be left alone with his Dallas Police custodians, Ruby became even more insistent about this request:

Mr. Ruby: All I want is a lie detector test, and you refuse to give it to me. . . . And they will not give it to me, because I want to tell the truth.

And then I want to leave this world. . . .

*Any hope that Warren's conduct had a reasonable explanation was quashed by J. Lee Rankin, chief counsel of the Warren Commission, in 1978 testimony during the House Assassination hearings. When asked about the Commission's strange denial of Ruby's persistent pleas, Rankin said, "We were all convinced that Ruby was interested in a trip to Washington rather than how much he could enlighten the Commission."[100] If, indeed, the Commission knew as little about Ruby's situation as Rankin claimed, then its investigatory incompetence was almost as appalling as the more sinister possibilities otherwise suggested.

Warren himself discussed the assassination in a May 1972 television interview.[101] His remarks were analyzed by a private researcher using the Psychological Stress Evaluator (PSE), a lie-detecting device that measures stress by voice pattern analysis.[102] Demonstrated reliable in several tests,[103] it is used by hundreds of U.S. law enforcement agencies and accepted as evidence in more than a dozen states.[104]

Warren's remarks in the interview were found to have been generally unstressed,[105] but when the conversation turned to the assassination, a completely different pattern emerged.[106] Warren answered a series of questions by contending the Commission had explored all angles and found no evidence of conspiracy.[107] "The PSE showed hard stress" in each response,[108] revealing at one point "a perfectly trimmed hedge"—the strongest possible indication of deception.[109]

> Chief Justice Warren: Mr. Ruby, I promise you that you
> will be able to take such a test.
>
> Mr. Ruby: When?[112]

Ruby put little stock in Warren's assurance:

> Mr. Ruby: . . . these things are going to be promised,
> but you see they aren't going to let me do these things.
>
> Because when you leave here, I am finished. My family
> is finished.
>
> Representative Ford: Isn't it true, Mr. Chief Justice, that
> the same maximum protection and security Mr. Ruby has
> been given in the past will be continued?
>
> Mr. Ruby: But now that I have divulged certain informa-
> tion . . .[113]

Ruby's skepticism persisted, and he repeated his request for a polygraph test in his last statement of the hearing[114] — even after both Warren and Ford had promised that he would be given such a test.[115]

Ruby's skepticism was not groundless. On June 11, 1964, FBI Director J. Edgar Hoover sent a letter to the Warren Commission denying its request to have the FBI administer a polygraph test to Ruby.[116] Hoover claimed the test was unreliable[117] (although the FBI had administered such a test to at least one other assassination witness[118]) and that Ruby's appeals were in progress[119] (they were still going on in late 1966[120]). The Warren Commission then sent Hoover a letter repeating its request,[121] and on July 13 Hoover refused again.[122]

Nevertheless, perhaps because of the unequivocal pledge that Ruby secured from it, the Commission scheduled the test for July 16, 1964.[123] A few days beforehand, however, the Commission received word from Ruby's sister and attorneys that they opposed the test.[124] They objected on the grounds that "his mental state was such that the test would be meaningless," and that the test "would affect Ruby's health and would be of questionable value."[125] But finally, on July 18, 1964, the test was administered to Ruby.[126]

There are two reasons why Ruby would have desired such a

test. First, it could have provided an avenue out of the clutches of the Dallas Police—although, as it turned out, it was administered in the Dallas County Jail,[127] as was his June 7 hearing.[128] Second, it could have allowed Ruby to appease anyone threatening him by relating his alibi, yet still expose the truth through the polygraph readings. He had to ensure only that the right questions were posed to him. Ruby probably did not realize, however, that the polygraph apparatus only measures stress, and that death threats could generate as much stress as considerations of integrity. In any event, as the House Assassinations Committee concluded, the results were impossible to interpret because of "numerous procedural errors made during the test."[129]

RUBY'S DISCLOSURES

Despite Ruby's failure to escape Dallas Police custody and to generate a mechanical record of the truth, he did succeed in putting valuable disclosures on record. In some cases, his statements were made in the guise of attempting to bolster his alibi,[130] as with this remark:

> How can we give me the clearance that the ads put in [announcing the closing of the Carousel and Vegas clubs November 22–24] were authentic, my sincerity, my feeling of emotionalism were sincere; that that Sunday morning I got carried away after reading the article, a letter addressed to Caroline and then this little article that stated Mrs. Kennedy might be requested to come back and face the ordeal of the trial?
>
> Also, *if there was a conspiracy, then this little girl that called me on the phone in Fort Worth then is a part of the conspiracy.*[131]

Yet in other cases, there was no such covering preface,[132] as with this additional statement about Oswald's murder, which also merits repeating:

> Who else could have timed it so perfectly by seconds. If it were timed that way, then someone in the police depart-

ment is guilty of giving the information as to when Lee Harvey Oswald was coming down.[133]

Especially noteworthy are Ruby's repeated requests during his polygraph session to be questioned about the underworld. At one point, Ruby mentioned, "I also had numerous phone calls, long-distance calls, all over the country," and asked to be questioned about organized crime contacts.[134] When Assistant District Attorney William Alexander then proposed the question, "Did any union or underworld connection have anything to do with the shooting of Oswald?" Ruby replied, "Very good."[135] Ruby later repeated, "How about the underworld? . . . There were a lot of phone calls."[136]

After further discussion, Ruby was asked whether he wished to be questioned about any other topic[137] Ruby replied, "Yes— whether or not I was ever mixed up with the underworld here or involved in any crime?"[138] Asked later whether he wished to be posed further questions, Ruby replied, "Oh, yes, sir. Has the underworld ever contributed money to me for my clubs, or was I put here as a front for the underworld or things to that effect."[139] He then commented that people thought

maybe I was put here as a front of the underworld and sooner or later they will get something out of me that they want done to their advantage.[140]

Additional disclosures by Ruby are considered later.

RUBY'S FINAL STATEMENT

Ruby got another brief chance for public contact on March 19, 1965, when he was met by reporters between the Dallas jail and the court.[14] His remarks were telecast that evening on CBS-TV, as reported by Sylvia Meagher,[142] the author of the only comprehensive index to the Warren Commission exhibits.[143] According to Meagher's notes, Ruby pleaded to be removed to federal jurisdiction and made a statement including the words "complete conspiracy . . . and the assassination too . . . if you knew the facts you would be amazed."[144]

In another television interview, which was concluded in the BBC special *The Kennedy Assassination: What Do We Know Now That We Didn't Then*, Ruby said:

> Everything pertaining to what's happening has never come to the surface. The world will never know the true facts of what occurred, my motives.[145]

When asked, "Do you think it'll ever come out," Ruby answered,

> No, because unfortunately the people [who] had so much to gain and had such an ulterior motive to put me in the position I'm in will never let the true facts come aboveboard to the world.[146]

Ruby's chance to elaborate appeared imminent when his long-standing request to be extricated from Dallas Police custody was finally granted. On December 7, 1966, a Texas court ruled favorably on his appeal and scheduled a new trial for him in Wichita Falls.[147] But three days later, Ruby was reported ill of lung cancer.[148] He died the following month, on January 3, 1967.[149]

Before his death, Ruby was thus able to indicate conspiracy in the Oswald shooting, and to hint boldly at Mafia involvement. Moreover, as Ruby's background surfaced, it became clear that he had indeed been "mixed up with the underworld"[150] and put in Dallas "as a front of the underworld."[151] But only a series of documents scattered in National Archives files could unravel his "numerous phone calls, long distance calls, all over the country,"[152] and resolve whether he had in fact been "used for a purpose"[153] to accomplish something the Mob wanted "done to their advantage."[154] Only these documents could reveal Jack Ruby's final legacy — the identification of President Kennedy's killers.

PART IV

Pilgrims
and
Pirates

With the exposure of Ruby's Syndicate connection and of the careful staging behind his murder of Oswald, a demonstration of the Mob's long-suspected[1] assassination role is now within reach. Yet such a demonstration will be most meaningful in the context of broader issues. Were other individuals or groups involved in the plot? Why was the Warren Commission so blind to evidence of conspiracy, so unresponsive to Ruby's attempts to speak freely? And most important, did the killing of President Kennedy effect a transformation in the political course of the United States?

Before following the final stretch of the trail to President Kennedy's killers, this part provides an interlude to begin exploring these questions. The journey sweeps through murky ground — from Cuban armaments to Southeast Asian heroin, from the Bobby Baker scandal to Watergate. Yet certain conclusions can be clearly drawn.

We will see that President Kennedy's policies after the Cuban missile crisis — the test ban treaty and announced armaments reductions, civil rights initiatives, the ordered withdrawal of one thousand troops from Vietnam and the escalated war against organized crime — marked a sharp departure from previous American policy. These initiatives aroused the wrath of a loose coalition including the Mob, extreme right wingers and elements of the CIA that had been drawn together in the early 1960s in a common campaign to eliminate Cuban Premier Fidel Castro. Increasingly frustrated in this campaign by a clamp-down on anti-Castro activity in 1963, this coalition came to focus its enmity on President Kennedy, as well.

We will see that Mobsters and others from the ranks of this coalition took steps to conceal evidence in the Kennedy assassination case. This cover-up, in addition to shielding the culprits, has obscured the larger political transformation that occurred as a result of the November 22 murder. Indeed, as will be shown in the book's final chapters on the assassination aftermath, much of President Kennedy's policy thrust was reversed in the Johnson Administration, contrary to popular belief, while both the Nixon and Reagan presidencies saw the specter of the anti-Castro coalition reemerge.

The policies, alliances and antipathies to be considered can perhaps be illuminated by brief reflection on their philosophical roots in American history. Since Columbus's voyage in 1492, two classes have settled and shaped the United States: pilgrims and pirates. The pilgrims sought sustenance: they planted, crafted and nurtured. The pirates sought plunder: they extorted, ravaged and murdered. In the nation's westward expansion, this dichotomy was reflected by industrious homesteaders, on the one hand, and by the feverish hordes of the gold rush, whose big winners were not the shrewdest prospectors but the best gunmen. Unfortunately, in some of the richest economic domains, where control of oil wells, watering holes and other natural resources was pivotal, the ruthless prevailed.

Twentieth-century America retained these noblest and basest of values, but often in a bewildering amalgamation. There were some, for example, steeped in the methods and profits of killing, who applied these in perverse quests to strengthen America. And others coupled the practices of exploitation, manipulation and deception with moral pronouncements, charitable donations and sponsorship of public television broadcasts in proper British accents.

Yet one group retained its ultimate, unadulterated commitment to extortion: the Mafia. Forged by the brutality of assorted conquerors during centuries of foreign subjugation in Sicily,[2] many of its members came to the United States at the turn of the 20th century seeking richer pastures of plunder.[3] They started out as henchmen and merchants of vice; by the end of World War II, they had regrouped into a new American confederation that dominated organized criminal activity.[4] And over the course of three postwar decades, the Mob completed its evolution from servant to master of America's darker side.

It no longer cracked skulls for ruthless labor bosses or country club executives — it controlled major unions[5] and elite country clubs.[6] It no longer robbed banks — it bought, sold, and drained them.[7] It no longer bribed just mayors and policemen—it dictated votes to Congressmen and hobnobbed with presidents.[8] One reflection of this post-war ascendancy of the Mob is its central role in the murky chronicle that follows.

Others might hate Kennedy. The mob was in a unique position to do something about it. Unlike Kennedy's other enemies, the Minutemen or the exiles, the Cosa Nostra was not a small band of fanatic zealots. It was a cool, well-disciplined conspiracy of enormous dimensions.[1]

Robert Sam Anson, TV producer and
political correspondent

15
The Anti-Castro Coalition

The Mafia has formed opportune alliances with parties across the political spectrum, ranging from labor bosses to industrial magnates, from American Communists to Italian Fascists.[2] And upon the 1959 victory of Castro's revolutionary forces in Cuba, it acquired bedfellows, as previously noted, of three persuasions: Cuban exiles, extreme right-wingers and certain elements of the CIA. All cooperated in efforts to eliminate the new Cuban premier, then refocused their antagonism on the chief obstacle to this and other objectives: President Kennedy. The antipathy that developed between the president and this anti-Castro alliance was drawn in part across conventional lines of political ideology. But vituperative rhetoric and murderous methods exposed it as primarily a Pilgrim-Pirate struggle.

"WANTED FOR TREASON"

Planned in the Eisenhower Administration under White House Action Officer Richard Nixon,[3] and approved by newly elected President Kennedy,[4] the Bay of Pigs invasion was touted by the CIA as an operation vital to U.S. security.[5] But from the first hours of the abortive April 1961 incursion into Cuba, it became clear that it could be salvaged only by American military intervention, in particular, by the air support that the CIA had promised the exiles;[6] President Kennedy refused.[7] The reaction of the

CIA and the exiles was bitter,[8] as reflected by sharp criticism of Kennedy in the memoirs of E. Howard Hunt, a CIA anti-Castro operative.[9] And the president, unhappy with the CIA's handling of the invasion, shook up its top leadership,[10] telling aides he wanted to splinter the CIA "into a thousand pieces and scatter [it] to the winds."[11] The continuing antagonism between President Kennedy and the CIA was exhibited and probably exacerbated just before his death, when he ordered a task force to review American intelligence activities.[12]

In October 1962, the discovery of Soviet missiles in Cuba precipitated a major crisis; President Kennedy averted nuclear war by pledging not to invade Cuba in return for removal of the Russian weapons.[13] The president subsequently ordered the CIA to cut off all support to the Cuban exiles.[14] And in 1963, after several CIA-sponsored raids were carried out despite this order, President Kennedy issued strong warnings against further such anti-Castro activity.[15] The Minutemen, an extreme right-wing group, partially tempered the effect of this ban, however, by providing arms and other assistance to the exiles.[16] In November 1963, President Kennedy further dissociated the United States from violent efforts against Castro by setting up preliminary talks on diplomatic accommodation with Cuba.[17]

Seeking a humane national posture on other fronts, President Kennedy took initiatives viewed radical and treacherous by those who thrived on racial subjugation, international polarization and the profits derived therefrom. His administration pioneered civil rights measures and sent federal troops to Alabama to enforce court-ordered integration.[18] In August 1963, after the Reverend Martin Luther King gave his famous "I Have a Dream" address to 250,000 Americans in front of the Lincoln Memorial, President Kennedy warmly greeted him at the White House.[19]

On June 10, 1963, President Kennedy shattered hopes for aggressive military action against the Communist bloc in a noteworthy address at American University, concerning "the most important topic on earth—peace."[20] Nikita Khrushchev responded on July 2 with a sharp departure from his own hard-line stance; the two leaders swiftly negotiated a test-ban treaty, signed on August 5.[21] At a reception for the signers, a Soviet band played Gershwin's "Love Walked In."[22] Later that year, a wheat sale agreement was concluded between the two superpowers.[23]

On November 18, 1963, Defense Secretary Robert McNamara told the New York Economic Club, as summarized in *Business Week*, that "a major cut in defense spending [was] in the works,"[24] similar to the cut proposed by Khrushchev in July.[25] McNamara made it plain that "a fundamental strategic shift" was involved, "not just a temporary slash."[26] Such a cut was poorly received by the armaments industry, which was heavily represented in Texas.[27]* And in a January 1963 tax message, President Kennedy affronted the oil industry by calling for a sharp reduction in the oil depletion allowance.[34]

In the spring of 1963, President Kennedy told aide Kenneth O'Donnell of his determination to withdraw American forces from Vietnam after the November election, commenting, "I'll be damned everywhere as a communist appeaser. But I don't care."[35] On October 2, 1963, Defense Secretary McNamara and General Maxwell Taylor reported that it was their objective to terminate the "major part" of U.S. military involvement in Vietnam by 1965.[36] Specifically, they predicted that 1,000 U.S. troops would be withdrawn from there by the end of 1963.[37] On October 31, in a news conference, President Kennedy reaffirmed his administration's intention to pull out these 1,000 troops.[38] The first 220 of them were withdrawn on December 3, 1963, as directed by Kennedy's prior order.[39]

Their Pirate sensibilities inflamed, some from the extreme right openly expressed their loathing of Kennedy. In April 1963, a flyer was sent to Cubans in Miami, which read:

Only through one development will you Cuban patriots ever live again in your homeland as freemen . . . [only] if an inspired Act of God should place in the White House within weeks a Texan known to be a friend of all Latin

*The Mafia too had a share in Pentagon dollars. For example, Medico Industries of Pennsylvania received a $3.9 million contract to produce 600,000 warheads for use in Vietnam.[28] The company's general manager, William Medico, was an associate of Russell Bufalino,[29] the northeastern Pennsylvania Mafia boss,[30] who frequently visited the Medico offices.[31] Company President Phillip Medico was described in an FBI wiretap as "a capo" (chief) in Bufalino's Mafia Family.[32] And a third Medico official was apprehended at the 1957 Mafia conclave in Apalachin, New York.[33]

Americans . . . though he must under present conditions bow to the Zionists who since 1905 came into control of the United States, and for whom Jack Kennedy and Nelson Rockefeller and other members of the Council of Foreign Relations and allied agencies are only stooges and pawns. Though Johnson must now bow to these crafty and cunning Communist-hatching Jews, yet, did an Act of God suddenly elevate him into the top position [he] would revert to what his beloved father and grandfather were, and to their values and principles and loyalties.[40]

The flyer was dated April 18, 1963, and signed "a Texan who resents the Oriental influence that has come to control, to degrade, to pollute and enslave his own people."[41]

Dallas oil magnate and extreme right-wing propagandist H. L. Hunt reportedly had similar designs for President Kennedy. During a party before the president's visit to Dallas, according to German journalist Joachim Joesten, several witnesses heard Hunt remark that there was "no way left to get those traitors out of our government except by shooting them out," referring to President Kennedy.[42] Edwin Walker, a well-known Dallas official of the John Birch Society, exhibited similar sentiments. Walker flew the flag in front of his house upside-down days before President Kennedy's visit, as a UPI dispatch reported.[43] But he flew it at full staff during President Johnson's proclaimed period of half-staff mourning.[44]

A few days before the assassination, handbills with President Kennedy's photo and a "Wanted for Treason" caption appeared on the streets of Dallas.[45] They were printed by Robert A. Surrey, a close associate of Walker.[46] And on the day of the president's visit, a local newspaper carried a full-page, black-bordered ad harshly critical of his policies.[47] The sponsors of the ad included Nelson Bunker Hunt, son of H. L. Hunt, and Birch Society members.[48]

ALIGNMENT AGAINST CASTRO

Thus President Kennedy secured the enmity of Cuban exiles, extreme right-wingers and elements within the CIA through his moderation toward Castro, his peace and civil rights initiatives, and his proposed reduction in the oil depletion allowance. At the same time, he incurred the wrath of the Mob through his administration's crusade against organized crime. But the issue that brought the Mob and these other groups together was Castro's disruption of a massive enterprise in Cuba: Mafia-controlled gambling.

The Mob's dealings in Cuba were chronicled in a report furnished to Congress in 1978 by the Cuban government.[49] "The Mafia began its activities in Cuba during the '20s, taking advantage of the corruption of the successive governments of that period."[50] During the 1940s, it infiltrated Cuban trade unions, while investing "in real estate companies and the building of luxury hotels, casinos and other tourist facilities."[51] The casinos were administered by "Cubans or foreign figures linked to the Mafia" and "directed by Mafia-appointed chiefs"; Florida chieftain Santos Trafficante "represented the Mafia leadership."[52] The Mafia "also controlled the traffic in drugs, jewels, the currency exchange, white slavery and pornographic film shows."[53] Indeed, by the mid-1950s, Havana had become a multibillion-dollar Mob center of gambling, narcotics and vice, equivalent to today's Las Vegas and Atlantic City combined.[54]

Like his friend Santos Trafficante and several other Mobsters, Carlos Marcello kept a finger in the Cuban pie through an interest in a gambling casino there.[55] Marcello was also heavily involved in the Cuban narcotics trade,[56] and was rumored to have associated with Cuban exiles and dealt in armaments.[57] The third member of the Mob's anti-Kennedy triumvirate, Jimmy Hoffa, likewise became involved in the Cuban scene by sponsoring an arms smuggling operation from southern Florida to Cuba.[58]

As Castro began making headway during the mid-1950s, the Mob followed the same strategy it used for domestic political challengers.[59] Certain Mob casino operators, including Norman Rothman, supplied Castro with guns and cash, while the bulk of the Mob payoffs still went to Batista.[60] A group of Mobsters even formed a corporation, Akros Dynamics, which sold a fleet of C-74 airplanes to the new Castro government; Hoffa tried unsuccessfully to secure a $300,000 Teamsters pension fund loan for the venture.[61]

So when Castro took power in 1959, only prominent Batista allies like Meyer Lansky fled, and the Mob as a whole was not alarmed.[62] In fact, an accommodation was worked out that permitted gambling to continue from March 1959 through September 1961.[63] Supervising was the Castro-appointed "Minister for Games of Chance," a casino operator who had run guns for Castro.[64] He was Frank Fiorini, alias Frank Sturgis of Watergate fame.[65] Along with Norman "Roughhouse" Rothman, Sturgis later became an important liaison between the CIA and Mafia in their anti-Castro collaboration.[66]

But Castro had little regard for the American hoodlums, and by September 1961 he had expelled all the Mob casino operators from Cuba.[67] Castro declared, according to Sturgis, "I'm going to run all these fascist mobsters, all these American gangsters, out of Cuba . . . Cuba for Cubans."[68] As Jack Anderson commented, this expulsion hit the Mob "as hard as the 1929 stock market crash rocked Wall Street."[69] Whereas *Fortune* magazine placed the largest loss from expropriation for a U.S. firm at $272 million,[70] the *New York Times* had estimated the Mob's annual gambling take from Cuba at between $350 and $700 million.[71]* It was not surprising, therefore, that Castro's distaste for the Mob was vociferously reciprocated.

THE CIA AND THE MAFIA

The common desire to eliminate the Castro regime eventually led to cooperative activity by the Mob and the CIA.[74] But such sinister collusion between the two groups was not unprecedented. During World War II, William Donovan, chief of U.S. Intelligence (OSS), decided that a "corps of skilled safecrackers, housebreakers and assassins" could further the war effort.[75] Donovan secured the best—Mafia boss Charles "Lucky" Luciano[76]—who used his influence to protect Mafia-infested American docks from Axis sabotage.[77] In return, Luciano was granted a commu-

---

*The enormous magnitude of the Mob's Cuban gambling profits was indicated by John Scarne, an American gambling expert, who spent five hours observing one dice table in a Havana casino.[72] He counted a fantastic $3 million change hands that evening at that single dice game in that one casino.[73]

tation of a long prison sentence, and was deported to Italy in 1946.[78] There he helped revitalize the Mafia's international narcotics ring,[79] later moving to Havana to control operations in that key American supply point.[80] Between 1946 and 1952, the number of heroin addicts in the United States tripled.[81]

While the details of Luciano's war involvements are hidden in classified files,[82] the better-known activities of fellow boss Vito Genovese reflect the Mafia's contribution to the war effort. In 1937, Genovese fled from New York to Italy after Brooklyn police secured two witnesses to his murder of a Mafia colleague.[83] Genovese ingratiated himself with the Mussolini regime,[84] reportedly contributing $250,000 to the construction of Fascist Party headquarters out of the take he was still drawing from American rackets.[85] Genovese also showed his friendship to the Mussolini government by ordering the January 1943 murder of Carlos Tresca, editor of the New York anti-Fascist newspaper *The Hammer*.[86]

When the Allies occupied Italy, Genovese got himself appointed translator-liaison for U.S. Army headquarters.[87] Based in a luxury apartment in Naples, traveling freely with government passes in his chauffeur-driven limousine,[88] Genovese traded in stolen American supplies and was a kingpin in Italy's black market.[89] He also served as whoremaster to certain top Allied officers.[90] In one of his more cunning ventures, Genovese used U.S. Army trucks, later found destroyed by fire, to steal flour and sugar from American supplies in Nola.[91]

Genovese's activities were finally uncovered by O. C. Dickey of the U.S. Army Criminal Investigation Division, who sought to return Genovese to the United States for his Brooklyn murder trial.[92] But Genovese used his influence to stay in Italy until one of two witnesses against him, Peter LaTempa, was murdered.[93] While in a maximum security cell in a Brooklyn jail on January 15,1945, LaTempa suffered from a gallstone condition and asked for medicine to relieve the pain.[94] Later that day he was dead; a city autopsy revealed enough poison in his body "to kill eight horses."[95]

The favoritism shown to Luciano and Genovese was representative of a broader Pentagon courtship of the Sicilian Mafia. Fearing potential Communist advances in postwar Italy, American military officials cut back support for the anti-Fascist underground and turned instead to this underworld organization.[96] The Mafia was glad to cooperate, having been purged almost to extinction by Mussolini.[97] With arrangements apparently made through intermediaries from the American branch, the Sicilian Mafia arranged enthusiastic welcomes, protected the road from snipers and provided guides for General George Patton's troops on their July 1943 march to Palermo.[98]

The Allied military command subsequently appointed many of the Mafiosi, including top don Cologero Vizzini, as mayors of towns in western Sicily.[99] These appointments led to a "recrudescence of Mafia activities," including homicides, noted British Major General Lord Rennell, chief of the Allied Military Government of Occupied Territories.[100] And thanks to this Allied benevolence, the Mafia soon regained its former power in Italy.[101]

Consolidated into the CIA by the National Security Act of 1947,[102] American intelligence forces formed a similar relationship with the Corsican syndicates in France,[103] close allies of the Sicilian Mafia.[104] In the first year of its existence, the CIA hired the Corsicans to disrupt a Communist-inspired dock strike at Marseilles;[105] it was broken after a number of strikers were murdered.[106] The CIA again called upon the Corsicans in 1950, with similar results, when Marseilles dock workers refused to ship war materials to Indochina.[107]

When the CIA and the Mafia cooperated during the early 1960s in Cuba, however, as considered below, a questionable relationship mushroomed into a monstrous alliance. One manifestation was noted by Seymour Hersh in the *New York Times*, based on a 1974 interview with a CIA undercover agent "whose knowledge of the CIA seemed extensive"; Hersh reported that "the Mafia was relied upon" to "assault targets selected by the CIA."[108] The extent of such cooperation was suggested when the Nixon Administration intervened for the defense—ostensibly to protect "intelligence sources and methods"—in at least 20 trials of organized crime figures.[109] A further example of this Mafia-CIA alliance run amok was a joint counterfeiting operation in Southeast Asia, reported in July 1975 by staff members of the Senate Permanent Investigations Committee.[110]

ANTI-CASTRO RAIDS AND
ASSASSINATION ATTEMPTS

Returning to the setting of Cuba—where Castro had expropriated a vast gambling empire and inflamed Cold War sentiments—the Mob, the CIA and extreme right-wing elements initiated a series of operations against the Cuban leader.[111] The Mob contributed in several capacities, supplying arms, ammunition and aircraft to the Cuban exiles, and launching its own paramilitary operations.[112] This involvement surfaced on July 31,1963, when the FBI raided a dynamite cache in Mandeville, Louisiana that was used to supply Cuban exiles; it had been stocked by the Mob.[113] Later in 1963, the Kennedy Administration learned of raids being launched into Cuba by six Americans, including CIA undercover agent Frank Sturgis and his friend Alexander Rourke.[114] According to Rourke's attorney, Hans Tanner, the anti-Castro group backing Sturgis was apparently "financed by dispossessed hotel and gambling room owners who operated under Batista."[115] The Mob also reportedly funneled millions of dollars from gambling receipts to one prominent exile leader, Dr. Paulino Sierra Martinez.[116]

The most infamous joint effort between the Mob and CIA in Cuba was a series of assassination plots against Premier Fidel Castro.[117] In December 1959, CIA Director Allen Dulles, who would later serve on the Warren Commission, approved a recommendation that "thorough consideration be given to the elimination of Fidel Castro."[118] In August 1960, CIA officials Richard Bissell and Sheffield Edwards initiated the recruitment of underworld figures to perform the murder.[119] By then, however, as noted in a staff report of the House Assassinations Committee, the Mob had "probably initiated independent assassination plots against Castro," which were to continue for a few years.[120] It was thus likely that the CIA "found itself involved in providing additional resources for an independent operation that the syndicate already had commenced."[121]

The collaboration between the CIA and Mob to kill Castro was most intense at its outset, between August 1960 and April 1961.[122] That stage was followed by more attempts on the Cuban leader between late 1961 and 1963, one of which, code named

"AMLASH," was in progress when President Kennedy was shot.[123] Although some operations never advanced beyond the planning stage, killers were supplied with weapons on two occasions.[124] As the Senate Intelligence Committee summarized, the proposed assassination devices "ran the gamut from high-powered rifles to poison pills, poison pens, deadly bacterial powders, and other devices which strain the imagination."[125]

The go-between who enlisted the Mafia's cooperation for the CIA was Robert Maheu, then an investigator for Washington attorney Edward Bennett Williams.[126] Maheu had conducted questionable investigations on behalf of Williams' Teamster clients, including Jimmy Hoffa.[127] The principal underworld figures involved were West Coast Mafioso Johnny Roselli, Chicago chieftain Sam Giancana and Florida boss Santos Trafficante.[128]

POSSIBLE CONNECTIONS TO THE KENNEDY ASSASSINATION

One member of this Cuban hit squad, Johnny Roselli, was reportedly later in contact with Jack Ruby, as will be discussed,[129] suggesting a possible connection between murder plots against Castro and plots against President Kennedy. Roselli claimed, in fact, that Castro arranged for President Kennedy's murder, in retaliation for American plots against him.[130] Roselli contended that Castro discovered Mobsters in Havana planning to kill him and persuaded them to switch targets; they then lined up Oswald to kill the president.[131] Yet this retaliation theory, which conveniently draws the main focus of attention away from the Mob, has been rejected on several grounds by both the House Assassinations Committee[132] and several private commentators.[133]

First, given Castro's knowledge about the murder plots against him,[134] it is questionable whether he would have blamed them on President Kennedy. For the evidence indicates that these plots were hatched before John F. Kennedy took office,[135] and were carried on without the authorization of either Kennedy brother.[136] Second, the notion that Oswald became involved with Castro is far-fetched. Although such a connection was suggested in letters discovered by the FBI, the Bureau's investigation revealed that they were fabricated.[137] Indeed, as noted in chapter 4, Oswald's proclaimed pro-Castro sympathies are questionable given his many anti-Castro associations.[138]

Finally, by the year 1963, Castro had reason to look favorably on a continued Kennedy presidency and displayed anything but murderous intent. The Cuban premier appeared genuinely dismayed at the news of Kennedy's death,[139] later expressing admiration and respect for his adversary,[140] as did Khrushchev.[141] Castro called him a "bold man" with "initiative," "imagination" and "courage."[142] Moreover, American and Cuban delegations had arranged preliminary talks on bilateral accommodation just before Kennedy's death;[143] ironically, Kennedy's emissary was meeting with Castro when the president was shot.[144] Thus, as summarized in a staff report of the House Assassinations Committee,

> with the prospects of renewed diplomatic relations in the air and the knowledge that Kennedy possessed a more favorable attitude toward Cuba than other military or political leaders, Castro would have had every reason to hope that Kennedy maintained the Presidency.[145]

Castro himself noted that he had nothing to gain by President Kennedy's assassination and wondered "if someone did not wish to involve Cuba in this."[146]

A more logical connection between Cuban events and the Kennedy assassination has been widely hypothesized. By the fall of 1963, the Mob was chafing under the Kennedy Administration's anticrime assault, with even more drastic action portended by the televised Valachi hearings.[147] The aspirations of the Mob's anti-Castro bedfellows were dashed by President Kennedy's steps toward détente, his civil rights initiatives, and the Vietnam troop withdrawals he ordered.[148] Thus, it is conjectured,[149] when their common efforts to eliminate the Cuban premier were frustrated with increasing firmness by the Kennedy Administration,[150] the target of assassination shifted to this more immediate obstacle— President Kennedy.

Supporting this thesis of an anti-Castro connection to organized crime in the Kennedy assassination is a Secret Service report from an informant about statements made by Homer Echevarria, a Cuban exile. According to the report, Echevarria stated at a meeting on November 21, 1963 that he was ready to proceed with an illegal arms purchase "as soon as we take care of Kennedy."[151] The report noted that Echevarria was an associate of militant anti-Castroite Juan Francisco Blanco-Fernandez and that Echevarria's arms purchases were being financed through Paulino Sierra Martinez by "hoodlum elements."[152]

A subsequent investigation by the House Assassinations Committee confirmed, as related by chief counsel G. Robert Blakey, that "Echevarria was one of the many Cuban exiles who had come to despise Kennedy as much as he did Castro."[153] The Committee also identified several sources who confirmed that underworld interests were behind the anti-Castro financing of Sierra Martinez.[154] Recall that a similar virulence toward Kennedy was expressed by another anti-Castro activist, David Ferrie, an associate of both Carlos Marcello and Lee Harvey Oswald. Ferrie admitted to the FBI that after the Bay of Pigs invasion, he severely criticized President Kennedy and "might have used an offhand or colloquial expression, 'he ought to be shot.' "[155]

Thus, although the Mob was most directly hurt by President Kennedy's policies, its partners in the anti-Castro coalition also shared its desire to see him out of the picture. Further insight into the germination and functioning of this coalition is provided by the Cuban involvements of another key assassination player, Jack Ruby.

By the late 1950s, according to his own Warren Commission testimony, Ruby had developed a particular affinity for all things Cuban. That was where the money was and that was where the Mafia was. It was through his Cuban intrigues that Ruby's trail crossed those of some of the most powerful organized crime bosses in America.[1]

William Scott Malone, journalist

Now they're going to find out about Cuba, they're going to find out about the guns, find out about New Orleans, find out about everything.[2]

Jack Ruby, in jail after his murder conviction, as reported by a visiting Carousel Club employee

16
Jack Ruby's Cuban Connection

While the Syndicate was engaged in the Cuban dealings described earlier, flying high with its rackets in the 1950s and desperately trying to reestablish them in the early 1960s, Ruby was right in on the action. The circumstances of his Cuban activities provide further insight into both his background and the events previously described.

ARMS SHIPMENTS FROM FLORIDA IN THE 1950s

Jack Ruby's first Cuban involvement was reported by FBI informant Blaney Mack Johnson, a pilot who had flown cargo to Cuba and had been affiliated with a Miami gambling casino.[3] According to Johnson, "in the early 1950's, Jack Ruby held [an] interest in the Colonial Inn" in Hallandale, Florida,[4] a famous night club and gambling house whose principals included several Mobsters.[5] At that time, Johnson told the FBI, Ruby "was active in arranging illegal flights of weapons from Miami to the Castro organization in Cuba."[6] Johnson furnished specifics about these operations, including the name of one of Ruby's collaborators—

Edward Browder[7]—whose Cuban entanglements were also reported by federal sources.[8]

A storage point in Browder's gunrunning operations was the Florida Keys,[9] where Ruby turned up later in connection with similar activity. According to an FBI report, around May 30, 1958, Mary Thompson took her daughter, Dolores, and her son-in-law to visit her brother, James Woodard, in Islamorada, on the eastern end of the Florida Keys.[10] The first night there, Dolores and her husband were put up in a nearby cottage owned by a friend of Woodard's named Jack.[11] This "Jack," as Mary Thompson later identified from a photograph, was Jack Ruby.[12] Dolores, too, said that photos of Ruby resembled this man.[13]

The two women's identification of Ruby was confirmed by details they learned of his background and life style. Mary Thompson told the FBI that "Jack" drove a car with Texas license plates, ran a drinking place in Dallas, was originally from Chicago and was said to have killed a couple of men.[14] She said that his actual first name was "Leon,"[15] which was Ruby's middle name.[16] And she related being warned by Woodard's wife to "get Dolores out of Jack's house, because Jack might try to rape her."[17] Dolores added that he wore a diamond ring and appeared accustomed to a high standard of living.[18] She also told the FBI that she had been led to believe Jack was part of the Syndicate[19]—a fact not generally known then outside underworld circles.

The witnesses gave the following descriptions of Ruby's smuggling activities. Dolores told the FBI that one night when Woodard got drunk, he mentioned that "he and Jack would run some guns to Cuba" and that Jack had several guns.[20] Mary Thompson reported that Woodard's wife told her that Jack had a trunk full of guns.[21] And Dolores saw several boxes and trunks in Jack's garage,[22] which Jack's girlfriend Isabel claimed "contained her furs."[23]

Federal reports concerning Ruby's attested collaborator, James Woodard, give every indication that Ruby's trunks indeed contained arms bound for Cuba. In an FBI interview in September 1963, Woodard admitted having "furnished ammunition and dynamite to both Castro and Cuban exile forces."[24] Included with the FBI report of this interview was a U.S. Customs official's description of Woodard as "armed and dangerous."[25] And on October 8, 1963, when questioned about stolen dynamite found at his residence, he told authorities that it was to be used by Cuban exile forces against Castro.[26] Given Woodard's background and the reported details about "Jack," therefore, the Thompson account of Ruby's Cuban gunrunning activity appears accurate.

Further confirmation of Ruby's arms dealings during the 1950s was contained in U.S. government files. In 1958, Ruby wrote a letter to the State Department's Office of Munitions Controls "requesting permission to negotiate the purchase of firearms and ammunition from an Italian firm."[27] And the name "Jack Rubenstein" was listed in a 1959 Army Intelligence report on U.S. arms dealers.[28] Although located by clerks of these two federal agencies in 1963, both documents are today inexplicably missing.[29]

DEALINGS AND TRAVELS IN 1959

On January 1, 1959, with the help of armaments and cash supplied by the Mob—which it also supplied to Batista—revolutionary leader Fidel Castro gained control of Cuba.[30] But Castro double-crossed his double-dealing benefactor by jailing some of its top emissaries and closing the casinos.[31] Although in late February he permitted operations to resume, extracting millions more from the Syndicate, the accommodation was shaky at best.[32] The Mob's panic following Castro's initial shutdown of the casinos and its dealings in the subsequent period of accommodation are illuminated by some of Jack Ruby's activities in 1959.

In his FBI interview of December 21, 1963, Ruby related that

at a time when Castro was popular in the United States he read of an individual in the vicinity of Houston, Texas, having been engaged in "gun running to Castro." He said he attempted by telephone to get in touch with this individual as he had in mind "making a buck" by possibly acquiring some Jeeps or other similar equipment which he might

221

sell to persons interested in their importation to Cuba. He said nothing came of this.[33]

Further details provided by Ruby[34] led the FBI to conclude that "the most logical individual to whom Ruby referred" was Robert McKeown[35] — a resident of Bay Cliff, Texas who had smuggled goods to Cuba and whose support Castro had publicly acknowledged.[36]

The FBI thus interviewed McKeown,[37] who related the following information. About a week after Castro's takeover on January 1, 1959, Deputy Sheriff Anthony "Boots" Ayo told McKeown that someone from Dallas was "frantically calling the Harris County Sheriff's Office in an effort to locate McKeown."[38] When questioned by the FBI, Deputy Sheriff Ayo also recalled this "exceedingly intent" caller from Dallas.[39] About an hour later, McKeown reported, a man identifying himself as "Rubenstein" from Dallas telephoned him.[40] The caller asked McKeown if he would use his influence with Castro to free three people held in Cuba.[41] He offered McKeown $5,000 for each person released, indicating that the money would come from Las Vegas.[42]

As McKeown told the FBI, a man who did not disclose his identity visited him three weeks later and offered him $25,000 to write a letter of introduction to Castro.[43] The visitor said that he had an option on a large number of jeeps in Shreveport, Louisiana, which he wished to sell in Cuba.[44] McKeown told the FBI that he made preliminary arrangements to carry out this deal but never heard from the man again.[45] After viewing photos of Ruby, McKeown told the FBI he felt "strongly that this individual was in fact Jack Ruby."[46] McKeown later told an interviewer, "Well I found out later through friends of mine that he did go to Cuba and he did use my name."[47]

Further information about this or a similar contact is provided in a February 24, 1964 memorandum by Warren Commission staff members Leon Hubert and Burt Griffin.[48] The memo states that "in about 1959, Ruby became interested in the possibility of selling war materials to Cubans and in the possibility of opening a gambling casino in Havana."[49] This squares with the statement by FBI informant Blaney Mack Johnson that Ruby left Miami after his gunrunning dealings "and purchased a substantial share in a Havana gaming house."[50]

But the most definite indication of Ruby's Cuban involvement was his travel to Havana in 1959, during the temporary period of accommodation between Castro and the Mob. One of these trips, a visit of eight or ten days in August with Ruby's friend Lewis McWillie, was reported by both Ruby[51] and McWillie.[52] Ruby noted that McWillie was "a key man over the Tropicana down there," adding, "that was during our good times."[53] Ruby also reported that during his Cuban visit he met with one of the owners of the Tropicana.[54] But he failed to mention that the Tropicana's top men, in addition to manager McWillie,[55] were Mobsters Meyer and Jake Lansky, Norman Rothman, Willie Bischoff, Giuseppe Cotrini and John Guglielmo.[56] He also failed to state that McWillie was a top man in Syndicate gambling operations,[57] who was associated with Santos Trafficante and the Lansky brothers.[58]

Ruby testified that his August visit with McWillie was strictly a vacation and insisted that it was the only trip he ever made to Cuba.[59] But several sources contradict this testimony. Records of the Cuban government show that a Jack Ruby of Dallas, Texas arrived in Cuba on August 8 and left on September 11, only to return September 12 and leave again September 13.[60] U.S. Immigration and Naturalization Service documents confirm Ruby's overnight trip to Cuba September 12–13,[61] hardly long enough to have been a casual visit. Three Chicago men saw Ruby at the Tropicana Night Club during the weekend of September 4–6,[62] one reporting that Ruby "appeared to know his way around and was familiar with the employees."[63] A girlfriend of Ruby's received a postcard dated September 8 written by him from Cuba,[64] and a former employee of his told the FBI that Ruby "vacationed in Cuba" the entire summer.[65] Yet bank and FBI records reveal that Ruby was in Dallas August 6, August 21, August 31, and September 4.[66] The House Assassinations Committee thus concluded that if the evidence were correct, "Ruby had to have made at least three trips to Cuba."[67]

Ruby's offhand comments provide the most credible indication of the purpose of his Cuban visits. One acquaintance of his told the FBI that Ruby had said he went to Cuba "trying to get some gambling concessions at a casino there."[68] During his official medical interview, Ruby discussed "his involvement with a deal in Cuba with one Mack Willey [sic], a gambler, and explained how this was a chance to make a quick dollar."[69] And according to a Dallas Police informant, Ruby had told his physician that he was bitter about a federal tax claim against him (amounting to $44,000[70]) and "was going to Cuba to 'collect' his income tax and take a 'breather.' "[71]

Also significant was the report of Elaine Mynier, a mutual friend of Ruby and McWillie, who worked at a car rental agency at the Dallas airport.[72] Mynier told the FBI that in May 1959, she visited Cuba and delivered a short coded message from Ruby to McWillie.[73] Mynier's credibility was demonstrated by the accuracy of details she furnished concerning McWillie's gambling operations.[74] It thus appeared that at least during his one-day visit to Cuba in September, Ruby "was most likely serving as a courier for gambling interests,"[75] as the House Assassinations Committee concluded. Chief counsel G. Robert Blakey later reported, "We came to believe that Ruby's trips to Cuba were, in fact, organized-crime activities."[76]

The House Assassinations Committee also deemed it "likely" that "Ruby at least met various organized crime figures in Cuba, possibly including some who had been detained by the Cuban government."[77] During the summer of 1959, in particular, one of those held by Castro was Mafia chieftain Santos Trafficante,[78] who later reciprocated by spearheading Mafia-CIA assassination plots against his former host.[79] Another reportedly involved in these plots,[80] Lewis McWillie, visited the Trescornia detention camp where Trafficante was held.[81] So too, apparently, did Jack Ruby.

When asked who went with him to the camp, McWillie testified, without prompting, that "Jack Ruby could have been out there one time with me."[82] In addition, British journalist John Wilson Hudson, who was also detained at Trescornia,[83] reported that he met "an American gangster-gambler named Santos" who "was visited frequently by an American gangster type named Ruby."[84] The House Assassinations Committee found that "the 'Santos' referred to by Hudson was probably Santos Trafficante."[85] And the Committee concluded that "there was considerable evidence" of a meeting between Trafficante and Ruby in Cuba.[86]

If the two Mobsters met in Cuba, their business was probably just routine underworld dealings. Mobster Johnny Roselli reportedly told a close friend that "Ruby was hooked up with Trafficante in the rackets in Havana."[87] And mercenary Gerry Hemming related that Ruby met with an American close to Castro, apparently to help secure Trafficante's release from Cuban detention;[88] this provided a possible follow-up to the McKeown incident.

ANTI-CASTRO ACTIVITY IN 1961

Although Trafficante was freed by the Cuban government in August or September 1959[89] and casino operations were temporarily resumed,[90] the Mob's days in Cuba were numbered. Lewis McWillie, for one, was expelled from Cuba, with all of his assets confiscated, around January 1, 1961[91] (two months after the departure of another of Ruby's Mob associates, Russell D. Matthews[92]). Ruby testified that McWillie "was the last person to leave, if I recall, when they had to leave, when he left the casino."[93] And in 1961, when the Mob embarked with other groups on a campaign to eliminate Castro,[94] Jack Ruby was once again involved. His activities in this phase of the Cuban scenario were described by just one witness, whose credibility could not be successfully impeached.

The testimony of Nancy Perrin Rich[95] belied the Warren Commission's denials of Ruby's ties to Cuba,[96] organized crime[97] and the Dallas Police.[98] And just as Mobster-attorney Sidney Korshak stepped forward to discredit informant Edward Becker,[99] as will be discussed in the next chapter, so an attorney, a Dallas policeman and others offered disparaging remarks about Rich.[100] One detractor was Dave Cherry, whom she described as a collaborator in Cuban gunrunning and a contact in a call-girl ring.[101] Cherry told the FBI that Rich was "mentally deranged" and "incoherent in her speech."[102] But Cherry's statements are less than reliable considering that he worked at a night club owned by Benny Bickers,[103] a Dallas underworld figure acquainted with Jack Ruby.[104] Another person who contradicted Rich[105] had a criminal re-

225

cord,[106] while a third[107] was a former dealer and manager at Las Vegas casinos.[108]

Also seeming to discredit Rich was a Secret Service report that concluded that "she told many stories about doing undercover work and working on counterfeiting cases which appeared to be obvious fabrications."[109] But these "stories" were in fact confirmed in a letter written by Oscar A. Kistle, the chief deputy district attorney of Sacramento County, California;[110] it was verified for the Warren Commission by the Sacramento County district attorney's office.[111] This letter, dated October 25, 1963, described undercover work Rich had performed for the Oakland Police Department that led to a criminal conviction.[112] It praised her "utmost cooperation" and "excellent judgment," relating that she "handled herself in the manner of an experienced investigator."[113] It also cited her qualifications "to be a success in the investigative field wherever her services can be used."[114] There is thus no reason to question the account she consistently related in an FBI interview of November 27, 1963,[115] in three subsequent FBI interviews[116] and in testimony of June 2, 1964.[117]

Rich reported that she had become involved in a Cuban smuggling operation through her former husband, Robert Perrin, with whom she had lived in Dallas during 1961.[118] Perrin had been a bodyguard for California Mafioso[119] Jack Dragna and had performed other services for the Mob, Rich admitted after some hesitation.[120] He was ideally qualified for an arms smuggling assignment, since he had been a gunrunner during the Spanish Civil War and was familiar with boats and Cuba, as described by Rich.[121] And Rich, too, had experience that proved significant: employment in mid-1961 at Ruby's Carousel Club,[122] as confirmed by a Dallas Police officer.[123]

In 1961,[124] Rich testified, she accompanied her husband to a Dallas apartment to meet with bartender Dave Cherry and a military officer in uniform.[125] At that meeting, her husband was offered $10,000 to pilot a boat bringing refugees from Cuba to Miami.[126] At a second meeting five or six days later, her husband was told that the deal would also involve bringing armaments into Cuba that the officer had stolen from a military base.[127] During this meeting, Rich related, "a knock comes on the door and who walks in but my little friend Jack Ruby."[128] Rich inferred that Ruby had brought money to the group, because he came with a "rather extensive bulge" in his jacket that was gone when he left ten minutes later.[129] Also, he received an enthusiastic reception, and plans suddenly became firmer after his arrival.[130]

Rich testified that after a third meeting, she became uneasy about the operation and persuaded her husband to drop out.[131] Her fears had magnified when a new man appeared at that meeting who so resembled Vito Genovese that she believed he might have been his son.[132] At that point,

> everything had fallen into place, because Ruby had had various characters visit him, both from New York, Chicago, even from up in Minneapolis. . . . I was introduced to some of them. I was asked to go out with some of them. . . . I saw them come and go.[133]

Her feelings were summarized in the following exchange:

> Q: And you came to the conclusion, then, that Vito Genovese and that group of people were involved in this matter.
> Rich: Within my own mind; yes. I thought — then I got thinking that perhaps the higher-up that the colonel spoke of was perhaps the element I did not want to deal with that was running guns in, and God knows what else.[134]

Her conclusion was hardly far-fetched, considering Ruby's Mob affiliation, his prior Cuban involvements and the Mob's central role in the anti-Castro campaign, which reached its peak of activity in 1961.[135]

A curious footnote to this period of Ruby's Cuban activity was a series of eight meetings between him and FBI agent Charles W. Flynn.[136] As reported by Flynn, Ruby initiated the contacts in March 1959, volunteering to supply confidential information about criminal activities.[137] But Flynn terminated Ruby's potential criminal informant file in November as Ruby had not been especially helpful.[138] G. Robert Blakey observed that "Ruby's behavior was consistent with the pattern of seasoned offenders, who often cultivate a relationship with a law enforcement agency . . . [hoping] to secure immunity from prosecution."[139]

TIES TO EXTREME RIGHT-WING ELEMENTS

It was perhaps through the anti-Castro campaign that Ruby formed certain ties with extreme right-wing elements. Suggesting such ties were three photographs of an "Impeach Earl Warren" sign that were found on Ruby's person after he shot Oswald.[140] As discussed, Ruby's explanation of how he obtained these photos is dubious.[141] Also found on Ruby was an envelope marked "box 1757,"[142] the box number that appeared on the "Impeach Earl Warren" sign.[143] On the back of this envelope were the name, address and phone number of Thomas Hill, a John Birch Society official from Belmont, Massachusetts.[144] Hill was listed in the February 24 memo of Warren Commission counsels Hubert and Griffin as among possible "sources of contact between Ruby and politically motivated groups interested in securing the assassination of President Kennedy."[145]

Two other persons listed in the same category as Hill in the February 24 memo were H. L. Hunt, the Dallas oil billionaire and extreme right-wing propagandist, and his son Lamar Hunt.[146] The Hunts were worthy of scrutiny; H. L. had reportedly spoken of shooting "those traitors out of our government,"[147] and his son Nelson Bunker had co-sponsored the black-bordered assassination-day ad attacking President Kennedy.[148] Also, a *Houston Post* reporter formerly employed at the Hunt Oil Company disclosed that Hunt personally approached him about plotting to kill either Fidel Castro or the prime minister of Guyana.[149] A participant in the murder plan, later scrapped, was notorious Mobster Russell D. Matthews[150]—an associate of Trafficante, McWillie and Ruby.[151]

According to an informant judged reliable by the Secret Service, Ruby had met H. L. Hunt in the early 1950s through some large football bets made between them.[152] Two other sources confirmed Hunt's fondness for high-stakes gambling,[153] and a third indicated that Ruby and Hunt had patronized the same Dallas gambling club in the 1940s.[154] Also, Lamar Hunt's name appeared in one of Ruby's notebooks.[155] And several transcripts of

"Life Line" radio broadcasts sponsored by H. L. Hunt were found among Ruby's personal articles.[156]

In summary, from the 1950s through the early 1960s, Cuba was a hub of Mob activity. And through all phases of this activity, Mobster Jack Ruby was right in the thick of things. Gambling, gunrunning, courting Castro and then conspiring with extreme right-wing elements to destroy him — Ruby was involved in the Mob's Cuban imbroglio every step of the way. Not as a principal, certainly, but not one to be left out either. And in 1963, when the Mafia redirected its efforts toward a critical new undertaking in Dallas, Jack Ruby was there.

A shocking crime was committed on the unscrupulous initiative of few individuals, with the blessing of more, and amid the passive acquiescence of all.[1]

Tacitus, the Roman historian, commenting 19 centuries ago
on the assassination of Emperor Galba

I believe that the Warren Commission was set up at the time to feed Pablum to the American people for reasons not yet known and that one of the biggest cover-ups in the history of our country occurred at that time.[2]

Former U.S. Senator Richard Schweiker.

17
The Warren Commission Cover-Up

The two fatal shootings generated unprecedented attention and controversy. A committee, named after its distinguished chairman, was charged to investigate. After several weeks of hearings and deliberations, it presented a report to the chief executive.[3]

The report found that two men characterized as maladjusted were responsible for the killings, and appeared to allay nagging suspicions that others were involved.[4] The *Boston Herald* reported that the misgivings of "serious and earnest minded people" were "dissipated by the calm and dispassionate recital of the evidence."[5] The *New York Times* concluded that the committee had done "a great public service" in "assuring the American people and the world that no intentional or notorious injustice [had] been done."[6] Another leading newspaper attributed to the report "the earmarks of fairness, consideration, shrewdness and coolness."[7] It seemed pointless, even presumptuous, to question the findings of a committee chaired by such an eminent figure: Harvard University President Abbott Lawrence Lowell.[8] And so in 1927, with all doubts dissolved by the lavishly acclaimed Lowell Committee's report, shoe worker Nicola Sacco and fish peddler Bartolomeo Vanzetti were sent to the electric chair.[9]

But history returned a radically different verdict on the Sacco and Vanzetti case. Over the years, it became clear that prejudice more than evidence had linked the two Italian "anarchists" to the April 15, 1920 robbery and murders at the Slater and Morill Shoe Company in South Braintree, Massachusetts.[10] In 1977, 50 years after their executions, the "very real possibility that a grievous miscarriage of justice occurred" was finally recognized by the State of Massachusetts.[11] In a proclamation signed by Governor Michael Dukakis, the state designated a Sacco and Vanzetti Memorial Day, stipulating that "any stigma and disgrace should be forever removed" from their names.[12]

The passage of time also revealed the identity of the real South Braintree killers. In 1920, before he became a top Mafia don, Frank "Butsey" Morelli and four brothers had specialized in rifling railroad cars filled with textiles and shoes.[13] The Morellis had been indicted in connection with a shipment of shoes stolen from, of all places, the Slater and Morill Company in South Braintree.[14] Within weeks after the April 15 robbery and murders at that factory, the Morelli brothers were put under police surveillance as prime suspects.[15] And a subsequent confession, physical evidence, eyewitness descriptions and factors of motivation all implicated the Morellis in the crime.[16]

This evidence was corroborated in 1973, with the publication of the memoirs of Mafia defector Vincent Teresa.[17] Teresa wrote that in the mid-1950s, he visited Butsey Morelli, who had terminal cancer, shortly after an article in the *Boston Globe* accused Morelli of the Slater and Morill robbery-murders.[18] During that visit, Morelli told Teresa "we whacked them out, we killed those guys in the robbery. Those two greaseballs [Sacco and Vanzetti] took it on the chin."[19] Teresa noted that Morelli "didn't brag about anything — ever."[20]

In 1964, the Warren Commission once again implicated two men deemed misfits, this time by no means innocent ones, in another case that had all the earmarks of Mafia culpability. This chapter will consider some factors behind this shameful misjudgment, including administration coercion, Commission credulity, Mob subversion, and the misconduct of the nation's top law enforcement officer.

231

Before the Kennedy assassination probe even began, certain top government officials had stipulated who the culprit would be. Reviewing the government's performance in that investigation, the Senate Intelligence Committee reported in 1976:

> Almost immediately after the assassination, [FBI] Director [J. Edgar] Hoover, the Justice Department and the White House "exerted pressure" on senior Bureau officials to complete their investigation and issue a factual report supporting the conclusion that Oswald was the lone assassin.[21]

Reflecting this bias in a telephone conversation of November 24, 1963, immediately following Oswald's murder, Hoover stated:

> The thing I am most concerned about, and so is Mr. Katzenbach, is having something issued so we can convince the public that Oswald is the real assassin.[22]

The next day, Deputy Attorney General Nicholas Katzenbach wrote a memo asserting:

> The public must be satisfied that Oswald was the assassin; that he did not have confederates who are still at large; and that the evidence was such that he would have been convicted at trial.[23]

Katzenbach continued, "Speculation about Oswald's motivation ought to be cut off."[24]

During early December, as the Warren Commission began its investigation, Hoover orchestrated press leaks proclaiming Oswald to be the "lone and unaided assassin."[25] According to William Sullivan, former number-three man at the FBI, Hoover's motive was "to blunt the drive for an independent investigation of the assassination."[26] On December 13, in harmony with Hoover's cues, *Time* magazine previewed a confidential FBI report to the Warren Commission.[27] The report would find, *Time* proclaimed, that "Oswald, acting in his own lunatic loneliness, was indeed the President's assassin."[28]

One official interview of an assassination witness reflected this administration predisposition toward the lone-assassin line. In his autobiography, former House Speaker Tip O'Neill recalls a dinner with two Kennedy aides, Kenneth O'Donnell and Dave Powers, who were both in the Secret Service follow-up car in Dallas.[29] O'Donnell told O'Neill, as did Powers, that "he was sure he had heard two shots that came from behind the fence."[30] Reminded by O'Neill that this was not what he had told the Warren Commission, O'Donnell replied, "You're right."[31] The Kennedy aide elaborated,

> I told the FBI what I had heard, but they said it couldn't have happened that way and that I must have been imagining things. So I testified the way they wanted me to. I just didn't want to stir up any more pain and trouble for the family.[32]

WITHHELD EVIDENCE

In line with the Hoover-Katzenbach quest for a simple solution and a satisfied public, evidence that contradicted official dogma was withheld or ignored. The Senate Intelligence Committee reported in 1976, as summarized by the *Washington Post*, that "senior officials of both the CIA and the FBI covered up crucial information in the course of investigating President Kennedy's assassination."[33] A similar conclusion was offered by Judge Burt W. Griffin, former assistant counsel for the Warren Commission. In 1978, Judge Griffin told the House Assassinations Committee that "evidence in the possession of government agencies was deliberately withheld from the Warren Commission."[34] He elaborated in a private interview:

> I feel betrayed. I feel that the CIA lied to us, that we had an agency of government here which we were depending upon that we expected to be truthful with us and to cooperate with us and they didn't do it.[35]

Particularly derelict in his performance was Commission member Allen Dulles—the former CIA chief who resigned following the Bay of Pigs invasion.[36] Curiously, at the Commission's first executive session, Dulles gave each of his colleagues a book purporting to show how American assassinations were always perpetrated by lone, demented men.[37] Then, throughout the Commission meetings, Dulles concealed his knowledge of relevant CIA-Mafia assassination plots against Castro, including the so-called "AMLASH" plot.[38] The Senate Intelligence Committee concluded in 1976 that the AMLASH operation "should have raised major concerns within the CIA about its possible connection with the Kennedy assassination" but that information on it "was not supplied to either the Warren Commission or the FBI."[39]

ACCOMMODATION

Although Chief Justice Earl Warren was heavily involved in his Commission's investigation,[40] the other Commissioners had little touch with its affairs,[41] while the staff members each explored limited areas.[42] And without an adequate grasp of even the limited evidence that the Commission had been provided, these Commissioners and staffers found themselves trapped by the FBI's predetermined conclusion. This dilemma was noted in executive session by J. Lee Rankin, the Commission's general counsel:

> Part of our difficulty . . . is that [the FBI officials] have no problem. They have decided that it is Oswald who committed the assassination, they have decided that no one else was involved. . . .[43]

The same complaint was expressed by Commission members Russell and Boggs.[44] Working under tight time constraints,[45] with no serious exploration of alternatives,[46] the Commission thus became increasingly committed to this simplistic solution.*

---

*Considering Chief Justice Warren's central role in the investigation and his amazing handling of Jack Ruby's testimony, it is more difficult to fathom an innocent explanation for his behavior. Whatever his role in the cover-up, however, it was not performed readily. For Warren initially declined President Johnson's offer to preside over the assassination investigation.[47] And when Warren finally acquiesced in a private meeting with LBJ, he emerged with tears in his eyes.[48]

Commission curiosity may have also been contained by fabricated national security concerns. Just such a situation occurred during the Watergate maneuvering, when a CIA directive citing bogus security considerations aborted an FBI probe of the White House "plumbers."[49] And, in fact, Hoover justified his opposition to an independent assassination probe by alluding to "aspects which would complicate our foreign relations."[50] No such "aspects" emerged, however, when the case was reviewed in the late 1970s by the Senate and House.[51] Also, the FBI discovered forged letters linking Oswald with Fidel Castro;[52] these may have been used to raise a smoke screen of national security for some unsuspecting Commission investigator.

The credulity required to swallow such a ruse was subsequently displayed by one Commission member, Gerald Ford. As reported in *Time* on February 4, 1974,

> After meeting with Nixon for nearly two hours, Vice President Gerald Ford declared that the White House was in possession of evidence that "will exonerate the President" of complicity in the conspiracy to conceal the origins of the Watergate wiretap-burglary.[53]

When asked what the evidence was, Ford replied that

> the President had offered to show it to him, but he had "not had time" to look at it.[54]

One glaring manifestation of the Warren Commission's lack of critical judgment was its infamous "single-bullet theory." To reconcile the filmed sequence of assassination events[55] with the capabilities of Oswald's rifle,[56] the Commission proposed that a single bullet fired from the Depository Building struck President Kennedy in "the base of the back of his neck," exited from his throat, and then passed downward through Governor Connally's back, chest, wrist and thigh.[57] But this proposition is incredible given the conclusions stated during Kennedy's autopsy by Dr. James Humes, the chief surgeon. As noted in FBI reports of November 23,[58] November 26,[59] December 9[60] and January 13,[61] and as subsequently reaffirmed by two agents present at the autopsy,[62] a bullet struck the president "just below the shoulder," at "an angle of 45 to 60 degrees downward." It "penetrated to a distance of less than a finger length," leaving "a hole of short depth with no point of exit," and apparently "worked its way out of the victim's back during cardiac massage."[63] Bullet holes in Kennedy's shirt and jacket in fact pinpointed the wound's position in the shoulder,[64] several inches below the neckline location invented by the Warren Commission.[65] It was thus unlikely that a bullet entering there at a downward angle passed upward through Kennedy's throat, flipped in midair, and plunged downward into Connally's back, as the Commission's hypothesis required.[66]

Continuing in its flight of fantasy, the Commission proposed that the body wounds to Kennedy and Connally were inflicted by one bullet, which was found on a stretcher at Parkland Hospital and matched to Oswald's rifle.[67] But it was difficult to explain how this bullet, in nearly perfect condition,[68] could have shattered Connally's fifth rib and right wrist and left metal fragments in his chest, wrist and thigh.[69] Indeed, two of the president's autopsy surgeons[70] and forensic experts[71] found it highly unlikely that this bullet could have inflicted all of this damage. And in U.S. Army ballistic tests simulating Connally's wounds, bullets fired in either rib or wrist bones were significantly deformed.[72]

In an attempt to salvage its single-bullet theory from this contrary evidence, the Commission tangled itself in a spectacular self-contradiction. The results of the Army ballistic tests did not apply, it proposed, because

> the bullet which entered the Governor's chest had already *lost velocity* by passing through the President's neck. Moreover, the *large* wound on the Governor's back would be explained by a bullet which was *yawing*. . . .[73]

Later in the report, however, the Commission addressed another dilemma: how could a bullet transiting Kennedy's neck have retained enough momentum to have penetrated five layers of Connally's skin and shattered two of his bones?[74] This time, citing the same Army ballistic tests, the Commission stated, "From these tests, it was concluded that the bullet *lost little of its velocity* in penetrating the president's neck."[75] Now, the bullet exiting his neck *"had retained most of its stability."*[76] This explained the character of Governor Connally's back wound, as noted elsewhere in the Warren Report:

> Because of the *small size* and clean-cut edges of the wound on the Governor's back, Dr. Robert Shaw concluded that it was an entry wound.[77]

The Commission's attempts to bend evidence to fit its desired conclusions thus reached schizophrenic proportions. Yet some of its representatives were bothered by the discrepancies. Staff member Wesley Liebler, for one, described the testimony of the chief witness against Oswald in the slaying of officer J.D. Tippit as "contradictory" and "worthless."[78] Liebler also wrote a 26-page memo criticizing the first draft of the Warren Report, calling Oswald's asserted capability to easily fire the assassination shots "a fairy tale."[79] Several staff members were skeptical of the testimony of Marina Oswald,[80] a key witness against her husband.[81] One was Norman Redlich, who wrote a memo stating that she had "lied to the Secret Service, the FBI, and this Commission repeatedly."[82]

BEYOND BLUNDERING

Thus, for the Commission's accommodation to the lone-assassin line there were many explanations. Administration pressure. Incomplete information. Credulity. And a misdirected initial focus on Oswald—a versatile mercenary, apparently, whose worldwide trail of involvements was difficult to untangle.[83] Indeed, it is tempting to write off the assassination cover-up as an unfortunate exercise in blundering—as senseless as the assassination was represented to be.

Benign excuses fail, however, to cover the Commission's gross mishandling of its second target of investigation, Jack Ruby. In early news reports and in voluminous FBI files, one fact plainly emerged: Ruby was affiliated with the Mob—the same organization with the clear motive and means to murder President Kennedy.[84] But amazingly, the Commission concluded that there was "no credible evidence that Jack Ruby was active in the criminal underworld."[85] This bizarre reversal of reality was noted by Congressman Stewart McKinney in a question to an FBI spokesman during the House Assassinations hearings:

> Wasn't it pretty well known to the FBI that Jack Ruby, No. 1, was a member of organized crime, No. 2, he ran a strip joint and had been somewhat commonly referred to as a supplier of both women and booze to political and police figures in the city of Dallas[?]
>
> Didn't you find it a little difficult to accept the Warren Commission's final output on Ruby with the knowledge that the FBI had put into the Commission?[86]

In a similar vein, *Time* noted how "the Warren Commission failed abysmally to pursue FBI leads linking Oswald's own assassin, Jack Ruby, to the Mob."[87]

Indeed, it was only by the crudest suppression and distortion of evidence that the Warren Commission could hide Ruby's Mob connection. Again and again, materials in National Archives files relating to organized crime were omitted from the 26 volumes of hearings and exhibits published by the Commission.[88] Sometimes, documents were published in the hearings and exhibits excluding the particular pages dealing with underworld involvement.[89] In one instance, the paragraphs reporting Ruby's frequent association with the Mafia boss of Dallas were blanked out of an otherwise perfect photoreproduction.[90]

Even after such censorship, however, many more clues to Ruby's Syndicate involvement remained in the published hearings and exhibits on which the Commission's report was based. For its absolution of Ruby, therefore, the Commission was forced into such audacious sleights-of-hand as this previously quoted gem: "Virtually all of Ruby's Chicago friends stated he had no close connection with organized crime."[91] The Commission neglected to report that one of the cited "Chicago friends" was in fact a top Mob executioner[92] and that five others had assorted criminal involvements.[93]

Without any legitimate explanation, therefore, glaring clues to Mafia assassination culpability were buried, distorted and disingenuously deflected in the Warren Commission's final report. The related roles and actions of three Mob-linked men indicate that calculated subversion was a factor in achieving this concealment.

One, who had direct access to all of the Commission's proceedings and files, was Walter E. Craig, then president of the American Bar Association.[94] As related in the Warren Commission report, Craig was designated "to participate in the investigation and to advise the Commission whether in his opinion the proceedings conformed to the basic principles of American justice. Mr. Craig accepted this assignment and participated fully and without limitation. He attended Commission hearings in person or through his appointed assistants. All working papers, reports, and other data in Commission files were made available. . . ."[95]

An episode a decade later, typifying organized crime's pervasive influence in America's legal system,[96] suggested a willingness on the part of Craig to subvert his professional duties for the Mob's benefit. His role this time was presiding judge in the 1972 murder conspiracy trial of Joe Bonanno, Jr., son of the top Mafia don. The prosecution's case was solid: five of Bonanno's co-defendants had already pleaded guilty to various charges.[97] But when U.S. attorney Ann Bowen questioned government witnesses in the Arizona courtroom, Judge Craig ridiculed her presentation by rolling his eyes, burying his face in his hands, laughing openly and mimicking one witness in a falsetto voice.[98] Juror Robert Clark noted that Craig "had incredulous looks" on his face and that "his conduct was anything but impartial."[99] Such conduct was not out of character for Craig, however, who was noted for questionable leniency and personal ties to Mob defendants in his courtroom.[100]

Despite Craig's grotesque efforts to discredit the prosecution's case, the jury found Bonanno guilty of conspiracy to murder as charged.[101] Six weeks after the conviction, however, Craig held a 70-minute hearing and freed Bonanno; he claimed that the jury might have mistakenly based its verdict on Bonanno's involvement in a shakedown attempt.[102] Juror Robert Clark subsequently filed a petition to the U.S. Supreme Court calling for Craig's impeachment.[103] Clark said Craig's speculations about the jury's basis for conviction were "as slanderous as they are false."[104] Prosecutor Ann Bowen was likewise incensed by Craig's peculiar reversal of the government's hard-fought conviction.[105] And jury foreman Jerry Boyd was "flabbergasted" by his action.[106]

As routine as the Mob's subversion of judges and prosecutors to avert adverse action is its manipulation of the news media. Secured through widespread payoffs to accommodating reporters,[107] intimidation[108] and control of many outlets of distribution,[109] Mob influence over America's press has been exhibited by censorship of organized crime coverage[110] and, in some cases, favorable publicity for Mobsters.[111] An example contemporaneous with the Warren Commission investigation was a New York Mafioso's comment to an FBI informant in 1964 that

money was being gathered to fight Valachi's testimony and the Senate [rackets] hearings. They are getting in touch with people in the news media and political figures to hold up any legislation which may result.[112]

Such Mob manipulation of media figures is illustrated by the involvements of three of Ruby's acquaintances in Dallas. One was Gordon McLendon, owner of the Liberty Broadcasting Network and of radio stations throughout the country, including KLIF in Dallas.[113] A friend of Jack Ruby[114] who gave him "a lot of free plugs,"[115] he reportedly offered assistance in 1971 to the Mob-Teamster campaign to spring Jimmy Hoffa from jail.[116] Matty Brescia, who headed a public relations firm and worked at one point for McLendon's Liberty Network, was also well-acquainted with Ruby.[117]

Rounding out the bunch was Tony Zoppi, a locally prominent entertainment columnist for the *Dallas Morning News*[118] who moved to Las Vegas after 1963.[119] Zoppi was close to Ruby, McLendon and Brescia.[120] He also knew Mobsters Joseph Campisi,[121] Russell D. Matthews[122] and Lewis McWillie,[123] sending "regards to McWillie" in a letter to Brescia.[124]

Of the journalistic services Zoppi performed for the Mob, most mundane were his repeated promotions of the Campisi-owned Egyptian Lounge,[125] a Dallas Mafia hangout.[126] Although Zoppi himself frequented that restaurant,[127] he assured the House Assassinations Committee that Dallas "had no syndicated or organized crime that he was aware of."[128] Zoppi also emphasized that Ruby "was not involved in gambling" and lamented that "quick buck artists are saying Jack went down there to plan the assassination. . . . All of a sudden he's a CIA agent, a Mafia don, etc, etc. Sickening."[129]

Zoppi stuck his neck out even further to mask Ruby's Mob connection in a 1973 column entitled "Ruby in Retrospect."[130] Attempting to provide an innocent explanation for Ruby's August 1959 trip to Cuba, discussed in the previous chapter, Zoppi wrote:

> Jack had a good friend named Lewis McWillie who was a casino executive at the Tropicana in Havana. He asked McWillie if he would like me to fly to Cuba and do a story on the Tropicana's show. Lew agreed. . . . The date was set for December 17, 1960. By coincidence, I received a call from . . . Las Vegas inviting me to the "summit meeting"— an unprecedented show featuring Frank Sinatra, Dean Martin, Sammy Davis, Joey Bishop and Peter Lawford. I called Ruby and told him I would have to postpone the trip. . . . He said he would depart as scheduled. . . .[131]

When questioned by the House Assassinations Committee in 1978, Zoppi repeated this story with major modifications,[132] and McWillie backed him up.[133] But the charade proved embarrassing to both, since in 1964 McWillie had detailed a totally different explanation for Ruby's visit to Cuba.[134] Moreover, that visit occurred five months before the "summit meeting" show Zoppi was to review, as pointed out by skeptical Committee interviewers.[135]

The man whose intervention in the Kennedy assassination case was most direct and sinister, however, was Los Angeles Mobster-attorney Sidney Korshak. Described in 1976 by senior Justice

Department officials as one of "the most powerful members of the underworld,"[136] Korshak acquired experience for this role by repeatedly intervening to conceal his own background. The *New York Times* noted, for example, that Chicago newspapers repeatedly mentioned Korshak's business and social dealings, but sidestepped his underworld affiliation by describing him "with such vague phrases as 'wheeler-dealer' and 'mystery man.' "[137] One senior Chicago reporter cited two instances in which editors deleted unfavorable references to Korshak, noting "you couldn't get a story about him in the paper."[138] And a friend recalled Korshak's boasts that he was able to influence the *Chicago Tribune* to softpeddle stories about him.[139]

Korshak was once again spared unfavorable publicity in 1979 when several California newspapers dropped a sequence of "Doonesbury" cartoons that satirized his links with then-Governor Jerry Brown.[140] The sequence mentioned, among other things, a $1,000 campaign contribution from Korshak to Brown.[141]

The assassination incident that called Korshak's skills at cover-up into play was Carlos Marcello's careless diatribe of September 1962, as discussed earlier, in which the Mafia boss outlined a plot to murder President Kennedy.[142] The incident was made public when informant Edward Becker described it to Pulitzer Prize-winner Ed Reid, who related it in *The Grim Reapers*, which was published in 1969.[143] The FBI, in turn, learned of Becker's account when Reid showed his manuscript to Los Angeles Bureau officials on May 6, 1967.[144]

But on May 7, the next day, the FBI's Los Angeles office received allegations discrediting Becker.[145] Specifically, the FBI was informed through an intermediary that Sidney Korshak

advised that Becker was trying to shake down some of Korshak's friends for money by claiming he is the collaborator with Reid and that for money he could keep the names of these people out of the book.[146]

Korshak further stated that "Becker was a no-good shakedown artist."[147] Subsequent FBI documents contain repeated references to the Bureau's use of Korshak's allegations, but no references to his own background, activities or possible motives in defaming Becker.[148] This was rather surprising, since Korshak had been repeatedly linked to organized crime in the FBI's own files.[149]

Although charged to pursue any new developments in the Kennedy assassination case,[150] the FBI accepted Korshak's allegations and took no action to investigate the Marcello threat.[151] Instead, as noted in a staff report of the House Assassinations Committee, it assisted the effort to suppress Becker's report, exhibiting "a strong desire to 'discredit' the information without having actually to investigate it."[152] On May 26, 1967, for example, the man who forwarded the Korshak allegations to the FBI contacted author Ed Reid; an FBI agent visited Reid five days later.[153] Their mission, as noted in a June 5 FBI memo to FBI Director Hoover, was to "discredit Becker to Reid in order that the Carlos Marcello incident would be deleted from the book by Reid."[154] The only FBI directive issued regarding the entire Becker affair was a handwritten notation by Assistant Director Cartha DeLoach; it requested the Bureau to "discreetly identify the publisher" of the Reid book.[155]

THE TWO FBIs

The FBI's handling of the Marcello assassination threat "had highly disturbing implications," noted a staff report of the House Assassinations Committee.[156] So, too, did the overall conduct of FBI Director J. Edgar Hoover and other top-level FBI officials in the Kennedy assassination probe. Hoover, who immediately mandated that Oswald was the lone assassin,[157] opposed the creation of any public commission to study the case.[158] After the Warren Commission was established, the Senate Intelligence Committee noted, it "was perceived as an adversary by both Hoover and senior FBI officials."[159] William Sullivan, former FBI assistant director, observed that Hoover "did not want the Warren Commission to conduct an exhaustive investigation."[160] And on two occasions, the Senate Intelligence Committee reported, Hoover "asked for all derogatory material on Warren Commission members and staff contained in the FBI files."[161]

The dichotomy between the diligent performance of agents and the questionable conduct of leadership—most notably

Hoover—extended to a broader area of FBI functioning. As observed by Ralph Salerno, retired organized crime expert of the New York Police Department,

> There are, in fact, two FBIs. . . . One is the splendid organization itself; the other is its long-time director.[162]

Salerno was referring, in particular, to J. Edgar Hoover's atrocious record on organized crime.[163]

Hoover directed the FBI to fight car thieves, bank robbers and the Communist menace decried by his friend[164] Joe McCarthy. But he left organized crime almost totally unscathed[165] and until the early 1960s steadfastly denied that a national crime syndicate existed.[166] Hoover refused to acknowledge that fact even after the spectacular police bust of the Mob's 1957 conclave in Apalachin, New York, which was investigated in depth by his own New York agents.[167] Illustrating his position, in 1958 he had an FBI report on the Mafia rescinded, calling it "baloney."[168] FBI personnel who probed the Mob found their work thwarted, their careers jeopardized.[169] Moreover, Hoover consistently opposed special efforts to fight the Mob;[170] it was largely his opposition that caused a federal task force on organized crime to disband in 1958, with its recommendations rejected.[171] Only after Robert Kennedy became attorney general in his brother's administration was Hoover prodded into action against the Syndicate.[172]

While ignoring the Mob in his official capacity, Hoover was less exclusive in his personal relationships. He often stayed for free at the Las Vegas hotels of construction tycoon Del E. Webb,[173] whose holdings were permeated with organized crime entanglements.[174] Hoover and Webb also met frequently on vacations in Del Mar, California.[175] During Hoover's annual trips to that city's luxurious Del Charro Motel, his bill was paid by its owner, Clint Murchison, Jr.,[176] Hoover's "bosom pal."[177] Murchison, a Texas oil tycoon who backed Lyndon Johnson,[178] was questionably involved with both the Teamsters and Bobby Baker,[179] the infamous LBJ aide whose misdeeds will be discussed. But Hoover continued to accept Murchison's hospitality, even while Murchison's dealings with Baker were being investigated by both the Senate[180] and Hoover's own FBI.[181]

Hoover's free vacations at the Del Charro, during which he often attended the nearby Murchison-owned Del Mar Race Track,[182] did not lead to the best of company. As Jack Anderson reported in 1970,

> The late Clint Murchison picked up Hoover's tab ($100-a-day suites) year after year at the . . . Del Charro near their favorite race track . . . at the same time some of the nation's most notorious gamblers and racketeers have been registered there.[183]

Given Hoover's position as the nation's top law enforcement officer, these and other contacts[184] with individuals linked to organized crime were certainly questionable. But most troublesome was his contact with Frank Costello, a top Mafia boss of the 1940s.[185] According to *Time*, in a 1975 cover story on Hoover, some FBI agents spoke of his "sometimes traveling to Manhattan to meet one of the Mafia's top figures, Frank Costello. The two would meet in Central Park."[186] Historian Arthur Schlesinger, Jr. reported, "The fact that Hoover met with Costello is confirmed by William Hundley, a former Justice Department official, and Edward Bennett Williams."[187] The impropriety was glaring—the FBI chief meeting the top Mafia chieftain, impeding efforts to fight the Mob, and resisting a proper investigation of the Mob's suspected assassination of a president.

Hoover's reluctance to confront organized crime was a possible factor in his considerable animosity toward Robert Kennedy,[188] who finally pushed him to do so. Hoover harbored similar enmity toward a friend of RFK, the Reverend Martin Luther King. Included among his large files of derogatory information[189] were tapes of an extramarital affair of King, which he sent to King's wife and played for reporters.[190] And Hoover demonstrated his contempt for RFK and the Reverend King, as reported by former assistant William Sullivan, by delaying the announcement of the capture of King's slayer "so he could interrupt TV coverage of Bobby's burial."[191]

Equally antagonistic toward Robert Kennedy was Clyde Tolson, Hoover's FBI deputy and companion,[192] who was extensively briefed on the FBI's activities during the Kennedy assassination probe.[193] According to Sullivan, Tolson once said of Robert Kennedy, "I hope someone shoots and kills the son of a bitch."[194]

BASE ALLIANCES IN THE WHITE HOUSE

Sharing Hoover's opposition to an independent assassination probe was President Lyndon Johnson. On November 29, 1963, a week after President Kennedy's death, Hoover told Johnson over the telephone that the FBI's report on the case, portraying Oswald as the lone assassin, was almost finished.[195] In a memo that day recounting the conversation, Hoover wrote:

> The President stated he wanted to get by just with my file and my report. I told him I thought it would be very bad to have a rash of investigations. He then indicated the only way to stop it is to appoint a high-level committee to evaluate my report and tell the House and Senate not to go ahead with the investigation.[196]

The same day, Johnson signed an executive order creating the Warren Commission,[197] which would so faithfully obey the Hoover-Katzenbach injunction to "convince the public that Oswald is the real assassin."[198]

The capability to coordinate the cover-up achieved by the Warren Commission was demonstrated early in Johnson's career. As reported by Pulitzer Prize-winner Robert Caro, Johnson "stole his first election in 1930" for a seat on the college senior council and won another school election by blackmail.[199] Through many such underhanded political tricks, Johnson became "so deeply and widely mistrusted" by his classmates that they called him "Bull," for "Bullshit" — the nickname recorded in his yearbook.[200] And Johnson's incessant lying earned him the reputation of being "the biggest liar on campus."[201]

Yet prior to 1981, not one biography of Johnson reported this information about his college years.[202] The reason, Caro explained, was that while still an undergraduate at the Texas State Teachers College at San Marcos, Johnson arranged to have excised (literally cut out) from hundreds of copies of the college yearbook certain pages that gave clues to his years there (luckily for history, some copies escaped the scissors). Issues of the college newspaper that chronicle certain crucial episodes in his college career are missing from the college library. A ruthless use thereafter of political power in San Marcos made faculty members and classmates reluctant to discuss those aspects of his career.[203]

If the skills to coordinate an assassination cover-up were honed in Johnson's college days, the motivation to do so was indicated by two allegations of payoffs to him from organized crime. One was reported by Jack Halfen, a Dallas gangster who had graduated from criminal exploits with desperados "Pretty Boy" Floyd, Bonnie Parker and Clyde Barrow to coordinating gambling during the 1940s and 1950s in the Houston area.[204] Bookmaking alone netted more than $15 million a year in Houston;[205] 40 percent went to Carlos Marcello, 35 percent to Halfen and 25 percent to police and politicians for bribes.[206] These arrangements were illuminated during Halfen's 1954 trial for income-tax evasion, which brought him a four-year prison sentence.[207] But prosecutor Charles Herring, a friend and former aide of Lyndon Johnson, never pressed the embarrassing issue of where Halfen's myriad payoff dollars stopped.[208]

Although Halfen never informed on his Mob associates, his loyalty to political collaborators wore thin as the months in jail rolled by.[209] And in conversations with U.S. Marshal J. Neal Matthews in 1956, Halfen provided incriminating information on several of them, including one of his closest political affiliates: Lyndon Johnson.[210] Halfen reported that his Mob-franchised gambling network had given $500,000 in cash and campaign contributions to Johnson over a ten-year period while Johnson was in the Senate.[211] In return, Senator Johnson repeatedly killed antirackets legislation, watered down the bills that could not be defeated and curbed Congressional investigations of the Mob.[212] For example, a U.S. Senate committee chaired by Estes Kefauver held hearings on organized crime in more than a dozen cities during the early 1950s.[213] But the committee never made it to

Texas, reportedly as a result of Johnson's intervention.[214] Halfen had concrete substantiation of his association with Johnson, including a letter from Johnson to the Texas Board of Paroles on his behalf[215] and photographs showing Johnson, Halfen and other Texas politicians on a private hunting expedition.[216]

Mob payoffs to Johnson were also indicated in sworn testimony by Jack Sullivan, a former administrative assistant to Senator Daniel Brewster of Maryland.[217] During a 1964 cocktail party at Teamster headquarters that Sullivan attended, Brewster and Teamster boss Jimmy Hoffa walked off to talk privately on the terrace overlooking Capitol Hill.[218] Afterward, Brewster told Sullivan that Hoffa had asked him to take $100,000 in cash for Johnson to presidential aide Cliff Carter.[219] The payoff was meant to enlist Johnson's support in blocking Hoffa's prosecution for jury tampering and pension fund fraud,[220] for which Hoffa was ultimately convicted.[221]

A few days after the party, Sullivan testified, Teamster lobbyist Sid Zagri came into Senator Brewster's office and gave Brewster a suitcase full of money.[222] Sullivan then accompanied Brewster to Cliff Carter's office and waited in the car as Brewster went into the office with the suitcase and left without it.[223]

Lending credence to Sullivan's testimony was Senator Brewster's indictment for corruption by a Baltimore grand jury in 1969 and subsequent conviction. And both allegations were consistent with further unsavory patterns in Johnson's political career. Johnson secured his first federal office, a U.S. Senate seat in 1948, by winning a Democratic primary election in Texas.[224] He won by 87 votes—when 203 new votes suddenly turned up in alphabetical order late in the ballot tabulation.[225] The federal government launched an investigation for vote fraud,[226] and suspicions were finally confirmed in 1977 when a Texas election judge, Luis Salas, confessed that the election had been stolen at Johnson's suggestion.[227]

During his years in Washington, Johnson retained his crooked habits, as disclosed by author Robert Caro:

For years, men came into Lyndon Johnson's office and handed him envelopes stuffed with cash. They didn't stop coming even when the office in which he sat was the office of the Vice President of the United States. Fifty thousand dollars (in hundred-dollar bills in sealed envelopes) was what one lobbyist—for *one* oil company—testified that he brought to Johnson's office during his term as Vice President.[228] [Emphasis in original.]

It was perhaps through such envelopes and the blatant use of political power to further his private business interests[229] that Johnson accumulated a $20 million fortune during his political career.[230]

A prime insight into Johnson's predilection for corruption, cover-up and organized crime was furnished by the Bobby Baker affair. Baker was secretary to Senate Majority Leader Johnson for eight years,[231] during which time he accumulated an estimated $2 million.[232] He resigned on October 7, 1963, a month after his grand-scale influence peddling was exposed by the *Washington Post*.[233] The ensuing scandal proved embarrassing to Johnson, his mentor and boss, who had called Baker "one of my trusted friends."[234] As a result of the scandal, in fact, Johnson had been expected to be dumped by President Kennedy from the second spot on the 1964 Democratic ticket.[235]

Baker's far-flung corruption eventually brought him a prison term on seven counts of tax evasion, theft and fraud involving nearly $100,000 in political payoff money.[236] Among the transactions unraveled were dealings with Mobsters and Teamsters in Texas, Las Vegas, the Caribbean and his home base of Washington, D.C.,[237] where he functioned as the Mob-Teamster "man in Washington."[238] But little information was obtained from Baker himself, who during his appearances before the Senate Rules Committee repeatedly invoked the Fifth Amendment.[239] And the day after Vice President Lyndon Johnson succeeded Kennedy as president, the Organized Crime Section of the Justice Department stopped receiving information on Baker from Hoover's FBI.[240]

The hush on Baker may be explained by a conversation between Johnson and House Speaker John McCormack as reported in *The Washington Payoff* by ex-Washington lobbyist Robert Winter-Berger.[241] On February 4, 1964, Winter-Berger was discussing public relations with McCormack in McCormack's

Washington office.[242] President Johnson then barged in and began ranting hysterically, Winter-Berger reported, oblivious to the lobbyist's presence.[243] During his long tirade, Johnson said:

> John, that son of a bitch [Bobby Baker] is going to ruin me. If that cocksucker talks, I'm gonna land in jail. . . . I practically raised that motherfucker, and now he's gonna make me the first President of the United States to spend the last days of his life behind bars.[244]

When Johnson finally noticed Winter-Berger's presence, McCormack explained that the visiting lobbyist was a close friend of Nat Voloshen,[245] who was a Mob fixer of enormous influence.[246] Johnson then became enthusiastic, exclaiming, "Nat can get to Bobby. They're friends. Have Nat get to Bobby."[247] When Winter-Berger volunteered that he had an appointment with Voloshen the next day, Johnson told Winter-Berger

> Tell Nat that I want him to get in touch with Bobby Baker as soon as possible—tomorrow if he can. Tell Nat to tell Bobby that I will give him a million dollars if he takes this rap. Bobby must not talk. I'll see to it that he gets a million-dollar settlement.[248]

Given a subsequent scandal involving intercessions for Mobsters from McCormack's office at Voloshen's behest,[249] the recounted tirade would hardly have been exceptional in that office. And the Baker case did indeed involve some close friends of LBJ, including Texas oil magnate Clint Murchison, for whose company Baker interceded to reverse a Department of Agriculture ruling prohibiting the importation of unsanitarily processed meat from Haiti to Puerto Rico.[250] Also, when Baker's problems began in September 1963, the attorney he chose was Johnson's close friend[251] Abe Fortas,[252] who later achieved notoriety as the first U.S. Supreme Court justice to resign under pressure.[253]

But in November 1963, Fortas was replaced as Baker's counsel by Edward Bennett Williams,[254] who specialized in clientele of Baker's ilk, including New York Mafia boss Frank Costello,[255] Teamster boss Jimmy Hoffa,[256] Chicago Mafia boss Sam Giancana[257] and Chicago Mafia "lord high executioner"[258] Felix Alde-risio.[259] Fortas had quit the defense of Johnson's protégé Baker to accept a new position, as described in a November 26, 1963 memo by Texas Attorney General Wagoner Carr:

> Mr. Fortas informed me that he has been assigned to coor-dinate the FBI, Department of Justice and Texas Attorney General's efforts regarding the assassination of President Kennedy.[260]

In conclusion, the Kennedy assassination cover-up fit the pat-tern that Tacitus had characterized earlier: "a shocking crime" committed "on the unscrupulous initiative of few individuals, with the blessing of more, and amid the passive acquiescence of all."[261] This time, the unscrupulous initiators included Lyndon Johnson and J. Edgar Hoover, who stressed the need to "con-vince the public that Oswald [was] the real assassin." Both ap-plied extraordinary pressure to stifle a thorough investigation of the case while maintaining questionable postures toward orga-nized crime. Assists were furnished by people like ex-CIA direc-tor Allen Dulles, journalist Tony Zoppi and Mobster Sidney Korshak, while Kennedy's enemies from the anti-Castro alliance undoubtedly gave their blessings. And the complacent multitudes were credulous members of the Warren Commission, uncritical journalists and other Americans who jumped on the lone-assas-sin bandwagon rather than seek the difficult truth behind the tragic killing.

For some participants, the driving force behind this mammoth cover-up may have been largely the desire to hide embarrassing secrets—the CIA, for example, its participation with the Mob in Cuban assassination plots, and the FBI its contacts with Oswald prior to the assassination.[262] The latter was one factor that led Hoover to fear, as Blakey and Billings noted, that "the Bureau would be charged with dereliction and his reputation would be ruined."[263]

Yet Korshak's intervention to discredit Becker and the coordi-nated perjury of Jack Ruby's underworld contacts, to be examined soon, demonstrate that calculated subversion by the underworld was a factor, as well. And the Mob indeed had much to conceal in the JFK murder case, as will be shown in the climactic part that follows.

PART V

A
Mafia
Contract

An objective investigation of the JFK assassination, which the Warren Commission obsequiously skirted, was finally carried out in the late 1970s by the House Select Committee on Assassinations. In 1979, after a two-year probe, the Committee reported that President Kennedy "was probably assassinated as a result of a conspiracy";[1] this conclusion was shared by 75 percent of assassination experts and 80 percent of the American public polled in the early 1980s.[2] The Committee also found that the Mafia had the "motive, means and opportunity" to kill him,[3] while its chief counsel, G. Robert Blakey, asserted his firm opinion that the Mob murdered President Kennedy.[4]

The evidence presented earlier certainly points to this conclusion. As established by acoustical and eyewitness evidence, a second gunman fired at President Kennedy from the grassy knoll. Three assassination suspects, Ferrie, Oswald and Brading, had ties to organized crime. Key Mob figures, including New Orleans Mafia boss Carlos Marcello, discussed plots to murder John and Robert Kennedy. And Jack Ruby, a Dallas Mobster, murdered Oswald as part of a carefully orchestrated conspiracy. Through the following steps, based largely on newly disclosed evidence, this part now completes a compelling case in support of Congressional indications that the Mafia killed President Kennedy.

First, after President Kennedy's trip to Dallas was announced, Ruby called and visited more than a dozen Mobsters across the nation, including several associates of Marcello, Trafficante and Hoffa. As November 22 approached, these Mob contacts sharply intensified and then shifted focus to Dallas. Second, the Mobsters called and visited by Ruby presented a collusively fabricated alibi to explain their contacts—directly exhibiting conspiracy and precluding an innocent explanation. And third, in the final days before November 22, Ruby's contacts with this Mob pack were punctuated by actions that exposed his participation in a contract to murder the president, including a November 21 trip to stalk Kennedy in Houston.

The Mafia assassination contract against President Kennedy, as exposed through the National Archives file on Jack Ruby, begins in a key Mob base: New Orleans.

Organized crime involves itself in the life of every single human being. It causes prices to be raised; it affects your pocketbook when you go to a laundry or dry cleaner; the price you pay for food in the market. I have been involved in and know of bad meat being purchased, unfit for human consumption, that has been converted into salami in delicatessens and forced to be sold through grocery stores. . . .

When I testified about Mr. DeCarlo, I, too, had the native feel of what organized crime was.

I saw photographs of graves dug in New Jersey, with over 35 bodies over a period of years, melted with lye. I sat and heard the voices at dinner talking over murdering a 12-year-old child and burying bodies in New Jersey. . . .

Narcotics, manipulation of businesses that cause prices to spiral, we can go on for a long, long time. . . . It goes on and on.[1]

Mob defector Gerald Zelmanowitz, testifying in 1973
before a U.S. Senate committee

18
Nationwide
Mob Contacts

A boss among bosses in the Mafia hierarchy,[2] Carlos Marcello of New Orleans had much to lose from the Kennedy crime crusade. Not only was his immensely profitable Louisiana fiefdom threatened, but also he found himself high on the attorney general's "hit list" of Mobsters targeted for prosecution.[3] Pushed to desperation, as informant Edward Becker testified, in 1962 the enraged Marcello "clearly stated that he was going to arrange to have President Kennedy murdered in some way."[4] In what Becker termed a deliberate plot, Marcello intended to use an outsider for the crime[5] to avoid implicating his own lieutenants. Available for this role was a local named Lee Harvey Oswald, whose uncle and surrogate father, Charles "Dutz" Murret, worked as a bookie in Marcello's criminal organization. Marcello's opportunity to implement his plan would come in November 1963, when President Kennedy entered his Gulf Coast domain for a motorcade ride through Dallas.

Yet, as also shown previously, Marcello was not the only Mafia power who had contemplated the murder of President Kennedy. During the summer months of 1962, Tampa Mafia boss Santos Trafficante, Jr. and the Mob-involved Teamster boss, Jimmy Hoffa, revealed similar assassination designs. "Kennedy is in trouble, and he will get what is coming to him," Trafficante raged, referring to the president. "He is going to be hit."[6] Hoffa targeted Robert Kennedy for murder, and considered having him killed by a lone rifleman somewhere in the South, where extreme segregationists could be blamed.[7] Noting Hoffa's rabid hatred of President Kennedy, a Hoffa aide found it quite possible that one Kennedy assassination plan by him developed into another.[8]

If Marcello, Trafficante and Hoffa, all close associates, did in fact join forces to assassinate President Kennedy, the progression of the conspiracy is easy to surmise. Powerful as they were, the two Mafia bosses and their Teamster ally would have required the nod for such a monumental undertaking from the full Mafia National Commission—particularly the key bosses representing New York, Chicago and the West Coast. A hit squad would have then been formed from the Mob's nationwide network of expert executioners. And someone would have been selected in Dallas to coordinate communications among the various elements of the conspiracy: associates of the instigating triumvirate, representatives of other top Mafia families and Mob executioners. For this local coordinator to leave an incriminating, documentary trail of precisely such contacts, however, hardly could have been part of the plan.

This chapter covers Ruby's activities for the period between April 23, 1963, the date President Kennedy's trip to Dallas was first reported,[9] and mid-November 1963. The trail of Mob contacts is laid largely by toll call records from Ruby's home and Carousel office telephones[10] plus other sources that identify the parties he called. Barring unidentified, freak exceptions, as discussed in Appendix 1, all such calls were placed by Ruby himself and will be referenced as such. Additional contacts that Ruby made during the latter part of November will be covered in chapter 20.

MAY THROUGH JULY 1963:
FOCUS IN NEW ORLEANS

Ruby's rate of toll calls from his Carousel office phone, the best available index of his activity in 1963,[11] is modest between January and April.[12] Telephone records covering most of this period, in fact, show only one out-of-state call from that phone.[13] But this pattern changes following an April 23 story in the *Dallas Times Herald* reporting the itinerary of a proposed trip by President Kennedy to Dallas.[14] A spree of telephone calls and visits begins between Ruby and Mafia associates in several cities, contacts that intensify with each update on the president's trip. For the first three months, these interactions occur in Marcello's turf, New Orleans, punctuated by a few others with Mobster Lewis McWillie in Las Vegas.

May 7, 1963. Ruby calls the Sho-Bar on Bourbon Street in New Orleans.[15] That establishment is then owned by Pete Marcello,[16] a brother and lieutenant of Carlos and a convicted narcotics felon.[17]

May 10. At Ruby's request, a .38 Smith and Wesson revolver is shipped to his friend Lewis McWillie in Las Vegas, according to records of the Dallas gun supplier.[18] Curiously, McWillie never picks up the gun, and it is returned to the supplier.[19] In his polygraph exam hearing, Ruby later repeatedly brings up another gun sent to McWillie and a message Ruby transmitted about it,[20] remarking, "This is incriminating against me very bad."[21] McWillie would claim he asked Ruby to ship the gun because he didn't know where to get one in Las Vegas: "I didn't even know you could buy a gun in a store."[22] Coming from a prominent Syndicate figure[23] described by Dallas Police as a "gambler and murderer,"[24] this explanation is less than credible.

May 12. Ruby places a 6-minute call to the Mob-owned[25] Thunderbird Hotel in Las Vegas.[26] This and many subsequent calls to that number are apparently to McWillie, who is then employed there[27] (McWillie acknowledged receiving calls from Ruby at the Thunderbird and at his home,[28] and Ruby's sister Eva Grant testified that Ruby called McWillie at least ten times in the latter part of 1963[29]). The explanations of Ruby's contacts with McWillie and other Mobsters will be examined in the next chapter.

Mid-May. Shortly after the call to McWillie, Ruby travels to New Orleans, the first of several trips there, where he visits the Old French Opera House on Bourbon Street.[30] That establishment is then owned by Frank Caracci,[31] a New Orleans Mobster closely affiliated with Carlos Marcello.[32] Ruby calls the club at least eight times during the next three months.[33]

June 5. President Kennedy, Vice President Johnson and Governor Connally meet in El Paso, Texas, and decide to proceed with the president's proposed November trip to the Lone Star State.[34] On the same day, Ruby places a 28-minute call to Caracci's Old French Opera House.[35] During the next few days, Ruby visits New Orleans, where he reportedly goes to another Caracci establishment, the 500 Club, of which the Marcello associate was part owner.[36] An FBI chronology states that Caracci "saw Ruby" in New Orleans during his visit there,[37] a charge Caracci denied.[38] (Another meeting between Ruby and Caracci, reported by a New Orleans Police detective, will be discussed shortly.) Also contacted on the New Orleans trip is Caracci's Mafia-involved[39] brother-in-law Nick Graffagnini.[40] Graffagnini converses with Ruby at the Sho-Bar, according to Graffagnini and three other witnesses.[41]

June 8. Many out-of-state Mobsters, including "one of the nation's top vice lords," begin to descend upon Dallas, according to a Dallas Police report cited by journalist Seth Kantor.[42] On June 9, they hold the first of a series of meetings with local colleagues.[43] Among their rendezvous sites: a Howard Johnson's restaurant on the Fort Worth Turnpike in Arlington and Jack Ruby's Carousel Club.[44] Ruby calls the Arlington Howard Johnson's on June 10 for one minute and on June 13 for seven minutes.[45] In between, Ruby also makes a 3-minute call, on June 11, to Pete Marcello's Sho-Bar in New Orleans.[46]

June 14. Ruby places a 7-minute call to the Old French Opera House, owned by Caracci.[47] This is the first of four calls Ruby will make to that establishment over the next week, which he has visited just days before. He follows those contacts with a call to Lewis McWillie at his Las Vegas home on June 27; they talk for seven minutes.[48] And in July, Ruby telephones Caracci's Old French Opera House twice, on the 6th and the 24th.[49]

AUGUST: THE WEST COAST AND NEW YORK

In August, Ruby's contacts with Marcello associates in New Orleans almost completely subside. At the same time, Ruby's phone and travel records for that month show intensified contacts in Las Vegas, New York and Chicago.

August 2. Ruby places a 3-minute call to the Thunderbird Hotel in Las Vegas,[50] presumably again to his friend Lewis McWillie.[51] The McWillie call marks the start of a busy week for Ruby: over the next five days, he calls four other underworld-linked men and visits two more in New York.

The same day, Ruby places a 2-minute call to the Los Angeles home of William Miller[52] and then a 7-minute call to Miller at a Beverly Hills residence where Miller is visiting.[53] Miller is a booking agent, night-club operator and one-time co-owner of the Riverside hotel-casino in Reno, Nevada.[54] He knows Lewis McWillie[55] and is close to Benjamin Dranow,[56] the latter convicted of helping to drain $1.7 million from the Teamster pension fund.[57] Miller himself applied for a $2.75 million Teamster loan for the Riverside, which was granted with unusual haste — just in time for the hotel to declare bankruptcy in 1962.[58]

Also on August 2, Ruby places two calls to Michael Shore, one at his home in Beverly Hills, California and the other at his office at the Reprise Record Company in Los Angeles.[59] Shore is then a very close friend and business partner of Irwin Weiner,[60] one of the most prominent Mafia associates in the Chicago area during that period.[61]

August 4. Ruby steps up his flurry of activity by placing a 5-minute call to the Thunderbird Hotel in Las Vegas,[62] presumably again to McWillie.[63] The same day a call is placed from the number 242–5431 in New Orleans to Ruby's telephone in Dallas.[64] The number is that of a telephone at the Tropical Tourist Court trailer park, in the private office of its manager, Nofio Pecora.[65] Pecora, according to the FBI, Justice Department and Metropolitan Crime Commission of New Orleans, is at the time "one of Marcello's three most trusted aides."[66]

Years later, when questioned by the House Assassinations Committee, Pecora first declined to respond, then claimed no recollection of a call to Ruby.[67] But Pecora admitted he was probably the only person who had access to his Tropical Court telephone in 1963.[68] "A multiple ex-convict in the heroin traffic," as described to Congress in 1970, Pecora dealt in narcotics with Marcello before the latter achieved his boss status.[69] Exemplifying their close relationship, Pecora received a telephone call from Marcello on June 24, 1963 — at the very same Tropical Court phone from which Pecora called Ruby a month later.[70]

Also on August 4, Ruby places a 3-minute call to a New York number listed to the Milton Blackstone Advertising Agency.[71] Then employed there, in "public relations," is Ruby's old buddy Barney Ross,[72] formerly a boxer and drug addict.[73] A slip of paper with the name "Barney Ross," that New York telephone number, and the message "Hurry north" is later found among Ruby's personal effects.[74]

Ruby does in fact "hurry north," taking American Airlines flight 186 to New York that same day[75] and checking into the New York Hilton at 10:59 p.m.[76] Ruby tells a fellow passenger, Walter Blassingame, that he is going to be met at the New York airport by a Barney Ross, as Blassingame would later tell the FBI.[77] When they arrive, Blassingame hears Barney Ross paged.[78] Ruby also tells another passenger on the flight, Alfred Lurie, that he is on his way to see Ross.[79] Another witness would testify that Ruby's New York trip "was to go see a friend," evidently Ross,[80] and Ruby himself would confirm contact with Ross during that trip.[81]

But later, when interviewed by the FBI, Ross said he last saw Ruby "accidentally" in Chicago around the end of 1961, and had only talked to him by telephone since then.[82] Equally dubious was Ross' account to the FBI of his former relationship with Al Capone. In that interview, Ross admitted that "about 1926," when he began his boxing career, he and his friends ran "innocuous errands" for Capone.[83] Ross claimed that he believed Capone gave them these errands only "to keep them from hanging around the streets" and that he did not realize Capone was a big-time racketeer until "about 1927."[84] Capone was in fact notorious by early 1925, however.[85] The report of Ross' FBI interview also noted a direct admission of his duplicity:

> Ross pointed out that in his autobiography although he stated that he had at one time worked for Al Capone, he never did actually work for Capone.[86]

Once in New York, Ruby wastes no time in calling Caracci's Old French Opera House[87] and the Los Angeles residence of Michael Shore.[88] Ruby's activities of the following day are also noteworthy.

August 5. Ruby visits Joseph Glaser in the New York office of Associated Booking Corporation, as reported by both Ruby[89] and Glaser.[90] Glaser is then president of Associated Booking,[91] the nation's third largest theatrical booking agency, whose clients have included Louis Armstrong, Duke Ellington and Barbra Streisand.[92] But the man who then has "virtually absolute control of Associated Booking," the *New York Times* would expose in 1976, is Mobster Sidney Korshak.[93] A year before Ruby's visit, in fact, Glaser transferred a major share of the company's voting rights to Korshak, paving the way for Korshak later to assume complete control.[94] And Glaser himself "probably could have been in rackets," Eva Grant later testifies,[95] offering similar gentle characterizations of three Mob killers.[96]

August 6. Ruby checks out of the Hilton at 4:40 p.m.,[97] preparing to head home. But one stop remains. On the return to Dallas he goes via Chicago, and members of his family join him briefly at O'Hare Field, the Chicago airport,[98] Ruby later tells the FBI. But in his apparent candor, Ruby neglects to mention that while in Chicago he stopped at Henrici's Restaurant, as reported by a woman who met him there.[99] Henrici's at the time served such patrons as Teamster official Gus Zapas and narcotics trafficker Vincent "Piggy Mack" Marchesi,[100] both Mob figures with long criminal records.[101]

August 15. Following up on his recent contacts, Ruby places two 3-minute calls to Joseph Glaser, Korshak's partner, in New York.[102] He then places three calls in four days, August 19–22, to the Thunderbird in Las Vegas.[103] Since Lewis McWillie would later acknowledge calls from Ruby at the club in August,[104] these again are probably to that Mob "gambler and murderer."[105]

Ruby's recorded activities in September are minimal—only three out-of-state calls, all to relatives, and no trips.[106] At the end of the month, however, a critical decision is reported in Washington: President Kennedy will in fact visit Texas, on November 21 and 22.[107] And in the following weeks, Ruby's intensive telephone activity and travel resume in earnest.

A compilation of Ruby's toll calls by date, as charted, provides a striking measure of this spurt in activity. In October, following the confirmation of the president's trip, Ruby's rate of out-of-state calls rises tenfold over September's rate. Among the people Ruby calls are several well-connected Mob and Teamster figures who serve as trusted go-betweens for the big-city Mafia patriarchs. As October folds into November, Ruby's rate of out-of-state calls continues its upsurge: in the week of November 3, the rate skyrockets to 25 times the average rate of January through September. Then, in the weeks before the assassination, this rate plummets just as dramatically—at the same time that Ruby receives several Mob visitors in Dallas, as will be discussed in chapter 20.

October 3. Ruby places a 13-minute call to the Shreveport, Louisiana home of Elizabeth Matthews,[108] who has been recently divorced from Russell D. Matthews.[109] Since Russell is an associate of Ruby,[110] and Elizabeth would later report having no acquaintance with Ruby nor recollection of any call from him,[111] it appears that Ruby is trying to contact Russell. Russell Matthews is described by federal sources at the time as "a burglar, armed robber, narcotics pusher and murderer."[112] An associate of Mafia boss Santos Trafficante,[113] Matthews visited Cuba in the late 1950s on Trafficante's behalf.[114] Matthews is then also a close associate of Dallas Mafioso Joseph Campisi.[115]

Besides calling Matthews, Ruby reportedly ventures into Trafficante's sphere twice as the assassination day approaches. Those visits are detected through federal surveillance of Johnny Roselli,[116] a notorious West Coast Mafioso and known principal with Trafficante and Chicago Mafia boss Sam Giancana in assassination plots against Castro.[117] According to federal sources cited in *New Times*,

Rate of Toll Calls from
Ruby's Carousel Office Phone During 1963

Calls per week

30 —

25 —

20 —

15 —

10 —

5 —

0 —

| 1,13 | 0,5 | 3,13 | 6,13 | 4,9 | 5,3 | 1,11 | | 10,11 | 9,12 | 16,15 | 4,15 | 0,1 |

1/17 THRU 3/1 — 4/10 THRU 4/30 — MAY — JUNE — JULY — AUG. — SEPT. — 10/1 THRU 10/26 — 10/27 THRU 11/2 — 11/3 THRU 11/9 — 11/10 THRU 11/16 — 11/17 THRU 11/22

X,Y ——— Numbers of out-of-state, in-state calls in period

——— In-state calls

——— Out-of-state calls

This chart shows toll calls from Ruby's Carousel office phone, compiled from telephone records subpoenaed by the FBI[119] and telephone bills found in Ruby's possession.[120] The less frequent calls from his home phone[121] are not included, as records for such calls prior to May 1963 are not available. There are smaller gaps in his Carousel toll call records, for the periods January 1–16 and March 2–April 9, 1963.

two Miami motel rooms have been identified as the locations of two meetings between Roselli and Jack Ruby. The meetings occurred during the two months preceding the Kennedy assassination.[118]

It is Roselli, the link between West Coast Mobsters, Trafficante and Giancana, who in the mid-1970s began telling associates and news contacts that Ruby was "one of our boys" and was lined up to kill Oswald.[122] Columnist Jack Anderson reported, "When Oswald was picked up, Roselli suggested, the underworld conspirators feared that he would crack and disclose information that might lead to them. . . . So Jack Ruby was ordered to eliminate Oswald."[123]

Amazing candor from a Mobster? The Mafia apparently thought so. A few months after he testified in secret session before the Senate Intelligence Committee in 1976, Roselli's dismembered body was found in an oil drum in Miami's Biscayne Bay.[124] He had last been seen on a boat owned by a Trafficante associate.[125]

On June 19, 1975, three days before Roselli had first been questioned by the Senate Intelligence Committee, staff members of the Committee arrived in Chicago to arrange for Mafia boss Sam Giancana's testimony about Cuban assassination plots.[126] That evening, Giancana was shot seven times and killed in his Oak Park home.[127] One of his daughters insisted that he was slain by the same people responsible for killing the Kennedys.[128] A staff report of the House Assassinations Committee noted that "Trafficante has most often been the person assigned responsibility" for the murders of both Giancana and Roselli.[129]

Around the time of the reported meeting with Roselli, Ruby pays a second timely visit to Marcello associate Frank Caracci in New Orleans.[130] The visit is witnessed by New Orleans Police Detective Frederick O'Sullivan of the department's intelligence unit. O'Sullivan tells the FBI on November 27, 1963 that six to eight weeks earlier, he saw a man he believed was Ruby.[131] O'Sullivan

felt fairly certain that he had seen Ruby in the French Quarter in the company of Frank Caracci, owner of the

500 Club, Bourbon Street. Also present was Nick Korano [Carno], partner of Frank Caracci.[132]

Two points corroborate O'Sullivan's account. First, Nick Carno is then in fact Caracci's partner at the 500 Club[133] and had been there with Caracci when Ruby visited in June.[134] Second, there are only two gaps of more than a day in Ruby's toll call records for October and November, 1963; they occur between October 3 and 7 and between October 8 and 12.[135] Both of these gaps fall within the period of October 1 to 15 estimated by Detective O'Sullivan for Ruby's encounter with Caracci. Also consistent with out-of-state travel by Ruby in early October is a notation in one of his notebooks: "American Airline[s], Tuesday October 9 – 985, 11–11:30 A.M."[136]

When questioned by the FBI on November 27, 1963, Caracci denied any contact with Ruby.[137] And four years later, when subpoenaed with Carlos Marcello during a grand jury probe of the Mob, Caracci would declare the probe "off base" and claim to know nothing about organized crime.[138] Caracci's level of credibility in such declarations, however, is perhaps indicated by his subsequent conviction for attempting to bribe a federal agent.[139]

October 26. Ruby places a 12-minute person-to-person call to Irwin S. Weiner at his Chicago home.[140] Weiner is then and now a prominent Chicago Mafia associate who is instrumental in coordinating the flow of cash among the Teamsters Union, Las Vegas casinos and the Chicago branch of the Mob.[141] He has been linked to arson, extortion, Medicare fraud, gambling, bribery and murder.[142] His close associates have included Trafficante, Giancana and Hoffa.[143]

When questioned by the FBI five days after the assassination, Weiner refused to discuss the call from Ruby;[144] he later provided a series of contradictory explanations.[145] Weiner was also curiously uncertain about what he was doing at the time of the assassination; he could not even remember what city he was in or how he first heard the news.[146] Weiner did confirm, however, that he met with Trafficante in Miami at about that date.[147] Their subject of discussion: "just trivialities."[148]

Ruby's brother Hyman testified that after Ruby "tried to call" Weiner he then "tried to call Lenny Patrick,"[149] whom Ruby had known as a young man in Chicago.[150] Ruby's sister Eva testified that Ruby did in fact call Lenny Patrick in 1963.[151] Patrick is a notorious Mob assassin[152] whom police credit with "masterminding some of the Syndicate's more important liquidations."[153]

October 30. At 9:13 p.m., Ruby places a 1-minute call to the office phone of Marcello lieutenant Nofio Pecora at the Tropical Court in New Orleans.[154] As discussed, Pecora's Tropical Court phone records show a prior call to Ruby, on August 4.

November 7. Ruby receives a collect call from "Barney Baker, Chicago, Illinois," and speaks for seven minutes.[155] Baker, who later admits telephoning Ruby in November,[156] is at that time a Hoffa aide described by federal sources as "a reported muscle and bagman" for the Teamster boss and "a hoodlum with organized crime and Teamster connections."[157] He had been released from prison in June 1963 after serving two years for shaking down a Pittsburgh newspaper.[158]

November 8. Ruby places a 4-minute call to the Eden Roc Hotel in Miami, person-to-person to Dusty Miller.[159] Murray W. "Dusty" Miller, who confirms this contact,[160] is the head of the Southern Conference of Teamsters in 1963 and later becomes the union's international secretary treasurer.[161] The House Assassinations Committee would disclose that Miller "was associated with numerous underworld figures."[162] Also on November 8, Ruby places a 14-minute call to Barney Baker, the Teamster goon, at Baker's Chicago residence.[163]*

November 12. Ruby places a 10-minute call person-to-person to Frank Goldstein in San Francisco.[166] Goldstein, who confirms the call,[167] describes himself as a "professional gambler."[168] Mob killers Russell Matthews,[169] Lewis McWillie[170] and Lenny Patrick[171] are also referred to as such by other Warren Commission witnesses.

November 17. Al Gruber of Los Angeles places an 8-minute call to Ruby.[172] Gruber, whose record shows six arrests under

---

*Baker's telephone records show two calls in November 1963 to the Denver number of boxer Sonny Liston.[164] These contacts lend credibility to the 1973 account of Mafia defector Patsy Lepera that Liston deliberately lost the 1964 championship match against Muhammed Ali on the Mob's orders: "This guy didn't just take a dive—he did a one and a half off the highboard."[165]

268

three different names,[173] also visits Ruby for several days in mid-November, as will be discussed in chapter 20.

These timely and intensive contacts of Ruby suggest that a Mob conspiracy was in progress. The existence of such a conspiracy is confirmed by the concertedly fabricated alibi presented to cover these contacts.

The mob is a cancer on this land. . . . They reach congressmen just as quickly as they reach state houses and police precincts. They corrupt businessmen and unions, you name it. . . . There isn't a state in the union where the mob doesn't have influence. They have stolen so many billions in securities that you can't dream that high, let alone count.[1]

Mob defector Vincent Teresa

19
The AGVA Alibi:
Mob Perjury

Lying is second nature for Mobsters; self-serving explanations of their activities are not to be taken seriously. The fabrications are sometimes improvised, such as the stories of several delegates to a 1957 Mafia conclave in Apalachin, New York. When surrounded there by police, Vito Genovese of New York City maintained that host Joseph Barbara was sick and that all of his visitors "just came to wish him speedy recovery."[2] Some of the conferees caught in the woods surrounding Barbara's house said that they had been "looking at real estate."[3] Two others picked up outside claimed that they had been "walking to the railroad station";[4] small matter that the nearest railroad station was 70 miles away.[5]

More sinister than such extemporaneous lying is the Mob's routine use of outsiders to bolster its fabrications. For example, the House Judiciary Committee reported that in 1966 an FBI bug recorded how Mafia underboss Jerry Angiulo planned to handle an assault charge. Angiulo schemed to thwart conviction by getting two men to perjure themselves and provide an alibi for him.[6]

In a similar case reported by sociologist Donald Cressey, some Mafia "soldiers" were indicted for killing a man.[7] At the trial, the Mafiosi were provided a false alibi by a hotel owner whom they had once assisted.[8] "He had to perjure himself or be killed," Cressey noted.[9] Cressey also described two cases in which witnesses against the Mob received death threats to recant their testimony; one was later murdered.[10]

Similarly orchestrated, like the accounts of Ruby's assassination weekend activities, were the explanations for his series of nationwide Mob contacts prior to November 22. In particular, the main cover story about Ruby's "AGVA" problem, recited by many of the Mobsters he contacted, is shown false by both multiple contradictions and critical flaws in its basic premises. This coordinated perjury is a prima facie demonstration of Mob conspiracy after the fact. It is also a strong indication that Ruby's underworld contacts were part of a plot to murder President Kennedy.

BACKGROUND ON AGVA

Recently, I had to make so many numerous calls that I am sure you know of. Am I right? Because of trying to survive in my business.

My unfair competition had been running certain shows that we were restricted to run by regulation of the union . . . and consequently I was becoming insolvent because of it.

All those calls were made with only, in relation to seeing if they can help out, with the American Guild of Variety Artists. Does that confirm a lot of things you have heard?[11]

To explain his many pre-assassination calls to Mobsters, Ruby testified, as quoted above, that he made them only to secure assistance in a problem with the American Guild of Variety Artists (AGVA).[12] This AGVA story, echoed by many of the Mobsters he called,[13] was rooted in two points of fact: AGVA had jurisdiction over Ruby's night club entertainers, and the parties he called included some officials of that union.[14] Furthermore, given pervasive Mob influence in many unions, the rationale offered for such contacts is superficially reasonable. An examination of AGVA's background, Ruby's relationship with it and the situation described, however, exposes this story as a total fabrication.

271

In 1962, the U.S. Senate Permanent Subcommittee on Investigations conducted a series of hearings on AGVA's treatment of the striptease dancers in its ranks.[15] The conditions revealed by union members and officials, law enforcement officials and other witnesses were summarized in a blistering closing statement by Senator John McClellan, the Subcommittee's chairman, as briefly excerpted below:

> For the past 2 weeks we have seen unfolded before us a sordid and distressing picture of a labor union which has miserably failed to meet its responsibilities to the profession of artists . . . and to the members whom it represents. . . .
>
> The so-called exotic dancers in the vicious and degrading establishments of the underworld . . . are required to mix with customers, induce customers to buy drinks, and assist their employers in relieving suckers of every cent that can be taken from them by whatever means may be effective, from short-changing and padded checks to prostitution, jackrolling, knockout drops, and every other means that can be devised or imagined. . . .
>
> The AGVA members employed in these clubs are under complete domination and control of hoodlum owners. . . .
>
> Because of the failure of AGVA to enforce its contracts, the rank and file members are deprived of social security, workmen's compensation, unemployment insurance and other benefits guaranteed them. . . .
>
> Hoodlums and racketeers are able to reap fantastic profits through the exploitation of AGVA members, who are required to work as "B" girls and worse simply because the union will not protect them. . . .[16]

AGVA's character in the early 1960s was perhaps most succinctly summarized by a Subcommittee member, Senator Karl Mundt:

> The testimony indicated yesterday . . . the AGVA dues-paying members get nothing but their receipt for their dues. It is purely a racket to collect money. . . .[17]

A Chicago Police official who interviewed almost a hundred members likewise concluded, "The union was merely a dues collecting agency."[18]

Its pattern of operation typical of a Mob-controlled union,[19] AGVA was found, not surprisingly, to have many Mob connections. Ernest Fast, former Midwest regional director of AGVA,[20] had meetings with several top Chicago gangsters[21] and admitted close association with Chicago Mafia kingpin James Allegretti.[22] Another Chicago AGVA representative was a reputed Teamster goon,[23] while a number of local AGVA booking agents were reportedly involved in vice operations.[24] In Philadelphia[25] and New Orleans,[26] more AGVA links to the Teamsters were discovered, and a federal official investigating AGVA was found to have been selling information to Hoffa associates.[27] When one active dissident, Penny Singleton, criticized official misconduct at union meetings, a series of false charges were drawn up against her by Irwin Mazzei, the West Coast regional director.[28] Later president of AGVA, Singleton characterized the union during that period as totally corrupt, its situation "abominable."[29]

AGVA's character in Texas was illustrated by the rap sheet of James Henry Dolan, described by the FBI as "one of the two most notorious hoodlums" in Dallas.[30] Although Dolan specialized in armed robbery, confidence swindles and shakedown rackets,[31] his seven-state trail of arrests and convictions indicates even more diverse criminal skills.[32] His associates included such Mob heavies as Santos Trafficante, Nofio Pecora, Irwin Weiner and James Fratianno.[33] In 1962, an informant reported, Dolan was in the "fire business"[34] — reflected by his one-to-three-year sentence for arson in December 1963.[35]

From 1958 to 1961, as the House Assassinations Committee noted, "Dolan was employed as the Dallas representative of the American Guild of Variety Artists."[36] Basically, "he was concerned with enforcing minimum standards for entertaining employees in the Dallas area."[37] Although one knowledgeable source labeled Dolan's post "a racketeer position,"[38] Dolan was apparently too busy planning armed robberies in Texas, Arkansas and Mississippi during his tenure[39] to extort payoffs with undivided attention.[40] Dolan might have clarified his AGVA duties to federal interviewers in 1978 had they not been interrupted by

Dolan's "pre-dinner 'lock-up' ritual" at the Atlanta Federal Penitentiary.[41]

RUBY'S CONTACTS WITH AGVA OFFICIALS

Predictably, it was several of the same AGVA officials cited for misconduct or underworld affiliation whom Ruby contacted in the months before the assassination. In the early fall of 1963, former AGVA official Dolan saw Ruby in a downtown Dallas restaurant.[42] This encounter punctuated a four-state crime spree by Dolan,[43] which may have included contacts with Marcello associates in May 1963.[44] On August 2 and November 9, Ruby called Irwin Mazzei,[45] the AGVA official who drew up charges against dissident Penny Singleton. In one of these calls, Mazzei later told the FBI, Ruby revealed that he was a friend of Chicago official Ernie Fast,[46] the close associate of a Mafia boss.

Also representative of Ruby's contacts in AGVA was Jack Yanover, one of the "officers of record" of the Dream Way Bar in Cicero, Illinois,[47] a reputed underworld strip joint and gambling front.[48] Ruby called the Dream Way Bar on May 12, 1963,[49] apparently for Yanover.[50] And on November 20, Ruby called another Chicago AGVA official, Alton Sharpe;[51] Sharpe telephoned a message for Ruby three days later.[52] Sharpe told the FBI that these contacts concerned a letter Ruby wished to send Sharpe about his AGVA problem.[53] But when questioned about Sharpe's explanation, AGVA's Dallas branch manager Tom Palmer replied, "I don't accept it."[54] Palmer testified, "I couldn't understand his [Ruby's] sending any pertinent data to Chicago, which was not a regional office and had no jurisdiction over this area. . . . I still cannot understand what was of importance, of such importance that would require a weekend transaction of AGVA business."[55]

An aura of legitimacy, on the other hand, was suggested by Ruby's pre-assassination calls to two national AGVA officials in New York: Joey Adams,[56] who was reputedly "well connected" with Joseph Glaser,[57] and Bobby Faye.[58] Ruby told of further contacts with these two men, spurred by his desperate concern about his AGVA problem:

I even flew to New York to see Joe Gla[s]er, and he called Bobby Faye. He was the national president. That didn't help. He called Barney Ross and Joey Adams.[59]

But the record shows little concern by Ruby for this purported problem during his New York visit. When he registered at the Hilton Hotel, the chief room clerk told the FBI, Ruby said only that he was there "looking for talent for his night club. . . . he was not going to go to any legitimate booking agents, but rather was going to look around the New York night clubs."[60] Barney Ross (whom Ruby did meet in New York[61]) also said that Ruby discussed talent searching in a call to Ross just before that trip.[62]

Ruby's claim that Glaser called AGVA President Bobby Faye for him, as quoted above, is likewise not supported. For Glaser told the FBI that when Ruby requested his assistance in New York, he refused to do anything and "immediately thereafter terminated the interview" with Ruby.[63] If Glaser was telling the truth, perhaps Ruby contacted Faye directly as described by AGVA official Irv Mazzei. Mazzei told the FBI that he received a call from Faye, and

learned from Faye that Ruby was dissatisfied and had flown from Dallas to New York to see Mr. Faye and was, in fact, sitting in Faye's office when the call was made by Faye.[64]

But Faye told the FBI that he "never had any personal contact with Jack Ruby."[65] Thus, the only credibly established contacts of Ruby during his New York trip were with Joseph Glaser, Mobster Sidney Korshak's partner, and with Capone-tied boxer Barney Ross.[66]

RUBY'S AGVA PROBLEM

In summary, AGVA was a Mob-infiltrated "dues collecting" agency, and Ruby's contacts with union officials were particularly questionable. It is consequently difficult to believe that these contacts, much less Ruby's numerous calls to underworld figures, concerned any legitimate union grievance. It is not surprising, therefore, that the story of Ruby's AGVA difficulty proves fraudulent in its basic premises.

The accounts of Ruby, his Mob contacts and some AGVA officials followed this basic line. Jack Ruby, along with night club operators Abe and Barney Weinstein, had been running "amateur strip shows" at their burlesque establishments for at least two years before the assassination.[67] These shows featured about five or six women paid $10 to $15 per show, and were presented about once a week at each of the clubs.[68] But Ruby ran such shows only to keep up with the competition,[69] believing the Weinsteins were scheduling them to destroy his business.[70] And since 1961 he had attempted to persuade AGVA officials to prohibit them.[71]

Early in 1963, when AGVA did ban amateur strip shows in unionized night clubs,[72] Ruby stopped running these acts.[73] The Weinsteins, on the other hand, continued them under various subterfuges.[74] Ruby, his business suffering,[75] then repeatedly called AGVA officials to complain about the Weinsteins.[76] Ruby also called numerous Mobsters, so the story goes, solely to request their intervention with AGVA.[77]

In fact, there is no facet of this AGVA alibi—the purported threat to Ruby's business, Ruby's concern over it or his method of solving it—that bears any relation to reality. First, Ruby was at no competitive disadvantage because of AGVA's policy on amateur strip shows. Although Abe and Barney Weinstein ran such shows at one club each,[78] Ruby ran them at both the Carousel and Vegas clubs.[79] And contrary to a key contention of his alibi,[80] Ruby continued to run such shows into the latter part of 1963,[81] well after AGVA issued its directive banning them.[82]

Second, the whole issue was old and inconsequential. According to a one-time Dallas board member of AGVA, the Weinsteins had run amateur strip shows for about 13 years,[83] long before Ruby professed concern over the matter. And AGVA regulations, if they had ever been enforced, merely required Ruby to pay his amateur strippers about $20 more per night to meet union scale.[84] These extra payments, once a week to six women,[85] could hardly have been significant to Ruby—a ranking Dallas gambling and narcotics operative[86] who carried thousands of dollars[87] and paid off hundreds of police officers.[88] Indeed, in November 1963, when his telephone activity peaked,[89] Ruby indicated anything but concern over his night club operations. For during that month, Ruby was constantly away from the Carousel Club, engaged in unknown activities,[90] in contrast to his regular presence there before November.[91]

Ruby's lack of concern over any night club problem was also indicated in the 1978 Congressional testimony of Andrew Armstrong, his handyman and assistant at the Carousel Club during 1963:[92]

> Q: Well, was there a time in the fall of 1963 . . . that the club was in financial trouble because the competition was doing a lot better because of their use of amateur nights?
> Armstrong: No.
> Q: They were drawing a lot more customers in and Jack's business was hurting. Do you remember that in the fall of 1963?
> Armstrong: No. We was using amateurs, too. . . .
> Q: Were there any problems that Jack and the club were encountering in the fall of 1963 that was different from before? Were there any special things that were bothering Jack Ruby or bothering the club?
> Armstrong: No.[93]

Armstrong noted, in fact, that Ruby's night club business was "picking up" during the fall of 1963.[94]

A third fallacy in the AGVA alibi is the absurd assumption that any such regulation issued by this Mob-tied racketeering outfit would be taken seriously. Indeed, Ruby habitually and flagrantly violated AGVA regulations far more significant than the amateur show directive. Ruby pandered his Carousel strippers[95] and expected them to mix with customers to promote the consumption of liquor.[96] Although he regularly funneled cash to AGVA,[97] Ruby was delinquent in paying welfare benefits to his AGVA-affiliated employees.[98] And Ruby physically abused his employees, as many witnesses reported.[99] In short, Carousel house rules included mixing with customers, prostitution, cash transactions, delinquent welfare payments and physical abuse—precisely the practices of hoodlum night club owners described in the Senate AGVA hearings.[100]

Despite his flagrant violations of AGVA regulations, however, Ruby maintained cozy relationships with local AGVA officials. Dallas branch manager Tom Palmer testified that his relationship with Ruby was "amicable in all instances."[101] Palmer explained that he "exercised extreme leniency" in his dealings with Ruby[102] and that he reacted only by "collecting data that indicated Jack was continuing to violate certain rules of AGVA that could have been awkward for him."[103]

Ruby had also enjoyed friendly relations with Palmer's infamous predecessor, James Henry Dolan. On one occasion, Dolan stood by while Ruby assaulted a band leader in Dolan's AGVA membership; Dolan then joined Ruby in appropriating the proceeds of the musician's act.[104] On another occasion, when a woman complained that Ruby had struck her at the Carousel Club, Dolan reportedly told her to "forget the incident."[105] Another AGVA official, Jack Cole, had similarly ignored a union member's complaint of abuse by Ruby.[106] Also indicative of Ruby's preferred treatment by AGVA was the report of one Carousel stripper that he had obtained a favorable AGVA rating, allowing him to pay lower salaries, "because he had connections."[107]

A particularly useful contact of Ruby in AGVA was Breck Wall, president of its Dallas council.[108] Responsible for reviewing complaints by performers against night club operators,[109] Wall told the Warren Commission that Ruby called him four times in November 1963 concerning a problem with AGVA.[110] But remarkably, given the purported urgency of Ruby's problem, Ruby's close friendship with Wall[111] and Wall's AGVA position, Wall could not remember what the problem was:

> Wall: . . . he was having some sort of problem with his girls and the union was going to make him do something, which I didn't think was right. I told him I would help him out and make sure his case was presented correctly.
>
> Q: What was the union trying to make him do?
>
> Wall: I don't recall.[112]

Later in his testimony, however, Wall did recollect the cause of the trouble with the AGVA: Ruby was not allowing enough break time between striptease acts.[113] Wall never mentioned any problem with amateur strippers.[114]

Even if the issue of amateur strip shows had been a genuine, timely or significant concern of Ruby's, however, it was not a reasonable explanation for his nationwide contacts with Mobsters. The incongruity was pointed out by Congressman Floyd Fithian to one such Chicago contact, Irwin Weiner, and applied equally to others:

> Doesn't that strike you as being a little curious . . . [for Ruby to have] bothered to call somebody in Chicago when his little difficulty over an amateur stripper was in Dallas?

Fithian added, "That does not seem to be a very credible story."[115]

Indeed, if some freak enforcement of AGVA regulations had caused Ruby any genuine concern, there was only one hoodlum whose intervention was needed. That was the man who had routinely subverted AGVA rules through "amicable" relationships with union officials: Dallas Mobster Jack Ruby.

OTHER ALIBIS

Two other alibis were presented to cover certain of Ruby's pre-assassination contacts with Mobsters, especially in New Orleans.

When questioned by the FBI about Ruby's June visit to New Orleans, half a dozen witnesses related that Ruby had been seeking entertainers for his night club.[116] In particular, they said that Ruby had inquired about Janet Conforto ("Jada"),[117] a striptease dancer who did, in fact, begin working at the Carousel Club in July 1963.[118]

This quest to hire Jada might be credible were talent scouting not the stock cover story for so many of Ruby's suspicious activities. During his August visit to New York, for example, as related earlier, he told a hotel clerk that he was there to seek night club talent.[119] But Ruby cited the AGVA story to the Warren Commission as the reason for this trip.[120] An associate provided the story of seeking night club talent for Ruby's 1959 trip to Cuba.[121] But

Ruby also gave a totally different explanation for this trip, mentioning nothing about night club talent, in his testimony before the Warren Commission.[122]

The night club alibi is further muddled by inconsistencies with a second, even more dubious one. All of Ruby's New Orleans telephone calls between May and November of 1963, so this story goes, were contacts between Ruby and just one New Orleans acquaintance: Harold Tannenbaum.[123] Reminiscent of "Harry Rubenstein," to whom all of Ruby's criminal dealings in the Chicago night club district were attributed,[124] Tannenbaum purportedly accounted for at least 18 calls between Ruby's phone and five New Orleans numbers.[125]

But the specifics of the Tannenbaum alibi reveal serious conflicts. In an unpublished FBI interview, Tannenbaum reported that he first met Ruby around May 15, 1963, when they struck up a conversation outside Frank Caracci's Old French Opera House.[126] An FBI chronology fixes the date precisely as May 15[127] by events which, according to Tannenbaum, occurred the following day.[128] But the name "Harold Tannenbaum" appears in an official log identifying Ruby's call to the Sho-Bar on May 7[129] — a week before Ruby was supposed to have met him. Another source indicates that Ruby and Tannenbaum made their introductions yet a third time. According to Jada, the striptease dancer, when she and Tannenbaum met Ruby in June, "Ruby had apparently never met Tannenbaum on any previous occasion."[130]

Whenever they purportedly first got together, however, Tannenbaum would surely have filled a pressing need for Ruby. For as noted earlier, Ruby claimed that his purpose in traveling to New Orleans in early June was to hire Jada. And it so happened that Ruby's new friend Harold Tannenbaum was a booking agent,[131] identified as such or as "Jada's agent" in handwritten notations on telephone logs.[132] In fact, Tannenbaum told the FBI that his phone calls to Ruby on May 16 and on June 5, just before Ruby's New Orleans trip, were "to discuss the hiring of Jada and Jada's contract."[133]

But as the FBI paraphrased it, Mob associate Nick Graffagnini reported that

Jack Ruby came into the Sho-Bar a few days before Janet Conforto (Jada) completed her engagement [on June 12[134]] and wanted to know how he could go about hiring Jada for a club he had in Dallas, Texas. Graffagnini said he told him he did not handle the hiring or signing of contracts with the entertainers and he sent him to the 500 Club on Bourbon Street.[135]

When Ruby came to the 500 Club, according to Marcello associate Frank Caracci, he inquired about hiring dancers, only for Caracci to communicate through his manager that none was available.[136] Thus, although Harold Tannenbaum was supposedly Ruby's close contact and "Jada's agent," Ruby nevertheless went on a wild-goose chase to hire Jada — in two bars which happened to be owned by criminal associates of Marcello.

Once again, this fundamental contradiction between two alibis — the night club talent search and the Tannenbaum story — indicate that neither was true. Indeed, it appears that Tannenbaum was a front for Ruby's Mob contacts in New Orleans; such a subterfuge would have been routine on a matter of sensitive underworld business, given the intensive electronic surveillance of the Mob conducted during the Kennedy Administration.[137]

Finally, it is significant to note, as disclosed by the House Assassinations Committee, that Tannenbaum ran "several Bourbon Street clubs controlled allegedly by the Marcello interests";[138] one was Frank Caracci's Old French Opera House.[139] Thus, whether Tannenbaum was only a front or an actual Ruby contact, his alibi hardly sanitizes the Marcello connection underlying Ruby's numerous New Orleans telephone communications.

MOB CONSPIRACY

While the talent search and Tannenbaum alibis are lame, it is the AGVA story, recited by so many of Ruby's underworld contacts and demonstrably fraudulent, which directly exhibits a Mob conspiracy to cover its trail in the Kennedy murder. This coordinated perjury is further revealed in the story's contorted renditions by Ruby's Mob contacts. Teamster goon Barney Baker, for one, told the FBI in 1964 that Ruby called Baker's Chicago home from Dallas in November 1963 and left a message with Baker's wife.[140] Baker related that he then called Ruby, a complete stranger to him, at which point Ruby complained that his "competitors through the help of the AGVA were 'giving [him] a fit.' "[141] Telephone records show, however, that Baker placed a collect call to Ruby *the day before*, not after, Ruby called Baker.[142]

When questioned by the House Assassinations Committee in 1978, Baker gave a rambling account of his contacts with Ruby,[143] punctuated by sudden bursts of recollection, dubious explanations and reversals.[144] At one point, however, Baker responded with unconscious candor when confronted with some of Ruby's testimony: "Yes, that refreshes me a lot in memorizing exactly what it was about."[145]

On June 1, 1964, Los Angeles felon Al Gruber told the FBI that during their mid-November contacts, Ruby often

> expressed concern about his business being poor. Ruby mentioned that he had been forced by the union to stop having amateur night at his club, and indicated that his competitors had continued having their amateur night programs.[146]

When initially questioned by the FBI on November 25, 1963, however, Gruber provided a detailed account of his conversations with Ruby that omitted any reference to such a problem.[147]

Questioned four days later in Los Angeles, William Miller apparently confused a hastily conveyed AGVA story with the talent-scouting alibi. A one-time Nevada casino owner and beneficiary of Teamster pension fund money, Miller told the FBI that Ruby had telephoned him and complained to him that AGVA "would not let him run the amateur strip nights, but that his competitors were doing so."[148] Yet Miller told the FBI that in the same call, Ruby had asked Miller "if he could obtain some girls to help sponsor an amateur striptease contest in his [Ruby's] Dallas clubs."[149]

The most flagrant fabrications came from Chicago Mobster Irwin Weiner. When questioned by the FBI on November 27, 1963, as agents noted, Weiner "refused to furnish any information concerning Jack Ruby."[150] In 1974, a private investigator seeking this information was threatened over the telephone by Weiner.[151] Later, Weiner told a reporter, "Ruby was a friend of mine. He called me. I talked to him. What I talked to him about was my own business."[152] And in January 1978, Weiner told an investigator that the call from Ruby had nothing to do with AGVA or any labor problem.[153]

Weiner finally came around to the AGVA line in May 1978, when questioned by the House Assassinations Committee. Weiner testified that his previous accounts had been false, and that he habitually lied to reporters.[154] Instead, he explained, Ruby had called and asked him to write a bond in connection with a lawsuit against a competitor who was running amateur strip shows.[155] But the Committee could not find any indication that Ruby was contemplating such a suit, nor any explanation "for his having to go to Chicago for such a bond."[156] Needless to say, "the Committee was not satisfied with Weiner's explanation of his relationship to Ruby."[157]

Other variations on the AGVA theme were presented by these pre-assassination contacts of Ruby: Lewis McWillie,[158] the Mob "gambler and murderer" and associate of Santos Trafficante;[159] Dusty Miller,[160] the Teamster executive and organized crime associate;[161] Frank Goldstein,[162] the "professional gambler";[163] and Joseph Glaser,[164] the Korshak partner who "probably could have been in rackets."[165] Similar stories were also provided by columnist Tony Zoppi,[166] and by three AGVA officials who were curiously fired within three days preceding the assassination of President Kennedy:[167] Alton Sharpe,[168] Irv Mazzei[169] and Bobby Faye.[170] Indeed, the widespread participation in presenting the phony AGVA story indicates how desperately the Mafia needed to conceal the incriminating trail left in the phone records of one Dallas conspirator, Jack Ruby.

The House Assassinations Committee noted that "AGVA has been used frequently by members of organized crime as a front for criminal activities."[171] As demonstrated in this chapter, Ruby's AGVA alibi typified this pattern. And further activities of Ruby in the final days before November 22, as examined next, remove any doubt as to his participation in a plot to murder President Kennedy.

I am now firmly of the opinion that the mob did it. It is a historical truth.[1]

> G. Robert Blakey, chief counsel to the House Assassinations Committee, referring to the assassination of President Kennedy

20
The Mafia Killed President Kennedy

Jack Ruby's meetings in New Orleans, New York, Chicago and Miami, four key Mafia bases, were behind him. After a remarkable, 25-fold peak in the first week of November, as charted earlier, his rate of out-of-state calls plummeted. Now, as November 22 approached, the focus of the Mob activity occupying Ruby shifted to Dallas.

One indication of Ruby's change in pattern during this final period was offered by Nancy Powell, a two-year employee of the Carousel Club.[2] Asked about Ruby's behavior "the couple of weeks or months before President Kennedy was shot," Powell testified:

> He became more relaxed about the club. At first, he would never leave the club. He was there all the time, but he got to where he would go out and come in later like at 10 o'clock or something.[3]

Larry Crafard, who worked full-time at the Carousel Club for one month in November 1963,[4] was more specific. Crafard told the FBI that during November, Ruby would typically spend one or two hours in the early afternoon at the club.[5] He would then leave for the day, return at about 10 p.m., and remain there until closing at about 1:30 or 2 a.m.[6]

Crafard amplified when subsequently questioned by Warren Commission counsel:

Q: So as I understand it . . . he would spend 8 or 10 [of] what would presumably be waking hours away from the club each day.

Mr. Crafard: Yes.

Q: Did he ever talk about what he was doing during that period of time?

Mr. Crafard: No.

Q: Did you ever hear anything or do you have any idea of what he was doing during that period of time?

Mr. Crafard: No.[7]

Crafard also testified that during November 1963, "people would come to the club to see him, he would go downstairs, leave with them, and sometimes would be gone the rest of the afternoon."[8]

By mid-November, however, Ruby no longer had time for routine Carousel-based racketeering; he no longer had any reason for placing calls from his night club office to Mobsters across the country. Now, as documented in National Archives files, Ruby was busy receiving Mob guests from out of town, meeting with other underworld figures from Dallas, and assisting in the final preparations for President Kennedy's murder.

VISITS OF PAUL ROLAND JONES AND AL GRUBER

"About a week before the assassination of President Kennedy," Paul Roland Jones told the FBI, he took a two-day trip to Dallas.[9] During that trip, Jones "stopped at Ruby's club and spoke to him just briefly and generally."[10] Living then in Alabama,[11] Jones was an old acquaintance of Ruby and a go-between for the Chicago Mob in the Dallas bribery negotiations of the 1940s.[12] His criminal credentials included convictions for bribery, narcotics smuggling and murder, plus an indictment for perjury.[13]

Al Gruber, another underworld acquaintance of Ruby, dropped in to see him about the same time. Based in Los Angeles, Gruber had six arrests in three states under his name and two aliases, with a conviction for grand larceny.[14] He listed himself as a self-employed scrap dealer working from his residence,[15] but the focus of his activity was probably reflected better by his management of a "card room" in the "Veteran's Cabin" during the 1960s.[16] Seth Kantor, a journalist in the White House press corps, reported further that Gruber was "running with Frank Matula, whom Hoffa had installed as a Teamster official shortly after Matula got out of jail on perjury charges. Gruber also maintained known connections with hoodlums who worked with racketeer Mickey Cohen."[17] Barney Ross, the Capone-tied boxer, was another associate of Gruber.[18]

In a 1964 interview, Gruber told the FBI that he had not been in touch with Ruby since 1947.[19] But about two weeks before the assassination, Gruber related,

> en route to Los Angeles from New York, where he attended a relative's wedding, he stopped at Joplin, Missouri, to get some information on a car wash facility. Since Dallas, Texas was about 100 miles from Joplin, he decided to visit Ruby in Dallas.[20]

When interviewed in 1978 by the House Assassinations Committee, however, Gruber insisted that he had not come from a wedding in New York: "From a wedding? No. . . . I might have said that, but that ain't true."[21] Gruber now explained that he was "driving a Cadillac across for somebody" when it broke down in Joplin, and he decided to visit Dallas,[22] which is actually 300 miles away. "And I figured I would just go see Jack I guess," Gruber related.[23] "I don't know why I went there really."[24]

Ruby, on the other hand, recalled exactly why Gruber visited: "He came to try to interest my brother, Sammy, in this new washateria deal to wash cars."[25] But Gruber testified that he never contacted Sam Ruby[26] and didn't even know him.[27] Similar flagrant contradictions characterized the date of Gruber's visit with Ruby (from a few days[28] to two weeks[29] before the assassination), its duration (one day[30] to several days[31]) and the subject of their conversations.[32] Gruber also provided sharply conflicting accounts[33] for another timely contact: a 3-minute call from Ruby to Gruber in Los Angeles two hours after the assassination.[34]

A MAFIA PARTY

Following the usual pattern, Ruby and two associates related conflicting innocuous activities to explain his whereabouts on the night of November 20.[35] This time, however, the cover was penetrated by detailed independent reports.

Beginning in the late evening of November 20, Frank T. Tortoriello held an all-night party at his residence in the Tanglewood Apartments in Dallas.[36] According to the FBI's first report of this party, Tortoriello's guests were Jada, the Carousel stripper, Jack Ruby, Joe F. Frederici, plus Frederici's wife, Sandy, and Tortoriello's next-door neighbor, Ann Bryant.[37] Subsequent FBI reports provided more information about the party and about the intriguing relationships of three of those present.

Frank T. Tortoriello, the host, was a partner in a Mob-linked construction company[38] and a buddy of Mafioso Joseph Campisi.[39] Another friend of Tortoriello was Jada, the Carousel stripper, who spent several nights in his apartment during and before November 1963.[40]

Joseph Frank Federici, aliases Frederici, Frederica and Frederico,[41] was described to the FBI as a nephew of Vito Genovese, the notorious former Mafia boss from New Jersey.[42] Federici's background was consistent with that relationship. For one thing, he was a New Jersey resident who lived in Dallas, at the Tanglewood Apartments, only between February 1963 and January 1964.[43] During that period, another Tanglewood resident reported, he was "allegedly employed in the management consultant business at Dallas for his father, who allegedly resides in Trenton, New Jersey."[44]

Federici confirmed that his position in Dallas was "Occupation Management Consultant"[45] — a sufficiently vague job title to cover a man with three aliases. And when asked by the FBI about his reported connection to Genovese, Federici admitted that he had told others he was Genovese's nephew.[46] But only "in jest," he explained.[47]

Given Federici's background, it is understandable that recollections about Tortoriello's Wednesday night party were blurred. Tortoriello and Federici denied that Federici attended the party.[48] So did Ann Bryant, who stopped in briefly from next door early

Thursday morning.[49] But another Tanglewood resident related that Bryant had told her that Federici had indeed been there.[50] And the resident apartment manager, who investigated complaints of noise from the all-night party, also told the FBI that Federici had attended.[51] As for Ruby's presence, Tortoriello denied it,[52] but Bryant observed a guest "who resembled Ruby's photograph."[53] Moreover, Bryant's description of this man's companion ("about twenty-five years of age, tall brunette," with "a theatrical appearance"[54]) characterized photos of Gloria Fillmon,[55] who was with Ruby late that evening.[56] The indicated presence of Ruby and Fillmon at the party is particularly credible given the conflicts in their alibis for that evening.[57] The most striking clue to Ruby's presence at Tortoriello's party, however, was his association with the others present. Jada, of course, was Ruby's employee and the alibi for his June visit to New Orleans.[58] Tortoriello was a close associate of Ruby, as Tortoriello told the FBI.[59] Finally, Federici's name was found among Ruby's personal effects,[60] and Federici confirmed his acquaintance with Ruby.[61]

Whatever the nature of Tortoriello's party—strictly a social function, a break from organization business, or a pre-assassination gala—it was another timely Mafia contact of Ruby covered by a suspicious maze of contradictory accounts. Timely, too, was Federici's departure from Dallas to Providence, Rhode Island "during the early morning of November 22, 1963."[62] Federici explained that he left Dallas with his wife "to visit relatives."[63]

"YOU PROBABLY DON'T KNOW ME NOW, BUT YOU WILL"

About 10:30 or 11 a.m. on Thursday, November 21, Ruby told the FBI, he drove a young friend, Connie Trammel, to the office of Lamar Hunt.[64] According to Trammel, who supported Ruby's account, she went to see Hunt, a son of oil tycoon H. L. Hunt, for an employment interview.[65] After dropping Trammel off, Ruby related, he met with one of two attorneys—he couldn't remember which one—in the building in which Lamar Hunt's office was located.[66] Ruby then waited around in the lobby for Trammel to come down, he reported, and finally left the building.[67] A more direct contact with Lamar Hunt, however, is indicated in the February 24, 1964 memo of Warren Commission counsel Hubert and Griffin: "Ruby visited his office on November 21. Hunt denies knowing Ruby. Ruby gives innocent explanation."[68]

The reported contact between Ruby and Lamar Hunt is consistent with the appearance of the name "Lamar Hunt" in one of Ruby's notebooks[69] and Ruby's acquaintance with Lamar's father, H. L. Hunt.[70] And it raises suspicion in view of the Hunts' sharp antagonism toward President Kennedy. During a party before the fateful Dallas visit, as previously noted, H. L. reportedly remarked that there was "no way left to get those traitors out of government except by shooting them out," referring to President Kennedy.[71] Also, H. L.'s son Nelson Bunker Hunt co-sponsored the black-bordered ad attacking President Kennedy that appeared in the *Dallas Morning News* on November 22.[72]

At about noon on November 21, Ruby was seen in City Hall by Dallas Police Officer W. F. Dyson.[73] According to Dyson, Ruby entered the sixth floor office of Assistant District Attorney Ben Ellis and handed out Carousel Club cards to Dyson and other policemen in the office.[74] Ruby introduced himself to Ellis, telling him, "you probably don't know me now, but you will."[75] Ruby also visited Assistant District Attorney Bill Alexander;[76] Alexander reported that they discussed some bad checks issued to Ruby.[77]

Also about noon, November 21, Eugene Hale Brading of Los Angeles checked in with Roger Carroll, the chief parole officer in Dallas.[78] Then on parole for embezzlement,[79] Brading was a Mobster with 35 arrests and three convictions under several aliases.[80] According to a report Carroll filed that day, Brading "advised that he planned to see Lamar Hunt and other oil speculators" while in Dallas.[81] Brading claimed that he never actually saw Hunt during that trip,[82] but confirmed that three underworld-involved associates of his did visit the Hunt Oil Company that day to see Lamar and Nelson Hunt.[83] According to Paul Rothermal, then chief of security for Hunt Oil, however, the company log for November 21 showed a visit by Brading's three associates, Bauman, Brown and Nowlin, "and friend."[84] Rothermal believed that this "friend" was Brading.[85]

On December 4, 1963, Secret Service agent Elmer Moore questioned Ruby "regarding his whereabouts and movements" on Thursday, November 21.[86] Ruby reported visiting the Merchants State Bank downtown;[87] according to Connie Trammel, he stopped in on the way to Lamar Hunt's office.[88] As for Ruby's activities that afternoon, however, the usual contradictions plagued his alibi.

The only other thing that Ruby could recall about his activities Thursday was that he "talked to a bartender named Mickey Ryan" at the Carousel Club, "probably in the early afternoon hours."[89] Andrew Armstrong, the Carousel's handyman, also reported that Ruby was at the club Thursday afternoon "with Mickey Ryan, a bartender who wanted to borrow money from Ruby."[90] But Ryan told the FBI he did not recall meeting Ruby at the Carousel Club that day.[91] In fact, Ryan believed that he "last saw Ruby approximately two weeks prior to November 22."[92] In further support of Ruby's alibi, Andrew Armstrong reported that he believed Ruby called some AGVA officials from the Carousel Club Thursday afternoon "regarding auditions of amateurs."[93] But telephone records show no calls from the Carousel Club that day.[94]

What was Ruby actually doing Thursday afternoon? His telephone records provide a further clue. Mrs. Billy Chester Carr, a Houston booking agent, told the FBI that Ruby called her on November 19, and again on November 21 between 2:30 and 3 p.m.[95] Ruby's toll call records show the reported call to Carr in Houston on November 19[96] but no such call on November 21.[97] By Thursday afternoon, however, Ruby did not have to place a toll call to reach Houston. For Ruby was there, monitoring President Kennedy's movements in preparation for the next day's assassination in Dallas.

On December 2, 1963, Secret Service agent Lane Bertram filed a detailed report of a three-day investigation conducted in Houston.[98] It opened with this synopsis:

Numerous witnesses identify Jack Leon Rubenstein [also known as] Jack Ruby, as being in Houston, Texas on November 21, for several hours, one block from the President's entrance route and from the Rice Hotel where he stayed.[99]

On November 26, as his report describes, Special Agent Bertram interviewed five witnesses who saw Ruby on the 400 block of Milam Street in Houston Thursday afternoon.[100] One was a Houston deputy sheriff, Bill Williams, who "saw the man on two or three different occasions and talked to him about 3 p.m."[101] Williams "was sure the picture of Ruby appearing in the paper was identical with the man he observed."[102] After conducting these interviews, Bertram secured police photographs of Ruby and presented them to the five witnesses.[103] "All agree[d] that in their opinion Jack Rubenstein was in Houston on November 21 from about 2:30 to 7:15 p.m., in close proximity to the President's route to the hotel and the Rice Hotel itself."[104]

It is noteworthy that Ruby was first sighted in Houston at about 2:30 to 3 p.m.,[105] the same time that Carr received a call from him.[106] This is also the time at which he would have arrived in Houston if he had left Dallas at about noon and driven the 243 miles on the freeway to Houston at an 80- to 100-mile-per-hour Texas clip. Such a speed would have been natural for Ruby given his many traffic violations, including four for speeding.[107]

The only conceivable doubt about the identifications of Ruby was introduced by Marshall Bradley, a witness who got a close view of Ruby from the left.[108] Bradley reported that on the left side of Ruby's face, which had a "one to three days' beard," he saw a very faint scar.[109] No other Houston witness observed a scar,[110] nor was such a mark visible under superficial observation of Ruby.[111]

Yet Ruby's medical history supports the possibility that he had some such faint scar, perhaps noticeable only in the background of heavy stubble. Dr. Martin Towler testified that in interviews with Ruby and his siblings, "numerous fights and 'brawls' were described during which the subject was frequently struck about the head and face."[112] For example, at age 14 or 15, Ruby recalled, he had "a fight with two grown men in which he sustained lacerations of his lip requiring sutures for repair."[113] At age 16 or so, Ruby was "pistol whipped" by two policemen, causing "bleeding from the scalp."[114] A medical document in the National Archives also describes several incidents in which Ruby was struck on the head or face.[115] In one he suffered a concussion, and in another he was cut by a jug of wine broken over his head.[116] And in 1956, according to a police informant, Ruby was treated by a private physician for abrasions of the head, eye and face received in a fight.[117]

The possible anomaly introduced by one witness, however, is more than offset by the positive identifications of Ruby by the other four. And hardly effective was a carelessly presented disguise: Ruby represented himself as an oil worker, wearing an army jacket and boots over his white shirt and dark striped trousers.[118] Indeed, his extroversion prevailing over prudence, Ruby reverted to the fast talking, big spending gangster that he was. The five Houston witnesses "advised that the subject was a smooth talker, but talked rather rapidly and appeared nervous."[119] One witness reported that the man said he had money and a Cadillac parked around the corner;[120] another said he exhibited some money.[121] Two said he asked about a club on Washington Street operated by a man named Jack,[122] a natural instant improvisation for Ruby in that circumstance.

Most telling, however, was the composite physical description of the man (the FBI's description of Ruby is inserted in brackets): "white male, 5-7 – 5-8 [5'9"], 180-210 [175 pounds], brown hair receding, thin on top ["brown hair thinning on top"], brown eyes [brown eyes], dark complexion [medium complexion]."[123] The witnesses also reported that the man was wearing "heavy material possibly making subject appear larger,"[124] accounting for the discrepancy in weight.

Ruby's interest in President Kennedy's movements was explicitly reported by one witness, Gloria Reece. Reece stated that

the subject asked her if she was going to the "President's dinner." She advised him that she had not been invited and asked him to buy her a beer and attempted to make a date with him. The subject declined, stating that he was in a hurry and departed going in the direction of the Coliseum where the President was to appear at the Albert Thomas Appreciation Dinner.[125]

It is therefore difficult to dispute Special Agent Bertram's conclusion that Ruby's visit "very probably had some connection with the President's appearance in Houston."[126]

Also in Houston on Thursday was Bruce Carlin, the reputed pimp,[127] who frequented the Carousel Club in November 1963.[128] Carlin claimed that he was there servicing motels with assorted drugs and sundries for the "Motel Drug Service,"[129] a firm with no office or telephone,[130] although Karen Carlin said that he was unemployed at that time.[131] Under intensive questioning, he could furnish virtually no specifics about his whereabouts that day.[132] And one of his few concrete claims was proven impossible, as discussed previously, by an early Thursday morning call he placed from Houston to Ruby's Carousel Club.[133]

THREE ASSASSINATION-EVE CONTACTS

At about 10 p.m., as reported by several sources, Ruby stopped in for about 45 minutes at the Egyptian Lounge,[134] a Dallas underworld hangout.[135] One of its owners was Joseph Campisi,[136] a top-ranking Dallas Mafioso close to Carlos Marcello and Marcello's Mafia-involved brothers.[137] When questioned by the House Assassinations Committee in 1978, Campisi said that he was not at the Egyptian Lounge on the night of November 21 and had not known Ruby was there.[138] But on December 7, 1963, Campisi had told the FBI of his "contact with Ruby" that Thursday night, "when Ruby came to the Egyptian Lounge for a steak."[139]

About midnight, Ruby stopped in at a restaurant in the Teamster-financed[140] Dallas Cabana Hotel.[141] With Ruby was Larry Meyers,[142] who had checked into the Cabana that day,[143] as had Mobster Eugene Brading.[144] A sales executive for a Chicago sporting goods firm, Meyers smoothly explained this contact with Ruby as a social encounter and cited specific business engagements to justify his presence in Dallas.[145] Yet there are hints of suspicion about Meyers and this rendezvous with Ruby.

Although married, Meyers traveled to Dallas from Chicago with "a rather dumb, but accommodating broad" named "Jean West,"[146] "Jean Aase"[147] or "Ann."[148] He was described by one of Ruby's strippers, with whom he had apparently had a similar,

$200 encounter,[149] as a "real swinger" with business interests in Chicago, Minneapolis and Las Vegas.[150] Meyers related in detail how Ruby "poured out his troubles" about the AGVA situation,[151] the phony alibi presented mainly by people tied to organized crime.[152] During interrogation by Warren Commission counsel, the mention of Meyers' name prompted a blank pause from Ruby's associate Ralph Paul[153] and a tirade about Ruby's racketeering acquaintances from his sister Eva, who denied knowing Meyers.[154] And in different interviews, Meyers presented detailed but totally contradictory accounts of subsequent contact with Ruby on November 23.[155] Meyers' accounts of activities Friday afternoon and Sunday morning were also inconsistent.[156]

Following his encounters with Joseph Campisi at the Egyptian Lounge and with Larry Meyers at the Cabana, Ruby met a third man at a third Dallas restaurant. At about 1:30 a.m. Friday, a young man walked into the Lucas B&B Restaurant and sat down at a table.[157] About an hour later, as recounted by B&B waitress Mary Lawrence, "Jack Ruby came into the B&B Restaurant and, after looking at the young man at the table, sat down at a table behind the cash register. He did not order his usual food, stating he didn't feel good, and ordered a large glass of orange juice. A few minutes later, the young man who was seated at the table went over to Ruby's table. Thereafter, Ruby paid the bill for both himself and the young man who had eaten."[158]

After President Kennedy was shot and Oswald arrested later that day, Lawrence was struck by a close resemblance between the man with Ruby and photographs of Oswald.[159] She told the FBI that both she and the night shift cashier "agreed that he appeared very similar to Lee Harvey Oswald."[160] She further reported that the man was "in his 20's, 5'7"-9", medium build, 140 lbs.," with "dark hair."[161] This exactly matched Oswald's characteristics: 24 years old, 5'9", 140 lbs., with brown hair.[162] Later in her FBI interview, however, Lawrence added one detail that seemed to preclude this man being Oswald—he had "a small scar near his mouth, either on the right or left side."[163]

When subsequently questioned by the Dallas Police, Lawrence provided a virtually identical account of the assassination morning encounter, and stated that the man with Ruby "was positively Lee Harvey Oswald."[164] Later in that interview, however, she backed down from her positive identification and once more reported a scar on Ruby's visitor.[165] Yet her initial positive identification is credible given other accounts of prior encounters between Ruby and Oswald at the Carousel Club,[166*] testimony by Ruby calling attention to that possibility[168] and contradictory reports by Ruby and an associate about his whereabouts early November 22.[169] It is also pertinent to note that on December 3, 1963, two days before her FBI interview, as she reported, an unknown male had called Lawrence and told her, "If you don't want to die, you better get out of town."[170]

Meanwhile, during the early Friday morning hours, ten Secret Service agents enjoyed liquid refreshments at the Cellar Door night club in Fort Worth.[171] As disclosed in a Secret Service report, among those present were five of the eight agents who would ride in the car directly behind President Kennedy's, plus two other members of the White House detail.[172] Most stayed until at least 2:45 a.m., and one stayed until 5:00 a.m.,[173] although many had to report for duty by 8:00 that morning.[174]

The agents went to the Cellar Door that night on the specific invitation of its owner, Pat Kirkwood.[175] Kirkwood provided them drinks on the house,[176] but he and his manager assured the Secret Service in subsequent interviews that these drinks were all non-alcoholic and that no alcoholic drinks were served in their club.[177] In 1978, however, Kirkwood volunteered to the *Dallas Morning News* that he would keep "several bottles of liquor re-

---

*Especially intriguing, although not probative, was the report of Dallas attorney Carroll Jarnagin, who was drinking heavily with his date at the Carousel Club on October 4. Jarnagin overheard Ruby speaking at an adjacent table to a man named "Lee," whom he later identified as Oswald from news photos, about a contract for Lee to kill Governor Connally of Texas. When Lee asked "what have you got against the Governor?" Ruby replied, "He won't work with us on paroles; with a few of the right boys we could really open up this State." Ruby lamented that they'd "clamped the lid down in Chicago" and that "Cuba was closed"; that the "boys from Chicago have no place to go, no place to really operate." Ruby explained that Connally had been in Washington too long, where "they get to thinking like the Attorney General. The Attorney General, now there's a guy the boys would like to get, but it[']s no use, he stays in Washington too much." When Lee interjected that killing the governor of Texas would put the heat on too, Ruby replied, "Not really, they'll think some crack-pot or communist did it, and it will be written off as an unsolved crime."[167]

served for special customers, like doctors, lawyers or off-duty policemen—people I figured I might have to depend upon later in life."[178]

As with his acquaintance[179] Jack Ruby, however, the habitual reason for Kirkwood's generosity to officials was apparently to cover criminal activity. Karen Carlin, who worked at the Cellar Door in the spring of 1963, testified that she

> told the police, the vice squad about him [Kirkwood] and identified some policemen that were being paid off by him and everything, and of course, he had so many friends he got out of it real easy.[180]

This alleged pattern of corruption complemented Kirkwood's underworld affiliations: his father, W.C., had operated an illegal, high stakes gambling club, and both were close friends with Mobster Lewis McWillie.[181]

The purpose of Kirkwood's hospitality to President Kennedy's Secret Service guards was suggested in the testimony of another Carousel stripper, Nancy Powell. After several hours of questioning, Powell mentioned Kirkwood's Cellar Door night club, "where the Secret Service men go."[182] She then threw out this comment: "Pat said he would probably be called to ask him about *getting them drunk on purpose*."[183]

A RINGSIDE VIEW

Between 9:00 and 9:30 a.m. on November 22, Dallas Police Officer T. M. Hansen, Jr. saw Jack Ruby outside the Dallas Police building.[184] Hansen told the FBI that Ruby was standing with four or five others "directly to the side of the stairway which leads to the basement" at the Harwood Street entrance.[185] As Hansen passed Ruby, whom he knew casually, Hansen "shook his hand and said good morning."[186]

Filling in Ruby's alibi for later that morning was Tony Zoppi, the entertainment columnist who lamented reports of "quick buck artists" linking Ruby to the Mob and the assassination.[187] At about 10:30 a.m. Friday morning, according to Zoppi and

Ruby, Ruby stopped in at Zoppi's office in the Dallas Morning News building.[188] Zoppi said that Ruby had come to discuss "an ESP expert he wanted Zoppi to plug";[189] Ruby testified that he picked up a brochure about a memory expert while in Zoppi's office that morning.[190]

Like Zoppi's preposterous alibi for Ruby's trip to Cuba,[191] however, this story was fatally flawed. For in a 1978 Congressional interview, Zoppi detailed his assassination morning conversation with Ruby; Zoppi noted that Ruby appeared "too calm that morning to have been involved in a conspiracy."[192] Ruby's script of events, however, included no actual meeting with Zoppi. Ruby told the FBI in 1963 that a few hours before the assassination, he "went to the office of Tony Zoppi, but Tony was not there."[193] Ruby subsequently testified that he "went down there Friday morning to Tony Zoppi's office, and they said he went to New Orleans for a couple of days."[194]

Ruby related that he remained in the Dallas Morning News building all morning to place his regular weekend ads for his night clubs.[195] Even after the noon deadline for the ads had passed, Ruby hung around another half hour,[196] although President Kennedy's motorcade was to drive by just a few blocks away.[197] It was especially curious that Ruby missed the chance to see his professed "idol,"[198] since two "partial" Wednesday newspapers showing the motorcade route were found in Ruby's car.[199] During his polygraph hearing of July 1964, Ruby himself noted this problem in his story:

> Oh yes; they didn't ask me another question: "if I loved the President so much, why wasn't I at the parade?"[200]

But in fact, Ruby observed the critical event of that day from a perfect vantage point. An FBI chronology summarized,

> Ruby was on the second floor, front of the Dallas Morning News Building which looks out at the TSBD [Texas School Book Depository] Building. At about the time the President was shot, Ruby allegedly would have a perfect view of the front of the TSBD Building. . . .
> [Ruby was] allegedly sitting in the only chair from which

he could observe the site of the President's assassination. . . .

Georgia Mayor, secretary in the Advertising Division, *Dallas Morning News,* advised that when she returned from lunch at approximately 12:30 p.m., Jack Ruby was sitting in a chair directly in front of her desk. She believes that Ruby had been looking out at the scene when the President was shot. . . .[201]

There is little to add to Ruby's own testimony on this matter:

Now, what about my being present in the News Building that morning? Here—the assassination took place across the street from there? . . . if I was in a conspiracy, wouldn't it start off with that point?[202]

LETHAL FINALE

At 12:30 p.m., as Ruby anxiously watched, a shot was fired at President Kennedy from the Texas School Book Depository; it inflicted a minor, shallow wound in Kennedy's shoulder.[203] In the limousine of Vice President Johnson, Secret Service Agent Rufus Youngblood reacted instantly; Johnson reported that Youngblood "turned in a flash, immediately after the first explosion, hitting me on the shoulder, and shouted to all of us in the back seat to get down."[204] During the next eight seconds, however, not even a warning was shouted from the agents in President Kennedy's follow-up car[205]—five of whom had been so solicitously hosted early that morning at Kirkwood's Cellar Door.[206] And then, a bullet was fired from behind the stockade fence in the grassy knoll; President Kennedy's skull splintered backward.[207]

Soon afterward, a man who identified himself as Jim Braden was arrested in the Dal-Tex Building opposite Dealey Plaza.[208] According to police reports, Braden was in the building "without a good excuse" when President Kennedy was assassinated.[209] Six years later, a trace of Braden's driver's license revealed that he was actually Eugene Hale Brading, a prominent California Mobster with 35 arrests and three convictions under six aliases.[210] Questioned then by Los Angeles Police, Brading provided a highly dubious alibi for his whereabouts at the time of the assassination.[211]

Dallas Mafioso Joseph Campisi reported that he was driving his car when he heard about the assassination, but could not remember where.[212] Campisi also had trouble remembering whether he had met with Ruby the night before,[213] but police records confirmed that he did meet with Ruby in jail on November 30.[214]

At 1:30 p.m., an hour after viewing Kennedy's shooting from his prime vantage point, Ruby dropped by Parkland Hospital to ascertain its outcome.[215] At about the same time, in the Oak Cliff section of Dallas, Police Officer J. D. Tippit, a close associate of Ruby,[216] was shot to death.[217] During the next two days, as detailed earlier, Ruby met with another Dallas Police crony, Harry Olsen,[218] and repeatedly visited the police building,[219] where Lee Harvey Oswald was being held. At 11:17 a.m. Sunday morning, as others established an elaborate alibi for him and coordinated the split-second timing, Ruby left the downtown Western Union office to pay another such visit.[220] And at 11:21 a.m., in the crowning action of his Mob career, Ruby fired the shot that ensured Oswald's everlasting silence.

Following a classic pattern, many others with potentially incriminating information were subsequently murdered or intimidated.[221] Representative was the fate of Karen Carlin, who Ruby hinted was "part of the conspiracy."[222] In a Secret Service interview the evening of Oswald's murder, hysterical with terror, Carlin stated that she was "under the impression that Lee Harvey Oswald, Jack Ruby and other individuals unknown to her, were involved in a plot to assassinate President Kennedy."[223] She feared that "she would be killed if she gave any information to authorities" and asked that "all information she had related be kept confidential to prevent retaliation."[224] Carlin also testified that after the president was shot, Cellar Door owner Pat Kirkwood called and told her, "I want you down here in about 20 minutes."[225] When she refused, Kirkwood told her, "If you're not down here, you won't be around too long."[226] Several months later, she was found shot to death in a Houston hotel.[227]

Yet some witnesses survived to present highly incriminating testimony. Three informants detailed assassination designs against the Kennedys that were expressed in 1962 by New Orleans Mafia boss Carlos Marcello, Tampa chieftain Santos Trafficante and their Teamster ally, Jimmy Hoffa.[228] Johnny Roselli, whose body was found floating in an oil drum after testifying in secret session before the Senate Intelligence Committee, reported that Jack Ruby was "one of our boys" and had been ordered to murder Oswald to silence him.[229] Crucial, too, was the testimony of this tormented conspirator, who had come to face the same sinister pressure for silence. On June 7, 1964, stating that he could not tell the truth in Dallas and repeatedly expressing fears for his life, Jack Ruby pleaded with Chief Justice Earl Warren for a hearing in Washington.[230] Although Warren inexplicably refused,[231] Ruby was able to slip in many candid disclosures during his testimony in Dallas.

Ruby mocked his canned alibi ("I must be a great actor"[232]) and indicated conspiracy in the Oswald murder ("If it were timed that way, then, someone in the police department is guilty of giving the information as to when Lee Harvey Oswald was coming down"[233]). He repeatedly called attention to his underworld connections,[234] his opportunity for contacts with Oswald and Tippit,[235] his "numerous phone calls, long-distance calls, all over the country."[236] And it was clearly his own confession, not another's accusation, when he said, "Maybe I was put here as a front of the underworld and sooner or later they will get something out of me that they want done to their advantage."[237]

Other witnesses filled in the details and reported further incriminating incidents: Ruby's visits with Caracci in New Orleans, with Ross and Glaser in New York, with Roselli in Miami; his mid-November contacts in Dallas with several more underworld figures; and his November 21 trip to Houston to preview the president's motorcade. Telephone records showed the striking, 25-fold increase in his out-of-state calls, peaking in early November and then plummeting during his final weeks of activity in Dallas. And covering all was the endless stream of fabrications issued by Ruby's local associates and his distant Mob contacts — some ad-libbed, others coordinated — precluding any last chance that this timely Mob confluence in Dallas was unrelated to the assassination.

And so, when the evidence is sorted and arranged, the pieces of the assassination puzzle fall neatly into place. Gracing the tableau are neither crackpots nor clowns, freak coincidences nor senseless crimes. Rather, coming sharply into focus is the vicious combine of killers suspected by Europeans from the start,[238] a group with the motive and capability to perform the assassination. Indeed, the conclusion is clear: the Mafia killed President Kennedy.

President John F. Kennedy and his attorney-general brother, Robert, launched an unprecedented crusade to eradicate organized crime in America. Walter Sheridan (right) was a key lieutenant to Robert Kennedy in this crusade, spearheading the Justice Department's investigation of Teamster boss Jimmy Hoffa.

On November 22, 1963, minutes after the photo was taken, shots were fired at the limousine carrying President and Jacqueline Kennedy (rear seat) and Texas Governor John and Nelly Connally (middle seat). President Kennedy was killed. Lee Harvey Oswald, who was in the Texas School Book Depository, was accused of the crime.

Several witnesses, however, saw smoke, cigarette butts and footprints behind the stockade fence in the grassy knoll, as denoted by a square in the figure below. In 1978, a team of acoustical experts determined from a sound tape of the shooting that a second gunman was positioned within seven feet away, as denoted by a circle. The House Assassinations Committee concluded that President Kennedy was "probably assassinated as a result of a conspiracy."

Texas School Book Depository Building

Dal-Tex Building

Railroad Yard

Railroad Parking Lot

Motorcade path

Stockade Fence

Houston St.

Grassy Knoll

The position of President Kennedy's limousine when the fatal shot struck his head

Elm St.

Railroad Overpass

Main St.

Approximate scale

25 50 75 100 ft. N

Commerce St.

David Ferrie, an associate of New Orleans Mafia boss Carlos Marcello and an old acquaintance of Oswald, was in contact with both men in the months before the Kennedy killing. Active in the anti-Castro movement, Ferrie had sharply criticized Kennedy and admitted that he "might have used an offhand or colloquial expression, 'He ought to be shot.'" Ferrie presented a highly dubious alibi to explain his whereabouts around the time of the assassination.

Lee Harvey Oswald, the accused assassin, was in close contact with Charles "Dutz" Murret, his uncle and surrogate father of sorts, in the months leading up to the November 22 assassination. Murret was a New Orleans bookie in the Marcello Mafia fiefdom and had probably met Marcello himself.

"Jim Braden" was arrested after the Kennedy shooting for his suspicious presence in a building facing the president's motorcade. Claiming to be an oil man, Braden was released by police. Six years later, however, a trace of his driver's license exposed his true identity: Eugene Hale Brading, a Mafia associate with 35 arrests.

In 1967, New Orleans District Attorney Jim Garrison, now a judge, launched a new investigation into the Kennedy assassination. Cozy with Carlos Marcello's Mafia clan, Garrison accused Cuban exiles, CIA agents, Minutemen and Nazis, but strangely avoided mention of one prime suspect: organized crime.

New Orleans Mafia boss Carlos Marcello, whose Gulf-area fiefdom included Dallas, was a prominent target of the Kennedy Administration's war on organized crime. In a September 1962 gathering at his estate, an enraged Marcello declared his intention to have President Kennedy murdered. According to a witness, Marcello spoke of hiring an outsider to do the job so that his lieutenants would not be implicated.

Also in September 1962, in a Miami Beach motel, Tampa Mafia boss Santos Trafficante, Jr. angrily declared that President Kennedy would be "hit" before the 1964 election. A close associate of Marcello, Trafficante was an international narcotics kingpin and principal in Mafia-CIA murder plots against Cuban Premier Fidel Castro. Later asked about his prediction, Trafficante pleaded the Fifth Amendment.

Around the same time, Teamster boss James Riddle Hoffa, a longtime associate of Marcello and Trafficante, spoke repeatedly about killing his arch-enemy, Robert Kennedy. One Hoffa plan, involving a lone gunman firing on a convertible in a Southern city, was strikingly similar to the JFK murder. The Hoffa aide who reported the plots, which the FBI found fully credible, said that one assassination plan could have developed into another.

Sam Giancana, Chicago's Mafia boss during the 1960s, was another principal in Mob-CIA plots to assassinate Cuban Premier Fidel Castro. Giancana dated Judith Campbell while she was romantically involved with President Kennedy. In the Mob's view, the affair may have compromised an otherwise untouchable President Kennedy.

On November 24, 1963, as Lee Harvey Oswald was being transferred from the Dallas Police station to the county jail, a Dallas night club operator named Jack Ruby fatally shot him in the abdomen. Ruby portrayed the killing as a spontaneous act of vengeance, but the evidence demonstrates a carefully staged conspiracy to silence Oswald. In testimony before the Warren Commission, Ruby strayed from his prepared story to provide several thinly veiled hints of complicity by the underworld, corrupt policemen and night club stripper Karen Carlin, the key prop in his alibi.

Jack Ruby, both in personality and preoccupations, fit the classic image of the free-wheeling gangster. Owner of the Carousel Club, a Dallas strip joint, Ruby had arrived in Dallas in 1947 with other Chicago hoodlums to stake out new rackets territory. Running illegal gambling, narcotics and prostitution operations out of his night club, he rose to become the Mob's police fixer in Dallas.

As Ruby advanced in his criminal career, he forged ties with Mobsters throughout the country, including Dallas Mafia boss Joseph Civello. On the following page is an FBI report, now in the National Archives, documenting Ruby's close contact with "Joseph Cirello," who is actually Civello. Opposite that is the same report as published by the Warren Commission, which was established by President Johnson to investigate the assassination.

Notice that in the Warren Commission version, the last three paragraphs, which report Ruby's contact with Civello, have been blanked out of an otherwise perfect photoreproduction.

West Coast Mobster Johnny Roselli was one of several underworld figures, chiefly associates of Marcello, Trafficante and Hoffa, whom Ruby contacted in the months before the assassination. In the mid-1970s, an aging Roselli began telling associates, journalists and Senate investigators that Ruby was "one of our boys" and had been delegated to silence Oswald. A few months after Roselli testified in secret session before the Senate Intelligence Committee in 1976, his dismembered body was found in an oil drum in Miami's Biscayne Bay.

FD-302 (Rev. 3-3-59)

FEDERAL BUREAU OF INVESTIGATION

CD 84

Date November 27, 1963

1

       BOBBY GENE MOORE, 865 43rd Street, Oakland, California, was interviewed at his home. He stated that he desired to furnish information regarding JACK RUBY, who he had known in Dallas, Texas. He stated that he had observed an interview on television with an associate of RUBY in which the associate said that RUBY had no gangster connections. MOORE furnished the following information:

      He was raised in Dallas, Texas, having been born in that city on December 12, 1927. About 1951 or 1952, he was living at a rooming house at 1214 Poll Street, Dallas. This house was at the rear of Hill's Liquor Store at the corner of Ross Avenue and Bell Street. This liquor store was a front for a bookie-type operation where bets were taken on all types of athletic events and horse races. It was operated by a man named HILL, first name unknown, and his son. This gambling place was patronized by most of the gambling element in Dallas and RUBY was a frequent visitor. MOORE did not know whether or not RUBY was actually connected with the operation of the gambling place or was merely a participant.

      During that time MOORE was employed by Cirello and LaMonte Italian Importing Company 3400 Ross Avenue. MOORE suspected that his employers, JOSEPH CIRELLO and FRANK LA MONTE, were engaged in racket activities because on occasion they would not allow him to open certain cartons containing cheese imported from Italy, although that was his alleged job. It was his opinion, based on this, that they might be importing narcotics. He had no additional information to substantiate this. RUBY was also a frequent visitor and associate of CIRELLO and LA MONTE.

      Two officers, CHARLIE SANSONE (PH), white, male, American, about 40, a detective in the Dallas Police Department, and MARVIN BLUNT, a Texas State Policeman, were regular patrons at Hill's Liquor Store and MOORE felt that they were obviously either aware of the gambling action if they were not actually involved.

      Judge O'BRIEN, a Municipal Judge in Dallas, was a friend of CIRELLO and LA MONTE and MOORE frequently put hams and other food stuffs in O'BRIEN's car at their request.

<table>
<tr><td>on <u>11/26/63</u> at <u>Oakland, California</u></td><td>File # </td><td>SF 44-494
DL 44-1639</td></tr>
<tr><td>by Special Agent <u>DONALD F. HALLAHAN &
THOMAS C. NG CES/cw/cah</u>   91</td><td>Date dictated</td><td>11/27/63</td></tr>
</table>

Date __November 27, 1963__

1

     BOBBY GENE MOORE, 865 43rd Street, Oakland, California, was interviewed at his home. He stated that he desired to furnish information regarding JACK RUBY, who he had known in Dallas, Texas. He stated that he had observed an interview on television with an associate of RUBY in which the associate said that RUBY had no gangster connections. MOORE furnished the following information:

     He was raised in Dallas, Texas, having been born in that city on December 12, 1927. About 1951 or 1952, he was living at a rooming house at 1214 Boll Street, Dallas. This house was at the rear of Hill's Liquor Store, at the corner of Ross Avenue and Boll Street. This liquor store was a front for a bookie-type operation where bets were taken on all types of athletic events and horse races. It was operated by a man named HILL, first name unknown, and his son. This gambling place was patronized by most of the gambling element in Dallas and RUBY was a frequent visitor. MOORE did not know whether or not RUBY was actually connected with the operation of the gambling place or was merely a participant.

> Note that the description of Ruby's close association with Dallas Mafia boss Joseph Civello ("Civello") was blanked out. See explanation earlier, with Civello photo.

on __11/26/63__ at __Oakland, California__   File #   SF 44-494   DL 44-1639

by Special Agent   DONALD F. HALLAHAN & ~~THOMAS G. MC GEE~~/rcw/cah   Date dictated __11/27/63__

91

COMMISSION EXHIBIT No. 1536

As published by the Warren Commission (Commission Exhibit 1536)

The day Oswald was shot, longtime FBI Director J. Edgar Hoover urged "having something issued so we can convince the public that Oswald is the real assassin." When the Warren Commission began its investigation, according to the Senate Intelligence Committee, Hoover orchestrated press leaks proclaiming Oswald to be the "lone and unaided assassin." The committee concluded that senior officials of the FBI and the CIA covered up crucial information in the assassination investigation.

Both despised by J. Edgar Hoover, Robert F. Kennedy and the Rev. Martin Luther King, Jr. were assassinated two months apart in 1968. Each had spoken out against the Mafia's abuse of the inner-city poor.

Sirhan's intention to murder Robert Kennedy was never in question, however. In private notebooks Sirhan repeatedly scribbled "RFK must die" and mentioned several payments. One entry indicated Sirhan was to receive money from Frank Donneroummas, alias Henry Ramistella, a criminal who was Sirhan's boss at the Corona horse-breeding farm.

On June 5, 1968, shortly after a speech accepting victory in the California Democratic presidential primary, Senator Robert F. Kennedy was killed by a bullet fired point blank from behind. Sirhan Bishara Sirhan was immediately captured and convicted of the murder. But Sirhan had fired at arm's length from the front. And FBI photos and witness accounts conclusively established that at least 13 bullets were fired, five more than could have fit in Sirhan's eight-chamber revolver.

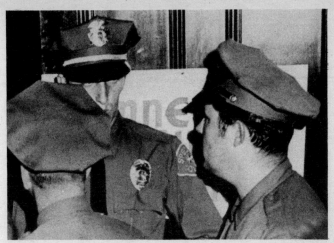

Security guard Thane Eugene Cesar (right) was standing directly behind Robert Kennedy when Sirhan began firing. Cesar admitted drawing his gun, and an eyewitness stated unequivocally that Cesar fired it. Cesar, a last-minute stand-in for a regular security guard, was linked to alleged Mobster John Alessio, one source suggests. The tie sprawled next to the dying Kennedy (see previous photo) is missing from Cesar's neck.

On the day of Sept 6, 1968 I recieved $15.00 from Jim Yalder. The Item involved is a H&R .22 pistol 9 shot serial No. Y 13332

Thane Cesar

Cesar claimed the gun he drew that night was a .38-caliber revolver, but he also owned a .22 like the one Sirhan fired. The security guard claimed he sold the .22 three months before Robert Kennedy was shot, but this note shows the sale took place three months after the shooting. The gun disappeared before it could be examined.

Called President Reagan's "First Friend," former Nevada Senator Paul Laxalt has been his perennial campaign head and confidant. Yet Laxalt's associates and political patrons have allegedly included several underworld figures. Indeed, the recently retired head of the FBI's Las Vegas office characterized Laxalt, in his perception, as "a tool of organized crime." Here, Reagan signs papers making Laxalt chairman of the president's reelection committee.

Teamsters President Jackie Presser (right) takes orders from the Mob and has been party to kickbacks, attempted bribery and racketeering, according to federal sources. He was under indictment for draining $700,000 from union coffers. Raymond Donovan, (left) vice president of a New Jersey construction firm, was repeatedly linked to organized crime by FBI sources and in taped surveillance of Mobsters. President Ronald Reagan named Presser, an eighth-grade dropout, a "senior economic advisor" on his 1980 transition team and made Donovan secretary of labor.

PART VI

Echoes
of
November 22

The assassination of President Kennedy succeeded in stopping his administration's crushing assault on the Mob. By 1967, the field time spent by the Justice Department's organized crime section had declined by 48 percent, the time before grand juries by 72 percent and the number of District Court briefs from that section by 83 percent.[1] Allegations discussed earlier of payoffs from the Mob[2] may explain Lyndon Johnson's generally poor record on organized crime.[3]

The assassination also aborted other initiatives of President Kennedy that the Mob's allies in the anti-Castro coalition found objectionable. The "major cut in defense spending" that Defense Secretary Robert McNamara had announced four days before Kennedy was shot,[4] similar to a cut proposed by Khrushchev in July 1963,[5] never occurred. President Kennedy's moves toward accommodation with Cuba were also promptly abandoned under Johnson.[6] According to *New York Times* columnist Tad Szulc, the CIA reactivated Cuban invasion and assassination plans in the following two years.[7] And in 1965, Johnson sent U.S. Marines to the Dominican Republic, the Mob's new Caribbean gambling base,[8] to prevent its former leader, Juan Bosch, from returning to power.[9] President Kennedy had supported Bosch, a democratic, non-Communist politician hostile to the Mob, who had been ousted by a coup in September 1963.[10]*

Also aborted by Johnson was President Kennedy's attempt in his last months, as outlined earlier, to pull America out of its Vietnam quagmire. Two days after his murder—the day Ruby shot Oswald—Lyndon Johnson called a meeting of his top advisers to discuss this issue.[14] The results of the meeting were em-

Life Magazine reported in 1967 that Rafael Trujillo, the dictator of the Dominican Republic until his assassination in 1961, had been "fast friends" with New Jersey Mafioso Joe Zicarelli.[11] According to *Life*, Zicarelli sold more than $1 million in arms to Trujillo and arranged the 1952 Manhattan murder of anti-Trujillo exile Andres Requena.[12] Zicarelli was also linked to the 1956 kidnapping and presumed killing of another exile, Jesus DeGalindez, a teacher at Columbia University.[13]

bodied in National Security Action Memorandum 273 of November 26, 1963, parts of which were released in the Pentagon Papers.[15] This memorandum pledged total commitment to "denying" Vietnam to communism, authorized "specific covert operations, graduated in intensity, against the DRV" (North Vietnam), and reversed President Kennedy's movement toward a military disengagement.[16] The remaining 780 of the 1,000 troops that Kennedy had ordered out of Vietnam were never withdrawn under Johnson.[17] And after Johnson won the 1964 presidential election by styling himself a peace candidate, his administration began to escalate American involvement.

Subsequent developments in Vietnam provided the first of several hints that the sinister alliance between the underworld and elements of the CIA that surfaced in assassination plots against Castro was resurrected after President Kennedy's death. The point of collaboration this time was narcotics, as noted by Robert Sam Anson, who was captured by Communist troops while covering the Vietnam War for *Time* magazine.[18] Anson observed that Southeast Asia was a domain "where CIA-supported dictators had allowed the syndicate to flourish. The Mafia's interest in Southeast Asia was heroin. . . ."[19]

Indeed, since the 1950s, the so-called Golden Triangle of Burma, Thailand and Laos had been a worldwide source of heroin — harvested by local underworld suppliers, processed by the Corsican Mafia and distributed by the closely allied American Mafia.[20] When Communist forces began making headway in the region, the CIA, with characteristic shortsighted pragmatism, organized and supported a small army of Laotian and Vietnamese heroin-dealing, anti-Communist mercenaries.[21] To stabilize this arrangement, the CIA courted local heroin overlords, a powerful factor in Vietnamese politics, as French intelligence had done before it.[22] And by the early 1960s, Anson wrote,

CIA money was indirectly financing a vast opium industry. CIA-employed troops grew it, harvested it, and shipped it to Vientiane and Saigon aboard planes of Air America, the CIA airline.[23]

The extension of this collaboration into the late 1960s was noted by Russell Bintliff, former special agent of the Army's Criminal Intelligence Command.[24] Bintliff said it was widely known in the Far East that the CIA had maintained a close working relationship with opium producers in Southeast Asia's "Golden Triangle."[25] He cited the case of an American soft drink company, Pepsi-Cola,[26] which set up a bottling plant in Vientiane, Laos, with U.S. government financing.[27] But the plant "never produced a single bottle," Bintliff said.[28] "It was for processing opium into heroin. I think this narcotics connection was responsible for most of the GIs who were turned into addicts during the Vietnam War."[29]

Other sources report that this plant, whose construction began in 1965, was used as a cover for purchases of chemicals vital to heroin processing.[30] One of its principals was Chinese narcotics merchant Huu Tim Heng, who was tied to the heroin distribution network of Vietnamese Vice President Nguyen Cao Ky.[31]

The war in Vietnam also opened up generally fertile ground for the American Mafia, which was still smarting from the loss of its Cuban empire. As Alfred McCoy noted in *The Politics of Heroin in Southeast Asia*,

> Attracted to Vietnam by lucrative construction and service contracts, the mafiosi concentrated on ordinary graft and kickbacks at first, but later branched out into narcotics smuggling as they built up their contacts in Hong Kong and Indochina.[32]

One Florida Mobster, Frank Carmen Furci, "became a key figure in the systematic graft and corruption that began to plague U.S. military clubs in Vietnam," as exposed in a lengthy Senate investigation.[33] In 1968, Tampa Mafia boss Santos Trafficante visited Furci in Hong Kong and proceeded to Vietnam, where he met with powerful Corsican gangsters.[34] It is suspected that the purpose of Trafficante's visit was "to secure new sources of heroin for Mafia distributors inside the United States."[35]

For all but the Mob heroin traffickers, the Vietnam War was thus one of the most unfortunate consequences of the murder of President Kennedy. Other tragic echoes of the November 22 shooting were the subsequent assassinations in the 1960s of Malcolm X, Martin Luther King and Robert Kennedy. Chapter 21 will consider hints of possible Mob complicity in each, strongest in the latter case, and review the stances against organized crime paralleling RFK's taken by the two martyred black leaders.

Yet perhaps the most disturbing benefit that the Mob derived from the murder of President Kennedy has been unprecedented influence at the highest levels of the American government. Chapter 22 will examine a frightening array of dealings, payoffs and favors between organized crime and one post-assassination president, Richard Nixon. And Chapter 23 will review several organized crime entanglements of officials in the Reagan Administration. Indeed, when President Reagan's "first friend," Paul Laxalt, admits working "closely" with a notorious Chicago Mafia affiliate, recently slain gangland style, it becomes clear that reverberations from the Mob-sponsored assassination of November 22, 1963 continue to undermine the nation's political process.

And now, as you can see,
the Sicilian ballad singer has arrived:
he has arrived to sing the story
of Turiddu Carnivali,
the young man who was killed
at Sciara, in the Province of Palermo,
who was killed by the Mafia. . . .
who died, murdered, like Christ.

> From the "Ballad of Turiddu Carnivali," by the popular Sicilian
> poet, Ignazio Buttitta[1]*

21
More
Assassinations

Following the assassination of President Kennedy, others carried on the courageous struggle against organized crime. Responding to the Mafia's brutal exploitation of the nation's inner cities, discussed briefly below by way of introduction, both Malcolm X and the Reverend Martin Luther King, Jr. in their different styles posed stark challenges to this lucrative empire. And a full-scale resurrection of the Kennedy anti-crime drive was portended by Robert Kennedy's promising campaign for the presidency in 1968.

Given the established precedent of Mafia culpability in the JFK murder, it is not unreasonable to consider a possible similar role in the subsequent killings of these three crusaders. A brief review of the Malcolm X and King assassination cases, though hardly conclusive, yields nothing to preclude these suspicions. As for the RFK murder, however, compelling considerations of motive and precedent plus several intriguing leads support a reasonable presumption that the Mob was responsible.

---

*Carnivali, the greatest of Sicilian postwar peasant heroes, became the 38th trade union victim of the Mafia when assassinated in 1955 at the age of 31.[2] His indiscretion: protesting the 11-hour day forced upon workers at a stone quarry operated by the Mafia in partnership with a feudal landlord.[3]

Civil rights activists of the 1960s braved bombings, beatings and killings to dislodge an entrenched system of segregation in the South. And when black American leaders focused on the North's inner cities, they came up against an equally vicious oppressor.

The Mafia's role in the ghetto was illuminated by a cash flow study of New York City's three main slum areas. The New York State Crime Committee determined that in 1968, the state spent $273 million for welfare payments in those areas.[4] And the Committee estimated that in the same year, the Mob drained $343 million in gambling and narcotics revenues from those same areas — $70 million more than the state welfare expenditure.[5]

John Hughes, chairman of the Crime Committee, observed that "the flow of money from the ghetto to organized crime is so great that there can be little meaningful economic improvement in New York City's ghettos until it is stopped."[6] And Congressman Joseph McDade of Pennsylvania concluded, "We are losing ground in the war on poverty because organized crime takes from the urban poor far more money than the government puts in."[7]

Yet economic plunder is only one aspect of the Mafia's devastation of the ghetto. As organized crime expert Ralph Salerno told Congress,

> Mr. Whitney Young . . . said that he thought it was laughable for anyone to suggest that there is violence in Harlem, for example, because television is showing "Gunsmoke." . . . He said if they really want to know what causes violence among young people in Harlem, let them study heroin trafficking and the reluctance of public officials to do something about the Mafia.[8]

Salerno related that after a 1967 riot in Newark, Floyd McKissick, then executive director of the Congress on Racial Equality (CORE), was asked in a television interview what caused it. "His answer was blame it on the Mafia, they controlled all of the narcotics, all of the gambling, all of the loan sharking in Newark."[9] Shortly before the riot, in fact, residents picketed City Hall with leaflets proclaiming, "We're tired of our Mafia government."[10] And two state commissions[11] concluded that residents' anger against the Mob and Mob-corrupted government was a major cause of the ghetto riots of the 1960s. As Salerno put it, "Organized crime has been raping the ghetto."[12]

No one understood the ghetto's problems better than its resident and spokesman, Malcolm X. A former regular numbers player, betting up to $20 a day,[13] Malcolm X observed that "practically everyone played every day in the poverty ridden black ghetto of Harlem."[14] In his autobiography, written with Alex Haley, he noted the large profits extracted from numbers operations, commenting, "And we wonder why we stay so poor."[15] Also, when he became a Muslim minister, Malcolm X often preached against the moral degradation wrought by the ghetto rackets.[16]

To combat the devastating effects of ghetto vice, Malcolm X attacked on two fronts, with striking success. First, he attracted hundreds of thousands of converts to the Black Muslim movement,[17] which forbade its members to gamble, use narcotics or patronize prostitutes.[18] Second, he exhorted the black community to deal directly with a root cause of its problems:

> Since the police can't eliminate the drug traffic, we have to eliminate it. Since the police can't eliminate organized gambling, we have to eliminate it. Since the police can't eliminate organized prostitution and all of these evils that are destroying the moral fiber of our community, it is up to you and me to eliminate these evils ourselves. . . .
> *We must declare an all-out war against organized crime in our community.*[19]

Neither such instructions nor the boycott of ghetto rackets he led was likely to have endeared Malcolm X to the Mob.

On February 21, 1965, Malcolm X was beginning a speech at the Audubon Ballroom in New York City when two men in the audience stood up and started an argument.[20] During the commotion, a man with a shotgun and others with pistols advanced toward Malcolm and fatally shot him.[21] One of the assailants, Talmadge Hayer, was shot in the leg and captured;[22] the others escaped.[23]

Suspicion immediately focused on the followers of Elijah Muhammad, the top Muslim leader with whom Malcolm X had split.[24] And when fire destroyed the Muslim mosque in Manhattan the night of the assassination, wreaking further havoc within the movement, it was written off as the retribution of Malcolm's followers.[25] Several days later, proceeding on the theory that Muslims were behind Malcolm's murder, police arrested Norman 3X Butler and Thomas 15X Johnson.[26] Hayer, Butler and Johnson were subsequently convicted of the homicide.[27]

But there were problems with the official reconstruction of the crime. Talmadge Hayer, the apprehended and admitted[28] assailant, had a criminal record[29] but no credibly established Muslim ties.[30] Butler and Johnson, on the other hand, were proud and well-known Muslims.[31] But they were picked up at home well after the fact,[32] maintained their innocence throughout[33] and were implicated by witnesses of dubious credibility.

Particularly questionable was the prosecution's star witness,[34] Cary Thomas, a one-time narcotics pusher with several arrests and Army courts-martial.[35] A bodyguard for Malcolm X at the fateful Audubon Ballroom engagement,[36] Thomas "stood there transfixed through the shooting . . . and then ignominiously ducked."[37] He did not furnish any information about the killing for six weeks,[38] and then presented contradictory accounts incriminating Hayer, Butler and Johnson.[39] Also shaky was the testimony of Charles X Blackwell, the only other witness who implicated all three men.[40] Blackwell first told police that he didn't know who did the shooting,[41] then rearranged the roles of the alleged assassins.[42] Finally, under cross-examination, he admitted that he had lied under oath.[43]

Another gap in the case against Butler and Johnson was the absence of any physical evidence implicating them.[44] The pistol allegedly fired by Butler was never found,[45] and the shotgun allegedly fired by Johnson could not be traced to him by either fingerprints or purchase history.[46] Further clouding the case was the failure of police to identify or apprehend others whom they believed ordered and abetted the killing.[47] According to *Newsweek* editor Peter Goldman, "Their guesses at the number of men actually involved ranged from four to six or seven—three guns, plus one or two people to create diversions and maybe get in the way of the bodyguards, plus one or two getaway drivers."[48]

Some of these suspects were apparently within Malcolm's organization;[49] as one investigator remarked, "He was definitely set up for it."[50] Malcolm's bodyguards were not armed, nobody was searched, police presence was limited, and no one was on stage with Malcolm at the time of his slaying.[51] All this was purportedly done on Malcolm's instructions yet was contrary to usual procedure.[52] Particularly suspicious was one bodyguard whom police described as a "professional hood,"[53] who suddenly came into money just before the assassination.[54] When the diversionary quarrel started, he left his post[55] and skipped town before police could question him.[56]

The theory that co-religionists killed Malcolm X suffered another setback when assailant Talmadge Hayer addressed the judge toward the end of his trial. Hayer stated he had just been telling Butler and Johnson

> that I know they didn't have anything to do with the crime that was committed at the Audubon Ballroom February 21, that I did take part in it and that I know for a fact that they wasn't there, and I wanted this to be known to the jury and the court, the judge.[57]

Hayer refused to name his confederates[58] but did furnish this information:

> Q: . . . did somebody ask you and others to shoot and kill Malcolm X?
> Hayer: Well, yes, sir. . . .
> Q: Did this person tell you why he wanted to hire you and these others to assassinate Malcolm X?
> Hayer: No, sir.
> Q: Were any of them, to your knowledge, Black Muslims?
> Hayer: No, they weren't. . . .
> Q: What was your motive?
> Hayer: Money.[59]

There was one organization that Hayer would not have fingered at any cost — the same organization known for using associates of the victim, perjured witnesses and corrupted officials[60] to assist and cover its murders. And given the crusade of Malcolm X against ghetto rackets, plus his exhortation to declare an "all-out war against organized crime," the same group had a clear motive for his murder. Indeed, the possibility that the Mafia killed Malcolm X was proposed by CORE leader James Farmer, as reported in *Ebony* magazine:

> Farmer had conferred with Malcolm in his Greenwich Village apartment shortly before the young firebrand departed for a trip to Mecca. Without revealing the content of their conversation, Farmer has since repeatedly hinted that Malcolm was killed because of his crusade against the drug traffic.
>
> In his book, *Freedom When?*, Farmer writes: "Malcolm's killers have not been convicted and I have a hunch that the real story of his death will surprise those who saw it as a case of Muslim revenge. Malcolm was warring on the international narcotic interests in Harlem and they were not pleased about it."[61]

If indeed the Mob was behind the Malcolm X murder, a choice of attorneys in the case was appropriate. For in the late 1960s and early 1970s, Talmadge Hayer's appeal was handled by Edward Bennett Williams.[62] Williams had defended the nation's most notorious Mafia members and associates, including New York boss Frank Costello,[63] Chicago boss Sam Giancana,[64] Teamster President Jimmy Hoffa,[65] Senate fixer Bobby Baker[66] and Chicago Mafia "lord high executioner"[67] Phil Alderisio.[68]

A poignant postscript to the Malcolm X slaying was provided by the fate of his protégé, Charles Kenyatta. As recounted by Frank Hercules in a *National Geographic* essay of 1977 on life in Harlem, Kenyatta "speaks of the overlordship of vice in the community" and of "the seduction of the community's children into using narcotics."[69] He excoriates the "overseers of vice." The suffering on his ascetic face deepens. "Why don't they leave our children alone?"

Some time ago, an automobile in which Kenyatta was riding was ambushed. His body was honeycombed by bullets, and he was left for dead. But, as by a miracle, the crusading idealist recovered.[70]

THE ASSASSINATION OF MARTIN LUTHER KING

The Reverend Martin Luther King, Jr. proclaimed:

> I have a dream . . . deeply rooted in the American dream . . . that one day this nation will rise up and live out the true meaning of its creeds — "we hold these truths to be self-evident that all men were created equal."[71]

Yet he realized that for the inner city resident, this dream was overshadowed by an ever-present nightmare:

> Permissive crime in the ghettos is the nightmare of the slum family. Permissive crime is the name for the organized crime that flourishes in the ghettos — designed, directed and cultivated by the white national crime syndicates operating numbers, narcotics and prostitution rackets freely in the protected sanctuaries of the ghettos. Because no one, including the police, cares particularly about ghetto crime, it pervades every area of life.[72]

The inherent risks of Dr. King's stance were noted by the well-known black journalist Louis Lomax:

> By making a national public issue of the plight of Chicago's Negroes, Martin was on the verge of exposing not only a corrupt political system but the influence of the underworld in ghetto economic life as well. I was surprised, and honestly so, that Martin did not disappear into Lake Michigan, his feet encased in concrete.[73]

Lomax continued,

> For this is the precise fate of those who threaten the nickel and dime numbers racket that rakes in millions of welfare dollars each year; this is the precise fate of those who threaten the millions reaped each year by white underworld czars who peddle dope as an antidote for despair.[74]

The Reverend King's commitment to nonviolence hardly mitigated the threat he posed to the Mafia's empire of exploitation in the ghetto.

On April 4, 1968, Dr. King was fatally shot in Memphis, Tennessee.[75] A massive manhunt led to the capture several weeks later of James Earl Ray,[76] a reputed narcotics and jewel smuggler,[77] who pleaded guilty to the slaying.[78] Ray acted alone, maintained attorney Percy Foreman at Ray's sentencing.[79] To support his claim, Foreman related that it had taken Ramsey Clark and J. Edgar Hoover "less than one day after the murder to conclude there was no conspiracy."[80] But Ray himself took issue with Foreman's pronouncement. "I can't agree with Mr. [Ramsey] Clark," Ray told the court.[81] "I don't want to add something on I haven't agreed to in the past."[82]

Ray, who of all people should have known, was not alone in this conclusion. His brother John was convinced there was a conspiracy.[83] Ray's first attorney, Arthur Hanes, said that there was "no question" in his mind that Ray did not act alone.[84] Judge W. Preston Battle, who presided over Ray's trial,[85] and Senator James Eastland[86] also doubted that Ray had been a lone assassin. Moreover, Canadian police found it probable that Ray "had important, perhaps underworld accomplices helping him to make his escape through Canada," the *New York Times* reported.[87] And in 1978, the House Assassinations Committee concluded "there is a likelihood that James Earl Ray assassinated Dr. Martin Luther King as a result of a conspiracy."[88]

A Mob conspiracy, in particular, two sources suggest. On February 1, 1975, comedian-activist Dick Gregory told a Boston University audience that Dr. King had once called him from a hotel room:[89]

I said, "what is it Martin," and he said, "could you explain to me what the Mafia is." And I did. And that was the only reason he was killed.[90]

Mafia culpability was also suggested in *The Two Kennedys*, an Italian documentary.[91] The film reported a rumor that the King murder was arranged by New Orleans Mafia boss Carlos Marcello as a favor to the Ku Klux Klan.[92]

The trail of the King case did in fact lead into Marcello's turf. On December 15, 1967, less than four months before the Memphis shooting, Ray and another man, Charles Stein, took a car trip from California to New Orleans[93] — the same city frequented by Oswald, Ruby, Ferrie and Brading in the months before the Kennedy assassination.[94] According to the House Assassinations Committee, Ray took the "possibly sinister"[95] trip with a specific and important objective,[96] accomplished it rapidly,[97] met with someone in New Orleans[98] and received money on the trip.[99] Ray himself admitted receiving $500 during this trip but provided a dubious account of how he obtained it.[100] His brother John explained the apparent limit to Ray's candor:

> If my brother did kill King he did it for a lot of money — he never did anything if it wasn't for money — and those who paid him wouldn't want him sitting in a courtroom telling everything he knows.[101]

The underworld involvement of Ray's traveling companion, Charles Stein, provides a possible clue to Ray's contact in New Orleans. A 38-year-old former resident of that city,[102] Stein had touched key bases there during his criminal career. In the mid-1950s, he worked at several bars in the French Quarter, including Marie's Lounge, where he managed and ran dice tables.[103] In the early 1960s, he ran a prostitution ring that included his wife.[104] During the same period, he was also reputedly involved in selling narcotics[105] — a favorite Mafia activity in New Orleans, along with gambling and prostitution.[106] Later, in 1974, Stein was convicted of selling heroin in California.[107]

When Stein and Ray arrived in New Orleans on December 17, 1967, they drove to the Provincial Motel, where Ray checked in on Stein's recommendation.[108] According to William Sartor, an independent researcher, both Stein and Ray subsequently met with three men: Salvatore "Sam" DiPiazza, Dr. Lucas A. DiLeo and Salvadore La Charda.[109] Sartor alleged that DiPiazza and La Charda had direct ties to Carlos Marcello and that all three were avid racists.[110] The site of the meeting was either the Provincial Motel, where Ray was staying, or Marcello's Town and Country Motel;[111] both were reputed underworld hangouts.[112]

When questioned by the House Assassinations Committee, Carlos Marcello, DiPiazza, DiLeo, Stein and two of Sartor's reported sources denied his allegations;[113] La Charda could not be interviewed since he had "committed suicide in June 1968."[114] Yet the Committee did confirm that DiPiazza was a bookmaker with reputed Marcello connections.[115] It also found that DiLeo, a practicing physician, "had a record for such minor offenses as disturbing the peace, resisting arrest, and assault."[116] And the Committee could establish nothing about the whereabouts of DiPiazza, DiLeo or La Charda during mid-December 1967 to preclude the alleged meeting with Ray and Stein.[117]

The complicity of Marcello Mobsters in the murder of Martin Luther King was further suggested by a report out of Memphis, Tennessee. On April 8, 1968, a witness told the FBI of a remark he had overheard four days earlier, the day of King's assassination, at the Liberto, Liberto and Latch Produce Store.[118] According to this source, as the House Assassinations Committee summarized, company president Frank Liberto "indicated that his brother in New Orleans, La., was going to pay $5,000 to someone to kill a person on a balcony."[119] The Committee noted that Liberto did in fact have a brother, Salvatore, in New Orleans, who was indirectly linked to the Marcello clan.[120] And researcher William Sartor alleged that Frank Liberto himself was connected with organized crime figures in both Memphis and New Orleans.[121] Frank Liberto denied any involvement in or knowledge of Dr. King's murder, but he admitted making disparaging remarks about King in the presence of his customers.[122]

THE ASSASSINATION OF ROBERT KENNEDY

On the night of June 4, 1968, Senator Robert Kennedy was at the Ambassador Hotel in Los Angeles celebrating his decisive victories in two Democratic presidential primaries.[123] Shortly after midnight, Kennedy finished a speech to campaign workers and was led out of the Embassy Room through the hotel pantry.[124] Suddenly, shots rang out; Kennedy and five bystanders were hit.[125] Kennedy fell to the floor, mortally wounded, his right hand clutched near a clip-on necktie.[126]

The assailant who held out his flashing gun, who drew the attention of dozens of witnesses,[127] was Sirhan Sirhan. And if an eight-shot gun cannot fire 13 bullets, evidence suggests that the man who wore the clip-on tie was Robert Kennedy's assassin.

The path to this startling conclusion begins with the counsel of the Roman Emperor Marcus Aurelius to observe "careful inquiry in all matters of deliberation," never satisfaction "with appearances which first present themselves."[128] If we ignore initial appearances in the Robert Kennedy shooting, for the moment, a natural suspect emerges once more with a motive, means and declared intention to kill.

A list of Robert Kennedy's enemies during the 1960s is conspicuously topped by one person: Jimmy Hoffa. During the summer of 1962, as discussed earlier, Hoffa had outlined plans to assassinate the attorney general.[129] But Hoffa deferred to the presidential assassination plan previewed by his associates Marcello and Trafficante, a plan that aborted the Kennedys' crime-fighting campaign and resolved the Mob's vendetta against them.[130] As for Robert Kennedy personally, Hoffa was content to gloat two days after the Dallas killing that his nemesis had become "just another lawyer."[131]

Over the next four years, the only reported plots against Robert Kennedy were initiated by Frank Chavez, the vicious boss of Puerto Rican Teamster Local 901.[132] During Kennedy's New York senatorial campaign of 1964, according to former Kennedy aide Walter Sheridan, Chavez traveled to New York to kill Kennedy but was dissuaded from going through with it.[133] Later, in March 1967, Chavez left San Juan for Washington, armed, after having sworn to kill Kennedy, Sheridan and witness Ed Partin if Hoffa went to prison.[134] Placed under surveillance, with police protection provided for his intended victims, Chavez did not follow through on his plan.[135]

But in 1968, when Robert Kennedy launched a promising campaign for the presidency, the situation required more than one thug's heroics. For the Mafia was not about to let its foremost antagonist reach the pinnacle of power to finish the job his brother's administration had left undone. Nor was it going to wait for the inconvenience of again penetrating a tight Secret Service cordon, when Kennedy could be hit on June 5 at the Ambassador Hotel with no police protection.[136] And the final green light to such an assassination plan would have been signaled by Kennedy's decisive primary victories that evening,[137] which left him a leading contender for the presidency.[138]

Robert Kennedy's curiosity about his brother's death posed a further threat to the Mob. As reported by William Turner and Jonn Christian in their book, *The Assassination of Robert F. Kennedy*, Kennedy had suspected from the beginning that "his archenemy Jimmy Hoffa might somehow have been responsible."[139] Robert Kennedy had, in fact, asked Assistant Secretary of Labor Daniel Moynihan to investigate this possibility.[140] Yet overcome by the tragedy of the event, Kennedy initially kept these suspicions in check. Journalist Tom Braden, who was with RFK at the Ambassador Hotel on June 5, had once asked him, "Why don't you just go on a crusade to find out about the murder of your brother?" Kennedy "shook his head," Braden reported, "and he said it's so horrible I don't want to think about it and I've just accepted what the Warren Commission said."[141]

As the years passed, however, Robert Kennedy again began to inquire about the painful matter. In 1967, Kennedy reportedly sent a former aide to meet with New Orleans District Attorney Jim Garrison,[142] whose sinister connection with Carlos Marcello had not yet been exposed.[143] And on May 28, 1968, a week before his death, Kennedy spent two hours in Oxnard, California checking out a reported lead to his brother's death.[144]

By June 1968, the Mafia's plans for Robert Kennedy were in fact well under way. As Turner and Christian reported, a recently released FBI document disclosed

that a wealthy Southern California rancher who had ties to the ultraright Minutemen and detested RFK because of his support of [Farm Workers' Union President] Cesar Chavez reportedly pledged $2,000 toward a $500,000 to $750,000

Mafia contract to kill the senator "in the event it appeared he could receive the Democratic nomination" for President.[145]

And Sirhan biographer Robert Blair Kaiser reported that

a fellow prisoner of Hoffa's in the Lewisburg, Pennsylvania Federal Penitentiary had told the FBI that he overheard Hoffa and his cronies talking in May, 1968, about a "contract to kill Bob Kennedy."[146]

One of these cronies may have been New York Mafia boss Carmine Galente, with whom Hoffa spoke frequently at Lewisburg.[147] Galente was the top boss of the prison's Mafia row[148] and an ally of both Carlos Marcello and Santos Trafficante.[149]

The Mafia's planned contract on Robert Kennedy would be academic, however, if Sirhan Sirhan had stood in with a timely, unassisted shooting. But an examination of Sirhan's background discounts the possibility that he acted alone.

Sirhan Bishara Sirhan, a Palestinian immigrant, claimed to have shot Kennedy because of the senator's support for Israel.[150] Yet Sirhan told an interviewer that he did not "identify with the Arabs politically or any other way."[151] Sirhan said that he did not go for Arab food, "their robes and all that bullshit," and that he was a Christian who could barely speak Arabic.[152] And curiously, Sirhan carried four $100 bills but no personal identification at the time of the shooting.[153] To Robert Houghton, chief of detectives of the Los Angeles Police Department, this suggested at first impression the pattern of a "hired killer."[154]

Also fitting this pattern was Sirhan's compulsive race track gambling and his heavy losses, particularly in the months before the assassination.[155] And this pastime brought him into contact with a rather notorious crowd. Between 1965 and 1967, following in the footsteps of Jack Ruby,[156] Sirhan worked and hung out at the Santa Anita track,[157] a Syndicate meeting place.[158] Sirhan had also worked at the Del Mar Race Track,[159] which was frequented by some of the nation's most infamous racketeers.[160]

A particularly suspicious racing acquaintance of Sirhan was Frank Donneroummas, alias Henry Ramistella, of New Jersey,[161] whose rap sheet showed several arrests in New York and Miami.[162] Donneroummas knew Sirhan at the Santa Anita Race Track[163] and in 1966 found him a job at the Corona Breeding Farm, where he was Sirhan's boss and close associate.[164] FBI agents attempted to question Donneroummas after the assassination, but it took them ten months to locate him.[165] And their desire to question him was far from idle, given the following passage in one of Sirhan's notebooks:

> happiness hppiness Dona Donaruma Donaruma Frank Donaruma pl please ple please pay to 5 please pay to the order of Sirhan Sirhan the amount of 5 . . .[166]

Several other notations containing the phrase "please pay to the order of Sirhan" were found in Sirhan's notebooks—references to Robert Kennedy or to "kill" always appeared on these same pages.[167]

Did someone in fact hire Sirhan to kill Robert Kennedy? The question is intriguing, but is overshadowed by a surprising ballistic conclusion: the fatal shot to Robert Kennedy's head was not fired from Sirhan's gun.

Three shots struck Robert Kennedy from point-blank range; a fourth passed through his suit coat.[168] This was the conclusion of both Los Angeles County Coroner Thomas Noguchi and police examiner DeWayne Wolfer, based on an autopsy examination of powder burns on Kennedy's body,[169] chemical tests performed on his jacket[170] and further ballistic tests.[171] In particular, Dr. Noguchi testified, the fatal bullet was fired with the gun tip within inches of Kennedy's right ear, and less than one inch from his head.[172] And a Los Angeles Police report concluded that "the muzzle of the weapon was held at a distance of between one and six inches from the coat at the time of all firings."[173]

But the forensically determined position of the Kennedy murder weapon was not the position of Sirhan's gun. In grand jury and trial testimony, many eyewitnesses fixed the closest distance between Sirhan's gun and Kennedy at roughly one yard;[174] not one witness reported this distance at less than one and one-half feet.[175] Furthermore, eyewitnesses uniformly reported that Sirhan fired at Kennedy from the front,[176] whereas the autopsy revealed that all shots struck him from behind, sharply below and to his right.[177]

Particularly adamant on Sirhan's position was Karl Uecker, assistant maitre d' at the Ambassador Hotel, who was the only person standing between Kennedy and Sirhan during the shooting.[178] In court testimony and subsequent interviews, Uecker positively asserted that Sirhan fired with his gun about two feet in front of Kennedy.[179] Uecker was also "a hundred percent sure" that he pushed Sirhan over the pantry steam table, completely out of point-blank range, just after the second shot.[180]

The apparent difference in the positions of Sirhan's gun and the murder weapon perturbed William Harper,[181] a nationally respected West Coast criminologist.[182] And when Harper compared the bullet removed from Kennedy's neck with one removed from a bystander, he observed another critical disparity. Harper found that the two bullets differed distinctly in rifling angle and all other characteristics he checked,[183] and in his opinion "could not have been fired from the same gun."[184] He concluded that "two 22 calibre guns were involved in the assassination": one fired by Sirhan, wounding the five bystanders behind Kennedy, and the other fired at Kennedy from behind.[185] Forensic expert Herbert MacDonnell discovered another significant difference between the two bullets and likewise concluded that they could not have been fired from the same weapon.[186]

In 1975, in response to calls from critics and the prestigious American Academy of Forensic Sciences, the California Superior Court commissioned a seven-member panel to review the ballistic evidence in the RFK case.[187] The panel's findings were inconclusive: although it uncovered "no substantive or demonstrable evidence" that more than one gun was fired, members noted "significant differences" between bullets recovered from the victims and those test fired from Sirhan's gun.[188] And the panel did not rule out the possibility of a second gun.[189]

But the coup de grace to the lone assassin assumption came with a count of the number of bullets fired in the Ambassador Hotel kitchen. For Sirhan's eight-chamber revolver could have fired at most eight bullets.[190] And eight bullets were accounted for: two recovered from Senator Kennedy, five from wounded bystanders, and another, police reported, lost in the ceiling interspace.[191]

Yet additional bullets lodged in ceiling panels, a door divider and a doorjamb were described by eyewitnesses.[192]* And a series of captioned FBI photographs taken at the Ambassador Hotel shortly after the shooting, released under the Freedom of Information Act in 1976,[198] clearly demonstrate that many more than eight bullets had been fired. As the FBI described, two of these photos show "two bullet holes, which are circled" in "the doorway leading into the kitchen."[199] Another photograph released by local authorities shows these same two bullet holes being examined and measured by Los Angeles County Coroner Thomas Noguchi.[200]

A third FBI photograph shows, as captioned, a "close-up view of two bullet holes located in the center door frame inside kitchen serving area."[201] In 1976, William Bailey, one of the FBI agents who had examined the RFK crime scene on June 5, told Los Angeles County Supervisor Baxter Ward that the presence of those bullet holes was "not even subject to speculation." Bailey told Ward, "I definitely recall closely examining those two holes, and they definitely were bullets."[202] Two bullet holes and a bullet were also reported in the same spot in affidavits by eyewitnesses Martin Patrusky[203] and Angelo DiPierro.[204]

More photographs, FBI notations and eyewitness accounts document that at least one more bullet was at the scene,[205] yielding a total of at least 13 bullets. At least five bullets, therefore, were not shot by Sirhan Sirhan. At least one additional gunman fired with Sirhan, accounting for the irregular bursts of sound heard by witnesses, like a string of firecrackers, rather than regularly spaced reports.[206] The evidence was well summarized by Vincent Bugliosi, the former Los Angeles district attorney who prosecuted the Charles Manson murders and who was active in the reexamination of the RFK case:[207]

*Following persistent requests by researchers to examine the objects in question,[193] District Attorney Evelle Younger promised in June 1969 that "tons of information" in police possession would be "made available."[194] But nothing was forthcoming until 1975, when the Los Angeles Superior Court began a probe of ballistic irregularities in the case.[195] It was then that a Los Angeles Police spokesman disclosed that the ceiling panels and door parts had been destroyed by police on June 27, 1969[196]—two weeks after Younger's pledge.[197]

Gentlemen, the time for us to keep on looking for additional bullets in this case has passed. The time has come for us to start looking for the members of the firing squad that night.[208]

The ballistics evidence provides a prime lead. As noted, Robert Kennedy's autopsy revealed that three closely grouped shots struck him and a fourth hit his jacket at point-blank range from behind, sharply below and to the right.[209] And standing directly behind and right of Kennedy was security guard Thane Eugene Cesar, who drew his gun after Sirhan began firing.[210] Cesar provided several conflicting accounts as to exactly when he pulled the gun out of his holster.[211] But he was perhaps most candid in a 1969 filmed and tape-recorded interview with journalist Theodore Charach:

Cesar: For some reason, I don't know why, I had a hold of his [Kennedy's] arm under his elbow here . . . his right arm. . . . And I was a little behind Bobby. . . . When the shots were fired, when I reached for my gun, and that's when I got knocked down. . . .

Charach: Did you see other guys pull their guns after you pulled your gun. . . . in the kitchen?

Cesar: No, I didn't see anyone else pull their guns in the kitchen area. . . . Except for myself. . . .

Charach: How far did you have it out?

Cesar: Oh, I had it out of my holster. I had it in my hand.[212]

The possibility that Cesar shot Kennedy accidentally was found highly unlikely by criminologist William Harper.[213] It was also ruled out by Cesar's response to Charach's subsequent question:

Charach: Is there any chance that that gun could have gone off?

Cesar: My gun?

Charach: Yea.

Cesar: [rapidly:] Ah, the only way it would've gone off is

[if] I'd'v pulled the trigger because the hammer wasn't cocked. (Pause.) It would have taken more pressure, I would'a had to, I would'a had to wanna fire the gun. . . .[214]

And the fact that Cesar did fire his gun—the only gun in the exact position to inflict Kennedy's wounds—is demonstrated by the report of CBS News employee Donald Schulman, who was standing behind Kennedy and Cesar at the time of the assassination.[215] Moments after the shooting, still apparently stunned, Schulman provided the following account to radio reporter Jeff Brent:

> Schulman: A Caucasian gentlemen [Sirhan] stepped out and fired three times, the security guard [Cesar] hit Kennedy all three times. Mr. Kennedy slumped to the floor. They carried him away. The security guard fired back.
> Brent: I heard about six or seven shots in succession. Is this the security guard firing back?
> Schulman: Yes, the man who stepped out fired three times at Kennedy, hit him all three times and the security guard then fired back . . . hitting him. . . .[216]

The same information was more coherently phrased in a broadcast on the Los Angeles CBS-TV affiliate minutes after the shooting:

> Don Schulman, one of our KNXT employees, witnessed the shooting that we've been telling you about. Kennedy was walking toward the kitchen and was en route out of the ballroom; a man stepped out of a crowd and shot Kennedy; Kennedy's bodyguard fired back. . . .[217]

A similar report appeared on June 6 in the Paris newspaper *France Soir*: "a bodyguard of Kennedy drew his gun, firing from the hip, as in a western."[218] And in an interview several months later with journalist Theodore Charach, Schulman confirmed that "the guard definitely pulled out his gun and fired."[219]

Although Cesar claimed that the gun he drew was a .38-caliber revolver,[220] it so happened that he also owned an H&R .22-caliber nine-shot revolver,[221] of the same caliber as Sirhan's pistol and the recovered bullets.[222] When questioned by police about this .22-caliber gun, Cesar said that he had sold it three months before the assassination.[223] Yet a bill of sale (see photo section) showed that Cesar sold it on September 6, 1968, three months *after* the assassination.[224] And when investigators tried to locate this gun in 1972, the purchaser reported that it had been stolen.[225]

But these irregularities concerning Cesar's .22-caliber revolver were not surprising. For the evidence suggests that Cesar's gun, and only Cesar's gun, was in position to pump four slugs point blank into Kennedy from behind, under cover of Sirhan's flashing pistol. Kennedy himself may have discerned this in his last moments of consciousness. For it was Cesar's necktie that was shown in photographs near the stricken senator's right hand[226] and missing from Cesar's neck;[227] it was this necktie that Robert Kennedy apparently ripped off before felled by the fatal head shot.[228]

As researchers uncovered the evidence implicating Thane Eugene Cesar in Robert Kennedy's murder, an all-too-familiar campaign of terror unfolded. In August 1971, the day before criminologist William Harper testified about the case, two men in a Buick tailed him; Harper then heard a loud explosion as a bullet from a high-powered gun struck his car's rear bumper.[229] Wald Emerson, a financial backer of research on the case, received threatening phone calls.[230] The wife of attorney Godfrey Isaacs, who assisted the probe, died under mysterious circumstances.[231] Journalist Theodore Charach, a leading investigator of the case who witnessed RFK's shooting, was accosted with a gun and asked to hand over evidence.[232] His assistant, Betty Dryer, was knifed.[233] And further incidents were described by Charach:

> You see the hotel also had Mafia connections too. Mr. Gardner, who was in charge of security, he disappeared, and Cesar told me, "well we've taken care of him; you'll never get an interview with him." Now I don't know whether he's in the bottom of the Pacific Ocean, or where

he is, but I haven't been able, you know, to locate him. And then another man, who was overall operations director, he committed suicide, and of course the files were destroyed, we found out, at the Ambassador Hotel.[234]

Of course, there is one organization for which this pattern of terror is routine. It was this combine of killers that repeatedly plotted to murder Robert Kennedy, had killed his brother and would stop at nothing to keep another Kennedy from the White House. It was this same group that had in fact been tied to the Ambassador Hotel since the 1940s, when Mickey Cohen ran a major gambling operation there with some of its personnel.[235] And it was again the Mafia, as one intriguing report suggests, that may have been linked to Thane Eugene Cesar.

Cesar was assigned to guard the Ambassador Hotel on the night of June 4 by the Ace Guard Service,[236] a firm that had protected the U.S. National Bank in San Diego; the bank collapsed in 1973 following several dealings with organized crime figures.[237] But as disclosed to the author by Alex Bottus, a crime investigator from Chicago, Cesar was only carried by Ace as a temporary employee.[238] According to California State records, Bottus reported, it had been "months and months" since Cesar had worked for Ace.[239] And Bottus claimed that Cesar was called in at the last minute to substitute at the Ambassador for a regular employee of the firm.[240] In a recent interview with investigative reporter Dan Moldea, the first journalist to speak with him in 12 years, Cesar admitted being called on June 4 for guard duty at the Ambassador but said he accepted the assignment reluctantly.[241]

Cesar's specialty in the field of crime, however, may not have been prevention. As Bottus told the author, Cesar had been arrested several times in Tijuana, Mexico,[242] though independent confirmation of these arrests has proven impossible. According to Bottus, Cesar's detention "was all fixed by none other than John Alessio,"[243] an alleged Mobster from California who had been a director of the conglomerate that controlled the U.S. National Bank.[244] And Cesar's organized crime ties, Bottus claimed, were demonstrated by "his whole track record."[245] "You trace him either through Missouri, Arkansas, and go down like I said into Chula Vista, you get down in University City, you get down into Tijuana, they all know about Cesar. And this guy's got connections like crazy."[246] Attempts to locate Bottus for follow-up during the last several years have been unsuccessful, although at least two other investigators have looked into a possible organized crime connection to Cesar.

These insinuations of Mafia contacts, attacks on those close to the assassination probe, Sirhan's notebook entry about payment from Donneroummas, alias Ramistella, documented Mafia threats to kill Robert Kennedy, plus compelling factors of motive and precedent — all of these support a reasonable presumption of Mob involvement. But the evidence is merely suggestive, and any definite links among Cesar, Sirhan and the Mob have yet to be found.

The key to unravelling this mystery may lie in thousands of documents collected during the investigation that for nearly twenty years were locked away in Los Angeles Police files. All that was released was a widely expurgated summary that is of no value to scholars. Finally, in December 1986, after calls to open these files from two Los Angeles newspapers and several concerned citizens, Los Angeles Mayor Tom Bradley fulfilled a promise to press for such disclosure, and the City Council passed a resolution to effect it. Although these RFK files have been turned over to the California State Archives, nothing has been released as of this writing. It is imperative that this evidence be expeditiously and fully disclosed.

If in fact hints of underworld involvement in the RFK killing are true, we have come full circle in the Mafia's contract on America. For recall that on February 15, 1933, Chicago Mayor Anton Cermak was shot together with several bystanders as Giuseppe Zangara stepped forward and fired his revolver.[247] Cermak, who died after accusing the Mob of the shooting,[248] had, like Robert Kennedy, aroused its wrath by intensive official action against it.[249] And Zangara, the conjectured victim of a Mafia squeeze play,[250] was, like Sirhan, a drifter who spent much of his time betting at race tracks.[251]

But most chillingly reminiscent of the Cermak slaying was the role of suspected second gunman Gene Cesar. For according to noted sociologist Saul Alinsky, the way Cermak was killed had "been commonly known for many years in many circles in Chicago."[252] As quoted earlier from *The Bootleggers* by Kenneth Allsop,

> In the crowd near Zangara was another armed man — a Capone killer. In the flurry of shots six people were hit — but the bullet that struck Cermak was a .45, and not from the .32-calibre pistol used by Zangara, and was fired by the unknown Capone man who took advantage of the confusion to accomplish his mission.[253]

COUNSEL AND PROSECUTOR

The backgrounds of counsel and the prosecutor in the RFK assassination case provide further suggestions of a broader plot. During the trial of Sirhan Sirhan, his defense lawyers repeatedly cut off prosecution testimony on the nature and position of Robert Kennedy's wounds.[254] And to avoid having the issue probed, chief defense counsel Grant Cooper magnanimously told the court he would stipulate that the fatal bullet to Kennedy's head was fired from Sirhan's gun.[255] Police expert DeWayne Wolfer later testified, however, that this point could not be positively determined.[256]

While Sirhan's trial was in progress, attorney Cooper also represented one of four codefendants of Mafioso Johnny Roselli in a gambling case.[257] All five were accused and all but one eventually convicted of running a card cheating scam at the Friar's Club in Beverly Hills, where Frank Sinatra and Dean Martin had sponsored Roselli for membership.[258] And in 1969, Cooper himself was convicted of an accessory crime: the unauthorized possession of secret grand jury testimony against the five defendants.[259] Cooper admitted to the court that he had lied about where he got the transcripts but refused to divulge their actual source.[260] It is pertinent to note that the Mafia uses leaked grand jury transcripts to prepare perjured testimony[261] and to determine the identities of witnesses who are subsequently murdered.[262]

As Cooper became increasingly preoccupied with underworld swindling and his own perjury, the burden of Sirhan's defense fell on co-counsel Russell Parsons.[263] Parsons had represented many Mob clients[264] and had once been investigated himself for hoodlum connections by the chief counsel of the Senate rackets committee: Robert Kennedy.[265] Although Parsons viewed Robert Kennedy as "a dirty son of a bitch,"[266] he had warmer feelings toward California Mobster Mickey Cohen. Parsons had written a letter of reference for Cohen to Cleveland authorities, recommending that his criminal probation be terminated.[267] The disclosure of this letter brought a quick end to a campaign by Parsons to become mayor of Los Angeles.[268]

Also pivotal in Sirhan's case was District Attorney Evelle Younger,[269] who unsuccessfully ran for the California governorship in 1978.[270] According to a 1979 report in the *Washington Monthly*,

> When Evelle Younger, the recently defeated Republican gubernatorial candidate in California, was asked during the campaign about well-documented charges that he was too friendly to the Mafia, he replied, according to *Rolling Stone*'s Greil Marcus, "I never said I was tough on crime."[271]

Younger perhaps exhibited this philosophy by repeatedly intervening to block examinations of conspiracy in the RFK case.[272] Also suspicious, as noted earlier, was the destruction of critical evidence in the case two weeks after Younger had pledged its release.[273]

Other, more successful candidates for the California governorship turned a blind eye to organized crime at various points in their political careers. The links of Jerry Brown, who defeated Younger, to Mobster Sidney Korshak were satirized in a 1979 series of Doonesbury cartoons;[274] that particular series was dropped by several major newspapers in California and Nevada.[275] An expert Mob fixer and media manipulator,[276] Korshak had supplied derogatory claims against a witness in an attempt to undermine evidence linking Carlos Marcello to the John Kennedy assassination.[277]

Edmund "Pat" Brown, Jerry's father, provided special treatment for Mobsters both before and after he governed in Sacramento. In 1949, as district attorney of San Francisco, Pat Brown mysteriously dropped a murder charge against Mafioso Sebastiano Nani.[278] And in 1977, Brown telegraphed a glowing recommendation for John Alessio,[279] Gene Cesar's alleged backer, who was then under examination by the New Mexico State Racing Commission.[280] Finally, Murray Chotiner, who managed campaigns for one-time California governor Earl Warren,[281] was a Mob-associated lawyer and alleged fixer.[282]

These peripheral relationships, however, are overshadowed by the shocking entanglements of two other competitors for the California governorship, both of whom moved upward and eastward to the White House.

The iron-fisted rulers who control the Mafia have locked a stranglehold on American politics. Using such tactics as bribes, campaign contributions, threats, blackmail, ballot box manipulation and delivery of large voting blocks, they have spread their tentacles of power through every level of government. From city halls to state capitols and from the halls of Congress even to the White House, no public official is regarded by the Mob as exempt from possible corruption.[1]

Michael Dorman, journalist and author

22
Richard Nixon and the Mob

In 1968, the year that Robert Kennedy was murdered and 15,000 American soldiers died in Vietnam, Richard Milhous Nixon was elected president of the United States. Following his prior losses to John Kennedy in 1960 for the presidency and to Edmund Brown in 1962 for the California governorship, the victory was a personal triumph for Nixon. Yet certain signs portended a less beneficial outcome for the nation.

Nixon was the first Republican presidential candidate to be supported by singer Frank Sinatra, and he made Sinatra a prominent guest at the White House. Sinatra had become *persona non grata* in the Kennedys' social circle after a 19-page Justice Department report detailed his extensive friendships and dealings with Mafia figures.[2] For his secretary of labor, Nixon selected Peter Brennan, boss of New York City's Mob-linked Building and Trades Council, who traveled around carrying a loaded gun, accompanied by a pack of bodyguards. And for his vice president, Nixon chose Spiro Agnew, a corrupt Maryland politician who became fast friends with Sinatra. Agnew pleaded no contest to income-tax evasion charges and resigned in 1973 following his implication in a kickback scheme.

If these circumstances gave cause for concern, however, Nixon's record was ultimately clarified — as summarized by Jeff

Gerth, now a *New York Times* reporter—through the "unparalleled panoply of organized criminal activity and offenses committed by his White House during his years in office."[3] Below is a sampling, progressing from questionable relationships to flagrant misconduct.

BEBE REBOZO, C. ARNHOLT SMITH AND MURRAY CHOTINER

Nixon's posture toward organized crime was perhaps modeled after those of his closest associates. A case in point was Bebe Rebozo,[4] one of Nixon's most faithful friends and most ardent supporters. Rebozo's underworld dealings were represented by his longstanding legal and financial ties with "Big Al" Polizzi, a Cleveland Mobster and drug trafficker.[5] Polizzi was characterized in the 1964 Senate narcotics hearings as "one of the most influential figures of the underworld in the United States."[6]

Both Nixon and Rebozo were prominent in the anti-Castro movement, Nixon as White House action officer under Eisenhower for the Bay of Pigs invasion[7] and Rebozo through heavy involvement with Cuban exiles in Mafia-sponsored activities against Castro.[8] And both had a murky series of financial entanglements in the Bahamas and Florida.[9] Among these were various real estate dealings in which the two were assisted by the Keyes Realty company, an underworld-linked business of which Watergate burglar Eugenio Martinez was vice president until 1971.[10] Nixon and Rebozo later bought Key Biscayne lots at bargain rates from Donald Berg, with whom the Secret Service later advised Nixon to stop associating because of Berg's background.[11] The lender for one of these Nixon properties was Arthur Desser, an associate of Meyer Lansky and Jimmy Hoffa.[12]

Both Rebozo and Nixon were friends of James Crosby,[13] chairman of the board of Resorts International,[14] a company that has been repeatedly linked to top Mob figures.[15] Rebozo's Key Biscayne Bank, which did a good deal of business with Resorts,[16] was a suspected conduit for Mob dollars skimmed from the firm's Paradise Island Casino in the Bahamas.[17] And in January

1968, Nixon appeared as Crosby's guest at the opening of the casino.[18] The previous year, *Life* had reported that it was to be controlled by "Lansky & Co."[19]

Nixon's relationship with Resorts proved rewarding to him in at least two ways. During the 1968 Republican national convention in Miami, the Paradise Island Casino's company yacht was put at Nixon's disposal.[20] And, as the *New York Times* reported, Crosby contributed $100,000 to Nixon's presidential primary campaign.[21]

As questionable as the Nixon-Rebozo relationship was Nixon's close friendship with another generous benefactor, San Diego millionaire C. Arnholt Smith.[22] This association proved rather embarrassing to Nixon in 1973 when the U.S. National Bank, controlled by Smith, collapsed.[23] The reason for the failure was that Smith had siphoned off $400 million of its assets into 86 shell companies.[24] The Internal Revenue Service subsequently filed a $22.8 million tax lien against Smith, the largest for a single year in its history.[25] Smith also drew fire from three other federal agencies and a federal grand jury,[26] and he was sentenced to one year in jail for grand theft and tax evasion in 1984.[27]

A major beneficiary of the U.S. National Bank scam was indicated in a front-page article of September 10, 1973 in the *New York Times*. In particular, the *Times* noted that "Mr. Smith and his enterprises [had] a long history of dealings with organized crime."[28] Lewis Lipton, for example, senior vice president of the U.S. National Bank, was "well-connected in the Southern California underworld."[29] Lipton, alias Felix Aguirre, helped a Mafia boss and a Mafia-controlled firm secure loans from the bank.[30]

And a one-time director of Smith's Westgate-California conglomerate was John Alessio, an alleged Syndicate figure convicted of income-tax evasion.[31] The *New York Times* cited "Mr. Smith's long business and personal relationship with John S. Alessio" as what federal agents considered "the most obvious example of Mr. Smith's connections to organized crime."[32] Alessio was the man who had reputedly fixed arrests for Thane Eugene Cesar, the suspected second gunman in the Robert Kennedy assassination.[33] Like Smith, Alessio was a benefactor of Nixon, contributing $26,000 to his 1968 presidential campaign.[34]

Another of Nixon's closest advisers and friends was Murray Chotiner,[35] a lawyer who had represented leading Syndicate figures during his career.[36] Dubbed "the one that made Nixon,"[37] Chotiner helped him achieve his first public position.[38] And Chotiner managed Nixon's political ascension from California congressman to vice presidential nominee during the same three-year period in which he and his brother defended Syndicate figures in a total of 221 prosecutions.[39] Chotiner also conceived the melodramatic "Checkers" speech when a secret fund scandal threatened to force Nixon off the Eisenhower ticket in 1952.[40] This close relationship continued throughout Nixon's presidency, as demonstrated by a private office Chotiner occupied in the Nixon White House.[41]

Chotiner's several Mob associates[42] included D'Alton Smith,[43] who was close with Carlos Marcello[44] and produced rock music festivals in California under Marcello's sponsorship.[45] Both Chotiner and Smith were instrumental in the last stage of the seven-year Mob-Teamster campaign to thwart Jimmy Hoffa's criminal prosecution.[46] This campaign was marked by a barrage of bribery, intimidation and perjury,[47] whose "audacity and sweep," as *Life* magazine noted, few Mob fixes "could top."[48] It finally succeeded, with the intervention of Chotiner and Smith,[49] when Nixon commuted Hoffa's prison term in December 1971.[50]

Walter Sheridan, a former Kennedy Justice Department official, had warned journalist Clark Mollenhoff earlier: "It's all set for the Nixon Administration to spring Jimmy Hoffa. . . . I'm told Murray Chotiner is handling it with the Las Vegas Mob."[51] The commutation was granted four months after a U.S. parole board unanimously rejected such a release.[52] It allowed Hoffa to serve just five years of a 13-year sentence for jury tampering and defrauding the Teamsters of almost $2 million.[53]

"NIXON, THE TEAMSTERS, THE MAFIA"

The *New York Times* called Nixon's pardon of Hoffa "a pivotal element in the strange love affair between the Administration and the two million-member truck union, ousted from the rest of the labor movement in 1957 for racketeer domination."[54] This strange kinship was further demonstrated by the Nixon Administration's repeated interventions to quash prosecutions and investigations of Teamster criminal activity, as outlined in a *Los Angeles Times* lead editorial entitled "Nixon, the Teamsters, the Mafia."[55]

One such intervention began with a conclave at La Costa Country Club, a "Mafia watering hole"[56] in Carlsbad, California.[57] The participants were Teamster President Frank Fitzsimmons, Allen Dorfman, Chicago Mafia boss Anthony Accardo and other Mob figures.[58] The meeting, which occurred February 9–12, 1973, soon turned to routine business: a massive scam of Teamster welfare funds.[59] The particular scheme under consideration called for Teamster members to be enrolled in prepaid medical plans, which would kick back 7 percent of their business to People's Industrial Consultants — a Los Angeles front for the Mob.[60] The take would then be divided among Mob and Teamster bosses.[61] The potential bonanza was huge, with $1 billion in projected annual business.[62] The conversations at La Costa outlining the scheme were disclosed by several sources — most notably FBI electronic surveillance of People's Industrial Consultants.[63]

On February 9, 1973, while the Mob-Teamster discussions were in progress, White House aides H. R. Haldeman, John Ehrlichman, John Dean and Richard Moore also met at La Costa Country Club, for about 12 hours, to discuss Watergate strategy.[64] Some of Nixon's own staff members found the proximity shocking.[65] On February 12, the last day of the Mob-Teamster discussions, Teamster boss Fitzsimmons flew back to Washington with President Nixon on Air Force One.[66] A month later, Attorney General Richard Kleindienst denied an FBI request to continue electronic surveillance of People's Industrial Consultants.[67] Through aides, Kleindienst characterized the surveillance as "unproductive," to the amazement of FBI agents.[68] On the contrary, as the *New York Times* reported, the surveillance "had begun to penetrate connections between the Mafia and the teamsters union."[69] The *Times* called the termination of surveillance an instance of "the perversion of justice that pose[d] as law and order" in the Nixon Administration.[70]*

Nixon's efforts on behalf of the Mob did not go unrewarded. Citing government informants and a secret FBI report, *Time* disclosed in 1977 that the White House had received a $1 million underworld bribe shortly before the dual conclaves at La Costa.[76] The principals in the payoff were Frank Fitzsimmons and Tony Provenzano;[77] Provenzano is a Mafia captain, former Teamster international vice president, and convicted murderer.[78] Also involved was Allen Dorfman,[79] a Chicago Mob associate, convicted labor racketeer and Teamster pension fund adviser[80] who was slain gangland style in 1983.[81] Dorfman's role in the Teamsters, noted author Dan Moldea, was to ensure that "every section of organized crime got its fair share of the union's billion-dollar pension and welfare funds."[82] *Time* reported that "the $1 million was intended as a payoff for the Administration's cooperation in preventing Jimmy Hoffa from wresting the union presidency from Frank Fitzsimmons."[83]

According to government informants, *Time* reported, Dorfman provided half of the bribe for Nixon on Fitzsimmons' orders.[84] The other $500,000 was handled by Provenzano, again at Fitzsimmons' behest, and delivered to a White House courier in Las Vegas.[85] Provenzano told government informants that the Nixon-Teamster intermediary was White House aide Charles Colson, and the FBI believed that Colson received the money in Las Vegas on January 6, 1973.[86] The FBI called the information on the million-dollar transaction "solid."[87]

One FBI agent commented, "This whole thing of the Teamsters and the mob and the White House is one of the scariest

---

*Kleindienst had quashed several prosecutions and investigations of the Mob and Teamsters.[71] As deputy attorney general, he had been offered a $100,000 bribe to stop prosecution of several underworld figures in a stock fraud case, but he reported it a week later only when he learned that federal agents were investigating the case.[72] He also lied to a Senate committee about an antitrust case and later drew a criminal conviction for that offense.[73]

After he left public office, Kleindienst collected $125,000 for a few hours' time arranging a health insurance contract between the Teamsters and an insurance firm of dubious reputation.[74] The outcome was classic: $7 million in union members' premiums were siphoned off into several shell companies.[75]

things I've ever seen."[88] Also ominous was the possibility, as *Time* reported, that Nixon may have desired the Dorfman-Provenzano cash to subvert the democratic process further: to provide hush money for the Watergate conspirators.[89] *Time* noted the "crucial timing" of demands for payoffs by Watergate burglar E. Howard Hunt in late 1972, and of a meeting between Hunt's lawyer and Colson on this matter on January 3, 1973.[90]

A Mob-Watergate connection was discussed, in fact, in the White House tape transcripts of March 21, 1973. Presidential aide John Dean told Nixon that $1 million in Watergate hush money was needed, to which Nixon responded,

> We could get that. . . . You could get a million dollars. You could get it in cash. I know where it could be gotten.[91]

Dean remarked that laundering money is "the sort of thing Mafia people can do."[92] Playing the innocent, Nixon replied, "Maybe it takes a gang to do that."[93]

In a second White House tape, Ehrlichman told Nixon that Hunt and Gordon Liddy had gone to Las Vegas for covert purposes,[94] supporting allegations that both had picked up cash from Mob gambling interests there.[95] And in a third tape of May 5, 1971, Nixon and Haldeman considered another role for the Mob—attacking anti-war protesters:

> Haldeman: . . . do it with the Teamsters. Just ask them to dig up those, their eight thugs.
> President: Yeah. . . . they've got guys who'll go in and knock their heads off.
> Haldeman: Sure. Murderers. . . . it's the regular strike-buster-types . . . and then they're gonna beat the [obscenity] out of some of these people.[96]

Some such "thug-type guy" was in fact used by Nixon's men to disrupt the Muskie presidential campaign of 1968, as mentioned by Haldeman on that White House tape of May 1971.[97]

A suggestion of an even broader underworld network enveloping the Nixon presidency was furnished by Charles Colson, another convicted Watergate conspirator. In a 1976 interview with *Village Voice* reporter Dick Russell, Colson stated that he heard one theory that the Las Vegas gambling empire of the eccentric billionaire Howard Hughes was

> really a headquarters of the Mafia's operation; that they owned Bebe Rebozo, they got their hooks into Nixon early, and, of course, that ties into the overlap of the CIA and the mob. . . . Don't say that's my theory, but I've heard it expounded as a possibility and, of course, it is.[98]

Having intervened on Nixon's behalf to aid one New York Mafia leader facing prosecution and arranged the early parole of a Teamster official in Miami, as the *Washington Post* reported in 1973,[99] Colson could hardly have been speculating idly.

Indeed, the early hooks into Nixon that Colson related were demonstrated by a longstanding flow of underworld cash. Mobster Mickey Cohen wrote in his memoirs that he had contributed $5,000 to Murray Chotiner for Nixon's first Congressional campaign in 1946.[100] For Nixon's 1950 senatorial race against Helen Gahagan Douglas, Cohen wrote, he had raised $75,000 from Las Vegas gamblers.[101] And in 1960, just before the first of the Kennedy-Nixon debates, Mafia boss Carlos Marcello funneled $500,000 in cash to Nixon through Jimmy Hoffa.[102] That bribe was reported by Edward Partin,[103] a former Hoffa aide turned government informant; Partin's information has been corroborated on several occasions,[104] and he has been found credible by both juries and federal officials.[105] Indeed, as noted by Army criminal investigator Russell Bintliff, "There were strong indications of a history of Nixon connections with money from organized crime."[106]

In short, in the words of one Justice Department official, Richard Nixon was "a man who pardoned organized crime figures after millions were spent by the government putting them away, a guy who's had these connections since he was a congressman in the 1940s."[107] And Nixon apparently maintained these connections after resigning his presidency. In October 1975, the *New York Times* reported Nixon's presence with Teamster President Frank Fitzsimmons in a golf tournament at La Costa Country Club.[108] Among Nixon's golfing companions that day was Jackie Presser,[109] a top Teamster official reputedly controlled by the Mob, who had allegedly helped dole out millions of dollars in Teamster loans to Mafia enterprises.[110] Two other golfing companions of Nixon that day were his million-dollar benefactors: Allen Dorfman, the Mob-Teamster financial coordinator who was later murdered gangland style, and Tony Provenzano, the former Teamster vice president and convicted Mafia killer.[111]

Nixon's involvement with men of Provenzano's and Dorfman's background drives home an important axiom. The Mafia's millions are extracted by murder. And its bribes are bathed in blood. Which brings us to the most revolting instance of Nixon Administration misconduct on behalf of the Mob.

THE PARDON OF ANGELO "GYP" DECARLO

Louis D. Saperstein was in debt to the Mob for $400,000 and could no longer make the interest payments of $5,000 per week.[112] On September 13, 1968, as Mob defector Gerald Zelmanowitz later testified, Zelmanowitz arrived at the headquarters of New Jersey Mafioso Angelo "Gyp" DeCarlo.[113] Zelmanowitz found Saperstein "lying on the floor, purple, bloody, tongue hanging out, spit all over him."[114] Zelmanowitz related,

I thought he was dead. He was being kicked by Mr. Polverino and Mr. Cecere. He was lifted up off the floor, placed in a chair, hit again, knocked off the chair, picked up and hit again.[115]

DeCarlo then instructed the men to stop the beating and told Saperstein to repay the loan by December 13 or he would "be dead."[116]

On November 26, 1968, Saperstein died of what was initially listed as gastric upset.[117] But the day before, he had written to the FBI describing how DeCarlo and his henchmen had threatened his life.[118] Saperstein wrote that they had "stated many times" that his "wife and son would be maimed or killed."[119] An autopsy prompted by Saperstein's letters disclosed enough arsenic in his body to kill a mule.[120]

The murder of Saperstein was just a day's work for Angelo DeCarlo, a captain in the Genovese Mafia Family[121] described by the FBI as a "methodical gangland executioner."[122] Some of his expertise was revealed in the "DeCavalcante Tapes" of the FBI's electronic surveillance of New Jersey Mafia hangouts during the early 1960s. This 1,200-page transcript was released to the public by court order in 1970,[123] providing a wealth of information about the Mafia.[124] In one conversation, DeCarlo told fellow Mobsters that a good way to handle a murder was to poison the victim and prop him behind the wheel of his auto.[125] DeCarlo then described how he had shot one victim to death: "Itchie was the kid's name. . . . I hit him in the heart."[126]

DeCarlo was finally forced to account, in part, for one of his crimes. In March 1970, he was sentenced to 12 years in prison for extortion against Saperstein, based upon the testimony of prosecution witness Gerald Zelmanowitz.[127] But less than two years later, DeCarlo, reportedly terminally ill,[128] was freed by Richard Nixon on a presidential pardon.[129] Shortly afterward, *Newsweek* reported that DeCarlo, though ailing, was "back at his old rackets, boasting that his connections with Sinatra freed him."[130]

According to FBI informants, as reported by the *New York Times*, the release was obtained through Frank Sinatra's intervention with Vice President Agnew; the details were arranged by John Dean and Agnew aide Peter Malatesta.[131] The release followed an "unrecorded contribution" of $100,000 in cash and another contribution of $50,000 forwarded by Sinatra to a Nixon campaign official.[132] The FBI dismissed these allegations,[133] but Senator Henry Jackson, chairman of the Senate Permanent Subcommittee on Investigations, charged that the pardon "bypassed normal procedures and safeguards."[134] Indeed, no one had taken the routine step of consulting officials involved in the prosecution.[135] Citing "serious and disturbing questions as to the reasons and manner" governing the release, Jackson declared, "Something smells and I want to know what."[136]

While DeCarlo was free and back at his rackets, Zelmanowitz, who had been relocated under a new identity,[137] was treated very differently by the Nixon Justice Department. In 1973, Zelmanowitz's cover was destroyed when a background check disclosed that the Justice Department had not filed any of the documents it had promised to supply for his relocation.[138] The Internal Revenue Service then enforced a tax lien against him, contrary to a prior agreement.[139] Amazingly, enforcing the lien were the very same IRS agents whom Zelmanowitz had previously identified to federal investigators as recipients of bribes in connection with his earlier Mob activity.[140]

The incredible conduct of the Justice Department was highlighted in Zelmanowitz's testimony in 1973 before Senator Jackson's Permanent Subcommittee on Investigations:

> While DeCarlo lives in luxury and leisure in his home, I and my family are once again dislocated with our property seized and in fear for our lives. Unfortunately, it seems that there is no one left but this committee to heed me.
>
> Even at this moment I still do not have protection from the U.S. Marshal's Service although it has been requested. I have been living for the last week, since last Saturday night, in a motel room. But for the courtesy of your staff, who picked me up this morning and brought me to this committee, armed, I was able to come here.[141]

At the conclusion of his testimony, Zelmanowitz stated,

> I don't know what happens now when I leave this committee room. . . . I am in fear of my life. I do not know where to go or what to do when this is over.[142]

Zelmanowitz had genuine reason for concern. For as *Newsweek* reported in 1977, four Mob defectors under the Justice Department witness protection plan were murdered between 1971 and 1977.[143] And six others died from "such ambiguous causes as drug overdoses, suicides and an auto accident."[144] The Justice Department conducted an 18-month investigation of corruption in the program, leading to the indictment of one U.S. marshal and the resignation of four others.[145] One marshal learned that "the word was you could buy the location of a witness for $5,000 in Jersey."[146] But these marshals were merely emulating their boss, Richard Nixon, who had well earned the appellation "the Syndicate's President."[147]

The extraordinary thing about organized crime is that America has tolerated it for so long.[1]

U.S. President's Commission on Law Enforcement
and Administration of Justice, 1967

23
The Reagan Administration

The reported Nixon-Mafia relationship heralded a political realignment that had long been brewing for organized crime. Following the pattern of other immigrant groups, the Mafia had found its political base during its first several decades in America with the big-city Democratic Party machines. The Kennedys' anti-crime crusade and the Mafia-CIA alliance against Castro put the first cracks in this longstanding allegiance. And the forces of upward social mobility and southwestern migration moved the Syndicate further toward the Republican Party in the post-assassination decades, resulting in a truly bipartisan orientation.

Indeed, with the Kennedy threat cleared by assassination, the Mob enjoyed unprecedented prosperity and capital acquisition, drawing an annual income of $100 billion[2] and gaining control of some 50,000 U.S. firms.[3] Especially significant was its major penetration of banking and finance,[4] resulting in a rash of U.S. bank failures beginning in 1964[5] and the nation's three largest bank collapses of the 1970s.[6] An estimated loss of $50 billion in stolen U.S. securities by 1973[7] was another manifestation of what Claude Pepper, chairing a House Crime Committee probe in 1971, described as the "pervasive influence of organized crime in the banking and securities industries."[8] Clearly, the Mob had found its niche in the monied class.

Given this socio-political realignment, it was thus not anomalous when another California Republican, Ronald Reagan, received apparent Mob backing in his 1980 bid for the presidency, as signaled once again by a warm endorsement from the Teamsters Union. Unfortunately, however, the Nixon parallel does not stop there. President Reagan reciprocated this support by appointing two men distinguished only by their reported Mob connections. And he kept as his closest friend and advisor a man whom the retired head of the FBI's Las Vegas office characterized, in his perception, as a "tool of organized crime."[9] At the same time, paradoxically and refreshingly, the Reagan Administration presided over the most sweeping series of prosecutions against the Mob since the Kennedy years. The irony sharpens with an examination of both sides of this record.

PAUL LAXALT

Paul Laxalt's relationship with Ronald Reagan was summarized by a senior aide to the President: "Paul Laxalt is both his closest friend and most trusted advisor."[10] Laxalt, who as a senator visited Reagan several times per week,[11] was described as the "First Friend"[12] and called the President's "eyes and ears"[13] in the Senate. He was also Reagan's campaign manager in 1976, 1980 and 1984[14] and nominated him for president in those three years.[15]

In contrast to Laxalt's White House connection, however, were several relationships of a less savory character. Most shocking was his longstanding association with Allen Dorfman, a convicted extortionist who presided over the drain of Teamster pension funds into Mob enterprises.[16] Laxalt acknowledged their close relationship in a 1971 letter to Richard Nixon requesting Jimmy Hoffa's release from prison:

Dear President Dick:
The other day I had an extended discussion with Al Dorfman of the Teamsters, with whom I've worked closely the past few years. . . . This discussion, which described in detail the personal vendetta that Bobby Kennedy had against Hoffa, together with other information provided

me over the years, leads me to the inevitable conclusion that Jim is a victim of Kennedy's revenge.[17]

Laxalt described Hoffa as a "political prisoner" and asked Nixon to release him. Laxalt then once again alluded to his connection with Dorfman, whom Justice Department officials cited as the person "most responsible" for turning the Teamsters pension fund "into a series of mob loans":[18]

while I don't know Mr. Hoffa personally, I have had occasion to have a great deal of contact with Mr. Dorfman. . . .[19]

Dorfman's Mob identity was brought home by his 1983 murder, a gangland-style slaying by ski-masked killers in a Chicago parking lot.[20] Standing at his side was Irwin Weiner, the highly placed Chicago Mobster whose pre-assassination contact with Jack Ruby has been discussed.[21]

Moe Dalitz, a Las Vegas Mobster,[22] is another longstanding friend of Laxalt.[23] After Laxalt's election to the U.S. Senate in 1974, Dalitz reportedly claimed, "Laxalt is my boy, I put him there."[24] Laxalt received a total of nearly $50,000 in his two Senate campaigns from Dalitz and several others linked by federal law enforcement agencies to organized crime.[25] Laxalt, quoted in the *Wall Street Journal*, said of Dalitz: "He's been so decent to me over the years, there's no way — I don't care what the political considerations would be — I would turn my back on him."[26]

Another criminal backer of Laxalt was Ruby Kolod, a key fundraiser for Laxalt's successful 1966 bid for the Nevada governorship.[27] Laxalt admitted that Kolod, who had been convicted of fraud and extortion in 1965,[28] "did help us tremendously."[29] Other supporters of Laxalt, who contributed to his campaigns for the U.S. Senate, included the late Sydney Wyman,[30] formerly an illegal gambling operator and partner of hoodlum Bugsy Siegel;[31] Allen Glick,[32] whom an FBI affidavit called a front for the Chicago Syndicate;[33] Frank "Lefty" Rosenthal,[34] another Chicago Mob front;[35] Morris Shenker,[36] who informants swore in an FBI affidavit did the Kansas City Mob's bidding;[37] and Benny

Binion, a rackets boss with reported ties to the Texas underworld.[38]

Laxalt also exhibited a disturbing toleration of the underworld in one of his key business partnerships. In 1970, after his term as Nevada governor expired, Laxalt and his brother Peter built the Ormsby House gambling casino in Carson City, Nevada.[39] A third partner in the venture and its chief source of investment capital was Bernard Nemerov, who by then had accumulated "a long, documented history of association with some of the most notorious members of the national crime syndicate."[40]

In November 1983, the *Sacramento Bee* published an investigative feature, as exhaustive as it was explosive, on Laxalt's questionable past. Written by Pulitzer Prize-winning journalist Denny Walsh, the story led with charges by IRS agents that substantial skimming took place at Ormsby House in the early 1970s and went on to say that those profits, some $2 million per year, were funneled to organized crime.[41] A year later, Laxalt sued the *Bee*'s parent company for $250 million; the case was settled out of court, with no monetary damages awarded, in June 1987.[42] Though the settlement agreement required the defense to concede that it could not prove the IRS agents' allegations of skimming at Ormsby House, the *Bee* retracted none of the story.[43] In fact, the feature's most important revelations—those concerning Laxalt's ties to reputed Mobsters, particularly in financing the Ormsby House—were left unchallenged in the settlement.[44]

Given the above entanglements, it is no surprise that as an elected official, Laxalt took steps to restrain federal action against the underworld. In 1981, Laxalt spoke with President Reagan and met three times with then-Attorney General William French Smith to protest aggressive investigations of the Mob by the FBI and the Justice Department's organized crime strike force in Las Vegas.[45] Claiming that the probes were hurting the city's casino industry, Laxalt complained to the *Miami Herald*: "We have far more bureau agents than we need."[46] According to organized crime expert Dan Moldea, Laxalt also pledged to use his influence on the Senate Appropriations Committee to rein in the federal investigators in Nevada.[47]

FBI Chief Webster refused to yield to Laxalt's pressure and in 1983 approved the installation of a political corruption hotline in the FBI's Las Vegas office, which proved highly effective.[48] Laxalt complained heatedly to Attorney General Smith, asking that the line be "immediately discontinued."[49] In the few years leading up to his departure from the Senate, Laxalt spearheaded Congressional opposition to a regulation, which was implemented in February 1985, aimed at reducing laundering of illicit drug profits through Las Vegas casinos.[50] He also sponsored Senate legislation to divert the focus of federal law enforcement efforts from organized crime to street crime.[51]

Laxalt's record on organized crime became the subject of two potentially explosive exposés by CBS's "60 Minutes" and ABC's "World News Tonight" that were scheduled to be aired in September 1984.[52] The networks' mutual on-camera source, Joseph Yablonsky,[53] had been chief of the FBI's Las Vegas office from 1979 until his retirement in 1983. Dubbed the "king of sting" for his prior successful undercover operations, Yablonsky had been hand picked for the post by FBI Director William Webster.[54]

A possible preview of the television reports was Yablonsky's comment, quoted in a prior magazine story: "Laxalt began to emerge in my mind as a tool of organized crime."[55] But both exposés were postponed, and not subsequently aired, after CBS and ABC received letters from Laxalt's lawyer threatening libel action.[56] The networks claimed, however, that they killed the pieces because they discovered that Yablonsky had promised each an exclusive.[57]

Two months after the Laxalt exposés were cancelled, President Reagan was reelected, and in 1987 Laxalt entered the race to become his successor. Undaunted by Laxalt's alleged underworld involvements, Reagan had told followers at a March 1986 dinner in Laxalt's honor, "Look to the son of the high mountains and peasant herders. . . . to a friend, to an American who gave himself so that others might live in freedom."[58] Laxalt pulled out of the presidential race later that year, citing lack of financial support and perhaps realizing that his past could not withstand the scrutiny of a national campaign.

In October 1975, as noted previously, Richard Nixon went to a golf tournament at La Costa Country Club in California, a "Mafia watering hole" built by Laxalt's friend and backer Moe Dalitz. Among Nixon's golfing partners that day were Teamster boss Frank Fitzsimmons; Allen Dorfman, the Mob-Teamster intermediary with whom Laxalt had "worked closely" and who would be murdered in 1983; and Tony Provenzano, a Mafia captain convicted of murder who had been a Teamster vice president. All three, as discussed, had reportedly been principals in a million-dollar bribe to the Nixon White House in 1973.

A fourth golfing partner of Nixon that October day was Jackie Presser, a Teamster official who would become the union's president in 1983. An eighth-grade dropout who never drove or loaded a truck for a living,[59] Presser was described in an internal Justice Department file as a "well known corrupt union leader" whose "fingers are out to pick whatever pockets he can."[60] Jackie's father, William Presser, a former Teamsters vice president, had been convicted for obstruction of justice, contempt of Congress and a shake-down scheme.[61]

The Justice Department file on son Jackie cites his alleged links to top Cleveland Mafia figures,[62] while the President's Commission on Organized Crime detailed allegations of kickbacks, payoffs, attempted bribery and racketeering in Presser's past.[63] Mafia informer Jimmy Fratianno testified that Presser told him, "I don't do nothing unless Blackie [Cleveland Mafia boss James Licavoli] tells me."[64] Fratianno also stated that, "Cosa Nostra runs the Teamsters,"[65] echoing Mafia boss Carlos Marcello's boast to an FBI bug[66] and the conclusions of the President's Commission on Organized Crime.[67]

Given his underworld credentials, it came as a shock when in 1980, Presser was appointed a "senior economic advisor" on newly elected President Ronald Reagan's transition team.[68] Then-Senator Paul Laxalt helped arrange the appointment,[69] and several in the Administration, including Attorney General Edwin Meese,[70] Reagan-Bush campaign manager Ed Rollins[71] and

Reagan himself,[72] maintained cordial relations with Presser in subsequent years. Presser's chief economic expertise consisted of allegedly draining his union's treasury into Mob enterprises, which he reportedly did as a trustee of the Teamsters' Central States Pension Fund.[73] Shortly before Presser's appointment to Reagan's transition team, in fact, New Jersey State Police officers testified in a state inquiry that Presser was a contact for arranging Mafia loans from the pension fund.[74] (Asked once about his ownership of a Cleveland sports complex that defaulted on a $1.1 million Teamster pension loan, Presser replied: "I am trying to find out how I became a stockholder."[75])

America had come a long way. Kennedy prosecuted a Teamster boss; Nixon pardoned him. Reagan went one better: he appointed Jackie Presser—a Mob-tied, eighth-grade dropout—to his transition team.

Prior to his death in 1988, Presser was awaiting trial in Cleveland on charges that he drained $700,000 from union coffers.[76] He joined more than 100 local Teamsters officials and consultants indicted or convicted for fraud, racketeering or embezzlement in the last five years.[77]

President Reagan's appointment of and cordiality to Jackie Presser was just one facet of an unnaturally cozy relationship between a Republican president and the mighty union, a strange love affair reminiscent of the Nixon Administration. Reagan launched his fall 1980 campaign with a speech to the Teamsters in Ohio, where he also met privately with Presser, Presser's father, and then-Teamster President Roy Williams.[78] Williams was later described in a Senate report as "an organized crime mole operating at senior levels of the Teamsters Union."[79] The day before this meeting with Reagan, Williams had taken the Fifth Amendment repeatedly when questioned by a Senate committee about his Mob involvements.[80] And when Reagan visited Washington after winning the election, one of his first stops was Teamster headquarters, where he met in closed session with Presser, Williams and other board members.[81]

The President was not as friendly to all labor unions; he crippled the Air Traffic Controllers, one of only two unions other than the Teamsters to support his 1980 candidacy, after its illegal strike in 1981. But he was unusually warm to the International Longshoremen's Association (ILA), becoming in 1983 the first U.S. president to address its national convention.[82] Expelled from the AFL-CIO, like the Teamsters, for underworld infestation,[83] the ILA is run by the Genovese and Gambino Mafia families.[84] The President's Commission on Organized Crime concluded that the historical assessment of the ILA as "virtually a synonym for organized crime in the labor movement" remains true today.[85] And NBC reported that through massive systematic hijackings, "the Mafia and the Longshoremen's Union have been able to put their own tax on every item moving in or out of the ports they control."[86] Over the past several years, more than 30 of the union's officials have been convicted on a variety of criminal charges.[87]

Typifying its style of leadership, ILA President Thomas Gleason, now retired, took the Fifth Amendment when questioned by a grand jury about corruption in his union.[88] In concert with Connie Noonan, a boss of a waterfront numbers racket, Gleason earlier in his career had allegedly engaged in a number of business deals, including selling armed planes to the Dominican Republic.[89] Like Presser, Gleason opposed an administration bill to force convicted felons out of union leadership positions.[90]

But when Reagan addressed the ILA on July 18, 1983, he had only praise for its boss. Gleason "sticks by his friends and he sticks by his country," Reagan declared, "the kind of integrity and loyalty that is hard to come by today."[91] Before the speech, the first by a U.S. president to the Mob-infiltrated union, Reagan had been given background material on corruption within the ILA.[92]

RAY DONOVAN

In December 1980, President Reagan named 50-year-old Raymond Donovan his secretary of labor. A vice president and labor liaison for New Jersey's Schiavone Construction Company, Donovan was the Teamsters' first pick for the labor position[93] but was unknown to most national labor leaders.[94] The appointment would prove reminiscent of Nixon's selection of Peter Brennan, boss of New York City's Mob-dominated Building and Trades Council, for the same Cabinet post.

The next month, the FBI presented the results of a ten-day investigation of Donovan to the Senate Labor Committee.[95] In its 19-page report, the FBI summarized allegations from six witnesses it judged reliable that the Schiavone company was "mobbed-up" and that Donovan "had social and business ties with organized crime figures."[96] One FBI informant alleged that in the 1960s Donovan had made periodic payments for labor peace to a trucking firm owned by a reputed Mafia hit man.[97] Amid these public charges, the FBI's New York office also sent Washington a secret memo revealing that the would-be labor secretary's construction company had given William "Billy the Butcher" Masselli, a soldier in the Genovese crime family, "preferential treatment on subcontracting projects" and conspired with him in "numerous, possibly fraudulent schemes."[98]

Oddly, the FBI's spokesman at the Donovan hearings, former Executive Assistant Director Bud Mullen, Jr., did not mention these assertions to the Senate committee.[99] Instead, he testified, FBI investigations of Donovan and his company had been "favorable."[100] Without the benefit of the complete picture, the Senate confirmed Donovan.

In February 1981, however, the Senate Labor Committee reopened its investigation of Donovan after new disclosures surfaced that linked him to the underworld and indicated that the FBI's initial report had been deficient.[101] One was an FBI tape recording in which William Masselli recalled to his son an invitation he had received to fly to a function with Donovan and Ronnie Schiavone, the president of Schiavone Construction.[102] In a newspaper interview, Masselli later recounted that he knew Donovan personally, had met him at two social events and had been his guest at a couple of football games.[103] But Donovan had testified that he had met Masselli only three times, "totally on a business basis."[104]

During the renewed probe, Senate aides working on the case received anonymous threats at the same time the Schiavone Company announced it was going to "investigate" the participating

Senators and staff. In December 1981, however, the Senate probe was halted due to the appointment of special prosecutor Leon Silverman to investigate the charges against Donovan; Silverman subsequently concluded that there was "insufficient credible evidence" of a crime to warrant prosecution.[105] But this finding was called into question by subsequent perjury convictions of two Mob-linked union leaders questioned in the probe.[106] Even more unsettling were a pair of gangland murders that precluded critical testimony linking Donovan to the Mob.

Fred Furino, a key government witness against Donovan, was found in June 1982 inside a car trunk with a bullet in his head.[107] A Mafia bagman alleged to have received payments from Schiavone, Furino had failed a lie-detector test on his denials that he knew Donovan.[108]

William Masselli's son Nat was shot to death, also in the head, the night before the elder Mobster was to testify before a New York grand jury investigating Donovan.[109] Mafia soldiers Salvatore Odierno and Philip Buono were convicted in the slaying.[110] In his closing argument, the New York state prosecutor charged that the Mafia murder was performed to "destroy" the Silverman probe and protect Donovan, whom the prosecutor called a "political connection" of organized crime.[111]

Supporting the prosecution's successful case, James Toohill, a prisonmate of Odierno, said Odierno admitted that the slaying had been carried out to prevent the testimony of Nat and William Masselli.[112] Toohill testified: "[Odierno] said that . . . if they [the Massellis] were allowed to testify or cooperate, that it would be 30-to-life federally, and everybody would go from the top down, whereas dead, the only thing could happen was two, maybe one [would go to prison] or if they were lucky, nobody would go."[113]

Less than a year later, largely based on FBI evidence that had been suppressed at his confirmation hearings, Labor Secretary Donovan was indicted, along with Masselli, a New York state senator and several top Schiavone executives on charges of larceny and fraud.[114] The prosecution charged that Schiavone Construction tried to defraud the New York City Transit Authority out of $7.4 million.[115] The alleged fraud involved payments to

Jopel Construction, which was owned by William Masselli and fronted by a black state senator, Joseph Galiber, who had made no capital investment in the firm.[116] When Schiavone first subcontracted to Jopel Construction, satisfying a minority contracting requirement, the latter had no money, equipment or experience; Schiavone gave the company a $250,000 loan and $1 million worth of equipment.[117]

Donovan, who resigned his Labor post several months after the indictment, was acquitted along with the other defendants of all charges in May 1987.[118] The acquittal was based on stringent instructions from the judge that, for a guilty ruling, the jury had to find that Schiavone intended to defraud the Transit Authority the day the contract was awarded, not merely that fraud took place.[119] Ample evidence of fraud was in fact provided by Masselli's admission, recorded by the FBI, that though he made no considerable investment, he would be "guaranteed" at least $250,000 in illegal payoffs from Schiavone.[120] And Galiber had been recorded describing how he and Masselli would backdate documents to legitimize Schiavone's subcontract to Jopel.[121] Galiber also expressed concern that the arrangement would be discovered and that an exposé of it would appear on the "60 Minutes" television program.[122]

Although Donovan was acquitted on the fraud-related charges, evidence scrutinized in the trial further suggested his Mafia ties. In 892 secret FBI tapes of William Masselli's phone and office conversations, for example, Donovan, his company and other Schiavone executives were mentioned 351 times.[123] Just before Donovan was acquitted, however, President Reagan called him "a man of great integrity."[124] Neither these unsavory connections, the murders of two witnesses in the Silverman probe nor the perjury of two others was of apparent concern to the president.

ROY BREWER

Roy M. Brewer is another Reagan appointee, once boss of another Mob-tied union. His role can best be understood against the backdrop of a pivotal event in the Mob infiltration of Hollywood.

In 1934, the Mafia took over the International Alliance of Theatrical Stage Employees (IATSE), which represented studio-crafters, as part of a massive post-Prohibition assault on labor unions. The conquest was achieved when Syndicate gunmen descended upon the union's convention in Louisville and installed their front man as president, without one dissenting vote.[125] Following this takeover, the Mob used the union to muscle into Hollywood's movie studios, gaining a major influence that continues today.[126]

In 1937, when Ronald Reagan arrived in Hollywood, he could hardly have been naive about such workings of organized crime. Coming of age in northern Illinois during the roaring twenties, Reagan had worked as a sportscaster out of Des Moines, Iowa, cavorting with a crowd that drank and gambled at local speakeasies.[127] Conspicuous in those surroundings was the Chicago Capone gang's Des Moines auxiliary, whose special interests included college athletes, sportswriters and Hollywood movie studios.[128]

It was during his tenure in the late 1940s and 1950s as president of the Screen Actors Guild, another major Hollywood union, that Ronald Reagan got to know Roy Brewer. The event that drew them together was a jurisdictional fight between the AFL's Conference of Studio Unions and the gangster-infested IATSE, whose Hollywood operations Brewer ran.[129] The Conference asked the Screen Actors Guild for assistance in its battle with the IATSE.[130] But Reagan rebuffed the Conference's request, with the result that it was crushed with the help of IATSE goons.[131]

Brewer explained that with Reagan's help, he prevented "an effort by a communist group" to take over the IATSE.[132] Brewer also cited anti-Communism to justify his role in killing a screenplay by Arthur Miller about waterfront corruption.[133] The arbiter of the Hollywood Blacklist during the McCarthy era, Brewer recalled that he and Reagan became "close friends."[134]

In 1984, President Reagan appointed former IATSE boss Brewer to a sensitive labor post in the federal government.[135]

FRANK SINATRA, WILLIAM CASEY
AND GILBERT DOZIER

President Reagan's questionable judgment with respect to organized crime is further indicated by the following involvements and actions.

As Nixon had before him, Reagan made Frank Sinatra a prominent guest at the White House.[136] Reagan also awarded the singer a Presidential Medal of Freedom[137] and wrote him a glowing letter of recommendation for a casino license hearing before the Nevada Gaming Commission.[138] In contrast, Sinatra had been declared *persona non grata* at the Kennedy White House because of his extensive Mafia associations and dealings.[139] These have been documented in an unpublished 19-page Justice Department report and other sources.[140] Reagan's former CIA director, William Casey, who served from 1981 until just before his death in May 1987, had been the partner of an organized crime figure in an agribusiness firm that went bankrupt in 1971, after deceiving investors.[141] Casey appointed Max Hugel and sponsored William McCann, both linked to organized crime, for government positions.[142] Hugel was forced to resign, and the nomination of McCann was withdrawn, after the connections became known.[143] A strong push to dump Casey himself was stopped with the help of a lobbying effort spearheaded by Senator Paul Laxalt.[144]

In June 1984, Reagan caused a storm of protest in Louisiana by commuting the 18-year sentence of Gilbert Dozier.[145] Dozier is a former state official convicted of extortion and racketeering—the first Louisiana official ever convicted on a federal racketeering statute.[146] During his trial, prosecutors introduced testimony that Dozier had inquired about contracting to kill an individual associated with the case and charged that he had tried to bribe a juror.[147]

Up to that point, Reagan had received 588 commutation requests.[148] The 10 he granted, including Dozier's, were all to embezzlers and other whitecollar criminals.[149]

But there is another, strikingly different side to the Reagan record on organized crime. During his terms as president, federal prosecutors have brought more than one thousand largely successful indictments against Mafia figures throughout the nation.[150] These prosecutions have crippled the Mob's leadership in Boston, Chicago, Cleveland, Kansas City, Los Angeles, New Orleans and New York, and have struck at most of its other centers of operations.[151]

Especially damaging were prison sentences of 40 to 100 years handed down to three Mafia family bosses and five key associates in New York City.[152] The convictions were secured by crusading U.S. Attorney Rudolph Giuliani through a bold application of the federal Racketeer Influenced and Corrupt Organizations (RICO) Act against the New York branch of the Mafia's National Commission, whose existence was admitted by the defense.[153] The eight were found guilty of a pattern of racketeering activity that included murders, loan sharking, labor payoffs, and extortion that pushed the price of concrete in New York to almost double that in Philadelphia.[154] In a further precedent-setting application of the RICO statute, federal prosecutors recently filed a civil suit to seize the assets of the entire Brooklyn-based Bonanno Mafia family.[155] Yet potentially most significant of all is a civil RICO suit now being prepared by the Justice Department to put the entire Mob-dominated[156] Teamsters Union under federal trusteeship.[157]

Although tempered somewhat by this sweeping federal assault, the Mob's arrogant power is hardly a relic. Its influence continues to plague several national unions, including the Laborers International,[158] at whose 1981 convention a member was beaten in public view for daring to run against the Mafia's designated candidate for president, Angelo Fosco.[159] And it is still active in a broad spectrum of illegal operations,[160] such as toxic dumping, in which Mob-controlled brokers dispose of poisonous chemicals in woods, farmlands or gasoline dispensed to motorists.[161] Yet, as RICO author G. Robert Blakey observed, "The cases that have been made recently are incredibly significant."[162] He predicted that "if this can be sustained for another decade," the government could "decimate" the Mob.[163]

Law enforcement officials and experts attribute the recent federal victories against organized crime to several factors, the *New York Times* noted, most dating back a decade.[164] The starting point was a redirection of the FBI under J. Edgar Hoover's successors, Clarence Kelley and William Webster, toward making quality cases against the underworld.[165] Beginning in the mid-1970s, consistent with this new posture, the FBI began using undercover agents to infiltrate the Mob.[166] Other tools used with increasing effectiveness beginning in that era were the federal witness protection program, the RICO statute and electronic surveillance, while greater cooperation among agencies further strengthened law enforcement's hand.[167] This new approach began to bear fruit during the Carter Administration, as investigations and indictments were launched in ten cities against more than a dozen top Mafia bosses, including Tony Accardo, Joseph Bonanno, Raymond Patriarca, Carlos Marcello and Santos Trafficante.[168]

Funding for federal probes of organized crime was reduced sharply during the budget cuts of the early 1980s,[169] yet President Reagan set the tone for the continued federal anti-crime crusade through his repeated vows to "break the power of the Mob in America."[170] In a July 1983 speech to the FBI he declared, "I ask you to redouble your efforts to break apart and ultimately cripple the criminal syndicates in America."[171]

The government's posture toward the underworld, however, has been partially compromised by the darker side of Ronald Reagan's record. As noted earlier, Paul Laxalt applied pressure to rein in federal investigations of organized crime in Las Vegas, which FBI chief William Webster resisted. And prosecutions of union officials declined by 30 percent during Raymond Donovan's tenure as secretary of labor; Republican Senator Orrin Hatch called this "policy of inaction and ineptitude" a "travesty."[172]

President Reagan's own Commission on Organized Crime,

which he established in 1983, criticized his amicable relationship with Jackie Presser. The commission warned that further contacts with the Teamster chief could "lead to an erosion in public confidence and dampen the desire to end racketeering."[173] The commission also voiced concern about whether Teamster support of Reagan in the 1980 and 1984 elections had delayed the Justice Department's criminal investigation of Presser after federal prosecutors in Cleveland had recommended indictment.[174] And several commission members criticized the Justice Department for failing to apply the RICO statute to its full potential[175] and for not responding to questions about the performance of its Organized Crime and Racketeering Section.[176]

Despite these limitations, however, the major strides against organized crime during the 1980s reflect credit on President Reagan. But the debits — his friendship with Laxalt, his appointments of Presser, Donovan and Brewer, and his nonchalant support of Donovan as two witnesses against the labor secretary were murdered and Senate probers were threatened — cannot be ignored. And whatever their most palatable explanation, they reveal the shocking extent to which the Mafia has penetrated and been publicly accepted at the highest levels of American government. These Reagan appointments stand in sharp contrast to the relentless, fully committed attack on the Mob mobilized by John and Robert Kennedy — a national direction that was reversed only by assassination.

An even more insidious web of Mob corruption, with links to both the Nixon and Reagan Administrations, has been unraveled through a series of scandals in the Mob's birthplace, Italy. During the past 15 years, several extraordinary prosecutions have exposed corrupt alliances involving top Italian officials, leading financiers and even the Vatican. At the heart of this sinister network is a collaboration between elements of the intelligence community and of the Mafia, analogous to a suspected continuing relationship in the U.S. that surfaced during the anti-Castro campaign. These shocking revelations from the Italian example offer a penetrating glimpse into Mafia methods of the 1980s.

MICHELE SINDONA, FRANCESCO PAZIENZA
AND LICIO GELLI

The saga begins with Michele Sindona, a lawyer and wartime trader in Sicily during the 1940s who within two decades became one of Europe's wealthiest financiers.[177] By the mid 1970s, his multibillion-dollar empire included six banks in four countries, Italy's largest hotel chain, the CIA-linked Rome *Daily American* and roughly 500 corporations around the world.[178] His most significant American holding, whose board of directors he chaired, was the Franklin National Bank of New York,[179] the nation's 19th largest.[180] Sindona shared his financial acumen in packed lecture halls at such schools as Harvard, MIT and the University of Chicago.[181]

He also had friends in high places, reportedly including Richard Nixon.[182] Before becoming president, Nixon referred several clients to Sindona.[183] Later, Sindona offered a $1 million contribution to the 1972 Nixon reelection drive on condition of anonymity[184] and oversaw efforts to get Nixon the Italian-American vote.[185] While president, Nixon authorized millions of dollars, funneled through Sindona's banks, to finance covert activities against the Italian left.[186]

Beneath his veil of power and prestige, however, Sindona was a Sicilian Mafioso of the highest rank. At a 1957 conclave of top-ranking Sicilian and American Mafiosi in Palermo, Sindona was named the Mob's head banker, in charge of investing profits from the trans-Atlantic heroin trade.[187] The American Mafia was always coming to Sindona, according to his son, and saying "Don Michele, you are the greatest of all Sicilians. . . . Tell us whom you want killed. Tell us who these bastards are. . . . We murder only for our friends."[188]

In 1974, the collapse of the Sindona-controlled Franklin National Bank of New York sent his empire crashing down. The largest bank failure in United States history,[189] this triggered the collapse of the Banca Privata Italiana of Milan and other lending institutions he controlled.[190] Authorities later detailed

the intricate steps by which Sindona allegedly looted the Milan banks he controlled to come up with the funds to buy Franklin National, then drained deposits from Franklin National to put funds back in his Italian institutions. All of the funds made the trip from Italy to the U.S. via Switzerland, most of the time through a Zurich bank that Sindona also controlled.[191]*

In 1980, Sindona was sentenced to 25 years in U.S. federal prison for fraud, misappropriation of funds and perjury in connection with the Franklin National draining.[197] Two years later, Italy indicted Sindona and 75 other Mafiosi in a massive heroin conspiracy.[198] He was then extradited to Italy and convicted in 1986 for yet another crime: ordering the gangland-style slaying of the Italian judge charged with liquidating Sindona's fortune.[199] Four days after receiving a life sentence for the killing, Sindona collapsed in his jail cell and died soon thereafter in a Milan area hospital; the cause of death, cyanide poisoning.[200]

The trail of Sindona's schemes led to another major scandal in Italy, involving the so-called Propaganda Due, or P2. A clandestine masonic lodge based in Italy, P2's membership included the heads of Italy's intelligence agencies, three government ministers, 43 members of Italy's Parliament, several Italian and South American generals and admirals, plus judges, journalists and businessmen.[201] Several top Mafiosi also belonged, including Italy's "boss of bosses" Michele Greco, the chairman of the Syndicate's ruling commission,[202] who is now under indictment for 90 murders.[203] Sindona, too, was among P2's ranks, handling its finances.[204] The lodge's membership roster was discovered in 1981, when police raided the villa of its grandmaster, Licio Gelli,[205] who had zealously supported the Italian dictator Benito

---

*Another Sindona financial scheme involved the Gulf & Western Corporation. In a 1970 transaction, Gulf & Western purchased 15 million shares of Società Generale Immobiliare, an Italian conglomerate dominated by Sindona, and listed them on its books at one-and-one-half times their market value.[192] Sindona, in turn, purchased a Hollywood holding from the American conglomerate at double its assessed value.[193] The SEC charged Sindona and Gulf & Western Chairman Charles Bludhorn with violating securities laws by trading worthless stock back and forth to create a false market; the two agreed to stop, and the commission dropped the charges.[194] Gulf & Western was involved in other questionable financial dealings,[195] and additional circumstances suggest links to organized crime.[196]

Mussolini.[206] The revelation was a fatal embarrassment to premier Arnaldo Forlani's government, causing it to topple the following year.[207]

P2 functioned as a "state within a state"[208] whose goal, according to an Italian parliamentary commission, was the surreptitious control of the nation.[209] With Sindona's financial backing, the fiercely anticommunist society conspired in at least three unsuccessful coups against leftist governments in Italy[210] and assisted dictators in Latin America.[211] Its fundraising activities have included kidnapping wealthy businessmen, drug trafficking in South America[212] and helping fascist fugitives smuggle their money out of Europe after World War II (for a 40 percent cut).[213] Wedding the Mafia and Italian intelligence, P2 can be seen as a formal analogue to U.S. Mob-CIA collusion, which has been virtually untraceable since the anti-Castro alliance of the early 1960s.[214]

This sinister web extended further still with the involvement of Sindona and possibly P2 in subversion of the Vatican. In the spring of 1969, Sindona received a private audience with Pope Paul VI,[215] who had been seeking to reform the Church's financial administration by diversifying its assets.[216] By the time Sindona had kissed the papal ring and departed, the Pope had given Sindona control over a large part of the Vatican's wealth.[217] And by January 1975, the Vatican had lost approximately $240 million from Sindona's financial manipulations.[218] Perturbed by these huge losses, and perhaps haunted by his meeting with Sindona, Pope Paul remarked, "perhaps only the hand of an oppressor can free Us and the Church from it all. Satan may overleap himself."[219]

Less than a decade later, the Vatican took another major loss through the machinations of two Sindona protégés,[220] Roberto Calvi and Archbishop Paul Marcinkus. Calvi, a member of P2, was a key financial advisor to the Vatican.[221] He was also president of Banco Ambrosiano, Italy's largest private bank,[222] which collapsed in August 1982 after "the apparent looting of $1.4 billion."[223] According to investigators, the money was funneled from Italy to Luxembourg, back to Italy, then to Nicaragua, Peru and finally Panama where it "seems to have disappeared."[224]

Archbishop Marcinkus, the head of the Vatican bank, facilitated the fraud by vouching for Calvi's transactions.[225] Also a freemason,[226] Marcinkus was a former papal bodyguard[227] from Cicero, Illinois with no prior experience in finance.[228]

As investigators closed in on Marcinkus' role in the Ambrosiano looting, William Wilson, ambassador to the Vatican and a close friend of President Ronald Reagan, intervened. In 1982, Wilson wrote a letter on behalf of the archbishop to Attorney General William French Smith to determine whether Marcinkus was being probed by the U.S. government and to vouch for his good character.[229] Wilson subsequently invited Smith to a breakfast in his Rome villa when Smith was in Italy, with Marcinkus to be present.[230] Smith declined, his aides alarmed at the impropriety of such a meeting.[231]

In 1984, the Vatican bank paid $244 million to Banco Ambrosiano creditors "as recognition of moral responsibility" for Marcinkus' involvement.[232] Three years later, despite Wilson's earlier efforts, Italian officials issued an arrest warrant for Marcinkus and two associates, charging them with conspiring to commit fraud in connection with the bank dealings.[233] But deferring to Vatican immunity from Italian law, Italy's highest court nullified the warrants,[234] allowing Marcinkus' continued silence. The silence of other parties privy to the Sindona and Calvi banking scandals had been assured: seven people met violent or untimely deaths, and one, Ambrosiano's vice president, narrowly escaped a murder attempt.[235] Bank president Roberto Calvi was found hanging from a London bridge in 1982.[236]

The one person who had the power and determination to put an early end to the Vatican bank's shady involvements was Pope John Paul I. Shortly after his ascent in 1978, as David Yallop's *In God's Name* reports, John Paul began a personal investigation of Marcinkus' handling of the Church's finances.[237] And on September 28, he made known his intention to remove Marcinkus and three other Calvi cronies in the Vatican bank and to replace several high-ranking Vatican officials with questionable involvements.[238]

On September 29, 33 days after becoming Pope, John Paul was found dead. No autopsy was performed, and the cause of death was obscured by contradictory reports and destroyed evidence.[239] John Paul, a recreational mountain climber, had been declared in excellent health just days before.[240] Yallop, two of whose previous books caused cases to be reopened in Britain, names P2 grandmaster Gelli as the mastermind of a plot to kill the Pope.[241]

Three years after the death of Pope John Paul, his successor, John Paul II, was the target of an assassination attempt. His assailant, Ali Agca, was a notorious terrorist affiliated with the extreme right-wing Turkish Gray Wolves.[242] According to the *Washington Post*, "a laborious three-year investigation by Italian authorities" established beyond doubt that shots fired by Agca were the workings of "a conspiracy to kill the pontiff."[243] Indeed, after first claiming that he acted alone, Agca changed his story to implicate two sponsors, upon which public suspicion then focused: the Bulgarian secret service and the Soviet KGB.[244] Yet there are several indications that the Bulgarian connection was fabricated through intelligence and Mob channels, with a possible assist from a future player in the Iran-Contra affair.

Giovanni Pandico, a Mafia defector who was turning state's evidence in a massive trial of gangsters, charged that while in a nearby prison cell, he witnessed a senior military intelligence agent and his deputy coach Agca on the story.[245] Pandico fingered the deputy, Francesco Pazienza, as the mastermind of the cover-up[246] and said the Naples branch of the Mafia was involved.[247] Pazienza, an Italian Mafia-intelligence liaison with reputed ties to the American Mob and the CIA,[248] was in fact a source for the leading journalistic exponent of Bulgarian culpability, Claire Sterling.[249] And he was convicted of misusing his intelligence position to blame the left for right-wing terrorism in an unrelated matter.[250] Also convicted of criminal association with Mobsters,[251] Pazienza is currently under indictment in several criminal cases, including the Ambrosiano scandal.[252]

Agca, the Pope's assailant, provided further hints that the Bulgarian connection was fabricated. Pressed by an Italian judge, Agca admitted inventing charges about the Bulgarians, although denying he was coached to do so,[253] but later testified that Pazienza had offered him favors to implicate them.[254] An Italian magistrate, however, dropped an investigation into charges that

Agca had been so coached, citing insufficient evidence.[255] Yet this possibility is supported by an Italian court's acquittal of the three accused Bulgarians in March 1986.[256]

A clue to the origin of the Bulgarian accusation was provided by Agca's alleged coach, Pazienza himself. According to *The Nation*, Pazienza said that Michael Ledeen, an American expert on Italian fascism, was the person responsible for inventing the Bulgarian connection.[257] This contention is plausible given the close collaboration of Ledeen, who became a Reagan Administration advisor, with all the key players in the alleged fabrication.

The *Wall Street Journal* reported that Italian military intelligence, closely linked to P2, paid Ledeen more than $100,000 for various services in 1980 and 1981, which Ledeen admits.[258] Several sources, including Alexander Haig,[259] former U.S. Ambassador to Italy Richard Gardner,[260] and an Italian indictment[261] have noted close and repeated collusion between Ledeen and Pazienza.[262] A friend of Claire Sterling, the prime proponent of Bulgarian culpability, Ledeen is also rumored to have worked for the CIA in Italy.[263] That intelligence agency was another apparent promoter of the Bulgarian story, sacking its Rome station chief when he refused to swallow it, according to a published account.[264]

Among other joint ventures between Ledeen and Pazienza, who later became Italy's number one fugitive,[265] was an effort to sabotage Jimmy Carter's 1980 reelection bid by discrediting his brother Billy.* Shortly after Ronald Reagan took office, the State Department appointed Ledeen a special advisor on international terrorism;[272] Pazienza had served the Italian government in the same capacity.[273] Ledeen later became a high-level consultant on

---

*Shortly before the 1980 election, an article appeared in *The New Republic* reporting that Billy Carter had met with leaders of the Palestine Liberation Organization and accepted $50,000 from Libya.[266] The article, which touched off the "Billygate scandal," was written by Michael Ledeen and now *Washington Times* Editor-in-Chief Arnaud de Borchgrave.[267] Their source: Francesco Pazienza.[268] Pazienza explained that he fed Ledeen the information because he and the P2-controlled intelligence service for which he worked wanted the election tilted against President Carter.[269] Pazienza was indicted in 1985 in Italy for fraudulently obtaining this information "in collaboration with Ledeen" and then having it published.[270] Ledeen was not charged and has refused to discuss Pazienza's version of events with the press.[271]

the National Security Council, where he was given a key role in arranging the infamous U.S. arms-for-hostages deal with Iran.[274]

While Ledeen was promoted, his collaborator was indicted, not only for the Billy Carter affair,[275] but also in connection with a bloody terrorist attack. On August 2, 1980, as resort-bound Italian and foreign tourists crowded Italy's Bologna railroad station, a massive bomb ripped through a waiting room.[276] The explosion left 85 people dead and 200 others injured.[277] It was the worst terrorist strike in postwar Europe.[278]

After a six-year probe, the Italian government indicted 15 people for the attack and subsequent cover-up, including two former secret service chiefs and several organized crime figures.[279] Investigating magistrates believe that the bombing was carried out to destabilize the Italian government and push it politically rightward.[280] The prosecution charged it was part of a broader conspiracy by organized crime, the secret services and P2 "to control the state's institutions."[281] Pazienza's role, according to the indictment, was planting false clues to subvert the investigation.[282] Another defendant in the pending trial is P2 grandmaster Licio Gelli, now a fugitive believed to be hiding in South America.[283]

In 1981, shortly before fleeing multiple criminal indictments, Gelli had been an honored guest at Ronald Reagan's inaugural ball.[284] He came at the invitation of Philip A. Guarino, who was then and remains national chairman of an Italian-American division within the U.S. Republican National Committee.[285] Guarino, who admitted that Gelli "had a better seat than I did,"[286] is also a member of P2.[287]

Further contact between the two P2 comrades was discovered when police raided Gelli's villa in 1981.[288] There they found an exchange of letters between Gelli and Guarino discussing ways to help "our brother, Michele," referring to Sindona, another P2 member.[289] Sindona, who had curried the Italian-American vote for Nixon as Guarino did for Reagan, was then on trial in New York.[290] Gelli also wrote a letter of support to Ronald Reagan offering to ensure favorable coverage for him in the Italian press.[291] The powerful Italian used his influence in a major publishing empire to do exactly that.[292]

The Reagan Administration's link to these Italian scandals, though at low levels, hints of deeper, troubling parallels. Like the schemers across the ocean, the president has countenanced the use of unsavory partnerships and methods to further a political agenda. Moreover, two policy developments of his presidency find disturbing counterparts in Mob ideology and perhaps reflect traces of the Mob's insidious, post-assassination influence in American politics.

A classic Mob scam is to assume control of a thriving business and drain its wealth through massive loans based on its previously good financial standing. During President Reagan's two terms, Americans have been steered along in an orgy of consumption that has tripled the national debt from $645 billion to $2 trillion and turned the world's largest creditor nation into the world's largest debtor.[293] As domestic investment dwindles and the nation's productive base stagnates, the indulgent charge toward more paper profits and foreign subsidies continues.[294]

Organized crime's "ultimate solution to everything is to kill somebody," as one defector observed.[295] During the early years of Ronald Reagan's presidency, military force became the prime instrument of U.S. foreign policy. Patterned after a perceived Soviet menace and financed by the ballooning deficit, the biggest peacetime weapons buildup in U.S. history was conducted.[296] This obsessive reliance on weaponry was no better exhibited than in the 1985 covert U.S. arms sales to Iran—ostensibly a good-will gesture—while that nation was known to be sponsoring terrorism against American citizens.

As with the record on organized crime, however, these disturbing trends may be overshadowed by a welcome development: President Reagan's signing of the INF treaty, with the hope of subsequent substantial reductions in U.S. and Soviet nuclear arsenals. This initiative recalls the national leadership of two decades earlier, when it was America that was charting the world's course with an enlightened agenda. By creating the Peace Corps, negotiating a nuclear test ban treaty, and working toward peaceful global coexistence, President Kennedy was establishing a new order that did not include killing as a problem-solving technique. And in his domestic crusade against organized crime, Kennedy was striving for a society that would not include killers in positions of power.

The killers struck back at President Kennedy, aborting his visionary program and reasserting their insidious national influence. The time has come for us to reclaim the America of our martyred leader.

Epilogue

Since *Contract on America* first appeared in hardcover, several striking developments have further exposed the Mafia's role in the murder of President Kennedy. These include a new book by historian John H. Davis and three television documentaries aired in the United States and Britain during the fall of 1988. I am gratified that each used my book to varying degrees and extended facets of the case against the Mob. The world-wide acceptance of these combined investigative achievements over the past year has been especially satisfying.

John H. Davis's book, *Mafia Kingfish: Carlos Marcello and the Assassination of John F. Kennedy* (New York: McGraw-Hill, 1989), focuses on the role of the New Orleans Mafia boss. It was Marcello, remember, who spoke in 1962 of his specific intent to have Kennedy killed and who was linked to several assassination suspects.

Among Davis' startling revelations is the testimony of Georgia businessman Gene Sumner. During a trip to New Orleans around March of 1963, Sumner dined at the Town and Country restaurant. That establishment was owned by the Marcellos and served as Carlos' headquarters. While eating there, Sumner observed the restaurant manager pass a wad of money under the table to a young man. The man left with his date soon afterward without ordering any food or drinks.

After the assassination, Sumner recognized the young man who had received the money as Oswald. He immediately contacted local police in Georgia, who transmitted his allegation to the Savannah FBI. The FBI interviewed Sumner and investigated further. The restaurant manager whom Sumner closely described turned out to be Joseph Poretto—a top lieutenant of Carlos Marcello.

Sumner's report that Oswald received money from a Marcello underboss early in 1963 was highly significant. It was also credible, since Sumner was a respected businessman who later became the mayor of Darien, Georgia. Yet, incredibly, the FBI dropped its probe after Poretto and Anthony Marcello denied any contact with Oswald. Equally shocking, FBI Director J. Edgar Hoover withheld from the Warren Commission the most significant documents related to Sumner's allegations.

More generally, Davis cites dozens of FBI documents suggesting Marcello's assassination culpability that Hoover withheld from the Warren Commission. In fact, the record shows that eight Marcello associates were questioned in connection with the JFK murder in the months following. But as a result of Hoover's censorship, the Commission learned virtually none of this.

Among other FBI information partially misreported by Hoover was an FBI interview of Eugene De Laparra. A generally reliable informant, De Laparra was a part-time worker at Tregle's Bar in New Orleans. In the spring of 1963, De Laparra overheard Marcello-connected bar owner Ben Tregle tell two other men: "There is a price on the President's head, and other members of the Kennedy family. Somebody will kill Kennedy when he comes down South."

De Laparra related this conversation to the FBI a few days after the assassination. He later recounted another incident, in which Tony Marcello had come to service the bar's pinball machine and announced to Tregle: "The word is out to get the Kennedy family."

More incriminating remarks from the Marcello clan were reported by Joseph Hauser, an undercover witness in an FBI sting operation (BRILAB), which put Carlos in prison in 1980. In one of many conversations with Carlos's brother Joe, Hauser brought up the presidential aspirations of Teddy Kennedy. Joe then boasted to Hauser, concerning the Kennedys: "Don't worry, we took care of 'em, didn't we?" On another occasion, during a session with Carlos Marcello and two underworld associates, Hauser heard one, Phillip Rizzuto, say: "Yeah, so we put *him* out of business!" referring to Robert Kennedy.

Hauser also elicited a significant admission from Mafia boss Carlos himself: that Oswald had worked in Marcello's bookmaking network during the summer of 1963. This admission squared with Oswald's close contacts in 1963 with two Marcello underlings, Dutz Murret and David Ferrie. Disturbingly, three tapes from the FBI's BRILAB investigation that are believed to contain further incriminating statements by Marcello about the JFK assassination were put under seal by a federal judge.

Davis presents additional evidence of conspiracy and cover-up related to a reported visit of Oswald to Mexico City. In late September of 1963, a man representing himself as Oswald visited the Soviet and Cuban embassies there seeking a visa to the Soviet Union. To the point of being obnoxious, the man repeatedly called attention to his purported identity and history of pro-Castro activism. Yet testimony by embassy personnel, photographs and background information about the visitor have convincingly indicated that he was an impostor, not Oswald.

Recent developments related by Davis render this conclusion inescapable. In a classified report, Edwin Lopez, an investigator for the House Assassinations Committee, determined that CIA surveillance photos covering three purported visits of Oswald to the Cuban Embassy did not show Oswald. In a follow-up interview for public TV's "Kwitny Report" (see below), Lopez explained that these strips of photos were complete sequential records for the times in question and positively precluded an Oswald visit.

Davis further discloses a top secret memo written by J. Edgar Hoover reporting a determination by FBI agents that the Mexico City visitor "was not Lee Harvey Oswald." Characteristically, Hoover withheld this critical finding from the Warren Commission. The record of the Mexico City incident thus shows a conspiracy to frame Oswald and link him to Cuba, compounded by a brazen Hoover cover-up.

Unfortunately, advocacy of this discredited Castro link to the JFK murder weakened an otherwise constructive documentary, "American Exposé: Who Murdered JFK?," by columnist Jack Anderson, which aired on November 2, 1988. Among Anderson's many disclosures indicating Mob culpability were statements by Esther Ann Mash, a former cocktail waitress at Jack Ruby's Carousel Club in 1962 and 1963. Consistent with several other accounts to the Warren Commission, Mash said that she saw Oswald and several well-dressed gangster types meet with Ruby at his club.

A second report of Ruby-Oswald contact was among the evidence presented in the British Central Independent Television documentary, "Viewpoint '88 Special: The Men Who Killed Kennedy," which aired on October 25. The source of this account was Beverly Oliver, a singer at the neighboring Colony Club who often visited Ruby's club during her breaks. Two weeks before the assassination, Oliver saw Jack Ruby there at a table with stripper Jada and another man whom Ruby introduced to Oliver as Lee. Oliver realized after the assassination that the man was Oswald.

Another witness who appeared on the British documentary, Dallas policeman Don Ray Archer, offered a chilling footnote to the final Ruby-Oswald encounter. Archer, who took Ruby into custody after he shot Oswald, was struck by Ruby's extremely nervous and agitated behavior. But then a policeman brought Ruby the news that Oswald had died: "Jack, it looks like it's going to be the electric chair." Ruby immediately relaxed, Archer recounted. Archer observed that it seemed as if Ruby's life had depended on killing Oswald.

The British documentary broke further new ground, including compelling photographic and eyewitness evidence of a shot from the grassy knoll. But most dramatic and controversial was its naming of three Corsican Mob figures, two of them still alive, as the gunmen in Dealey Plaza. The three allegedly had intelligence ties and were hired by the American Mafia to kill Kennedy.

Prior to the airing of the program, American investigator Steve Rivele was threatened by one of the accused, whom he tried to question. Afterward, the two living suspects supplied alibis for their whereabouts on November 22, 1963, but one later changed his story. The documentary's producer, Nigel Turner, stood by his report; Rivele went into hiding. A year earlier, Rivele had furnished these accusations to the U.S. Justice Department, which did nothing about them.

The third television documentary about the JFK killing was a special by public TV's "Kwitny Report" that aired on November 1, 1988. The program concluded that the Mob killed Kennedy based upon many significant disclosures, including an on-camera statement of Kefauver Committee counsel Joe Nellis. Nellis said that during the Congressional committee's probe of interstate organized crime in the 1950s, Jack Ruby's name came up in connection with hijackings in several states. The committee found after briefly questioning Ruby that he never did anything in Chicago without the Mob's approval. The Kwitny Report also featured an audiotape made by journalist Dan Moldea in which James Hoffa, Jr. stated that his father had known Ruby since 1939.

Ruby's victim, Lee Harvey Oswald, was also the subject of recent attention. In a November *Ladies' Home Journal* interview, his widow, Marina, said that the Warren Commission had manipulated her to portray Lee as the lone assassin. Marina expressed her belief that Lee was part of a broader assassination plot that included organized crime.

Yet my best insight into the Warren Commission's workings was provided by Judge Burt Griffin, the staff attorney who investigated Jack Ruby. In a lengthy and cordial October 1988 interview, Griffin told me that his probe of Ruby had been severely restricted by lack of time, staff and information. Given just six months to conduct his probe, Griffin told me he had complained to Commission chief counsel J. Lee Rankin: "There's no way we're going to do this job in the period of time we're talking about."

Griffin felt particularly frustrated by the lack of cooperation he received from the FBI and CIA. Indeed, without the benefit of key FBI documents withheld by J. Edgar Hoover, Griffin had no framework from which to consider the Mob as a serious suspect. And when he queried the CIA in a February 1964 memo about Ruby's numerous underworld contacts, he received no response. Equally outrageous was the Warren Commission's exclusion of Griffin, its only staffer who knew anything about Jack Ruby, from Ruby's June 1964 hearing in Dallas.

This exclusion of Griffin from Ruby's interrogation was protested vigorously by another staff attorney, David Belin. While Judge Griffin has neither accepted nor ruled out JFK conspiracy theories, Belin, however, has staunchly defended the Commission's lone-assassin conclusion. Belin recently advanced this position in *Final Disclosure: The Full Truth About the Assassination of President Kennedy* (New York: Charles Scribner's Sons), published in November 1988.

Although sincere, Belin's strident arguments repeatedly depart from the record. For example, he asserts that Jack Ruby's polygraph test cleared him of conspiracy. But in fact, a panel of polygraph experts commissioned by the House Assassinations Committee found that Ruby's test "was not validly conducted."

Because of "numerous procedural errors," the panel concluded, the test was impossible to interpret. Moreover, the House committee determined from conflicting testimony and records that Ruby lied at least twice during the polygraph session.

Amazingly, Belin advances two alibis that Ruby told his rabbi, Hillel Silverman—both of which Ruby himself later admitted fabricating! One was Ruby's account to Silverman that he had killed Oswald to spare Jacqueline and Caroline Kennedy the anguish of a trial. But in a note smuggled from his jail cell, published in 1967 by *Newsweek* (see chapter 12), Ruby flatly admitted inventing that story to bolster his trial defense.

The second story Belin heard through Silverman was that Ruby had been carrying a gun at the assassination-night press conference and could have killed Oswald then if he were part of a conspiracy. But when asked about carrying a gun that night in his subsequent June hearing, Ruby testified: "I will be honest with you. I lied about it. It isn't so. I didn't have a gun."

Another previously quoted statement from that June hearing was especially noteworthy. If the shooting of Oswald were timed "so perfectly by seconds," Ruby told the Warren Commission, "then someone in the police department is guilty of giving the information as to when Lee Harvey Oswald was coming down." This possibility is ominously credible, as noted earlier, given that two police friends of Ruby with key roles in the Oswald transfer—Sheriff Bill Decker and Sergeant Patrick Dean—were closely linked to Joseph Civello, Dallas Mafia boss of that era.

Sergeant Dean had in fact dined with Civello shortly after Civello returned to Dallas from the Apalachin Mafia convention in 1957 (an observation of the House Assassinations Committee that I had overlooked). Recall that Dean, the officer in charge of security when Oswald was shot, flunked a polygraph test on how Ruby entered the police basement. And according to a Dallas acquaintance, the recently deceased Dean was evasive about his actions on November 24, 1963.

The 1968 assassination of Robert Kennedy has also been the focus of recent developments. On April 19, 1988, the State of California finally opened to the public the police files on that killing. But the state's chief archivist disclosed, amazingly, that 2,400 photographs of the crime scene and other crucial evidence had been destroyed by police. These photos might have revealed who pumped four bullets into RFK point blank from behind, under the cover of Sirhan Sirhan's flashing revolver.

In chapter 21, I related an allegation of Mob ties to Thane Eugene Cesar, the substitute security guard who drew his gun directly behind Robert Kennedy during the shooting. I also noted that Sirhan was close to Mobster Frank Donneroummas, alias Henry Ramistella, and had written in his diary about receiving money from Donneroummas. Author John Davis alludes to additional indications of organized crime connections to both Cesar and Sirhan.

In summary, these recent developments reconfirm that the Mafia killed President Kennedy and very possibly his brother Robert as well. The evidence mandates that the U.S. government finally render justice for these assassinations and stop the ongoing subversions of its sovereignty. Our martyred leaders and new generations of idealists deserve no less.

Recommendations

On November 22, 1963, President John F. Kennedy was assassinated in Dallas, the victim of a Mafia conspiracy. Five years later, his brother Robert, who had spearheaded the Kennedy anti-crime crusade, was also murdered. The Mob prospered with their deaths, and policies the brothers had tried to pursue perished with them. The circumstances of both killings were long shrouded by cover-up.

These revelations mandate a national response. To begin, the following measures are urged:

- That, as a first step toward an eventual indictment, the Department of Justice conduct a thorough investigation of all evidence suggesting the involvement of Carlos Marcello, the one suspected principal still alive, in a conspiracy to assassinate President John F. Kennedy.
- That the files on the Robert F. Kennedy assassination, now being processed at the California State Archives, be opened to the public as expeditiously as possible in their uncensored versions[1] and that an objective official reexamination of the case be conducted.
- That the federal Racketeer Influenced and Corrupt Organizations (RICO) Act be aggressively applied against the Mafia with the eventual goal of eliminating it from our national life.
- That, in the event of another presidential assassination in which underworld complicity is indicated, the government take strong and immediate measures to neutralize the Mob. If necessary, this counterattack could include use of military force, as sanctioned under title 10, sections 332 and 333 of the U.S. Code.[2]
- That Americans support political candidates who promote effective action against organized crime. It is further urged that

Americans refuse to patronize Mob-tainted enterprises, including certain casinos in Las Vegas and Atlantic City. Through these and other democratic options, it is within our power to overcome the pernicious repercussions of the November 22, 1963 assassination in Dallas and fulfill the promise of the Kennedy years.

Appendix 1
Additional Background
on Jack Ruby

FURTHER UNDERWORLD
CONTACTS OF JACK RUBY

Bobby Joe Chapman was a Dallas bookmaker who reportedly operated in partnership with James Dolan,[1] a notorious Mafia associate.[2] Chapman was one of 11 men arrested by the FBI on January 18, 1972 in a series of gambling raids in Dallas.[3] An envelope marked "The Dallas Cowboys Football Club," containing $10,000 in $100 bills, was returned to Chapman after charges against the 11 men were dropped "to protect confidential informants."[4]

Contacts with Ruby. On December 13, 1963, Chapman told the FBI that he had known Ruby for "about ten or twelve years."[5] The notation "Bobby Chapman, DA4-4139" was found on a slip of paper with four other names in Ruby's auto.[6]

An FBI report described James Henry Dolan as one of the two most notorious hoodlums in Dallas.[7] Dolan boasts an arrest record spanning seven states, with convictions for operating a racetrack swindle, impersonating a federal officer, violating parole, possessing burglary tools, and arson.[8] Although his record does not reflect the judicial immunity given a ranking organized crime figure, his roster of associates includes Mob heavies Santos Trafficante, Nofio Pecora, Irwin Weiner, James Fratianno, Russell D. Matthews, and Eugene Hale Brading.[9] From 1958 to 1961, Dolan served as the Dallas representative of the American Guild of Variety Artists (AGVA), a union representing night club entertainers.[10]

Contacts with Ruby. Dolan saw Ruby frequently during his term as Dallas AGVA representative.[11] Dolan and Ruby even produced one musical together, which they expropriated from a musician in Dolan's AGVA membership.[12] Dolan also met Jack Ruby in Dallas about two months before the assassination.[13]

Joseph Locurto, alias Joseph Bonds,[14] had a criminal record dating back to 1930.[15] It shows six arrests in three states on charges including assault to murder, attempted grand larceny, rape, and sodomy, with a conviction and jail sentence on the last charge.[16]

Contacts with Ruby. Joseph Locurto and Jack Ruby were partners in the Vegas Club in the early 1950s and were close associates between 1948 and 1954, according to Ruby, Locurto, and other sources.[17]

Isadore Max Miller, whose name appeared on the Seidband list of Dallas gamblers,[18] was a principal in one of Dallas' three most important bookmaking operations.[19] Among the men Miller hired as collectors were hoodlums Russell D. Matthews and James Dolan.[20] Although Miller had been engaged in illicit gambling operations since the 1930s,[21] he was first convicted in 1965, on federal gambling charges.[22]

Contacts with Ruby. Miller told the FBI that he had known Jack Ruby since 1949.[23] Both his name and his brother's (Dave L. Miller) were found among Ruby's personal effects.[24]

Meyer Panitz made a full swing in the Mob-dominated[25] gambling circuit, from bookmaker[26] to box man in Dallas crap games for Lewis McWillie;[27] then from employee of the Capri Hotel in Cuba,[28] in which Santos Trafficante held a major interest,[29] to box man in the Lansky-owned[30] Thunderbird Hotel in Las Vegas.[31] Panitz was "a very close friend" of Mobster Lewis McWillie.[32]

Contacts with Ruby. Panitz told the FBI he was a "good friend of Ruby's," from 1947 to 1958, when Panitz lived in Dallas.[33] McWillie concurred that Panitz was a "close friend" of Ruby.[34] In the summer of 1959, Panitz met Ruby in Miami on two occasions.[35] These meetings were arranged as a result of a phone call to Panitz from McWillie in Cuba.[36] Panitz told the FBI he called Ruby in mid-1963 "while passing through Dallas, Texas."[37]

Johnny Ross Patrono owned a Dallas liquor store[38] and operated a night club.[39] He was also bookmaker,[40] reportedly in partnership with Bobby Chapman and James Dolan.[41]

Contacts with Ruby. In an FBI interview of December 18, 1963, Patrono said that he had "known Jack Ruby for about seven or eight years," and had once received a $500 loan from him.[42] Joseph Campisi and another witness described Patrono as a friend of Ruby.[43] Patrono told the FBI that he visited Ruby at the Carousel Club "about the middle of November, 1963." [44]

The FBI identified Jack Yanover and Pasquale Stella as co-owners of the Dream Way Bar in Cicero, Illinois,[45] a strip joint and gambling operation run by Chicago hoodlums.[46] Ruby's sister Eva Grant testified that Yanover had "upped himself from racketeering" to a position with the American Guild of Variety Artists in Chicago.[47] But given the widespread collusion between this union and the Mob, exposed in 1962 Senate hearings,[48] it is more likely that Yanover's position represented a rise in, rather than out of, racketeering.

Contacts with Ruby. Telephone records show an 11-minute call placed on May 12, 1963 from the Carousel Club to the Dream Way Bar in Cicero, Illinois.[49] Since Ruby's brother Hyman[50] and his sister Eva Grant[51] reported that they knew Yanover, it appears that this call was from Ruby to Yanover.

Considered in chapter 6 were amazing statements by the Warren Commission claiming denials of Ruby's Mob connections by "virtually all of Ruby's Chicago friends" and by "numerous persons." Of similar character was the following Commission assertion: "Both State and Federal officials have indicated that Ruby was not affiliated with organized crime activity."[52] When the evidence is examined, this claim proves equally flimsy.

One of the state officials cited by the Warren Commission was Charles Batchelor, assistant chief of the Dallas Police, whose pertinent statement was that "Ruby's operation has not been a troublesome one for the Dallas Police Department."[53] Indeed, as already shown, Ruby's operations and other Syndicate activities were quite rewarding to much of the force. Batchelor's additional assertion that "the crime and vice problem in Dallas was not a substantial one"[54] called his judgment further into question.

The other state reference cited by the Commission was William F. Alexander, a Dallas assistant district attorney,[55] whose signed Carousel pass card was found among Ruby's possessions,[56] and who spoke with Ruby the day before the assassination.[57] Alexander told the FBI that he didn't know of any connection between Ruby and the underworld.[58] If there was such a connection, he believed that "it would have come to the attention of his office."[59] This is remarkably similar to a statement of Dallas Police Detective E. E. Carlson concerning Ruby's ties to hoodlum Joseph Locurto, alias Joseph Bonds.[60] Detective Carlson advised the FBI he knew "more about Ruby than any other officer in the Dallas Police Department," and asserted that "he [knew] of no association whatever between Bonds and Ruby and [felt] certain if there was such an association, he, Carlson, would be aware of it."[61] Yet Bonds and Ruby were business partners and close associates until Bonds left Dallas in 1954;[62] this relationship was reported by Ruby,[63] Bonds,[64] and several other witnesses.[65] So much for the cited state officials.

The remaining references provided for the quoted Commission assertion were two federal sources which discussed the clientele of Ruby's Carousel Club.[66] An FBI report asserted that the Carousel was not "frequented by any known criminal element."[67] And FBI Director J. Edgar Hoover testified that it "wasn't any so-called 'Joint. . . .' It was just another night-club."[68]

Although hardly relevant to the issue of Ruby's criminal affiliation,[69] Hoover's observation was quite correct. The Carousel Club certainly was no joint (unlike one of Ruby's earlier clubs, the Silver Spur—a Mob hangout[70] where "you could get exonerated for murder easier than you could for burglary"[71]). The Carousel was a classy establishment, where prostitution dates ran $100 a night.[72] Its patrons were generally well-dressed, as was customer Lewis McWillie, who could pass for "a doctor or a lawyer."[73] Visitors to the Carousel were not unmannerly, two-bit thugs, but prominent underworld figures: including McWillie,[74] a Mob "gambler and murderer";[75] James Dolan,[76] one of the most notorious hoodlums in Dallas;[77] Joseph Campisi,[78] a Mobster close to the Marcellos;[79] Paul Roland Jones,[80] a Chicago underworld liaison convicted of murder;[81] and other Syndicate men from across the country who dropped in to see Ruby.[82]

BACKGROUND ON JACK RUBY'S
TELEPHONE RECORDS

A telephone with unpublished number WH1-5601 was listed to Jack Ruby from November 1962 through November 1963 at his residence, 223 South Ewing Street, Apartment 207, Dallas.[83] A telephone with number RI7-2362 was listed from November 1959 through November 1963 to the Carousel Club, 1312 1/2 Commerce Street, Dallas,[84] which was owned and operated by Ruby;[85] the phone was in Ruby's office.[86] A third telephone with number LA8-4775 was listed from March 1956 through November 1963 to the Vegas Club, 3508 Oak Lawn, Dallas, and to Jack Ruby.[87] But since the Vegas Club was managed by Ruby's sister Eva Grant,[88] and there is no indication that calls from that phone were placed by Ruby, the small number of long distance calls placed from that phone in the latter part of 1963[89] have been ignored.

Toll calls placed from Ruby's home phone (WH1-5601) and his Carousel phone (RI7-2362) are itemized in telephone company records subpoenaed by the FBI[90] and in some telephone bills found in Ruby's possessions.[91] Included are toll calls from Ruby's Carousel phone from January 17 through March 1 and April 10 through November 22, 1963.

There are several indications that virtually all of the out-of-state calls from both Ruby's home and Carousel phones were placed by Ruby. Ruby testified he "had numerous phone calls, long-distance calls, all over the country."[92] Many of the persons called from Ruby's home and Carousel phones reported that the party who placed the calls in question was Jack Ruby.[93] Neither Ruby's roommate,[94] George Senator, nor his Carousel Club live-in handyman,[95] Larry Crafard, recalled making any out-of-state calls from these phones.[96] In fact, only one call among those from these phones appears to have been placed by a party other than Jack Ruby.[97] And there are gaps in Ruby's telephone records[98] corresponding to three periods during which Ruby was away from Dallas: the New York-Chicago trip of August 4–6,[99] the New Orleans trip the week of June 5,[100] and a trip to Houston and Edna, Texas, beginning on May 9.[101]

Appendix 2
Sources on the Mafia

Following are highlights from selected references on the Mafia, grouped by subject. Citations beginning with the prefix "U.S.–" are abbreviations for government documents listed in the bibliography. Any phrase in quotes, unless tagged with a footnote or identified parenthetically, is from the first reference subsequently cited.

Most of the sources on the Mob cited in this appendix and throughout this book are dated from the 1960s, the era of the Kennedy anti-crime crusade and assassinations, through the 1980s. The similarity in the material spanning these three decades is a consequence of historical context. The Mafia began its mass migration from Sicily to America in the late 1800s;[1] by 1890, a New Orleans grand jury could conclude, "the existence of a secret organization known as the Mafia has been established beyond doubt."[2] Over the last century, despite proclamations of its imminent demise after the 1931 conviction of Al Capone[3] and after the 1957 bust of the Apalachin Mafia convention,[4] its structure and character have been largely preserved.

Appendix 2: Sources on the Mafia

I. A LOOK AT THE MENACE
1. Introduction
2. Infiltration of the food and drug industries and toxic dumping
3. The worst victims: the poor and the Black
4. Louisiana: the Mafia's sovereign domain

II. GENERAL DESCRIPTION AND HISTORY
5. Structure
6. Modus operandi
7. Roots in Sicily
8. Migration to America

III. CRIMINAL OPERATIONS
9. Gambling
10. Loan sharking
11. Narcotics
12. Extortion
13. Securities theft and fraud
14. Cargo theft
15. Other activities
16. The Mafia and street crime

IV. ECONOMIC PENETRATION
17. Infiltration of business
18. Infiltration of labor
19. Estimated annual income

V. CORRUPTION
20. Scope and methods of corruption
21. Police corruption
22. Corruption of the judiciary
23. Corruption of local government
24. Corruption of state government and statewide networks of corruption
25. Corruption of federal government
26. Subversion of the press
27. From the Redwood Forests to the Gulf Stream waters

I. A LOOK AT THE MENACE

1. Introduction

1.1 "The Mob . . . it poisons us all." Photos show 24 bosses of Mafia families across the country; a cartoon depicts Mafia activities, including gambling, murder, loan sharking, corruption, narcotics, bankruptcy fraud, union embezzlement, extortion, strike-breaking, prostitution, and business infiltration. *Life*, September 1, 1967, pp. 15, 20–21.

1.2 The Mafia in the 1980s. "They have gone the way of sophisticated corporate America, and they've done it successfully," commented one FBI agent to the *New York Times*. The Mafia's newest methods can involve Swiss bank accounts and all the other financial, legal and technical "accouterments of a global business cartel." But its expanding infiltration into legitimate business—everything from pizza restaurants to disposal of toxic wastes—is countered by increasing trouble with the law: the past few years have been marked by major Mafia trials and the convictions of a number of top bosses. Robert D. McFadden, "The Mafia of the 1980's: Divided and Under Siege," *New York Times*, March 11, 1987, pp. 1, B2; *U.S.–President's Commission on OC, The Impact*, pp. 46–47.

1.3 Congressional action: a public law "to seek the eradication of organized crime." The Organized Crime Control Act of 1970 included the Racketeer Influenced and Corrupt Organizations (RICO) statute, which "criminalize[d] the pattern of conduct characteristic of organized crime"(B) and provided for civil suits as well as criminal prosecutions and forfeiture. Twenty-three states have similar statutes.(B) A–*U.S.–OC Control Act of 1970*. B–*U.S.–President's Commission on Organized Crime, The Impact*, pp. 130, 133, 209.

2. Infiltration of the food and drug industries and toxic dumping

2.1 "Mafia war on the A&P." Several major food chains agreed to carry a Mafia-promoted detergent described by the FDA as "extremely dangerous, toxic, and hazardous"(B), but A&P refused. A&P, at the time the world's largest food retailer, was subsequently almost put "out of business on the East Coast" through $60 million in damage from arson and the murders of two grocery store managers. A–*Reader's Digest*, July 1970, pp. 71–76; B–Dorman, *Payoff*, pp. 242–48; also, C–*Good Housekeeping*, August 1971, pp. 68ff.

2.2 "The Mafia in the Supermarket": "Mob control down every aisle." *Newsday* (1971), reproduced in Gage, *Mafia, U.S.A.*, pp. 323–34; update in *Newsday*, September 8, 1986, p. 11.

.3 Mafia infiltration of the legitimate drug industry. From $50 to $100 million annually in counterfeit drugs are distributed nationwide. They include subpotent, contaminated, or totally inert facsimiles of lifesaving medicines. Operations are dominated by the Mob and characterized by traditional Mafia tactics. From the Congressional testimony of Margaret Kreig, an author who worked with FDA undercover investigators, in *U.S.-House, Federal Effort Against OC*, pp. 137–64.

2.4 "How the Mafia Drives Up Meat Prices. . . . it reeks—just reeks with rottenness." The Mafia adds $1 million a week to meat bills in the New York City area alone through labor racketeering. This is probably more profit than is made by the supplying farmers. *Farm Journal*, August 1972, pp. 18–19.

2.5 "How the Mafia Gets Its Cut. . . . as many as a hundred murders." Mafia violence in connection with labor extortion in the food industry was described to Congress in 1972 by Clarence Adamy, president of the National Association of Food Chains. Adamy testified: "We are suspicious, at least, that some store manager deaths, some food company employee deaths, some warehouse fires, some store fires were the result of reprisals by organized crime." And he added: "Mr. Chairman, a man from my staff disappeared on May 10, 1971, under the most peculiar circumstances." *Farm Journal*, September 1972, pp. 24, 48.

2.6 Mafia extortion adds 15 percent to meat prices in New York. *New York Times*, May 9, 1972, p. 1.

2.7 Mafia frankfurters from "carcasses of diseased cows, horses, and sheep."

The Mafia's heavy hand falls on key people. . . . Here is a chemist who is having financial trouble. Let him know how he can make a buck and then lean on him. . . .

A pharmacist does not like their pills? Then they offer to throw him down the cellar stairs or through his front window. . . .

"Joe's Truck Stop won't stock our Bennies? Break Joe's legs!" That has happened. . . .

Is it an exaggeration to talk of criminal takeover of segments of the legitimate drug industry when:

A major manufacturer sold only a few bottles of a leading drug in one of our largest cities because black-marketeers got there first?

At least one company has already been driven into bankruptcy because its most heavily advertised drug was counterfeited?

Countless pharmacies are forced out of business by unfair competition from unethical druggists who buy on the black market?

Mafia leaders from a number of states have little Apalachin-type "sitdowns" to discuss getting into chemicals and pharmaceuticals to avoid the heat of narcotics trafficking?

Hoodlum enforcers use muscle to persuade reluctant collaborators—and there is more than a whiff of suspicion that labor racketeers have engineered splendid drug-selling deals in various parts of the country by forcing union members to trade in pharmacies supplied and controlled by mob members?

Margaret Kreig, in *U.S.-House, Federal Effort Against OC*, pp. 148–49.

These were sold to supermarkets — with no returns allowed — by a formerly reputable meat company infiltrated by the Mob. Gage, *The Mafia is not an Equal Opportunity Employer*, pp. 175–77.

2.8 Dumping truckloads of toxic chemical wastes in the New England countryside. The chemical industry produces large quantities of toxic and radioactive waste material that, sometimes even in trace amounts, can cause severe illness, birth defects, or death. The U.S. Environmental Protection Agency requires that these wastes be disposed only in carefully controlled dumping sites. With large profits at stake, however, the Mob has established less exacting procedures.

"With the aid and precision of organized crime, authorities say, gypsy truckers are hauling toxic chemicals from factories in the mid-Atlantic and Western States and illegally dumping the hazardous waste in the woods and farmland of Northern New England. . . . Their trucks loaded with rusting, often leaky drums of solvents, cyanide solutions, pesticides and acids, the truckers operate with apparent immunity. . . . It is common talk among truckers that the brokers represent organized crime. They say that those who question turn up with broken arms or collarbones." Noted Dennis Roberts, Rhode Island's attorney general, "It's clear to us that the shipping is being arranged by people with organized-crime involvement."

One illegal Mafia dumping operation in Elizabeth, New Jersey, came to light in April 1980, when sixty thousand 55-gallon drums of toxic chemicals exploded. Only favorable winds kept huge clouds of toxic smoke from floating over New York City.

Albuquerque Journal, March 17, 1980, p. C11; *Newsweek*, January 5, 1981, pp. 35, 39.

2.9 "[H]azardous wastes flushed into suburban sewer systems, poured into garbage landfills, dumped into waterways, mixed into heating oil, stacked in warehouses and buried in unmarked pits" by companies under Mob control. The Mob used its traditional control of the garbage carting industry in New York and New Jersey to gain a foothold in the growing and profitable field of toxic waste disposal. In one incident, a Mob-controlled company charged Ford Motor Company $50 to $150 a cubic yard for disposing of chemical wastes such as paint sludge, which it then dumped at a New Jersey garbage landfill not designated for toxic wastes at "the standard garbage fee" of 50¢ a cubic yard. It is common practice among Mob-controlled companies to mix toxic wastes with ordinary garbage and even with fuel oil.

The characters and techniques are typical of Mob involvement with legitimate industry. The Mafia ordered the formation of a waste haulers association in New Jersey. The Mafia rigs bids for waste disposal contracts. The president of what was at one point "the country's largest hazardous-waste treatment company" (SCA Services Inc. of Boston) was identified as "an associate member of organized crime"; he resigned. The business agent of Teamsters local 945, Ernest Palmieri, was on the payroll of a New Jersey wastehandling company that was among the three largest nationally; he was also a leader in the Genovese Mafia family and was sentenced to seven years in jail on racketeering and kickback charges.[5]

Ralph Blumenthal and Ben A. Franklin, "Illegal Dumping of Toxins Laid to Organized Crime," *New York Times*, June 5, 1983, pp. 1, 44.

3. The worst victims: the poor and the Black

3.1 "How the Mafia Preys on the Poor." Narcotics, numbers racketeering and loan sharking drain and degrade the nation's urban ghettos. *Reader's Digest*, September 1970, pp. 49–55.

3.2 "Organized crime takes from the urban poor far more money than the government puts in." The New York State Joint Legislative Committee on Crime found that in 1968, organized crime extracted $343 million in narcotics and gambling revenues from New York City's three main slum areas. That was $70 million more than the state spent on welfare in those areas that year.

The quoted phrase was stated by Congressman Joseph McDade and appears in Cressey, *Theft of the Nation*, p. 196. The figures are from the *New York Times* (1970–71), reprinted in Gage, *The Mafia is not an Equal Opportunity Employer*, p. 150. These figures are also cited in *U.S.–House, OC Control*, p. 423.

3.3 "Cosa Nostra is comparable to an invading army." Wide-open gambling, narcotics, and vice operations directed by the Mafia frustrate federal antipoverty programs and make law enforcement a mockery to ghetto youth. From a statement to Congress by sociologist Donald Cressey, in *U.S.–House, Criminal Justice Hearings*, pp. 446–51.

3.4 Pushing Mafia-imported dope to pay the Mafia loan shark to cover debts from Mafia-controlled gambling. From the *New York Times* (1970–71), reprinted in Gage, *The Mafia is not an Equal Opportunity Employer*, pp. 149–61.

3.5 "We must declare all-out war on organized crime in our community." From a speech by Malcolm X, transcribed in *By Any Means Necessary*, pp. 50–51.

3.6 Organized crime: "the nightmare of the slum family." Martin Luther King, Jr., "Beyond the Los Angeles Riots: Next Stop, The North," *Saturday Review*, November 13, 1965, p. 34.

3.7 Organized crime: "Raping the ghetto." The similar positions of Whitney Young, Floyd McKissick, the Hughes Commission, and organized crime expert Ralph Salerno. As summarized in the Congressional statement of Salerno in *U.S.–House, Criminal Justice Hearings*, pp. 150, 163–65. Also see Cressey, *Theft of the Nation*, pp. 275–77.

3.8 Mafia control of ghetto numbers rackets. From the testimony of Detroit Police Chief George Edwards in *U.S.–Senate, OC and Narcotics Hearings*, pp. 412–15; see also *New York Times*, March 15, 1986, p. 29.

3.9 Corrupt policemen help the Mob eliminate black competition. Cressey, *Theft of the Nation*, pp. 197–99.

It is to be hoped that those politicians who profess concern for our poor and the crisis in our cities will soon realize that one powerful solution is before them—*all-out attack against organized crime.*

Eugene Methvin, Washington correspondent, *Reader's Digest*, September 1970, p. 55.

3.10 The Mob opposes urban renewal in Mount Vernon: "more money out of a Harlem than a Scarsdale." Salerno and Tompkins, *Crime Confederation*, p. 377.

3.11 No link between ghetto problems and organized crime was noted by the National Advisory Commission on Civil Disorders, chaired by Governor Otto Kerner of Illinois. (The report did make the token observation that "the Mafia was reputed to control much of the organized crime" in Newark.) But Kerner had apparently acquired a peculiar blindness toward organized crime during his stint as U.S. Attorney of Chicago. At a law-enforcement conference in 1950, Kerner stated that there was "no organized gambling" in Chicago. He also told the conference that he "did not know that the Capone syndicate exist[ed]. I have read about it in the newspapers. I have never received any evidence of it." In 1973, Kerner was sentenced to three years in prison for accepting $150,000 in bribes from horse racing interests. *Report of the National Advisory Commission on Civil Disorders* (New York: Dutton, 1968), p. 59, see summary and index; Blakey and Billings, *The Plot to Kill the President*, p. 181; *Newsweek*, April 30, 1973, p. 41.

3.12 "One part of the answer to improved conditions for the urban poor must be a war on organized crime." This is the conclusion of Congressman Joseph McDade, with supporting information, in a 1967 report on organized crime and the poor, prepared by McDade and 22 Republican colleagues in the House. Cressey, *Theft of the Nation*, pp. 196–97; Salerno and Tompkins, *Crime Confederation*, pp. 271–73.

4. Louisiana: The Mafia's sovereign domain

4.1 Carlos Marcello "controlled the State of Louisiana." *Life*, April 10, 1970, p. 31, summarizing *Life*, September 8, 1967, pp. 94–97 and September 29, 1967, pp. 34–36.

4.2 Mob actions in Louisiana "are more flagrant than ever." Marcello's political control has been maintained, his economic penetration extended. *Life*, April 10, 1970, pp. 31–36. See also Mollenhoff, *Strike Force*, pp. 164–65; Dorman, *Payoff*, pp. 102–3, 115–17; Cook, *Two-Dollar Bet*, p. 162.

4.3 Growth of the Mob in Louisiana: capitalizing on "Huey Long's welcome to [Mafia boss Frank] Costello." *U.S.–Senate, Kefauver Report, Third Interim*, pp. 77–83, 89–90.

4.4 Carlos Marcello: from thug to Mafia boss. Statement of Aaron Kohn, director of the New Orleans Metropolitan Crime Commission, in *U.S.–Senate, Gambling and OC*, pp. 509–13.

4.5 Marcello's influence spans the United States. Marcello's nationwide influence is indicated by his control of organized crime in the Gulf Coast area,[6] close ties in Dallas and other parts of Texas,[7] representation in Las Vegas,[8] former interest in a Cuban casino,[9] control of a racing wire service in several states,[10] nationwide phone contacts,[11] and attendance at the 1966 Mafia mini-conclave at La Stella Restaurant in New York City.[12] Gambling warehouses in Louisiana, Mississippi and Oklahoma,[13] a gambling book in Houston,[14] rock festivals in California,[15] and an extortion scheme in Indiana[16] were also linked to him. Marcello is currently considered the nation's top-ranking Mafia boss.[17]

a. How Louisiana's first family enriches its treasury

4.6 The Mob's annual income in New Orleans "runs to $1,114,000,000, making it by far the state's largest industry." Half of the Mob's income in New Orleans comes from wide-open illegal gambling operations; fourteen Mob casinos in Gretta were visible in one aerial photograph. Bill Davidson, "Cosa Nostra's Wall Street," *Saturday Evening Post*, February 29, 1964, pp. 15ff.

4.7 Dun and Bradstreet estimates that 50 percent of New Orleans area hotels are financially backed by Marcello. From the *Wall Street Journal* (1968–70), reproduced in Gartner, *Crime and Business*, pp. 10–15.

4.8 Mafia business interests in Louisiana range from banks to whiskey distributorships, from bus lines to shrimpboat fleets, plus traditional illegal operations. Most of its income comes from infiltration of legitimate businesses, and its power is mostly gained through political influence. The family "serves as an example" to Mobsters across the nation in the infiltration of businesses. Dorman, *Payoff*, pp. 100–101; *U.S.-President's Commission on OC, The Impact*, p. 46.

4.9 Marcello enterprises are "scattered through surrounding states and include thousands of acres of oil leases on federal land." Reid, *Grim Reapers*, pp. 152–53.

4.10 By 1980, net profits from Marcello's operations were said to total "more than $1 billion a year." But in 1981, the Louisiana boss was convicted on bribery and racketeering charges. The conviction was the result of an FBI sting, codenamed Brilab, for bribery-labor, in which Marcello arranged bribes to public officials. In 1982, Marcello was sentenced to 10 years in prison for trying to bribe the judge who was scheduled to preside over a racketeering trial in Los Angeles. *Newsweek*, June 30, 1980, p. 22; *U.S.-President's Commission on OC, Appendix to The Edge*, p. 227; *New York Times*, April 15, 1982, p. 23.

b. From corruption to political control

4.11 "They're all in deathly fear of Carlos Marcello because he's got the law, all the politicians in the state, right in his hip pocket." Teresa, *My Life in the Mafia*, p. 357.

4.12 A unique interview with Carlos Marcello and an aide. Rackets provided the main source of campaign funds in Louisiana and other Southern states. "We picked the candidates; we paid for their campaigns; we paid them off; we told them what to do. We even provided the poll-watchers and vote-counters." Dorman, *Payoff*, pp. 103–4, 109–10.

4.13 New York Mafia boss Frank Costello was received in New Orleans in 1955 by a police honor guard. From the testimony of Metropolitan Crime Commission Director Aaron Kohn in *U.S.-House, OC in Sports*, p. 886.

4.14 Jefferson Parish Police harassed bar owners who didn't buy Marcello jukeboxes. Cook, *Two-Dollar Bet*, pp. 160–61; *Saturday Evening Post*, February 29, 1964, p. 16.

4.15 Marcello's criminal enterprise "required, and had, corrupt collusion of public officials at every critical level including police, sheriffs, justices of peace, prosecutors, mayors, governors, judges, councilmen, licensing authorities, state legislators and at least one member of Congress." Statement of Aaron Kohn in *U.S.-House, OC Control*, p. 433.

4.16 Ninety-eight percent of Louisiana legislators will accept bribes. Reported by Peter Hand, a former Mob-affiliated bookmaker, close friend of Governor Earl Long, and member of the Louisiana legislature for eight years. Cook, *Two-Dollar Bet*, pp. 167–69.

4.17 A Mob gambler was convicted of bribery, then pardoned by Governor Earl Long, his graft money returned. Cook, *Two-Dollar Bet*, p. 158; *U.S.-House, OC Control*, p. 435.

4.18 A "cozy relationship" between underworld figures and the New Orleans office of the Small Business Administration. This relationship "resulted in millions in Federal funds going to persons with known Mafia backgrounds and their associates." *New York Times*, February 28, 1974, p. 24.

II. GENERAL DESCRIPTION AND HISTORY

5. Structure

a. Conclusions of the U.S. government

5.1 Kefauver Committee, 1951: "There is a nationwide crime syndicate known as the Mafia." It controls the most lucrative rackets and resorts to murder, political influence, bribery and intimidation. *U.S.-Senate, Kefauver Report, Third Interim*, p. 150.

5.2 McClellan Committee, 1964: The Mafia "operates vast illegal enterprises that produce an annual income of many billions of dollars." It consists of separate families structured along military lines, and is run by a national commission. *U.S.-Senate, OC and Narcotics Report*, p. 117.

5.3 U.S. President's Task Force on Organized Crime, 1967: The U.S. government "is being seriously challenged, if not threatened" by the Mob. The Mafia is comprised of approximately 5,000 members of Italian descent, grouped into 24 families, and is governed by a national commission. It works with large numbers of nonmember associates from all ethnic groups. It uses specialists in murder and corruption. *U.S.-Task Force Report*, pp. 1, 6–8.

5.4 U.S. Departments of Justice and Transportation, 1972: the Mafia's "existence, structure, activities, personnel . . . have been confirmed and reconfirmed beyond rational dispute." Confirmation of these facts and such terminology as "boss," "captain," "family," "soldier," and "commission" has been achieved "through interceptions of phone conversations and other oral communications at different times and places between [Mob] members and associates." *U.S.-Cargo Theft and OC*, p. 24.

5.5 President's Commission on Organized Crime, 1986: The Mafia's "undertakings range from multi-million dollar heroin shipments to storefront numbers operations, from extortion by violence to sophisticated infiltration of legitimate businesses." Testimony confirmed the structure and hierarchy of Mafia families and the existence of a national commission. The FBI's minimum estimate of Mafia affiliation is 1,700 members and 17,000 associates. Wharton Econometric Forecasting Associates estimated about 8,800 to 14,600 members and 39,400 to 63,100 associates, based on a survey of law enforcement agencies. *U.S.-President's Commission on OC, The Impact*, pp. 35–36, 425–26, 476.

b. Conclusions of individual commentators

5.6 Donald R. Cressey, member of the President's Commission on Law Enforcement and Administration of Justice: Mafia families, united under a national commission, control gambling, loan sharking, narcotics importation and wholesaling, and "own several state legislators and federal congressmen and other officials in the legislative, executive, and judicial branches of government at the local, state, and federal levels." Cressey, *Theft of the Nation*, pp. x-xi.

5.7 Charles Grutzner, reporter for the *New York Times*: Five thousand Mafia members in 24 families work with at least 50,000 associates. Grutzner, "How to Lock Out the Mafia," *Harvard Business Review*, March-April 1970, p. 47.

5.8 Aaron Kohn, director of the New Orleans Metropolitan Crime Commission: Although directed by "only 3,000 to 5,000 hard-core members," the Cosa Nostra "burdens, frightens and, in one way or another, victimizes everyone in the United States." *U.S.-House, OC Control*, pp. 437-38.

5.9 Nicholas Gage, reporter for the *New York Times*: The Mafia consists of 5,000 full-fledged members in 26 families based in 21 metropolitan areas across the United States. Gage, *Mafia, U.S.A.*, p. 16.

c. Conclusions of law enforcement agencies

5.10 Findings of a New Orleans grand jury in 1890 upon indictment of 19 Mafia gangsters for the murder of Police Chief David Hennessey: "The existence of a secret organization known as the Mafia has been established beyond doubt." Sondern, *Brotherhood of Evil*, pp. 58-62; Reid, *Grim Reapers*, pp. 146-50.

5.11 William J. Duffy, director of the Intelligence Division of the Chicago Police Department: The Mafia is "aggressively engaged in attempts to subvert the process of government by well-organized endeavors"; it is "dedicated to commit murder and other acts of violence." *U.S.-Senate, OC and Narcotics Hearings*, pp. 506-8.

5.12 E. Michael Kahoe, FBI Agent: "The Affiant has learned through numerous conversations with other Agents of the FBI and through a comprehensive review of confidential information furnished by reliable informants to Agents of the FBI in Cleveland, Ohio, and elsewhere, that there exists within the United States an organized crime conspiracy which is exclusively Italian. Geographical areas of the United States are apportioned to the members of this conspiracy for the conduct of illegal activities. . . . The said criminal organization in the United States is controlled by a policy group known as the 'commission.' The 'commission' members are actually the various bosses of the 'families.' This criminal organization is engaged in the conduct of gambling, loan sharking, extortion, murder, labor racketeering, and other violations of federal and state law."

From an affidavit filed by FBI agent E. Michael Kahoe on December 27, 1977 in an Ohio Court, in connection with a case involving organized crime. *U.S.-House, Assassination Hearings, JFK*, vol. 5, p. 389.

5.13 Tampa, Florida Police Chief Neil Brown: "It is our considered conclusion that the Mafia exists in Tampa, that it controls most illegal gambling in Tampa and central Florida, and that its members have interstate and international ties to other Mafia groups." This conclusion is "based upon personal knowledge, criminal records, surveillance reports, personal histories, familial relationships, statistical analyses, reports from confidential informants, information from Federal and local law enforcement agencies, and other customary police intelligence sources." *U.S.–Senate, OC and Narcotics Hearings*, p. 522.

5.14 A 1961 Kansas City grand jury report: "It is an indisputable fact that the professional criminals in Kansas City are highly organized. This criminal group is ruled by an 'inner circle' commonly called 'the syndicate.' The 'syndicate' functions like a board of directors, formulating policy and giving orders to the other members. . . . Based on sworn testimony it is the belief of this jury that the Kansas City 'syndicate' is probably connected with the Mafia or Black Hand Society.

"Beginning in Kansas City in the early 1900's there was a small group of thugs, mostly of foreign descent, who started by preying upon members of their own national group. By means of threats of arson, bombing, beatings and murder, this parasitical element established a flourishing extortion racket. . . . Based on sworn testimony presented to this jury, it now seems apparent that sometime in 1953 a 'deal' was made between the 'syndicate' and certain members of the Kansas City, Missouri, Police Department which led to the 'syndicate' being permitted to operate a number of gambling and after-hours liquor establishments, control prostitution, and fence stolen merchandise in Kansas City."

The grand jury also observed: "From the days of prohibition the 'syndicate' has had an active interest in politics and exerted considerable influence in both city and county elections. Many citizens of this community will still recall the 'bloody' election of March 27, 1934, when 'syndicate' hoodlums roamed the city in unlicensed black sedans slugging and killing. According to the *Kansas City Star* of the next day the result was four dead, 11 critically injured and countless numbers severely beaten."

From a 1961 Kansas City grand jury report, reproduced in Tyler, *Organized Crime in America*, pp. 296–98.

5.15 Detroit Police Chief George Edwards: Chief Edwards named 66 members and 18 associates of the Detroit Mafia family, and described its organizational structure, blood and marriage interrelationships, criminal arrests and convictions, and connection to the nationwide Mafia organization. He presented a chart of its infiltration into 98 businesses, histories of gambling, prostitution, and narcotics cases involving several of its members, and synopses of 69 gangland murders committed in the Detroit area. *U.S.–Senate, OC and Narcotics Hearings*, pp. 400ff.

5.16 Charts of 11 Mafia families from the 1963–64 Senate Organized Crime and Narcotics Hearings. Included were charts of five families in New York City and of families in Chicago, Detroit, Tampa, Rhode Island, Boston, and Buffalo, New York. Charts gave the names, aliases, FBI numbers, photos, and criminal activity codes of known family members. They were prepared using information from local police files, the FBI, the Federal Bureau of Narcotics, the testimony of Joseph Valachi, and other sources. The average number of arrests for each of the 356 identified members of the five New York families was seven. *U.S.–Senate, OC and Narcotics Hearings*, pp. 259, 410, 508, 522, 550, 580, 652.

5.17 The Commission trial: On November 19, 1986, eight members and key associates of the Mafia's ruling national commission were convicted under the RICO statute.[18] They included Genovese boss Anthony "Fat Tony" Salerno, Lucchese boss Anthony "Tony Ducks" Corallo, and Colombo boss Carmine

"Junior" Persico. Prosecutors showed that the commission exists and that it divides territory between members, plans and parcels out rackets, resolves disputes, and sometimes orders executions.

The defense also admitted the Mafia's existence. "I tell you now, plainly and simply and directly, that there is [the Mafia], right here in New York City," said one of the Mob's attorneys. The unique defense strategy also conceded the existence of a national commission of Mafia leaders.

Paragraphs respectively from Robert D. McFadden, "The Mafia of the 1980's: Divided and Under Siege," *New York Times*, March 11, 1987, pp. 1, B2; *Newsday*, September 19, 1986, p. 3.

5.18 The first-ever civil action against an entire Mob family: In August 1987, the federal government hit New York City's Bonanno crime family with a civil RICO suit that would bar members from doing business with one another and prohibit induction of new members. The government also asked that a trustee assume control of an alleged Bonanno enterprise—Teamsters Local 814, the city's van drivers, packers and furniture handlers union. The suit stated: "Immeasurable damage is being done to legitimate business and innocent people by the Bonanno family. . . . Preliminary and forceful relief is necessary to stop this ongoing depravity." *Newsday*, August 27, 1987, p. 3ff.

d. Information from electronic surveillance

5.19 The Taglianetti Airtels: publicly released transcripts of FBI eavesdropping on the Mafia's Rhode Island headquarters between 1962 and 1965. These voluminous transcripts, released in connection with the tax evasion trial of Louis Taglianetti, provide a detailed, inside look at Mafia operations. They confirmed the existence of Mafia families, formal members, a military chain of command ("boss," "caporegime," "soldier," etc.), and the governing national commission. They also provided evidence of diverse criminal activities, including infiltration of business, corruption of high-ranking officials (the state attorney general, for one) and a dozen murders performed under the orders of boss Raymond Patriarca. All types of crime in his territory, including robberies, hijackings, kidnapping, thefts and arson, were cleared with Patriarca. (The FBI bug in Patriarca's office allowed police to thwart repeated murder attempts against two gangsters out of favor with Patriarca. Within two years after the bug was removed as a result of Johnson Administration orders, both men were murdered—one in Providence and the other in Miami.[19]) Cressey, *Theft of the Nation*, pp. 120–26; *Life*, September 1, 1967, p. 44.

5.20 The "DeCavalcante Tapes": 2,000 pages of publicly released transcripts of FBI surveillance of New Jersey Mafia hangouts between 1961 and 1965. Detailed descriptions of Mafia operations. Mollenhoff, *Strike Force*, chapter 2; *Newsweek*, June 23, 1969, pp. 37–38; *Life*, September 1, 1967, pp. 44–45.

5.21 The "Gold Bug": from a police bug in a Mafia base of operations in Brooklyn, New York, in the early 1970s. It yielded 300 miles of taped conversations, plus 36,000 feet of color movie film and 54,000 photographs. The bug recorded the visits of 100 New York policemen and deals involving arson, assault, auto theft, bookmaking, burglaries, coercion, corruption, counterfeiting, extortion, forgery, hijacking, insurance frauds, labor racketeering, loan sharking, narcotics sales, policy, possession and sale of weapons, receiving stolen property, and robbery. *Time*, October 30, 1972, pp. 26, 28.

5.22 FBI electronic surveillance. The House Assassinations Committee released numerous segments from FBI surveillance of the Mob during the early 1960s. Two excerpts are quoted below.

Buffalo Mafia boss Stefano Magaddino to members of his Family on June 3, 1963, about the FBI: "They know everybody's name. They know who's Boss. They know who is on the Commission. . . . The FBI said, 'What was your caporegime doing here?' . . . To Carlo Gambino they said 'This is your underboss, this is your caporegime, this is your consiglieri.' "

Detroit Mafia Captain Anthony Zerilla to Nick Ditta on December 4, 1963: "You are a friend of ours [a Mafia member] and you belong to my Regime. If I tell you to jump off a 20-story building, you jump off and you jump off any time I tell you to."

U.S.–House, Assassination Hearings, JFK, vol. 5, pp. 424–26, see pp. 437–53.

5.23 The FBI bugged the headquarters of New England Mafia underboss Gennaro "Jerry" Angiulo. In January 1981, the FBI planted microphones in the Boston apartment from which Angiulo and his Mafioso brothers operated. Agents listened to discussions of gambling, bookmaking, and loan sharking operations (including "lucrative Las Vegas nights" supposedly for the benefit of retarded children) and plans to murder a grand jury witness. The bug resulted in Angiulo's conviction on racketeering charges more than five years later. "A World of Violence Captured by the FBI," *Boston Globe,* April 6, 1987, pp. 1, 8–9. From series "An Anatomy of the Angiulo Case," April 5–9, 1987.

5.24 Several other publicized transcripts of electronic surveillance of Mafia operations. See *U.S.–Senate, Kefauver Hearings,* vol. 5, pp. 1175–87; *Life,* August 9, 1968, pp. 20–27; *Life,* May 30, 1969, pp. 45–47; Dorman, *Payoff,* pp. 45–49; *Saturday Evening Post,* November 9, 1963, p. 20.

e. Information from Mob defectors

5.25 Inside information spanning 50 years, from Mobsters Tony Notaro, Nicola Gentile, Joseph Valachi, and Joseph Luparelli. Gage, *Mafia, U.S.A.,* pp. 15–16; see also *U.S.–House, Assassination Appendix, JFK,* vol. 9, p. 44.

5.26 The testimony of Tony Notaro. During his lengthy testimony in 1918, Notaro described his initiation into the Mafia. Gage, *The Mafia Is Not an Equal Opportunity Employer,* pp. 31–32.

5.27 The confessions of Sicilian Mafioso Dr. Melchiorre Allegra. Obtained by Italian authorities in 1937, they were discovered and published by *L'Ora* in 1962.

When you go on a thing like that [a Mafia initiation ceremony], they bring you in front of the family. You sit down and take the oath. Then you're officially made. . . .

I remember when [Colombo Family underboss Joseph Yackovelli] was made. . . . The family boss and the consigliere and all the captains were there. It was supposed to be secret, but everyone in the neighborhood knew about it.

Colombo Family member Joseph Luparelli, who defected and became a government witness in 1972, in Meskil, *Luparelli Tapes,* pp. 80–81, 123.

Allegra described the structure and modus operandi of the Mafia, and the high positions in society of its members. He also recounted his initiation into the organization. Cook, *Secret Rulers*, pp. 59–61.

5.28 The memoirs of Sicilian Mafioso Nicola Gentile. Written during the 1950s, these were supported by the subsequent testimony of Joseph Valachi. Gage, *The Mafia Is Not an Equal Opportunity Employer,* pp. 32–33.

5.29 Information provided in 1945 by Mafia associate Charles Wall. Wall was forced to accept Mafioso Santos Trafficante, Sr. as a partner in his large-scale gambling operations after three Mafia murder attempts. Wall described the structure of the Mafia and its tremendous power in the United States. Related by Tampa Police Chief Neil G. Brown in *U.S.–Senate, OC and Narcotics Hearings,* pp. 531–33.

5.30 The testimony of Joseph Valachi. In appearances before the U.S. Senate in the fall of 1963 (see chapter 5, "An Attorney General Fights Crime" in text), Mafia defector Joseph Valachi provided extensive information about the organization. He gave "detailed accounts of approximately three dozen murders that were directly linked with Mafia activities, and police officials specifically corroborated his information in dates, locations, and circumstances." *U.S.–Senate, OC and Narcotics Report,* pp. 12–13, 118–19; see Valachi's testimony in *U.S.–Senate, OC and Narcotics Hearings,* i.e., pp. 180–84.

5.31 An exhaustive description of the Mafia from a former top-ranking insider, Vincent Teresa. Teresa was the number-three man in the New England Mafia organization. He operated throughout the East Coast, the Caribbean, and Europe, and was one of the Mob's leading moneymakers. When he defected in 1970 and testified in Senate hearings and court trials, he became perhaps the most important single source of information on the Mob. His remarks are often cited in this volume. See, for example, Teresa's testimony in *U.S.–Senate, OC and Stolen Securities, 1971,* pp. 777–78; and his memoirs, *My Life in the Mafia,* pp. 1, 86–89, 216–17.

5.32 The Senate testimony of Mob money-mover Michael Raymond (appearing under the name "George White"). Raymond worked for Peter LaPlaca, a New Jersey Mafia boss, who told Raymond he had bodies "planted like potatoes in New Jersey." Raymond explained how in one deal, Mobsters from another family planned to relieve him of $500,000 in stocks and then kill him, until he mentioned his connection to LaPlaca. Carmine Lombardozzi, a Gambino Family captain who attended the Apalachin Mafia conclave,[20] later said to Raymond, "why didn't you tell us? I was going to drink your blood," adding "other charming euphemisms." Raymond, like Vincent Teresa and several other witnesses against the Mob quoted in this volume,[21] testified under a grant of immunity from U.S. District Court Judge John Sirica. *U.S.–Senate, OC and Stolen Securities,* 1971, pp. 637, 656–64, 956, 1245–46.

5.33 Information to prosecutors and newsmen from former Detroit Mafia Lieutenant Eugene Ayotte. Love nests and bodies in concrete were among the subjects covered in his disclosures. *Chicago Daily News,* September 17, 1974; Jack Anderson, "Stories of Mafia Operations in Detroit Area Business," *Detroit Free Press,* September 19, 1974.

5.34 The Senate testimony of Robert Cudak and James Schaeffer. Cudak and Schaeffer were airport mail thieves who dealt frequently with the Mob. They noted that organized crime is controlled by the Mafia, and described a Mafia "sitdown." *U.S.-Senate, OC and Stolen Securities, 1971*, pp. 224–25, 228–29, 584–85.

5.35 James Fratianno, former acting boss of the Los Angeles Mafia Family, became a government witness. Fratianno's testimony at various trials had resulted in approximately forty convictions by the time he testified before the President's Commission on Organized Crime in 1984, including convictions of bosses and underbosses in New York, Cleveland, and Los Angeles. *U.S.-President's Commission on OC, OC and Money Laundering*, p. 19.

5.36 The House testimony of Joseph Barboza, former killer for the New England Patriarca Mafia Family. Bookmaking in Massachusetts operates "like a big wagon wheel with Patriarca in the center." Excerpts from Barboza's testimony are quoted at several points in this appendix. *U.S.-House, OC in Sports*, pp. 764, 731.

5.37 The testimony of Sicilian Mafioso Tommaso Buscetta at the "Pizza Connection" trial in NY. Buscetta, a high-ranking figure in the Sicilian Mob who participated in the formation of a commission in Palermo around 1959, testified in Italy and in the U.S. after "two of his sons, a son-in-law, two brothers, and two nephews" were killed in a Mafia war. *U.S.-President's Commission on OC, The Impact*, p. 56; *New York Times*, November 1, 1985, p. B3.

5.38 The testimony of former Cleveland underboss Angelo Lonardo. Two million dollars skimmed from Mob-controlled casinos in Las Vegas was divided among families in Milwaukee, Cleveland and Kansas City. Chicago boss Joseph John Aiuppa arbitrated a dispute over the money in exchange for 25 percent of the take. "Kansas City and Milwaukee belong to Chicago," explained Lonardo. "Cleveland reports to New York." Lonardo is the highest ranking U.S. Mafioso to defect so far. *New York Times*, November 24, 1985, p. 37; "Hitting the Mafia," *Time*, September 29, 1986, p. 22.

f. Mafia conclaves

5.39 Cleveland, 1928. Police stumbled upon a meeting of 21 Mafiosi in a Cleveland hotel, several of whom later became top bosses. Cook, *Secret Rulers*, p. 77; Salerno and Tompkins, *Crime Confederation*, p. 278.

5.40 Atlantic City, 1929. Informants described a large meeting of Mobsters from cities across the Eastern United States, including such notables as Frank Costello, Lucky Luciano, Frank Nitti, and Al Capone. Cook, *Secret Rulers*, pp. 77–79.

5.41 Apalachin, New York, 1957. In November 1957, New York State Police arrested 58 persons from across the country meeting at the estate of Joseph Barbara in Apalachin, New York. Most were identified Mafia members and several were top national bosses. Fifty had arrest records, 35 had convictions, 22 were involved in labor-management relations, and most were active in business enterprises. Roughly half of the arrested delegates were related by blood or marriage. Salerno and Tompkins, *Crime Confederation*, pp. 297–99; Kennedy, *Enemy Within*, pp. 228–29; McClellan, *Crime Without Punishment*, pp. 119–21; Sondern, *Brotherhood of Evil*, pp. 35–37; Tyler, *Organized Crime in America*, pp. 23–27; *U.S.-Senate, McClellan Labor Hearings*, pp. 12194–201, vol. 32 exhibit 5; *U.S.-House Assassination Appendix, JFK*, vol. 9, pp. 7–9.

5.42 Forest Hills, New York, 1966. On September 22, 13 men sitting around a table at La Stella Restaurant in Forest Hills, New York, were arrested. They were Carlo Gambino, boss of the Gambino Family; Carlos Marcello, boss of New Orleans; Santos Trafficante, Jr., boss of Tampa, Florida; Anthony Corollo and Frank Gagliano of the Marcello Family; Joseph N. Gallo, caporegima in the Gambino Family; Anthony Carillo, soldier in the Genovese Family; Aniello Dellacroce, caporegima in the Gambino Family; Joseph Marcello, Jr., member of the Marcello Family; Dominick Alongi, soldier in the Genovese Family; Thomas Eboli, acting boss of the Genovese Family; Joseph Colombo, boss of the Colombo Family; and Michael Miranda, consiglieri in the Genovese Family. Reid, *Grim Reapers*, pp. 329, 158–59.

g. *Mafia response to criminal charges: the Fifth Amendment*

5.43 The consistent use of the Fifth Amendment by Mobsters in Congressional testimony. McClellan, *Crime Without Punishment*, pp. 132–37. For other examples, see *U.S.-Senate, McClellan Labor Hearings*, p. 14035; *U.S.-House, OC in Sports*, pp. 970–72, 1496; *U.S.-President's Commission on OC, OC and Labor-Management Racketeering*, pp. 45–67.

6. Modus operandi

a. *Murder and violence*

6.1 "The ultimate solution to everything is to kill somebody." The ability "to commit murder and other acts of violence without compunction" is the "one single characteristic which is most responsible for the success and continuity" of the Syndicate. From the testimony of former Chicago Police Intelligence Director William Duffy in *U.S.-Senate, OC and Narcotics Hearings*, pp. 512–13. The title phrase is from testimony by Mob defector Michael Raymond ("George White") in *U.S.-Senate, OC and Stolen Securities*, 1971, p. 672.

6.2 The testimony of defected Mob killer Joseph Barboza, formerly "the most feared rackets enforcer in New England." Barboza gave details of several murders he committed for New England Mafia boss Raymond Patriarca, naming his victims and describing the methods used. In some cases he got the contract through channels: "Peter Lemoine was the one who gave me the contract, and I got the ok from [underboss] Henry Tameleo, who subsequently got all the final ok's from Raymond Patriarca." In other cases he got "the ok to kill people" directly from Patriarca. Barboza also related how he severely beat a candidate for office in the baker's union in Boston whom the Mob did not want to run. Barboza "left him in a heap, a bloody heap in the middle of the street." *U.S.-House, OC in Sports*, pp. 731–34, 740–41, 767–69.

6.3 Comments of Mafia defector Vincent Teresa. Each Mafia family "has its own assassination squads who are available for lend-lease assignments." Teresa described several Mob murders in which hit men were imported from one Mafia family to perform a job for another. He also discussed the various side activities of Mob hit squads, such as selling machine guns, hand grenades, and mines. One killer mentioned by Teresa was "Ice Pick Barney" of "Anastasia's Old Murder, Inc." who would puncture his victims through the ear with an ice pick, leaving them to die of what would be ruled a cerebral hemorrhage. Teresa, *My Life in the Mafia*, chapter 17, especially pp. 180–87.

6.4 A Mafia hit squad on tape. The conversation of Chicago Mobsters John Cerone, Fiore Buccieri, Dave Yaras, and others was picked up by an FBI bug while they were in Miami to kill Chicago union boss and political bigwig Frank Esposito. They discussed plans for killing Esposito and reminisced about their previous contracts, including the sadistic murder of FBI informant William Jackson. The FBI bug saved Esposito's life. Excerpts from the transcripts of a February 11, 1962 conversation of the Mob hit squad in *Life*, May 30, 1968, pp. 45–47; Demaris, *Captive City*, pp. 60–63.

6.5 The Mafia murder of a government witness, disguised by rape and robbery. In 1970, Sol Landie furnished information to authorities on the gambling activities of Kansas City, Missouri, Mafia boss Nick Civella and other local Mafia figures, leading to an indictment against Civella and associates on October 22. One month later, four young men robbed Landie's house, shot him dead, and then raped his wife. Three men were arrested for the murder, and they confessed that it was a contract killing; "they had received instructions through intermediaries to make it appear that robbery was the motive for the murder." Mob associate Tony Lee, who assigned the contract, was convicted of murder. *U.S.-House, Assassination Report*, p. 163; *U.S.-House, Assassination Appendix, JFK*, vol. 9, pp. 51–52; Mollenhoff, *Strike Force*, pp. 150–52, 237.

6.6 The arrangements for a typical Mob contract. A Mob murder is usually a methodical job, performed by a coordinated team of specialists. Up to 15 gunmen, drivers, spotters, and other backup personnel, plus several cars, are used on some jobs. Tyler, *Organized Crime in America*, pp. 229–31; Meskil, *Luparelli Tapes*, p. 13, passim, *U.S.-House, Assassination Appendix*, vol. 9, pp. 44–47.

6.7 The efficient disposal of bodies was a frequent topic of conversation in the DeCavalcante tapes (these tapes were recordings of FBI surveillance of Mafia hangouts in New Jersey during 1961–65). One idea discussed was a pulverizing device capable of turning a human body into a "meatball." *Time*, June 20, 1969, pp. 22–23.

6.8 Joseph Valachi: "You are there for that purpose." Valachi testified how he performed several murder contracts for the Mob without pay as part of the obligations of membership. *U.S.-Senate, OC and Narcotics Hearings*, pp. 192–93.

6.9 The murder of Detroit radio commentator Gerald Buckley. In 1930 Buckley was shot to death after he "had threatened to reveal the identity of the gangland's overlords and their connections with city government." Four men, including Mafiosi Joe Bommarito and Pete Licavoli, were indicted for the murder; Licavoli fled the state until his three codefendants had been acquitted. Police later found the gun used to kill Buckley at the home of Mafioso "Cockeyed Joe" Catalanotte. From the testimony of Detroit Police Chief George Edwards in *U.S.-Senate, OC and Narcotics Hearings*, pp. 428–29; see also Reid, *Grim Reapers*, p. 76.

6.10 "A trail of murder from Tampa to San Francisco": Mafia murders in various American cities were described by the Kefauver Committee. In one case, government witness Carl Carramusa was shot to death in front of his 15-year-old daughter in Chicago, "where he had gone to escape retribution

From the 1971 hearings of the Permanent Subcommittee on Investigations of the Senate Government Operations Committee, in *U.S.–Senate, OC and Stolen Securities, 1971*, pp. 633–35, 616:

Mr. Gallinaro [Committee investigator]: Information received from law enforcement intelligence agencies states that Gregory Scarpa is a member of the Joseph Colombo crime family in Brooklyn, N.Y. . . .

Scarpa is involved in gambling, policy, and fencing stolen property. He has met on a frequent basis with alleged LCN [Cosa Nostra] members of the Colombo family, including Joseph Colombo himself, at the Cantalupo Realty Co., located at 1434 86th Street, Brooklyn, N.Y.

Chairman McClellan: Do you want to deny whether you met with Colombo?

Mr. Scarpa: I respectfully decline to answer the question, Senator, on the ground it may tend to incriminate me.

Chairman McClellan: Proceed.

Mr. Gallinaro: Scarpa has taken the fifth amendment before the Federal grand jury in the Eastern District of New York, to all questions concerning the Colombo crime family in the past. . . .

Chairman McClellan: You mentioned two people were killed. . . . They were killed after testifying where?

Mr. Gallinaro: Before a grand jury in the City of New York. . . . Richard [LoCicero], after he testified, was stabbed 100 times and killed. . . . [The other murdered man, Richard's uncle, was a "very close associate" of Scarpa.]

Chairman McClellan: There is some information that frequently witnesses are disposed of, prospective witnesses, in this fashion by the organized crime elements. Would you have any information about that that you would care to tell us, Mr. Scarpa.

Mr. Scarpa: No, Senator.

Chairman McClellan: You don't have any information? Or do you?

Mr. Scarpa: I respectfully decline to answer the question, Senator, on the ground that it may tend to incriminate me. . . .

Senator Percy: Do you consider yourself a "made man" [full-fledged member] in Mob circles?

Mr. Scarpa: I respectfully decline to answer the question, Senator, on the ground it may tend to incriminate me. . . .

Senator Gurney: . . . I did notice that you were laughing uproariously at the exchange I had on [dumping Mob counterfeit money at] the church bazaar. Were you listening at that time?

Mr. Scarpa: I respectfully decline to answer the question, Senator, on the ground that it may tend to incriminate me.

by the Mafia." The killing occurred three years after his testimony in a Kansas City narcotics trial. The Kefauver Committee concluded that it had been performed by Chicago Mobsters "on orders from the Kansas City group." Government witness Thomas Buffa was likewise killed after he fled to California. *U.S.–Kefauver Report, Third Interim*, pp. 38, 148–49.

6.11 "Let's take Joey's share." Airport mail thief Robert Cudak testified that in one $125,000 deal, Mafioso[22] Billy Ricchiuti suggested that the two increase their share by setting a murder contract on Cudak's partner Joe Russo. *U.S.–Senate, OC and Stolen Securities, 1971*, pp. 227–28.

6.12 The acid blinding of noted labor columnist Victor Riesel. Mafioso[23] Johnny Dioguardi escaped a conviction for this crime after a prosecution witness refused to testify, but he was later sentenced to two years in prison on an extortion charge. According to U.S. Attorney Paul Williams, the man who splashed the acid on Riesel, Abraham Telvi, was paid $500 and subsequently murdered on Dioguardi's orders. Reid, *Grim Reapers*, p. 174; *U.S.–House, Assassination Appendix, JFK*, vol. 9, pp. 47–49.

6.13 The shooting of New York Mob boss Joseph Colombo. Colombo irked the conservative Mob leadership by drawing attention to the Mafia in a ludicrous campaign which portrayed it as "a myth." The farce was rudely shattered at one of his rallies in New York's Columbus Circle in 1971, when he was gunned down by an assailant who was shot to death immediately afterwards. Colombo was taken to the hospital, whose corridors were ringed with Mafia guards in an "almost surrealistic parody"(B) of a scene from *The Godfather*. A–Dorman, *Payoff*, pp. 276–86; B–*Time* (1971) reprinted in Gage, *Mafia, U.S.A.*, pp. 179–87; C–*U.S.–House, Assassination Appendix, JFK*, vol. 9, pp. 50–51.

6.14 Specialists from New England. "So feared are the New England Mafia specialists in violence that Mafia families in other cities frequently send for the Boston or Providence boys to do their dirtiest work." For example, the FBI learned that Jackie Nazarian of Providence was assigned to kill New York Mafia underboss Albert Anastasia; Nazarian gunned him down in 1957 in a barber's chair in a Manhattan hotel. Anastasia was the founder of "Murder, Incorporated," a Mafia hit squad which itself exported killers out of town. Another New Englander, Joe Puzzangara, is often assigned to out-of-state bombing contracts. Bill Davidson, "The Mafia: How it Bleeds New England," *Saturday Evening Post*, November 18, 1967, p. 28; see Teresa, *My Life in the Mafia*, p. 178.

6.15 The murder of Ferdinand Boccia. Mafia boss Vito Genovese assigned a contract to a friend of the intended victim and then lined up an assassin to take care of the killer. Maas, *Valachi Papers*, pp. 155–56.

6.16 "Kill your wife." Joseph Yackovelli, New York Colombo Family underboss, told Family member Joseph Luparelli, as Luparelli later related: "You shouldn't be with your kids so much. You're not paying attention to Our Thing." He then said to Luparelli, "Your wife is a cancer to you. I want you to cut her out of your life. I want you to kill her." It was this order and the suspicion engendered in Yackovelli when Luparelli refused to carry it out that led to Luparelli's defection. In a similar case, related by Vincent Teresa, New England Mafia boss Raymond Patriarca ordered old-time Mafioso Joe Modica to murder Modica's son, who had stolen $200,000 from a Mafia-controlled finance company.

Meskil, *Luparelli Tapes*, pp. 212–13; Teresa, *My Life in the Mafia*, pp. 97–98.

6.17 The abortive contract on Joseph Barboza. Vincent Teresa described how, on orders from New England Mafia underboss Henry Tameleo, he procured weapons from the New Jersey Mob and joined a hit squad which prepared to kill Barboza. The contract plans also called for the murder of

Guy Frizzi, an associate of Barboza who was delegated to set him up. When Barboza got wind of the plan, Tameleo wanted Teresa to assure Barboza that everything was okay, explaining to Teresa that they would later "whack him when he least expect[ed] it." Teresa, *My Life in the Mafia*, pp. 245–47.

6.18 Between 1919 and 1963, 976 gangland-type slayings were charted in Chicago. Of these, just two were cleared by the arrest and conviction of the killers. "These executions were usually committed by hired guns often imported from other cities for this specific purpose." From the testimony of Chicago Police Chief O. W. Wilson in *U.S.-OC and Narcotics Hearings*, p. 487.

6.19 The murders of four Mob defectors under federal protection and more than a dozen murders of FBI informants. Between 1971 and 1977, four Mob defectors under federal protection were murdered, while six others died unnatural deaths as the apparent result of corruption in the witness protection program. Between 1976 and 1977, almost 20 FBI informants were murdered, when their covers were blown by FBI agents. *Newsweek*, November 28, 1977, p. 66; NBC Evening News, "Segment 3," December 16, 1977.

6.20 A special Mafia hit squad murders 20 victims. In 1977 Gino Gallina, a Manhattan district attorney who became a lawyer for the Mob, was killed gangland style in Greenwich Village. Gallina had testified to a Newark grand jury about a Mafia hit squad armed with .22-caliber automatics complete with silencers. This squad had murdered at least 20 persons in the previous two years, including six FBI informants and witnesses. Federal officials think that a leak from the grand jury led to Gallina's slaying; other leaks from government files and court records have led to similar murders. *Time*, November 21, 1977, p. 39.

b. Various other methods of operation

6.21 Recruitment and training. Convicts and college graduates. *U.S.-Task Force Report*, pp. 55–56.

6.22 Counterintelligence. Salerno and Tompkins, *Crime Confederation*, pp. 172–73.

6.23 Silence and insulation. Orders are given through intermediaries; "each man is a wall protecting the next guy higher up." Teresa, *My Life in the Mafia*, pp. 87–88.

6.24 Mafia "licenses" to unaffiliated allies. In New England, where the resident Mafia family is relatively small, "non-Mafia allies hold Mafia 'licenses'" to be bookies, loan sharks or fences. The Mafia takes 25 to 40 percent of the receipts. Some allies have Mafia licenses for whole territories. The aging town of Somerville, Massachusetts, was the haven of Howie Winter, the last of the Irish gang leaders who once ran the Boston underworld. A 1967 report stated: "Winter pays tribute regularly to Angiulo's men"; they met in the Nautical Cafe, a Boston night club. Bill Davidson, "The Mafia: How it Bleeds New England," *Saturday Evening Post*, November 18, 1967, p. 28.

6.25 Feigning illness to evade the law. Both Al Capone and Meyer Lansky pleaded serious or terminal illness in the 1920s to duck grand jury subpoenas. The Taglianetti airtels revealed that New England Mafioso[24] Louis Taglianetti was "considering feigning a heart attack in order to postpone his tax case." Doctors on the hook with the Mob sometimes cooperate. Mollenhoff, *Strike Force*, p. 122; Gage, *The Mafia is not an Equal Opportunity Employer*, pp. 59–60; Teresa, *My Life in the Mafia*, p. 192; Allsop, *The Bootleggers*, p. 321.

6.26 Mafia treatment of nonmember employees. "They bleed you dry and . . . when your mind and body aren't any use to them—they throw you out and have you killed." Testimony of Mob defector Patsy Lepera in *U.S.-OC and Stolen Securities, 1973*, pp. 453–54, 470.

6.27 Dirty tricks, Watergate style. A New York Mafioso hired blacks and Puerto Ricans to build white backlash against a referendum to authorize a new race track in Secaucus, New Jersey. The hired men passed out leaflets in support of the referendum stating that it would "bring full integration to Secaucus," and went door to door trying to rent rooms as future track employees. The referendum was defeated. Salerno and Tompkins, *Crime Confederation*, pp. 267–68.

6.28 Colombo Family activities. Eleven members and associates of the Colombo crime family were tried in Manhattan in 1985 on racketeering and other criminal charges. The prosecutor said in his opening statement that the jury would hear "about people who build buildings in the city paying the family, people who run restaurants in the city paying the family, unions run by the family, money loaned at illegal interest rates by the family, illegal gambling run by the family, businesses burglarized by the family, prison officials and tax agents bribed by the family." *New York Times*, November 5, 1985, p. B1.

6.29 Framing the FBI. New Jersey Mobsters obtained copies of classified FBI documents concerning a loan sharking case and attempted to implicate the FBI in illegal activities. *Newark* [N.J.] *Star Ledger*, August 8, 1974, p. 1.

6.30 Anti-Mafia prosecutors were fired, threatened and libeled in New Jersey. Several New Jersey district attorneys suffered political setbacks, including dismissal, when they vigorously prosecuted the Mafia. In the 1960s, when U.S. Attorney Frederick Lacey was securing indictments and convictions against top New Jersey Mafiosi and politicians, his family was threatened, and he was smeared with absurd charges of communist collaboration. "Is the power of organized crime in America now so great that any man who tries to stand up to it must expect to become the victim of threats, lies and vilification?" Fred Cook, "New Jersey: The State of Mafia," *Nation*, May 11, 1970, pp. 560–63, 574.

6.31 Maintaining Family traditions. On July 20, 1973, two men dropped off a third man at the emergency room door of Wyckoff Heights Hospital. He was "clad only in charred shorts and burned over 90 percent of his body." Moments before, the Vic Construction Company six blocks away had burst into flame after an explosion. The fire marshal's office called it arson. The burned man, who later died of his injuries, was Leonard Vario, the 23-year-old son of New York Mafia boss Paul Vario. *New York Times*, October 11, 1973, p. 12.

6.32 Laundering money through foreign banks. Cash from Mafia illegal activities, such as narcotics or loan sharking, is funneled into banks in Switzerland, the Bahamas and other foreign countries, and returned as loans. This hides Mafia income from law enforcement authorities and the IRS. Foreign banks are also used to facilitate such illegal transactions as sales of stolen stocks. And the Mob has gone a step further in its foreign bank dealings, noted former U.S. Attorney Robert Morgenthau: "Today, numerous banks in Switzerland and the Bahamas are owned and controlled not only by Americans, but in some cases by American hoodlums closely linked to loan sharking, gambling rackets, and other illegal businesses." Dorman, *Payoff*, pp. 255–58; testimony of former Mob money-mover Gerald Zelmanowitz in *U.S.–Senate, OC and Stolen Securities, 1973*, pp. 73–74.

6.33 A Mafioso's prayer. When Chicago Mafioso Sam DeStefano was troubled, reported informant Charles Crimaldi, he would kneel down and "smash his fists against the floor in frustration and rage. The drool would pour from his mouth in streams. . . . His gravelly voice would become a croak so guttural that his words were barely comprehensible." He would then pray to the devil: "I'm your fuckin' disciple. You put me where I am. How can you do this thing and cause me all this goddamned heat—all this fuckin' agitation. What do you want me to do? Kill somebody? Can't you tell me in another way instead of handin' me all this fuckin' aggravation?" John Kidner, *Crimaldi: Contract Killer* (Washington, D.C.: Acropolis Books, 1976), pp. 134–35.

6.34 Philosophy behind the methods. The Mafioso "believes he has the right to steal, corrupt, even murder." Reid, *Grim Reapers*, pp. 1–2.

c. Public relations and the affectation of respectability

6.35 Polite demeanor characterized a Mafia hit man. Gage, *Mafia, U.S.A.*, p. 21.

6.36 Aping an upstanding citizen. Gifts to charity and a professional public relations firm were used to bolster a Mobster's image. Dorman, *Payoff*, p. 276; Cressey, *Theft of the Nation*, p. 274.

6.37 Buffalo, New York "Man of the Year," prominent in business and politics, was exposed as Mafia member. John Montana, a one-time Buffalo City Councilman, owner of the largest taxicab company in western New York State and a member of civic and fraternal organizations, was one of those arrested at the Apalachin Mafia conclave in 1957. He was found to be a lieutenant in the Buffalo Magaddino Family, with close ties to several area Mafia figures. Joseph Valachi, who knew Magaddino well, confirmed this in his Congressional testimony. *U.S.–Senate, OC and Narcotics Hearings*, pp. 591–92, 196, 299.

6.38 The glad hand. "The Mafia front men are characterized by the smile, the glad hand, the tuxedo and the ticket to the charity ball. But the basic Mafia tools are still money, murder, and corruption." From the testimony of Detroit Police Chief George Edwards in *U.S.–Senate, OC and Narcotics Hearings*, pp. 400–401.

7. Roots in Sicily

7.1 Origins of the Mafia. "The taproots of the criminal organization known as the Mafia lie deep in the troubled history of the island of Sicily, which was overrun by invaders and conquerors for almost 2,000 years." During this period, Sicilian slave labor enriched a succession of foreign powers, including the Romans, Normans, Germans, French, Aragonese, Spaniards and Bourbons. The last stretch of brutality was imposed by the Inquisition, which disbanded in Sicily at the end of the 18th century. Under the direction of Sicilian barons, Sicilians were tortured and stripped of their property for a variety of vaguely defined offenses or philosophical positions. The Duke of Merindaceli, the Spanish Viceroy, wrote: "It would take a year to describe the things they do. Unheard of things—the most hideous and frightful enormities."(B)

"The precise origins and development of the secret criminal society on the island are uncertain, but it is probable that the Mafia came into being to fight the excesses of absentee feudal landlords in their harsh treatment of the peasantry on the island. Historians who have traced the growth of the organization from medieval times into the modern era are generally agreed that the Mafia was conceived in rebellion against Sicily's conquerors. In modern times, the Sicilian Mafia has almost entirely lost its ancient aura of revolutionary and patriotic lawlessness and has become primarily a criminal combine specializing in fraud and extortion, among other crimes." A—*U.S.-Senate, OC and Narcotics Report*, p. 5; B—Gage, *Mafia, U.S.A.*, pp. 65–67.

7.2 From Robin Hoods to hoods. A tradition of revenge and silence developed under foreign oppression. But by 1945 the Mafia had become the worst oppressor of the peasants. The Mafia imposed its own tax on all forms of agriculture, industry, and commerce. It virtually replaced the police department. It secured the election of puppet candidates through rigged balloting. It took over the manufacture of religious relics to make huge profits from facsimiles. Lewis, *The Honored Society*, reprinted in Gage, *Mafia, U.S.A.*, pp. 67–77.

7.3 No subtlety in its approach. Scores of political and trade union leaders in Sicily have been murdered by the Mafia. Eighteen bystanders were wounded in 1944 when the Mafia fired into the crowd at an anti-Mob political rally. A Mafia-backed political candidate declared, "I am a friend of the Mafia." A Mafia physician poisoned a murder witness. Mafiosi bombed facilities of a leading Sicilian newspaper. Pantaleone, *Mafia and Politics*, pp. 73, 88, 115–16, 127, 202–6.

7.4 The Mafia in Sicily in the 1920s. It "dominated and controlled the whole social life . . . in big cities and in small centres, . . . forced its way into every kind of business, and got its way by means of threats and intimidation." From a January 19, 1931 report of the Procurator-General of Palermo, reprinted in Cook, *Secret Rulers*, p. 55.

7.5 The Mafia in Italy in the 1960s. "The Mafia doctor got all the patients" and the "Mafia advocate had all the briefs he could handle." The Mafia got the government contracts and arranged the elections of members of Parliament. Lewis, *The Honored Society*, p. 84; Luigi Barzini, *The Italians* (New York: Atheneum, 1964), pp. 259–60.

7.6 The Mafia in Italy in the 1970s. The Mafia has managed to "survive and prosper" in changing times with its standard techniques "including terror, extortion and bribery." In Palermo, "there's good reason to believe that not a single traffic light goes up these days without its ok." Mafia operations have been extended to the mainland; Mafia hit men are sent from Sicily to the mainland and vice versa. Close ties and "mutual dependence" exist between the Mafia and the ruling Christian Democratic Party, as documented in a 270-page 1971 report by the Italian Parliament. *Newsweek*, October 23, 1972, p. 58; July 26, 1971, p. 38.

7.7 The Mafia in Italy in the 1980s. The Italian Mob operates a $625 million-per-year extortion racket against merchants and businessmen. It owns or is associated with nearly half of the 6,000 companies involved in public works projects in Sicily. It has threatened an estimated 10 percent of Italy's merchants to pay protection money, often regularly. This and other evidence, authorities say, shows the Mob to be stifling the Italian economy. *Washington Post*, May 24, 1984, p. E2.

7.8 The Palermo Connection. In the early 1970s, when international drug agents broke the "French Connection," the multibillion-dollar heroin industry based in Marseilles, the Sicilian Mafia took over the trade. Authorities estimate that two tons of heroin are produced in Palermo alone each year. Sixty percent of the Mafia's $1 billion in yearly profits in Sicily come from narcotics trafficking. It is also estimated that the Sicilian Mob oversees 60 percent of the American heroin trade. Because of the Mafia's sophisticated trans-Atlantic smuggling ring, heroin produced in Sicily on Monday can be bought in Times Square, New York, on Wednesday. *Newsweek*, October 15, 1984, pp. 56–60; *Time*, October 15, 1984, pp. 42–51.

7.9 Wholesale slaughter. The Mafia's chief foe in Italy was executed in broad daylight. Judge Cesare Terranova, age 58, was caught in Palermo's rush-hour traffic on September 24, 1979, when two men opened fire on his car. His murderers fled, "having demonstrated publicly the fate that awaited those who dared oppose them." Terranova "had an encyclopedic knowledge of the connections between the Mafia and politicians, the police, judges, Government officials, the nobility, the Vatican, and captains of industry. . . ." He was about to have been given more power when he was murdered. An appeals court threw out a lower court conviction in the case, which had rested largely on testimony from Italy's highest-ranking Mafioso ever to defect.

Other Mafia victims in 1979 alone included the provincial secretary for the Christian Democrats in Palermo, the vice commandant of Palermo's police force, the chief of Palermo's strike force against narcotics, the investigator of Italy's largest bank failure, "in which the Mafia was believed heavily involved," and a police colonel who had sent dozens of Mafiosi to jail. Italian murder victims of the Mafia in the 1970s, according to police estimates, number at least 1,000.

Klaus Schwidrowski, "Italy's Mafia Blight," *Die Zeit* (Hamburg), translated and reprinted in *World Press Review*, March 1980, p. 56; *Manchester Guardian*, April 17, 1987, p. 5.

7.10 Murder for power. The next year, prosecutor Gaetano Costa was ordered murdered because Salvatore Inzerillo, a chief heroin exporter, "wanted to demonstrate that he was very powerful." From the testimony of Mafia defector Tommaso Buscetta, in *Newsweek*, October 15, 1984, pp. 58, 60.

7.11 The slaying of Italy's top antiterrorist policeman. In 1982, recognizing the intolerable threat posed by the Mafia, the Italian government commissioned its senior antiterrorist policeman, General Carlo Dalla Chiesa, to investigate the Cosa Nostra. On September 3, Dalla Chiesa and his wife were murdered by gunshots fired at their car in Palermo, Sicily; a police escort was also killed. Italian Prime Minister Giovanni Spadolini blamed the Mafia for the killings, commenting: "General Dalla Chiesa, who had made an immense contribution to the struggle against terrorism, has fallen at a moment when he was putting into action, with intelligence and courage, a battle plan against the Mafia terror." The prime minister called the murders "a mortal challenge launched by the Mafia against the democratic state, a challenge that for some time has turned into open warfare." *Washington Post*, September 4, 1982, p. A24.

7.12 A crusading magistrate is car-bombed. Judge Rocco Chinnici had put more than 100 Mafiosi in jail in just nine months and made frequent speeches vocally denouncing the Mafia heroin trade. One morning in 1983, surrounded by guards on a sealed-off street, Chinnici left his apartment for his bullet-proof car. Apparently these precautions were not enough; a remote-control bomb planted under his car was detonated, killing the judge, his bodyguards and a concierge in front of the apartment. *Newsweek*, August 8, 1983, p. 49.

7.13 The biggest Mafia trial in decades. Seventy-four Mafiosi, including top members of the Gambino, Inzerillo and Buscetta families, were convicted and sentenced in June 1983. The trial illuminated the financial workings of the trans-Atlantic drug trade. *Newsday*, June 9, 1983.

7.14 A pre-dawn roundup. In October 1984, on the day honoring St. Michael, the patron saint of police, authorities carried out a massive series of early-morning raids, capturing 53 gangsters and issuing arrest warrants for another 313. The raid was sparked by information from Tommaso Buscetta, a top-level Sicilian Mobster who became the first of his stature to break the code of silence. *Time*, October 15, 1984, pp. 42–51.

7.15 The Mafia on trial. In February 1986, 467 alleged Mafiosi went on trial in Italy for scores of crimes, including the slaying of antiterrorist policeman Carlo Dalla Chiesa and 96 other murders. Not since Benito Mussolini's pre-war scourges had there been such a crackdown on the Mob in Italy. The indictment, 8,636 pages long, took a team of constantly guarded judges three years to prepare. The defendants were housed in 20 separate microphone-equipped cages inside a special courtroom erected next to a prison, while the Mafiosi turning state's evidence sat behind a bullet-proof glass screen 30 yards away. Just after the trial got underway, police captured "boss of bosses" Michele Greco, the chairman of the Syndicate's ruling commission. He and his brother, Salvatore, already had been convicted in absentia and sentenced to life in prison in 1984 for murdering a tough anti-Mafia judge; both Grecos were also charged in the 8,636-page indictment with drug trafficking and multiple murders, including the assassination of Dalla Chiesa. The indictment defined its intent to stage "the trial of the

Mafia organization called Cosa Nostra." *Washington Post*, February 21, 1986; *Manchester Guardian*, April 17, 1987, p. 5. (Update, December 1987: most were convicted).

8. Migration to America

8.1 Black-Hand extortion letters and dock racketeering at the turn of the 20th century. Investigation of these led to the Mafia murders of New Orleans Police Chief David Hennessey in 1890 and of New York Police Lieutenant Joseph Petrosino in 1909. Sondern, *Brotherhood of Evil*, pp. 56–65; Reid, *Grim Reapers*, pp. 146–50.

8.2 Description of the Mafia in the early 1900s from the memoirs of Mafioso Nicola Gentile. Gage, *The Mafia Is Not an Equal Opportunity Employer*, pp. 32–35; Messick and Goldblatt, *The Mobs and the Mafia*, pp. 7–9.

8.3 The Capone era: an example of Mafia operations in the 1920s and 1930s. "All restraints were lifted." Dozens of citizens were murdered, including a newspaper reporter and assistant state's attorney William McSwiggin. The homes of Senator Beneen and political candidate John Swanton were bombed. From the testimony of Joseph Morris, Chicago deputy superintendent of police, in *U.S.-Senate, OC and Narcotics Hearings*, pp. 502–3.

8.4 Post-Prohibition adjustments. "The underworld turned to industry, labor, and real estate." From "servant" to "master" in labor relations. Tyler, *Organized Crime in America*, pp. 152–53.

8.5 The birth of a unified nationwide organization. The "Castellammarese war" of 1930–31 between Mafia factions was ended with a mass meeting in New York. Presiding boss Salvatore Maranzano laid out a national structure unifying the various Mafia gangs in America. Maas, *Valachi Papers*, pp. 104–7; *Time*, August 22, 1969, p. 19; *U.S.-House, Assassination Appendix, JFK*, vol. 9, pp. 5–6.

III. CRIMINAL OPERATIONS

9. Gambling

9.1 "The meat and potatoes of the Mafia." Gambling is the Mob's "largest single source of income" in the Northeast. Gage, *Mafia, U.S.A.*, pp. 17–18; *U.S.-President's Commission on Organized Crime, OC and Gambling*, p. 4.

9.2 A Massachusetts crime commission found that state residents spent more on gambling than on food. A 1957 commission report, which focused on organized crime's corruption of police, found that in 1954, the state's illegal gambling turnover was $2 billion, almost double its food sales. Cook, *Two-Dollar Bet*, pp. 6–7.

a. Mafia control of gambling

9.3 Mafia members "control all but a tiny part of the illegal gambling in the United States." Those illegal betting and lottery operations that they do not own "they control, or provide with essential services." Cressey, *Theft of the Nation*, pp. xi, 75; *U.S.–Task Force Report*, pp. 2–3.

9.4 Bookmakers in Chicago pay a "street tax" to the Mob "for the privilege of operating" there. The "Outfit" establishes a fifty-fifty partnership with the bookmakers and supplies wire rooms, clerks and telephones. Eventually, the Mob drains the bookmaker's finances and takes over the business. From the testimony of Sergeant Donald Herion of the Chicago Police Department before the President's Commission on Organized Crime. *U.S.–President's Commission on OC, OC and Gambling*, p. 148.

9.5 Mob protection for illegal gambling operations is mandatory—for a 50 percent cut. From the testimony of defected New England Mob killer Joseph Barboza in *U.S.–House, OC in Sports*, p. 751.

9.6 Kefauver Committee findings: "The committee was repeatedly struck by the magnitude of the gambling business and by the pattern of domination in this business by an interlocking group of gangsters, racketeers, and hoodlums." *U.S.–Senate, Kefauver Report, Third Interim*, p. 90.

9.7 Independent gambling operations are eliminated. Carlton O'Brien ran a bookie network in Rhode Island independent of Mafia boss Raymond Patriarca. "O'Brien's bookies were held up, bookie parlors wrecked, and telephone lines pulled out, bookmakers slugged and robbed." Finally, in 1951, O'Brien was murdered by a shotgun blast. From the testimony of Col. Walter E. Stone, superintendent of the Rhode Island State Police, in *U.S.–Senate, OC and Narcotics Hearings*, p. 552.

b. Improving the odds

9.8 A Mafia–licensed Detroit numbers operation was "completely crooked." Winning numbers were changed when heavily bet. From the testimony of Detroit Police Chief Edwards in *U.S.–Senate, OC and Narcotics Hearings*, pp. 412–415.

9.9 Rigging the number in New York City. The winning number of a Mob-controlled New York numbers game was based on the daily volume of the Cincinnati Clearinghouse. Police wiretaps and a confession of the clearinghouse secretary revealed that this figure was adjusted daily by the secretary for a $1,000-a-month payoff to match the number least heavily bet. Tyler, *Organized Crime in America*, pp. 274–81.

c. Examples of Mob-controlled bookmaking, casino and numbers operations

9.10 The Mob's Las Vegas casino operations. They are characterized by concealed ownerships and millions of dollars skimmed annually, transported to Swiss banks by international couriers. *Life*, September 8, 1967, pp. 98–100.

9.11 The casino trial. In 1974, Mafia bosses from Kansas City, Milwaukee and Cleveland influenced trustees of a Teamsters pension fund to grant $87.75 million in loans to Allen R. Glick. The 32-year-old entrepreneur,[25] who used the money to acquire the Stardust and Fremont casinos in Las Vegas, soon discovered he had "partners" in business: the Mafia. The Mob skimmed over $2 million in gambling proceeds from the four casinos owned by Glick's Argent Corporation. The money was distributed among the Midwestern Mafia Families; Teamsters officials and trustees who helped swing the loans also got a cut of the profits.

Convicted felon and Mafia associate Frank Rosenthal managed the operation from his top position at Argent. Rosenthal employed a "known slot cheat"(B) to run the slot operations at the casinos, "embarked on a 'reign of terror' that resulted in the resignation of many casino employees," and told Glick to "drop dead, and if that's necessary, that can be arranged."

Glick was threatened by higher-ranking Mobsters than Rosenthal. Once, long past midnight in a darkened hotel room, Kansas City boss Nick Civella told him "it would be my choice that you never leave this room alive."(C) In 1979, Glick sold his company after Civella's underboss, Carl DeLuna, threatened to murder his sons.

John Cerone, Joseph Lombardo, Angelo Pietra, Milton Rockman and Chicago boss Joseph Aiuppa were convicted in 1986 of skimming money from the casinos. DeLuna and Frank Balistrieri pleaded guilty; Balistrieri's sons were acquitted. Nick Civella died of cancer in 1983 and was not indicted.

A–*New York Times*, January 16, 1986, p. A19; B–*U.S.-President's Commission on OC, OC and Gambling*, pp. 493–94; C–*New York Times*, April 3, 1986, p. A22; also *Washington Post*, January 22, 1986, p. A6.

9.12 The numbers racket: bleeding the poor. A majority of the adult residents in New York's and Chicago's major slum areas played Mob-controlled numbers games. A New York State committee found that the average resident bet $150 to $250 a year; Malcolm X reported that he used to bet up to $15 to $20 per day. Gage, *The Mafia Is Not an Equal Opportunity Employer*, pp. 150–51; *U.S.-Senate, Kefauver Report, Third Interim*, p. 56; Eugene Methvin, "How the Mafia Preys on the Poor," *Reader's Digest*, September 1970, pp. 51–52; Malcolm X, *The Autobiography of Malcolm X*, pp. 84–85.

9.13 A booming business in industrial plants and office buildings. In Washington, D.C., for example, elevator operators, car pool drivers, and messengers often double as numbers runners and bookies in federal buildings "not excluding the FBI section of the Department of Justice." The IRS has conducted gambling raids on government buildings including the Pentagon. King, *Gambling and Organized Crime*, p. 29; Cook, *Two-Dollar Bet*, p. 129; Tyler, *Organized Crime in America*, pp. 262–63.

9.14 Anatomy of a bookmaking ring. Vincent Teresa testified about a small Massachusetts bookmaking ring employing 60 to 70 agents that he once operated with Mobster[26] Robert Visconti. The ring, which was run with an okay from Mafia boss Patriarca, layoffs to the Mob and payoffs to police, grossed about $5 million per year. *U.S.-Senate, OC and Stolen Securities, 1971*, pp. 814–15.

9.15 How the Mob took over numbers operations in New York. "They 'persuaded' people with lead pipes, wet cement, baseball bats, brass knuckles, fists, feet, and blackjacks." Malcolm X, *The Autobiography of Malcolm X*, p. 87; *The New York Post* (1960), reprinted in Tyler, *Organized Crime in America*, pp. 260–74.

412

> Gambling is the single most important activity for organized crime. They control it all over the country and all over the world. . . . From it comes the corrupt politicians and policemen, the bribes and the payoffs, and sometimes murder . . . .
>
> There is no bookmaker that can do business by himself; he couldn't survive. The mob would turn him over to the police, give him a few beatings, or even kill him if he's real stubborn. He has to go with them, because they run everything.
>
> . . . There isn't one casino in the world, outside of the Communist countries, that doesn't have the mob involved in some way. . . . As an example of how the mob's control stretches everywhere, I can tell you about George Raft's Colony Sportsmen's Club in London. . . . Dino Cellini is involved in that club and so is Meyer Lansky. I know, because I ran gambling junkets, and we couldn't put a junket in there without their ok. It's the same at Paradise Island in the Bahamas. . . .
>
> When you lose $50,000 in London on credit, you don't come home and send the money to London. You pay Cellini and Meyer Lansky.
>
> Mafia defector Vincent Teresa, in *U.S.–Senate, OC and Stolen Securities, 1971*, pp. 813–14.

10. Loan sharking

10.1 Loans at exorbitant interest—the borrower's body is collateral. Small loans are characteristically made at "six for five," or 20 percent interest *per week*. Larger loans are made at lower rates. *Time*, August 22, 1969, p. 20; *Reader's Digest*, September 1970, p. 52; *U.S.-President's Commission on OC, The Impact*, p. 452.

10.2 Loan shark victims often turn to crime. "He gets in deep, and he can't pay, and they beat him up. He gets out of the hospital, and they beat him up again. Then he either turns to crime to get the money—say he is a truckdriver and starts hijacking trucks, or else he runs away. He leaves his wife and his kids and his home and runs away." From the testimony of Mafia defector Vincent Teresa in *U.S.-Senate, OC and Stolen Securities, 1971*, p. 815.

10.3 Case studies of Mafia loan sharking transactions. The "objective is to take every dime the borrower can lay his hands on." Threats and beatings often drive victims to crime or force them to become inside men for the Mob in a variety of crimes. Cressey, *Theft of the Nation*, pp. 78–91.

10.4 Mafia loan sharking exposed by testimony in a 1966 Illinois state investigation. Victims became caught in an unending nightmare of threats, beatings, and murders. "They may torture you, squeeze you—that's what it is—they squeeze you until there's no juice left. It destroys a man." Demaris, *Captive City*, pp. 50–59.

10.5 The testimony of former Mob loan shark collector Louis Mastriana. Mastriana told the Senate how he collected loans in the Washington, D.C. area for New Jersey Mafioso[27] Charlie Tourine. "I would give them a week

> If a man is three weeks late in his vigorish [interest payments], he gets a broken arm or leg. If he's six to eight weeks late, he has an accident. We fix the brakes of his car or we run him off the road, or we blow up his house or his business. Sometimes we go to his house and beat up his wife, or we break a leg on his kid on his way home from school. If the guy owes more than $15,000, or if he's arrogant about falling behind in his vigorish, he gets death.
>
> As described to an undercover agent by Phil Waggenheim, enforcer for Mafia loan shark Larry Baioni. Quoted in Davidson, "The Mafia: How it Bleeds New England," *Saturday Evening Post*, November 18, 1967, p. 29.

to pay. Then if he didn't pay, you whacked them ... break his head." *U.S.-Senate, OC and Stolen Securities, 1973*, pp. 167, 138–39.

10.6 Two-thirds of murders and maimings in New England involve Mafia loan shark victims. Charles Rogovin, the Massachusetts attorney general's expert on organized crime, stated that "all other Mafia families" usually "stop short of killing, on the theory that a dead man can't pay. But not here. They're totally ruthless about loan sharking debts. Two-thirds of the murders and maimings in New England involve people who have surrendered the collateral of their bodies to the loan sharks." Reid, *Grim Reapers*, p. 67.

11. Narcotics

11.1 Mafia control of most U.S heroin traffic was reported by the Federal Bureau of Narcotics in 1963 and 1969. *U.S.-Senate OC and Narcotics Report*, p. 56; *U.S.-House, Criminal Justice Hearings*, p. 333.

11.2 Non-Mob elements are moving into high-risk street sale of narcotics. "But the fact is that the Mafia is still bankrolling the drug traffic and pocketing most of the profits." Gage, *Mafia, U.S.A.*, p. 17.

11.3 The Mob still plays "a significant role" in the U.S. heroin trade in the 1980s, controlling 15.9 percent of the heroin traffic within organized crime. Much of this heroin comes to the U.S. by way of Sicily and the Sicilian Mafia. *U.S.-President's Commission on OC, America's Habit*, p. 126.

11.4 A Sicilian-American Mafia ring using pizzerias to disguise its operations "smuggled tons of heroin and cocaine into the country between 1979 and 1984." The conspiracy included "elaborate money-laundering routes" through which $50 million was transferred "to secret accounts in Switzerland, Bermuda and other locales overseas." Seventeen men, including Salvatore Catalano and former Sicilian boss Gaetano Badalamenti, were convicted in the conspiracy on March 2, 1987, after a seventeen-month trial during which one defendant was killed and another shot and paralyzed. Robert D. McFadden, "The Mafia of the 1980's: Divided and Under Siege,"

New York Times, March 11, 1987, p. B2; "Pizza Penance," *Time*, March 16, 1987, p. 34.

11.5 The Mafia reaps additional profits through fencing operations. Addicts spend about $2 billion a year on heroin, most of which is raised by stealing. The goods stolen to buy the drugs are usually taken from homes and stores in slum neighborhoods, and are often converted into cash (at 20 percent of value) through Mob fencing networks. Gage, *The Mafia Is Not an Equal Opportunity Employer*, pp. 158–59, 164–65.

12. Extortion

12.1 Self-proclaimed business partners. Cressey, *Theft of the Nation*, pp. 103–105.

12.2 Shaking down Boston-area bars not owned by the Mob. Notorious killer Joseph Barboza and his men "would go into these places and tear the joints apart. They'd bust up a few people, break the furniture, smash the bar, and storm out." Soon, 20 clubs were doling out $1,000 a month each to keep Barboza in check. Barboza and his men got 25 percent of this money while three top New England Mafiosi—Raymond Patriarca, Henry Tameleo and Vincent Teresa—split the other 75 percent. As described by Teresa and Barboza, who both became government witnesses, in Teresa, *My Life in the Mafia*, pp. 116–17; and *U.S.–House, OC in Sports*, pp. 745–47.

12.3 "A reverse twist of the old Black Hand technique." Detroit Mafioso Santo Perrone first bombed his victim with a small explosive device, then demanded extortion money. From the testimony of Detroit Police Criminal Intelligence Director Vince Piersante in *U.S.–Senate, OC and Narcotics Hearings*, p. 476.

13. Securities theft and fraud

13.1 Volume of thefts: from $9.1 million in 1966 to $50 billion in 1973. Wall Street and government estimates of securities thefts show an astronomical increase: $9.1 million in 1966,[28] $37 million in 1967,[29] $400 million in 1969 and 1970,[30] and $494 million in the first six months of 1971.[31] But the real shocker was the figure for 1973, as presented in the Senate's Organized Crime and Stolen Securities hearings. Henry DuPont, chairman of the board of the Securities Validation Corporation, estimated from a data base of 10 percent (in dollar value) of U.S. securities that the value of securities stolen or otherwise lost as of June 1973 was $50 billion, or 48 percent of all outstanding stocks. *U.S.–Senate, OC and Stolen Securities, 1973*, pp. 9–11, 20, 35, 42–43.

a. Mafia control of securities thefts

13.2 Organized crime elements "control the theft, distribution and conversion" of stolen securities. This conclusion is noted on a government chart showing the "Pattern of Organized Crime Perpetration of Thefts and Conversion of Securities." It was prepared by the Senate Government Operations Committee. Following is an excerpt, with punctuation modified: "Factors Involved in Thefts: 1. Direct Infiltration By The Mob; 2. Persons Under Pressure to Steal Securities [through] A. Gambling Debts, B. Loan sharking Debts, C. Narcotics Addiction, D. Strong Arm; 3. Thieves Who Depend On Mob For Conversion." The Senate chart similarly outlined Mob conversion and distribution of stocks. *U.S.-Senate, OC and Stolen Securities, 1971*, pp. 62–63.

13.3 The Mobsters "came to Wall Street with their same 'bag of tricks,' and . . . were more than able to breach the flimsy fortress of Wall Street security." From the testimony of New York Assistant District Attorney Murray Gross in *U.S.-Senate, OC and Stolen Securities, 1971*, pp. 72–77, 90–91.

13.4 Control through terror. "Utilizing terror as their usual practice, utilizing all of their normal techniques, they control the production of counterfeit securities, they control the theft of the securities. . . . On the street, and it has been known for years, they [Mobsters] look to get [securities] runners and customers, men on juice [in debt to loan sharks]. They look to get them with girls. They look to get them with narcotics, any way they can, to control the situation." From the testimony of Michael Raymond, a financial operator who worked closely with the Mafia, in *U.S.-Senate, OC and Stolen Securities, 1971*, p. 681; for background on Raymond, see pp. 659–64, 956, 1245–46.

House Crime Committee Chairman Claude Pepper, opening the Committee's 1971–72 hearings on worthless securities, in *U.S.-House, OC and Worthless Securities*, pp. 1–2:

This is the first of a series of hearings designed to show how extensively organized criminal elements have infiltrated the banking, securities, and insurance industries. The evidence uncovered thus far shows that important racketeers have combined with lawyers and accountants in developing schemes which have defrauded the general public as well as companies in the banking, securities, and insurance industries of hundreds of millions of dollars each year.

. . . The tremendous amounts of money they are able to amass . . . enables them to facilitate their operations by offering substantial bribes to bank presidents, insurance company executives, and stock brokerage management. . . .

These individuals move across State lines—from coast to coast and internationally—bankrupting small banks, insurance companies and stock brokerage institutions. Local law enforcement is entirely inadequate to cope with a scheme which is planned in California, prepared in New Jersey, and executed in Ohio. . . .

In addition to the bribery of banking and securities officials, these criminals are associated with corrupt lawyers and accountants. Evidence developed during our investigation shows that corrupt lawyers have been able to bribe judges in order to obtain preferential treatment. . . . This disclosure demonstrates the pervasive influence of organized crime in our State courts.

13.5 "The major portion of stolen securities" was controlled by organized crime. When asked by Senator Gurney "how to get at the organized crime people who run the show," a former Mob securities fence suggested, "if you started a program of rounding these people up from the top to the bottom eventually you might make a big dent." From the testimony of Edward Wuenche, in *U.S.-Senate, OC and Stolen Securities, 1971*, pp. 868–69; background on Wuenche, pp. 842–46.

13.6 The Mafia's role in the stolen securities business: "It is total." Stocks stolen-to-order within 24 hours. From the testimony of Pasty Lepera, former Mob securities fence, in *U.S.-Senate, OC and Stolen Securities, 1973*, pp. 474–75; background, pp. 389–90.

b. Cases of Mob securities thefts and racketeering activities on Wall Street

13.7 The Wall Street connection. A Mafia-controlled international stolen securities ring was uncovered by police in 1973. Twenty-five persons, including Genovese Family member Vincent Rizzo and other high-level Mobsters, were indicted on "charges ranging from narcotics smuggling to extortion to attempted murder." *Newsweek*, July 23, 1973, pp. 62–63.

13.8 A witness was murdered after the robbery of "a fortune in negotiable securities." A securities messenger, a nephew of a Mafioso, was robbed. He subsequently testified several times before the grand jury looking into whether the robbery was staged. During the investigation, "the messenger's corpse was found, covered with stab wounds." Grutzner, "How to Lock Out the Mafia," *Harvard Business Review*, March-April 1970, p. 56.

13.9 The theft and nationwide distribution of $21 million in securities stolen in 1968 from a mail pouch at New York's JFK airport. The theft was committed by Mafioso[32] William Ricchiuti and Mob associate[33] James Schaeffer. The principal fences were Gus Cangiano and Anthony Garafola, both Mafia members.[34] Within two years, securities from the pouch turned up in San Diego, Houston, Miami, Oklahoma City, Phoenix, Los Angeles, Boston, Mexico City, Chicago, New York, Toronto, and other cities. Also in that period, two associates of Cangiano and another man linked to the 1968 JFK theft were murdered (Cangiano invoked the Fifth Amendment when questioned about the murder[35]). From the testimony of U.S. Chief Postal Inspector William J. Cotter in *U.S.-Senate, OC and Stolen Securities, 1971*, pp. 108–19, 247–49, 611–12.

13.10 Selling millions in worthless stocks at securities firms owned by the Gambino Family. Meskil, *Don Carlo*, pp. 191–92; Cook, *Secret Rulers*, pp. 363–65.

14. Cargo theft

14.1 Excerpts from a U.S. government publication on cargo theft and organized crime. Cargo theft amounted to more than $2 billion in 1972, causing major economic dislocations. Losses are passed on to consumers. The increase in crime costs "has outpaced any corresponding increase in tonnage or revenue."

"Organized crime has a direct hand in the *execution* of cargo thefts, in *the distribution* of this cargo . . . and *in the actual consumption* of the stolen goods through the businesses it owns or otherwise controls." The Mafia "is the inner core of organized crime." Up to 80 percent of the thefts are committed by employees, often enlisted through Mob loan sharking activities, threats, and Mob-union collusion.

Guards are "frightened away" from stopping thefts. "Attempts to control theft on the waterfront have frequently resulted in personal injury through 'accidents' or direct assaults." "More portwatchmen were apprehended for stealing cargo . . . than they—the portwatchmen force—apprehended."

"What would alleviate the cargo theft problem is to break up organized crime." *U.S.–Cargo Theft and OC*, pp. 5–11, 15–19, 23–29.

14.2 Hijackings are arranged by the Mob, from staged "holdup" to disposition of the goods. "Most so-called hijacks with guns never happened that way. It was all set up before by the Mob." The truck driver, often in debt to the Mob, turns over his cargo to "some fringe punk" lined up to handle the theft. The Mob disposes of the goods and gets "the lion's share" of the profits. From the comments of Mafia defector Vincent Teresa in *My Life in the Mafia*, pp. 134–39.

14.3 Recent estimates. In 1986, Wharton Econometric Forecasting Associates estimated that losses from trucking, air, and railroad cargo theft alone amounted to between $796 million and $1.105 billion per year. *U.S.–President's Commission on OC, The Impact*, p. 463.

14.4 "The mob takeover of the air freight trucking industry at Kennedy Airport, N.Y. . . . annual thefts jumped 100-fold in 5 years, from $45,000 to 4.5 million." The Mob gained control of the union, Teamsters Local 295, and the industry association, the National Association for Air Freight (NAAF), handling air freight at JFK Airport. It then pressured trucking companies at JFK to join the NAAF, sign contracts with Local 295, and obey its dictates. Companies were induced to comply by Teamsters strikes and extensive sabotage.

"Trucking rackets, mail thefts, hijacking, flagrant pilferage, loan sharking, illegal gambling and other crimes are still flourishing at JFK, gangland's Open City."(B) Cargo is stolen with the help of cargo handlers, truckers, and even U.S. Customs employees on the Mob payroll, who are often hooked by loan sharking debts. Mob rackets at Kennedy and other New York airports still cost businesses and insurance companies millions of dollars. "Rampant Mob rule at Kennedy Airport is typical of the underworld's role at airports across the country." Reported *Harvard Business Re-*

Most of the drivers and a lot of the warehousemen are gamblers. They lose their salaries at Mob card and dice games, and the games are usually rigged. They get in a hole, and they start borrowing from the loan sharks. Then you have them. They can never get even, never pay off all they owe, because the juice mounts up. That's when you start the squeeze. They have a choice. Broken legs or arms, a threat against the family, or provide us with information on truckloads of goods they're hauling.

Vincent Teresa, in *My Life in the Mafia*, p. 138

view: "Ground operations at international airports are at present permeated by the syndicate or by men under its control."(C) In 1986, two top members of the Lucchese Mafia Family, several associates, a president and vice president of two Teamster locals were all indicted on charges of running shakedowns and trucking rackets at Kennedy Airport. A former vice president of an air transport company and a Lucchese Family associate pleaded guilty to involvement in the conspiracy. Eventually, almost two dozen people were convicted in connection with the JFK rackets.

A–Senator John McClellan, from testimony in *U.S.–House, OC Control*, p. 87; *Newsday*, September 29, 1986, p. 7; *Wall Street Journal*, March 10, 1987, p. 22.; B–Meskil, *Don Carlo*, pp. 154–59; also *Newsday*, September 8, 1986, p. 8; Dorman, *Payoff*, pp. 272–76; C–Grutzner, "How to Lock Out the Mafia," *Harvard Business Review*, March-April 1970, p. 58.

14.5 The nation's biggest armed robbery. In December 1978, $5,850,000 in cash and jewelry was seized from a Lufthansa cargo facility at Kennedy Airport. According to *Time*, members of the Mafia Family of the late Tommy Lucchese probably masterminded the crime. Officials suspected that the Mob had secured the cooperation of airline employees "by the time-honored method of inducing them to gamble, pressuring them to pay up, loaning them money at exorbitant rates, and, finally, pointing out that they could cancel their debts by helping out with the heist." In 1986, *Newsday* wrote that the robbery "was facilitated by a $15,000-a-year freight handler desperate to pay off his $20,000 debt to Luc[c]hese . . . loan sharks."(B) The FBI suspects that the loot was laundered "through a maze of Mafia business channels." .

A–*Time*, March 5, 1979, p. 23; B–*Newsday*, September 8, 1986, p. 13.

15. Other activities

a. Pornography and vice

15.1 "The Mafia now dominates the manufacture and distribution of pornographic books, magazines and movies." Volume of business: $2.2 billion a year. "The Mafia: Big, Bad and Booming," *Time*, May 16, 1977, pp. 33–34.

15.2 "The Gambino Mafia Family has a large interest in the child pornography business." The Mafia is moving back into prostitution. Genovese Family members allegedly control many nude bars in New York where girls are recruited for prostitution. *Time*, November 28, 1977, p. 23.

15.3 The Mafia takeover of the pornography industry is marked by traditional methods: terror, intimidation and murder. Ralph Blumenthal and Nicholas Gage, "Crime 'Families' Taking Control of Pornography," *New York Times*, December 10, 1972, pp. 1, 82; George Denison, "Smut: The Mafia's Newest Racket," *Reader's Digest*, December 1971, pp. 157–60.

15.4 The report of former Mafia operative James Barrett. Barrett, who worked for the Mafia in pornography ventures, became an FBI undercover informant and later a government witness. He reported that through muscle and payoffs to police and politicians, the Mafia ensures that no pornography enters any city in the United States without some payment to the local family. The Mob, he summarized, "has an iron grip on the smut industry." James Barrett, "Inside the Mob's Smut Rackets," *Reader's Digest,* December 1973, p. 128.

15.5 The Mafia-supplied prostitute "almost invariably is in league with the electronically equipped extortionist." Police estimate that the take from sex blackmail is far more than that from the prostitution itself. Federal agents raided one Chicago sex-blackmail ring directed by Mafia associate[36] Dominic Galiano in which "victims were drugged, robbed and shaken down for five-figure payoffs." Indictments were handed down against two Mobsters and seven associates in a similar ring in Detroit. In New York, police found a concealed television monitor and tape recording facilities in a massage parlor in the Mob-infested midtown vice district. Demaris, *Captive City,* pp. 96–97; *Time,* May 16, 1977, p. 35; *New York Times,* August 27, 1972, p. 1.

b. Rigged sporting events

15.6 "Banana" races in New England. "There was hardly a race track in New England where the mob didn't put the fix in at one time or another. . . . The races were so crooked you couldn't get them into the ground with a corkscrew." Vincent Teresa, *My Life in the Mafia,* pp. 152–63.

15.7 Mobsters "control" horse racing. Fixes were always placed with Mob consent. An estimated 60 percent of race horses in America are owned by Mobsters through fronts. Loan sharking debts, drugs, women, and bribes are routinely used by the Mob to hook jockeys into cooperating in fixes. From the testimony of Bobby Byrne, a former top horse racing fixer well connected with the Patriarca and Gambino families, who operated at tracks across the country, in *U.S.–House, OC in Sports,* pp. 1086–87, 1123, 1127–28, 1131–33, 1136; background, pp. 1083ff., 1117.

15.8 Mafia approval was needed to cash counterfeit twin double tickets at New York's Roosevelt Raceway. From the testimony of Nassau County, N.Y. District Attorney William Cahn in *U.S.–House, OC in Sports,* p. 1025.

[A jockey] owed a $1,500 tab in the Ebb Tide [a Mafia hangout]. He owed it to Richard Castucci. He [Mafia underboss Henry Tamello] said, "Bring him in and start to pressure him . . . and I will come in there and I will stop you. Don't hurt him, but just really come on strong."

So I went in there and said, "You owe $1,500. . . ." I pulled out a knife and put it at his throat and said I was going to slice it. And Henry came in and said, "What's this? What's going on? . . ." Henry Tamello says, "I want to pay for him. I am telling you, don't bother this kid any more. . . ." I walked out of the cloakroom. Henry Tamello stayed there with the jockey maybe 15–20 minutes, and he came out, and he had a jockey that was going to pull horses for him.

Defected New England Mob killer Joseph Barboza, in *U.S.–House, OC in Sports,* pp. 737–38. [Barboza testified that Tamello used a similar technique on other jockeys (ibid., p. 753).]

15.9 Mafia boss Raymond Patriarca was connected with Scarborough Downs, the Berkshires, and "owned about fifty percent of the horses that ran in New England." So Mob defector Joseph Barboza learned from Mob sources, including New England Mafia underboss[37] Henry Tamello [also spelled Tameleo]. Barboza named three persons who fronted ownership of horses for the Mafia. From Barboza's testimony in *U.S.-House, OC in Sports*, pp. 750–51.

15.10 Contacts between Mobsters and half the Boston Patriots football team. "Half" the team frequented Arthur's Farm, a vegetable store, Mafia meeting place, and outlet for stolen merchandise in Revere, Massachusetts. Team members bought merchandise and associated with the Mobsters who hung out there. Reported in *Life*, September 8, 1967, p. 93, and also by Vincent Teresa in *My Life in the Mafia*, p. 143. Mob defector Joseph Barboza reported one occasion when Patriots quarterback Babe Parilli and Celtics player Gene Conley met with Mafia underboss Henry Tamello at the Ebb Tide, after which "Tamello came out and said, 'Take the Lakers with four points.'" *U.S.-House, OC in Sports*, pp. 738–39; see also *Saturday Evening Post*, November 18, 1967, p. 29.

15.11 "A full squad of hoods, including a Cosa Nostra boss, was operating in Joe Namath's night club." The criminals, including Mafiosi Carmine Tramunti, Carmine Persico and Thomas Mancuso, worked gambling operations from phones in the club. Namath continued to associate with the hoods even after a federal agent revealed their identities. In 1969, when the gangster infestation of Bachelor's III was disclosed by football commissioner Pete Rozelle, Namath threatened to quit the Jets rather than sell the night club. *Life*, June 20, 1969, pp. 22ff.

15.12 Personal and business contacts were reported between Mobsters and players on the New Orleans Saints football team. In addition, federal officials proved the Mob "had attempted to influence, through payments of money to players," the scores of four L.S.U. football games in September and October 1966. From the testimony of New Orleans Metropolitan Crime Commission Director Aaron Kohn, *U.S.-House, OC in Sports*, pp. 953–55.

15.13 Top lightweight boxer Frank DePaula was shot by his Mafia friends. DePaula was friendly with New Jersey Mafia boss Joseph Zicarelli and was a regular at Namath's Bachelor's III bar. When DePaula was indicted with his manager for an $80,000 dock theft and interrogated by federal agents, the Mafia suspected he talked and ordered him hit. DePaula recovered from the bullets in his back and arm; "Mafia insiders were surprised that the slaying had been fumbled." *Newsweek*, June 8, 1970, pp. 67–68.

c. The music business

15.14 The Mafia moves in on "Rare Earth" and "Three Dog Night." After its first album sold two million copies in 1969, the rock group "Rare Earth" faced declining fortunes in the 1970s. And then, with ready cash, entered Joe Ullo: a reputed Mob enforcer from New York who had moved into the rock music business. By 1976, reported NBC, Ullo was boasting to associates that he "had taken over a hidden interest" in Rare Earth, by providing "Mob money and Mob muscle" to take care of their debts. The members of the group said "all they knew was that their manager was making deals with people who carry guns."

In 1978, noted NBC, Ullo was arrested "for the murder of former basketball star Jack Molinas—and police say members of Rare Earth are lucky no one got hurt." But it was a different story with Ullo's involvement in "Three Dog Night." The group's accountant "was shot in the arm and paralyzed in what police believe was a dispute over control of Three Dog Night." NBC News, "Segment 3," May 7, 1979.

15.15 "Payola and the Mob." A federal investigation of "payola, sex, drugs, and organized crime in the recording industry" began when Pasquale Falcone, a Mafia-connected talent manager for three Columbia artists, was indicted for heroin trafficking. "Sources close to the investigation say that at least one Columbia artist was driven into Falcone's stable with the help of Mafia muscle." *Newsweek*, July 30, 1973, p. 62.

15.16 "Payoffs to some disc jockeys, the use of threats by Mafiosi to keep performers in line and the use of drugs as payola." *New York Times*, June 15, 1973, p. 31.

15.17 The Mob is heavily involved in promoting rock concerts. The "Super Bowl of Rock" in Chicago featured some of the biggest rock stars and sold more than $2 million in tickets. According to NBC, "A federal grand jury is now investigating allegations that the Mob ran these concerts." Mobsters were suspected of paying city officials to get exclusive use of Soldier Field for concerts, booking rock stars through fronts, and forcing up ticket prices—"all part of a huge Mob scheme to make big money in the rock concert business." Terry Bruner, of the Chicago Better Government Association, noted, "This kind of thing goes on all over the country." NBC News, "Segment 3," May 8, 1979.

15.18 A hidden interest of New Jersey Mafia boss Angelo DeCarlo in Roulette Records and the Four Seasons singing group. From the testimony of defected Mob money-mover Gerald Zelmanowitz, in *U.S.–Senate, OC and Stolen Securities, 1973*, p. 60.

15.19 A gangland murder and two bombings characterized "organized crime's growing role" in the illegal bootleg cassette industry. Of $600 million spent on tape recordings in America in 1972, $200 million went for pirated tapes. *Chicago Tribune*, May 22, 1973, p. 10; *Newsweek*, July 30, 1973, p. 62; *New York Times*, June 15, 1973, p. 31.

15.20 "The Mafia has become one of the biggest producers of records and tapes in this country." In November 1978, FBI agents raided 23 warehouses of a counterfeit tape operation run by New York's Colombo Mafia Family. This network was just part of the Mob's massive bootleg record and tape operations, whose volume is approaching the $4 billion annual sales of the legitimate recording industry. For example, RSO Records sold 23 million copies of the sound track from the movie, "Saturday Night Fever." According to NBC, however, "Federal investigators say Mob counterfeits made and sold at least that many." The bootleg copies were virtually identical to the originals, but the recording artists got no royalties from their sales. One undercover agent in the Mob's record business said, "I don't think there's a store in the country you can go into and not find some counterfeit product on a given day." NBC News, "Segment 3," May 9, 1979.

d. The medical industry

15.21 Underworld Medicaid fraud in New York City. A federal grand jury "heard secret testimony that some mobsters have used fraud, extortion, arson, assault and other strong-arm tactics against Medicaid practitioners." According to one doctor who was shot and wounded shortly after testifying, the Mob extorted monthly payments from owners of Medicaid clinics with threats of beatings and arson, together with promises of political assistance and protection from competition. Its monthly take from some clinics reached several thousand dollars; other clinics were forced to use the services of Mob-controlled businesses. "Notorious mobsters like Meyer Lansky and Joe Colombo reportedly have been linked to nursing homes, hospitals, and clinical laboratories." Jack Anderson, "The Mob Taps Into Medicaid," *Miami Herald*, March 3, 1978, p. 7A.

15.22 Underworld Medicaid fraud in Chicago. In Chicago, an investigation of underworld Medicaid fraud was punctuated by five violent incidents. Among these were the murders of two Mob-affiliated partners who owned a medical syndicate that had "a virtual monopoly over welfare medicine on the south and west sides." A Chicago police spokesman asserted that underworld elements "control a lot of the pharmaceutical business and are probably heavy into Medicaid in Illinois." Jack Anderson, "Medicaid Inquiry Hit by Violence," *Washington Post*, April 6, 1978, p. VA19.

15.23 Mafia links to health-care providers. According to officials in Dade County, Florida, the Miami Heart Institute is "a regular meeting place for a number of organized crime figures," such as Mafia don Sam DeCavalcante, who was monitored going there almost daily.(A) In Boston, ownership of the Kenmore Hospital was traced to Mafia underboss Jerry Angiulo; an investigator "identified eight known bookies who entered the building in the course of a single afternoon."(B) Mafia defector Vincent Teresa remarked, "With what I knew about doctors on the Mob payroll in Boston, I wouldn't have gone near a Boston hospital if I was on my deathbed."(C)

A–NBC Evening News, "Segment 3," December 12, 1977; B–Davidson, "The Mafia: How It Bleeds New England," *Saturday Evening Post*, November 18, 1967, p. 29; C–Teresa, *My Life in the Mafia,* p. 336, see p. 192.

e. Miscellaneous

15.24 Mafia control of fuel distribution in parts of New England and sales of stolen gasoline in New York City. *Hartford Courant*, January 22, 1974; *Time*, December 10, 1973, p. 34.

15.25 Gasoline at a Gas Value service station on Long Island mixed with toxic chemicals in a Mob conspiracy. The altered gas saved wholesalers 30 to 40 cents a gallon and disposed of toxic waste. But, since it was 25 percent industrial solvent, the gas did not work very well in automobiles: they "sputtered and stopped, choked with a thick sludge." Profits were passed on to organized crime. In another operation, the Mob worked with oil distributors in a scheme to avoid paying up to $1 billion in federal and state gasoline taxes. And the Mob practice of diverting cargos of gasoline and crude oil before they can be taxed, which resulted in indictments in 1981 and 1986, was estimated to cost $3 billion a year in state and federal taxes. *Newsday*, September 8, 1986, p. 7; *Washington Post*, July 16, 1986, p. A5.

15.26 The Mafia is "siphoning off as much as $50 million a year" from cigarette smuggling. The figure peaked at $400 million in nationwide revenues lost in 1978, when smuggling was made a federal offense. In 1986, organized crime earnings from cigarette smuggling were estimated at between $193 million and $388 million. Reid, *Grim Reapers*, p. 44; *U.S.-Cargo Theft and OC*, p. 39; *Newsday*, September 8, 1986, p. 7; *U.S.-President's Commission on OC, The Impact*, p. 463.

15.27 The Mob is active in the multimillion-dollar "chop shop" business. Late-model cars are stolen on order and cut up for parts. NBC Evening News, "Segment 3," January 19, 1978.

15.28 Counterfeiting and credit card fraud. Counterfeit securities, passports, postage stamps, driver's licenses and money are printed by Mafia experts in any quantity members can use. Millions of dollars in counterfeit bills are routinely passed. Credit cards are counterfeited, stolen from the mail, or obtained from inside sources at credit card companies. Cards are used for airline tickets, hotel and restaurant bills, loans, jewelry, clothing, tires, and cars that are rented and then stolen. From the testimony of Mafia defector Vincent Teresa in *U.S.-Senate, OC and Stolen Securities, 1971*, pp. 808–13, also see p. 142.

15.29 Defrauding the Veterans Administration. Boston underworld figures "rented" veterans' names or addresses to receive fraudulent benefits. Two men involved in the scheme were slain gangland style. It was believed that "many veterans were denied benefits, even though they were eligible, because of the widespread fraud." *Boston Globe*, August 17, 1974, p. 1; August 16, 1974, p. 1.

15.30 Fencing stolen art. In 1976, Detroit Mafioso Peter Licavoli was convicted in Tucson for trying to sell a stolen 400-year-old painting for $80,000 to an FBI agent working undercover. Until then, officials had assumed Licavoli had retired in Arizona to operate an art gallery. NBC Evening News, "Segment 3," March 13, 1978.

15.31 A partial list of Mob activities. "The list of organized crime's activities would include gambling, usury, bribery, perjury, fraud, extortion, kidnapping, murder, labor racketeering, forgery, counterfeiting, narcotics, burglary, hijacking, fencing, monopoly, prostitution, terrorism, and tax evasion, among many others." It was noted that "the predominant group and inner core of organized crime" is the Mafia. *U.S.-Cargo Theft and OC*, pp. 23, 25.

16. The Mafia and street crime

16.1 "Almost every bit of crime we study has some link to organized crime." Statement of Milton Rector, director of the National Council on Crime and Delinquency, in *Time*, August 22, 1969, p. 18. See similar statements by Congressman Richard Poff, Senator John McClellan and Congressman Joseph McDade in *U.S.-House, OC Control*, pp. 80, 86, 594.

16.2 Mob corruption nullified law enforcement. "Cosa Nostra's ability to flout the law makes preachment of law and order a joke" to the urban poor. Police busy collecting payoffs cannot effectively stop any kind of

> Drug addiction turns your little sister into a prostitute before she gets into her teens; makes a criminal out of your little brother before he gets in his teens. . . .
>
> When a person is a drug addict, he's not the criminal; he's a victim of the criminal. The criminal is the man downtown who brings this drug into the country.
>
> Malcolm X, from a speech transcribed in *By Any Means Necessary*, pp. 50–51.

crime. *Time*, August 22, 1969, p. 18; *New Republic*, July 18, 1970, p. 13; *U.S.-House, Criminal Justice Hearings*, p. 150; Maas, *Serpico*, passim.

a. Mob heroin promotes crime

16.3 Half of street crime in large Eastern cities is committed by heroin addicts. As estimated by Congressman Joseph McDade, by authorities in the District of Columbia, and by New York Police organized crime expert Ralph Salerno. The drugs are supplied by organized crime (see section 11). *U.S.-House, OC Control*, pp. 423, 594; *U.S.-House, Criminal Justice Hearings*, p. 158.

16.4 $5 billion in stolen goods per year supports heroin addiction in New York City alone. Most of the victims of the robberies and thefts are inner city residents and stores. *Reader's Digest*, September 1970, pp. 50–51.

16.5 Mob narcotics, gambling, and loan sharking are behind much crime. Hearst newspapers (March 1970) reprinted in *U.S.-House, OC Control*, pp. 423–24.

b. Mafia directs robberies, burglaries and thefts

16.6 The Mob is "responsible for much crime against property—burglary, automobile theft, bank robbery, arson." Salerno and Tompkins, *Crime Confederation*, p. 93.

16.7 The Mob lines up the market, assembles a burglary crew. Mafia defector Joseph Luparelli described how he operated during his apprentice years as a burglar. "On most of the jobs, we already had the stuff sold before we took it. Usually a businessman would contact a made guy [Mafia member] and say he wanted a certain type of merchandise, like wool cloth or machine parts. A deal would be made on the price. Then the made guy would put a crew together and send them out to get the stuff. He'd tell them where to go and what they'd find there." Meskil, *Luparelli Tapes*, p. 42.

16.8 The Mob turns out the lights. Colombo captain Frank Melli was accused of "arranging to cut off electricity to the entire town of Carlstadt, N.J., in November 1979 to facilitate the burglary of $2.2 million worth of Swiss watches at a warehouse. Police communications were disrupted during the blackout." *Washington Post*, November 18, 1985, pp. A7–8.

16.9 A Mafia-backed burglary ring brutally murdered the daughter of a former U.S. senator during a robbery of his home. One morning in 1966, Charles H. Percy, then candidate for senator, was awakened by his wife's screams. He then entered the bedroom of his 21-year-old daughter, Valerie, and found her "agonizingly near death—her face, chest and stomach mutilated by stab wounds." By 1973, authorities were "all but certain" that Valerie Percy's murderers were members of a Mafia-backed band of thieves that flourished nationwide from 1965 to 1967. The gang, which operated with "almost military precision," would forward two-thirds of its take to the Mafia in return for planning expertise and the fencing of stolen merchandise. *Time,* December 10, 1973, p. 29.

16.10 A Mafioso stole $475,000 in furs; the store went bankrupt. New England Mafia defector Vincent Teresa described how, while perpetrating sophisticated multimillion-dollar stolen stock schemes, he was always out for an easy score. In two burglaries of the same furrier on Boylston Street in Boston, Teresa and criminal associates stole $475,000 in furs, for which they received $100,000 in cash from Mafia underboss Henry Tameleo. Earlier, Teresa had twice burglarized a high-volume supermarket across from a night club he owned, netting $31,000. Teresa, *My Life in the Mafia,* pp. 102–3.

16.11 New York Mafia boss Carlo Gambino was arrested for conspiring to commit a $6 million armored-car robbery. The plan was foiled when a leader of the robbery gang was arrested for a similar crime in Boston. Mollenhoff, *Strike Force,* p. 234.

16.12 Twelve Mob-tied criminals were convicted of stealing $1 million in goods in four truck hijackings. *U.S.–Cargo Theft and OC,* p. 38.

16.13 One hundred murders and five robberies were charged in a November 1973 indictment to ten members of a New Jersey Mafia gang. The gang, associated with the Genovese Family, coupled robberies with traditional gambling and narcotics operations, including "the manufacture and distribution of cocaine and heroin." The murder victims included rivals, disloyal associates, suspected police informants and potential prosecution witnesses. "The gang used bribery and threats of violence to influence jurors and witnesses." *New York Times,* November 30, 1973, pp. 1, 41.

c. The Mob's fencing network

16.14 One hundred million dollars from airport mail robberies was fenced with the Mob; the Mob got 85 percent of the take. Robert Cudak testified that between December 1967 and September 1970, he and his partners committed 125 mail thefts, stealing about $100 million in stocks, bonds, jewelry, cash, furs and other items. This was confirmed by one of his partners, James Schaeffer, and by post office figures which showed that $34 million was lost in just 14 of the thefts. Both Cudak and Schaeffer testified that the fences to whom they passed the goods were always affiliated with the Mob, and that they received from the fences at most 15 percent of the value of the goods.

Cudak reported that the most important of his partners in the thefts was Mobster William Ricchiuti, and that a gang led by Mobster Anthony Capucci was also active in airport mail thefts. Cudak testified that his thefts would not have been profitable without the Mob fences. *U.S.–Senate, OC and Stolen Securities, 1971,* pp. 210–17, 227, 230–31, 246–47, 250–54, 565–70.

16.15 Mob fences in action. In one Mob-engineered theft, a load of coffee was hijacked in New York at 4:30 p.m. and on sale at a supermarket by 5:15 p.m. the same day. One Mob fence operating in New York, Mike Jace, dealt in "silver bars, cash, credit cards, securities, jewels, rare coins, art treasures, and trailer loads of cigarettes, liquor, razor blades, furs, 'you name it.'" In monitored phone conversations, he discussed sales of driver's licenses, 3,800 airline tickets, 500,000 acres of land and a $500,000 diamond, and he inquired about the progress of a $340,000 cargo theft two days before it occurred.

During one conversation involving a casino transaction, Jace explained that the Mafia families appoint bosses "like a government." "The only ones other than [those with a certain ethnic background] who can get involved with them is one who gains their respect." *U.S.–Cargo Theft and OC*, pp. 38–42.

IV. ECONOMIC PENETRATION

17. Infiltration of business

17.1 "The rodents in charcoal suits." "The Mafia muscles its way into thriving businesses, milks their assets, and then drives them into bankruptcy. Thousands of working men and women are forced to settle for starvation wages under sweetheart contracts between unions and companies dominated by the Mob. Insurance rates rise because of thefts, frauds, and acts of violence committed by the Mafia to wipe out competition and advance its supposedly legitimate business interests. And consumers suffer when the Mob gains a business monopoly and boosts prices as high as the traffic will bear."(B) A–Cook, *Secret Rulers*, p. 2; B–Dorman, *Payoff*, p. 238.

a. Extent of infiltration

17.2 Organized crime "owns or has decision-making influence in 50,000 commercial or industrial companies," including two multinational conglomerates. Grutzner, "How to Lock Out the Mafia," *Harvard Business Review*, March-April 1970, p. 49; *U.S.–Cargo Theft and OC*, pp. 28–29.

17.3 "Seventy separate types of businesses into which countless hoodlums had infiltrated." They were listed by the Kefauver Committee in 1951: "Advertising, amusement industry, awnings, automobiles, bakeries, ballrooms, banking, baseball, bonding, . . . shipping, slot machines, steel, surplus property, tailoring, television manufacturing and sales, textiles, theaters (stage and movies), trucking, transportation, unions, and washing machines." Kefauver, *Crime in America*, reprinted in Tyler, *Organized Crime in America*, p. 292.

17.4 Legitimate businesses infiltrated by the Mafia include "liquor and food purveyors, restaurants, construction, banking, vending, jewelry, meat packing, sanitation and toxic waste disposal, import/export, tobacco, and laundry, among many others." *U.S.–President's Commission on OC, The Impact*, pp. 46–47.

17.5 The Boston area: The Mafia owns "25 or 30 percent" of motels and restaurants. "They have their fingers in just about everything." From the testimony of Vincent Teresa in *U.S.–Senate, OC and Stolen Securities*,

1971, p. 816; also see Davidson, "The Mafia: How it Bleeds New England," *Saturday Evening Post*, November 18, 1967, p. 29.

17.6 The Mob controls most of the school bus contracts in New York City. Mob-linked bidders can save on labor costs because they know the unions won't bother them. From the testimony of Mob lawyer Martin Light before the President's Commission on Organized Crime. *U.S.-President's Commission on OC, The Impact*, pp. 391–92.

17.7 Pennsylvania: "More than 375 major businesses," including a large defense contractor, "are controlled by the Mob." Medico Industries, a multimillion-dollar corporation in Luzerne County, received a $3.9 million Pentagon contract to produce 600,000 warheads for use in Vietnam. Company president Phillip Medico was described by northeastern Pennsylvania Mafia boss Russell Bufalino, in an FBI-recorded conversation, as a capo in his Mafia family. Bufalino was also an associate of company general manager William Medico, and "frequently visited the Medico offices."(B) A third Medico official, James Osticco, was a delegate to the 1957 Apalachin Mafia convention.(C) Peter Maggio, a captain in the Angelo Bruno Family, was "a partner in Michael's Dairies, Inc., one of the largest dairy companies in Philadelphia." Michael's Dairies received contracts to provide milk to two military bases, and three other companies owned by Philadelphia Mafia figures received sizable government contracts. A–Dorman, *Payoff*, pp. 254–55; B–*Time*, March 6, 1978, p. 21; C–*U.S.-Senate, McClellan Labor Hearings*, p. 12199.

17.8 New York: "In every kind of business." The businesses controlled by the Gambino Family include "insurance and real estate companies, a labor relations firm, construction, fuel oil distribution, dress factories." Private garbage disposal throughout New York City and several suburban areas is reportedly controlled by the Gambino Family, too. Meskil, *Don Carlo*, pp. 59–60. Also see *Newsday*, September 8, 1986.

17.9 Detroit: 100 Mafia-controlled businesses named in a chart prepared for the U.S. Senate by the Detroit Police. Businesses "owned, infiltrated, or influenced" by the Mafia, whose names and addresses were listed, include a 960-acre motel and restaurant complex and four other motels; several bars, restaurants, bakeries, car washes and food companies; the Hazel Park Race Track, 23 dry cleaning shops, a barber college and barber supply company; steel, aluminum, metal finishing and nickel surplus companies; extensive real estate holdings, including the Chrysler Office Building in Detroit and several properties in Arizona, Canada and Chicago; and construction, trucking, insurance, vending, concrete paving, die casting, cold storage, oil, linen, bus, and printing companies. *U.S.-Senate, OC and Narcotics Hearings*, p. 472.

17.10 Mob money movers are "constantly searching for new areas" to sink burgeoning profits. Grutzner, "How to Lock Out the Mafia," *Harvard Business Review*, March-April 1970, p. 49.

b. Methods of infiltration and operation

17.11 "Thievery is their way. Their executives are extortionists. Some of their salesmen are killers." Mob business operations are intricate, international in scope, but true-blue Mafia in character. Skimming receipts to avoid taxes is common. *Life*, September 8, 1967, p. 98.

> Mob defector Patsy Lepera described how a fraudulent financial statement based on stolen securities was used by some contractors who "belong[ed] to" Philadelphia Mafia boss Angelo Bruno. From Lepera and Goodman, *Memories of a Scam Man*, pp. 82–83:
>
> What these apartment house guys do shows you how the mob operates. First, they borrow $200,000 on the statement, which of course is phony to begin with. Then they steal $100,000 right off the top and whack it up. With the rest, they break ground, put the footing in. It looks great — but they're murdering the subcontractors. They're not paying them. A subcontractor's got fifty coming . . . they give him ten. He's hooked. They're paying off the inspectors. The inspector comes around, collects, reports back to the mortgage company everything is going along perfect. They borrow another $200,000 cash. They steal some of that and deduct the interest from their taxes. They ain't paying the subcontractors. Who are the subcontractors going to sue — Angelo Bruno? They're afraid they'll get put away. Most of the subcontractors who worked on those buildings went out of business. . .
>
> Now you go to a legitimate buyer to sell this thing. . . . These buildings are easy to sell. These buildings will make money, if they stay up.

17.12 "They take their habits with them wherever they go." "If things don't go right off the bat, they want to break somebody's head. . . . Or they will put a gun to your head and say 'Here, sign this. Here is a buck. That makes it legal.' " From the testimony of Mafia defector Vincent Teresa in *U.S.-Senate, OC and Stolen Securities, 1971*, p. 837.

17.13 "True American corporate competition does not include breaking legs" — unless the Mafia is involved. Robert D. McFadden, "The Mafia of the 1980's: Divided and Under Siege," *New York Times*, March 11, 1987, p. B2.

17.14 Failure of store owners to rent Mafia vending machines in New England "resulted in the wrecking of the store, fixtures, and bodily harm." The legitimate business people who were thus intimidated declined out of fear to testify against the Mafia hoodlums. From the testimony of Col. Walter E. Stone, superintendent of the Rhode Island State Police, in *U.S.-OC and Narcotics Hearings*, p. 552.

17.15 Some Mob business practices described by the U.S. Chamber of Commerce. "Included among these methods are the forcing of businessmen to join 'dummy' or fraudulent associations; the use of planned bankruptcy to make fast profits and leave legitimate creditors 'high and dry'; the establishment of gambling operations within plants and elsewhere; the infiltration of labor unions and the formation of phony labor organizations as a means to intimidate legitimate businesses; the lending of money at extortionate rates (loan sharking); the use of all types of practices — violent and otherwise — to reduce competition and secure monopoly in a given field (through threats, bribes, arson, personal and property assaults, etc.); and the illegal use of stocks, bonds, and cards." *U.S.-House, OC Control*, pp. 409–10.

17.16 Cash "being put into constructive purposes. . . . made them crazy." Defected Mob money mover Michael Raymond testified how the Mafia pressured him to milk the assets of one successful company for a few hundred thousand dollars in immediate gain, when millions could have been earned legitimately. And top Mafia defector Vincent Teresa provided an inside view into such thinking with his description of the attempted bust-out of a night club: "the night club was making money, but it was strictly a grind, and who needs a grind when there's easy money to be made?"(B) A–*U.S.-OC and Stolen Securities, 1971*, pp. 656–64; background, pp. 637, 956, 1245–46; B–Teresa, *My Life in the Mafia*, p. 102.

17.17 A medical center in Florida and a Mafia-owned hospital in Boston serve as Mob meeting places. *Saturday Evening Post*, November 18, 1967, p. 29; *U.S.-OC and Stolen Securities, 1971*, p. 816; NBC Evening News, "Segment 3," December 12, 1977.

17.18 Drain the assets and leave the shell to the public. From the testimony of Mob-connected securities fence Edward Wuenche in *U.S.-Senate, OC and Stolen Securities, 1971*, pp. 880–81.

17.19 Using captive unions to take over businesses. Meskil, *Don Carlo*, p. 21. Also see *Newsday*, September 8, 1986.

17.20 A loan shark debt leads to a silent partner. Cressey, *Theft of the Nation*, pp. 102–3.

17.21 "Once brought under the Mob's umbrella, a business almost always ceases to operate legitimately." From kickbacks to arson and murder. "The Mafia v. America," *Time*, August 22, 1969, p. 21.

17.22 Case studies of Mafia business methods. Several cases of Mafia infiltration, takeover, and draining of multimillion-dollar businesses are described in detail. For example, the Mafia took over and bankrupted the Progressive Drug Company of New York, a formerly reputable $10 million-a-year wholesale business. It accomplished this using Twentieth Century Industries, a large conglomerate that owned drug, plastics, metals, mining, and soft-drink companies. The conglomerate was deeply involved with the Mafia, with Gambino Family underboss Aniello Dellacroce on its payroll;[38] its vice president took the Fifth Amendment when questioned by the New York State Investigation Commission. The first step in the Mafia takeover of Progressive was a switch in its labor contract from a reputable AFL-CIO union to a Teamsters local.

There can "no longer be any doubt in the minds of perceptive business executives that there has been a massive infiltration of the national economy by members of organized crime."

Grutzner, "How to Lock Out the Mafia," *Harvard Business Review*, March-April 1970, pp. 45–58; see Dorman, *Payoff*, p. 253.

17.23 A classic case: draining, intimidation, and deception. The dealings of LBJ aide Bobby Baker and some other Mobsters in the late 1960s were described in 1972 hearings of the House Select Committee on Crime. The focus of the hearings was a multimillion-dollar scam of the Datacomp and Dumont corporations of New Jersey, spearheaded by New York Mafioso Salvatore Badalamente and front man Seymour Pollock. It was a classic case of the Mafia takeover of a business: The companies' assets were drained, their stocks manipulated, and their offices turned into meeting places for Badalamente's criminal associates, who on one occasion discussed robbing the bank next door to Datacomp.

Datacomp President Norman Forsythe testified that Bobby Baker was introduced to him through Pollock, who indicated that Baker could possibly help the company. Baker did indeed help—help siphon off the company's assets, that is—by taking an extensive tour of Europe paid for by Datacomp. Baker also helped at one point when death threats from Badalamente and Pollock failed to silence a Datacomp vice president, Dorothy O'Halloran. O'Halloran had been describing the hoodlums' transactions to Roger Nichols, an attorney representing a defrauded Los Angeles brokerage firm. After the Mobsters threatened O'Halloran, Nichols related to the Committee, Baker "engaged in a softer sell technique to get her to keep quiet." O'Halloran was unable to testify about the threats herself, because "she died under very strange circumstances in New York City about March of 1969."

Continuing along the trail exposed by the House Crime Committee, it turned out that the Datacomp-Dumont scam was perpetrated using worthless stock of the Baptist Foundation of America. Amazingly enough, this so-called foundation was just another shell for Badalamente and his Mafia crew. Its only activity was collecting money, which it accomplished with the help of a corrupt minister, a corrupt certified public accountant and a brochure describing a nonexistent hospital, retirement home and pension plan. Through this foundation, the Mob drained the American public of $26 million.

As Chairman Claude Pepper summarized the situation, "The organized crime crowd had a ripe plum ready for picking." The Baptist Foundation of America "went into receivership about 1970, about 1 1/2 or 2 years from the time it was started, with assets of $15,000 and outstanding notes that people had given value for in the amount of $26 million." But "the benefit would come not to the foundation . . . the gain derived to this organized crime crowd that manipulated all of this."

U.S.-OC and Worthless Securities, pp. 1–3, 9–26, 27–35, 193–94, 197, 223–25, 242.

c. Examples of Mob infiltration: banking and finance

17.24 The "pervasive influence of organized crime in the banking and securities industries" was noted by House Crime Committee Chairman Claude Pepper, who also pointed out the Mob's extensive infiltration of the insurance industry. U.S.-House, OC and Worthless Securities, pp. 1, 242.

17.25 A rash of bank collapses in the 1960s, plus the nation's three largest bank failures in the 1970s, were caused by Mob infiltration and draining (see chapter 22, "Bebe Rebozo, C. Arnholt Smith and Murray Chotiner," in text). Cook, Secret Rulers, p. 367; Jeff Gerth, address at The Politics of Conspiracy, workshop on organized crime (Boston University, George Sherman Union, East Ballroom), February 1, 1975, tape-recorded by author; New York Times, September 10, 1973, pp. 1ff.

17.26 "Hoodlum connections with some of the biggest banks in the country" were noted by former House Banking Committee Chairman Wright Patman. Representative Patman added that "criminal control of banks is widespread. It reaches from New York to Miami to Chicago, and even to some small towns. I would say there are dozens of banks influenced or owned by hoodlums." Cook, *Secret Rulers*, pp. 367–68.

17.27 Draining banks instead of robbing them. Reid, *Grim Reapers*, p. 21.

17.28 Hundreds of depositors lost their savings in the collapse of a Louisiana Loan and Thrift Company. "About one third of the deposits had been loaned to, or through, organized crime enterprises." In 1970, federal prosecution was pending against Louisiana Attorney General Jack Gremillion, State Representative Salvatore Anzelmo, and others, who were charged with fraudulent acts contributing to the bankruptcy. *U.S.–House, OC Control*, p. 431.

17.29 "Substantial infiltration of the banking, brokerage, insurance, and other financial communities by many persons who are directly or indirectly connected with organized crime." Details were reported from first-hand experience in the 122-page testimony of Michael Raymond, a defected Mob money mover. Raymond described numerous instances in which Mob financial transactions were aided by corrupt judges, police, and regulatory personnel. *U.S.–Senate, OC and Stolen Securities, 1971*, pp. 636–757, especially 712–13, 734–37; background, pp. 637–38, 659–64, 956, 1245–46.

17.30 Top Mobster Meyer Lansky took steps in 1968 to form a Miami stock exchange. Ex-Washington lobbyist Robert Winter-Berger described how he was paid $500 to do some research for the project, which was being handled by his associate, Mob-tied Washington lobbyist Nathan Voloshen. Winter-Berger learned that Voloshen "had met with Lansky at least three times to discuss the project," and that his fee had been paid by Lansky. Winter-Berger, *Washington Payoff*, pp. 130–31.

17.31 The numerous benefits derived by the Mob from controlling a bank. Dorman, *Payoff*, p. 260; Grutzner, "How to Lock Out the Mafia," *Harvard Business Review*, March-April 1970, p. 51.

17.32 A friendly banker. New York Mobsters[39] Lou Shomberg and Stanley Polley "could reach in any direction that they wanted. Polley set up a loan for me at Bankers Trust Co. It took me 15 minutes to walk in and walk out with $50,000. . . . It was a hook loan. The banker belonged to me." From the testimony of defected Mob money mover Michael Raymond in *U.S.–Senate, OC and Stolen Securities, 1971*, p. 665.

17.33 Mob penetration of the financial industry "underpins the whole economy of the United States, virtually all private ownership." As noted by Senator Charles Percy, who also commented, "as the mob moves in and extends its tentacles . . . you get a reaction of terror, of intimidation, of extortion and murder." *U.S.–Senate, OC and Stolen Securities, 1971*, p. 737.

d. Examples of Mob infiltration: trucking, garbage collection and garment manufacture in New York

17.34 The remarkable success of the Ross Trucking Company. The Ross Trucking Company, whose underworld connections were suspected by a member of the New York Waterfront Commission, hauled half the bananas imported into the New York area—despite its "exorbitant" rates and the lack of protective insulation in its trucks. Some jobbers questioned about the arrangement complained about being forced to use Ross, while others refused to comment or expressed fear of discussing the subject. From a series of articles by Stanley Penn in *The Wall Street Journal* (1969), reprinted in Gage, *Mafia, U.S.A.*, pp. 340–43.

17.35 "The destroyers move into your town." "Dangerously unsound buildings or highways or vehicles," at "outrageously high costs" characterize city contracts obtained by Mafia-controlled businesses. An example: garbage collection in Mount Vernon, New York. Gage, "How Organized Crime Invades the Home," *Good Housekeeping*, August 1971, pp. 68ff.

17.36 Murdering to monopoly. In the early 1950s, two companies were competing for the multimillion-dollar garbage removal business of New York's Westchester County. One was Rex Carting Company, a reputable firm which had a labor agreement with Teamsters Local 456, a legitimate union run by Everett Doyle and John Acropolis. The other was Westchester Carting Company, which was operated by Mafia soldier[40] Nick Ratteni, who spent 7 1/2 years at Sing Sing Prison, and by Joey Surprise, also a Sing Sing alumnus, with several arrests and a reversed first-degree murder conviction. Westchester Carting had a labor contract with Teamsters Local 27, run by Secretary-Treasurer Joe Parisi, a Mobster with 11 arrests and one rape conviction, and Bernard Adelstein, with five arrests and a reversed extortion conviction.

Westchester Carting Company expanded its operations as "businessmen were threatened, equipment of competitors was burned and destroyed, and reluctant store keepers were picketed." In 1952 at a Teamster convention, legitimate union leader Acropolis was threatened by Mobster Parisi. "Three weeks after the convention, Acropolis was shot to death as he opened the door to his house. A month later, Rex Carting sold out to Westchester Carting, which now had monopoly control of the garbage removal business in Westchester County."

The Rex-Westchester episode is typical of the Mob's style of competition. Between 1959 and 1983, at least 14 New York area murders were linked to Mob "trash wars."(B)

A–Robert F. Kennedy, *The Enemy Within*, pp. 230–32. B–Ralph Blumenthal and Ben A. Franklin, "Illegal Dumping of Toxins Laid to Organized Crime," *New York Times*, June 5, 1983, p. 44.

17.37 "Customers ended up footing the bill." A leading dress manufacturer found its existence threatened by hijackings and sabotage when it refused to use a trucking firm owned by one of Mafia boss Thomas Lucchese's relatives. When the dress company finally switched to the recommended firm, its troubles stopped, but its trucking costs rose 10 percent. The increase was passed on to consumers. Gage, "How Organized Crime Invades the Home," *Good Housekeeping*, August 1971, p. 118.

17.38 A Mafia interest in 20 percent of firms in the New York garment industry. "The first choice a New York dress manufacturer has to make, outside the high fashion field, is whether he wants a racketeer as a partner, creditor or competitor. No matter which way he turns, he will probably have a racketeer as his trucker." Mafia garment firms characteristically pay low wages to workers, often blacks and Puerto Ricans in nonunion shops. Hutchinson, *Imperfect Union*, pp. 91–92. Also see *Newsday*, September 8, 1986, p. 5.

e. Bankruptcy fraud

17.39 At least 200 Mob bankruptcy frauds are discovered each year, "each leaving up to 250 creditors holding the bag." Total debts in each case "usually run upward of $200,000." Dorman, *Payoff*, pp. 238–39.

17.40 Six bust-outs by Vincent Teresa: "We took manufacturers and insurance companies for more than five million bucks." Teresa and underworld partners would first set up a company, fronted by someone with a good credit rating, and lease a store or large building. The company would build up a credit line by ordering and paying for merchandise, then place huge orders a few months before Christmas. They would sell as much of this merchandise as they could, then surreptitiously send all the remaining goods to a fence. All that was left were a few broken toys, crates, or appliances they hauled in from a junk pile. Then they would "hire a torch, a good arsonist." After the building burned, they would "collect the insurance and declare bankruptcy."

Teresa used this technique on Auction City in Somerville, Massachusetts, and on Joseph's Department Store in Boston, a five-story building before it was torched. From these bust-outs, as well as from every one of Teresa's operations, New England Mafia boss Raymond Patriarca and underboss Henry Tameleo got a percentage of the proceeds. Teresa, *My Life in the Mafia*, pp. 99–101.

17.41 The bust-out of Murray Packing Co. The Mafia muscled into the prosperous family meat business when the owners borrowed from a finance company that proved to be a Gambino Family loan shark operation. In eight days the Mafia siphoned $745,000 out of the company, and it soon went into bankruptcy, leaving $1.3 million in debts. Grutzner, "How to Lock Out the Mafia," *Harvard Business Review*, March-April 1970, p. 53; Dorman, *Payoff*, pp. 239–41.

17.42 Fifteen underworld figures, including three Mafia captains, were arrested by the FBI in a bankruptcy fraud operation in the Detroit-Toledo area. Mollenhoff, *Strike Force*, p. 234.

17.43 Five reputed Mob figures, including a cousin of Carlo Gambino, were arrested in a New York bust-out scheme. The same five men had been indicted five months earlier in an almost identical case. *New York Times*, August 22, 1973, p. 17.

17.44 Some operations of the versatile king of scam, Chicago Mafioso Phil Alderisio. Among the incidents tied to Alderisio and associates were a $600,000 scam of an auto dealership and a $1 million fire that destroyed the Fullerton Metals Company. Four Alderisio associates were convicted of a $50,000 scam of Vogue Credit Jewelers, based on the testimony of one witness, Joseph Polito. Polito was murdered by four shotgun blasts on March 7, 1967. Demaris, *Captive City*, pp. 80–83.

17.45 "About a half-billion dollars a year goes to Cosa Nostra as profits" from bankruptcy frauds. More individual cases are described. Cressey, *Theft of the Nation*, pp. 105–6.

18. Infiltration of labor

18.1 The Mob's entry into the labor field. In the early 1930s, the Syndicate's income was sharply reduced by the repeal of Prohibition and the

Depression, while some of the "biggest and most solvent treasuries in the world were in the labor unions." The Capone gang, with years of experience in supplying thugs to break strikes for employers, turned its attention to the unions. The Syndicate began applying "steamroller pressure": murders and bombings were used to take over unions and capture their treasuries. By 1932, as Chicago Crime Commission President Frank Loesch reported, the Chicago Mob controlled or extracted tribute from two-thirds of all Chicago area unions, while the AFL conceded that 28 of its Chicago locals were dominated by the underworld. From *The Stolen Years*, by ex-Chicago gangster Roger Touhy and Ray Brennan, reprinted in Tyler, *Organized Crime in America*, pp. 193-95; also Hutchinson, *Imperfect Union*, pp. 116-17.

18.2 The Mafia "kept cropping up in almost every investigation that was made into improper activities in labor and management." Of the 58 delegates apprehended at the 1957 Mafia conclave at Apalachin, 23 "were directly connected with labor unions or with labor-management bargaining groups." John McClellan, *Crime Without Punishment*, p. 116.

18.3 "Control through strictly muscle." Mob defector Louis Mastriana, who was president of one union in New Jersey and ran another "paper" local, testified that he knew of few unions "that are not controlled by the [crime] families." When asked to explain how the Mafia controlled unions, he explained: "You got a goon squad. A lot of people want to go home at night but they don't want to go home all busted up." When asked by Senator Huddleston, "Do you mean this is still going on?" Mastriana replied, "Of course it goes on. It goes on every day." *U.S.–Senate, OC and Stolen Securities, 1973*, p. 168.

18.4 Methods of extortion and embezzlement using labor unions. Paper locals, sweetheart contracts, neglect of health and safety standards, extortion through threat of labor strike, and embezzlement of union funds are basic Mob labor practices. Cressey, *Theft of the Nation*, pp. 95-99; Steven Waldman, "The Best and the Worst of American Unions," *Washington Monthly*, July-August, 1987, p. 38.

18.5 "Underworld infiltration into labor-management affairs . . . a shocking pattern across the country." The Mob is "increasing its effort to seize control of legitimate businesses and unions," leading to "monopoly control" in some industries. Robert Kennedy, *The Enemy Within*, pp. 228-29.

18.6 Mobster officials in the unions. Two union officials—John J. De-Ross, officer in Locals 6 and 100 of the Hotel and Restaurant Employees Union and Ralph Scopo, former president of the Concrete Workers District Council—were among the defendants in the 1985 Colombo family racketeering trial. The family was charged with dominating "two locals of the Concrete Workers of the Laborers' International Union of North America, two [Teamsters] locals . . . and three locals of the Hotel & Restaurant Employees Union." *Washington Post*, October 25, 1984, pp. A1, A20; *U.S.–President's Commission on OC, The Edge*, pp. 82, 225.

a. The International Brotherhood of Teamsters

18.7 "The Most Controlled Union." The President's Commission on Organized Crime report included a chapter on the Teamsters titled "The Most Controlled Union." Former Teamsters International president Roy L. Wil-

435

liams testified that, "Every big Teamster local union had some connection with organized crime." Between 1979 and 1984, Teamster officials were indicted by federal authorities at an average rate of one every eight days. "The 225 indictments ranged from racketeering, arson, and aggravated assault to extortion, bribery, and pension fund embezzlement." Methods by which the Mob profits from the Teamsters include kickbacks for sweetheart contracts and, until the government took over the union's main pension fund in 1983, providing multimillion-dollar loans to Las Vegas casinos out of members' retirement benefits. In fact, Mob control over the pension fund was so blatant that the fund was commonly referred to as "the mafia bank." Steven Waldman, "The Best and Worst of American Unions," *Washington Monthly*, July-August, 1987, pp. 34–35.

18.8 Controlling the union: the election of Roy Lee Williams. Williams' election to the presidency of the Teamsters was engineered by the Mob, in particular by Kansas City boss Nick Civella. In a demonstration of how ineffective prison sentences can be in stopping the Mob, Civella held meetings to plan the 1981 election, which Williams won by acclamation, in the visiting room at Leavenworth federal prison. Tapes of the meetings were introduced as evidence in the 1985 casino-skimming trial of several top Midwestern Mafiosi, at which Williams testified for the government. *Washington Post*, November 6, 1985, p. A4.

18.9 Controlling the union: "Including murdering people?"—"Yes, sir." In 1986, Teamster Bruno Bauer was found murdered, gangland-style, several months after he had filed a complaint with the National Labor Relations Board. The complaint concerned wages lower than those agreed upon in the union contract. Bauer's union, Local 707, is controlled by New York's Colombo Mafia Family.

Charles Allen was a killer and strong arm man for Mafiosi Russell Bufalino and Tony Provenzano. He described his work, keeping legitimate unions and union leaders out of Teamsters and Hotel and Restaurant Employees locals in Delaware and Atlantic City, for the Senate Permanent Subcommittee on Investigations. Allen's duties ranged "from murder to selling drugs, from extortion to beating up people, hijacking."

U.S.-President's Commission on OC, The Edge, p. 118; *Newsday*, January 31, 1987.

18.10 Controlling New York's moving-and-storage industry. The Mafia used a Teamsters local to run the quarter-billion-dollar industry for more than 20 years. Starting in 1964, Mobsters who dominated Teamsters Local 814 extorted payoffs from moving companies who wished to avoid "work problems, labor problems, money problems, [and] life-and-limb problems." The Mob also arranged bid-rigging schemes among companies. Victims included the FBI, which moved its New York offices in 1979 and was overcharged on a rigged bid from which $5,000 went to a Teamsters "slush fund." And when nonunion workers refused to honor the local's picket lines, former union official Anthony Giliberti and fellow Mobsters "cut their tires, burned their trucks and gave them a whack."(B)

In 1986, union officials, owners of moving companies and Bonanno family leaders, including boss Philip Rastelli, were convicted of labor racketeering for the operation. That same year, Carmine Persico, Anthony Salerno, and Anthony Corallo, bosses of the Colombo, Genovese and Lucchese

Families respectively, were convicted of membership in the Mafia's national commission. They were each sentenced to 100 years in prison. RICO was among the charges in both trials.

But John Gotti, powerful boss of the Gambino Family was acquitted in March 1987 with six lieutenants of charges involving racketeering, gambling, loan sharking, truck hijacking and murder.

A–New York Times, May 13, 1986 p. B3; B–*New York Times*, May 16, 1986, p. A19; also *New York Times*, October 16, 1986, p. B9; *New York Times*, January 14, 1987, p. A1; *Washington Post*, March 14, 1987, p. A1.

18.11 Exploiting union members: labor-leasing companies return workers to "plantation days." Mob muscle was essential to Eugene Boffa's operation of more than 30 labor-leasing companies across the United States. Corporations that contracted with Boffa's companies fired their truck drivers and then rehired them, at reduced wages and under unsafe or unfair conditions, from Boffa. Boffa, who received a percentage on his contracts, also guaranteed labor peace, and union dissidents or troublemakers were not rehired.

Boffa was an associate of Mafia boss Russell Bufalino and worked with the Provenzanos in New Jersey. Mob-tied Teamster officials, including Sam Provenzano, Sam Ancona, Frank Sheeran and Jackie Presser, assisted Boffa with bribes to local officials who would sell out their membership, supported him against honest officials, and arranged labor peace or labor problems to persuade corporations to use his companies.

Boffa was convicted under RICO in 1981; he was sentenced to 20 years in prison, and his companies were forfeited. But he apparently continues to operate and profit from new and similar companies while in jail.

U.S.–President's Commission on OC, The Edge, pp. 110–11, 132–37.

18.12 Local 560. Teamsters Local 560 in Northern New Jersey was ruled by the Mafia, in particular by Anthony "Tony Pro" Provenzano and his

---

Glimco, Joseph Paul [profile of a Mafia labor leader]

Record dates back to 1923, more than 38 arrests: disorderly conduct, vagrancy, assault with auto, . . . armed robbery, assault with gun with intent to murder, murder. Prime suspect in at least 4 murders. . . . Tried for murder in 1928 after a deathbed statement by victim, acquitted. A 17-count indictment for violations of Taft-Hartley Act was dismissed by Federal Judge Michael L. Igoe in August 1965. Convictions: larceny, . . . conspiracy to violate the Volstead Act. . . . Citizenship granted in 1943 by Federal Judge Michael L. Igoe after State Representative Andrew A. Euzzino had subject's police record destroyed. Took Fifth 80 times before Kefauver Committee, and 152 times before McClellan Committee. . . .

Modus Operandi: The Syndicate's top labor czar; boss of at least 15 Teamster locals; a power in the jukebox and coin machine industry, and a hidden owner of a wide variety of legitimate enterprises—a front for top Syndicate bosses, who in turn uses fronts. A Mafia don with a reputation as a vicious and brutal gangster who enforces his edicts with violence and murder.

Ovid Demaris, *Captive City*, pp. 342–43.

brothers. Their activities included violence, extortion, sweetheart contracts, and embezzlement; in the early 1960s the salaries of Provenzano and business agent Stephen Andretta exceeded Jimmy Hoffa's. In 1984, Local 560 became the first union ever placed in trusteeship by the federal government under the civil provisions of RICO. *U.S.-President's Commission on OC, The Edge*, pp. 123–26.

18.13 Bribing a U.S. Senator. Teamsters President Roy L. Williams was convicted along with Allen Dorfman and Joseph Lombardo in 1982 for conspiring to bribe Nevada Senator Howard Cannon with land owned by the Central States Pension Fund. The conspiracy apparently succeeded in blocking critical trucking deregulation legislation sponsored by Senator Edward Kennedy. *U.S.-President's Commission on OC, Appendix to The Edge*, pp. 40–41.

18.14 The Mafia's bank. The Teamsters Central States Pension Fund "served as a virtual bank for the mob." The Mafia controlled the fund through members of its Board of Trustees. In 1977, 60.6% of its $1.59 billion in assets was invested in real estate; $260.6 million of this was in Nevada, mostly in casinos. The fund was put in trusteeship by the federal government in 1983; by 1985 assets were $5.3 billion, of which only $34.7 million was in Nevada real estate.(B) A–*New York Times*, April 3, 1986, p. A22. B–*U.S.-President's Commission on OC, The Edge*, p. 140.

18.15 A RICO suit against the entire union. In June, 1987, the federal government announced preparations for a civil lawsuit under RICO to place the entire Teamsters union under federal control because of Mafia influence. The Teamsters countered by garnishing support to block this move, scoring a victory in October, when the AFL-CIO voted to allow it back into the labor federation. The merger was publicly described as an effort to reunify the trade union movement, but one underworld informant saw it as the Mob's doing. Indeed, one of the three principal negotiators was Edward T. Hanley, president of the Hotel and Restaurant Employees International Union, described in a 1986 President's Commission on Organized Crime report as one of the "big four" unions "substantially influenced and/or controlled by organized crime." The merger came thirty years after the Teamsters was expelled from the AFL-CIO for corruption and just months before the scheduled trial of Teamster President Jackie Presser on charges of fraud and racketeering.

Washington Post, June 10, 1987, p. A1, October 25, 1987, pp. A1, A9; *U.S.-President's Commission on OC, The Edge*, p. xvi.

b. The construction unions

18.16 Extracting millions of Pentagon dollars through a Mafia-controlled union. During the late 1960s, a Pentagon construction contract in St. Louis was handled by the Mafia-controlled Laborers Local 42. At the time, the local was led by Lou Shoulders, a Mob killer who was himself murdered gangland-style in 1972. Among those who turned up on the government payroll were "a small army of Mob soldiers, relatives and high-rankers," some of whom actually showed up at the construction site—to run gambling operations, shake down workers for kickbacks, and instill terror into project supervisors. Millions of dollars were siphoned off in phony overtime payments and paychecks to ghost workers.

One of those who drew $8,000 in a four-month period was Mike Trupiano, a nephew of St. Louis Mafia boss Tony Giardano, who had been arrested for burglary and brandishing a deadly weapon. Trupiano, who never came close to the plant while under surveillance during a five-work-day period, later became business agent of Laborers Local 110, with a fat salary and expense account. More than a dozen other named Mafia members and associates were on the payroll, including "a Syndicate arsonist," Joseph Scalise. Not surprisingly, the cost of the Pentagon contract came to $22 million, almost triple the original estimate.

The Mafia-controlled Laborers Local 42 also had jurisdiction over the construction of a St. Louis bridge. This job, too, was characterized by terror and inflated costs: Two union officials who protested the arrangements were brutally beaten, and one union member was murdered on the construction site. Indeed, St. Louis unions in general have been plagued with racketeering, "in which the Mafia-dominated crime syndicate has played the major role. Mob-controlled unions hold much of the available labor in a virtual hammerlock." It was thus not surprising that the 25- to 50-percent productivity at the Pentagon project was shrugged off by Army brass as "typical of the St. Louis area."

Denny Walsh, "The Mob: It Racks Up Overtime on a Government Payroll," *Life*, February 14, 1969, pp. 52–56; for background on Local 42 boss Lou Shoulders see "Shoulders Bid $7,000 on Contract to Kill," *St. Louis Post Dispatch*, March 1, 1974.

18.17. Extorting $35,000 from a New Jersey contractor. Mafia boss Nick Delmore offered labor relations assistance to developers of a large apartment complex. "Within weeks, pickets from a Cosa Nostra-controlled union had shut down the entire project." The developers then paid $35,000 to Delmore and his Mafia partner, Sam DeCavalcante, to settle the strike. William Schultz, "The Mob's Grip in New Jersey," *Reader's Digest*, February 1971, p. 113.

18.18 Pervasive Mafia extortion in New Jersey construction. The De-Cavalcante tapes bore out the boast of New Jersey Mafia boss Sam De-Cavalcante that no new apartment units were built in his territory without his approval. DeCavalcante, in cooperation with construction unions and the Teamsters, would guarantee labor peace for a hefty fee, permitting builders to save $1,000 a unit through the use of nonunion workers. As one union leader told DeCavalcante, "Right now the picture is ideal for you, Sam. . . . I told the guy he's gotta be one hundred percent union. . . . I got the pickets ready and everything. . . . He knows if he doesn't go your way, he's gotta go one hundred percent." DeCavalcante associate Gaetano Vastola explained, "When I sit down with the boss [the builder] I tell him how much it's gonna cost him in welfare, hospitalization and all that. . . . [I'll say] 'It's gonna cost one hundred thousand dollars a year. Let's cut it in half, and forget about it.' " Not content with shaking down contractors, DeCavalcante and his associates also formed their own union — Warehouse-men's Local 242 — to pocket the $5 a month in dues paid by the members. Mollenhoff, *Strike Force*, pp. 8–18.

18.19 Concrete prices: Philadelphia–$45 per cubic yard; Brooklyn and Queens–$60 per cubic yard; Manhattan–nearly $85 per cubic yard. According to *Newsday*, the particularly expensive Manhattan variety "is produced by Transit-Mix Concrete Corp. and Certified Concrete Co.—two firms under common ownership and organized-crime domination."(B) The same two companies supplied concrete for 94 out of 108 Manhattan jobs examined by investigators for the President's Commission on Organized Crime between 1977 and 1984.

The Mob controlled all concrete contracts in the city worth more than $2 million, and claimed two percent of the value of each contract by means of a "club" of contractors which it ran. Mob-run unions, such as Ralph Scopo's Cement and Concrete Workers (he served as president of the union's New York District Council and of Local 6A) provided a good base for extortion, since they were responsible for the presence or absence of labor peace at a job site; the Mob's control of the concrete supply also gave it leverage. Club members were allowed "to dispense with such requirements as the payment of union-scale wages or benefits to workers at a job site," and corrupt union officials frequently served as a conduit for payoffs to the Mob.

It has been estimated that as much as 20 percent of the cost of construction in New York goes to benefit the Mob.

A-*U.S.-President's Commission on OC, The Edge*, pp. 218-19, 225, 228, 231; B-*Newsday*, September 8, 1986, p. 11.

18.20 Description of a New York Mafia union leader's operations. Bobbie Cervone was business agent of Mason Tenders Local 13, which the New York State Investigation Commission identified as Mob-dominated. Cervone was also a Mafia associate and loan shark, who was questioned in a number of murders and arrested three times but never convicted.

Cervone's union operation was described by a former Mob associate, Vincent Siciliano, who had worked in the union. Cervone drew an official salary of $175 per week from the union but owned a Rolls-Royce, a Cadillac, houses in Long Island and Florida, a couple million dollars in a Swiss bank account, and several million dollars in assets in the U.S. Much of this loot came from his union's welfare funds. Collecting 8 percent of his members' salaries, Cervone amassed $1 million a year in welfare payments. Little of this was ever disbursed to the membership. Siciliano explained, "If one of the union members get hurt or something, Bobbie can just make a deal—maybe throw in a few bucks for the doctor. Who is the guy going to kick to? He could end up dead instead of sick if he tried."

"Do you think that *people* build all those buildings around New York? *Ghosts* build most of them—that's people who just aren't." [Emphasis in original.] Whenever contractors hired workers from Cervone's Mason Tenders Union, the steward would record workers who were not there, sometimes more "ghosts" than workers; the paychecks went to Cervone. "The contractor expects this. He already has raised his prices to take care of it. . . . And you wonder why it costs so much to put up a building? Besides all of this, every time a guy wants to build, he also has to pay something straight out to Bobbie."

Cervone made additional income from "concession money," a cut from bookmaking, loan sharking, prostitution, and dope operations on construction sites under his jurisdiction. This income covered large bribes, which secured him top political and police connections. Cervone was eventually suspended from the union post when his racketeering involvements were publicized. But "he never for a second lost control"; his replacement was his former chauffeur.

Vincent Siciliano, *Unless They Kill Me First*, pp. 123, 134–37. See also *Newsweek*, January 5, 1981, p. 37.

18.21 Cervone indicted for "bleeding" the Queens construction industry. Bobbie Cervone, his two sons and 17 others were indicted in August 1987 for labor racketeering and corruption. Through their schemes they forced those renting or buying property in Queens to pay a "racketeering tax." The head of the Justice Department's organized crime task force in Brooklyn said the construction trade is "in a virtual stranglehold of organized crime and a group of labor racketeers and their willing business accomplices." The U.S. attorney in Eastern New York noted: "It is widely recognized that organized crime has a pervasive influence in the construction industry." *New York Times*, August 19, 1987, p. B1.

18.22 A Mafia representative serves as labor troubleshooter for one of the world's largest construction firms. Stephen Broccoli, alias "Peanuts the Dwarf," was shop steward for Local 251 of the Laborers Union in Providence. He was also employed by the Gilbain Building Company, "one of the largest construction companies in the world," where he acted as an intermediary between labor and management. Broccoli had been convicted three times for armed robbery and according to information from Rhode Island police, was placed on the Gilbain payroll by New England Mafia boss Raymond Patriarca. From the testimony of Colonel Walter Stone, superintendent of Rhode Island State Police, in *U.S.–Senate, OC and Narcotics Hearings*, p. 557.

18.23 Extent of Mafia infiltration of the Laborers. Mobsters literally own Laborers locals in New York City, through which they dominate construction there. For example, Laborers International Union Locals 731, 20, 18, 394, 1298, 66, and 95; Concrete Workers District Council Local 6; and Mason Tenders Union Local 23 are all controlled by or have ties to organized crime. Laborers national president Angelo Fosco appointed Chicago Mafioso Al Pilotto and St. Louis boss Matthew Trupiano as "special international representatives" for the union. And in 1986, a Laborers local, Local 6A, became the first AFL-CIO union to be placed in court trusteeship because of thorough Mafia infiltration. *U.S.–President's Commission on OC, OC and Labor-Management Racketeering*, pp. 74–75. *Newsday*, September 10, 1986, p. 26; Steven Waldman, "The Best and the Worst of American Unions," *Washington Monthly*, July-August, 1987, p. 38.

18.24 Some Laborers dissidents. National vice president Robert Powell, the highest-ranking black in the mostly non-white Laborers Union, had considered running against national president Angelo Fosco in 1981. Powell received telephoned death threats, and a dead rat and two dead pigeons were planted in his car. He also got a personal message from Fosco: "Powell, you're dead. You're dead. You're dead."(B) Powell moved his wife to another city for more than a year, began wearing a bullet-proof vest and carrying a handgun, and decided not to run. Shortly afterward, he retired from his union post.

Member Dennis Ryan did attempt to challenge Fosco—who, according to one President's Commission witness, is simply a figurehead for the Mob—

in the 1981 election. Ryan was beaten on the convention floor, in full view of the other delegates.

Ben Medina, a friend of Powell's and recording secretary of Laborer's Local 332, was murdered in 1982—days after resigning his post to run for business agent of the local. Five masked men came to his house in the middle of the night and beat him to death.

During the President's Commission hearings, when these incidents were exposed, the union complained of "a massive campaign of government harassment . . . and a vicious display of anti-Italian bias and prejudice."(B)

A—*U.S.-President's Commission on OC, The Edge*, pp. 158–60; B—*Washington Post*, April 23, 1985, p. A3.

18.25 The International Union of Operating Engineers is plagued with multimillion-dollar embezzlement, undemocratic management, violence, and murder; its leadership is allied with the Mafia. The McClellan Committee reported that "literally millions of dollars have vanished from the IUOE treasury, often reappearing in the form of improved living standards for union bigwigs." The Committee described kickbacks, collusion with employers, and sweetheart contracts, some officials owning the very companies with which they negotiated. It found rule by intimidation and violence, with little democratic control by the 280,000 members. And the Committee reported connections and joint extortion ventures between International president William Maloney and Chicago Mobsters. The situation was summed up by Dennis Ziegler, who led a dissident movement that was subjected to armed violence by Maloney and Teamster-Syndicate figures. Ziegler noted the union's reputation of "being dominated and controlled by the worst forms of racketeers, hoodlums, and murderers in America." He was later murdered after having received a death threat from Maloney. Hutchinson, *Imperfect Union*, pp. 189–94.

18.26 "The hidden wiring that links politicians, trade union leaders and the crime syndicate." In the early 1960s, *Chicago Tribune* reporter George Bliss wrote a Pulitzer Prize-winning series on the Chicago Metropolitan Sanitary District. He wrote that through faking time sheets, padding payrolls, inflating wage scales, kicking back insurance money, and rigging contracts and real estate leases, Mob-connected employees were bilking Chicago taxpayers of "at least $5 million a year." Richard B. Ogilvie, then candidate for sheriff, charged that the district was "a rest home and haven for relatives and friends of the Chicago crime syndicate," and listed 36 district workers connected to the Mob. A new district superintendent, appointed in the heat of the scandal, then probed deeper and committed what the *Chicago Daily News* termed "the unforgivable political sin": exposing "some of the hidden wiring that links politicians, trade union leaders and the crime syndicate." A few hours after the superintendent asked for evidence in his probe, he started his car and escaped death only when four sticks of dynamite "failed to detonate because a wire had slipped off a spark plug."

One item investigated was a $3 million sewer, built under a contract questionably awarded to a construction firm reputed to have close ties to the Mob. Because of "serious construction defects," the sewer caused $5 million in damages to a nearby water treatment facility and had to be replaced. Demaris, *Captive City*, pp. 207–13.

18.27 "Administrative costs" of 68 percent on a union dental plan were siphoned to the Mob. The plan was administered by Robert J. Cantazaro, who obtained the contract from the Laborers' Central States Joint Board Health and Welfare Trust Fund after himself reviewing the proposals of competing bidders. He did open a clinic as specified by the contract, but it closed fifteen months after it began operations — "just when there were complaints that more clinics were needed to improve service to the membership." Of the more than $5.1 million Cantazaro received in insurance premiums, 68 percent went to "corporate overhead and profits for Cantazaro's companies. . . . approximately $2.5 million was directly traced to Cantazaro and his family." But Cantazaro was only a front man for the Mob. He had originally been introduced to the trustees of the Fund by none other than Mob-labor figure John Serpico. The executive director of the Teamsters Central States Pension Fund, which has been reformed under the supervision of the federal government, characterized the 68 percent figure as "outrageous. . . . I would tell you 25 percent was a ripoff. There is nothing to describe 68 percent in my opinion." *U.S.–President's Commission on OC, The Edge*, pp. 153–56.

18.28 "The Mafia and its associates inside labor": "looting some pension funds, terrorizing officials, rank-and-filers and employers alike, shaking down contractors and extorting millions of dollars annually." Covering a conference of federal officials from strike forces against organized crime, noted labor columnist Victor Riesel wrote: "It was reported that anyone looking too closely at some New York construction unions would get 'a bullet in the back. . . .' Despite gory killings and car bombings of St. Louis pipefitters (plumbers) union local 562, 'the racketeering surface hasn't been scratched there. . . .' national AFL-CIO construction union chiefs . . . can't control many of their locals. Frequently, trustees aren't put in because there are few men who'll dare attempt to take over a Mafia-controlled local union until there is a conviction."

Riesel declared that the time has come to confront racketeers "from New York with its complex construction unions to Mafiosi now surveying 'open' cities reaching from Atlanta to Los Angeles." *New Orleans Times-Picayune*, September 27, 1973, p. 11.

18.29 Terrorism in the building trades. A sickening barrage of dynamitings, arson, vicious beatings, and murders against nonunion contractors was related in a four-part series in *Reader's Digest*. Cases from across the country were described. In June 1971, for example, 16 goons descended upon a nonunion construction site near Philadelphia and attacked workers with baseball bats. Six men were left "a mass of bloody flesh, broken arms and fractured skulls"; one was nearly blinded. An assailant who expressed remorse over the vicious attacks was found in a ditch, shot in the head, the next morning. Bloody baseball bats left behind after the beatings bore the emblem of Roofers Local 30; this was one of four unions cited by the *Philadelphia Inquirer* as "suspected by police of being involved with the Mafia."(B)

This was representative of "172 separate instances of violence, vandalism and similar harassment" against contractors reported in 1972 alone. The violence allowed the racketeer-infested unions to continue "wholesale shakedowns of the contractors, while stealing from and cheating their own members." As one union member explained, "it is a standing phrase in construction work that the Mafia has taken over, thus the violence—and the kickbacks and bullying systems so obvious to the workers."

A–Charles Stevenson, *Reader's Digest*, June 1973, pp. 89–94; July 1973, pp. 79–83; August 1973, pp. 153–57; December 1973, pp. 85–90; B–*Philadelphia Inquirer*, January 22, 1974.

c. Restaurant workers' unions

18.30 The Mafia takeover of both the unions and business association in the restaurant field in Chicago; 124 bombings and arsons by 1965. "Goon squads smashed windows, slugged owners and patrons with baseball bats, slashed tires, dumped sugar in gasoline tanks, tossed stinkbombs, set fires and planted black-powder and dynamite bombs, and when everything else failed, resorted to murder." In sweetheart contracts arranged by the unions—one of which was operated by a Mafia lieutenant without even the pretext of a front—everyone but the workers benefited. After a new epidemic of bombing and arson in the early 1960s, the *Chicago Daily News* declared that the risk to Chicagoans had "passed the point of toleration," while the *American* deemed the situation an emergency. Demaris, *Captive City*, pp. 22–29; McClellan, *Crime Without Punishment*, pp. 138–46.

18.31 Mafia 'paper' unions in New York. Mafia representatives "organized" New York restaurants using intimidation, picketing, and sabotage. Restaurant owners or employees paid monthly union "dues" without receiving union cards, union scale wages or any benefits whatsoever. From the *Wall Street Journal* (1968–70), reprinted in Gartner, *Crime and Business*, pp. 194–96.

d. The International Longshoremen's Association

18.32 The "Mob runs the docks in this country." The International Longshoremen's Association (ILA) is run by the Genovese, Gambino, and Marcello Mafia families. One International vice president, Tony Scotto, is a captain in the Gambino Family; Scotto took the Fifth Amendment when asked in 1970 by New York State's joint legislative committee on crime whether he was a member of the Mafia.[41] He was convicted on a federal racketeering count in 1979.[42] Through the cooperation of ILA officials, the Mob carries out massive systematic hijackings at U.S. docks. "In effect, the Mafia and the Longshoremen's Union have been able to put their own tax on every item moving in or out of the ports they control." NBC Evening News "Segment 3," September 6, 1977, and September 7, 1977.

18.33 The Mob "has treated the waterfront as its own money machine" for most of this century. The New York Mafia has "extracted tribute from companies doing business on the waterfront: kickbacks from employers grateful for sweetheart contracts, payments extorted from union members in return for work and pilferage that amounts to millions of dollars a year." In one racket, international vice president and Gambino capo Anthony Scotto received cash payments totaling $210,000 from the president of McGrath Service, Inc., a national stevedoring company, to halt a flood of false claims by union members seeking compensation for injuries.

"Compensation payouts dropped 400 percent" after the payoffs were made.

The Mafia maintains total control over the Brooklyn, Staten Island, Manhattan and New Jersey waterfronts; its influence extends as far south as the piers in Miami.
Newsday, September 8, 1986, pp. 8–9, 13.

18.34 "In the upper echelons there is an amalgamation" between the Mafia, Teamsters, and ILA. As stated in 1967 by Henry Peterson, then chief of the Justice Department's organized crime and racketeering section. Reid, *Grim Reapers*, p. 275.

18.35 Mafia control of New York docks is a longstanding tradition. A special waterfront investigation by the Brooklyn district attorney's office in 1940 revealed that Mafia boss Albert Anastasia "had been stealing hundreds of thousands of dollars from unions" and that there had been "crimes of extortion, larceny of union funds, destruction of union books and falsification of new ones, kickbacks in wages for the benefit of racketeers." And the New York State Crime Commission, after an investigation in the early 1950s that logged 4,000 interviews and 30,000 pages of testimony, found that "at least thirty percent of officials of the ILA longshore locals have police records. . . . Through their powers as union officials, they place their confederates in key positions on the docks, shake down steamship and stevedoring companies by threats of work stoppages, operate the lucrative public loading business, and carry on such activities as pilferage, loan-sharking and gambling."

The membership was found to be "virtually disenfranchised." The Commission cited 22 ILA hiring bosses who participated in or encouraged "assault, organized theft, pilferage, extortion, kickbacks, loan-sharking, gambling, payroll padding, other criminal activities and even murder." The Commission named a number of Mobsters behind the criminal network at the New York docks, and noted that the steady deterioration of the competitive position of the New York port was due mostly to "criminal or quasi-criminal practices."
U.S.–Senate, Kefauver Report, Third Interim, pp. 130–32; Hutchinson, *Imperfect Union*, pp. 98–107.

18.36 Mafia control of New York docks in the 1960s and 1970s. Despite changes in leadership and image, the Mafia still maintains ironclad control of the New York and New Jersey docks and the area locals of the ILA. *Life*, September 8, 1967, pp. 101–3; Meskil, *Don Carlo*, pp. 159–66.

18.37 Port Newark is "a flat Cosa Nostra concession." Gambling, loan sharking, and cargo theft are rampant. *Life*, September 8, 1967, p. 103; *Reader's Digest*, February 1971, p. 113.

18.38 The ILA, like the Teamsters, was ousted from the AFL for infestation by "gangsters, racketeers and thugs." In 1953, the ILA was expelled by the AFL, which reported that the ILA "has permitted gangsters, racketeers and thugs to fasten themselves to the body of its organizations, infecting it with corruption and destroying its integrity, its effectiveness and its trade-union character." The union was readmitted in 1959 after an attempt to found a new longshoremen's union failed. Hutchinson, *Imperfect Union*, p. 297. *U.S.–President's Commission on OC, The Edge*, p. 37.

e. Motion picture and theatrical workers' unions

18.39 Chicago Mafia members and associates were convicted in the 1940s for multimillion-dollar labor extortion in the motion picture industry. After Chicago Mobsters captured one local of the International Alliance of Theatre Stage Employees (IATSE), they decided to take control of the International. So in 1934, top Syndicate figures and their gunmen descended upon the International's convention in Louisville, and Mob front George Browne was elected president without one dissenting vote. The Mob then persuaded the Hollywood studios to give the IATSE jurisdiction over its employees by closing every theatre from St. Louis to Chicago.

With the entire motion picture industry now in the Mob's grip, Mob representative Willie Bioff contacted industry spokesman Nicholas Schenck, president of Loew's, and demanded $2 million against the threat of a nationwide strike. A deal was arranged in which major studios would pay the Mob $50,000 a year, minor companies $25,000; the payments were to continue indefinitely. But federal investigators uncovered the scheme and sent several Chicago Mafia members and associates to prison. From the essay "Crime on the Labor Front" by Malcolm Johnson (1950), reprinted in Tyler, *Organized Crime in America*, pp. 199–205; also see Hutchinson, *Imperfect Union*, pp. 134–37.

Note: According to investigative reporter Jeff Gerth, "the movie industry since the 1930s has been controlled by organized crime."[43] For current material on Mob-Hollywood connections see *New York Times*, June 27, 1976, p. 20; *New York Times Magazine*, December 26, 1976, pp. 18ff; *Public Affairs Series Special Report 13: The Mafia Today* (Los Angeles: Knight Publishing, 1977), pp. 54–61.

18.40 A 72-year-old projectionist opposing a syndicate union boss was murdered. In 1960, Herman Posner, a 72-year-old projectionist, attempted to lead a rebel movement in the Mafia-controlled IATSE Chicago Local 110. But Posner was knifed to death a few days before he was to turn over to federal investigators evidence of shakedowns and kickbacks. His killers fled with the evidence. "Posner's murder was the seventh in the bloody history of the union." Demaris, *Captive City*, p. 35.

f. Unions in New York and surrounding states

18.41 Unskilled workers are exploited by sweetheart contracts and embezzlement of union funds. In one case discussed, the New York State Investigating Commission exposed the workings of a New York local of the Laborers International union. Electronic surveillance revealed that it was controlled by a Mafia soldier on orders from Carlo Gambino. "Union members, under sweetheart contracts, were forced to work for wages below union scale." The welfare and pension funds were so thoroughly plundered that they went bankrupt. Union stewards ran loan sharking and gambling on job sites. "Mafia rule was enforced with threats, shootings, even bombings." In factories under the jurisdiction of other Mafia unions, employees worked for poverty wages in substandard conditions. Methvin, "How the Mafia Preys on the Poor," *Reader's Digest*, September 1970, p. 53; Kennedy, *The Enemy Within*, pp. 215–16.

18.42 Mafia labor czar Frank Costello gave New Yorkers a puppet show. Costello was asked by the night manager of a Manhattan hotel to avoid using the hotel's steam baths. The next day, not one waiter, custodian, maid, or elevator operator came to work at the hotel. Within hours, the hotel's manager was "frantically begging him to return." Gage, *Mafia, U.S.A.*, p. 19.

18.43 Mafioso Johnny Dio straightened out any union problems. "Senator, I had a dress shop, a negligee and dress contract, on Prospect Avenue. I never belonged in any union. If I got in trouble, any union organizer came around, all I had to do was call up John Dio or Tommy Dio and all my troubles were straightened out." From the testimony of Mafia defector Joseph Valachi in *U.S.-Senate, OC and Narcotics Hearings*, p. 227.

18.44 The S.G.S. labor relations firm was hired by leading New York businesses; the "G" stood for Mafia boss Carlo Gambino. When service and maintenance men struck the Chrysler Building in 1960, the owners hired Gambino's S.G.S. Associates. The strike was soon settled after armed goons arrived in Cadillacs and ran the elevators. Grutzner, "How to Lock Out the Mafia," *Harvard Business Review*, March-April 1970, pp. 53–54. Similar services rendered by Gambino Family underboss[44] Carmine Lombardozzi are described in Kennedy, *The Enemy Within*, pp. 229–30.

18.45 Profile of a New York Mafia labor boss. Tony "Ducks" Corallo, a caporegime in the New York Lucchese Family,[45] controlled five Teamster locals and locals of such other unions as the Toy and Novelty Workers Union, the Painters and Decorators Union, the Food Handlers Union, the Conduit Workers Union, and the United Textile Workers. Workers in many of Corallo's unions were victimized by sweetheart contracts, substandard wages and poor working conditions. Corallo served six months in prison on a narcotics violation, and was described by a New York Police official as involved in "gambling, labor racketeering, extortion, strongarm and murder."(B) During 1963 Senate rackets hearings, he invoked the Fifth Amendment 120 times. A-Dorman, *Payoff*, pp. 76–77; B-*U.S.-Senate, OC and Narcotics Hearings*, pp. 282–83.

18.46 Goons, bombs, embezzlement, and extortion in Mafia-controlled unions in New Jersey. As usual, everyone benefited but the captive members of the Mafia-controlled unions. Schulz, "The Mob's Grip on New Jersey," *Reader's Digest*, February 1971, p. 113.

19. Estimated annual income

In 1986, Wharton Econometric Forecasting Associates estimated the annual gross receipts of organized crime to be between $41.6 billion and $106.2 billion.[46] The following additional estimates of Mob income are listed by source, year, and annual amount (figures in parentheses represent value in 1987 dollars, adjusted for inflation using the consumer price index): Congressman Dante B. Fascell, former chairman of the Legal and Monetary Affairs Subcommittee of the House Committee on Government Operations, 1969, "at least $60 billion" ($208 billion);[47] organized crime expert, Ralph Salerno, 1969, at least $40 billion ($139 billion);[48] journalist Stanley Penn, in the *Wall Street Journal*, 1969, "as much as $50 billion" ($174 billion);[49] Congressman Robert McClory, 1970, "between $50 to $60 billion" ($163 billion to $196 billion);[50] *Time*, 1977, "at least $48 billion" ($107 billion);[51] *Newsweek*, 1981, estimates "begin at $120 billion" ($160 billion).[52] Experts in Chicago and New Orleans estimated in 1964 that the Mob's combined annual income in just those two cities was $3.1 billion ($12.7 billion).[53]

Time magazine estimated that fully half of the Mob's huge annual income is realized as profit[54]—money pocketed by Mafia members and top associates. The rest goes mainly to lower level functionaries and outside assistants: a bookie or numbers runner,[55] a truck driver who sets up a hijacking,[56] a Wall Street clerk who pilfers stock certificates,[57] a businessman who fronts a bankruptcy fraud,[58] or a nonmember associate who assaults and murders for the Mafia.[59] One of the Mob's largest expenses is corruption of police and politicians at all levels of government. In expert estimates and case studies in several U.S. cities, the percentage of Mob income paid out in bribes has been found to average at least 15 percent.[60] Applying that percentage to a conservative income estimate of $100 billion per year yields an annual corruption expenditure of $15 billion.[61]

V. CORRUPTION

20. Scope and methods of corruption

20.1 "Organized crime is, in the vernacular, taking us over." U.S. Attorney Frederick B. Lacey, commenting on Mob corruption in New Jersey, quoted in Dorman, *Payoff*, p. 53.

20.2 The Mafia has "locked a strangle hold on American politics." Mafia political operations "tear at the fabric of American society" to an extent "greater than ever before in our history." Dorman, *Payoff*, pp. 13–14.

20.3 The Mob cannot operate without corruption. Former Mob money mover Michael Raymond: "There is no area in organized crime that can operate without the duplicity of the police, the agencies involved. I have had enormous experience in the area. I have seen it. . . . [for example] there is no numbers operation in the world that can operate without police protection. It doesn't exist. Anyone who tells you that is lying." *U.S.– Senate, OC and Stolen Securities, 1971*, pp. 670–71.

20.4 "A war on organized crime is inseparable from a war on political corruption. In this fact may lie hidden the reason why it is so difficult for political leadership to wage a comprehensive war on organized crime—for to do so would be to risk severe political consequences." From a 1967 report by 23 Republican members of the U.S. House of Representatives, quoted in Cressey, *Theft of the Nation*, p. 275.

a. Some methods of corruption

20.5 Each Mafia family has at least one specialist in corruption who "bribes, buys intimidates, threatens, negotiates, and sweet-talks himself into a relationship with police, public officials, and anyone else who might help 'family' members maintain immunity from arrest, prosecution, and punishment." Cressey, *Theft of the Nation*, p. 250.

20.6 An anti-Mob candidate for sheriff in Newport, Kentucky, was drugged, put to bed with a stripper, arrested by cooperative police. The

At the heart of every successful gangster's operation is the Fix—the working arrangement with key police and elected officials and business and union executives. . . .It can be accomplished by putting in fear, through means as unsubtle as a crack over the head, an arm broken by twisting, an implied disclosure of family skeletons, a hoarse voice on the phone, a timely murder. It can be accomplished by campaign "contributions" or by outright bribes. It can be attained through employment of public relations counsels. . . . It can be helped immeasurably with cheap devices like easy "loans" to a reporter whose tastes outrun his income.

Life, September 1, 1967, p. 22

residents of Newport, Kentucky, became fed up with the wide-open gambling and vice operations in their city, "recognized the relation of crime to politics, and decided the only chance for reform was to elect some honest officials." Ex-football star George Ratterman was persuaded to run for sheriff, and despite the frame against him, which city residents did not swallow, was elected in 1961. Soon after Ratterman took office, as Attorney General Robert Kennedy reported, gambling "virtually ceased" in Newport. Hank Messick and Burt Goldblatt, *The Mobs and the Mafia* (New York: Ballantine, 1972), pp. 184–87.

20.7 Sexual blackmail used to help lure a politician to Hollywood. A Mob corrupter described how one captive politician became excessively greedy and had to be removed from office. "Some of our guys wanted to put out a 'contract' on him, but I persuaded them that knocking him off would just bring us more heat than we could afford. . . .I had created him and now I had to eliminate him."

The corrupter played on the politician's secret desire to be a movie star, with the help of a leading actor and Mobster with a secret interest in a movie studio. To blackmail the actor into cooperating, a party was arranged for the actor and politician which was "stocked with whores" and wired with "a half-dozen hidden microphones." The corrupter then played tapes of the party for the actor, who quickly agreed to offer the politician a Hollywood contract. The politician "bit like a fish on a worm . . . resigned from office, packed his stuff and left. . . . We picked out another guy we could control and elected him to the vacant office." Dorman, *Payoff*, pp. 91–93.

20.8 Hooking a policeman or official through minor bribes and favors. One official who ignored the criminal record of a Mafia soldier in a liquor license application was threatened with exposure of that transaction if he did not approve other licenses for the Mob. Soon, the official was deeply involved in corruption. He was discovered and indicted, but he was murdered before the trial began. Another compromised officeholder related, "I forgot that those gangsters are animals. When I gave them my hand, they began nibbling at my fingertips. Before I knew it, they had swallowed my arm and were gnawing on my shoulders." Cressey, *Theft of the Nation*, pp. 288–89.

20.9 Getting out the vote for a Mob candidate. To elect their chosen slate

> Let's say, for example, you have a judge or a senator along on your junket, and plenty of them went on mine. You arrange for him to be with a hooker, to get a blow job in the suite you've rented. At the same time, the place is set up so that you can get pictures and tape recordings of what is going on. Then, when one of your people gets in trouble with the law, or the mob needs votes on a bill they want passed, a copy of that photograph or tape recording is sent to him.
>
> > Vincent Teresa, who ran gambling junkets to casinos in Las Vegas and abroad, *My Life in the Mafia*, p. 232.

of candidates, some New York Mobsters offered a free play on the numbers to all neighborhood residents who voted, and provided Mob-employed chauffeurs and babysitters to assist the voters. A record turnout resulted, and the Mob candidates were elected. Dorman, *Payoff*, p. 15.

20.10 The systematic use of politics by a Mafia underboss. New England Mafia underboss Henry Tameleo "used politics to get the things [boss Raymond] Patriarca wanted. He could reach out to a governor's office or a police precinct or a city council or a state legislature, even a congressman to get the things the mob needed." Teresa, *My Life in the Mafia*, p. 81.

20.11 "Official cover-up: A flagrant case in point." *Life* magazine noted that cover-up inevitably accompanies Mob corruption. One example *Life* cited was the censored report on organized crime by President Johnson's crime commission (U.S.–Task Force Report). Among the suppressed items, from a section by Notre Dame Professor G. Robert Blakey:

"The success of the Chicago group [of the Mob] has been primarily attributable to its ability to corrupt the law enforcement processes, including police officials and members of the judiciary. . . .

"Control, sometimes direct, has been exercised over local, state and federal officials and representatives. Men have been told when to run or not run for office or how to vote or not to vote on legislative issues or [for judges] how to decide motions to suppress evidence or judgments of acquittal." *Life*, September 8, 1967, p. 103.

21. Police corruption

21.1 Police corruption, almost always tied to Mob-controlled illegal gambling, has been uncovered again and again throughout the country. The New York City Police Department, the oldest in the nation, has been repeatedly rocked by major scandals involving massive firings, resignations and reorganizations. Such scandals have occurred in the early 1930s, 1950, 1959, 1964, and 1971, each involving gambling or other Mob-controlled operations. Similar scandals have shaken police departments in cities throughout the country, including Albany, Atlanta, Baltimore, Chicago, Denver, Detroit, Kansas City, Louisville, New Orleans, Newark, Philadelphia, Reading, Reno, San Francisco and Seattle. Maas, *Serpico*, pp. 11,

137–40, 299–302, passim; Methvin, "How Organized Crime Corrupts Our Law Enforcers," *Reader's Digest*, January 1972, pp. 85–89.

21.2 Organized crime cannot operate without police protection—Malcolm X. "Wherever you have organized crime, that type of crime cannot exist other than with the consent of the police, the knowledge of the police and the cooperation of the police. You'll agree that you can't run a number in your neighborhood. . . . A prostitute can't turn a trick on the block. . . . A man can't push drugs anywhere along the avenue without the police knowing it. And they pay off the police so they will not get arrested. I know what I'm talking about—I used to be out there." Malcolm X noted, "The police are all right. . . . there's some good ones and some bad ones. But they usually send the bad ones to Harlem." From a speech by Malcolm X, transcribed in *By Any Means Necessary*, p. 50.

21.3 A Yale University study showed that one out of five policemen "was observed in a criminal violation." The 1966 study monitored the actions of 597 policemen selected at random in Boston, New York, and Washington, D.C. Twenty percent of the policemen committed crimes, *even though they knew they were being watched*, including "actual theft, receiving protection payoffs, and accepting money to alter sworn testimony." Maas, *Serpico*, pp. 138–39.

21.4 The rookie policeman is faced with a climate of corruption. After a 1971 investigation of police corruption in New York City, the Knapp Commission concluded that "the underlying problem is that the climate is inhospitable to attempts to uncover acts of corruption and protective of those who are corrupt. The rookie is faced with the situation where it is easier for him to become corrupt than to remain honest." Defected Mob killer Joseph Barboza described the situation this way: "Every other cop is taking money, and a new police officer gets on the force and his partner is taking money, his zeal kind of leaves him, and then, also, probably because of the low pay. The enticement of big money."(B) A–Methvin, "How Organized Crime Corrupts Our Law Enforcers," *Reader's Digest*, January 1972, p. 88; B–*U.S.–House, OC in Sports*, p. 765.

21.5 The Mob got data from a national police intelligence association. The Law Enforcement Intelligence Unit, established to exchange information on crime among local police departments, has been plagued with leaks to the Mob since its inception in 1956. Its Pueblo, Colorado, chapter was expelled in 1960 for passing sensitive intelligence to the underworld and its Denver and Kansas City chapters were expelled in ensuing years on corruption charges. In 1966, a former Dallas policeman stole a photocopy of an FBI file on the Mafia. In September 1978, the Las Vegas chapter was thrown out when FBI wiretaps revealed that an intelligence specialist with the Las Vegas police had leaked information to reputed Mob figures. *Washington Post*, November 24, 1978, pp. A1, A8.

a. Chicago

21.6 "Corruption Behind the Swinging Clubs. Walker Report: Chicago Cops Rioted; Life Report: Mob Payoffs to Police." Summarizing the Walker Report, *Life* magazine noted that during the 1968 Democratic Convention, several Chicago police units "simply dissolved in violent gangs and attacked protesters, press and bystanders indiscriminately" in "what can only be called a police riot." *Life* concluded that discipline under pressure requires trust and morale. "And it is clear that such trust and morale could not exist in Chicago, where an important section of the police structure, from patrolman to high rank in headquarters, has been—and is today—seriously corrupted by payoffs and favors from the Mob."

Following are highlights from this lengthy *Life* magazine report:

Chicago Police Captain William Duffy, head of the intelligence division, was a "superb cop" of "national stature in law enforcement." In September 1964 Duffy led a raid by police and FBI agents on a numbers operation. Police found a list of payoffs containing names and badge numbers of 469 Chicago policemen in three districts. Police headquarters took no action.

In January 1968, Duffy's men and federal officials raided a numbers operation run by Mob racketeers. In this raid of "one of a score" of Mob numbers operations in Chicago, "ice lists" were confiscated, as reproduced in *Life*, showing payoffs to police "in 10 of Chicago's 21 police districts." Also shown were 38 special payments, supplementing standard-scale graft, to individual policemen for extra services. Again no action was taken on the graft. Six weeks after a Mob gambling boss boasted publicly that "we got a promise that Duffy will go," Captain Duffy was relieved of his command of the intelligence division and transferred.

In 1963, the U.S. Justice Department filed an 18-page report which "named 29 policemen alleged to be trafficking with or taking payoffs from the Mob." Nothing was done about the charges and most of the 29, including six with high positions, were still on the force in 1968. One on the list, Lt. Paul Quinn, was a top Chicago police liaison to City Hall in 1968.

A number of policemen actually worked for the Mob. One detective talked almost daily with a Mafia killer, Phil Alderisio, and moonlighted for Alderisio by tapping the phones of bookies suspected of cheating the Mob. Gambling boss Angelo Volpe kept another detective as a confidant and occasional chauffeur-bodyguard. As *Life* summarized, "there is a climate around Chicago police in which organized crime thrives like jungle shrubbery."

Sandy Smith, "Corruption Behind the Swinging Clubs," *Life*, December 6, 1968, pp. 35–43; see also Demaris, *Captive City*, pp. 233–320, for dozens of similar cases.

21.7 A policeman suspended for service to a Mobster became chief of police of a Chicago suburb. When Rocco Salvatore was tried for a speeding violation in 1966, Melrose Park Police Sergeant Dominic Cimino attested to Salvatore's fine character and told the court that Salvatore needed his driver's license for his business. Cimino was later temporarily suspended from the Melrose Park Force when it surfaced that Salvatore's "business" was acting as chauffeur and bodyguard for Chicago Mafioso[62] Sam Battaglia. But in 1967, Dominic Cimino became chief of police of Melrose Park. Shortly afterward, reports surfaced that Cimino often met with Charles (Chuck) Nicoletti, a Mob enforcer and terrorist. "News accounts related that Chief Cimino was observed conferring with Nicoletti almost daily." Cressey, *Theft of the Nation*, pp. 262–63.

21.8 Comments of an informant on the Chicago Police Force. "The going rate for promotions to sergeant today [in the Chicago Police Force] runs around $3,000 to $5,000—depends on how much they think they can take off the man." Lieutenancies cost about $10,000 and captaincies at least $15,000. The bribes are usually paid by sponsors in "the Party or the Outfit [Mafia]."

The informant cited the case of "an Outfit hood by the name of Mike Glitta, who owns the Shore club on North Clark Street." His brother-in-law, Vince Serritella, became a police sergeant, "and Glitta bragged it cost him five grand." Glitta intended to have Serritella assigned to the state's attorney's office where he could be of maximum service to Glitta. The informant mentioned other cases of Outfit-connected cops. "Believe me, there are a lot of sleepers in the department. I mean policemen who are Outfit connected, hoodlum related."

The informant noted that some police captains ask Mobsters for tips to make an arrest. The Mobsters "give them a stick-up team or something that's not Outfit connected. Or they'll pinch some free-lancing whore or knock over a little Negro-operated policy wheel."

From a lengthy interview with an unnamed informant on the Chicago Police Force, transcribed in Demaris, *Captive City*, pp. 257-61.

b. Detroit

21.9 "The continual brazen effort of the Mafia to secure their immunity from law enforcement by direct briberies of police officials." Detroit Police Chief George Edwards related several examples of this effort. He also noted that in 1939 "we saw the former mayor of the city of Detroit, the former prosecuting attorney, the former sheriff, the former superintendent of police, and roughly 250 police officers all go to jail for the acceptance of graft in order to let gambling operate in the city of Detroit." *U.S.–Senate, OC and Narcotics Hearings*, pp. 402–5.

21.10 Six of Detroit's top 12 policemen were found on a Mafia bribe list. In 1965, agents under Detective Vince Piersante arrested a Mafia member in the act of giving a Detroit cop his monthly payoff. Piersante confiscated a notebook showing bribes to 134 Detroit policemen, including six of the top 12 members of the force. The arrested Mafioso was sentenced to just 60 days in prison of a possible five-year term. But Piersante "was hounded by his superiors with reprisals ranging from an attempt to frame him on a charge of stealing seized property to harassment and transfers of his men." In 1971 federal and local law enforcement officials arrested 151 persons, including 16 Detroit policemen, for participating in illegal gambling. *Reader's Digest*, January 1972, p. 86.

c. Philadelphia

21.11 A Pennsylvania crime commission reported in 1974 that "police corruption in Philadelphia is ongoing, widespread, systematic, and occurring at all levels of the police department." In every police district and every rank, from patrolman to inspector, corruption was found. Gamblers, racketeers, prostitutes, and night club owners often paid off the police, as detailed in the report. More than 400 policemen were identified as having received cash, goods, meals or sex. Raymond C. Brecht, "Gamblers Pay and Flourish, Probers Find," *Philadelphia Evening Bulletin*, March 10, 1974.

d. Boston, Providence and other New England cities

21.12 "Crooked cops were the mainstay of the New England Mob." Mafia defector Vincent Teresa reported that overall police protection was handled by New England Mafia underboss[63] Jerry Angiulo, who claimed he could control 300 of Boston's 360-odd detectives. Providence, Rhode Island boss Raymond Patriarca "had half the city on his payroll."

Teresa related how in several New England cities, dozens of cops would go into Mob hangouts "to get their presents and their envelopes at Christmas time." Teresa described how he cultivated one particular Boston policeman, who for "a G-note" ($1,000) ignored $160,000 in stolen furs in Teresa's possession, and for $2,500 blocked a police investigation of $50,000 in fraudulent bank loans. The policeman fed Teresa information regularly and performed similar favors in exchange for payoffs.

"There were so many cops on the mob's pad, it's really hard to remember them all." When a policeman gave the Mafia a hard time, Patriarca would call Angiulo, who would get in touch with one of the high-ranking officers on the pad. Soon the policeman would be transferred to another district where he would be out of the Mob's way.

"People have got to understand that there are lots of Reveres, lots of Bostons in this country." Policemen are on the take, Teresa noted, because they don't earn much and get disillusioned when they see the politicians taking and judges dismissing cases they've slaved over. "It don't take long for a cop to get the message. Everyone's making money and he isn't, so he just joins the parade."

Teresa, *My Life in the Mafia*, pp. 146–51.

f. New York City

21.13 The pad: payoffs as systematic as paychecks in every one of New York's 80 police precincts. In a series of speeches to Congress in 1960, preacher-politician Adam Clayton Powell charged that the Mob was wiping out black numbers operators in Harlem, detailed the mechanics of Mob-police payoffs, and pinpointed some specific numbers games and persons involved. Monthly payoffs for one typical numbers game ran as follows (punctuation changed from original list format): "Division–$420, Borough Headquarters–$275, Police Commissioner–$275, 1st Deputy Commissioner–$275, Chief Inspector–$275 [these categories referred to departments and not necessarily to individuals]. Precinct: Captain–$50, 23 sergeants at $10–$230, 8 lieutenants–$260, uniformed officers on post–$192, radio cars (2 shifts)–$192. Detective squad: 33 detectives–$330, Detective Lieutenant–$50, Detective Sergeant–$25. Total: $2,749."

In 1960, the same year that Powell publicized the situation in Harlem, the *New York Post* published a series of investigative reports on the numbers game that furnished a monthly breakdown of payoffs similar to that described by Powell. The *Post* reported that there were 90 numbers spots in a single section of Harlem, each of which paid off about $2,500 a month, yielding an annual police payoff of $2,500,000 in just that one Harlem area from numbers alone. The *Post* concluded that the numbers racket was controlled by "call them what you like—the East Harlem Mob, the Syndicate, the Mafia." And it quoted one expert source who noted "there are 80 precincts in New York City, and in all my experience in all five boroughs, I have not found a single one in which a Pad for policy isn't maintained in one form or another."

Cook, *Two-Dollar Bet*, pp. 134–36; Ted Poston, "The Numbers Racket," *New York Post* (1960) reprinted in Tyler, *Organized Crime in America*, pp. 260–71. The same systematic and pervasive corruption was described from first-hand experience by the heroic New York policeman, Frank Serpico, in Maas, *Serpico*, passim.

21.14 Mobster Stanley Polley "had enormous contact with the Police Department in New York, with political figures." Defected Mob money mover Michael Raymond testified about one of his former associates, Stanley Polley, a fixer for the Mob. "When I met Stanley and as the relationship developed, I had met many high police officials in New York. I sat in front of more police stations in New York waiting for Stanley to come out than I even knew existed. . . . This was virtually a nightly occurrence. At all odd hours of the morning we would meet with high police officials. I have been witness to conversations with high police officials involving many, shall we say, breaches of security in the police world." *U.S.–Senate, OC and Stolen Securities, 1971*, p. 649.

21.15 A 1972 investigation of a police gambling unit in Brooklyn revealed that "70 percent of the police in the special unit were taking payments from organized-crime gamblers." In 1973, 16 policemen were convicted in the Brooklyn Supreme Court of accepting "protection money from gamblers linked to organized crime." Payoffs averaged more than $10,000 per year.(B) A–Gage, *Mafia, U.S.A.*, p. 14; B–*New York Times*, June 10, 1973, p. 43; see also Meskil, *Luparelli Tapes*, p. 168.

(See chapter 10 of text for material on police corruption in Dallas.)

g. Beyond malfeasance: cases of Mob-police criminal complicity

21.16 "The creeping paralysis of law-enforcement" from gambling-tied corruption "contributes to a breakdown in connection with other fields of crime." It was also noted that "wherever organized criminal gangs are entrenched in a particular community and have been given the green light to operate, it is not unusual to see the forces of law enforcement being used against their competitors, while protected operations are left alone." Such selective enforcement was found in New York, Miami and Los Angeles, forcing one bookmaking syndicate in Miami "to capitulate to the demands of the Accardo-Guzik-Fischetti crime syndicate." *U.S.–Senate, Kefauver Report, Third Interim*, p. 182.

21.17 A New York policeman made dumdum bullets for the Mafia to kill federal "stool pigeons." A New York policeman agreed to make "dumdum bullets" for a Mafia soldier, knowing that they would be used to kill federal informants. A transcript of a bugged conversation between the Mafioso and policeman provides details of the arrangement. After the policeman promised to supply bullets which would make a hole "you can put your fist through," the Mafioso informed him that they would be used to shoot federal informers: "Nobody else. Only stool pigeons. I mean, like, the cops like stool pigeons when they go, especially if they're federal stool pigeons, right?" Cressey, *Theft of the Nation*, pp. 191–93.

21.18 "Involvement in corruption by dozens of Indianapolis policemen . . . has led some members in the department to criminal activities." The *Indianapolis Star*, the FBI, and a federal organized crime strike force investigated widespread corruption among Indianapolis police. A murder and a car bombing shortly after the *Star*'s disclosures were believed linked to the investigation. *New York Times*, March 4, 1974, p. 19.

21.19 "Some officials bend over backwards to help their Mafia friends." A sheriff in Florida some years ago furnished "special policing" for some illegal gambling casinos; the sheriff "even deputized the men who drove the armored cars carrying the casino's profits to the bank." Gage, *Mafia, U.S.A.*, p. 269.

21.20 New York policemen were charged in the disappearance of $70 million worth of confiscated heroin and cocaine. State special prosecutor Maurice Nadjari charged that "less than 10" policemen planned it, "and then solicited the underworld for aid" in selling the 400 pounds of narcotics. Fifty-seven pounds of heroin were from the "French Connection" case. *New York Times*, October 15, 1973, p. 41.

21.21 Two Baltimore policemen were suspended in connection with the disappearance of 248 bags of heroin. The narcotic theft scandal broke during an investigation of illegal gambling payoffs that led to the indictments of six city policemen. *New York Times*, January 28, 1973, p. 39, June 15, 1973, p. 13.

21.22 The Chicago Police in the Capone era: a private army for the underworld. It was officially estimated that in 1923, 60 percent of Chicago policemen were engaged in bootlegging, "not in connivance, but actually." Allsop, *The Bootleggers*, p. 17.

21.23 The Chicago Police: regularly committing every crime, including Mafia-directed murder. "Policemen still regularly commit burglary, robbery, felonious assault, bribery, auto theft, extortion, larceny, brutality and murder. They still moonlight for the Syndicate as procurers, narcotics peddlers, bootleggers, collectors and assassins. Cases are made against policemen in nearly all these categories monthly. In the majority of the incidents, they are exonerated by the courts and continue on the police payroll."

One case, which led to what Intelligence Division Chief William Duffy described as "the first crime-syndicate murder conviction in my memory," involved four Chicago policemen who were also members of a Syndicate narcotics ring. One member of that ring, Chicago Policeman Thomas N. Durso, was convicted with Syndicate terrorist Michael Gargano of the murder of federal narcotics informant Anthony Moschiano. Durso and Gargano were each sentenced to 100 to 150 years in prison. Demaris, *Captive City*, pp. 65–68, 264–65.

22. Corruption of the judiciary

22.1 Some standard Mob judicial procedures. Bribe the police and the district attorney. "Get to the witnesses"; some "can be intimidated, some can be bought, and some must be liquidated." Hit the jury with "the usual round of bribes and threats." Provide unlimited funds for the best lawyers. If all else fails, arrange soft jobs, special treatment, and financial support for Mobsters sent to prison. Tyler, *Organized Crime in America*, pp. 231–33.

a. Intimidation and murder of witnesses

22.2 Prosecutions against the Mob have too often failed "because essential witnesses have been killed, bribed or intimidated into forgetfulness." In connection with a prosecution for embezzlement of union funds, based upon a Teamsters-Mafia alliance in Kansas City, key federal witness Robert Williams had to be preserved by shipping him to the Canal Zone in 1962." In the same case, "one of the codefendants was Floyd Hayes, who was convicted and then became a cooperative government witness. He made a series of statements to prosecutors about unsolved syndicate crimes which had extended over many years. . . . his cooperation surfaced as a witness in a perjury trial. About six weeks later he was murdered. Five or more prosecutions died with him." From the statement of New Orleans Metropolitan Crime Commission Director Aaron Kohn in *U.S.–House, OC Control*, pp. 430–31.

22.3 Twenty-two observers, no witnesses in a Mob murder in Providence. Jackie Nazarian, an assassin for New England Mafia boss Raymond Patriarca, murdered George Baletto in the Bella Napoli Cafe in Providence. Of the 22 patrons there, one man, an ex-boxer named Eddie Hannan, considered testifying, but he was garroted by Nazarian and left in a dump. Reid, *Grim Reapers*, p. 66.

22.4 Mob slayings are difficult to solve primarily because of reluctance of witnesses to furnish information to law enforcement officials. From the testimony of Tampa Police Chief Neil Brown in *U.S.–Senate, OC and Narcotics Hearings*, p. 536.

b. Corruption of judges and prosecutors

22.5 Extensive Mob corruption in the nation's largest court system. A federal report named 16 circuit court judges in the Cook County, Illinois, Judiciary who had "at one time or another been contacted by various representatives of the crime syndicate to handle specific cases." The report found that the Mob routinely used its political clout to assign its cases to such judges. Specifically, it noted that 90 percent of all cases in one year involving arrests in Loop strip joints were brought before five judges, who handed down "very few, if any," guilty verdicts.

One blatant example was the trial of George Ammirati, the 45-year-old son of a former Mob boss, who described himself to police as a "self-employed bookie" and boasted of his top Syndicate contacts. On December 3, 1962, Ammirati shot a man who tried to disarm him in a barroom brawl. Ammirati followed his victim outside, and fired a second, fatal shot into his back. Ammirati then hired an attorney specializing in Mob clientele, "which automatically assured him of a dozen continuances in the quest for a sympathetic judge."

The case was finally heard before Judge George B. Weiss, who dispensed with a jury at Ammirati's request, tried the case in one day, and dismissed the charges of murder and voluntary manslaughter. Judge Weiss found Ammirati guilty of only involuntary manslaughter, carrying a one- to ten-year prison term, and suspended his sentence to just 90 days in jail plus five years probation. The judge defended his decision to newsmen by claiming that Ammirati was "a good family man" and that the shots "were on the accidental side."

Demaris, *Captive City*, pp. 296–98.

22.6 a. The judicial and political connections of Colombo Family members Joseph Yackovelli and Carmine Persico. Yackovelli and Persico "had a lot of connections with politicians and judges." Persico's contacts included both state and federal judges. Reported by Mafia defector Joseph Luparelli in Meskil, *Luparelli Tapes*, p. 217.

22.6 b. A Mobster killed a black couple at a party before 30 guests; Yackovelli and Persico secured his freedom. Charles Shepard and his common law wife, Shirley Green, were hired to serve at a New Year's Eve party at the Wayne, New Jersey, home of Mobster Joseph (Fatty) Russo. During the party, Shepard angered Russo by drinking and dancing with one of the guests. Russo then got his gun and fired six shots into Shepard. Shirley Green "was screaming and fighting to get out of there but a couple of guys held on to her. Fatty went back upstairs and reloaded. Then he came down and shot her too." The bodies were found in a roadside snow bank on the morning of January 1, 1971.

Russo later went to Colombo Family underboss Joseph Yackovelli for assistance, as described by their mutual associate, Joseph Luparelli, who was present during the conversation. Yackovelli told Russo, "I know the chief of police out there" and "probably could get in touch with the judge. But it would cost you." Russo said he would "go as high as a hundred thousand dollars." Yackovelli then discussed the matter with another Colombo Family member, Carmine Persico, assuring Persico "the guy's all right. He just blew his top and killed two blacks." Persico told Yackovelli, "We'll see what we can do."

In Russo's December 1971 trial, one of the 30 guests at the party gave an eyewitness account of both murders. But the trial was aborted when Passaic County Court Judge Louis Schwartz dismissed the jurors after 15 hours of deliberations, claiming that they were exhausted. In June 1972 Russo was again tried, and Judge Schwartz again declared a mistrial, explaining that one of the jurors felt ill and that the two alternate jurors said they had discussed the case. Russo totally escaped punishment for the two murders.

Meskil, *Luparelli Tapes*, pp. 217–23.

22.6 c. Yackovelli and Persico were indicted for obstruction of justice; then freed through suspicious judicial maneuvers. Colombo Family members Joseph Yackovelli and Carmine Persico, along with Joseph Russo and Carmine DiMase, were indicted for conspiracy to thwart the Shepard-Green murder prosecution of Russo. On September 24, 1973, Federal Judge John Bartels, presiding over the trial of Persico and Russo, made the unusual request that the press refuse to report the backgrounds of the defendants. The next day, after the press ignored the order, Judge Bartels "declared a mistrial . . . dismissed the jury and began trying the case himself." One week later, Judge Bartels dismissed the indictment against all four defend-

458

ants. *New York Times*, September 25, 1973, p. 24; September 26, 1973, p. 43; October 3, 1973, p. 50.

22.7 New York Mafia boss Thomas Lucchese "was for many years a patron of a number of public officials in New York City." Twenty-two judges were guests of Lucchese in just two of the many charity dinners he attended. And the tables were turned on one occasion when an assistant U.S. attorney, Armand Chankalian, picked up Lucchese's hotel tab. Reid, *Grim Reapers*, p. 41.

22.8 New York State Supreme Court Justice Dominic Rinaldi investigated for alleged judicial misconduct in "wrist-slapping" sentences to Mafia hoodlums. The New York State special prosecutor's office investigated the cases of Lucchese captain Paul Vario, who received a $250 fine from Rinaldi on a bribery conviction, instead of the maximum sentence of a year in jail, and of Mafia associate Salvatore Agro, who received only a suspended sentence on charges connected with a million-dollar swindle. Rinaldi also gave a conditional discharge to a narcotics dealer who had a long criminal record and had violated parole by continuing to sell narcotics. The New York State Committee on Crime found that this conditional discharge was "illegal" and resulted in "no punishment whatsoever" for the narcotics trafficking conviction. Assistant District Attorney Edward Panzarella, who prosecuted the Agro case and appeared to approve of Rinaldi's sentence, "later resigned in a controversy over an alleged failure to prosecute another drug case."

In Rhode Island, impeachment hearings were begun against state Supreme Court Chief Justice Joseph A. Bevilacqua for questionable financial practices and for his admitted ties to organized crime. Bevilacqua resigned during the impeachment proceedings. Some of his finances were handled by Stephen Fusco, an E.F. Hutton broker whose shady practices were spotlighted in a probe of the company by the New England Organized Crime Strike Force. The strike force in October 1987 recommended that the government seek an indictment against E.F. Hutton for allegedly helping organized crime figures launder hundreds of thousands of dollars. The company had been convicted in 1985 for a massive check-kiting scheme.

New York Times, November 13, 1973, pp. 1, 36; *Washington Post*, October 10, 1987, pp. 1ff.

22.9 A line to a federal judge. Defected Mob money-mover Gerald Zelmanowitz testified, "I was in Florida with [New Jersey Mafioso[64]] Ray DeCarlo and [John V.] Kenney, another gentleman from New Jersey, now currently in prison, or I believe he has been released since then. He was head of the Democratic Party in Union County, NJ." Zelmanowitz related that a call was made in his presence to a federal judge, who in this instance refused to perform the favor asked, stating that "it is too hot a potato for me to touch." Zelmanowitz advised, however, that at other times the judge had been "cooperative with Mr. Kenney and Mr. DeCarlo." *U.S.–Senate, OC and Stolen Securities, 1973*, p. 99.

22.10 Widespread Mob corruption in New York courts. The New York Joint Legislative Committee on Crime documented cases of court fixes, political interference in Mob trials, and leniency towards racketeers by many judges. The corruption was described to the committee by several witnesses, who wore hoods to hide their identities. One testified that Mafia superiors had told him there would be no problem if he were arrested in Brooklyn, because "we got judges on the payroll that can straighten it out one-two-three."

The criminal record of New York Mafia enforcer Dominick "Mimi" Scialo exemplified this corrupt pattern. "Since 1944, Scialo has been arrested fourteen times on charges ranging from felonious assault and rape to first degree murder. But he has never been sent to jail." In Scialo's murder case, the Mafioso and accomplices were accused of beating two young men to death with snow-tire chains. Scialo had previously hired the victims— Bartholomew Garafalo, age 18, and Alexander Menditto, age 19—to torch a dance hall in Boston. In his hospital bed, before he died, Menditto signed a police statement implicating Scialo. Based on this and other evidence, Scialo was charged for the murders. But later, "Menditto's deathbed statement was said to have mysteriously disappeared from the district attorney's office. The charges were then dismissed."

Michael Dorman, *Payoff*, pp. 122–24.

22.11 New York State Supreme Court Justice Thomas Aurelio thanked Mafia boss Frank Costello profusely for obtaining the judgeship for him. Aurelio added, "I want to assure you of my loyalty for all you have done. It's undying." Costello told Aurelio, "When I tell you something is in the bag, you can rest assured." Although the wiretap of the conversation was made public and investigated by a grand jury, Aurelio retained his Supreme Court position. Dorman, *Payoff*, p. 122; or see *U.S.–Senate, Kefauver Report, Third Interim*, p. 122.

22.12 Flagrant misconduct on behalf of the Mob by a top Arizona judge. U.S. District Court Judge Walter E. Craig, a former president of the American Bar Association, had a reputation for exceptional leniency in cases involving organized crime. In one case, for example, Judge Craig dismissed a tax evasion charge against a gambler whom Craig admitted having known for many years. And Judge Craig was criticized for the light sentences and unusually low bonds he granted to a man with a long criminal record and two others accused of sizable narcotics operations.

When questioned about his conduct, Craig protested, with perhaps unintentional irony, "I don't remember individual cases. These cases go through here like money through a slot machine." Craig also proclaimed, "I don't know of any organized crime in Arizona."

In 1972 Judge Craig presided over the murder conspiracy trial of Joe Bonanno, Jr., son of the top Mafia boss. Five of Bonanno's codefendants had already pleaded guilty to various charges. When the intended murder victim testified against Bonanno, as juror Robert Clark later described, Judge Craig had "incredulous looks" on his face and made gestures indicating disbelief. Clark noted that "his conduct was anything but impartial", and "his reaction to various witnesses and their testimony left little doubt as to what he thought of them." U.S. Attorney Ann Bowen, who prosecuted the case, charged that during her presentation, Judge Craig buried his face in his hands, openly laughed, mimicked one government witness in a falsetto voice and "generally ridiculed her entire presentation by rolling his eyes and gesturing."

In May of 1972, the jury convicted Bonanno of conspiracy to murder as charged. After the verdict, a window of the gas station owned by the jury foreman was shot out. Another juror's car was struck by a truck which careened out of control; the truck was found to have been stolen and the driver was never located. And six weeks after the verdict, Judge Craig overturned the conviction, claiming that the jury might have reached its decision unjustly because of Bonanno's participation in a shakedown attempt. The jury was "flabbergasted" by Craig's reversal, reported foreman Jerry Boyd. Another juror stated that Craig's speculations concerning how the jury reached its verdict were "as slanderous as they are false," and petitioned for the impeachment of Craig.

Craig's behavior, however, was not unique in Arizona judicial circles. One former State Supreme Court justice furnished a liquor license reference for an associate of Detroit-based Mafioso[65] Pete Licavoli. Another state judge, who socialized with a Phoenix bookmaker, was believed to have met several underworld figures at a restaurant and discussed drug importation. Former State Attorney General Gary Nelson, who became a state appellate judge, was under a federal probe concerning his conduct in office. And Arizona authorities investigated an attorney tied to Mafioso Pete Licavoli suspected of high level narcotics dealings, along with another lawyer believed to be providing cover for a major heroin supplier.

From the Investigative Reports and Editors (IRE) series on organized crime in Arizona, *Albuquerque Journal*, April 3, 1977, pp. A1, A6.

22.13 The Mob coaches a captive judge on responding to corruption charges. An FBI bug placed in Chicago First Ward Democratic headquarters, a hangout for Chicago gangsters, recorded a conversation between Illinois Circuit Judge Pasqual Sorrentino and Pat Marcy, "a friend of the Chicago LCN [La Cosa Nostra] family." When Judge Sorrentino asked Marcy what to reply if questioned by federal agents about his associations with gangsters, Marcy responded: "Stand on your dignity. Don't answer those questions. Tell them they're trying to embarrass you. Stay on the offensive." "The Mafia v. America," *Time*, August 22, 1969, p. 19.

c. Criminal lawyers and lawyer criminals

22.14 Some techniques of Mob lawyers. "The courtroom antics of Mob mouthpieces are more often staged than spontaneous. Witnesses experience lapses in memory, policemen make reversible slip-of-the-tongue errors, prosecutors ignore valuable evidence, judges rule improperly, and jurors are bribed, intimidated or just plain hate to commit their childhood heroes to prison." In one case, for example, a lawyer worked out a small change in the story of the arresting officer, which would justify acquittal on a legal technicality. The lawyer could hardly have failed to realize that the policeman would be bribed to incorporate this change. Demaris, *Captive City*, p. 308; Cressey, *Theft of the Nation*, pp. 255–57.

22.15 A Syndicate lawyer orchestrated perjury, bribed a juror. Richard Gorman, a former Chicago policeman and federal prosecutor, specialized in defending Syndicate figures against federal raps. An expert on legal loopholes, Gorman once freed a client in a tax evasion case by arguing that the $900,000 in question was embezzled from the Laundry Workers Union and therefore not taxable income; Gorman charged his $15,000 fee to the Laundry Workers Union.

In 1959, Gorman defended Mobster Gerald Covelli in a hijacking case which ended in a hung jury when one member, Robert Saporito, held out against conviction. Covelli later became a government witness and testified that Gorman had instructed him to lie, had rehearsed the perjury with him, and had shown him a list of jury members with Saporito's name marked with an X. Saporito confessed to accepting the bribe offered via his brother Michael, who was on the Chicago Police force. "The boys have approached me on this," Michael told his brother. Michael was in fact promised a promotion to the police narcotics detail by his Mob sponsor in return for his intercession. In 1962, Gorman, Chicago Mafioso[66] Joseph DiVarco and Charles Hudson were indicted by a federal grand jury for jury tampering.

The outcome of the case was classic. The Saporitos' bond was posted by a cousin of Chicago Mafioso[67] John Cerone. Robert was given only a suspended sentence after pleading no contest; Michael disappeared and was presumed murdered. Gerald Covelli, the Mob defendant turned witness, was killed when a bomb exploded in his car in 1967 in Encino, California. And after the notoriously corrupt federal judge Michael Igoe appeared as character witness for Gorman, Gorman and the other defendants were acquitted. Gorman, however, was later convicted and sentenced to two years in prison for income-tax evasion.

Demaris, *Captive City*, pp. 309–16.

d. Accommodating the few who get sent to prison

22.16 Royal treatment for Mobsters in jail. The Mob's influence helps secure the most comfortable facilities, quick parole, and special privileges for members in jail, while dependents receive weekly cash payments. Not atypical was the case of Chicago Mafioso Sam DeStefano, moved by court order in 1968 from an Illinois penitentiary to a hospital for surgery. "Three weeks later it was discovered that he was operating a loan shark business from his guarded room and enjoying fine foods, vintage wines, card games with underworld friends, and visits from women." Salerno and Tompkins, *Crime Confederation*, p. 183.

22.17 Carrying the power of the organization behind bars. From James D. Horan, *The Mob's Man*, reproduced in Tyler, *Organized Crime in America*, pp. 237–44.

22.18 Mafia operations behind bars. Some bosses "can keep operating from prison, dispatching orders through their lawyers and visiting relatives. They may use other, less watched inmates to send messages. Prison mail is rarely read by censors." For example, Mafioso Philip Rastelli not only received kickbacks and retained control of a Teamsters local while in jail, but regained his position as head of the Bonanno family while he was there. "Hitting the Mafia," *Time*, September 29, 1986, p. 22; *New York Times*, May 17, 1986, p. 31.

e. The end result: corruption neutralizes law enforcement

22.19 In 1965, 5,116 adults were arrested for gambling felonies in New York State; four were sent to prison. In 1966, .3 percent of those arrested on gambling charges were convicted. Salerno and Tompkins, *Crime Confederation*, pp. 164–65.

22.20 "Years of dedicated investigation nullified." Judges often give light sentences to Mobsters "because of corruption, political considerations or lack of knowledge." In Pennsylvania, for example, Mafia corrupter Walter Plopi gave a $300 bribe to a state senator while being tape-recorded with the senator's consent. Plopi asked the senator to influence a prosecutor to ignore gambling violations, promising $2,000 a month to the prosecutor, plus $200,000 a year. Plopi also promised the senator 50 percent of the gambling profits, and money for any political campaigns "if you really want to play ball on a county-wide basis." Plopi could have received a year in jail for the corruption conviction. But he was fined only $250—and then reimbursed his $300 bribe.

In New York, John Lombardozzi, brother of a Gambino Family captain, drew no jail term on convictions for smuggling and bankruptcy fraud. Lombardozzi also received far less than the maximum sentences in convictions for assaulting an FBI agent, whose skull he fractured with Mafia accomplices, and for the theft of more than $1 million in securities.

In Chicago, the FBI and federal prosecutors spent four years to convict Mafioso Joey Glimco on a union extortion charge. Yet Glimco, with 36 previous arrests on charges including robbery and murder, got only a $40,000 fine instead of a possible four years in jail. Assistant U.S. Attorney David Shippers commented, "When Glimco got a kiss and went free, it was devastating to us all."

In Boston, Mafia underboss Jerry Angiulo was convicted of assaulting a federal officer. "FBI agents, electronically monitoring boss Patriarca's headquarters, recorded how Angiulo discussed his pending prosecution in detail, plotting to defeat it by procuring a blind man to perjure himself and establish an alibi, then getting a second 'standup' witness to lie that he, too, saw the phantom encounter." Angiulo got only 30 days in jail out of a possible three-year sentence. Other similar cases are cited.

John McClellan, "Weak Link in Our War on the Mafia." *Reader's Digest*, April 6, 1970, reprinted in *U.S.-House, OC Control*, pp. 111–13.

23. Corruption of local government

23.1 "A Two-Faced Crime Fight in St. Louis: Both the mayor and his new crime commissioner have personal ties to the underworld." A year-long investigation by *Life* magazine in 1969–70 disclosed that "Mayor Cervantes himself has business and personal ties with the gangsters that operate in his city. Any real drive against organized crime in St. Louis could start with a number of the mayor's own associates."

The new crime commissioner, Morris Shenker, was one of the Mob's leading lawyers in the U.S. His relations with prominent hoodlums went "far beyond mere legal representation. . . . Shenker, in fact, would have to do little more than tell what he already knows about organized crime to go a long way toward breaking its back in St. Louis and several other places as well."

As an example of Mayor Cervantes' Mob ties, *Life* magazine cited Tony Sansone, "the man closest to Cervantes, as friend, business associate, campaign manager and unofficial but forceful influence around city hall." Sansone is also Cervantes' liaison with the Mafia and the Syrian Mob "that coexists these days as an 'ally by treaty' with the Sicilian Mafia family headed by Anthony Giardano." In December 1964, two days before Cervantes announced his candidacy for mayor, he met with Sansone and the late Syrian Mob leader Jimmy Michaels to plan campaign strategy at a Mob-controlled business incorporated by Shenker. Three months later, after Cervantes had won the primary, Sansone, Michaels, and Mafia boss Giardano met at the same place to discuss his prospects for the general election.

Denny Walsh, "A Two-Faced Crime Fight in St. Louis," *Life*, May 29, 1970, pp. 25–31.

23.2 How the Mob ran Reading, Pennsylvania in the 1950s and early 1960s. The Mob's complete control of the city government and its wide-open rackets operations was detailed in a 19-page study included as an appendix to the 1967 U.S. Task Force Report on Organized Crime. Mob control was broken in the mid-1960s, at least temporarily, when the mayor and rackets boss were convicted of extortion, several other city figures jailed, and a reform administration elected. John A. Gardiner, "Wincanton: The Politics of Corruption," *U.S.-Task Force Report*, appendix B, pp. 61–79. See also Dorman, *Payoff*, pp. 18–32, which identifies some whose names were fictionalized in the Gardiner report, and identifies the specific Mafia families involved.

23.3 An Atlantic City mayor owned by the Mob. The Mob used the considerable influence of Hotel and Restaurant Employees Local 54 in Atlantic City to buy the mayor's office there. This local itself is dominated by the Mob and its officers "boast convictions for murder, arson, extortion, drugs, bribes, kickbacks and racketeering." Before he ran for mayor, Michael Matthews approached several officers of the local, in their capacity as representatives of Atlantic City Mafia boss Nicodemo Scarfo, to solicit an illegal $125,000 campaign contribution. In exchange, he promised to help them acquire land on which to build a casino. Matthews was eventually convicted after accepting payoffs from an undercover FBI agent in connection with the sale of millions of dollars worth of publicly owned land. *U.S.-President's Commission on OC, OC and Gambling*, pp. 243, 249, 276, *The Edge*, p. 79.

23.4 Two mayors refuse Mob bribes. Mayor Richard Hatcher of Gary, Indiana, disclosed that the Mob offered him $100,000 to withdraw from a

---

Chairman Pepper: What are the reasons why local officials in areas where mob operations are carried on over a period of years, are unable to break up the mob and protect the community and other people against their operations? Why is it that they are not able to do it?

Mr. Barboza [defected New England Mob killer]: Well, they don't really want to. In other words, they are getting money from them. . . .

From *U.S.-House, OC in Sports*, p. 760

Democratic primary contest against the machine candidate. It then offered him the same amount after the election for an "understanding" to permit gambling and other rackets. Meanwhile, the forces of Hatcher's predecessor, who was jailed for income-tax evasion, started to undermine the reform program. Hatcher asked Gary citizens to resist "a machine which bought votes wholesale and stole the rest; a machine which exploited blacks and Latins and ignored their just demands; a machine greased with the millions which float from rackets, gambling, and prostitution."

In Newark, "even after Mayor Hugh Addonizio was convicted in an extortion conspiracy and defeated at the polls, the greedy Mafia overlords tried to perpetuate their empire."(B) Shortly after reform Mayor Kenneth Gibson took office in 1970, he revealed in outrage how he had been offered $15,000 to appoint a particular police director and encouraged to follow the former practice of pocketing 10 percent of monies on all city contracts.

A-Dorman, *Payoff*, pp. 32–33; B-Methvin, "How Organized Crime Corrupts Our Law Enforcers," *Reader's Digest*, January 1972, p. 87.

23.5 Chicago in the Capone era: Mafia control of government. In 1931, Albert R. Brunker of the Chicago Civic Safety Committee stated that "there are six thousand city, State and Federal officials in Capone's pay," and "eighty per cent of Chicago's magistrates and judges are criminals."(A) Representative was James Adduci, who was described by the press as a "hoodlum," "gangster," "vice monger," "West Side gambler," and "notorious member of the murderous Capone gang." Adduci "was arrested eighteen times between 1920 and 1934—the year he was first elected to the state legislature."(B) A-Allsop, *The Bootleggers*, pp. 314–15; B-Demaris, *Captive City*, p. 173.

23.6 Chicago in recent years: venal and pervasive Mafia corruption. In 1962, an internal FBI document noted "the almost complete influence and control of politicians, police, and even courts in the Chicago area by the underworld." (E) *Life* Magazine observed that in Chicago, "the connection between the Mob and the politicians remains extensive and arrogant." Below are a few examples.

When *Life* investigated the situation in 1967, Mafia boss Sam Giancana and his lieutenants were "firmly in control of both the Democratic and the Republican political organizations in Chicago's famous First Ward." That ward includes City Hall, the Cook County court house, the federal court house, police headquarters, the Chicago Stock Exchange and Board of Trade, the city's largest office buildings and hotels, and its commercial center. Giancana's main liaison with the First Ward politicians was Pat Marcy, secretary of the First Ward Democratic organization, who previously served a prison term for bank robbery.

Chicago's city treasurer in 1967 was Marshall Korshak, brother of powerful Mafia representative[68] Sidney Korshak. Treasurer Marshall Korshak had "an especially warm relationship" with Giancana lieutenant Gus Alex, and was listed on an apartment application as Alex's employer.

"La Cosa Nostra exerts major influence in a dozen Chicago wards and dictates the votes of as many as 15 state legislators. . . . The Mob opposes anticrime bills in the state legislature, forces gangsters onto the payroll of Mayor Richard Daley's Chicago machine, and corrupts the city police department."(B) Richard Cain, former chief investigator for the Cook County

Sheriff's office, once gave lie detector tests to five robbery suspects. He "was not after the guilty man but in search of the FBI informant among the five. The tipster, Guy Menolia, Jr., was subsequently murdered."(B) Cain later became a "chauffeur and courier" to Chicago Mafia boss Sam Giancana. Eventually he became an FBI informant, and "admitted that he had worked covertly for Giancana and been on his payroll while he was a member of the Chicago Police Department from 1956-60, director of a private intelligence agency from 1960-62, and chief investigator for the Cook County Sheriff's Office from 1962-64."(E)

Ben Lewis, boss of Chicago's 24th Ward, was praised by the late Mayor Richard Daley as a "superior alderman."(D) A secret federal report differed: "Advised in 1961 that Ben Lewis . . . is Lenny Patrick's boy and that he does not do anything without Patrick's O.K. Anyone who operates a book in the 24th Ward is required to give Patrick 50 percent. . . . Advised that Patrick could not be stopped in his gambling and other illicit activities since he was backed politically by [Chicago politicians] Jake Arvey, Sidney Deutsch and Arthur X. Elrod."(C) Lenny Patrick was a top Syndicate killer.[69] Patrick's captive alderman, Ben Lewis, was later slain gangland-style at his political headquarters.

A former assistant U.S. attorney general who headed the Justice Department's Organized Crime Section reported on the fate of federal agents sent to investigate Mafia-political ties in Chicago. "We had a great deal of evidence of payoffs to protect syndicate gambling and other rackets. The Mob had connections all the way to the top—at the Chicago City Hall, the Illinois State House, and in Congress."(D) According to the official, who resigned in protest over the handling of the probe, it was impeded at every turn by Chicago officials, staff members of the local U.S. attorney, federal judges, and finally called off on direct orders from the White House.

A–*Life*, September 1, 1967, pp. 42b–43; B–*Time*, August 22, 1969, pp. 18–19; C–Demaris, *Captive City*, pp. 151–53, 168–69; D–Dorman, *Payoff*, pp. 52–53; E–*U.S.–House, Assassination Appendix, JFK*, vol. 9, pp. 14–15; vol. 10, p. 172.

23.7 New York in the 1960s. In 1961, Lucchese Family caporegime Tony "Ducks" Corallo, a New York State Supreme Court justice and a U.S. attorney were each sentenced to two years in prison. The conviction arose from a bribe by Corallo to the two high officials to free a Mob associate in a bankruptcy fraud case. After his prison stay, Corallo went back to work by extending an exorbitant interest loan to James Marcus, Mayor Lindsay's water commissioner. Marcus was steered to Corallo by Daniel Motto, an exconvict and a top official in the Bakery and Confectionery Workers Union. Once on the hook, Marcus was forced to award an $835,000 city reservoir drainage contract to a scandal-ridden firm, which in turn gave kickbacks to Corallo, Marcus, Motto, and another individual. Mafia lieutenant Corallo, Tammany Hall boss Carmine DeSapio, and Water Commissioner Marcus were each sentenced to jail after the reservoir contract and similar deals were exposed. The trial was marked by a plot to murder the chief prosecution witness. Fortunately, this political penetration by the Mafia was discovered before another scheme to extort $5 million on a $100 million contract for a nuclear power plant could be realized.

The crime problem in the Miami area . . . has existed here for decades. Since the days of Al Capone, crime if not welcomed has been tolerated.

In order to exist, crime has corrupted our public life. Not only public officials have cooperated with the mob, but many of our businessmen have been associated in syndicate activity. . . .

Recently we had an election in Miami Beach. More than half the candidates running had criminal arrest records. A candidate for mayor had just been acquitted on a grand larceny charge. An incumbent city councilman had just escaped a bribery charge. . . .

Under the circumstances it isn't surprising that there should also be an increase in such nonorganized crime fields as juvenile delinquency and crime on the streets. When organized crime creates a climate of cynicism, of disrespect for law and justice, it is sure to be recognized by the young, by the petty hood. Indeed, much of the discontent on the part of our young people today stems from the fact that they recognize the hypocrisy of our generation which pays lip service only to the ideals of justice.

. . . I assure you, the public will respond to an intelligent, fearless, aggressive investigation that penetrates beyond the appearance of things and gets to the reality.

> Bayard Strell, president of the Miami Beach Taxpayers Association, from a statement in *U.S.-House, Crime in America*, pp. 403-4.

Salerno and Tompkins, *Crime Confederation*, p. 254; Dorman, *Payoff*, pp. 77-91; Gage, *Mafia, U.S.A.*, pp. 271-90.

23.8 An Iowa Mobster makes friends in high places. Luigi Fratto, alias Lew Farrell, whose record included 20 arrests and convictions, became the Chicago Mafia's ambassador to Iowa in 1939. While he continued his involvement in illegal gambling, shakedowns and counterfeiting, Fratto cultivated and exploited the friendship of top-ranking politicians and law enforcement officials in Iowa. Among Fratto's many friends was Judge Edwin Moore, who wrote a letter praising Fratto as a reference for a liquor permit. A few months later, Judge Moore dropped an illegal gambling charge against Fratto. Moore later became Chief Justice of the Iowa Supreme Court.

Journalist Clark Mollenhoff of the Des Moines Register described how Fratto and his associates could reverse IRS decisions at the highest levels. Mollenhoff also "watched the tentacles of Lew Farrell reach into the Des Moines Police Department to promote his friends; into the Sheriff's Office for a gun permit; into the Prosecutor's Office to kill a criminal indictment; into the local courts to manipulate decisions on evidence; and into the state political arena." Fratto was also close with top Teamster officials, including Jimmy Hoffa and the notorious goon Barney Baker.

Mollenhoff, *Strike Force*, pp. 34-54.

467

24. Corruption of state government and statewide networks of corruption

a. New Jersey

24.1 Mafia domination of New Jersey government. Mafia control of political figures at every level—from police chiefs, judges and mayors, to political party leaders, a congressman and a governor—has been exposed in dozens of court convictions and in a 2,000-page transcript of FBI electronic surveillance of Mafia hangouts. A good sampling of such information, which is too extensive to summarize adequately in this short review, is provided in the following sources: *Newsweek*, June 23, 1969, p. 37, January 19, 1970, p. 23; Dorman, *Payoff*, pp. 53–74; William Schulz, "The Mob's Grip on New Jersey," *Reader's Digest*, February 1971, pp. 111–15; Fred Cook, "New Jersey: The State of Mafia," *Nation*, May 11, 1970, pp. 560–74. State official William Brennan summarized, "organized crime in New Jersey manages to work its way into . . . almost every area of our society except the church." [70]

b. Massachusetts and Rhode Island

24.2 Excerpts from the Taglianetti Airtels (publicly released FBI summaries of electronic surveillance of Mafia headquarters in Providence, Rhode Island). When a murderer was identified by a witness, "a payoff of $5000.00 was necessary to 'square the rap away.' $5000.00 was furnished to a Lt. Dunn (phonetic) for this purpose and the charge was dropped. The individual was released. . . . (10/26/64)

". . . Joe Modica, Boston, Mass. contacted [Mafia boss] Patriarca specifically concerning the Berkshire Downs Race Track in which Raymond Patriarca allegedly has a financial interest. Patriarca told Modica to contact his friend who is allegedly extremely close to Attorney General Edward W. Brooke of Massachusetts and have him arrange to release the $100,000 bond that is being held by the Massachusetts Court in connection with civil suits that have been heard in Massachusetts courts.(1/25/65)

"[Mafia underboss] Henry Tameleo advised he contacted George Kattar and reiterated to Kattar that in order to operate he 'must have the State.' Kattar told him that he has arranged to pay off the State Police and that he would furnish Tameleo the identities and the amounts paid to individual members of the State Police. . . . (1/28/65)"

Providence Journal, May 20, 1967, quoted in Cressey, *Theft of the Nation*, pp. 269–70.

24.3 The New England Mafia Family's "impressive list of allies among the area's politicians." Informants said that a high-ranking state official, a court administrator, a police chief, two licensing officials, and several powerful state legislators are all "in the bag." Such officials grease the Mob's path: ignoring its crime, allowing its bars and clubs to stay open late, giving its trials to lenient judges, and arranging pardons and paroles for its convicts.

In 1963, FBI agents observed Mafia boss Patriarca meeting with the high-ranking state official in the parking lot of a Boston hospital. Patriarca later commented on the FBI surveillance of the meeting; his words were picked up by an FBI bug in his office. Patriarca stated that he had contacted the official to obtain the parole of two of his lieutenants, Leo Santaniello and Larry Baioni, who had been convicted of loan sharking extortion.

The Taglianetti Airtels also revealed that the Mafia had tried to present $100,000 bribes to Massachusetts ex-Lieutenant Governor Francis Bellotti during his campaign for governor and attorney general in the mid-1960s. When Bellotti refused the bribes, the Mob countered by spreading the word that he *had* accepted them; "these rumors were a major factor in Democrat Bellotti's defeat in both campaigns."

Bill Davidson, "The Mafia, How It Bleeds New England," *Saturday Evening Post*, November 18, 1967, p. 28.

c. Illinois

24.4 Eulogies marred by $800,000 in cash. When Illinois Secretary of State Paul Powell died in 1970, he was given a funeral befitting a state politician of the greatest stature, with flowery homage from leaders of both political parties. The accolades ended, however, when it was discovered that Powell had accumulated an estate of $3 million including $800,000 in cash found in shoe boxes, envelopes, a closet and an office safe. Powell's salary had never exceeded $30,000 a year in the 36 years he had held state office. Federal and state agents discovered "that one of the chief sources of his riches was an alliance with Illinois gambling interests." Demonstrating this alliance, for example, Powell had once issued a special unlisted license plate to Chicago Mafia boss Sam Giancana. Dorman, *Payoff*, pp. 136–37.

d. California

24.5 "Mr. Big" in California. The Kefauver Committee Report devoted several pages to the activities of lobbyist Adrian Samish, who it said could "safely be called 'Mr. Big' in California" and whose power "nearly defie[d] description." The Committee found that while Samish acted as a corrupt intermediary between liquor interests, state legislators, and other parties, he had visits and phone contacts with several Mobsters and Mob-owned businesses across the country. His diverse contacts included ties to both Meyer Lansky and J. Edgar Hoover.[71]

The Kefauver Report found it "even more incredible" that such disclosures about Samish's corrupt activities had been made in a 1938 report of the California legislature, which "strangely enough . . . was almost immediately expunged from the record." Copies disappeared "to the extent that the report became a virtual collector's item." In that report, Samish was quoted as saying, "I am the governor of the legislature, to hell with the Governor of the State." Samish served 26 months in prison for income-tax evasion in the late 1950s, only to resume his previous activities upon release.

U.S.–Senate, Kefauver Report, Third Interim, pp. 100–106; Reid, *Grim Reapers*, pp. 177–81.

24.6 A district attorney dropped a murder indictment against a Mafioso, became governor. Nick DeJohn was a member of the Chicago Mob delegation involved in the Dallas bribe attempt.[72] In 1947, he was murdered.

After a diligent investigation by two San Francisco police inspectors, Frank Ahern and Thomas Cahill, three men were indicted for the murder: New York Colombo Family Mafioso[73] Sebastiano Nani, convicted narcotics dealer Leonard Calamia, and Scappatora Abati. At the conclusion of the murder trial, the jury spent more than 30 hours considering the verdict. But the district attorney then dropped the charges against the three men, assuring Ahern and Cahill that it would be legally advantageous to do so and reinstate charges at a later date. No subsequent charges, however, were ever pressed. And the district attorney, Edmund "Pat" Brown, later became governor of California.

In 1977, then ex-Governor Brown got another chance to demonstrate his loyalties. John Alessio was a convicted felon, described by federal agents as a member of organized crime.[74] Alessio and relatives were being scrutinized by the New Mexico state racing commission in connection with a race track license. During the investigation, Brown sent a telegram to the commission proclaiming that he had, as governor of California, "met Mr. John Alessio" and his relatives under scrutiny, and had found them "very helpful in many matters affecting our state." Brown declared he had "no hesitation in recommending them."

Paragraphs respectively from Reid, *Grim Reapers*, pp. 202–4; *Albuquerque Journal*, March 9, 1977, p. 1.

e. Ohio

24.7 "The Governor and the Mobster": commutation of a murder sentence. Mafia boss Thomas "Yonnie" Licavoli had engaged in bootlegging, gambling, and extortion, deserted the Navy, and killed for the Mob. In 1934, he and four underlings were convicted of murdering three men and a woman, and were sentenced to life imprisonment. During his term in prison, his record was "outrageously bad." He received regular visits from Mafia members and associates, such as Teamster boss Jimmy Hoffa; he continued to run Toledo numbers rackets from prison; and he received special favors which led to the firing of two wardens and the resignation of another. Licavoli, in fact, became "the prison's 'inside boss,'" banking an internal numbers game, heading a narcotics and liquor ring, and receiving special food."

For more than a decade it was common knowledge among the underworld and police that anyone who helped Licavoli out of prison would receive $250,000 from a "spring Yonnie" fund. Indeed, one former governor acknowledged that overtures had been made to him to consider Licavoli's case, while another reported repeated attempts to bribe him to commute the Mobster's sentence. In 1969, "the underworld-grapevine began humming with the word that the [Spring Yonnie] fund had risen to $300,000—and that Yonnie would be released shortly." The pivotal official was now Ohio Governor James Rhodes, whose "financial shenanigans," detailed by *Life* magazine, culminated in IRS claims against Rhodes for more than $100,000 in tax interest and penalties on unreported income. In January 1969, everything fell into place when Governor Rhodes commuted the sentence of Mafia boss Licavoli. Rhodes refused to answer questions or comment on *Life* magazine's story about the commutation.

Denny Walsh, "The Governor and the Mobster," *Life*, May 2, 1969, pp. 28–32A; *U.S.–Senate, OC and Narcotics Hearings*, p. 425.

25. Corruption of federal government

25.1 Leading organized crime expert Ralph Salerno estimated in 1969 that the votes of about 25 Congressmen can be delivered by Mob pressure. "Others say that estimate is far too low."(B) A–"The Mafia v. America," *Time*, August 22, 1969, p. 19; B–Dorman, *Payoff*, p. 178.

25.2 A prominent Congressman was a "tool and collaborator of a Cosa Nostra gang lord." Cornelius Gallagher was a prominent representative of New Jersey's 13th District in Congress between 1958 and 1972. Lyndon Johnson considered him a possible running mate. He served as the second-ranking Democrat on a House subcommittee that investigated organized crime in the late 1960s, in which position he disparaged efforts against the Mafia.

Using wiretaps suppressed for years by the LBJ Justice Department, *Life* magazine exposed regular contacts between Gallagher and New Jersey Mafia boss Joe Zicarelli. *Life* presented excerpts from the transcripts of several such conversations, citing the place and date of each call. Gallagher's dealings with the Mafia boss encompassed everything from fixes of local police to Caribbean politics to bogus cancer cures.

On June 21, 1960, for example, Zicarelli called Gallagher at his unlisted law office phone. The Mafia boss complained to the Congressman that Bayonne police had staked out key stations of his gambling network, and that his business was being disrupted by a top police official. Gallagher replied, "O.K. Let me get hold of him right now." In a conversation a few hours later, Gallagher told Zicarelli, "I got hold of a friend who said [the police official] was jumping. I got hold of the little guy in Jersey City and told him to reach out for him." In a conversation of June 22, Gallagher told Zicarelli that his request to call off the state police from Zicarelli's gambling operations "has already been taken care of. On June 25, Gallagher reported to Zicarelli that he had "laced into" the Bayonne police over Zicarelli's complaint. And a few days later in Washington, Gallagher quickly left the House floor to answer a telephone call from Zicarelli.

When Gallagher denied the reported contacts with Zicarelli in a pre-publication interview, his attorney suggested that *Life* "test its sense of fairness" by having Gallagher take a lie detector test. But Gallagher quickly cut in: "Hey, let me say something. I don't believe in lie detector tests. They're snake oil." After publication, Gallagher "never bothered to sue *Life* for its disclosures about him."(B) Yet Gallagher retained his positions on two House committees, including the one that conducted hearings on organized crime, for three years after the *Life* disclosures.[75] [In contrast, in 1973, 27 out of 30 members of an Italian parliamentary anti-Mafia commission "resigned to protest the membership on the commission of Giovanni Matta, a Christian Democratic deputy who ha[d] been linked to the Mafia."(C)]

In the early 1970s, Gallagher served a 17-month prison term for tax evasion.(D)

> George Jackson rotted in jail for nearly a decade for heisting $70. Jimmy
> Hoffa cops a million, bribes juries, runs with the most dangerous gangsters
> in America and, thanks to the intervention of his good friend Dick Nixon,
> does an easy five. This, after the parole board had rejected Hoffa's appeal
> three times in a row.
>
> Budd Schulberg, from the introduction to *The Fall and Rise of*
> *Jimmy Hoffa* by Walter Sheridan.

A–Sackett, Smith and Lambert, "The Congressman and the Hoodlum,"
Life, August 9, 1968, pp. 20–26; B–*Time*, August 22, 1969; C–*Washington*
Post, January 19, 1973, p. A22; D–*Washington Post*, May 2, 1982, p. A7.

25.3 Top-secret Justice Department information was leaked to the Mafia.
"Among political favors rendered by paid-for officials to Cosa Nostra are
the passing along of information that comes over their desks, and the sending up of storm signals whenever official action against the Mob is threatened." In 1962, for example, a top-secret list of gangsters compiled by the
Justice Department turned up in a Chicago office used by Mafiosi Sam
Giancana and Gus Alex.

In 1977 and 1978, the FBI conducted a massive investigation of waterfront corruption. The investigation revealed that the International Longshoremen's Association is controlled by the Genovese, Gambino, and
Marcello Mafia families and that it has extorted multimillion-dollar payments from shipping company executives. Among the sources of information were an undercover agent who served as a courier for such payoffs,
and a shipping company executive who became a government witness. Another source was a court-approved bug of the office of top ILA official
Anthony Scotto, who was identified in a 1969 Justice Department report as
a captain in the Gambino Mafia Family.[76] The FBI, via the same bug, then
learned to its astonishment that Scotto's men had gotten hold of secret FBI
reports summarizing the information from the bug. The leak caused the
convening of "one of the largest Mafia gatherings since the celebrated Apalachin, N.Y. meeting." More than 20 prominent Mafiosi met in Miami to
discuss underworld business and consider ways to undermine the FBI
probe.

Time magazine reported another use made by the Mafia of secret government documents. In 1977, a gangland slaying silenced Gino Gallina. He
had been testifying before a Newark grand jury on Mafia executions of
informants and potential witnesses against the Mob. "Federal officials
blame his slaying on a leak from the grand jury; leaks from secret Government files and sealed court records have led to the deaths of other informants."(D) Also, several times during the 1960s and 1970s, as discussed in
entry 21.5, corrupt police officials have leaked federal intelligence on the
Mob to underworld figures.

A–*Life*, September 1, 1967, p. 43; B–*Time*, March 20, 1978, p. 19;
C–NBC Evening News, "Segment 3," September 6, 1977 and September 7,
1977; D–*Time*, November 21, 1977, p. 39; E–*Washington Post*, November
24, 1978, pp. A1, A9.

25.4 A Congressman from Illinois "not only represented the Syndicate but gave all appearances of being a Mafioso himself." Roland Libonati went beyond even the norms of Illinois politics by posing for a photograph with Al Capone at a baseball game, and by dubbing Mafiosi Tony Accardo and Paul DeLucia (alias Ricca) "charitable" and "patriotic" fellows. Other notorious Chicago Mobsters were among 20 gangsters and politicians bagged in a police raid of Libonati's campaign headquarters in 1931. The Kefauver Report offered this assessment of his political leanings: "Roland Libonati, Democratic State Senator from the West Side, and a close associate of Capone's, spearheaded the opposition to the reform [anti-racketeering] legislation proposed by the Chicago Crime Commission and Governor Stevenson and backed by the bar."(B)

Libonati maintained this record as a U.S. Congressman between 1958 and 1964. Federal agents monitoring visits to Washington, D.C., of Murray Humphreys, a Chicago Mafia associate,[77] reported several contacts during the early 1960s between Humphreys and Libonati. Humphreys, "the master fixer of the Chicago Mob, . . . frequently delivered messages and packages to Libonati and other members of the Illinois Congressional Delegation."(C) Another of Humphreys' contacts was Illinois Congressman Thomas O'Brien, who earned the nickname "Blind Tom" O'Brien while Cook County sheriff. It was O'Brien who sponsored Libonati in a successful "vigorous behind-the-scene movement" to place Libonati on the powerful House Judiciary Committee.

On August 24, 1960, according to a federal informant, Libonati visited Chicago Mafioso[78] Paul DeLucia at the U.S. Penitentiary at Terre Haute, Indiana. When DeLucia and Libonati met, there was "a disgusting display of affection with hugging and kissing." (E) A secret federal report noted that in November of 1960, "Humphreys was apparently in frequent communication and personal contact with Congressman Libonati . . . to expedite the early release of Paul DeLucia" from prison.

On October 23, 1962, as monitored by an FBI bug, Libonati spoke with Pat Marcy, a "Giancana political underling," and John D'Arco, another political stooge of the Mafia boss. Libonati's words, as quoted by the House Assassinations Committee, again demonstrated his total subservience to the Mob: "Last time you guys built me up to 98,000 votes, and the other guy to 23,000. Who ran against me last time?" Libonati also discussed Robert Kennedy: "I killed six of his bills. That wiretapping bill, the intimidating informers bill." (E) Before Libonati left office in 1964, he distinguished himself by introducing a bill to prevent federal agents from keeping gangsters under surveillance.

A–Demaris, *Captive City*, pp. 142–50; B–*U.S.–Senate, Kefauver Report, Third Interim*, p. 59; C–*Life*, September 1, 1967, pp. 42B–43; D–Dorman, *Payoff*, pp. 178–83; E–*U.S.–House, Assassination Appendix, JFK*, vol. 9, pp. 22–25.

25.5 Libonati's successor: current Congressman Frank Annunzio. In 1963, Libonati announced that he would not seek reelection. A secret federal report assessed the situation: "Congressman Roland V. Libonati stepped down on orders from Sam Giancana. . . . Giancana has already selected Frank Annunzio to replace Libonati. Annunzio will follow dictate of Mob." It appeared that Giancana wanted someone whose subservience to the Mafia was less obvious; another secret federal report had stated: "Advised in February, 1962 that Sam Giancana has emphatically instructed his associates and lieutenants not to call 'these politicians' or meet them at their houses. . . . because if they [the Mob] lost these men they 'were dead'. Among the individuals indicated by Giancana were Frank Annunzio. . . . "

Annunzio demonstrated his loyalty to Giancana by retaining Libonati's top congressional aide, Anthony P. Tisci, with a hefty hike in salary. A son-in-law of Chicago Mafia boss Sam Giancana, Tisci resided at Giancana's Oak Park mansion between 1959 and 1963. Tisci also represented Giancana in court while on the Congressional payroll. Annunzio refused to fire Tisci even after Tisci took the Fifth Amendment in three appearances in 1965 before a federal grand jury investigating organized crime in Chicago. Seven weeks after Tisci finally resigned under pressure, he was bagged by St. Louis Police in a raid of what was believed to be a high-level Mob conclave. The St. Louis raid also picked up Mobster-politician[79] John D'Arco—a partner in a Chicago insurance business with Congressman Annunzio.

Annunzio currently heads the House Banking Committee.

Demaris, *Captive City*, pp. 144–45, 147–51; Dorman, *Payoff*, pp. 182–84; *Life*, September 1, 1967, pp. 42B–43.

25.6 Hundreds of private bills are introduced in Congress to aid the Mob. "Hundreds of private bills have been slid through at the tail end of congressional sessions to forestall deportation proceedings against Syndicate men who entered the country illegally or who made false statements on their naturalization applications." Salerno and Tompkins, *Crime Confederation*, pp. 250–51.

25.7 Prominent guests at a West Coast Syndicate retreat. Moe Dalitz is a leading Mafia associate and the founder of La Costa Country Club, a "Mafia watering hole" whose membership list includes Mobsters from across the country.[80] Massive surveillance of La Costa by local and federal law enforcement officers disclosed numerous prominent politicians and judges freeloading at La Costa, with Moe Dalitz footing the bill. They included "a prominent United States Senator from the East Coast, known in politics as an ardent liberal, a Federal Court appeals judge from Washington, D.C., and a member of the State Supreme Court of Nevada." Noyes, *Legacy of Doubt*, pp. 243–44.

25.8 The "Flood-Medico-Bufalino triangle." U.S. Congressman Daniel Flood of Pennsylvania was investigated "by at least eight separate U.S. Attorney's offices" and appeared headed for a federal indictment with "175 possible cases" pending against him. According to former aide Stephen Elko, who testified against Flood, he was "Congress's most successful 'muscler,' an official who used his considerable influence to direct federal contracts to people and companies that said 'thank you' in cash."

The first instance of Flood's questionable conduct cited in *Time* magazine's "Floodgate" article centered on the "Flood-Medico-Bufalino triangle." Medico Industries was a large Pennsylvania corporation that received a $3.9 million Pentagon contract to produce 600,000 warheads for use in Vietnam. Northeastern Pennsylvania Mafia boss Russell Bufalino, who frequented Medico's offices, was an associate of company general manager William Medico. And according to FBI intelligence, company President Phillip

Medico was "a capo (chief) in his Mafia family." *Time* reported that "the FBI discovered more than a decade ago that Flood steered Government business to the Medicos and traveled often on their company jet."

Time, March 6, 1978, p. 21; Dorman, *Payoff*, pp. 254–55.

25.9 No trouble from the Securities and Exchange Commission. "During both the Red-O-Lier deal and the Wavetronics deal [when] we were skirmishing constantly with the Securities and Exchange Commission, [Mobster[81]] Stanley Polley seemed to be able to handle any problems with the SEC without trouble. He claimed that he was able to reach anybody and pay the appropriate amount to reduce the pressure on us." From the testimony of defected Mob money mover Michael Raymond in *U.S.–Senate, OC and Stolen Securities, 1971*, p. 669.

25.10 "We can do anything in Washington—anything short of murder." Nat Voloshen was a close associate of several top Mob figures and Washington lobbyists. His record of contacts and dealings illustrates a mind-boggling morass of Mafia corruption.

Some of Voloshen's activities were exposed in 1970, when he was indicted with Martin Sweig, chief aide to House Speaker John McCormack. They were charged with perjury and conspiracy to misuse McCormack's office for the benefit of Voloshen's clients—including several members and associates of the Mafia. Sweig was convicted of perjury, acquitted on the conspiracy count, and sentenced to two-and-a-half years in prison; Voloshen pleaded guilty.

Among the alleged actions of the pair was a call by Sweig to New York State Parole Board Chairman Russell Oswald, as Oswald testified at Sweig's trial. Sweig asked Oswald to release Voloshen's client Manuel Bello, a close criminal associate of Mafia boss Raymond Patriarca. Trial testimony also established that Sweig had intervened with federal officials on behalf of another imprisoned Voloshen client, New York Lucchese Family member[82] Salvatore Granello. When Speaker McCormack was called to the witness stand, he professed ignorance of the activities of Sweig and Voloshen, explaining, "I'm not an inquiring fellow." But McCormack admitted that he was a long-time friend of Voloshen, whom he generally saw once or twice a week.

As Congressman Gerald Ford told a lobbyist in 1967, noting the difficulty of investigating Voloshen's gangland connections, "You can only go so far on the man and then the walls of protection come down before you can really get at him."(B) Indeed, it appears that the Sweig-Voloshen indictment merely scratched the surface of their activities. Robert Winter-Berger, a former Washington lobbyist and associate of Voloshen, wrote of his firsthand observations of the corrupter at work. Winter-Berger reported that he often heard McCormack tell Voloshen's clients, "Nat can take care of that for you. Nat's my dear friend and I will do anything I can for him."(B) Winter-Berger described how he once heard Voloshen and Sweig discuss the $2,500-a-month "rent" Voloshen paid McCormack for use of his office. He related, "Twice I saw [New York Mafia boss Frank] Costello with Nathan Voloshen in House Speaker McCormack's offices."(B)

Winter-Berger described Voloshen's ties with other members of Congress, too. In October 1968, he accompanied Voloshen to a fund-raising party at the Overseas Press Club in New York for Congressman John Rooney, the chairman of one House committee and ranking member of another. During the party, Winter-Berger saw Voloshen hand Rooney a white envelope, which Winter-Berger had watched Voloshen stuff with twenty $100 bills before the party. Voloshen told Rooney, "John, as you know, it isn't the first and it won't be the last." Rooney replied, "Nat, anything you want is yours. You're a dear, dear friend. I'm proud to know you."(B) (It was this same Congressman Rooney who requested and received petty "dirt" on a political opponent from FBI Director J. Edgar Hoover, as revealed in FBI memos released in 1978.)[83] Winter-Berger noted that Voloshen, in addition to being close to Congressman McCormack and Rooney, "was also the vest-pocket lobbyist-friend of House Majority Leader Carl Albert; House Majority Whip Hale Boggs; former Representative James Roosevelt of California; and former Representative Adam Clayton Powell of New York."(B)

A—Dorman, *Payoff*, pp. 189–97; B—Winter-Berger, *Washington Payoff*, pp. 50–51, 105–14.

25.11 The Voloshen-Sweig-McCormack combine and the Parvin-Dohrmann case. The stock of the Parvin-Dohrmann Company, a conglomerate, was enjoying a meteoric rise. But on May 5, 1969, it was suspended from trading by the Securities and Exchange Commission because of suspected illegal stock manipulation and underworld connections. The company enlisted the aid of Mob lobbyist Nathan M. Voloshen. Working with Martin Sweig, Speaker McCormack's top aide, Voloshen arranged a meeting between Parvin-Dohrmann officials and Hamer T. Budge, chairman of the Securities and Exchange Commission. Sidney Korshak, Parvin-Dohrmann's counsel, saw to it that Parvin-Dohrmann paid Voloshen $50,000 for his assistance.On May 12, 1969, six days after the meeting, the injunction against trading Parvin-Dohrmann stock was lifted. Two weeks later, Washington lobbyist Robert Winter-Berger went to McCormack's Washington office to meet Voloshen. Winter-Berger saw McCormack hold an envelope and tell Voloshen: "Many thanks for this, Nat. I appreciate it. I will salt it away. Glad you succeeded with Hamer Budge. Let me know if Martin [Sweig] can be of any further help to you."(B) The next day, Winter-Berger learned from Voloshen that $15,000 of Voloshen's $50,000 fee had gone to McCormack and $10,000 to Sweig.

The Parvin-Dohrmann company had been the subject of other federal probes. The company's investments in Las Vegas hotels linked to the Mob and Teamsters, and its mysterious multimillion-dollar transactions with Swiss banks suggested Mafia ties. The Parvin Foundation and Albert Parvin, a key figure in both the company and foundation, were also under federal scrutiny. Specifically, journalist Clark Mollenhoff summarized, a 1971 federal indictment of Meyer Lansky alleged that a $200,000 "finder's fee" paid to Lansky was actually "part of the Hotel Flamingo conspiracy involving the Albert Parvin Foundation."(C) And "according to the indictment, Albert Parvin . . . was believed by the Internal Revenue Service, the FBI, and Strike Force lawyers Mike DeFeo and Robert Thaller to be a front for the Lansky group."(C)

In 1976, the *New York Times* published a four-part series on Mob attorney Sidney Korshak, which confirmed the major Mob influence in the Parvin-Dohrmann company. After acquiring sealed SEC records under the Freedom of Information Act, the *Times* concluded that Korshak, one of the most powerful Mobsters in America, had "dominated the affairs of the Parvin-Dohrmann corporation in the late 1960's."(A) The *Times* reported that corporate chairman Delbert Coleman had served merely as a front for Korshak and was excluded from at least one important company meeting which Korshak attended. And the *Times* disclosed a secret Parvin-Dohrmann payment of $500,000 to Korshak — a payment not disclosed to shareholders in violation of SEC rules — for Korshak's role in the company purchase of the Las Vegas Stardust Hotel and Casino. "Federal officials concluded that it was Mr. Korshak's influence with organized crime figures rather than the extent of his activity that earned him his high fee."(A)

A–Seymour Hersh, in collaboration with Jeff Gerth, "Major Corporations Seek Korshak's Labor Advice," *New York Times*, June 29, 1976, pp. 1, 16; B–Winter-Berger, *Washington Payoff*, pp. 77–79; C–Mollenhoff, *Strike Force*, pp. 90–91, 189–92, 195–96.

26. Subversion of the press

26.1 Planting and suppressing newspaper stories. "A Fix . . . can be attained through employment of public relations counsels who stress things like the good name of a city or the amount of money donated to charity by Mob enterprises, or who plant in newspaper columns evidences of the charm, wit and good connections of key mobsters as they are seen about the spots where expensive people gather. It can be helped immeasurably with cheap devices like easy 'loans' to a reporter whose tastes outrun his income. . . .

"It is a matter of particular pride to [Mafia boss] Giancana and his boys that they are firmly in control of both the Democratic and the Republican political organizations in Chicago's famous First Ward. . . . [C]ertain journalists are part and parcel of the First Ward Fix. The First Ward Democratic organization, if it serves the gangsters needs, can — and on occasion does — swing enough influence in city rooms to get a story killed or softened to the point where it is almost an apology." *Life*, September 1, 1967, pp. 22, 42B.

Under any just and fair system of government it would seem that his [Robert Kennedy's] persecution of Hoffa should cease, since the only "crime" that Hoffa seems to be guilty of is that he will not knuckle under to the Kennedys and give them slavish obedience. . . . The fight of James Hoffa against the Kennedys is becoming the fight of all Americans who want to stay free men and women.

William Loeb, in a front page editorial in the *Manchester Union Leader*, May 13, 1963, quoted in Sheridan, *Fall and Rise of Jimmy Hoffa*, p. 280. A year after the editorial appeared, Hoffa was convicted of jury tampering and defrauding the Teamster pension fund of $2 million; five weeks earlier, the *Manchester Union Leader* had received a $500,000 loan from the Teamsters pension fund.

26.2 Information about a top Mob figure was consistently suppressed. In June 1976, the *New York Times* ran a four-part series on attorney Sidney Korshak. It described him as "the most important link between organized crime and legitimate business," and one of the most powerful Syndicate figures in the country. Korshak's "name has come up in at least 20 investigations of organized crime." His clout in the outfit was indicated one day in 1961, when Korshak arrived unexpectedly at the Riviera Hotel in Las Vegas; Teamster boss Jimmy Hoffa was thrown out of the hotel's presidential suite and moved to smaller quarters to make room for Korshak.

The *Times* found that in Chicago—Korshak's nurturing ground—the papers repeatedly lauded him for his charitable activities and mentioned him in gossip columns. But there has been no real reporting on him, and articles always skirted his underworld ties "with such vague phrases as 'wheeler-dealer' and 'mystery man.'" One veteran Chicago reporter cited two instances when top editors deleted unpleasant references to Korshak. The reporter noted, "You couldn't get a story about him in the paper." And "a former close Korshak friend recalled that he often heard Mr. Korshak boast that he was able to influence the *Chicago Tribune* to soften or tone down stories about him."

Seymour Hersh, in collaboration with Jeff Gerth, series on Sidney Korshak, *New York Times*, June 27, 1976–June 30, 1976; information on press coverage in June 30, 1976, p. 14.

26.3 A weekend "you won't forget." Pulitzer Prize-winning journalist Clark Mollenhoff had covered Iowa Mobster Luigi Fratto (alias Lew Farrell) and associates as a police reporter on the *Des Moines Register*. Mollenhoff wrote that they had displayed "a fondness for newsmen and police, and had a special interest in college athletes and sports writers. Lew even offered to pick up the tab for me for a weekend 'you won't forget' in St. Louis or Chicago. I am sure now that I never would have forgotten that weekend; I wouldn't have been permitted to do so." Mollenhoff, *Strike Force*, p. 39.

26.4 Corruption of reporters by the Teamsters. The McClellan Committee learned during its late-1950s labor probe that "Teamsters Union money had contaminated a few reporters, a few columnists, a few feature writers. We found that in a number of cases Hoffa's union had paid cash or given gifts or 'expenses' to get favorable press coverage." Robert Kennedy, *The Enemy Within*, p. 226.

26.5 A leading syndicated columnist was reportedly on the Mob payroll. "The Mob had on its payroll one of the nation's best-known syndicated newspaper columnists—who secretly lobbied in Washington on behalf of racket interests. Every six months, racketeers throughout the country set aside one day's take from slot and pinball machines and delivered it to the columnist—half in cash and half in a check to his favorite charitable foundation." From information furnished by Jack Halfen, a Texas Mobster and political fixer, reported in Dorman, *Payoff*, p. 156.

26.6 "A major newspaper in this country is controlled by the Mob. Columnist Jack Anderson reported that the "rather sensationalist" newspaper, which he did not name, is controlled and financed by the Mob and keeps retired Mobsters, who do no work for the paper, on its payroll. Jack Anderson on "The Diane Rehm Show," WAMU, Washington, D.C., June 16, 1987.

26.7 A Mob boss bans the word "Mafia." Joseph Colombo was boss of a New York Mafia family and member of the Mafia National Commission.[84] In 1970, he formed the Italian-American Civil Rights League, thereby performing, as *New York* magazine commented, "a feat of traditional 17th-century Sicilian sleight of hand," making "allies of his own victims." The absurdity of the Mafia's public relations campaign was highlighted when Colombo was gunned down at a League rally in 1971.[85] Yet the League succeeded in pressuring Attorney General John Mitchell to ban the words "Mafia" and "Cosa Nostra" from all Justice Department and FBI reports; several governors and other officials followed suit. League officials also managed to convince "Godfather" producer Al Ruddy to delete all references to the Mafia and Cosa Nostra from the film, and to donate revenues from the movie's premier performance to the League. A League-orchestrated campaign featuring "close to 100 letters of protest . . . from Senators, Congressmen and New York State Legislators"(B) had failed to stop production of the movie.

Perhaps most disturbing, however, was the censorship Mafia boss Colombo's organization exerted over the press. In 1970, after League members led by Colombo's son Anthony picketed the *New York Times*, the newspaper stopped using the words "Mafia" and "Cosa Nostra." The next day's issue referred to a notorious Mafioso as a "reputed member of organized crime." When New York City's *Staten Island Advance* refused to comply with Colombo's censorship or to cancel a series of articles on local Mobsters, the League picketed the Advance building and attempted to stop the newspaper's deliveries. One delivery truck carrying 10,000 papers "was forced off the road and set afire by four Colombo goons who pulled the driver and a circulation manager out of the truck and beat them with tire irons."(C)

A–Meskil, *Don Carlo*, pp. 203–4; B–*Time*, March 13, 1972, p. 57; C–Meskil, *Luparelli Tapes*, pp. 154–55; D–Dorman, *Payoff*, p. 281.

26.8 A movie on the Mob that never appeared. One of the most powerful books ever written about the Mob was Robert Kennedy's 1960 best seller, *The Enemy Within*. The book summarized the wholesale Mafia extortion, embezzlement, and violence in the labor movement revealed in the McClellan Committee hearings. At the prompting of Attorney General Kennedy, Budd Schulberg wrote a motion picture script based on the book, to be produced by Jerry Wald of 20th Century-Fox, "who alone had the courage to produce it."

But Jerry Wald died suddenly. The new studio head refused to handle it after a labor tough walked into his office and threatened to prevent delivery of prints to theaters if the movie were ever produced. As Schulberg related, "there have been ever-increasing ties between the Mob and some of the film studios and, of course, those studios rejected it out of hand." Schulberg then attended a meeting with several interested Columbia executives, but that studio turned it down after everyone at the meeting received an implicitly threatening letter from Mob-Teamster lawyer William Bufalino. When Schulberg tried to produce the film himself with Robert Kennedy's encouragement, one film star initially phoned Schulberg to say he loved the script. Schulberg related, he "then came to my house drunk to tell me he was afraid he might be killed if he did it."

From Budd Schulberg's introduction to *The Fall and Rise of Jimmy Hoffa* by Walter Sheridan.

26.9 Mob-Teamster shakedowns of several major newspapers. As Robert Kennedy summarized, "in a series of hearings [of the McClellan Committee] beginning in May 1959, . . . it was disclosed that associates of Mr. Hoffa had practiced shakedowns on management people engaged in newspaper distribution. The papers were: The *New York Times*, the New York *Daily Mirror*, the Detroit *Times*, the Pittsburgh *Sun-Telegraph*, and the *American Weekly*." Senator McClellan wrote that the Committee hearings revealed "gangster infiltration and dominance of the newspaper and magazine distribution business" in New York City during the 1950s, and "reported payoffs made to union officials by news publications who sought union peace by yielding to shakedowns and extortion."(B) Senator McClellan commented, "[O]nce more the venal coalition was revealed: hoodlums, collusive management, and union leaders, all working together."(B)

A–Kennedy, *The Enemy Within*, pp. 220–26; B–McClellan, *Crime Without Punishment*, p. 215; C–Hutchinson, *Imperfect Union*, pp. 274–76.

26.10 Murder and corruption in Arizona. Don Bolles, an Arizona reporter, was nominated for a Pulitzer Prize in 1965 and named the state's "Newsman of the Year" in 1974. In June 1976, Bolles set out to pursue a lead on his main investigative interest — Mob ties to business and politics. But when Bolles turned the ignition of his car, he was mutilated by the blast of a bomb planted under the floor-board. Before he died, Bolles told firemen "they finally got me — the Mafia."(D)

The Mob's timing was bad, however, for the bombing occurred just one week before the national meeting in Indianapolis of the Investigative Reporters and Editors Group (IRE). In response to the murder of Bolles, the IRE sent 36 reporters to Arizona under the direction of Pulitzer Prize winners Bob Greene and Dick Cady. The IRE sought to complete Bolles' work through an intensive investigation of organized crime in that state.

In a 23-part newspaper series that appeared nationwide in March and April 1977, the IRE exposed the pervasive influence of the Mob in Arizona. It detailed the penetration in Arizona's businesses, courts, and political establishment of more than 200 representatives of Mafia families from New York, Boston, Detroit, St. Louis, Chicago, Cleveland and other cities. And it reported that three of the state's leading political figures "have dominated Phoenix and much of Arizona while maintaining friendships and other alliances with Mob figures."(B)

Investigative Reporters and Editors Inc., Phoenix Project (IRE series), *Albuquerque Journal*, March 13 through April 3, 1977, especially A–March 13, p. A1; B–March 14, p. A1; C–March 15, pp. A1, A6. Also D–*Newsweek*, June 14, 1976, pp. 83–84; E–*New York Times*, March 17, 1977, p. A26; F–Reid and Demaris, *The Green Felt Jungle*, pp. 47, 50, 51.

27. From the Redwood Forests to the Gulf Stream waters

Following are miscellaneous references grouped alphabetically by state, concluding with a brief selection of sources on Mafia activities outside the United States.

27.1 Alabama: liquor profits. The Mob has been "making a fortune" in liquor distribution in Alabama. Dorman, *Payoff*, pp. 124–25.

27.2 Alaska: a piece of the oil pipeline action. The well-paid, free-spending workers on the Alaska pipeline represented a golden opportunity for the Mob. Salvatore Spinelli and Jerome Max Pasley, who are associated with Arizona Mafia boss Joseph Bonanno, quickly moved in. "Today, Bonanno's influence is strong in that state." IRE series on organized crime in Arizona, *Albuquerque Journal*, March 27, 1977, p. A4; also see Grutzner, "How to Lock Out the Mafia," *Harvard Business Review*, March–April 1970, p. 58.

27.3 Arizona: Mafia infestation. "Organized crime is staging a blitzkrieg invasion of Phoenix, Tucson and other Arizona cities. . . . There is a historic and continuing relationship between underworld chieftains and leading power-brokers of both the Republican and Democratic parties." Former U.S. Attorney William Smitherman commented, organized crime "has Arizona by the throat." IRE series on organized crime, *Albuquerque Journal*, March 13, 1977, pp. A1, A4; also see succeeding articles, from March 14, 1977 to April 2, 1977.

27.4 California, northern: "infiltration of crime into state business." An investigator for the State Department of Consumer Affairs was offered bribes and threatened to lay off an investigation of a Mob-infiltrated San Francisco Bay area employment agency. He continued the probe and then, following a break-in at his office, was "beaten to a pulp" outside a San Francisco restaurant. State Consumer Affairs Director John Kehoe noted, "profits from prostitution, gambling and other rackets are being 'laundered' in seemingly legitimate businesses." *Los Angeles Times*, October 19, 1973, p. 3.

27.5 California, southern: "The Mafia . . . has zeroed in." While advance elements of the Mob settled into Los Angeles, Orange and San Diego counties, Mafia bosses from Chicago, New York, Detroit and Las Vegas secretly convened and sent underlings scurrying about with messages and money. A seven-count federal indictment against 12 Southern California Mafia members and associates revealed "a widespread pattern of extortion, loansharking and racketeering."(B) A–Bill Hazlett, "Mafia Infiltrates Southland with Men and Money," *Los Angeles Times*, June 1, 1973, pp. 1, 18, 19; B–Hazlett, "12 Indicted Here in Crackdown on Mafia," *Los Angeles Times*, July 10, 1974, pp. 1, 19.

27.6 Colorado: Mafia operations for decades. Chicago Crime Commission Director Virgil Peterson described Mob gambling activities and business ventures in Blend, Canon City, Central City, Colorado Springs, Denver, Pueblo, and Trinidad, Colorado. Peterson named several Mafia members and associates from Kansas City, Los Angeles, and New York as well as local Mobsters who were involved in Colorado operations. *U.S.-Senate, Kefauver Hearings*, vol. 2, pp. 186–87.

27.7 Florida: "An expanding base of operations" for 14 of the 24 Mafia families. Extensive Mafia operations and real estate interests throughout the state are detailed by state and federal officials. *U.S.-House, Crime in America*, pp. 192–93, 317–56; *Life*, October 24, 1969, p. 62; Reid, *Grim Reapers*, p. 102; *U.S.-Senate, Kefauver Report, Third Interim*, pp. 30–36, 63–67.

27.8 Georgia: "11 Mafia families are represented." "Mafia racketeers from across the country are moving into Atlanta in increasing numbers" from cities across the nation. They move into gambling, drugs, liquor, prostitution, real estate, and commercial businesses. Mobsters have taken over "office buildings and night clubs, real estate, auto leasing and other ventures." Francis Kent, "Mafia Moving Into Atlanta — City Called 'Peach' Ripe for Picking," *Los Angeles Times*, July 1, 1974, p. 14; also see *Atlanta Journal*, March 22, 1974.

27.9 Illinois (Chicago): "A city in the grip of the Mob." "The situation today is nearly the same as it was . . . even in 1930, at the height of Al Capone's reign of terror. . . . The Syndicate is so solidly entrenched there and so monolithic in structure that it is almost impossible to root out. It has worked its way into nearly every facet of the life of the city. . . . you may be doing business with the Syndicate when you subscribe to a diaper service, hire a scavenging firm to haul your garbage away, buy a neon sign, park your car in a downtown garage, purchase bread in a supermarket, order a carpet, contract for plumbing work, get airline tickets through a travel agency, take out a loan at a bank or even go to the polls to vote." Bill Davidson, "How the Mob Controls Chicago," *Saturday Evening Post*, November 9, 1963, pp. 17–27.

27.10 Michigan: Mafia business interests. The *Detroit Free Press* revealed that Mafia boss Vincent Meli "apparently runs" J&J Cartage Company, one of Detroit's largest steel cartage companies. *Detroit Free Press*, April 11, 1974; see also "When the Mafia Takes Over a City; Detroit," *U.S. News and World Report*, October 21, 1963, p. 6.

27.11 Mississippi: Mob contracts "all over the state." One major Mob corrupter says he makes "as much money in Mississippi and Alabama as [he does] anywhere else." As an indication of his involvements there, he showed a business card that lists him as a construction company official in Jackson, Mississippi. Dorman, *Payoff*, p. 124.

27.12 Missouri: Mafia stronghold in Kansas City. *U.S.–Kefauver Hearings*, vol. 2, pp. 185–86; Tyler, *Organized Crime in America*, pp. 296–98.

27.13 Nevada: "In some cases . . . top Mob leaders have dominated both gambling and political operations." Pierre La Fitte, an undercover investigator hired by the *Las Vegas Sun*, impersonated a big-time racketeer and was able to bribe county and state officials to secure protection for his pretended operations. In a tape-recorded conversation with Lt. Governor and Democratic National Committee member Clifford Jones, La Fitte, using the name Louis Tabet, told Jones he'd "taken care of the county" and named several county officials whom he had agreed to pay off. Jones replied, "You're with the right people. I talk for the state. Louie Wiener, my [law] partner, takes care of the legal end of the deals and the finances." Tabet asked Jones for help in obtaining a gambling license, despite his admitted criminal record ("a few things when I was young — a little narcotics, bootlegging, murder, manslaughter"). When assured that Tabet had no recent convictions, Jones told him, "you're all right, but not until after the first of the year when [Gubernatorial candidate Vail] Pittman takes office."

Following the *Las Vegas Sun's* exposure of the exploits of "Louis Tabet," Jones resigned his position on the Democratic National Committee, but not his lieutenant governor post. Jones, who held interests in three Las Vegas casinos, later become involved with LBJ aide Bobby Baker in negotiations for gambling casinos in the Caribbean.

Dorman, *Payoff*, pp. 139–44.

27.14 New England states: vicious and prosperous Mafia operations. The Mob owns "diaper services, linen services, auto agencies, car-repair firms, drugstores and garbage collecting firms. . . . It controls numerous night clubs, bars and restaurants — ranging from dives . . . to some of the finest gourmet eating places in New England. The mob owns, or has owned, cemeteries, dude ranches, a New Hampshire ski resort and a country club north of Boston." Bill Davidson, "The Mafia: How it Bleeds New England," *Saturday Evening Post*, November 18, 1967, pp. 27–31; also see *U.S.-House, OC in Sports*, pp. 764–65.

27.15 New Jersey: versatile goons. DeCavalcante Family Mafioso Gaetano Vastola has a number of business interests in neighboring New York, including a leading booking agency for entertainment figures, and was convicted of extorting $500,000 from a rug company in Georgia. Genovese Family member Anthony Russo, after organizing bookmaking and loan sharking operations in the North Jersey Shore area, became owner of a number of construction firms, secured extensive horse racing interests, was hired as a labor consultant by two large resort hotels, and served a 3- to 5-year prison sentence for perjury. Mafia associate Michael Stavola, with convictions for assaulting an officer and bribery, owns or is the principal in more than 40 corporations "involved in road materials and construction, contracting equipment, condominium apartments, horseracing, refuse collection, landfill, beach clubs, soft drinks, and real estate. He does business in New Jersey, New York, Florida, Pennsylvania, Delaware, and owns a farm in Maine." From the testimony of New Jersey Police Captain William Baum in *U.S.-House, OC in Sports*, pp. 570–76.

27.16 New York: gambling, robbery, perjury, and extortion. After a series of raids in upstate New York and Scranton, Pennsylvania, indictments on these charges were handed down against northeastern Pennsylvania Mafia boss Russell Bufalino, 15 underlings and 8 others, three of whom were already in prison for possession of incendiary devices. Bufalino and his associates were also charged with conspiring to assault two competitors of a Mob cigarette vending firm in Binghamton, New York, which, not surprisingly, gained monopoly control of business in that area. According to affidavits by Mafia defector Joseph Zito, who was held in protective custody, Mob henchmen beat one competitor over the head with baseball bats. *New York Times*, April 22, 1973, p. 30; May 1, 1973, p. 46; May 6, 1973, p. 51.

27.17 Ohio: a Mafia reign of terror in Youngstown. During the 1950s and early 1960s, friction between rival Mob factions in Youngstown, Ohio, resulted in 81 gangland bombings and several murders. A settlement was imposed following a November 8, 1959, meeting of 150 Mafia dons in a Worcester, Massachusetts, hotel, as was reported by Massachusetts Attorney General Edward McCormack. Yet rivalries persisted. This was brought home to Youngstown residents on November 22, 1962, when a bomb exploded in the car of Mafia boss Charles Cavallaro, killing him and his 11-year-old son, Thomas, and crippling his 12-year-old son, Charles, Jr.

The violence finally led voters to oust Mayor Frank Franko, a defrocked judge and disbarred lawyer, for a reform administration. But after 40 years in which the underworld had "controlled politics, the police, and sometimes even the courts," traditions died hard. Police Chief William Golden, who had substituted merit for graft as a basis for promotions and had tripled the city's gambling arrests, found dynamite fuses wired to his car. Mobster Joey Naples, who was caught with gambling slips, stolen goods, and an arsenal of weapons at his home, almost escaped conviction when incriminating evidence was stolen right out of the courtroom. Finally, Naples' conviction was reversed when his lawyer raised a technical point concerning a search warrant and, to everyone's surprise, prosecutor John Cianflona agreed to the defense motion. Cianflona, an assistant Ohio attorney general, was fired for this action by State Attorney General William Saxbe, who suggested that a $20,000 slush fund to spring Naples may have contributed to the reversal.

Cook, *Secret Rulers*, pp. 26–54; Dorman, *Payoff*, pp. 94–96.

27.18 Wisconsin: "The Mafia has several footholds in Wisconsin businesses." The Grande Cheese Company was a large Mob-owned firm in Leroy, Wisconsin, founded in 1941 by Chicago Mafia boss Ross Prio. In 1973, it became the beneficiary of a $2.5 million industrial revenue bond issue voted in illegal and secret sessions of the town's board of supervisors.

In Forrestville, Wisconsin, associates of the New York Gambino Mafia Family bought their way into the Badger State Cheese Company. By 1977, eight months after the Mafia took over, Badger Cheese was bankrupt. The new owners skipped town with the company's assets, leaving a debt of more than $500,000 to the dairy farmers who supplied milk to the plant. "Fifty-five people lost their jobs. One bank is out $200,000 in loans to Gambino and his associates. And the economy of a small town was hurt badly. . . . The dairy farmers around here now know what it's like to do business with the Mob."(B)

A–Madison, Wisconsin *Capital Times*, February 4, 1974; B–NBC Evening News, "Segment 3," December 13, 1977. NBC also reported that the Mob has a virtual monopoly on cheese sold to pizzerias on the East Coast; it supplies the cheese at inflated prices.

27.19 Mafia tentacles around the world. Following are a scattering of references to Mafia activities and dealings outside the United States. Australia: Bob Wiedrich, "Aussies are wary of Mafia Invasion," *Chicago Tribune*, September 18, 1973, p. 14; Salerno and Tompkins, *Crime Confederation*, p. 385. The Bahamas: Reid, *Grim Reapers*, pp. 125–45; Salerno and Tompkins, pp. 385–87. Brazil: Reid, pp. 281–82. Canada: Salerno and Tompkins, p. 285. Dominican Republic: *Life*, September 8, 1967, p. 101. Great Britain: Salerno and Tompkins, pp. 382–83. Haiti: Teresa, *My Life in the Mafia*, pp. 222–30; Salerno and Tompkins, pp. 386–87. Italy: see section 7. For general information on international Mob activity, see Messick, *Syndicate Abroad*.

27.20 A series of indictments typify the Mafia's worldwide activities. Nineteen federal and state indictments were handed down against 25 persons, including high-ranking Mobsters. Among the crimes charged were narcotics smuggling, extortion, loan sharking, sale and distribution of counterfeit money and airline tickets, and attempted murder. The alleged principals in this web of crime were Mafiosi Matteo DiLorenzo and Vincent

> Mafia-controlled companies having branches in Latin America and interests in Europe serve as conduits for the outflow of profits from illicit operations in the United States. Some of the funds go to the smugglers of raw opium from the Near East; some to the refiners of heroin in France and Italy; others to coded accounts in Swiss Banks, or in the form of untraceable investments in major American corporations or equally untraceable "loans" to the very underworld bosses who started the funds on their roundabout journey.
>
> Charles Grutzner, "How to Lock Out the Mafia," *Harvard Business Review*, March-April 1970, p. 51.

Rizzo, of New York's Genovese Family. DiLorenzo reputedly controls criminal activities at Kennedy International Airport in New York City.

"The indictments . . . talk of threats and beatings, of people being thrown through windows and men traveling thousands of miles to make payments for drugs and other items. . . . They tell of deals in Buffalo, Las Vegas, New York, Argentina, Chile and Japan, of smuggling counterfeit money into the United States from Canada and then distributing the bills throughout the United States and into Japan and South America. . . . " Among the crimes charged was the attempted murder by two Genovese Family members of a boy, whom they beat up, breaking his skull, and then tossed out a window, for no apparent reason. The indictments reveal "a complex narcotics smuggling operation throughout Latin America." They describe "a number of incidents involving loan-sharking, extortion, and threat of bodily harm." *New York Times*, December 8, 1972, pp. 1, 90.

Notes

Abbreviations and Conventions

Citations with the prefix "*U.S.--*" are abbreviations for government documents, as listed in the bibliography. Citations that omit the author's first name also generally refer to sources listed in the bibliography.

The standard conventions used in this volume for citing material released by the Warren Commission are best demonstrated by the following examples:

"CD 123" refers to Commission Document 123 in the collection on the assassination of President Kennedy in the National Archives. National Archives documents are generally cited only when they are omitted or not reproduced faithfully in the published 26-volume Hearings and Exhibits.

"23H 99" refers to volume 23, page 99 in the Hearings and Exhibits.

"CE 1234" refers to Commission Exhibit 1234 in the Hearings and Exhibits.

Citations of the form "Smith Exhibit 8" refer to exhibits categorized by name in volumes 19–21 of the Hearings and Exhibits.

"WR 99" refers to page 99 of the Warren Commission Report.

Complete titles and publication information for the Warren Commission materials are listed in the bibliography under *U.S.-Warren Commission*.

"JFK microfilm" refers to *Files of Evidence Connected With the Investigation of the Assassination of President John F. Kennedy* (Washington, D.C.: Microcard Editions, 1967). It is a collection of 21 volumes of documents from the Texas Attorney General's investigation of the JFK assassination. A copy is held in the Library of Congress rare book collection, catalog number E842.9.F47.

Material released by the House Assassinations Committee is cited as follows:

"HAH 3H 99" refers to volume 3, page 99 of the House Assassinations Committee hearings on the assassination of President Kennedy, or of the appendix to those hearings (volumes 1–5 comprise the hearings, 6–12 the appendix).

"HAH-MLK 13H 99" refers to volume 13, page 99 of the appendix to the House Assassinations Committee hearings on the assassination of Martin Luther King.

"HAR 99" refers to page 99 of the House Assassinations Committee Report.

Complete titles and publication information for the House Assassinations Committee materials are listed in the bibliography under *U.S.-House, Assassinations*.

1. HAR 95.
2. Buchanan, *Who Killed Kennedy?* (London: Secker and Warburg, 1964), pp. 136–37; see Buchanan (New York: Putnam, 1964), p. 150, for date and author.
3. Buchanan, British edition, p. 130.
4. *Ibid.*, p. 139.
5. *Ibid.*, pp. 137–38.
6. Buchanan, British edition, pp. 137–39, cf. American ed., especially pp. 151–53, which begin and end as the text surrounding the deleted portion. Ironically preserved was a passing allusion to Groussard's thesis, with the promise that it would be "examined in detail a little later" (American ed., p. 131; British ed., p. 120).
7. Buchanan, British edition, pp. 140–41, cf. American ed., especially pp. 151–53, which begin and end as the text surrounding the deleted portion.
8. Buchanan, British edition, p. 135; American ed., p. 152.
9. Buchanan, British edition, p. 24; American ed., p. 25.
10. Buchanan, British edition, p. 26; American ed., p. 26.
11. Buchanan, British edition, p. 137; see American ed., p. 150.
12. Buchanan, American edition, p. 151.
13. WR 790; see chapter 6, "The Fine Reports of Ruby's Chicago Friends."
14. See chapter 6, "The Fine Reports of Ruby's Chicago Friends."
15. 5H 206; see chapter 14.
16. HAR 161; see HAR 169, 173, 176; chapters 2 and 17.
17. See chapter 21, in which possible underworld complicity in the assassination of Malcolm X is also discussed.

Chapter 1
Precedents

1. Salerno and Tompkins, *The Crime Confederation*, p. 72.
2. See chapter 5, "An Assassination Plan by Carlos Marcello," "An Assassination Prediction by Santos Trafficante," and "Assassination Plots by Jimmy Hoffa."
3. Lyle, *The Dry and Lawless Years*, p. 254. See also Demaris, *Captive City*, pp. 116–19; Gottfried, *Boss Cermak of Chicago*, pp. 318–19; Lyle, pp. 261, 265.
4. Allsop, *The Bootleggers*, p. 219; Lyle, p. 265; Demaris, p. 118; Gottfried, p. 319.
5. Lyle, p. 265; see also Allsop, p. 170.
6. Allsop, pp. 216–20; Demaris, pp. 116–19; Kobler, *Capone*, p. 322; Gottfried, pp. 318–19.
7. Expressed during the 1931 Chicago mayoral campaign by Democratic candidate Cermak to Republican contender John H. Lyle, quoted in Lyle, p. 260.

8. Gottfried, p. 320; Lyle, p. 261.
9. As cited in the prior note.
10. Allsop, pp. 219–20; Demaris, p. 118; Gottfried, p. 319; Lyle, pp. 265–66.
11. Demaris, p. 121; Gottfried, pp. 320–21.
12. Demaris, p. 119; Gottfried, pp. 320–21.
13. Demaris, p. 119; Gottfried, pp. 320–21; Lyle, p. 264.
14. Gottfried, pp. 320, 424.
15. Allsop, p. 220; Demaris, pp. 119–20; Kobler, p. 322.
16. As cited in the prior note.
17. As cited in the prior note.
18. Demaris, p. 120; Gottfried, pp. 318, 321–22.
19. As cited in the prior note.
20. Demaris, p. 121.
21. WR 463.
22. *Ibid.*
23. Demaris, p. 120.
24. *Ibid.*, p. 121.
25. *Ibid.*
26. *Ibid.*
27. Lyle, p. 267.
28. Demaris, p. 120.
29. *Ibid.*, p. 111.
30. *Ibid.*, p. 120.
31. *Ibid.*
32. Lyle, p. 267; Gottfried, pp. 320, 424.
33. Lyle, p. 268.
34. *Ibid.*, pp. 254, 258–61; Allsop, p. 216.
35. Lyle, p. 21.
36. Kobler, p. 322; Allsop, pp. 170, 220; Demaris, pp. 119–22.
37. Demaris, p. 121; Gottfried, p. 321.
38. Gottfried, p. 326; Demaris, p. 121.
39. Kobler, p. 322.
40. Allsop., pp. 168–69.
41. *Ibid.*, pp. 168–70.
42. *Ibid.*, pp. 169–70.
43. *Ibid.*, p. 170.
44. Robert F. Kennedy, *The Enemy Within*. The Committee was the Senate Select Committee on Improper Activities in the Labor or Management Field, chaired by Senator John McClellan.
45. *Ibid.*, pp. 237–38.
46. *Ibid.*, p. 238.
47. *Ibid.*
48. *Ibid.*, p. 239.
49. *U.S.–Senate, OC and Narcotics Hearings*, p. 652, chart F.
50. Kennedy, *The Enemy Within*, p. 79.
51. *Ibid.*, pp. 79–85.
52. Reid, *Grim Reapers*, p. 174; HAH 9H 47–50.
53. HAH 9H 47–49.
54. HAR 163.
55. *U.S.–President's Commission on OC, Appendix to The Edge*, p. 2; see

also the federal finding cited in Herbert Hill, "Thieves in the House of Labor," *Nation*, June 27, 1981, p. 793.

56. Cormier and Eaton, *Reuther*, pp. 13–17.
57. Gould and Hickok, *Walter Reuther: Labor's Rugged Individualist*, pp. 46–48, 384.
58. *Ibid.*, pp. 61–63.
59. Cormier and Eaton, p. vii.
60. *Ibid.*, p. 276.
61. *Ibid.*, p. 342.
62. Gould and Hickok, pp. 135–37, see also p. 139.
63. *Ibid.*, p. 134; Cook, *Walter Reuther*, p. 101; see also Reid, *The Grim Reapers*, p. 76.
64. Gould and Hickok, pp. 97, 134.
65. *U.S.–Senate, Kefauver Report, Third Interim*, p. 73.
66. *U.S.–Senate, OC and Narcotics Hearings*, p. 248, Chart A.
67. *U.S.–Senate, Kefauver Report, Third Interim*, p. 73; Cook, *The Secret Rulers*, p. 122.
68. Cormier and Eaton, pp. 128–29; Gould and Hickok, p. 139.
69. Gould and Hickok, pp. 254–56.
70. *Business Week*, August 21, 1948, pp. 92–94.
71. *U.S.–Senate, Kefauver Report, Third Interim*, p. 71.
72. *Ibid.*
73. Gould and Hickok, p. 256.
74. Cormier and Eaton, p. 255; Cook, *Walter Reuther*, p. 167; Gould and Hickok, p. 261.
75. Cook, *Walter Reuther*, p. 167; Gould and Hickok, p. 263.
76. Cook, *Walter Reuther*, p. 167.
77. Gould and Hickok, p. 269.
78. *Ibid.*
79. *Business Week*, August 21, 1948, p. 92.
80. Gould and Hickok, p. 256.
81. Cormier and Eaton, pp. 262–66.
82. *Ibid.*, p. 262.
83. *Ibid.*, pp. 266, 252.
84. Kennedy, *The Enemy Within*, p. 281; Cormier and Eaton, *Reuther*, p. 266.
85. *U.S.–Senate, OC and Narcotics Report*, p. 40.
86. Gould and Hickok, p. 271; Cormier and Eaton, pp. 262–63.
87. Gould and Hickok, p. 272.
88. Cormier and Eaton, pp. 263–64; *U.S.–Senate, Kefauver Report, Third Interim*, p. 74.
89. Cormier and Eaton, pp. 263–64; *U.S.–Senate, Kefauver Report, Third Interim*, pp. 74–75.
90. As cited in the prior note.
91. As cited in the prior note.
92. Cormier and Eaton, pp. 262, 264; Gould and Hickok, pp. 271–72; *U.S.–Senate, Kefauver Report, Third Interim*, p. 76.
93. *U.S.–Senate, Kefauver Report, Third Interim*, pp. 74–76; Cormier and Eaton, p. 264.
94. *U.S.–Senate, Kefauver Report, Third Interim*, p. 76.

95. *Ibid.*

96. *Ibid.*

97. *Ibid.*

98. Cormier and Eaton, p. 275.

99. *Ibid.*, pp. 274–75.

100. Cormier and Eaton, pp. 267, 271.

101. *Ibid.*, p. 267.

102. *Ibid.*, p. 269.

103. Gould and Hickok, p. 271.

104. Cormier and Eaton, p. 270.

105. *Ibid.*; Gould and Hickok, p. 275.

106. Cormier and Eaton, p. 270.

107. *U.S.–Senate, OC and Narcotics Hearings*, p. 410, Exhibit No. 18.

108. Cormier and Eaton, pp. 270–71.

109. Reported in the *New York Times*, January 10, 1954, and the *Detroit News* January 9, 1954, as cited in Cormier and Eaton, p. 272.

110. Cormier and Eaton, pp. 272–73.

111. *Ibid.*, p. 273; Gould and Hickok, pp. 276–77.

112. *U.S.–Senate, Kefauver Report, Third Interim*, p. 128; see chapter 14, "Would you rather I just delete what I said and just pretend that nothing is going on?"

113. During the McClellan Committee hearings in the fall of 1963, Detroit Police Commissioner George Edwards cited examples of what he described as "the continual brazen effort of the Mafia" to corrupt police officials (*U.S.–Senate, OC and Narcotics Hearings*, p. 404). Edwards testified that under a reform administration in 1939 "we saw the former mayor of the city of Detroit, the former prosecuting attorney, the former sheriff, the former superintendent of police, and roughly 250 police officers all go to jail for the acceptance of graft in order to let gambling operate in the city of Detroit" (*Ibid.*, p. 405). In 1965 and 1971 flagrant cases of Mob-police corruption were again exposed.

114. Cook, *Walter Reuther*, p. 173.

115. Hutchinson, *The Imperfect Union*, p. 313.

116. *Ibid.*, p. 314; *U.S.–Senate, OC and Narcotics Hearings*, pp. 479–80.

117. Hutchinson, p. 314; Demaris, p. 31; see also Hutchinson, pp. 156–59.

118. Demaris, pp. 30–31; Hutchinson, pp. 156–59.

119. The UAW-AFL was renamed the Allied Industrial Workers of America in 1956 (Hutchinson, p. 314).

120. *U.S.–Senate, OC and Narcotics Hearings*, p. 479; Demaris, pp. 30–31.

121. *U.S.–Senate, OC and Narcotics Hearings*, p. 479; Demaris, pp. 30, 33.

122. Demaris, pp. 30–32; *U.S.–Senate, OC and Narcotics Hearings*, p. 479.

123. Demaris, pp. 30–31.

124. *Ibid.*, p. 31.

125. *U.S.–Senate, OC and Narcotics Hearings*, p. 479.

126. *Ibid.*; Demaris, p. 31.

127. *U.S.–Senate, OC and Narcotics Hearings*, pp. 479–80.

128. *Ibid.*; Demaris, pp. 32–33.

129. *U.S.–Senate, OC and Narcotics Hearings*, p. 480.

130. Demaris, p. 33; *U.S.–Senate, OC and Narcotics Hearings*, p. 487; Navasky, *Kennedy Justice*, p. 47.

131. Demaris, p. 31.
132. *Ibid.*, p. 32.
133. *Ibid.*, pp. 31–32.
134. See chapter 5.
135. Anslinger, *The Protectors*, p. 216.

Part I
Assassins at Large

1. WR 1–2.
2. WR 2, 4.
3. WR 3.
4. WR 3. The Warren Commission described the location of President Kennedy's first wound as the "back of his neck" (WR 3, 19), mandated by its infamous single bullet theory. Actually, according to eyewitness accounts of the autopsy and several items of physical evidence, the wound was in the shoulder, several inches below the neckline (see Thompson, *Six Seconds in Dallas*, pp. 40–51). Both the bullet holes in the president's clothing (5H 59–60; see Thompson, pp. 48, 222–23) and Commission photos depicting "the point where the bullet entered" (WR 97, 102–3) show the wound location in the shoulder, well below the neckline.
5. WR 4.
6. WR 6–7.
7. WR 8–9.
8. *New York Times*, November 24, 1963, p. 1; WR 8–9, 16–19.
9. Kantor Exhibit 3, p. 366.
10. WR 17.
11. WR 17, 219.
12. WR 17–18.
13. *U.S.–Senate, Intelligence Report, JFK Assassination*, p. 32.
14. *Ibid.*, p. 33.
15. *Ibid.*, p. 23.
16. *Ibid.*
17. WR ix.
18. WR v.
19. *U.S.–Senate, Intelligence Report, JFK Assassination*, pp. 34–35, see also p. 23. The quoted phrase is from *Time*, December 13, 1963, p. 26.
20. WR vii, 18–22, 374.
21. Among the best such books that were published within five years of the assassination are *Accessories After the Fact* by Sylvia Meagher; *Inquest* by Edward J. Epstein; *Six Seconds in Dallas* by Josiah Thompson; *Forgive My Grief* by Penn Jones; and *Rush to Judgment* by Mark Lane. For articles, see the literature review by U.S. Representative Thomas Kupferman, 89th Congress, 2nd session, September 28, 1966, *Congressional Record*, vol. 118, pp. 24160–61. Also Cyril Wecht, "JFK Assassination: A Prolonged and Willful Cover-up,'" *Modern Medicine*, October 28, 1974, pp. 40X–40FF. A list including many other credible critiques of the Warren

Commission's conclusions is provided in the *Assassination Bibliography,* compiled and published by Robert A. Phillips.

22. *New Times,* August 8, 1975, p. 32; *Life,* October 7, 1966, p. 38.
23. *Time,* January 10, 1977, p. 17. A 1978 Harris Poll reported a similar finding (*Washington Post,* December 4, 1978, p. A7).
24. Statement of Representative Thomas Kupferman, 89th Congress, 2nd session, September 28, 1966, *Congressional Record,* vol. 118, p. 24157.
25. HAR 9–10.
26. HAH 5H 553–695.

Chapter 2
Crossfire in Dealey Plaza

1. WR 71.
2. HAR 1.
3. HAH 1H 40; WR 48.
4. As cited in the prior note.
5. This figure is derived from topographical maps (Thompson, *Six Seconds in Dallas,* pp. 252–53; HAH 5H 562) and aerial photographs (Thompson, front endpaper; HAH 5H 501, WR 33) of Dealey Plaza, and from a figure published by the House Assassinations Committee (HAH 8H 29). The map and photograph in Thompson (pp. 252–53, front endpaper) are particularly clear, and should be checked concerning matters of placement not apparent in the diagram. The scale of the diagram is determined from Thompson, pp. 252–53, 275.
6. Manchester, *Death of a President,* p. 154.
7. Holland Exhibit D; 6H 239–45.
8. Holland Exhibit D; 6H 243–44; Thompson, p. 115; see map, p. 166, in photo section, and note 5.
9. As cited in the prior note.
10. Holland Exhibit D.
11. 6H 243–44.
12. Filmed and tape-recorded interview of Dodd by Mark Lane, Decatur, Texas, March 24, 1966, cited in Lane, *Rush to Judgment,* pp. 40, 420.
13. CE 1422.
14. CE 2003, p. 41.
15. Tape-recorded interview of Murphy by Stewart Galanor, Dallas, May 6, 1966, cited in Lane, pp. 40, 420.
16. CE 1416; filmed and tape-recorded interview of Simmons by Lane, Mesquite, Texas, March 28, 1966, cited in Lane, pp. 40, 420.
17. Tape-recorded interview of Winborn by Stewart Galanor, Dallas, May 5, 1966, cited in Lane, pp. 40, 420.
18. CE 1422.
19. Tape-recorded interview of Holland by Josiah Thompson, November 30, 1966, cited in Thompson, p. 138.
20. Thompson, p. 138.
21. Meagher, *Accessories After the Fact,* p. 19n; HAH 1H 138.

22. HAH 7H 373; see also HAH 12H 24–25; HAH 1H 138.
23. Hurt, *Reasonable Doubt*, p. 117.
24. Thompson, pp. 252–53; HAH 8H 21, 173. Note that each uncircled number on the Thompson map represents the frame on the Zapruder film which was taken when President Kennedy was at the designated location. Note also that the last shot was fired at about the time that Zapruder frame 313 was filmed (HAH 5H 722), and that the Zapruder film ran at 18.3 frames per second (WR 97; *New York Times*, December 8, 1966, p. 40; see Thompson, pp. 293–94).
25. *Texas Observer*, December 13, 1963, cited in Lane, pp. 44, 421.
26. *Ibid.*; CD 205, cited in Thompson, p. 124. Smith indicated that he searched directly behind the picket fence (7H 535; see aerial photograph in Thompson, front endpaper).
27. 7H 535.
28. 6H 244; tape-recorded interview of Holland by Thompson, November 30, 1966, cited in Thompson, pp. 121–22; filmed and tape-recorded interview of Holland by Lane, Dallas, March 23, 1966, cited in Lane, pp. 34–35, 419; filmed and tape-recorded interview of Simmons by Lane, Mesquite, Texas, March 28, 1966, cited in Lane, pp. 34, 419; tape-recorded interview of Dodd by Lane, March 24, 1966, cited in Thompson, pp. 122, 138.
29. For location, see 6H 245–46; also see diagram by Holland in Thompson, p. 123.
30. 6H 246.
31. 6H 245–46.
32. 6H 246.
33. Filmed and tape-recorded interview of Simmons by Lane, Mesquite, Texas, March 23, 1966, cited in Lane, pp. 34, 419.
34. Tape-recorded interview of Dodd by Lane, March 24, 1966, cited in Thompson, pp. 122, 138.
35. HAR 87–91, 605–6; HAH 8H 139–41; Thompson, p. 25; Lane, p. 39, see pp. 399–402.
36. CE 2003, p. 45; CE 1431; see Thompson, Appendix A.
37. CE 2003, p. 45; see also Thompson, p. 126.
38. CE 1431; CE 2003, p. 43.
39. 24H 520; see Thompson, Appendix A.
40. *Dallas Morning News*, November 23, 1963, section 1, p. 3.
41. See Thompson, Appendix A.
42. Thompson, p. 193. See photographs in HAH 5H 507, 632; Thompson, pp. 103, 126, Appendix A.
43. Hurt, pp. 111–13.
44. 17H 461, see p. 492.
45. *Ibid.*
46. 19H 515.
47. Reports: 2H 181; 6H 244, 246–47, 288; 19H 502, 508, 514, 528, 530, 540; CE 1421. Photographs: Thompson, pp. 100, 119; HAH 5H 507. Note that the grassy knoll was almost deserted before the shots were fired (Thompson, pp. 186, 188).
48. 6H 247, 288, 294; CE 1416, 1417; see HAH 5H 507–8.
49. 6H 288.
50. HAH 5H 505–6; CE 1421.

51. 2H 181; 6H 288.

52. 19H 516; CD 5, cited in Thompson, p. 119; 19H 514, 530.

53. CD 5, quoted in Thompson, p. 119.

54. *Ibid.*

55. 7H 109.

56. *Ibid.*

57. 7H 107.

58. 6H 284–86; WR 72–73.

59. 6H 285.

60. 6H 285–86.

61. *Ibid.*

62. 6H 286.

63. 6H 287; tape-recorded interview of Bowers by Lane, Arlington, Texas, March 31, 1966, cited in Lane, pp. 30–31, 418. See Thompson, front end-paper and pp. 115, 121, for position.

64. Tape-recorded interview of Bowers by Lane, Arlington, Texas, March 31, 1966, cited in Lane, pp. 31, 418.

65. 6H 288; Tape-recorded interview of Bowers by Lane, Arlington, Texas, March 31, 1966, cited in Lane, pp. 32, 418.

66. 19H 492.

67. *Ibid.*

68. Filmed and tape-recorded interview of Price by Lane, Dallas, March 27, 1966, cited in Lane, pp. 32–33, 419.

69. 7H 535.

70. *Ibid.*

71. Hurt, p. 112.

72. CD 3, p. 44; CE 1024; WR 52; see Meagher, p. 25.

73. Thompson, pp. xv–xvii, 6–10, 273–74.

74. Thompson, pp. 115–29. The preceding discussion of these points in the text was greatly influenced by Thompson's presentation of the evidence.

75. Thompson, pp. 115–29.

76. *Ibid.*, pp. 82–86, 120–23.

77. *Ibid.*, pp. 83–85; 6H 243–45.

78. Thompson, pp. 120–21; 6H 243–45. Holland indicated that the smoke moved out from the fence corner toward the grassy knoll, as it would have with the 15-mile-per-hour wind blowing from the west at that time (HAH 8H 21, 173). In Holland's November 22 affidavit, the shot at which the smoke appeared, which sounded like a firecracker, is reported as the first shot (Holland Exhibit D, see 6H 245). But this designation may be an error attributable to the excited atmosphere Friday afternoon in which the affidavit was prepared and signed.

79. Thompson, p. 121. The westerly direction is implicit in his description; see the photograph of Holland's view in Thompson, p. 121 and the map in Thompson, pp. 252–53.

80. Thompson, p. 122.

81. *Ibid.*

82. *Ibid.*

83. *Ibid.*, pp. 194–95.

84. *Ibid.*, p. 195.

85. *Ibid.*

86. HAR 66–67; HAH 2H 16–17, 107–10; HAH 5H 637.
87. As cited in the prior note.
88. HAH 8H 5, 11.
89. HAH 5H 638; see HAR 67.
90. HAH 8H 70–74; WR 48–49.
91. HAR 66.
92. HAR 66–67; HAH 2H 17; HAH 5H 644, 674–75.
93. HAR 69, 72.
94. HAH 5H 555, 644; HAR 69.
95. HAR 67–72; HAH 2H 17–105.
96. HAH 5H 690, 723; HAH 8H 49–50; HAR 68.
97. HAH 5H 690; HAH 8H 49–50; HAR 79.
98. HAR 68–69.
99. HAH 2H 94; HAR 72.
100. HAR 72, 69; HAH 5H 593; HAH 8H 4.
101. HAH 8H 6–10; HAH 5H 557–58; HAR 72–73.
102. HAR 73; HAH 5H 673.
103. HAH 5H 555–72. Within a "coincidence window" of plus or minus .001 seconds, 10 of the 12 computed echo spikes appeared on the dictabelt. The remaining two also appeared, but below the noise threshold selected (HAR 73–74; HAH 8H 10, 26–32; HAH 5H 569–70, 586). The shape of each recorded echo spike was the mirror image of the shape of the muzzle blast spike, further demonstrating that the recorded spikes were the echo pattern of a gunshot (HAH 5H 581).
104. See HAR 68–69.
105. HAH 5H 555–615.
106. HAH 5H 556, 583; see HAR 74; HAH 8H 32.
107. HAH 5H 593.
108. HAH 5H 672–74.
109. HAH 5H 652–73.
110. *Washington Post*, October 26, 1983, p. A2; *Newsweek*, November 14, 1983, p. 58.
111. HAH 5H 671–72.
112. HAR 480–82.
113. *Washington Post*, July 7, 1981, p. A6.
114. *Ibid.*
115. Telephone conversation with Paul Hoch, June 28, 1987.
116. *Ibid.*
117. *Washington Post*, May 15, 1982, p. A3; *Report of the Committee on Ballistic Acoustics* (Washington, D.C.: National Academy Press, 1982), p. 34.
118. *Report of the Committee on Ballistic Acoustics*, pp. 6–7, 14–15; *Washington Post*, May 15, 1982, p. A3; see HAH 5H 656–57.
119. HAH 5H 671; *Washington Post*, May 15, 1982, p. A3.
120. *Washington Post*, May 15, 1982, p. A3; W. Anthony Marsh, "A Brief Rebuttal to the Ramsey Report," *The Third Decade* 2, no. 2 (January 1986), pp. 15–19. For example, the critical Weiss-Aschkenasy conclusion of a 95-percent probability of a grassy knoll shot was treated only in a sketchy three-page appendix that made one outright error—there was only one degree, not two, of freedom associated with the position of the shooter along the grassy knoll fence. This appendix also recalculated the probabil-

ity by subtracting degrees of freedom adjusted in the Weiss-Aschkenasy analysis from matches obtained, an arbitrary approximation to a complex mathematical calculation, akin to computing the volume of a cube as three by adding its dimensions. The appendix itself included the admission that this critical calculation was "possibly overconservative" and "may be unduly conservative" (*Report of the Committee on Ballistic Acoustics*, Appendix A-3, pp. 38–40).

121. Barger to G. Robert Blakey, February 18, 1983, copy in author's files.
122. HAR 71; HAH 2H 64–67, 70; see HAH 2H 49, 89.
123. The officer was H. B. McLain (HAH 5H 617–41). For the motorcycle position, see HAR 76; HAH 8H 29; HAH 5H 616–17, 628–30, 636–37, 717. For the relative position of the microphone on the motorcycle, see HAR 74; HAH 5H 582, 618, 631. See also HAH 5H 630, 636–37; HAH 8H 11 for confirmation of other implicit predictions about the microphone.
124. HAH 5H 171; HAR 74–75. The detected supersonic shock waves did not rule out pistol fire, since both pistols and pistol ammunition were available in 1963 to fire supersonic bullets (HAH 5H 614, 574). The House Assassinations Committee also determined, from test firings, that pistols could be fired virtually as accurately as rifles over the short range from the grassy knoll to the presidential limousine at the time of the third shot (HAH 5H 614).
125. HAH 8H 29. A radius of error of approximately five feet was associated with this placement (*ibid.*, HAH 5H 570).
126. Thompson, pp. 121–22; see text above.
127. See map, p. 166, in photo section, and note 5 above.
128. As cited in the prior note.
129. WR 3.
130. HAR 1.
131. HAR 97.
132. HAH 6H 121–25; Thompson, p. 34; Model and Groden, *JFK: The Case for Conspiracy*, pp. 143–44.
133. HAH 6H 122, 123.
134. HAH 6H 124.
135. *Ibid*.
136. See photos in HAH 6H 122.
137. HAH 6H 123.
138. HAH 6H 125.
139. See, for example, HAR 79–83; Thompson, pp. 82–111; HAH 6H 298–302; *Washington Post*, June 18, 1979, pp. A1, A6, June 19, 1979, p. A2, June 29, 1979, p. A3; *New York Times*, August 27, 1972, pp. 1, 57.
140. See Thompson, pp. 86–90; the left rearward snap is clear in a viewing of the film.
141. 2H 141; see WR 104; 6H 290, 292, 294–95; 7H 518; Thompson, pp. 86–102. The calculations presented in HAH 1H 412–14 are of little relevance, since they are based on a bullet fired from a Mannlicher-Carcano rifle. A high-powered, larger caliber rifle would fire a bullet with much greater momentum. The "jet-effect" theory (HAH 1H 428–442) is totally negated by the observed left-rearward motion of the bulk of the impact

debris. Other explanations are equally dubious (see Thompson, pp. 90–94).

142. Thompson, p. 100.
143. Interview shown in the British Broadcasting Company (BBC) Panorama special, "The Kennedy Assassination: What Do We Know Now That We Didn't Then," March 1978.
144. John Sparrow, *After the Assassination: A Positive Appraisal of the Warren Report* (New York: Chilmark Press, 1967), p. 39, see p. 10.
145. Turner and Christian, *The Assassination of Robert F. Kennedy*, p. 215.

Chapter 3
A Telltale Trail of Murder

1. *U.S.–Senate, OC and Stolen Securities, 1971*, p. 672. Raymond testified under the name "George White" (p. 956).
2. HAH 5H 345.
3. Dorman, *Payoff*, pp. 58–59.
4. *Ibid*.
5. *Ibid*.
6. *Ibid*.
7. *Ibid*.
8. *Ibid*.
9. See Appendix 2 for many other similar examples.
10. See the Introduction.
11. CE 2887.
12. *Ibid*.
13. *Ibid*.
14. See part II.
15. *Midlothian* (Texas) *Mirror*, June 3, 1965, reprinted in Jones, *Forgive My Grief*, vol. I, p. 5.
16. *Ibid*.; see also Joachim Joesten, *Oswald: The Truth* (London: P. Dawney, 1967), pp. 124–26.
17. JFK microfilm, vol. I, p. 394; National Archives, entry 45, Ruby-Oswald chronology, p. 861.
18. *San Francisco Chronicle*, April 24, 1964, p. 9; Jones, vol. I, p. 6.
19. As cited in the prior note.
20. Jones, vol. I, p. 6.
21. *Dallas Times Herald*, September 22, 1964, cited in Lane, *Rush to Judgment*, p. 284; Jones, vol. I, p. 6.
22. Jones, vol. II, p. 13.
23. *Ibid*., pp. 8–9.
24. *New York Times*, March 29, 1965, p. 33; Jones, vol. I, p. 6.
25. Jones, vol. I, p. 6.
26. 14H 256–57.
27. *Ibid*.
28. See text below.
29. Jones, vol. II, pp. 12–13.

30. Joesten, *Oswald: Assassin or Fall Guy?*, p. 102.
31. Ruby stated in his medical interview, "I did like Dorothy Kilgallen until she wrote a column saying I was a gangster so I don't like her now" (JFK microfilm, vol. 5, p. D24).
32. Jones, vol. II, p. 13.
33. *Ibid*.
34. *Ibid*.
35. WR 363.
36. *New York Times*, February 23, 1967, p. 22; CE 2882.
37. *New York Times*, February 23, 1967, p. 22; Jones, vol. I, p. 8; Jones, vol. II, p. 2.
38. *New York Times*, February 23, 1967, p. 22.
39. *Ibid*.
40. *Ibid*.
41. *Ibid*.
42. *Ibid*.
43. *Ibid*.
44. *Ibid*.
45. Jones, vol. II, p. 2.
46. *New York Times*, February 23, 1967, p. 22.
47. *Ibid*.
48. HAH 10H 199.
49. *Ibid*.
50. *Ibid*.
51. "The Bizarre Deaths Following JFK's Murder," *Argosy*, March 1977, p. 52; Jones, vol. II, p. 22; HAH 10H 199–204.
52. HAH 10H 200–203.
53. *Ibid*., p. 200.
54. *Ibid*., pp. 200–201.
55. *Ibid*., p. 199.
56. *Ibid*.
57. 6H 284.
58. See chapter 2.
59. Filmed and tape-recorded interview with Mark Lane, cited in Lane, p. 32; see chapter 2.
60. Reprinted in Jones, vol. II, p. 27.
61. *Ibid*.
62. *Ibid*.
63. WR 169–71.
64. WR 171.
65. *Ibid*.
66. CE 2523.
67. CE 2589.
68. *Ibid*.
69. *Ibid*.
70. 11H 438.
71. CE 2589.
72. 11H 437.
73. CE 2589.
74. *Ibid*.

75. *Ibid.*
76. CE 2587.
77. 11H 434–42.
78. CE 2587; 11H 438–40.
79. CE 2587.
80. 11H 441.
81. 11H 442.
82. CE 2587; 11H 441–42.
83. 11H 435.
84. Filmed and tape-recorded interview of Clemons by Lane, Dallas, March 23, 1966, cited in Lane, pp. 193–94.
85. Lane, p. 194.
86. 21H 139; 24H 7.
87. Lane interview, March 23, 1966, cited in Lane, p. 280.
88. *Ibid.*
89. 10H 352.
90. 10H 353–54.
91. 10H 353.
92. *Ibid.*
93. 10H 353–55; 26H 451.
94. As cited in the prior note.
95. As cited in the prior note.
96. 26H 577, 682–83.
97. 10H 340–51, 355; 26H 685, 702; WR 321.
98. CE 3091, 3092.
99. 10H 354; 26H 685.
100. WR 321.
101. *Ibid.*
102. See Lane, chapter 27; Anson, *"They've Killed the President!"* chapter 7.
103. WR 252; 2H 256; *Fort Worth Star Telegram*, December 19, 1965, cited in Lane, p. 333; Jones, vol. II, p. 12.
104. As cited in Lane, p. 333.
105. *San Francisco Chronicle*, November 18, 1973, p. 8A; Jones, vol. II, p. 37.
106. As cited in the prior note.
107. 6H 260–73.
108. *Ibid.*; 23H 817; see Noyes, *Legacy of Doubt*, pp. 84–94.
109. Noyes, p. 84.
110. *Ibid.*; Hurt, *Reasonable Doubt*, p. 125.
111. Noyes, pp. 95–96; Hurt, p. 125.
112. Hurt, p. 125.
113. *Ibid.*
114. *Dallas Morning News*, May 16, 1975, p. 5D.
115. Noyes, p. 84.
116. *Dallas Morning News*, May 16, 1975, p. 5D; *Dallas Times Herald*, May 16, 1975, p. B3.
117. As cited in the prior note.
118. *Dallas Morning News*, May 16, 1975, p. 5D.
119. *U.S.-Senate, Intelligence Report, Foreign Assassinations*, pp. 75–77; HAH 10H 151.

120. Malone, "The Secret Life of Jack Ruby," *New Times*, January 23, 1978, p. 51.
121. *Ibid.*; Jack Anderson, *Albuquerque Journal*, September 8, 1976.
122. Jack Anderson, *Albuquerque Journal*, September 8, 1976; Jack Anderson, *Washington Post*, January 3, 1979, p. B15; Davis, *The Kennedys: Dynasty and Disaster 1948-1984*, p. 790.
123. Jack Anderson, *Albuquerque Journal*, September 8, 1976; HAH 10H 155, 186; Moldea, *The Hoffa Wars*, p. 433.
124. WR 282.
125. For example, see indices in the Warren Report; Anson; and Meagher, *Accessories After the Fact*.
126. *Albuquerque Tribune*, March 30, 1977.
127. *Ibid.*
128. Meagher, pp. 293-302; Jones, vols. I-III.

Chapter 4
Intrigue in New Orleans

1. Noyes, *Legacy of Doubt*, p. 160.
2. Anson, *"They've Killed the President!"* chapter 4; Noyes, chapter 8; Garrison interview and background, *Playboy*, October 1967, pp. 59ff.
3. Rogers, "The Persecution of Clay Shaw," *Look*, August 26, 1969, pp. 54-55; *New York Times*, February 23, 1967, p. 22; Noyes, pp. 105, 109-10; *Playboy*, October 1967, p. 59; Hurt, *Reasonable Doubt*, pp. 263-64; see below for tie to Marcello.
4. Hurt, p. 264.
5. Rogers, in *Look*, pp. 54-55; *New York Times*, February 23, 1967, p. 22; Noyes, pp. 105, 109-10; *Playboy*, October 1967, p. 59; Hurt, p. 264.
6. Rogers, in *Look*, p. 56.
7. *Ibid.*; HAH 10H 111-12; HAR 143-45, 170.
8. Rogers, in *Look*, p. 56.
9. *Ibid.*; HAH 10H 112; *Los Angeles Times*, September 4, 1970; Noyes, pp. 144-45.
10. HAH 10H 12; see text below.
11. Blakey and Billings, *The Plot to Kill the President*, p. 50.
12. HAH 10H 107, 109, 112.
13. Noyes, p. 128.
14. HAH 10H 112; Blakey and Billings, p. 169.
15. CD 75, p. 199; HAH 10H 107, 111.
16. CD 75, p. 199; HAR 170.
17. CD 75, p. 199.
18. HAH 10H 113, 114.
19. CD 75, p. 220; HAH 10H 114.
20. HAH 9H 70-71.
21. *Ibid.*; see *U.S.-House, OC in Sports*, p. 970.
22. HAH 10H 114, note 5.
23. HAH 10H 114; CD 75, p. 220.

24. CD 75, p. 288; Rogers, in *Look*, p. 56.
25. As cited in the prior note; also HAH 10H 113; Anson, p. 106.
26. Anson, p. 106.
27. *Ibid.*; CD 75, p. 288.
28. HAH 10H 113.
29. CD 75, p. 291.
30. HAH 10H 113.
31. HAH 10H 113; Marcello's ownership of the Alamotel was reported in Paris Flammonde, *The Kennedy Conspiracy* (New York: Meredith, 1969), p. 28.
32. CD 75, p. 287; HAH 10H 112.
33. CD 75, p. 287.
34. CD 75, p. 307.
35. *Ibid.*
36. HAH 10H 113, 122; Rogers, in *Look*, p. 56.
37. CD 75, p. 291.
38. Rogers, in *Look*, p. 56.
39. CD 75, p. 292.
40. WR 670, 711, 736, 738.
41. WR 191, 375–76, 422–23; see Lane, *Rush to Judgment*, pp. 123–24.
42. See, for example, Meagher, *Accessories After the Fact.*
43. Kantor Exhibit 3, p. 366.
44. WR 287–92.
45. HAH 10H 3; see below.
46. HAH 10H 123.
47. *Ibid.*
48. WR 406–7, 375–76.
49. HAH 10H 132; HAR 180; HAH 4H 482.
50. HAH 10H 3.
51. WR 290–92.
52. HAR 170; see CD 75, p. 160.
53. HAR 170.
54. HAH 4H 565.
55. HAR 170.
56. Blakey and Billings, p. 342.
57. See below.
58. HAH 9H 95; Blakey and Billings, pp. 340–41.
59. As cited in the prior note.
60. As cited in the prior note.
61. As cited in the prior note.
62. Blakey and Billings, p. 341.
63. *Ibid.*; HAH 9H 95.
64. HAH 9H 95; Blakey and Billings, pp. 341–42.
65. National Archives, entry 45, Ruby-Oswald chronology, p. 615; see CD 75, p. 159; WR 728; Blakey and Billings, p. 342.
66. Blakey and Billings, p. 342.
67. WR 728.
68. HAH 9H 95–99; Blakey and Billings, p. 343–44.
69. HAH 9H 97–98.
70. HAH 9H 96–99.

71. HAH 9H 95–99, 116.
72. HAR 170.
73. HAH 9H 93.
74. HAH 9H 94.
75. HAH 9H 115–16; Blakey and Billings, pp. 344–45.
76. As cited in the prior note.
77. HAH 9H 115.
78. See Appendix 2, section 4b.
79. See Appendix 2, section 21a.
80. HAH 9H 117.
81. HAH 10H 19–32.
82. Tape-recorded interview of a witness who asked not to be named, July 12, 1983.
83. HAR 137–39; Blakey and Billings, p. 163.
84. WR 321–24; HAH 10H 20–23; HAR 137–39.
85. HAR 137–39.
86. *Ibid.*; Blakey and Billings, pp. 162–65.
87. HAH 10H 132.
88. HAH 9H 113–14.
89. HAR 142.
90. HAH 10H 132; HAR 142–43; HAH 4H 482.
91. Thompson, *Six Seconds in Dallas*, pp. 129–33.
92. *Ibid.*, pp. 132–33.
93. *Ibid.*, p. 193n.
94. As described in a tape-recorded interview of the family of retired Air Force Major Phillip Willis with Dr. Josiah Thompson, November 29, 1966, cited in Thompson, pp. 132, 139. For background of Willis, see Model and Groden, *JFK: The Case for Conspiracy*, p. 143.
95. As cited in the prior note.
96. 20H 499; see Thompson, pp. 132, 139.
97. Thompson, p. 132.
98. Decker Exhibit 5323, pp. 469, 527.
99. *Ibid.*
100. *Ibid.*
101. *Ibid.*
102. *Ibid.*
103. *Ibid.*; see Noyes, pp. 20–23.
104. Decker Exhibit 5323, pp. 469, 527.
105. Noyes, p. 27.
106. *Ibid.*, p. 28.
107. *Ibid.*, p. 29.
108. *Ibid.*, pp. 24, 80.
109. *Ibid.*, pp. 26–39.
110. *Ibid.*, pp. 37–39.
111. *Ibid.*, pp. 27, 30, 72.
112. *Ibid.*, pp. 30, 38.
113. Houghton, *Special Unit Senator*, p. 158.
114. Noyes, pp. 47–48.
115. Noyes, pp. 48, 57. Information on the Mob backgrounds of Fratianno, Meltzer and Sica is provided in Reid, *The Grim Reapers*, pp. 181, 184, 191–92, 299 and Noyes, pp. 56–57.

116. Noyes, pp. 28–29.
117. *Ibid.*, pp. 39, 40, 58.
118. *Ibid.*, pp. 58–59.
119. *Ibid.*, p. 33.
120. *Ibid.*, p. 72.
121. *Ibid.*, p. 73.
122. *Ibid.*
123. *Ibid.*, p. 74.
124. *Ibid.*, p. 73.
125. *Ibid.*, p. 79.
126. *Ibid.*, pp. 71–72, 81.
127. *Ibid.*
128. *Ibid.*, p. 72.
129. *Ibid.*, pp. 72–73, see p. 75.
130. *Ibid.*
131. *Ibid.*, pp. 65–66, 72–73.
132. *Ibid.*, p. 75.
133. *Ibid.*
134. *Ibid.*
135. Joachim Joesten, *The Case Against Lyndon Johnson in the Assassination of President Kennedy* (Munich: Dreischstr. 5, Selbstverlag, 1967), p. 9.
136. Noyes, pp. 157–58.
137. *Ibid.*, p. 158.
138. *Ibid.*
139. *Ibid.*
140. Statement of Representative Thomas Kupferman, 89th Congress, 2nd session, September 28, 1966, *Congressional Record*, vol. 118, pp. 24157–59.
141. *New Times*, August 8, 1975, p. 32; *Life*, October 7, 1966, p. 38.
142. Louis Harris Poll, reported in the *Washington Post*, October 3, 1966, p. A21, and the *New York Post*, October 3, 1966, p. 4.
143. As cited in the prior note.
144. Anson, pp. 105, 119, 301.
145. *Ibid.*, p. 119.
146. *Ibid.*, pp. 110–12; Epstein, *Counterplot*, pp. 67–69.
147. Anson, pp. 113–14; *Playboy*, October 1967, p. 59.
148. As cited in the prior note.
149. Rogers, "The Persecution of Clay Shaw," *Look*, August 26, 1969, p. 53. Shaw, however, may have known Ferrie and been linked to the CIA (Anson, pp. 121–22).
150. Sheridan, *The Fall and Rise of Jimmy Hoffa*, p. 416.
151. *Newsweek*, May 15, 1967, pp. 36–40.
152. *New York Times*, June 12, 1967, p. 1.
153. Rogers, in *Look*, pp. 53ff.
154. James Phelan, "Rush to Judgment in New Orleans," *Saturday Evening Post*, August 26, 1969.
155. *The JFK Conspiracy: The Case of Jim Garrison*, NBC, June 19, 1967, cited in Sheridan, p. 420.
156. Epstein, *Counterplot*; see also Anson, chapter 4 and Noyes, chapters 7–8.
157. As cited in notes 151–56.

158. *Newsweek*, May 16, 1967, pp. 35–40.
159. *New York Times*, June 12, 1967, p. 1.
160. Epstein, *Counterplot*, pp. 50, 57.
161. Garrison interview, *Playboy*, October 1967, pp. 59ff.; Epstein, *Counterplot*, p. 71; Noyes, p. 105.
162. Rogers, in *Look*, p. 56; Noyes, p. 106.
163. Garrison interview, *Playboy*, October 1967, p. 174.
164. *Ibid*.
165. 14H 330–64.
166. 14H 334, 353–55; see CE 3061, p. 627.
167. Rogers, in *Look*, p. 56; Noyes, p. 106.
168. Rogers, in *Look*, p. 56.
169. *Ibid*.; *Life*, September 29, 1967, p. 35.
170. James R. Phelan, "The Vice Man Cometh," *Saturday Evening Post*, June 8, 1963, p. 71.
171. *Life*, September 29, 1967, p. 36.
172. *Ibid*.
173. *Ibid*.
174. Sheridan, p. 417.
175. "The Mob," part 2, *Life*, September 8, 1967, p. 96.
176. Sheridan, p. 417.
177. "The Mob," part 2, *Life*, September 8, 1967, pp. 94–95.
178. *Ibid*.
179. *Life*, September 29, 1967, p. 35.
180. Chandler, "The 'Little Man' is Bigger Than Ever," *Life*, April 10, 1970, p. 33.
181. Noyes, p. 106.
182. Sheridan, p. 417; *Playboy*, October 1967, p. 60.
183. Sheridan, p. 417.
184. Chandler, in *Life*, p. 33.
185. *Ibid*.
186. *Ibid*.
187. *New York Times*, August 20, 1973, p. 15; see *New York Times Index*, 1973, pp. 856–57.
188. *New York Times*, September 28, 1973, p. 30.
189. *New York Times*, August 20, 1973, p. 15.
190. *New York Times*, September 7, 1973, p. 15; see *New York Times Index*, 1973, pp. 856–57.
191. *New York Times*, September 28, 1973, p. 30.
192. *New York Times*, September 21, 1973, p. 25.
193. Mollenhoff, *Strike Force*, pp. 160–61; see chapter 5, "An Assassination Plan by Carlos Marcello."
194. Noyes, p. 106; Chandler, in *Life*, p. 33; Rogers, in *Look*, pp. 56–58; *U.S.-House, OC Control*, pp. 410–38; Sheridan, pp. 417, 432; *Life*, September 29, 1967, p. 34; Lawson, "Carnival of Crime," *Wall Street Journal*, January 12, 1970, p. 1; "The Mob," part 2, *Life*, September 8, 1967, p. 94; NBC Evening News, September 7, 1977; Salerno and Tompkins, *The Crime Confederation*, p. 290.
195. Correspondence of early 1987 from a colleague who asked not to be named, reporting a direct observation.

196. Noyes, pp. 95–103, 159–61.
197. *Ibid.*, p. 97.
198. *Ibid.*, pp. 97–103.
199. *Ibid.*, pp. 102–3, 161.
200. "The Mob," part 1, *Life*, September 1, 1967, p. 22; Sheridan, chapter 12.
201. Sheridan, pp. 411–12, see pp. 415, 427, 429, 457 for similar actions by Gill in the spring-Hoffa campaign.
202. *Ibid.*, p. 411.
203. Playboy, October 1967, pp. 60, 74; James A. Autry, "The Garrison Investigation: How and Why It Began," *New Orleans*, April 1967, p. 8; Rogers, in *Look*, p. 54.
204. See chapter 9, "Frank Caracci."
205. Sheridan, pp. 411–12.
206. *Ibid.*, p. 423.
207. *Ibid.*

Chapter 5
The Why and the Wherewithal

1. Anson, *"They've Killed the President!"* p. 327.
2. Kennedy, *The Enemy Within*, p. 18.
3. *Ibid.*
4. *Ibid.*, p. 16.
5. *Ibid.*, pp. 15–16.
6. *Ibid.*, passim.
7. *Ibid.*
8. Mollenhoff, *Strike Force*, p. 3.
9. Navasky, *Kennedy Justice*, pp. 44–46; Anslinger, *The Protectors*, pp. 214–15.
10. See chapter 17, "The Two FBIs."
11. Navasky, p. 72, see pp. 47, 62–63; see also HAH 9H 31–35.
12. Navasky, pp. 62–63.
13. *Ibid.*, p. 48.
14. Anslinger, *The Protectors*, pp. 215–16.
15. Navasky, p. 53; Salerno and Tompkins, *The Crime Confederation*, p. 308.
16. Navasky, p. 55.
17. One hundred sixty racketeering convictions in the first half of 1963 versus 35 in the first half of 1960, as reported by Robert Kennedy in "Robert Kennedy Defines the Menace," *New York Times Magazine*, October 13, 1963, p. 106. See also HAH 9H 11–43, especially p. 21.
18. Kennedy, in *New York Times Magazine*, p. 106.
19. *U.S.-Senate, OC and Narcotics Hearings*, pp. 181–83.
20. See Appendix 2, section 5e.
21. Salerno and Tompkins, pp. 311, 315–16; HAH 9H 37–39; HAH 5H 449–53.
22. Salerno and Tompkins, pp. 311, 315–16; *U.S.-Senate, OC and Narcotics*

Report, p. 118; see Valachi testimony in *U.S.-Senate, OC and Narcotics Hearings*.

23. Reid, *The Grim Reapers*, p. 162.
24. Anson, p. 317.
25. McClellan, *Crime Without Punishment*, p. 282.
26. *Ibid*.
27. Navasky, p. 50.
28. *Ibid.*, p. 51.
29. Sheridan, *The Fall and Rise of Jimmy Hoffa*, p. 300.
30. HAH 5H 448.
31. *Ibid*.
32. HAH 5H 437-38, 440, 447.
33. HAH 5H 443.
34. HAH 5H 446.
35. *Ibid*.
36. Jack Anderson, "The Life and Trials of Carlos Marcello," *Parade*, August 10, 1980, pp. 4-5; HAH 5H 416.
37. HAH 9H 65-66.
38. HAH 9H 66, 69; Noyes, *Legacy of Doubt*, p. 143; *U.S.-House, OC Control*, p. 412; Anderson, in *Parade*, pp. 4-5.
39. HAH 9H 61, 64-65.
40. Davidson, "New Orleans: Cosa Nostra's Wall Street," *Saturday Evening Post*, February 29, 1964, p. 15.
41. *U.S.-House, OC Control*, p. 433.
42. Chandler, "The 'Little Man' is Bigger Than Ever," *Life*, April 10, 1970, p. 31; see also "The Mob," *Life*, September 8, 1967, pp. 94ff; *Life*, September 29, 1967, pp. 34ff.
43. See Appendix 2, entry 4.10.
44. Lawson, "Carnival of Crime," *Wall Street Journal*, January 12, 1970, p. 1.
45. Noyes, pp. 142-44.
46. Reid and Demaris, *The Green Felt Jungle*, pp. 85, 88, 91.
47. Reid, *The Grim Reapers*, p. 160; Dorman, *Payoff*, p. 100.
48. Meskil, *Don Carlo*, p. 137.
49. *Dallas Morning News*, March 28, 29, 30, and 31, 1973, p. A1.
50. *Houston Post*, April 20, 1975, p. 2A; *U.S.-Senate, Kefauver Report, Third Interim*, p. 82; *U.S.-Senate, OC and Narcotics Hearings*, pp. 1097-98; "The Mob," part 1, *Life*, September 1, 1967, p. 20; see chapter 9, "Joseph Francis Civello."
51. See chapter 9, "Joseph Campisi" and "Joseph Francis Civello."
52. HAH 9H 62.
53. *Ibid.*; Reid, *The Grim Reapers*, p. 151.
54. HAH 9H 62.
55. *Ibid*.
56. HAH 9H 63.
57. *U.S.-Senate, McClellan Labor Hearings*, pp. 17265-67; HAH 9H 64; Mollenhoff, *Strike Force*, p. 159.
58. HAH 9H 63; Mollenhoff, *Strike Force*, p. 159.
59. HAH 9H 63. The case was still pending in 1979 (*ibid.*).
60. HAH 9H 69-70.
61. HAH 9H 71-72; Reid, *The Grim Reapers*, pp. 151-53; Mollenhoff, *Strike*

Force, p. 159. Marcello's lawyers had fabricated records listing that country as his birthplace to minimize inconvenience to him in the event of such action to deport him (Reid, *The Grim Reapers*, p. 152; HAH 9H 72).

62. HAR 169.
63. HAH 9H 74; Mollenhoff, *Strike Force*, p. 160.
64. HAH 9H 74.
65. *Ibid*.
66. HAH 9H 74–75; Mollenhoff, *Strike Force*, pp. 160–61.
67. *New Orleans Times-Picayune*, November 23, 1963, p. 1; HAH 9H 74.
68. Reid, *The Grim Reapers*, pp. 160–62; HAH 9H 75.
69. HAH 9H 81–84.
70. HAH 9H 77, 80–82.
71. HAH 9H 80–82, 85.
72. Reid, *The Grim Reapers*, pp. 160–61; HAH 9H 75.
73. Reid, *The Grim Reapers*, pp. 161–62.
74. HAH 9H 82.
75. HAH 9H 82–83.
76. HAH 9H 83.
77. HAH 9H 77; "New President" instead of "new President" in the source.
78. HAH 9H 82–83.
79. HAH 9H 83.
80. *Ibid*.; Reid, *The Grim Reapers*, p. 162.
81. HAH 9H 83.
82. HAH 9H 84.
83. *Ibid*.
84. HAR 9H 69–70.
85. *Ibid*.
86. HAH 9H 84.
87. *Ibid*.
88. CD 75, p. 287.
89. HAH 9H 81.
90. HAH 9H 76.
91. HAH 9H 83, 85.
92. HAH 9H 80–81, 85.
93. HAH 9H 82–83.
94. HAH 9H 83.
95. *Ibid*.
96. Reid, *The Grim Reapers*, p. 300; Moldea, *The Hoffa Wars*, pp. 178–79.
97. Reid, *The Grim Reapers*, pp. 93, 95, 115, 290; HAR 152; McCoy, *The Politics of Heroin in Southeast Asia*, p. 27.
98. Reid, *The Grim Reapers*, pp. 93, 95, 115, 132.
99. *U.S.-Senate, McClellan Labor Hearings*, pp. 12194–12201 (see "Louis Santos" on p. 12200); see Appendix 2, entry 5.41 for background on the Apalachin convention.
100. Reid, *The Grim Reapers*, pp. 158, 329; HAH 9H 66–67.
101. As cited in the prior note.
102. HAH 5H 295, see 257–58; see also Crile, "The Mafia, the CIA, and Castro," *Washington Post*, May 16, 1976, p. C1.
103. HAR 152, 173.

104. HAR 173; Moldea, *The Hoffa Wars*, p. 352; Scott, *Crime and Cover-Up*, p. 21.
105. Reid, *The Grim Reapers*, p. 300.
106. See part VI introduction.
107. HAH 5H 441.
108. HAR 173.
109. Crile, "The Mafia, the CIA, and Castro," *Washington Post*, May 16, 1976, p. C4.
110. *Ibid.*
111. *Ibid.*
112. *Ibid.*
113. *Ibid.*
114. *Ibid.*
115. *Ibid.*
116. *Ibid.*
117. *New York Times*, March 17, 1977, p. A23.
118. *Ibid.*
119. *Ibid.*
120. HAR 173.
121. HAH 5H 345–48, 373–77.
122. HAH 5H 304–5.
123. HAH 5H 305.
124. HAR 174; HAH 5H 323, 345.
125. HAH 5H 306.
126. HAH 5H 314, 317–20; HAR 174.
127. HAH 5H 317.
128. HAH 5H 319.
129. See, for example, Kennedy, *The Enemy Within*; Sheridan, *The Fall and Rise of Jimmy Hoffa*; Mollenhoff, *Tentacles of Power*; Moldea, *The Hoffa Wars*; and Brill, *The Teamsters*.
130. Anson, p. 325.
131. *Time*, August 25, 1975, p. 55; Brill, pp. 248–57; see Anson, pp. 317–25.
132. Moldea, *The Hoffa Wars*, pp. 5–6.
133. *Ibid.*, p. 178; *Life*, September 29, 1967, p. 34; "The Mob," part 1, *Life*, September 1, 1967, p. 22.
134. Moldea, *The Hoffa Wars*, p. 169.
135. HAR 176.
136. Sheridan, p. 300.
137. HAR 176; Moldea, *The Hoffa Wars*, pp. 148–49.
138. As cited in the prior note.
139. Moldea, *The Hoffa Wars*, p. 149.
140. *Ibid.*, p. 148.
141. Sheridan, pp. 224–25, 227, 229–45, 247–51, 257; Moldea, *The Hoffa Wars*, p. 142. Partin was found credible by the jury that convicted Hoffa on a jury tampering charge in 1964 (Moldea, *The Hoffa Wars*, pp. 171–73).
142. *New York Times*, April 12, 1964, pp. 1, 35; HAR 176; Sheridan, p. 217.
143. Sheridan, pp. 216–17; HAR 176; Moldea, *The Hoffa Wars*, p. 148.
144. Sheridan, p. 217.
145. *Ibid.*

146. *Ibid.*; see Benjamin Bradlee, *Conversations With Kennedy*, pp. 124–27.
147. Moldea, *The Hoffa Wars*, p. 149.
148. Sheridan, p. 7.
149. HAR 176–77.
150. HAR 176; Moldea, *The Hoffa Wars*, p. 148.
151. HAR 176.
152. *Ibid.*
153. Moldea, *The Hoffa Wars*, pp. 5–6.
154. HAH 9H 77, 82–83.
155. Moldea, *The Hoffa Wars*, p. 150.
156. *Ibid.*
157. *Ibid.*
158. HAR 176; Sheridan, p. 217.
159. HAR 176.
160. Brill, p. 374.
161. Blakey and Billings, *The Plot to Kill the President*, p. 375.
162. *Ibid.*, pp. 376–77.
163. *Ibid.*, p. 377.
164. *Ibid.*, p. 378.
165. *Ibid.*, p. 379.
166. *Ibid.*
167. *Ibid.*
168. *Ibid.*, pp. 379–81.
169. *Ibid.*
170. *Ibid.*, pp. 379–80.
171. *Ibid.*, p. 380.
172. *Ibid.*, p. 381.
173. *Ibid.*
174. *Ibid.*, p. 382.
175. Teresa, *My Life in the Mafia*, p. vii; Vincent Teresa, *Vinnie Teresa's Mafia* (Garden City, N.Y.: Doubleday, 1975), p. 39.
176. Teresa (this and subsequent references are to *My Life in the Mafia*), p. 180; Tyler, ed., *Organized Crime in America*, comments by Tyler on p. 229; *U.S.-Senate, OC and Narcotics Hearings*, pp. 192–93; see Appendix 2, section 6a.
177. Teresa, p. 182.
178. *Ibid.*, p. 180.
179. *Ibid.*, p. 186; HAR 163.
180. Mollenhoff, *Strike Force*, p. 151; HAH 9H 51–53.
181. *New York Times*, June 21, 1973, p. 18.
182. See Appendix 2, section 6a.
183. Teresa, p. 182.
184. Maas, *The Valachi Papers*, pp. 155–57.
185. *U.S.-Senate, OC and Narcotics Hearings*, pp. 428–29.
186. *Newsweek*, June 14, 1976, pp. 83–84.
187. Reid and Demaris, pp. 71–72.
188. See chapter 1, "The Shooting of UAW President Walter Reuther."
189. Salerno and Tompkins, p. 388; "The Mob," part 2, *Life*, September 8, 1967, p. 101.
190. See Appendix 2, section 6a.

191. Teresa, pp. 180, 182.
192. *Ibid.*, p. 180.
193. *Ibid.*, pp. 179–80, 183–86.
194. *Ibid.*, p. 183.
195. Rogers, "The Persecution of Clay Shaw," *Look*, August 26, 1969, p. 56.
196. HAR 161, 169, 173, 176.

Part II
Mob Fixer in Dallas

1. *New York Times*, quoted in *U.S.-House, Criminal Justice Hearings*, p. 149; for further background on Salerno, see *U.S.-Senate, OC and Narcotics Hearings*, pp. 121–22.
2. HAH 5H 427–28.
3. Sondern, *Brotherhood of Evil*, p. 60.
4. *U.S.-Cargo Theft and OC*, p. 24.
5. See Appendix 2, section 5.
6. See Appendix 2, section 5g.
7. See Appendix 2, entry 26.7.

Chapter 6
Molding of a Mobster

1. Stated at "The Politics of Conspiracy," conference at Boston University, workshop on organized crime, George Sherman Student Center, February 1, 1975, tape-recorded by author.
2. WR 780.
3. *Ibid.*
4. WR 781–83; C. Ray Hall Exhibit 3, p. 12.
5. CE 1288; CE 2980, p. 6; 15H 20–21; 14H 409.
6. CE 1288.
7. *Ibid.*
8. *Ibid.*
9. CE 1289.
10. 14H 409–10; CE 1289; CE 2980, p. 6; CE 1208.
11. WR 789; CE 1289; CE 1208.
12. CE 1289; Landesco, *Organized Crime in Chicago*, p. 173; Allsop, *The Bootleggers*, p. 71.
13. Landesco, p. 173; Kobler, *Capone*, pp. 80, 98.
14. 14H 409–10.
15. CE 1288.
16. *Ibid.*
17. *Ibid.*
18. CE 1258.

19. *Ibid.*
20. *Ibid.*
21. CE 1247.
22. *Ibid.*
23. *Ibid.*
24. *U.S.-Senate, OC and Narcotics Report*, p. 37; Reid, *The Grim Reapers*, p. 326.
25. *Newsweek*, August 15, 1977, p. 22.
26. 14H 533–34; JFK microfilm, vol. 5, p. D26.
27. JFK microfilm, vol. 5, p. D26.
28. WR 785.
29. CE 1217.
30. WR 786–87; C. Ray Hall Exhibit 3, p. 13.
31. *U.S.-Senate, Kefauver Hearings*, part 5, pp. 391, 399–400.
32. C. Ray Hall Exhibit 3, p. 13; CE 2980.
33. CE 2328; 14H 458.
34. CE 2328.
35. CE 1753; CE 1242.
36. CE 1289.
37. WR 788.
38. JFK microfilm, vol. 5, pp. R2–3.
39. CE 1293; CE 1321; C. Ray Hall Exhibit 1.
40. CE 1279.
41. *Ibid.*
42. JFK microfilm, vol. 5, p. D19.
43. WR 785.
44. *Ibid.*; 14H 470.
45. See chapter 9, "Paul Roland Jones."
46. CE 1184; see chapter 9, "Paul Roland Jones."
47. CE 1184.
48. Model and Groden, *JFK: The Case for Conspiracy*, p. 243.
49. CE 1292.
50. *Chicago Tribune*, December 9, 1939, p. 1.
51. CE 1184.
52. Sheridan, *The Fall and Rise of Jimmy Hoffa*, pp. 15–16; Kennedy, *The Enemy Within*, p. 87; WR 788.
53. WR 788; CE 1289; CE 1236; see text below.
54. CE 1289.
55. 14H 445.
56. *U.S.-Senate, McClellan Labor Hearings*, pp. 16082–87; Kennedy, *The Enemy Within*, pp. 87–89.
57. Sheridan, p. 15; CE 2980; Kennedy, *The Enemy Within*, p. 87.
58. *New York Times*, November 26, 1963, p. 15.
59. *U.S.-Senate, McClellan Labor Hearings*, pp. 16086–87.
60. CE 1293.
61. *New York Times*, interview with Dorfman, November 26, 1963, p. 15.
62. JFK microfilm, vol. 5, pp. R2–3; Ruby told his medical interviewer that he was held there overnight (*ibid.*, p. D26).
63. CE 1202.
64. JFK microfilm, vol. 5, p. R3.

65. Demaris, *Captive City*, pp. 189, 340, 350, 352.
66. *Ibid.*, p. 259.
67. Tampa: *U.S.–Senate, Kefauver Report, Third Interim*, p. 65. New York: Cook, *A Two-Dollar Bet Means Murder*, p. 132; *U.S.–Senate, Kefauver Report, Third Interim*, p. 129. Miami: Salerno and Tompkins, *The Crime Confederation*, pp. 287–88. Cleveland: Reid, *Mickey Cohen: Mobster*, p. 42.
68. JFK microfilm, vol. 5, p. D19; C. Ray Hall Exhibit 1.
69. CE 1279.
70. WR 788.
71. CE 1236.
72. CE 1236; WR 788.
73. CE 1236.
74. JFK microfilm, vol. 5, pp. R2–3; CE 1235.
75. CE 1321.
76. *Ibid.*
77. C. Ray Hall Exhibit 3, p. 13; 14H 370, 442.
78. WR 788–91; C. Ray Hall Exhibit 3, p. 13; 14H 370, 442.
79. CE 1184.
80. *Ibid.*
81. CE 1193.
82. *Ibid.*
83. Demaris, p. 84.
84. *Ibid.*, p. 85.
85. CE 1240.
86. *Ibid.*
87. Landesco, pp. 33, 173–74.
88. CE 1240.
89. *Ibid.*
90. *Ibid.*
91. CE 1277.
92. *Ibid.*
93. CE 1245.
94. CE 1505.
95. *U.S.–Senate, OC and Narcotics Report*, p. 37; Reid, *The Grim Reapers*, p. 326.
96. CE 1247.
97. CE 1211, 1212, 1321.
98. CE 1211.
99. CE 1321.
100. *Ibid.*
101. CE 1210.
102. *U.S.–Senate, AGVA Hearings*, p. 208; CE 1212.
103. CE 1212.
104. *Ibid.*
105. *Ibid.*
106. *Ibid.*
107. CE 1262.
108. *Ibid.*
109. CE 1277, 1245, 1240.

110. CE 1213, 1758, 1517.
111. WR 790.
112. CE 1287.
113. 15H 22.
114. CE 1201.
115. *Ibid.*
116. CD 1193, p. 89.
117. WR 790.
118. WR 779–92.
119. WR 790.
120. CE 1321.
121. CE 1210.
122. CE 1212; see *U.S.-Senate, AGVA Hearings*, p. 208.
123. CE 1321, 1210, 1212.
124. CE 1202.
125. *U.S.-Senate, OC and Narcotics Report*, p. 37; Demaris, p. 349.
126. *U.S.-Senate, OC and Narcotics Report*, p. 37.
127. Demaris, p. 349.
128. CE 1246.
129. CE 1193.
130. CE 1201; 15H 22.
131. CE 1241, 1203, 1242, 1288, 1289.
132. CE 1200; C. Ray Hall Exhibit 3, p. 13.
133. WR 801.
134. CE 1748.
135. See chapter 9, "Joseph Campisi."
136. CE 2322.
137. CE 1229.
138. 14H 14–15; CD 84, p. 152; CE 1322, pp. 727, 773; CE 1567; 14H 13–14; CD 722, pp. 3–5.
139. See chapter 10, "Mob-Police Liaison," displayed footnote.
140. CE 1543.
141. *Ibid.*, p. 195.

Chapter 7
The Move to Dallas

1. Cook, *The Secret Rulers*, p. 2.
2. Dorman, *Payoff*, pp. 151–62.
3. Reid and Demaris, *The Green Felt Jungle*, pp. 184–211.
4. *U.S.-Senate, Kefauver Hearings*, part 2, p. 193; see also Reid and Demaris, pp. 184–211.
5. CE 1251.
6. *Ibid.*
7. Reid, *The Grim Reapers*, pp. 73–74.
8. *Ibid.*, pp. 74–75.
9. *U.S.-Senate, Kefauver Hearings*, part 2, pp. 184–86.

10. *Ibid.*, vol. 5, pp. 1175–87.
11. *U.S.–Senate, McClellan Labor Hearings*, pp. 12519–27.
12. *Ibid.*, p. 12520.
13. *U.S.–Senate, McClellan Labor Hearings*, pp. 12520–23.
14. *Ibid.*, p. 12523.
15. *Ibid.*, pp. 12523–26.
16. *U.S.–Senate, Kefauver Hearings*, part 5, pp. 1181–87.
17. *Ibid.*, pp. 1179–81.
18. CE 1184.
19. *U.S.–Senate, McClellan Labor Hearings*, p. 12524.
20. *Ibid.*
21. *U.S.–Senate, Kefauver Hearings*, part 5, pp. 1180–81.
22. *Ibid.*
23. *Ibid.*
24. Dorman, *Payoff*, p. 155.
25. *U.S.–Senate, Kefauver Hearings*, part 5, p. 1178.
26. *Ibid.*, p. 1181.
27. *Ibid.*, pp. 1182–83.
28. *Ibid.*, p. 1183.
29. *Ibid.*, pp. 1182–86.
30. WR 792–93.
31. Blakey and Billings, *The Plot to Kill the President*, p. 288.
32. CE 1251.
33. *Ibid.*
34. WR 793.
35. HAH 9H 519, 524.
36. CE 2416.
37. CE 1321.
38. *U.S.–Senate, McClellan Labor Hearings*, pp. 12520–21.
39. Viorst, "The Mafia, the CIA, and the Kennedy Assassination," *Washingtonian*, November 1975, p. 116.
40. Anthony Summers, *Conspiracy* (New York: McGraw-Hill, 1980), p. 458.
41. *U.S.–Senate, McClellan Labor Hearings*, p. 12520.
42. *Ibid.*
43. *U.S.–Senate, OC and Narcotics Hearings*, p. 1098.
44. *U.S.–Senate, McClellan Labor Hearings*, p. 12196.
45. Salerno and Tompkins, *The Crime Confederation*, p. 323.
46. WR 793; CD 86, p. 278.
47. *Ibid.*
48. C. Ray Hall Exhibit 1; C. Ray Hall Exhibit 3, p. 14.
49. CE 1265; WR 793.
50. JFK microfilm, vol. 5, p. D20.
51. WR 794; C. Ray Hall Exhibit 1; C. Ray Hall Exhibit 3, p. 14.
52. WR 794.
53. JFK microfilm, vol. 5, p. D20; C. Ray Hall Exhibit 1; C. Ray Hall Exhibit 3, p. 14; WR 799.
54. CE 1228.
55. *Ibid.*
56. JFK microfilm, vol. 5, p. D26.
57. CE 1228.

58. *Ibid.*; CD 1102c (identifies "Bonds" as Locurto).
59. CD 1102c; WR 794.
60. WR 794.
61. *Ibid.*
62. WR 795; C. Ray Hall Exhibit 2.
63. As cited in the prior note.
64. As cited in the prior note.
65. As cited in the prior note.
66. WR 799; JFK microfilm, vol. 5, pp. D20–26.

Chapter 8
Jack Ruby's Criminal Activities

1. *U.S.-House, OC Control*, p. 437.
2. See Appendix 2, section 9a.
3. CE 1693.
4. *Ibid.*
5. *Ibid.*
6. CD 86, p. 278.
7. *Ibid.*
8. *Ibid.*
9. *Ibid.*
10. *Ibid.*
11. *Ibid.*
12. *Ibid.*
13. CE 1750.
14. CD 86, p. 278.
15. *Ibid.*
16. CD 86, pp. 278–82.
17. CD 86, p. 278.
18. *Ibid.*
19. CE 1763.
20. *Ibid.*
21. *Ibid.*
22. Hardee reported that Ruby was well acquainted with a "Sol," who operated and owned Sol's Bar and Restaurant on either Main or Elm Street in Dallas (CE 1763). Several sources established that Ruby knew Dallas gambler E. R. Solomon, known as "Sol," who operated Sol's Turf Bar on Commerce Street, directly between Main and Elm Streets (CD 4, p. 366; CD 86, pp. 248–49; CE 2980; see CE 1693). And Hardee's account of Ruby's "hustling the strippers" of his club while keeping half of the prostitution earnings was confirmed by other witnesses (CE 1763, 1227, 1251, 2822; 15H 432; see chapter 8, "Prostitution and Other Criminal Activities").
23. The Secret Service report of Hall's interview states: "Harry Hall was an informant for the Los Angeles Office several years ago, giving information which resulted in the seizure of a counterfeiting plant. He has since given

information to the Intelligence Division of the Treasury and the Federal Bureau of Investigation. . . . his information in many cases has been reliable" (CE 1753).

24. *Ibid*.
25. *Ibid*.
26. *Ibid*.
27. HAH 5H 70–71, 170; HAH 9H 428.
28. CE 1753.
29. CE 2980.
30. CE 1708.
31. CE 2980.
32. *U.S.–Senate, Kefauver Hearings*, part 5, p. 1177.
33. CE 1761.
34. *Ibid*.
35. *Ibid*.
36. *Ibid*.
37. CE 1762.
38. *Ibid*.
39. *Ibid*.
40. *Ibid*.
41. *Ibid*.
42. As related above; see also CE 1240.
43. See chapter 9, "Joseph Francis Civello."
44. CE 1761.
45. CE 1251.
46. CE 1763.
47. CE 1606; 15H 625–26. The cited interpretation of this transaction is supported by the conflict between the accounts of Larry Meyers (15H 625–26) and Dale (CE 1606) concerning this payment, and by the fact that Meyers, although married (15H 621), traveled to Dallas on another occasion with a woman he described as "a rather dumb but accommodating broad" (CE 2267).
48. °CE 2822.
49. *Ibid*.
50. CE 1227.
51. 15H 432.
52. CE 1772.
53. *Ibid*.
54. Crafard Exhibit 5226; 15H 224; CE 1549; CE 1507; CE 1322, pp. 738, 746, note razor blades.
55. CE 1762.
56. Razor blades: Teresa, *My Life in the Mafia*, p. 135. Pornographic materials: see Appendix 2, section 15a.
57. CD 86, p. 278.
58. CE 1763.
59. CE 1753.
60. CE 1761.
61. 24CE 1762.
62. CE 2822.
63. These include Carlos Malone in Louisville, Kentucky (CE 1559); Bobby

Gene Moore in Oakland, California (CD 84, p. 91); Blaney Mack Johnson in Atlanta (CE 3063); and Nancy Perrin Rich in Hanover, Massachusetts (14H 331).

64. See chapter 6, "Racketeering in the Chicago Night Club District," and "The Fine Reports of Ruby's Chicago Friends.'"
65. See chapters 12, 13, 19.

Chapter 9
Jack Ruby's Underworld Contacts

1. *U.S.-Senate, OC and Stolen Securities, 1973*, p. 453.
2. Mollenhoff, *Strike Force*, p. 54.
3. Kennedy, *The Enemy Within*, p. 91.
4. Sheridan, *The Fall and Rise of Jimmy Hoffa*, p. 194.
5. Sheridan, p. 20; HAH 9H 276; *U.S.-Senate, McClellan Labor Hearings*, pp. 14059–61.
6. Kennedy, *The Enemy Within*, p. 91.
7. *Ibid.*, pp. 91–92.
8. *U.S.-Senate, McClellan Labor Hearings*, pp. 14052–53.
9. *Ibid.*, pp. 14059–61; HAH 9H 274.
10. Sheridan, p. 21.
11. Hutchinson, *The Imperfect Union*, p. 247.
12. *Ibid.*; HAH 9H 274–75.
13. Mollenhoff, *Strike Force*, p. 54.
14. Kennedy, *The Enemy Within*, p. 91.
15. CE 2331.
16. HAH 9H 274.
17. *U.S.-Senate, McClellan Labor Hearings*, pp. 14047–48, 14080; Hutchinson, p. 248; HAH 9H 274–76.
18. CE 2303.
19. *Ibid.*
20. CE 1322, p. 738.
21. HAH 9H 1146.
22. HAR 171; HAH 9H 335–36; JFK microfilm, vol. 5, p. G12; *Houston Post*, April 20, 1975, p. 2A.
23. HAH 9H 392.
24. *U.S.-Senate, McClellan Labor Hearings*, p. 12196; *U.S.-Senate, OC and Narcotics Hearings*, p. 1098.
25. HAH 9H 1146.
26. HAH 9H 336.
27. HAH 9H 335, 412.
28. HAH 9H 336.
29. *Ibid.*
30. HAH 9H 335.
31. *Ibid.*
32. *Houston Post*, April 20, 1975, p. 2A.
33. *Ibid.*; HAH 9H 392–97.

34. *Houston Post*, April 20, 1975, p. 2A.

35. HAH 9H 396.

36. *Houston Post*, April 20, 1975, p. 2A.

37. HAH 9H 392–97.

38. JFK microfilm, vol. 5, p. G12.

39. CD 106, p. 89.

40. CE 2259.

41. HAH 9H 343–48, 355–62, 366–67, 382–87.

42. HAH 9H 359.

43. CE 2259; CE 1748; see HAH 9H 336.

44. CE 2259.

45. CD 86, pp. 138–39.

46. CE 2259.

47. HAH 9H 363–64, 374.

48. *U.S.-House, OC Control*, p. 430.

49. Chandler, "The 'Little Man' is Bigger Than Ever," *Life*, April 10, 1970, p. 33.

50. Lawson, "Carnival of Crime," *Wall Street Journal*, January 12, 1970, p. 18.

51. Chandler, in *Life*, p. 31.

52. *Ibid*., p. 33; *Houston Post*, April 20, 1975, p. 2A.

53. As cited in the prior note.

54. As cited in the prior note.

55. Chandler, in *Life*, p. 33.

56. *Ibid*., pp. 33–34; Sheridan, pp. 458–59.

57. Chandler, in *Life*, pp. 33–34; Sheridan, pp. 458–59.

58. Chandler, in *Life*, pp. 33–34.

59. *Ibid*., p. 33.

60. *New York Times*, February 28, 1974, p. 24.

61. Chandler, in *Life*, pp. 33–34.

62. *Houston Post*, April 20, 1975, p. 2A.

63. Chandler, in *Life*, p. 34.

64. HAH 9H 72; Marcello has successfully fought deportation for more than 25 years, spending more money in the process than in any other such case in American history (HAH 9H 63).

65. Chandler, in *Life*, p. 34.

66. *Ibid*.

67. *Ibid*.

68. *U.S.-House, OC in Sports*, p. 954.

69. *Ibid*.

70. *Ibid*.

71. *Ibid*.

72. *Ibid*.

73. *Ibid*.

74. *Ibid*., p. 949.

75. See chapter 18.

76. Sheridan, pp. 202, 274, 356, 406–8; Moldea, *The Hoffa Wars*, p. 151; *U.S.-Senate, McClellan Labor Hearings*, p. 16642.

77. Sheridan, pp. 406–7; Moldea, *The Hoffa Wars*, p. 151.

78. Reid and Demaris, *The Green Felt Jungle*, pp. 104–5; Moldea, *The Hoffa Wars*, p. 151.
79. As cited in the prior note.
80. Sheridan, p. 356.
81. Sheridan, pp. 406–8; see chapter 21, "The Assassination of Robert Kennedy."
82. Sheridan, p. 408.
83. *New York Times*, January 14, 1987, p. 1
84. *Washington Post*, January 14, 1987, p. A1
85. *New York Times*, January 14, 1987, p. 1
86. *Washington Post*, January 8, 1987, P. A3
87. *New York Times*, January 14, 1987, p. 1
88. CD 86, p. 558; Reid and Demaris, p. 104.
89. CD 86, p. 558.
90. *Ibid.*
91. Moldea, *The Hoffa Wars*, p. 163.
92. *Ibid.*, pp. 163–64; Scott, *Crime and Cover-Up*, pp. 45–46.
93. Moldea, *The Hoffa Wars*, p. 112; Brill, *The Teamsters*, p. 131.
94. Sheridan, p. 282; Mollenhoff, *Strike Force*, p. 225.
95. Moldea, *The Hoffa Wars*, p. 417; NBC Evening News, "Segment 3," June 14, 1978.
96. See chapter 6, "Union Official."
97. *U.S.-Senate, OC and Narcotics Hearings*, p. 1098; *U.S.-Senate, Kefauver Report, Third Interim*, p. 82; "The Mob," part 1, *Life*, September 1, 1967, p. 20.
98. *U.S.-Senate, McClellan Labor Hearings*, p. 12195; *U.S.-Senate, OC and Narcotics Hearings*, p. 1098.
99. *Houston Post*, April 20, 1975, p. 2A.
100. *U.S.-Senate, OC and Narcotics Hearings*, p. 1098; *U.S.-Senate, McClellan Labor Hearings*, p. 12196.
101. *Houston Post*, April 20, 1975, p. 2A.
102. *U.S.-Senate, Kefauver Report, Third Interim*, p. 82.
103. CD 302, p. 16.
104. See chapter 9, "Joseph Campisi."
105. CD 84, pp. 91–92.
106. *Ibid.*
107. *Ibid.*
108. Compare CD 84, pp. 91–92, with Golz, *Dallas Morning News*, April 26, 1972, p. D1. See also CE 1506, 1585, 1618, 1652, 1757, 1758 concerning the friendship between Ruby and "Candy Barr" that Moore reported.
109. CD 84, p. 91.
110. *Ibid.*
111. Golz, *Dallas Morning News*, April 26, 1972, p. D1; see HAH 9H 390.
112. Sondern, *Brotherhood of Evil*, p. 240.
113. *U.S.-Senate, OC and Narcotics Hearings*, p. 1098.
114. CD 84, p. 91.
115. CD 302, p. 30.
116. Blakey and Billings, *The Plot to Kill the President*, p. 314.
117. CD 84, pp. 91–92.
118. CD 84, p. 92.

119. WR 801.
120. 14H 446.
121. 14H 445.
122. *Ibid.*
123. 14H 444.
124. See chapter 9, "Lewis J. McWillie," "Lenny Patrick" and "Dave Yaras."
125. Hersh, *New York Times*, June 27–30, 1976.
126. *Ibid.*, June 27, 1976, p. 1.
127. *Ibid.*, June 27, 1976, p. 20.
128. *Ibid.*, June 28, 1976, p. 1.
129. *Ibid.*, June 27, 1976, p. 20.
130. *Ibid.*, June 29, 1976, p. 16.
131. 5H 200; CE 1765.
132. CE 2308; CE 1322, p. 742.
133. CE 2284.
134. *Ibid.*
135. CD 1144, pp. 5–6.
136. *Ibid.*
137. Kantor, *Who was Jack Ruby?*, p. 22.
138. CE 2243, 2284.
139. As cited in the prior note; also 5H 185–86.
140. CE 2303.
141. CE 2243, 2284; see chapter 20, "Visits of Paul Roland Jones and Al Gruber."
142. *U.S.-Senate, Kefauver Hearings*, part 5, pp. 1175–87; *U.S.-Senate, McClellan Labor Hearings*, pp. 12519–27; see chapter 7, introduction.
143. *U.S.-Senate, Kefauver Hearings*, part 5, p. 1177; *U.S.-Senate, McClellan Labor Hearings*, p. 12520.
144. As cited in the prior note.
145. As cited in the prior note; also HAH 9H 513.
146. *U.S.-Senate, Kefauver Hearings*, part 5, p. 1177.
147. CE 1184; HAH 9H 514–18.
148. CE 1184; HAH 9H 518.
149. *U.S.-Senate, Kefauver Hearings*, part 5, p. 1177; CE 1184.
150. CE 1184.
151. CE 1184, 1300.
152. As cited in the prior note.
153. CE 1184, 1708, 2980.
154. CE 1184, 1300.
155. HAH 9H 527.
156. CE 2989; HAH 9H 525; *New York Times*, January 4, 1959, p. 6.
157. HAH 9H 527–30.
158. *Dallas Morning News*, January 12, 1974, p. 1.
159. *Ibid.*
160. HAH 9H 525.
161. HAR 173; HAH 9H 529, 380–81.
162. HAH 9H 528–29.
163. HAH 9H 529.
164. CE 2988; CE 1748; CE 1752; CD 86, p. 147.
165. CE 2303; CE 2989.

166. CE 1693.
167. CD 686d, p. 2.
168. *U.S.–Senate, Kefauver Hearings*, part 2, p. 193; Reid and Demaris, pp. 184–85, 187.
169. CE 1692.
170. Reid and Demaris, p. 188; *U.S.–Senate, OC and Narcotics Hearings*, p. 891.
171. As cited in the prior note.
172. CE 1692, 1693, 1184; *U.S.–Senate, Kefauver Hearings*, part 2, p. 194; 14H 445.
173. CE 1692, 1184; *U.S.–Senate, Kefauver Hearings*, part 2, p. 194.
174. 14H 445.
175. CE 1693.
176. CE 1691; CE 1697, p. 1; HAH 5H 3.
177. *U.S.–Senate, OC and Narcotics Hearings*, p. 569; Scott, "From Dallas to Watergate," in Blumenthal and Yazijian, eds., *Government by Gunplay: Assassination Conspiracy Theories from Dallas to Today*, p. 126; *New York Times*, January 4, 1959, p. 6; Anson, *"They've Killed the President!"* p. 309.
178. CE 1691; CE 1697, p. 1.
179. *Life*, March 10, 1958, p. 33; HAH 5H 161.
180. CD 686d, p. 2.
181. CE 1690, 1691, 1697; see chapter 15, "Alignment Against Castro."
182. HAH 5H 19–20.
183. CE 1692; HAH 5H 3.
184. Wallace Turner, *Gambler's Money*, pp. 159–65, 295; Demaris, *Captive City*, p. 11.
185. CE 1692, 1544.
186. Reid, *The Grim Reapers*, p. 75.
187. Wallace Turner, pp. 240–42.
188. CE 1692; CE 1697, p. 4.
189. HAH 5H 4.
190. Wallace Turner, p. 127.
191. CE 1692; CE 1697, p. 4.
192. HAH 5H 18.
193. 5H 201; JFK microfilm, vol. 5, p. D31; CE 1697, p. 1; HAH 4H 549–50; CE 1655.
194. CE 1697, p. 1; C. Ray Hall Exhibit 3, p. 15; 5H 201.
195. 5H 201.
196. CD 5, pp. 413–14; CE 1697, p. 4; HAH 5H 33.
197. See chapter 18, "May Through July, 1963: Focus in New Orleans," "August: The West Coast and New York."
198. Sheridan, p. 292.
199. *Time*, December 10, 1973, p. 30.
200. HAH 4H 566.
201. CE 2303; CD 360, p. 149; HAH 4H 566.
202. *U.S.–Senate, OC and Narcotics Report*, p. 37; HAH 9H 943–48.
203. As cited in the prior note.
204. Demaris, pp. 348–49.
205. *Ibid.*

206. HAH 9H 948, 945; Demaris, pp. 348–49.
207. HAH 9H 942; Demaris, p. 169.
208. HAH 9H 942.
209. HAH 9H 948; HAH 4H 567.
210. Reid, *The Grim Reapers*, p. 292.
211. HAH 9H 948.
212. Demaris, pp. 348–49.
213. CE 1202.
214. *Ibid.*
215. 14H 445; see 15H 29, HAH 4H 567.
216. *U.S.-House, OC Control*, pp. 416, 434.
217. HAH 4H 565.
218. *New York Times*, February 28, 1974, p. 24.
219. CE 2303; CD 84, pp. 131–32; *U.S.-House, OC Control*, p. 434; see chapter 18, "August: The West Coast and New York," "Fall: Intensive Nationwide Contacts."
220. HAR 155; HAH 4H 565; see Appendix 1, "Background on Jack Ruby's Telephone Records."
221. Reid, *The Grim Reapers*, pp. 188, 299.
222. *Ibid.*, p. 299.
223. *Ibid.*, pp. 216, 258–59.
224. See Appendix 2, entry 18.39.
225. *U.S.-Senate, Intelligence Report, Foreign Assassinations*, pp. 75–77; HAH 10H 151.
226. HAH 10H 186.
227. Malone, "The Secret Life of Jack Ruby," *New Times*, January 23, 1978, p. 51.
228. *Ibid.*
229. Malone, in *New Times*, p. 47; WR 786–87.
230. Malone, in *New Times*, p. 51.
231. *Chicago Tribune*, April 22, 1973, p. 5; HAH 9H 1040.
232. HAH 9H 1040–42.
233. *Washington Post*, April 6, 1978, p. VA19.
234. HAH 9H 1040.
235. Demaris, pp. 64, 324.
236. HAH 4H 564; HAH 9H 1041–42; *Chicago Tribune*, April 22, 1973, p. 5.
237. HAH 9H 1041–42.
238. HAH 9H 1042.
239. *Ibid.*
240. Sheridan, pp. 137–38; HAH 9H 1041.
241. HAH 9H 1041.
242. Sheridan, p. 364.
243. HAH 9H 1042.
244. HAH 9H 1040–41.
245. See chapter 16.
246. HAH 9H 1042.
247. HAH 9H 1041.
248. *Washington Post*, January 21, 1983, p. 1.
249. Sheridan, pp. 137–38.
250. *Ibid.*

251. *New York Times*, February 20, 1974, p. 14; *Boston Globe*, January 3, 1974, p. 31; Brill, pp. 219–28; see also *Chicago Tribune*, April 22, 1973, p. 5; HAH 9H 1041.
252. As cited in the prior note.
253. Brill, pp. 252–55.
254. HAH 9H 1041; see Brill, pp. 223–28; *Wall Street Journal*, July 24, 1975; Investigative Reporters and Editors Inc., Phoenix Project (IRE series), *Albuquerque Journal*, March 15, 1977, pp. 1, 14.
255. HAH 9H 1043.
256. CE 2303.
257. CD 84, p. 229.
258. See chapter 19, "Mob Conspiracy."
259. HAH 9H 948, 961.
260. *U.S.-Senate, OC and Narcotics Report*, p. 37.
261. Demaris, p. 354.
262. *Ibid.*; HAH 4H 567.
263. *Life*, May 30, 1969, pp. 45–47.
264. *Ibid.*
265. *Ibid.*
266. Moldea, *The Hoffa Wars*, pp. 178–79.
267. *Ibid.*, p. 155.
268. *Ibid.*, pp. 123–24; *U.S.-Senate, McClellan Labor Hearings*, pp. 7416, 12522.
269. Moldea, *The Hoffa Wars*, p. 124.
270. Marcello: Meskil, *Don Carlo*, p. 137. Trafficante and Roselli: *U.S.-Senate, Intelligence Report, Foreign Assassinations*, pp. 75–77; HAH 10H 151. Hoffa: Moldea, *The Hoffa Wars*, pp. 122–23. Ruby: see chapter 16. Matthews: CE 2989; HAH 9H 525; *New York Times*, January 4, 1959, p. 6. McWillie: see chapter 9, "Lewis J. McWillie." Patrick: HAH 9H 948. Weiner: HAH 9H 1042.
271. *U.S.-Senate, McClellan Labor Hearings*, p. 12522; Moldea, *The Hoffa Wars*, p. 124.
272. Moldea, *The Hoffa Wars*, pp. 124, 42.
273. HAH 4H 567.
274. *U.S.-Senate, Kefauver Report, Third Interim*, pp. 150–60; *U.S.-Senate, Kefauver Report, Second Interim*, pp. 11, 16–17; see also Appendix 2, section 9a.
275. *U.S.-Senate, Kefauver Report, Third Interim*, pp. 153, 155, 81.
276. *Ibid.*, pp. 154–55.
277. *U.S.-Senate, McClellan Labor Hearings*, pp. 12524–25.
278. *U.S.-Senate, Kefauver Report, Third Interim*, p. 155; *U.S.-Senate, Kefauver Hearings*, part 2, p. 189.
279. Reid and Demaris, p. 25.
280. *U.S.-Senate, McClellan Labor Hearings*, p. 12525.
281. Demaris, pp. 130, 354.
282. *Ibid.*
283. Reid and Demaris, pp. 71–72.
284. *Ibid.*
285. *Ibid.*
286. *Ibid.*; *U.S.-Senate, OC and Narcotics Hearings*, p. 504.

287. Demaris, p. 130.
288. CE 1268.
289. *Ibid.*
290. *Ibid.*
291. CE 2303; see chapter 9, "Barney Baker," and chapter 18, "Fall: Intensive Nationwide Contacts."
292. CE 2332.
293. *Ibid.*
294. *Ibid.*
295. CE 1559.
296. *Ibid.*
297. *Ibid.*
298. *Ibid.*
299. *Ibid.*
300. *Ibid.*
301. 14H 340–41.
302. CE 3061, p. 627.
303. *Ibid.*
304. 14H 354.
305. 14H 353–55. For example, pursuing this line of questioning, counsel asks, "and you came to the conclusion, then, that Vito Genovese and that group of people were involved in this matter." (14H 355).
306. 14H 359; see next chapter.

Chapter 10
Jack Ruby and the Dallas Police

1. *U.S.-Senate, Gambling and OC*, p. 31.
2. *Ramparts*, May 1968, p. 27.
3. See Appendix 2, sections 19, 23–25.
4. See Appendix 2, section 21.
5. Quoted by Fred Cook, in *Two-Dollar Bet Means Murder*, p. 7.
6. Rufus King, *Gambling and Organized Crime*, p. 28.
7. Reid and Demaris, *The Green Felt Jungle*, pp. 187, 197.
8. CE 1754; HAH 9H 527–28.
9. *Dallas Morning News*, March 29, 1974.
10. CD 1102d.
11. *Dallas Morning News*, January 12, 1974.
12. HAH 9H 529.
13. Demaris, *Captive City*, pp. 257–61.
14. *Ibid.*, pp. 264–65.
15. Smith, "Corruption Behind the Swinging Clubs," *Life*, December 6, 1968, pp. 35–43.
16. *Ibid.*, p. 42.
17. CE 1693; 14H 445; CE 1692; CE 1184; HAH 5H 20–23.
18. *Dallas Morning News*, April 26, 1972, p. D1.
19. *Ibid.*

20. HAH 9H 517.
21. Reid and Demaris, chapter 10; *U.S.–Senate, Kefauver Hearings*, part 2, p. 193; HAH 9H 530.
22. HAH 9H 517.
23. *Ibid*.
24. HAH 9H 527.
25. HAH 9H 412.
26. WR 43.
27. WR 209.
28. CD86, pp. 138–39; WR 809; note that Decker was the Dallas County sheriff and that Ruby was in the Dallas County jail.
29. CE 1697.
30. WR 801.
31. CE 1535.
32. 14H 603.
33. CE 1592.
34. CE 1467.
35. CE 1228.
36. CE 1615.
37. CE 1632.
38. CE 1624.
39. CE 1659.
40. CE 1735.
41. WR 801.
42. CE 1322, p. 750.
43. CE 1322, p. 748.
44. CE 1322, p. 741.
45. CE 1322, p. 735.
46. CE 1322, p. 736.
47. JFK microfilm, vol. 5, pp. R35–38.
48. *Ibid*.
49. *Ibid*.
50. *Ibid*.
51. JFK microfilm, vol. 5, p. R32.
52. Demaris, p. 115.
53. JFK microfilm, vol. 5, p. R32.
54. CE 1636.
55. CE 1515.
56. CE 1659.
57. CE 1657.
58. CE 1649.
59. CE 1646, 1615, 1632.
60. CE 1659.
61. 14H 341.
62. *Ibid*.
63. CE 1505.
64. CE 1624, 1632, 1636, 1696; JFK microfilm, vol. 5, pp. C7–9.
65. CE 1515.
66. CE 1659.
67. *Ibid*.

68. *Ibid.*
69. *Ibid.*
70. CE 1652.
71. CE 1646.
72. *Ibid.*
73. CE 1696.
74. CD 5, pp. 413–14.
75. Alice Nichols Exhibit 5355; CE 1227; CE 2887; C. Ray Hall Exhibit 3, p. 16; CE 1745; Sam Ruby Exhibit 1; CE 2392; CD 84, p. 106.
76. CD 302, pp. 128–29.
77. CE 1612.
78. CE 1184; *Dallas Times Herald*, November 25, 1963, p. 24A; *Austin* (Texas) *American*, November 25, 1963, p. 8; CE 2980.
79. WR 804–5.
80. CE 1184, p. 29; *Austin* (Texas) *American*, November 25, 1963, p. 8; *Dallas Morning News*, November 25, 1963, section 4, p. 1; CE 1543; CE 1651; CD 104, p. 64.
81. CE 1756.
82. CE 1300.
83. CE 1684.
84. CE 1561.
85. CE 2980, p. 4.
86. CE 1672.
87. *Ibid.*
88. *Ibid.*
89. *Ibid.*
90. CD 4, p. 533.
91. *Ibid.*
92. 14H 343.
93. 14H 358.
94. *Ibid.*
95. CE 1543.
96. CE 1528.
97. *Ibid.*
98. *Ibid.*
99. CE 1518.
100. CE 2980.
101. CE 1608; CE 1528.
102. CE 1608.
103. JFK microfilm, vol. 5, p. D25.
104. CE 1610.
105. *Ibid.*
106. CE 1611, 1612.
107. JFK microfilm, vol. 5, p. B1.
108. CE 1517.
109. CE 1515.
110. See chapter 12, "At the Dallas Police Building," chapter 20, "You probably don't know me, but you will."
111. 14H 359.
112. CD 4, p. 529. Al Bright, who reported this assertion by Ryan, also re-

ported Ryan had told him that Ruby was friendly with Jimmy Hoffa (*ibid*.); Ryan denied this, too (CE 1229). Supporting Bright, however, is a recent statement by Hoffa's son, James Hoffa, Jr.: "I think my dad knew Jack Ruby, but from what I understand, he [Ruby] was the kind of guy everybody knew. So what?" [Anthony Summers, *Conspiracy* (New York: McGraw-Hill, 1980), p. 472].

113. CE 1229.
114. Crafard Exhibit 5226; CD 84, p. 152; CE 1322, pp. 727, 773; CE 1567; CD 722, pp. 3–5; 14H 14–15; 13H 370–71; CE 2322.
115. CE 2322.
116. 15H 418.
117. *Ibid*.
118. *Ibid*.
119. CE 2322; 13H 370–71.
120. CD 722, p. 3.
121. CE 1753.
122. CE 1750.
123. CE 1763.
124. See Appendix 2, section 20a.

Chapter 11
Jack Ruby, Mobster

1. *Time*, December 19, 1977, pp. 18, 23.
2. HAH 3H 494.
3. See chapter 6, "The Fine Reports of Ruby's Chicago Friends.'"
4. CE 1322, pp. 725–26; Rossi Exhibit 1.
5. CE 1672.
6. CE 1184; *Dallas Times Herald*, November 25, 1963, p. 24A; *Austin* (Texas) *American*, November 25, 1963, p. 8; CE 2980.
7. CE 1322, pp. 746–47.
8. CD 86, pp. 279–80.
9. 14H 605–7, 611–12; 14H 602.
10. 14H 617.
11. CD 86, pp. 278–80.
12. CE 1505.
13. CE 1753.
14. C. Ray Hall Exhibit 3, p. 16; CE 1772; CD 86, p. 273.
15. 13H 428.
16. JFK microfilm, vol. 5, p. B10.
17. 13H 318.
18. CE 1469.
19. CE 1322, p. 754. The first page was evidently included since the copy bore a mailing label (*ibid*.).
20. *Wall Street Journal*, November 18, 1963, p. 1.
21. CE 1322, p. 755.
22. *New York Mirror*, September 8, 1963, p. 11.

23. *Ibid.*
24. *Dallas Morning News*, November 25, 1963, p. 7. The sum of $256.80 was found, according to police accounting (CE 1322, pp. 762–63).
25. CE 1322, pp. 725–26.
26. CE 2417, p. 260.
27. CE 1567.
28. CD 86, p. 486.
29. CD 86, p. 488.
30. 15H 477–78.
31. CE 1271; CE 1237.
32. Demaris, *Captive City*, p. 119.
33. CE 1318.
34. WR 788.
35. WR 798–99.
36. Messick, *Lansky*, p. 182.
37. *Ibid.*
38. "The Mafia v. America," *Time*, August 22, 1969, pp. 21–22.
39. Messick, *Lansky*, pp. 222–23, 253–54.
40. *Ibid.*, pp. 180–83.
41. Teresa, *My Life in the Mafia*, pp. 125–26.
42. *Ibid.*, p. 130.
43. Reid, *The Grim Reapers*, p. 151.
44. WR 355.
45. CD 86, p. 486.
46. CD 86, p. 488.
47. CE 1322, pp. 732, 757.
48. 13H 213; CD 4, p. 612.
49. C. Ray Hall Exhibit 3, p. 16; CD 86, p. 488.
50. C. Ray Hall Exhibit 3, p. 16; CE 1753.
51. CE 1753.
52. *Ibid.*
53. CE 1625–27.
54. CE 1584, 1753; C. Ray Hall Exhibit 3, p. 16.
55. CE 1772; C. Ray Hall Exhibit 3, p. 16.
56. CE 1559.
57. CE 1586, 1588–89, 1600–1601; CD 86, p. 459.
58. CE 1521–26; CD 84, pp. 131, 219–20.
59. CE 3063; CE 3065; see chapter 16, "Arms Shipments from Florida in the 1950s."
60. C. Ray Hall Exhibit 3, p. 15; 15H 201, 205; CE 1697, pp. 1–2; see chapter 16, "Dealings and Travels in 1959."
61. Sam Yaras: *U.S.–Senate, McClellan Labor Hearings*, p. 12522; CE 1268.
62. Nick DeJohn, Paul Labriola and Jimmy Weinberg: *U.S.–Senate, McClellan Labor Hearings*, p. 12524.
63. Danny Lardino: *ibid.*, p. 12526. Marcus Lipsky: *ibid.*, p. 12520; Demaris, p. 245. Paul Roland Jones: CE 1184.
64. CE 1251.
65. *U.S.–Senate, OC and Narcotics Hearings*, p. 1098; *U.S.–Senate, McClellan Labor Hearings*, p. 12196.
66. CE 1708; CE 2980; See chapter 8, "Narcotics."

67. CE 1761.
68. See Appendix 2, section 9.
69. Reid, *The Grim Reapers*, chapters 2–5; see Appendix 2, section 5.
70. Messick, *Lansky*, passim; Reid, *The Grim Reapers*, pp. 223–24; Reid, *Mickey Cohen: Mobster*, passim; George Carpozi, Jr., *Bugsy* (New York: Pinnacle, 1973), passim.
71. See Appendix 2, section 5.
72. Teresa, pp. 216–17; see Messick, *Lansky*.
73. Teresa, pp. 216–17.
74. Reid, *The Grim Reapers*, p. 316.
75. 14H 566.

Part III
Murder on Cue

1. WR 208, 16.
2. WR 354, 357.
3. 5H 199; 13H 204–5, 211–12; CE 2298.
4. WR 354, 357.
5. WR 209–16.
6. *Ibid*.
7. *Ibid*.
8. 13H 7, 17; WR 216; 4H 233.
9. 13H 28–29.
10. 13H 17.
11. WR 216.
12. C. Ray Hall Exhibit 2; C. Ray Hall Exhibit 3; 5H 181–213.
13. CE 2298.
14. WR 354, 357.
15. *Ibid*.
16. Buchanan, *Who Killed Kennedy?* (London: Secker and Warburg, 1964), p. 137. See Buchanan (New York: Putnam, 1964), p. 150.
17. Malone, "The Secret Life of Jack Ruby," *New Times*, January 23, 1978, p. 51; Jack Anderson, *Albuquerque Journal*, September 8, 1976.
18. See chapter 3, "Johnny Roselli and George DeMohrenschilt."
19. 5H 206.

Chapter 12
Perjury and Premeditation

1. Buchanan, *Who Killed Kennedy?*, British edition, p. 25.
2. C. Ray Hall Exhibit 2; C. Ray Hall Exhibit 3; 5H 181–213; see text below.
3. 5H 184–85; C. Ray Hall Exhibit 3, p. 4.
4. 5H 207; C. Ray Hall Exhibit 3, p. 5.

5. Kantor Exhibit 7.
6. Kantor Exhibit 8.
7. 15H 71–96.
8. Kantor Exhibit 7, 8; 15H 71–96.
9. 15H 72.
10. Kantor Exhibit 8.
11. 15H 88; see also Kantor Exhibit 8.
12. Kantor Exhibit 7.
13. 15H 392–94.
14. HAR 158.
15. WR 340–42.
16. *Ibid.*; 5H 188–89. Ruby later explained that he had gone to the police station that night to get the unlisted "hot line" number of the newsroom at radio station KLIF, so he could bring sandwiches to the employees there (5H 187–88; C. Ray Hall Exhibit 3, p. 6). Yet that telephone number (RI7–9319) appeared on two lists found on Ruby after he shot Oswald (CE 1322; pp. 727, 729; see 15H 437, Dowe Exhibit 1 for an identification of that number). On both, the number was followed by several names and phone numbers of people whom Ruby had contacted before November 22. In particular, in the first list (CE 2308; CE 1322, p. 729), following the KLIF entry, were the name and Minneapolis address of Smokey Turner, whom Ruby called in Minneapolis on November 16 (CE 2302), and the name and address of Connie Trammel, whom he saw on November 21 (CE 2270). In the second list (CE 1322, pp. 729–30), following the KLIF entry, were the names and numbers of Joe Severeign, Frank Goldstein and Irv Mazzei, whom Ruby called at the listed numbers respectively on July 18 (CE 2308; CE 1322, p. 729), November 12 (CE 2303), and November 9 (CE 2303), 1963.
17. Eberhardt Exhibit 5026.
18. 13H 187; Eberhardt Exhibit 5026.
19. 15H 615.
20. *Ibid.*
21. *Ibid.*
22. Robertson Exhibit 1.
23. 15H 348–51.
24. *Ibid.*
25. CE 2249, p. 14.
26. Jenkins Exhibit 1; National Archives, entry 45, Ruby-Oswald chronology, pp. 844–47.
27. CE 2276.
28. JFK microfilm, vol. 5, p. D28.
29. 15H 588–89.
30. *Ibid.*
31. 15H 356–57.
32. *Ibid.*
33. CE 2326.
34. CE 2327.
35. National Archives, entry 45, Ruby-Oswald chronology, pp. 844–47.
36. 5H 187–88; C. Ray Hall Exhibit 3, pp. 5–10.
37. Robertson Exhibit 2.

38. 15H 487–88.
39. 15H 257.
40. 15H 477–78.
41. C. Ray Hall Exhibit 3, p. 12.
42. 5H 185.
43. C. Ray Hall Exhibit 2, p. 14.
44. 5H 198.
45. C. Ray Hall Exhibit 2, pp. 14–15.
46. *Ibid.*
47. *Ibid.*; 5H 198–99.
48. HAR 158.
49. *Newsweek*, March 27, 1967, p. 21; HAR 158; Blakey and Billings, *The Plot to Kill the President*, p. 333.
50. CE 1753.
51. *Ibid.*
52. CE 1245.
53. CE 1184.
54. 5H 198.
55. *Ibid.*
56. *Ibid.*
57. 14H 564.
58. *Ibid.*
59. *Ibid.*
60. 14H 567.
61. CE 2161.
62. C. Ray Hall Exhibit 3, p. 8.
63. *Ibid.*
64. Ruby, disc jockey Russ Knight and another KLIF employee conflict sharply on how Ruby got into the newsroom that night. Ruby testified that he came into KLIF with disc jockey Russ Knight (5H 190; C. Ray Hall Exhibit 3, p. 8). This account was confirmed by KLIF employee Glen Duncan, who testified that he saw Ruby enter the newsroom with Knight (15H 486). Yet Knight testified that Ruby arrived at KLIF about 15 or 20 minutes after Knight, and that Knight was with Glen Duncan when Ruby came in (15H 256–57). Still another KLIF employee reported that he was the one who let Ruby into the station (McCurdy Exhibit 1; 15H 532). Also see below.
65. McCurdy of KLIF testified that Ruby "spent the majority of the time in the newsroom with our newsman, Glen Duncan, . . . and also a gentleman named Pappas" (15H 529–30). Also note that Pappas testified that he spent all of his time at KLIF in the newsroom (15H 366), and three KLIF employees placed Ruby in the newsroom during most of his visit (15H 257–58, 261, 486, 529–30; see also 5H 190). And Russ Knight testified that Ruby listened in on a conversation between himself and Pappas (15H 257–58, 261). But Pappas, who had met Ruby briefly at the midnight news conference, (15H 364–65) emphatically denied that Ruby was in the KLIF newsroom while he was there (15H 365).
66. Ruby was well-acquainted with Gordon McLendon (C. Ray Hall Exhibit 1; HAH 5H 87, 172), the owner of KLIF and many other radio stations throughout the United States (C. Ray Hall Exhibit 1; HAH 5H 172; Sheri-

dan, *The Fall and Rise of Jimmy Hoffa*, p. 503). McLendon gave Ruby "a lot of free plugs," Ruby reported (5H 187), and Ruby called McLendon's home the night of the assassination (5H 188). According to government witness Ed Partin, radio magnate McLendon was later named by Marcello associate D'Alton Smith as someone lined up to assist the Mob's spring-Hoffa campaign (Sheridan, p. 503; for background on Smith see Sheridan, p. 492). Ruby's ties to KLIF personnel were also demonstrated by more than a dozen entries of their names and phone numbers in documents found among his possessions (CE 1322, pp. 727, 730, 735–37, 771; Andrew Armstrong Exhibit 5305-K). Of particular interest was the phone number of Ruby's friend (15H 530. The number was DA1–0467), Russ "Knight" Moore (CE 1322, p. 727), the KLIF disc jockey, written on the back of an envelope found in Ruby's pocket when he shot Oswald (CE 1322, p. 730). The other notation on the back of that envelope was the name, address, and phone number of Thomas Hill of Belmont, Massachusetts, a John Birch Society official (*ibid.*; CE 2980, p. 12).

67. C. Ray Hall Exhibit 3, p. 8.
68. 5H 194.
69. 14H 631, 633, 646–48.
70. 14H 646–48.
71. 14H 631, 633, 646–48.
72. 14H 631–32.
73. CE 2418.
74. *Ibid.*
75. *Ibid.*
76. *Ibid.*
77. 5H 191.
78. *Ibid.*
79. 5H 193.
80. CE 23 18.
81. 14H 631.
82. CE 2418.
83. 14H 629–30.
84. *Ibid.*
85. *Ibid.*
86. 14H 645–46.
87. *Ibid.*
88. 14H 630–31 vs. 14H 646; 14H 635 vs. 14H 649.
89. 14H 635, 645, 649.
90. 14H 635, 649.
91. C. Ray Hall Exhibit 3, p. 5.
92. 14H 636–37.
93. *Ibid.*
94. 14H 650.
95. 14H 650–51.
96. 14H 635–36, 650.
97. 15H 214; 14H 653.
98. 14H 653.
99. 15H 214.
100. *Ibid.*

101. 14H 653; 14H 634.
102. 14H 637.
103. 14H 626, 642, 653.
104. C. Ray Hall Exhibit 3, p. 8; 5H 193.
105. C. Ray Hall Exhibit 3, pp. 8-9; Crafard Exhibit 5226; 5H 203; 13H 463-66, 504; 14H 219, 220, 324.
106. C. Ray Hall Exhibit 3, p. 8.
107. As cited in note 105.
108. 14H 219-20 vs. 13H 463-66, 504, and Crafard Exhibit 5226; 13H 251-52 vs. 13H 463 and Crafard Exhibit 5226.
109. C. Ray Hall Exhibit 3, pp. 8-9; 5H 203; 14H 324.
110. 14H 233; Senator Exhibit 5401, p. 3.
111. Senator Exhibit 5401, p. 3.
112. Senator Exhibit 5400.
113. 14H 300-303.
114. *Ibid.*
115. CE 1322, p. 725.
116. Senator Exhibit 5401.
117. CD 360, p. 132; JFK microfilm, vol. 5, p. R83; National Archives, entry 45, Ruby-Oswald chronology, p. 851.
118. Reid and Demaris, *The Green Felt Jungle*, p. 188; also note the employment at the Southland Hotel of Mobsters Lester Binion and Lewis McWillie (CE 1692).
119. Reid and Demaris, p. 188.
120. WR 371-72.
121. HAH 9H 985-88.
122. 14H 256; 14H 256-57.
123. 14H 257.
124. *Ibid.*
125. CE 3024, p. 5.
126. *Ibid.*, p. 6.
127. Jones, *Forgive My Grief*, vol. I, p. 5.
128. 14H 256-59.
129. 13H 468-69; 14H 39-40; Crafard Exhibit 5226.
130. Crafard Exhibit 5226.
131. 5H 206.
132. 13H 17, 28-29.
133. CE 2341.
134. *Ibid.*
135. 15H 490-91.
136. *Ibid.*
137. *Ibid.*
138. 15H 433-34.
139. *Ibid.*
140. See notes 64-66.
141. Dowe Exhibits 1, 2; 15H 432-34.
142. Dowe Exhibit 2.
143. 15H 432.
144. 15H 491.
145. 15H 397-98.

146. CE 2302, p. 15; WR 358, 795.
147. 15H 397–98.
148. 15H 398–99.
149. 15H 399.
150. *Ibid.*
151. 15H 402.
152. C. Ray Hall Exhibit 3, pp. 11–12; C. Ray Hall Exhibit 2, p. 16.
153. C. Ray Hall Exhibit 3, p. 7; WR 356–57.
154. C. Ray Hall Exhibit 2, p. 16.
155. C. Ray Hall Exhibit 3, p. 7.
156. 5H 205.
157. 5H 207–8.
158. 13H 311–12, 343–44; 14H 83–85; 14H 147; Wright Exhibit 1; CE 1623.

Chapter 13
Conspiracy

1. 14H 567.
2. 15H 620.
3. See chapter 13, "A $5 Loan to Karen Carlin."
4. WR 353.
5. 13H 206–7.
6. See chapter 8, "Prostitution and Other Criminal Activities."
7. 15H 216; JFK microfilm, vol. 5, pp. B9, B17, D30.
8. 13H 206.
9. 15H 619–20.
10. *Ibid.*
11. *Ibid.*
12. *Ibid.*
13. *Ibid.*
14. JFK microfilm, vol. 5, p. B17.
15. 15H 660.
16. Sybil Leek and Bert Sager, *The Assassination Chain* (New York: Corwin, 1976), p. 206; "Houston Hotel" in the source.
17. CD 722, p. 7.
18. 13H 202.
19. JFK microfilm, vol. 5, p. D30.
20. JFK microfilm, vol. 5, p. B17.
21. *Ibid.*; CE 2313, p. 264.
22. 15H 427.
23. 15H 216.
24. *Ibid.*
25. CE 2313.
26. 15H 642–43.
27. CD 722, p. 7.
28. 15H 642–44.
29. 15H 643.

30. *Ibid*.
31. 15H 643–47.
32. 15H 646; 13H 209.
33. 15H 643–44; see WR 42 concerning JFK trip to Houston.
34. 15H 642–43.
35. 15H 643–44.
36. CE 2313.
37. *Ibid*.
38. 15H 661.
39. HAH 1H 55–56.
40. See text below.
41. 13H 209.
42. 13H 209–10.
43. *Ibid*.
44. *Ibid*.
45. 13H 210–11; 15H 663.
46. As cited in the prior note.
47. 13H 209.
48. 13H 208.
49. Armstrong Exhibit 5310G.
50. 13H 505.
51. 13H 333.
52. 13H 334.
53. 13H 209.
54. Karen Carlin Exhibit 5318.
55. *Ibid*.
56. 13H 210, 245–46; 15H 651; CE 2334.
57. CE 2334.
58. *Ibid*.
59. *Ibid*.; 13H 247.
60. 13H 246.
61. 15H 423.
62. 15H 421–24, 653.
63. 15H 423–24.
64. 15H 423.
65. *Ibid*.
66. C. Ray Hall Exhibit 3, p. 10.
67. 13H 209.
68. 13H 333.
69. 15H 335.
70. 15H 423.
71. *Ibid*.
72. C. Ray Hall Exhibit 2, p. 13.
73. 15H 423.
74. 15H 411, 424.
75. WR 358.
76. See chapter 12, "Planning the Oswald Killing."
77. 15H 335.
78. 13H 248.
79. 13H 244–45, 249.

80. 15H 335.
81. *Ibid.*
82. 15H 335; 14H 455–56.
83. 15H 335.
84. *Ibid.*
85. CE 2298. The phone numbers, respectively, were JE4–8525 and WH1–5601.
86. 13H 204–5, 211–12; 5H 199.
87. 14H 236–40.
88. C. Ray Hall Exhibit 3, pp. 10–11; 5H 199.
89. As cited in the prior note.
90. Senator Exhibit 5401, pp. 3–4.
91. *Ibid.*
92. *Ibid.*
93. 13H 292–95.
94. 13H 293.
95. *Ibid.*
96. 13H 295.
97. As noted in 13H 295.
98. 13H 256–58.
99. *Ibid.*
100. *Ibid.*
101. 13H 279–84.
102. *Ibid.*
103. 13H 282.
104. 13H 283.
105. *Ibid.*
106. CD 85, pp. 501, 517.
107. CD 85, p. 502.
108. *Ibid.* In typically lame fashion, the Warren Commission attempted to dismiss the three crewmen's observations. First, it noted that neither saw Ruby "for an extended period" or "on a previous occasion" (WR 352), rather stringent criteria that it never applied to purported identifications of Oswald (i.e., WR 62–64, 143–46, 166–71). Second, it claimed that "Richey described Ruby as wearing a grayish overcoat," but "Ruby did not own an overcoat" (WR 352). In fact, witnesses described Ruby carrying (15H 488) and wearing (15H 508) an overcoat during the assassination weekend. And an overcoat was indeed appropriate for the 32-degree temperature at 8 a.m. Sunday [CE 2415. Ruby apparently discarded his overcoat in the late morning, when the temperature reached 48 degrees (*ibid.*)]. Third, the Commission related that Smith had described Ruby as "unkempt," but Ruby was characteristically well-groomed (WR 352), and "Senator testified that Ruby shaved and dressed before leaving their apartment that morning" (*Ibid.*). It failed to recall, however, that Ruby had scurried around Dallas the preceding two days with virtually no sleep (see chapter 12) and that it had itself found Senator an unreliable witness (WR 371–72). Finally, the Commission mentioned a man near the TV van "who might have been mistaken for Ruby" (WR 353). But the photo on which this assertion is based shows a man of little resemblance to Ruby (CE 3072. See Meagher, *Accessories After The Fact*, pp. 449–51).

109. 12H 75–79.
110. *Ibid.*
111. *Ibid.* For example, Revill introduced the matter of Rushing's visit with the remark, "by the way, he rode up on the elevator with Jack **Ruby**" (*ibid.*).
112. 12H 75–79.
113. 13H 230–31.
114. *Ibid.*
115. *Ibid.*
116. 13H 231.
117. *Ibid.*
118. CE 2002, p. 73.
119. *Ibid.*
120. CD 85, p. 271.
121. *Ibid.*
122. *Ibid.*
123. ABC-TV newsreel no. 9145, Dallas, November 24, 1963, cited by Mark Lane, in *Rush to Judgment*, p. 216.
124. CD 85, p. 480.
125. CD 85, p. 484.
126. *Ibid.*
127. CD 85, p. 483.
128. CD 84, p. 88.
129. *Ibid.*
130. *Ibid.*
131. 15H 350–51; CE 2249, p. 14; see chapter 12, "At the Dallas Police Building."
132. CD 84, p. 89.
133. WR 43.
134. WR 209.
135. CD 86, pp. 138–39; WR 809; note that Decker was the Dallas County sheriff and that Ruby was in the Dallas County jail.
136. HAH 9H 517.
137. HAH 9H 412, 527.
138. Blakey and Billings, *The Plot to Kill the President*, p. 322.
139. See chapter 12, "An Encounter with Dallas Policeman Harry Olsen."
140. *Ibid.*
141. 12H 432–33; See C. Ray Hall Exhibit 2 and Hall Exhibit 3, p. 11.
142. Blakey and Billings, p. 322.
143. *Ibid.*
144. *Ibid.*
145. 5H 206.
146. 14H 567.

Chapter 14
Jack Ruby's Startling Testimony

1. 5H 190.
2. 5H 194.

3. 5H 196.
4. 5H 211.
5. CE 1528.
6. *U.S.-Senate, Kefauver Hearings*, part 5, p. 1177; *U.S.-Senate, McClellan Labor Hearings*, p. 12520.
7. See chapter 9, "Dave Yaras."
8. John Kaplan and Jon Waltz, *The Trial of Jack Ruby* (New York: Macmillan, 1965), p. 20.
9. C. Ray Hall Exhibit 2.
10. *Ibid.*
11. *Ibid.*
12. *Ibid.*
13. C. Ray Hall Exhibit 3.
14. Meagher, *Accessories After the Fact*, p. 452.
15. 5H 190, 197.
16. 5H 181.
17. 5H 183–91, 193–94, 197–200; C. Ray Hall Exhibit 3.
18. 5H 182.
19. 5H 182–91, 193–94, 197–200.
20. 5H 207.
21. *Ibid.*
22. 5H 185.
23. 5H 192.
24. 5H 198.
25. 5H 199.
26. 5H 190.
27. *Ibid.*
28. *Ibid.*
29. 5H 191.
30. 5H 192.
31. 5H 194, see p. 193.
32. 5H 194.
33. *Ibid.*
34. *Ibid.*
35. C. Ray Hall Exhibit 3.
36. Reid, *Mickey Cohen: Mobster*, p. 103.
37. HAH 9H 1051, 1073–74, 1078, 1061, 1044; 14H 473, 400–403.
38. CE 1507.
39. HAH 9H 1050, 1078, 1044; CE 1507.
40. 5H 194.
41. 5H 195.
42. *Ibid.*
43. 5H 195–96.
44. 5H 196–97.
45. 5H 198.
46. 5H 209–13.
47. 5H 208.
48. 5H 210–13; see also 14H 531, 546.
49. 5H 210.
50. 5H 211–13.

51. HAH 10H 201.
52. HAH 10H 199.
53. CD 86, p. 558; see chapter 9, "Frank Chavez."
54. CD 86, p. 558.
55. See chapter 3, "Roger Craig."
56. *Ibid.*
57. See chapter 3, "Three Journalists."
58. *Ibid.*
59. 14H 256–57; see chapter 3, "Three Journalists" and chapter 12, "A Photography Excursion."
60. See chapter 12, "An Encounter with Dallas Policeman Harry Olsen" and "A Photography Excursion" and chapter 13, "The Carlins."
61. 15H 619–20.
62. See chapter 13, "The Carlins."
63. *U.S.-Senate, Kefauver Report, Third Interim*, p. 128.
64. Reid, *The Grim Reapers*, pp. 32–33; see chapter 15, "The CIA and the Mafia."
65. Pantaleone, *The Mafia and Politics*, pp. 155–57.
66. *Newsweek*, November 28, 1977, p. 66.
67. NBC Evening News, "Segment 3," December 16, 1977.
68. CD 86, p. 138.
69. HAH 9H 517.
70. *Houston Post*, April 20, 1975, p. 2A; see chapter 9, "Joseph Campisi."
71. CE 2259; CD 86, pp. 138–39.
72. See chapter 17.
73. 5H 181, 190, 197.
74. 5H 192, 197, 210.
75. 5H 192.
76. 5H 196–97.
77. CE 2980.
78. *Ibid.*
79. *Ibid.*
80. *Ibid.*
81. *Ibid.*
82. See chapter 18.
83. *Ibid.*
84. 5H 181–213.
85. 5H 193–98.
86. See WR 345–52.
87. WR 345–52.
88. 5H 198.
89. 5H 181–213.
90. 5H 190, 192, 193.
91. 5H 197.
92. 5H 194–95.
93. 5H 198.
94. *Ibid.*
95. 5H 199.
96. *Ibid.*
97. 5H 196.

98. *Ibid.*
99. 5H 197.
100. HAH 3H 622.
101. George O'Toole, "The Assassination Tapes," *Penthouse*, June 1973, pp. 45ff.
102. *Ibid.*
103. *Ibid.*
104. *TV Guide*, April 8, 1978, p. A5.
105. O'Toole, in *Penthouse*, June 1973, pp. 45ff.
106. *Ibid.*
107. *Ibid.*
108. *Ibid.*
109. *Ibid.*
110. 5H 212.
111. 5H 181, 182, 190, 191, 193, 196, 211–13.
112. 5H 211.
113. 5H 212.
114. 5H 213.
115. 5H 212.
116. CE 2728.
117. *Ibid.*
118. CE 3062, 3061.
119. CE 2728.
120. Meagher, pp. 452–53.
121. CE 2729.
122. CE 2730.
123. WR 808.
124. *Ibid.*
125. *Ibid.*
126. *Ibid.*
127. 14H 504.
128. 5H 181.
129. HAR 159.
130. 14H 565–67.
131. 14H 567.
132. See chapter 12, "Not Grieving" and chapter 14, "Would you rather I just delete what I said and just pretend that nothing is going on?"
133. 5H 206.
134. 14H 543.
135. *Ibid.*
136. 14H 548.
137. 14H 565.
138. *Ibid.*
139. 14H 566.
140. *Ibid.*
141. Meagher, pp. 452–53.
142. *Ibid.*
143. Sylvia Meagher, *Subject Index to the Warren Report and Hearings and Exhibits* (New York: Scarecrow Press, 1966).
144. Meagher, *Accessories After the Fact*, pp. 452–53.

145. British Broadcasting Company (BBC), Panorama special, "The Kennedy Assassination: What Do We Know Now That We Didn't Then," March 1978.
146. *Ibid*.
147. *Ibid*.
148. *Ibid*.
149. *Ibid*.
150. 14H 565.
151. 14H 566.
152. 14H 543.
153. 5H 211.
154. 14H 566.

Part IV
Pilgrims and Pirates

1. G. Robert Blakey and Richard N. Billings, "An Expert's Theory," *Parade*, November 16, 1980, pp. 5–6; Carl Oglesby and Jeff Goldberg, "Did the Mob Kill Kennedy?" *Washington Post*, February 25, 1979, pp. B1, B4; "Hints of the Mob," *Newsweek*, October 9, 1978, pp. 44, 47; William Scott Malone, "The Secret Life of Jack Ruby," *New Times*, January 23, 1978, pp. 46–51; *Time*, January 10, 1977, p. 17; George Crile III, "The Mafia, the CIA, and Castro," *Washington Post*, May 16, 1976, pp. C1, C4; Milton Viorst, "The Mafia, the CIA, and the Kennedy Assassination," *Washingtonian*, November 1975, pp. 113–18; Robert Anson, *"They've Killed the President!"* pp. 327–28; Peter Noyes, *Legacy of Doubt*, pp. 222–28; Dan Moldea, *The Hoffa Wars*, chapter 8.
2. See Appendix 2, section 7.
3. Reid, *Grim Reapers*, p. 6.
4. See Appendix 2, section 8.
5. See Appendix 2, section 18.
6. Noyes, *Legacy of Doubt*, p. 34; Demaris, *Captive City*, pp. 61–63; *Los Angeles Times*, May 31, 1973, p. 22.
7. See Appendix 2, section 17c.
8. See Appendix 2, section 25, and chapters 17, 22, 23 of text.

Chapter 15
The Anti-Castro Coalition

1. Anson, *"They've Killed the President!"* p. 327.
2. See chapter 1, "The Shooting of UAW President Walter Reuther" and chapter 15, "Alignment Against Castro," "The CIA and the Mafia."
3. Scott, "From Dallas to Watergate," in Blumenthal and Yazijian, eds.,

Government by Gunplay: Assassination Conspiracy Theories from Dallas to Today, p. 114; HAH 10H 7–8.

4. Wise and Ross, *The Invisible Government*, pp. 35–36, 185.
5. *Ibid.*, p. 36.
6. *Ibid.*, pp. 39, 67–70.
7. *Ibid.*, pp. 67–70, 188–89.
8. HAH 1H 3, 9; Anson, pp. 269–70, 278.
9. Cited in Anson, p. 269.
10. Wise and Ross, pp. 184–86.
11. Taylor Branch and George Crile III, "The Kennedy Vendetta," *Harper's*, August 1975, p. 50; see also HAH 1H 6.
12. Harry Ransom, "Containing Central Intelligence," *New Republic*, December 11, 1965, p. 13, cited in Scott, "The Death of Kennedy and the Vietnam War," in Blumenthal and Yazijian, p. 166.
13. HAH 1H 7; HAH 10H 12; Wise and Ross, pp. 297–98; Khrushchev, *Khrushchev Remembers*, p. 553.
14. HAH 10H 3, 12–13; Anson, p. 265.
15. HAH 10H 13; Scott, "The Death of Kennedy and the Vietnam War," in Blumenthal and Yazijian, p. 161.
16. Anson, p. 270.
17. *U.S.–Senate, Intelligence Report, Foreign Assassinations*, pp. 173–74; *U.S.–Senate, Intelligence Report, JFK Assassination*, p. 20; William Attwood, *The Reds and the Blacks* (London: Hutchinson, 1967), pp. 142–44.
18. Schlesinger, *A Thousand Days*, pp. 959, 962–63; see also HAH 1H 8.
19. Schlesinger, *A Thousand Days*, pp. 972–73.
20. *Ibid.*, pp. 900–901; see also HAH 1H 7.
21. Scott, "The Death of Kennedy and the Vietnam War," in Blumenthal and Yazijian, p. 159.
22. *Ibid.*
23. Schlesinger, *A Thousand Days*, p. 920.
24. *Business Week*, November 23, 1963, p. 41; Scott, "The Death of Kennedy and the Vietnam War," in Blumenthal and Yazijian, p. 159.
25. Scott, "The Death of Kennedy and the Vietnam War," in Blumenthal and Yazijian, p. 159.
26. *Business Week*, November 23, 1963, p. 41.
27. Anson, p. 16.
28. Dorman, *Payoff*, pp. 254–55.
29. *Ibid.*
30. *Ibid.*
31. *Time*, March 6, 1978, p. 21.
32. *Ibid.*
33. See "James Osticco" in *U.S.–Senate, McClellan Labor Hearings*, p. 12199.
34. Joesten, *Oswald, Assassin or Fall Guy?*, p. 149.
35. O'Donnell and Powers, *Johnny We Hardly Knew Ye*, p. 16.
36. *Public Papers of the Presidents*, John F. Kennedy, 1963 (U.S. Government Printing Office, 1964), pp. 759–60.
37. *Ibid.*
38. *Ibid.*, p. 828.

39. Scott, "The Death of Kennedy and the Vietnam War," in Blumenthal and Yazijian, pp. 153–54.
40. Manchester, *Death of a President*, p. 46.
41. *Ibid.*
42. Joachim Joesten, *The Case Against Lyndon Johnson in the Assassination of President Kennedy* (Munich: Dreischstr. 5, Selbstverlag, 1967), p. 9.
43. UPI, Dallas, December 20, 1963, cited in Joesten, *Oswald: Assassin or Fall Guy?*, p. 150.
44. *Ibid.*
45. WR 298.
46. *Ibid.*
47. WR 292–97.
48. WR 296–97.
49. HAH 5H 258, 295–96.
50. *Ibid.*, p. 296.
51. *Ibid.*
52. *Ibid.*
53. *Ibid.*
54. *Life*, March 10, 1958, pp. 32ff; Jack Anderson, "How Castro Double-Crossed the Gambling Syndicate," *Parade*, April 28, 1963, pp. 4–5; *New York Times*, January 4, 1959, p. 6; Salerno and Tompkins, *The Crime Confederation*, p. 386; Anson, p. 313.
55. Meskil, *Don Carlo*, p. 137.
56. Moldea, *The Hoffa Wars*, p. 87.
57. *The Two Kennedys*, an Italian documentary film, shown at the Orson Welles Theatre, Cambridge, Mass., March 14, 1976.
58. Moldea, *The Hoffa Wars*, pp. 122–23.
59. See Dorman, *Payoff*, p. 101; see also Moldea, *The Hoffa Wars*, p. 122.
60. Crile, "The Mafia, the CIA, and Castro," *Washington Post*, May 16, 1976, p. C4; Anson, pp. 312–13; see also Moldea, *The Hoffa Wars*, p. 122.
61. Moldea, pp. 122–23.
62. Anson, pp. 312–13; Crile, "The Mafia, the CIA, and Castro," *Washington Post*, May 16, 1976, pp. C1, C4.
63. HAH 5H 296; *Time*, March 2, 1959, pp. 22, 25; Malone, "The Secret Life of Jack Ruby," *New Times*, January 23, 1978, pp. 47–50; Anderson, in *Parade*, pp. 4–5.
64. Anson, pp. 312–13; HAH 10H 156; Scott, "From Dallas to Watergate," in Blumenthal and Yazijian, pp. 126–27; Malone, in *New Times*, p. 48.
65. As cited in the prior note.
66. Malone, in *New Times*, p. 49; see HAH 10H 156–57, 176.
67. HAH 5H 296; Crile, "The Mafia, the CIA, and Castro," *Washington Post*, May 16, 1976, pp. C1, C4; Anson, p. 313.
68. Malone, in *New Times*, p. 48.
69. Anderson, in *Parade*, p. 4.
70. As cited in Anson, p. 313.
71. *New York Times*, January 4, 1959, p. 6.
72. Anderson, in *Parade*, April 28, 1963, p. 4.
73. *Ibid.*
74. See chapter 15, "The CIA and the Mafia."

75. Miles Copeland, *Without Cloak or Dagger* (New York: Simon and Schuster, 1974), p. 235, cited in Anson, p. 291.

76. Thomas Sciacca, *Luciano* (New York: Pinnacle Books, 1975), p. 180, cited in Anson, p. 291.

77. Anson, pp. 291–92; Sondern, *The Brotherhood of Evil*, reprinted in Gage, *Mafia, U.S.A.*, pp. 154–57; see Rodney Campbell, *The Luciano Project* (New York: McGraw-Hill, 1977).

78. As cited in the prior note.

79. McCoy, *The Politics of Heroin in Southeast Asia*, pp. 23–27; Anson, pp. 238, 292, 308–9.

80. As cited in the prior note.

81. McCoy, p. 24; see pp. 7–8, 16, 23–28, 31.

82. Sondern in Gage, *Mafia, U.S.A.*, pp. 155–56; see Campbell.

83. Reid, *The Grim Reapers*, pp. 30, 32.

84. Meskil, *Don Carlo*, p. 77; Reid, *The Grim Reapers*, p. 30; Frank J. Prial, "Vito Genovese—Power to Spare," in Gage, *Mafia, U.S.A.*, pp. 166–67.

85. Prial, in Gage, *Mafia, U.S.A.*, pp. 166–67.

86. *U.S.-Senate, McClellan Labor Hearings*, pp. 12411–12, 12417; Reid, *The Grim Reapers*, p. 30.

87. McCoy, pp. 22–23; Reid, *The Grim Reapers*, p. 31.

88. Prial, in Gage, *Mafia, U.S.A.*, p. 167; Reid, *The Grim Reapers*, p. 32.

89. Reid, *The Grim Reapers*, p. 31; Meskil, *Don Carlo*, p. 77; Prial, in Gage, *Mafia, U.S.A.*, p. 167; Pantaleone, *The Mafia and Politics*, p. 63.

90. Reid, *The Grim Reapers*, p. 31.

91. *Ibid.*, p. 32.

92. *Ibid.*; Prial, in Gage, *Mafia, U.S.A.*, p. 167; Meskil, *Don Carlo*, p. 77.

93. Meskil, *Don Carlo*, p. 77; Prial, in Gage, *Mafia, U.S.A.*, pp. 167–68.

94. *U.S.-Senate, McClellan Labor Hearings*, pp. 12367, 12412; Reid, *The Grim Reapers*, p. 32.

95. *U.S.-Senate, McClellan Labor Hearings*, pp. 12367–68, 12412; Reid, *The Grim Reapers*, p. 33; Meskil, *Don Carlo*, p. 77.

96. McCoy, pp. 7, 22–23; see text below.

97. McCoy, pp. 19–20; Salerno and Tompkins, pp. 276–77.

98. McCoy, pp. 20–21; Pantaleone, pp. 52–58.

99. McCoy, p. 22; Pantaleone, p. 53.

100. Harry L. Coles and Albert K. Weinberg, *United States Army in World War II. Civil Affairs: Soldiers become Governors* (Washington, D.C.: Office of the Chief of Military History, Department of the Army, U.S. Government Printing Office, 1964), p. 210.

101. Pantaleone, p. 52.

102. Wise and Ross, pp. 94–95.

103. McCoy, pp. 30–31; see below.

104. Anson, p. 326; McCoy, p. 31.

105. McCoy, pp. 31, 44–46; Anson, p. 293.

106. McCoy, pp. 44–45; Anson, p. 293.

107. McCoy, pp. 45–47; Anson, p. 293.

108. *New York Times*, March 10, 1975, p. 49.

109. Anson, pp. 295–96.

110. Anson, pp. 296–97.

111. HAH 10H 10–15, 151, 157, 170–71; *U.S.-Senate, Intelligence Report,*

Foreign Assassinations, pp. 71-90, 257; *U.S.-Senate, Intelligence Report, JFK Assassination*, pp. 2, 99; Scott, "The Death of Kennedy and the Vietnam War," in Blumenthal and Yazijian, pp. 161-65.

112. HAH 10H 157, 170-71; Anson, p. 313; Scott, *Crime and Cover-Up*, pp. 16-17; Malone, in *New Times*, p. 49.

113. *U.S.-Senate, Intelligence Report, JFK Assassination*, p. 100; Scott, "The Death of Kennedy and the Vietnam War," in Blumenthal and Yazijian, p. 164; Anson, pp. 268, 313.

114. Scott, "From Dallas to Watergate," in Blumenthal and Yazijian, p. 117; Scott, "The Death of Kennedy and the Vietnam War," in Blumenthal and Yazijian, p. 161; HAH 10H 13.

115. Hans Tanner, *Counter-Revolutionary Agent* (London: G. T. Foulis, 1972), p. 127.

116. HAH 10H 95-101.

117. *U.S.-Senate, Intelligence Report, Foreign Assassinations*, pp. 71-85, 97; *U.S.-Senate, Intelligence Report, JFK Assassination*, pp. 99-104; HAH 10H 151-57, 161-89.

118. *U.S.-Senate, Intelligence Report, Foreign Assassinations*, p. 92.

119. *Ibid.*, pp. 74, 94-97; *U.S.-Senate, Intelligence Report, JFK Assassination*, p. 99; Moldea, *The Hoffa Wars*, p. 128.

120. HAH 10H 176; Malone, in *New Times*, p. 49; Gage, *The Mafia Is Not an Equal Opportunity Employer*, p. 78; Anson, pp. 298, 313.

121. HAH 10H 171, see pp. 156-57.

122. HAH 10H 151-52; *U.S.-Senate, Intelligence Report, Foreign Assassinations*, pp. 74-82.

123. HAH 10H 151-52, 157-58; *U.S.-Senate, Intelligence Report, Foreign Assassinations*, pp. 82-86.

124. *U.S.-Senate, Intelligence Report, Foreign Assassinations*, p. 71.

125. *Ibid.*

126. *Ibid.*, pp. 74-85; Scott, *Crime and Cover-Up*, p. 22; HAH 10H 166-67.

127. Scott, *Crime and Cover-Up*, p. 22.

128. *U.S.-Senate, Intelligence Report, Foreign Assassinations*, pp. 75-77; HAH 10H 151.

129. See chapter 18, "Fall: Intensive Nationwide Contacts."

130. HAH 10H 154; Jack Anderson's column, *Albuquerque Journal*, September 7, 1976 (reprinted in HAH 10H 159-60).

131. As cited in the prior note. Former LBJ staff member Leo Janos wrote in the *Atlantic Monthly*, July 1973, that LBJ had proposed such a theory.

132. HAH 10H 164-66, 181-82.

133. "Dousing a Popular Theory," *Time*, October 2, 1978, p. 22; Vivian Cadden, "The Murder of President Kennedy," *McCall's*, March 1977, p. 172; Anson, pp. 260-65; Kirby Jones, "Unlikely Assassin," *New Republic*, July 3, 1976, pp. 5-6; Viorst, "The Mafia, the CIA, and the Kennedy Assassination," *Washingtonian*, November 1975, p. 118.

134. *U.S.-Senate, Intelligence Report, Foreign Assassinations*, p. 71n.

135. *Ibid.*, pp. 74-75, 92; *U.S.-Senate, Intelligence Report, JFK Assassination*, p. 99.

136. *U.S.-Senate, Intelligence Report, Foreign Assassinations*, pp. 151-52; HAH 10H 187; Tad Szulc, "Cuba on our Mind," *Esquire*, February 1974; *New York Times*, March 10, 1975.

137. *Time*, December 19, 1977, p. 23.
138. HAH 10H 3.
139. Schlesinger, *A Thousand Days*, p. 1029; HAH 3H 184–85.
140. Anson, pp. 262–65.
141. Khrushchev, pp. 507–8, 555, 557.
142. Anson, pp. 263–64.
143. *U.S.-Senate, Intelligence Report, Foreign Assassinations*, pp. 173–74; *U.S.-Senate, Intelligence Report, JFK Assassination*, p. 20; HAH 10H 165.
144. *U.S.-Senate, Intelligence Report, Foreign Assassinations*, p. 174; HAH 3H 184–92.
145. HAH 10H 165–66, 182.
146. Anson, pp. 264–65. Castro gave what *Time* magazine called "eloquent testimony" against the theory that he was behind the JFK killing in a four-and-one-half-hour interview in April 1978 with members of the House Assassinations Committee (*Time*, October 2, 1978, p. 22). See also Jones, in *New Republic*, pp. 5–6; HAH 10H 164–65.
147. See chapter 5, "An Attorney General Fights Crime."
148. See chapter 15, "Wanted for Treason."
149. Anson, p. 272; Cadden, in *McCall's*, p. 172; Viorst, in *Washingtonian*, p. 114.
150. HAH 10H 3, 13; Scott, "From Dallas to Watergate," in Blumenthal and Yazijian, p. 117; Scott, "The Death of Kennedy and the Vietnam War," in Blumenthal and Yazijian, p. 161.
151. HAR 133–34; Blakey and Billings, *The Plot to Kill the President*, pp. 170–73.
152. *Ibid.*
153. Blakey and Billings, p. 171.
154. *Ibid.*, p. 172; HAR 133–34.
155. CD 75, p. 199; HAR 170.

Chapter 16
Jack Ruby's Cuban Connection

1. Malone, "The Secret Life of Jack Ruby," *New Times*, January 23, 1978, p. 47.
2. HAH 9H 162.
3. CE 3063.
4. *Ibid.*
5. Reid, *The Grim Reapers*, pp. 11, 92; *U.S.-Senate, McClellan Labor Hearings*, p. 14060.
6. CE 3063.
7. *Ibid.*
8. HAH 10H 161; Malone, in *New Times*, pp. 47–48.
9. Malone, in *New Times*, p. 48.
10. CE 3065.
11. *Ibid.*

12. *Ibid.*
13. *Ibid.*
14. *Ibid.*
15. *Ibid.*
16. WR 788.
17. CE 3065.
18. *Ibid.*
19. *Ibid.*
20. *Ibid.*
21. *Ibid.*
22. *Ibid.*
23. *Ibid.*
24. *Ibid.*
25. *Ibid.*
26. *Ibid.*
27. Malone, in *New Times*, p. 48.
28. *Ibid.*
29. *Ibid.*
30. Jack Anderson, "How Castro Double-Crossed the Gambling Syndicate," *Parade*, April 28, 1963, p. 5; Malone, in *New Times*, pp. 47–48; see chapter 15, "Alignment Against Castro."
31. Anderson, in *Parade*, pp. 4–5; *Time*, March 2, 1959, pp. 22, 25; Malone, in *New Times*, pp. 48–50; see chapter 15, "Alignment Against Castro."
32. As cited in the prior note.
33. C. Ray Hall Exhibit 3, p. 15.
34. 5H 202.
35. CE 1688.
36. CE 1688–89; HAH 9H 178.
37. CE 1689; see HAH 9H 178.
38. CE 1689.
39. *Ibid.*
40. *Ibid.*
41. *Ibid.*
42. *Ibid.*
43. *Ibid.*
44. *Ibid.*
45. *Ibid.*
46. *Ibid.* When questioned by the House Assassinations Committee in 1976, McKeown confirmed the essential features of this account, although he provided several new details that appeared confused and inconsistent (HAH 9H 180–82). Given the consistent initial accounts of McKeown, Ruby and Deputy Sheriff Ayo, however, a contact between Ruby and McKeown concerning some Cuban dealing appears well established.
47. Interview shown in British Broadcasting Company (BBC) Panorama special, "The Kennedy Assassination: What Do We Know Now That We Didn't Then," March 1978.
48. CE 2980.
49. *Ibid.*
50. CE 3063.
51. C. Ray Hall Exhibit 3, p. 15; 5H 201, 205.

52. CE 1697, pp. 1–2.
53. 5H 201.
54. C. Ray Hall Exhibit 3, p. 15.
55. CE 1691; CE 1697, p. 1.
56. *U.S.-Senate, OC and Narcotics Hearings*, p. 569; Scott, "From Dallas to Watergate," in Blumenthal and Yazijian, eds., *Government by Gunplay: Assassination Conspiracy Theories from Dallas to Today*, p. 126; Anson, *"They've Killed the President!"* p. 309; *New York Times*, January 4, 1959, p. 6.
57. See chapter 9, "Lewis J. McWillie."
58. CD 686d, p. 2.
59. 5H 201, 205, 207, 208; C. Ray Hall Exhibit 3, p. 15; see also CE 1697, pp. 1–2 and HAH 9H 164.
60. HAH 9H 172.
61. CE 1442–43; HAH 9H 175.
62. CE 1773–74.
63. CE 1773.
64. HAH 9H 162.
65. CE 2329.
66. HAH 9H 175.
67. HAR 151; see also HAH 9H 176.
68. CE 1440; see HAH 9H 159, 161.
69. JFK microfilm, vol. 5, p. D47.
70. WR 798–99.
71. JFK microfilm, vol. 5, p. G5.
72. CD 84, p. 215.
73. *Ibid.*
74. *Ibid.*; see chapter 9, "Lewis J. McWillie."
75. HAR 152; see also HAH 9H 177.
76. Blakey and Billings, *The Plot to Kill the President*, pp. 293–94.
77. HAR 152.
78. HAH 9H 172–73; HAR 153.
79. HAR 152.
80. Malone, in *New Times*, p. 51.
81. HAH 9H 166–67; HAH 5H 162–65.
82. HAH 5H 167; see also HAH 5H 147 and Malone, in *New Times*, p. 50.
83. HAR 153; HAH 9H 173–74, 169–70.
84. HAR 153.
85. HAH 9H 164.
86. HAR 173.
87. Malone, in *New Times*, p. 50.
88. *Ibid.*
89. HAH 9H 173; HAR 153.
90. Malone, in *New Times*, p. 49; *Time*, March 2, 1959, pp. 22, 25; Anderson, in *Parade*, pp. 4–5.
91. CE 1690; CE 1697, p. 1.
92. CE 2988; see chapter 9, "Russell D. Matthews."
93. 5H 201.
94. HAH 10H 10; see chapter 15, "Alignment Against Castro," "Anti-Castro Raids and Assassination Attempts."

95. 14H 330–64; see also CE 3061.
96. WR 369.
97. WR 663.
98. WR 801.
99. See chapter 17, "Mob Subversion."
100. CE 3058–62.
101. 14H 360–61; CE 3061, pp. 629–31; CE 3059, p. 618.
102. CE 3059, p. 618.
103. *Ibid.*; CE 3061, p. 631; CE 1517.
104. *U.S.–Senate, Kefauver Hearings*, part 2, p. 193; CE 1517.
105. CE 3061, p. 630.
106. CE 3059, pp. 624–25.
107. CE 3059, p. 619; cf. CE 3061, p. 630.
108. CE 3059, p. 619.
109. CE 3060, p. 627.
110. CE 3058, p. 615.
111. *Ibid.*
112. *Ibid.*
113. *Ibid.*
114. *Ibid.*
115. CE 3061, p. 627.
116. CE 3061, pp. 628, 630, 633.
117. 14H 330–64.
118. 14H 340–41.
119. Reid, *The Grim Reapers*, p. 167.
120. 14H 333–34.
121. 14H 334–35, 345.
122. 14H 340–41.
123. CE 3059, p. 618.
124. 14H 336, 340.
125. 14H 345–49. For identification of Dave Cherry, see 14H 360–61; CE 3059, p. 618; CE 3061, pp. 629–31.
126. 14H 345–48.
127. 14H 348–49.
128. 14H 349.
129. 14H 349–50.
130. *Ibid.*
131. 14H 353.
132. *Ibid.*
133. 14H 354.
134. 14H 355.
135. HAH 10H 10; Anson, pp. 257–60, 313; Moldea, *The Hoffa Wars*, pp. 126–33.
136. Blakey and Billings, pp. 295–96.
137. *Ibid.*
138. *Ibid.*
139. *Ibid.*
140. CE 1322, p. 725.
141. See chapter 12, "A Photography Excursion."
142. CE 1322, p. 730.

143. C. Ray Hall Exhibit 3, p. 8; 5H 203.
144. CE 1322, p. 730.
145. CE 2980, pp. 9, 12.
146. CE 2980, p. 13.
147. Joachim Joesten, *The Case Against Lyndon Johnson in the Assassination of President Kennedy* (Munich: Dreischstr. 5, Selbstverlag, 1967), p. 9.
148. WR 296; see chapter 15, "Wanted for Treason."
149. HAH 9H 532.
150. *Ibid.*
151. See chapter 9, "Russell D. Matthews."
152. CE 1753.
153. HAH 5H 170; HAH 9H 428.
154. HAH 5H 70–71; CE 1546. Although McWillie reported in 1978 that he was "almost positive" that he met Ruby after the Top of the Hill club closed (HAH 5H 71), McWillie told the FBI in 1963 that Ruby had visited that club (CE 1546).
155. CE 2980, p. 13.
156. CE 1322, pp. 734, 754, 757.

Chapter 17
The Warren Commission Cover-Up

1. Tacitus, *The Histories*, translated by Kenneth Wellesley (New York: Penguin, 1964), p. 38.
2. Interview shown in the British Broadcasting Company (BBC) Panorama special, "The Kennedy Assassination: What Do We Know Now That We Didn't Then," March 1978.
3. Feuerlicht, *Justice Crucified*, pp. 269, 339–59, 374–75, 410.
4. *Ibid.*, pp. 374–75, 380–81, 409.
5. *Boston Herald*, August 9, 1927, cited in Feuerlicht, p. 380.
6. *New York Times*, August 8, 1927, p. 16.
7. *New York World*, August 8, 1927.
8. Feuerlicht, pp. 358–59.
9. *Ibid.*, p. 409.
10. Felix Frankfurter, *The Case of Sacco and Vanzetti* (New York: Grosset and Dunlap, 1962), passim.
11. *Boston Globe*, July 19, 1977, p. 3, July 20, 1977, pp. 1, 6.
12. As cited in the prior note.
13. Teresa, *My Life in the Mafia*, pp. 43, 45; Feuerlicht, p. 316.
14. Teresa, p. 45; Feuerlicht, p. 318; Francis Russell, *Tragedy in Dedham* (New York: McGraw-Hill, 1962), pp. 288–89.
15. Ehrmann, *The Case That Will Not Die*, pp. 412–13.
16. *Ibid.*, pp. 404–49, 23, 43–44, 191–94, 399–400; Ehrmann, *The Untried Case*, chapter 5; Feuerlicht, pp. 312–22.
17. Teresa, pp. 45–46.
18. *Ibid.*, pp. 43, 45.
19. *Ibid.*, p. 45.

20. *Ibid.*, p. 46.
21. *U.S.-Senate, Intelligence Report, JFK Assassination*, p. 32.
22. *Ibid.*, p. 33.
23. *Ibid.*, p. 23.
24. *Ibid*. When asked by Congress fifteen years later why he had so hastily issued these rash pronouncements, Katzenbach's reply underscored the absence of any satisfactory explanation: "Because, very simply, if that was the conclusion that the FBI was going to come to, then the public had to be satisfied that that was the correct conclusion" (HAH 3H 652).
25. *U.S.-Senate, Intelligence Report, JFK Assassination*, p. 34, see p. 23.
26. *Ibid.*, pp. 34–35.
27. *Time*, December 13, 1963, p. 26.
28. *Ibid.*
29. Thomas P. O'Neill, *Man of the House*, excerpted in *Washington Post*, September 16, 1987, p. D1.
30. *Ibid.*
31. *Ibid.*
32. *Ibid.*
33. *Washington Post*, June 24, 1976, p. A1.
34. HAH 5H 475.
35. BBC special, "The Kennedy Assassination: What Do We Know Now That We Didn't Then."
36. Wise and Ross, *The Invisible Government*, p. 186.
37. Warren Commission Executive Transcript, December 5, 1963, cited in Anson, *"They've Killed the President!"* pp. 41, 368.
38. *U.S.-Senate, Intelligence Report, JFK Assassination*, pp. 67–68, 70.
39. *Ibid.*, pp. 74–75.
40. John D. Weaver, *Warren: The Man, the Court, the Era* (Boston: Little, 1967), p. 302; Epstein, *Inquest*, pp. 20–21.
41. Epstein, *Inquest*, pp. 20–21.
42. *Ibid.*, pp. 13–14, xiii.
43. Warren Commission Executive Session Transcript, January 27, 1964, p. 171, cited in Scott, *Crime and Cover-Up*, p. 4, and excerpted in Peter Dale Scott, Paul L. Hoch and Russell Stetler, eds., *The Assassinations* (New York: Vintage Books, 1976), p. 138.
44. *Ibid.*
45. Epstein, *Inquest*, pp. 81–84.
46. The Warren Commission based its investigation largely on the FBI summary report of December 9, 1963 (WR xi, see *U.S.-Senate, Intelligence Report, JFK Assassination*, p. 46), which affirmed Hoover's immediately drawn conclusion that Oswald was the lone assassin (*U.S.-Senate, Intelligence Report, JFK Assassination*, pp. 32–35).
47. Weaver, p. 302.
48. *Ibid.*
49. *Facts on File*, 1974, pp. 634–36, 939–40.
50. HAH 3H 472.
51. *U.S.-Senate, Intelligence Report, JFK Assassination*, passim; HAR, passim.
52. *Time*, December 19, 1977, p. 23.
53. *Time*, February 4, 1974, p. 13.

54. *Ibid.*
55. WR 98, 105–6; Thompson, *Six Seconds in Dallas*, chapters 3 and 4.
56. WR 97, 193–94; 3H 403–7.
57. WR 3, 19, 105–7.
58. CD 5, quoted in Thompson, pp. 40–41.
59. CD 7, quoted in Epstein, *Inquest*, pp. 169–70.
60. National Archives, FBI summary report of December 9, 1963, reproduced in part in Epstein, *Inquest*, p. 149.
61. National Archives, FBI supplemental report of January 13, 1964, reproduced in part in Epstein, *Inquest*, p. 162.
62. National Archives, Presidential Commission Administrative Records, J. Lee Rankin, December 1963 to March 1964, cited in Thompson, p. 45; see CD 7, quoted in Epstein, *Inquest*, pp. 169–70.
63. As cited in notes 58, 60 and 61.
64. 5H 59–60; CE 393–94; see Thompson, pp. 48–50, 201–2, 214, 222–23.
65. WR 3.
66. See Thompson, pp. 222–23, 281.
67. WR 18, 94–95.
68. 17H 49; 4H 121; see photos in Thompson, pp. 151–52.
69. WR 56, 92–93; 2H 375–76; 4H 113, 120, 125; 6H 111; CE 392.
70. 2H 374–76, 382; Note that Colonel Finck stated that this bullet could not have inflicted the wound on Governor Connally's wrist (2H 382), whereas the Warren Commission reported that "ballistic experiments and medical findings established that the missile which passed through the Governor's wrist and penetrated his thigh had first traversed his chest" (WR 94).
71. Thompson, pp. 152–54.
72. 5H 79–82; WR 582–84; CE 856, 857; see Thompson, pp. 151–52.
73. WR 109.
74. WR 582; see WR 56, 92–94; Thompson, p. 283.
75. WR 582.
76. *Ibid.*
77. WR 92.
78. Epstein, *Inquest*, p. 109.
79. *Ibid.*, pp. 111–20, quoted phrase on p. 119.
80. *Ibid.*, pp. 77–78.
81. 1H 1–264.
82. Epstein, *Inquest*, p. 78.
83. See, for example, Anson, chapters 6–7.
84. See part II and chapter 5.
85. WR 663; see also WR 785, 801.
86. HAH 3H 494.
87. *Time*, December 19, 1977, p. 18.
88. For example: CD 75, p. 491 (Caracci); CD 686d (McWillie); CD 86, p. 558 (Chavez); CD 4, p. 366 (association with Dallas gambling circle); CD 1193, p. 89 (offer of numbers job); CD 1102c (Joe Bonds); CD 84, p. 229 (Weiner); CD 4, p. 529 (Teamsters).
89. CD 86, pp. 278–82, cf. CE 1750; CD 1144, cf. CE 2284. See Commission Document 86, page 278, in the National Archives. The first and most significant page of a five-page FBI report dated December 7, 1963, it was omitted when the rest of this report was published in the Warren Commis-

sion Hearings and Exhibits as Commission Exhibit 1750.

90. CD 84, pp. 91–92, cf. CE 1536; see photo section, pp. 174–75.
91. WR 790.
92. *U.S.-Senate, OC and Narcotics Report*, p. 37; Demaris, *Captive City*, p. 349; see chapter 6, "The Fine Reports of 'Ruby's Chicago Friends.' "
93. See chapter 6, "The Fine Reports of 'Ruby's Chicago Friends.' "
94. IRE series, *Albuquerque Journal*, April 3, 1977, p. A1; WR xiv.
95. WR xiv-xv.
96. See Appendix 2, section 22.
97. IRE series, *Albuquerque Journal*, April 3, 1977, p. A6.
98. *Ibid.*
99. *Ibid.*
100. *Ibid.*, pp. A1, A6.
101. *Ibid.*
102. *Ibid.*, p. A6.
103. *Ibid.*
104. *Ibid.*
105. *Ibid.*
106. *Ibid.*
107. See Appendix 2, section 26.
108. See Appendix 2, entries 6.12, 26.7 and 26.8.
109. See Appendix 2, entry 26.9.
110. See Appendix 2, entries 26.1, 26.2, 26.7, 26.8; also see text below.
111. See Appendix 2, entries 26.1, 26.2 and the Loeb quotation following.
112. HAH 5H 453.
113. HAH 5H 172; Sheridan, *The Fall and Rise of Jimmy Hoffa*, p. 503.
114. C. Ray Hall Exhibit 1; HAH 5H 87.
115. 5H 187.
116. Sheridan, p. 503.
117. HAH 5H 172; see also CE 1322, p. 767.
118. HAH 5H 26–27, 120; HAH 9H 544.
119. HAH 5H 30, 169.
120. HAH 5H 27–30, 120, 170, 172.
121. HAH 9H 378.
122. HAH 9H 544.
123. HAH 5H 120, 169.
124. HAH 5H 28, 168.
125. HAH 9H 378.
126. *Houston Post*, April 20, 1975, p. 2A.
127. HAH 9H 378.
128. HAH 5H 169.
129. HAH 5H 168, 170.
130. HAH 9H 168.
131. HAH 9H 168–69.
132. HAH 9H 167–69.
133. HAH 5H 120–25.
134. CE 1697; HAH 5H 125–29, 133–34.
135. HAH 9H 168–69; HAH 5H 173. Zoppi claimed that he never checked his 1973 story with McWillie, which Committee interviewers found "very surprising" (HAH 5H 170–71).

136. Hersh, "The Contrasting Lives of Sidney R. Korshak," *New York Times*, June 27, 1976, p. 20.

137. *Ibid.*, June 30, 1976, p. 14.

138. *Ibid.*

139. *Ibid.*

140. *Washington Star*, July 12, 1979, p. 1.

141. *Ibid.*

142. See chapter 5, "An Assassination Plan by Carlos Marcello."

143. Reid, *The Grim Reapers*, pp. 160–62; HAH 9H 75–76.

144. HAH 9H 77.

145. HAH 9H 78.

146. *Ibid.*

147. *Ibid.*

148. HAH 9H 86.

149. HAH 9H 79.

150. HAH 9H 86.

151. HAH 9H 78, 85, 86.

152. HAH 9H 85.

153. HAH 9H 79, 85–86.

154. *Ibid.*

155. HAH 9H 78.

156. HAH 9H 85.

157. *U.S.–Senate, Intelligence Report, JFK Assassination*, p. 33.

158. *Ibid.*, pp. 34, 35, 46.

159. *Ibid.*, pp. 5, 47.

160. HAH 3H 489.

161. *U.S.–Senate, Intelligence Report, JFK Assassination*, p. 5, see p. 47.

162. Salerno and Tompkins, *The Crime Confederation*, p. 306.

163. *Ibid.*, pp. 306–7; William Turner, *Hoover's FBI*, pp. 44, 59, 167, 177–85; Navasky, *Kennedy Justice*, pp. 44–45; Viorst, "The Mafia, the CIA, and the Kennedy Assassination," *Washingtonian*, November 1975, pp. 113–14; William Turner, "Crime is Too Big for the FBI," *The Nation*, November 8, 1965, pp. 322–28; NBC Evening News, "Segment 3," December 16, 1977; HAH 3H 460; Hank Messick, "The Schenely Chapter," *The Nation*, April 5, 1971, pp. 428–31; Schlesinger, *Robert Kennedy and his Times*, pp. 283–86, 288, 289.

164. William Turner, *Hoover's FBI*, p. 79.

165. As cited in note 163.

166. Navasky, pp. 44–45; Salerno and Tompkins, pp. 306–7; see also HAH 3H 460.

167. As cited in the prior note.

168. Navasky, p. 44.

169. William Turner, *Hoover's FBI*, pp. 177–85; Salerno and Tompkins, pp. 306–7.

170. Navasky, pp. 44–45; William Turner, *Hoover's FBI*, pp. 19, 44, 59, 167, 177–85.

171. Navasky, pp. 44–46.

172. *Ibid.*, pp. 45–46.

173. IRE series, *Albuquerque Journal*, March 19, 1977, pp. A1, A9.

174. *Ibid.*

175. *Ibid.*, p. A9.
176. William Turner, *Hoover's FBI*, pp. 80–81, 97; Jack Anderson, *San Francisco Chronicle*, December 31, 1970, p. 25.
177. William Turner, *Hoover's FBI*, p. 97.
178. *Ibid.*
179. Scott, *Crime and Cover-Up*, pp. 11, 34–35, 38; Reid, *The Grim Reapers*, pp. 141–42.
180. *U.S.-Senate, Bobby Baker Hearings*, pp. 1864–67.
181. Navasky, p. 30.
182. Fred Cook, *The FBI Nobody Knows* (New York: Pyramid, 1964), p. 240.
183. Jack Anderson, *San Francisco Chronicle*, December 31, 1970, p. 25.
184. William Turner, *Hoover's FBI*, p. 80; Dorman, *Payoff*, pp. 212–14, 220, 223, 231–32, 235–36; Messick, in *The Nation*, pp. 428–31. For background on Joe Fusco, Alfred Hart and their liquor companies, see Reid, *The Grim Reapers*, p. 254; Demaris, p. 224; and *U.S.-Senate, Kefauver Hearings*, part 5, p. 539.
185. For Costello's background, see *U.S.-Senate, Kefauver Report, Third Interim*, pp. 111–24; Reid, *The Grim Reapers*, pp. 10–11; *U.S.-Senate, OC and Narcotics Hearings*, p. 652, chart B.
186. *Time*, December 22, 1975, p. 20.
187. Schlesinger, *Robert Kennedy and his Times*, p. 286n.
188. HAH 3H 646.
189. *Time*, December 22, 1975, p. 14; William Turner, *Hoover's FBI*, p. 96.
190. *Time*, December 22, 1975, p. 20; Joseph Nocera, "The Art of the Leak," *Washington Monthly*, July-August, 1979, p. 25.
191. *Newsweek*, July 9, 1979, pp. 35–36.
192. *Time*, December 22, 1975, pp. 15–16.
193. *U.S.-Senate, Intelligence Report, JFK Assassination*, see notes on pp. 23, 33, 34, 41, 46–48, 50–55.
194. *Newsweek*, July 9, 1979, p. 35.
195. *U.S.-Senate, Intelligence Report, JFK Assassination*, pp. 33–34.
196. *Ibid.*, p. 34.
197. WR ix.
198. *U.S.-Senate, Intelligence Report, JFK Assassination*, pp. 23, 33.
199. Robert A. Caro, *The Years of Lyndon Johnson*, excerpts from *Atlantic Monthly*, October 1981, p. 44, see p. 63.
200. Caro, in *Atlantic Monthly*, p. 42.
201. *Ibid.*
202. *Ibid.*
203. *Ibid.*
204. Dorman, "LBJ and the Racketeers," *Ramparts*, May 1968, pp. 27–28 (most of the information in this article is also furnished in chapter 7 of Dorman's book, *Payoff*). Dorman developed an unusual knack for cultivating Mobsters and obtained selective information on their political dealings during his ten years as a reporter for the *Houston Press*, his subsequent term with *Newsday* and his work as an author (*Ramparts*, May 1968). Dorman secured a unique on-the-record interview with Mafia boss Carlos Marcello (*Payoff*, pp. 103–4, 109–10), assisted federal investigators in the Hoffa case (*Payoff*, pp. 151, 229), assisted a New York State organized crime probe (*Payoff*, p. 226), and testified as an expert witness be-

fore a Texas grand jury investigating organized crime (*Payoff*, p. vii).

205. *Ibid.*, p. 27.
206. *Ibid.*
207. *Ibid.*, pp. 28–30.
208. *Ibid.*
209. *Ibid.*, p. 30.
210. *Ibid.*, p. 34.
211. *Ibid.*
212. *Ibid.*
213. *U.S.–Senate, Kefauver Report, Third Interim.*
214. Dorman, in *Ramparts*, p. 34.
215. *Ibid.*, pp. 30, 34.
216. *Ibid.*, p. 34.
217. Sheridan, pp. 380–81.
218. *Ibid.*
219. *Ibid.*
220. *Ibid.*
221. *Ibid.*, p. 7.
222. *Ibid.*, p. 381.
223. *Ibid.*
224. *Newsweek*, August 8, 1977, p. 27; Messick, *Secret File*, pp. 257–58.
225. As cited in the prior note.
226. *Newsweek*, August 8, 1977, p. 27.
227. *Ibid.*
228. Caro, in *Atlantic Monthly*, p. 44.
229. *Ibid.*, p 43.
230. *New York Times*, January 28, 1973, p. 43.
231. Winter-Berger, *The Washington Payoff*, pp. 53–54.
232. *Ibid.*
233. *Ibid.*, pp. 58, 60.
234. *Ibid.*, p. 54; Reid, *The Grim Reapers*, p. 133; Mollenhoff, *Strike Force*, p. 82.
235. Winter-Berger, p. 61.
236. *Ibid.*, p. 69; Mollenhoff, *Strike Force*, p. 115.
237. Mollenhoff, *Strike Force*, pp. 102–5, 186; Reid, *The Grim Reapers*, pp. 133–45; Dorman, *Payoff*, pp. 143–48; Winter-Berger, p. 68.
238. Anson, p. 324.
239. Winter-Berger, p. 68.
240. William Turner, *Hoover's FBI*, p. 185; Mollenhoff, *Strike Force*, p. 5.
241. Winter-Berger, pp. 61–66.
242. *Ibid.*
243. *Ibid.*, p. 62.
244. *Ibid.*, pp. 62–63.
245. *Ibid.*, p. 65.
246. *Ibid.*, passim; Dorman, *Payoff*, pp. 189–97.
247. Winter-Berger, p. 65.
248. *Ibid.*, pp. 65–66.
249. See Appendix 2, entries 25.10 and 25.11.
250. Reid, *The Grim Reapers*, pp. 140–42.
251. Mollenhoff, *Strike Force*, pp. 6, 110.

252. *Ibid.*, p. 110.
253. *Ibid.*, pp. 117–18.
254. *Ibid.*, pp. 110, 112–13.
255. Mollenhoff, *Strike Force*, p. 113.
256. *Ibid.*
257. Demaris, p. 14.
258. *Ibid.*, pp. 77, 324.
259. *Life*, May 30, 1969, p. 45.
260. National Archives, Texas Supplemental Report, November 26, 1963; also see Mollenhoff, *Strike Force*, p. 6.
261. Tacitus, p. 38.
262. Blakey and Billings, *The Plot to Kill the President*, pp. 26–27, 361–62; Hurt, *Reasonable Doubt*, pp. 250–53.
263. Blakey and Billings, p. 26.

Part V
A Mafia Contract

1. HAR 1.
2. Washington Post (weekly edition), July 16, 1984, p. 37.
3. HAR 161; see HAR 169, 173, 176; chapters 2 and 17.
4. *Newsweek*, July 30, 1979, p. 38.

Chapter 18
Nationwide Mob Contacts

1. U.S.-Senate, OC and Stolen Securities, 1973, pp. 120–21.
2. See chapter 5, "An Assassination Plan by Carlos Marcello."
3. HAH 9H 69; see chapter 5, "An Assassination Plan by Carlos Marcello."
4. HAH 9H 82; see chapter 5, "An Assassination Plan by Carlos Marcello."
5. Reid, *The Grim Reapers*, p. 162; HAH 9H 83.
6. Crile, "The Mafia, the CIA, and Castro," *Washington Post*, May 16, 1976, p. C4; see chapter 5, "An Assassination Prediction by Santos Trafficante."
7. See chapter 5, "Assassination Plots by Jimmy Hoffa."
8. Moldea, *The Hoffa Wars*, p. 150.
9. National Archives, entry 45, Ruby-Oswald chronology, p. 519.
10. Ruby's home phone number was WH1-5601; the Carousel Club RI7-2362. See Appendix 1 for a discussion of those telephone records.
11. Telephone records covering all but six weeks of the period January 1 through November 24, 1963 from Ruby's Carousel Club office phone, used almost exclusively by him (see Appendix 1), provide the only objective index of his activity throughout that year. Calls from his home phone are much less frequent (CE 2302, 2308; compare with CE 2303, 2309), and records are not available for that telephone prior to May 1963.
12. See chart later in this chapter.
13. CE 1322, pp. 758–59, 764–66.
14. National Archives, entry 45, Ruby-Oswald chronology, p. 519.

15. CE 2308; JFK microfilm, vol. 5, p. T16.
16. Reid, *The Grim Reapers*, p. 155; Lawson, "Carnival of Crime," *Wall Street Journal*, January 12, 1970, p. 1; "The Mob," part 2, *Life*, September 8, 1967, p. 95.
17. As cited in the prior note.
18. CD 5, pp. 413–14.
19. *Ibid.*
20. 14H 542–43, 567.
21. 14H 543.
22. HAH 5H 33; see also CE 1697, p. 4.
23. More detailed background on McWillie and other Ruby contacts is provided in chapter 9.
24. CE 1693.
25. Wallace Turner, *Gambler's Money*, p. 127; Reid and Demaris, *The Green Felt Jungle*, pp. 141, 147.
26. CE 2309 (735–4111); JFK microfilm, vol. 5, p. T12; CD 722, p. 6.
27. CE 1692; CE 1697, p. 4.
28. CE 1697, pp. 4–5; CD 86, p. 474.
29. 14H 459.
30. CD 84, pp. 131–32.
31. *Ibid.*, p. 233.
32. See chapter 9, "Frank Caracci."
33. CE 1244; CE 1581–83; CE 2308–9; JFK microfilm, vol. 5, p. T16. Note that area codes cited in CE 1244 and CE 1581 are incorrect; e.g., the number of the Bull-Pen in Arlington, Texas, 275–4891, which Ruby called frequently (see CE 2303) is prefixed with area code 807, which corresponds to Ontario, Canada. The call to 523–0930 is presumably to the Old French Opera House, a New Orleans bar with that number (JFK microfilm, vol. 5, p. T16), since Ruby called that number often that summer (CE 2308–9) and since he called another New Orleans number on August 4 (CE 2309).
34. WR 28.
35. CE 2308 (523–0930); JFK microfilm, vol. 5, p. T16; CD 84, p. 233.
36. CD 4, p. 666; CD 86, p. 487.
37. CD 86, p. 487.
38. CD 4, p. 666.
39. *U.S.–House, OC in Sports*, p. 949.
40. CE 1525, 1526; CD 86, p. 487.
41. CE 1524–26; CD 86, p. 487.
42. Kantor, *Who Was Jack Ruby?*, p. 20.
43. *Ibid.*
44. *Ibid.*; see JFK microfilm, vol. 5, p. T10; CD 86, p. 542.
45. CE 2309 (275–4321); JFK microfilm, vol. 5, p. T10; CD 86, p. 542.
46. CE 2309 (523–9468); JFK microfilm, vol. 5, p. T11; Reid, *The Grim Reapers*, p. 155; Lawson, in *Wall Street Journal*, p. 1.
47. CE 2309 (523–0930). JFK microfilm, vol. 5, p. T10; CD 86, p. 542. JFK microfilm lists the date of the call as June 15.
48. CE 2309 (735–4303); JFK microfilm, vol. 5, p. T12; CD 722, p. 6.
49. CE 2308, 2309 (523–0930); JFK microfilm, vol. 5, pp. 11, 16.
50. CE 2309 (735–4111); JFK microfilm, vol. 5, p. T12; CD 722, p. 6.
51. See notes 27–29.

52. CE 2308 (464–4785); JFK microfilm, vol. 5, p. T16; CE 1544.
53. CE 2309 (271–9722); JFK microfilm, vol. 5, p. T13; CE 1544.
54. CE 1544; Wallace Turner, pp. 240–41.
55. CE 1544, 1545.
56. Wallace Turner, pp. 240–41.
57. Sheridan, *The Fall and Rise of Jimmy Hoffa*, pp. 7, 361–62.
58. Wallace Turner, pp. 240–42.
59. CE 2308 (274–0043; 466–8211); JFK microfilm, vol. 5, pp. T16–17; CE 1507.
60. HAH 9H 1050, 1078.
61. See chapter 9, "Irwin Weiner."
62. CE 2308 (735–4111); JFK microfilm, vol. 5, p. T17; CD 722, p. 6.
63. See notes 27–29.
64. CD 84, pp. 131–32.
65. *U.S.-House, OC Control*, p. 434; HAH 4H 565.
66. HAH 4H 565.
67. *Ibid*.
68. *Ibid*.
69. *U.S.-House, OC Control*, p. 416.
70. HAH 4H 565; see note 64.
71. CE 2308 (247–4915); JFK microfilm, vol. 5, p. T16; CE 1261.
72. CE 1261; CE 1288.
73. CE 1288; Kantor, pp. 92, 98.
74. CE 1322, p. 741.
75. National Archives, entry 45, Ruby-Oswald chronology, p. 622.
76. CE 1581.
77. CD 106, p. 259.
78. *Ibid*.
79. National Archives, entry 45, Ruby-Oswald chronology, p. 622.
80. HAH 9H 251.
81. C. Ray Hall Exhibit 3, p. 16.
82. CE 1244.
83. CE 1288.
84. *Ibid*.
85. Allsop, *The Bootleggers*, pp. 61–64, 88–90.
86. CE 1288.
87. CE 1581 (523–0930); CD 84, p. 233; see note 33.
88. CE 1581; CE 1507.
89. 5H 200.
90. CE 1765.
91. *Ibid*.
92. Hersh, "The Contrasting Lives of Sidney R. Korshak," *New York Times*, June 29, 1976, p. 16.
93. *Ibid*., June 27, 1976, p. 20.
94. *Ibid*., June 29, 1976, p. 16.
95. 14H 446.
96. See chapter 9, "Joseph Glaser."
97. CE 1581.
98. C. Ray Hall Exhibit 3, p. 16.
99. An FBI chronology reports that Cheryl Aston saw Ruby at Henrici's Res-

taurant around the first or second week in August and was subsequently called by Ruby (CD 86, p. 488). Ruby's toll records show a 34-minute call on August 7 from Ruby's home phone to the Chicago number 631–1489, listed to Dewey Aston (CE 2308 JFK microfilm, vol. 5, p. T17).

100. *U.S.–Senate, McClellan Labor Hearings*, pp. 13915, 13921.
101. Background on Zapas, including more than 40 arrests in Chicago: *ibid.*, pp. 13900–922; Sheridan, p. 57. Background on Marchesi, including his invocation of the Fifth Amendment when asked if he was a member of the Mafia: *U.S.–Senate, McClellan Labor Hearings*, pp. 13915, 14034–36, 14080; Kennedy, *The Enemy Within*, p. 92.
102. CE 2308 (582–7700); JFK microfilm, vol. 5, p. T16; CE 1322, p. 742.
103. CE 2308 (735–4111); JFK microfilm, vol. 5, p. T17; CD 722, p. 6 (JFK microfilm does not list the August 22 call).
104. CE 1697, pp. 4–5; CD 86, p. 474.
105. CE 1693.
106. CE 2308, 2309; JFK microfilm, vol. 5, pp. T9–18; CD 86, pp. 488–89.
107. *Dallas Morning News*, September 26, 1963, p. 1. National Archives, entry 45, Ruby-Oswald chronology, pp. 667ff.
108. CE 2303 (661–3753); CE 2989.
109. CE 2989; HAH 9H 545–46.
110. See chapter 9, "Russell D. Matthews."
111. CE 2989.
112. HAH 9H 527.
113. HAR 173; HAH 9H 529.
114. HAH 9H 529.
115. HAH 9H 528, 529, 531.
116. Malone, "The Secret Life of Jack Ruby," *New Times*, January 23, 1978, p. 51.
117. *U.S.–Senate, Intelligence Report, Foreign Assassinations*, pp. 75–77; HAH 10H 151.
118. Malone, in *New Times*, p. 51.
119. CE 2303, 2309.
120. CE 1322, pp. 758–59, 764–66.
121. CE 2302, 2308; compare with CE 2303, 2309.
122. *Ibid.*; Jack Anderson, *Albuquerque Journal*, September 8, 1976; Jack Anderson, *Washington Post*, January 3, 1979, p. B15.
123. Jack Anderson, *Albuquerque Journal*, September 8, 1976.
124. *Ibid.*; HAH 10H 155, 186; Moldea, *The Hoffa Wars*, p. 433.
125. Moldea, *The Hoffa Wars*, p. 433.
126. G. Robert Blakey and Richard N. Billings, "An Expert's Theory," *Parade*, November 16, 1980, p. 6.
127. *Ibid.*; Brashler, *The Don*, pp. 321–23; HAH 10H 155, 186.
128. Brashler, p. 324.
129. HAH 10H 186.
130. CD 75, p. 491.
131. *Ibid.*
132. *Ibid.*
133. CD 4, p. 666.
134. *Ibid.*
135. CE 2302, 2303.

136. CE 1322, p. 771.
137. CD 4, p. 666.
138. *U.S.-House, OC Control*, p. 430.
139. *U.S.-House, OC in Sports*, p. 949.
140. CE 2303 (743-6865); see chapter 19, "Mob Conspiracy."
141. See chapter 9, "Irwin Weiner."
142. *Ibid.*
143. *Ibid.*
144. CD 84, p. 229.
145. See chapter 19, "Mob Conspiracy."
146. HAH 9H 1069, 1071.
147. HAH 9H 1055-56, 1061, 1069.
148. HAH 9H 1056.
149. 15H 29; see below and chapter 9, "Irwin Weiner," for a definitive identification of this Chicago bail bondsman as Weiner.
150. CE 1202.
151. 14H 445; HAH 4H 567. Ruby's telephone records show no calls to numbers listed to Patrick (CE 2302, 2303, 2308, 2309; JFK microfilm, vol. 5, pp. T9-18), but he could have called Patrick collect, or from a pay phone, or at any of the six Chicago numbers shown in his phone logs not listed to relatives: 236-5561, 728-4031, 427-3172, 652-9658, 631-1489 or 743-6865.
152. See chapter 9, "Lenny Patrick."
153. Demaris, *Captive City*, pp. 348-49.
154. CE 2309 (242-5431); CD 84, p. 132; *U.S.-House, OC Control*, p. 434; HAH 4H 565.
155. CE 2303
156. CE 2331.
157. *Ibid.*; HAH 9H 274; see chapter 9, "Barney Baker."
158. HAH 9H 276; Moldea, *The Hoffa Wars*, p. 118.
159. CE 2303 (532-2561).
160. CD 360, p. 149; HAH 4H 566.
161. Sheridan, p. 292; *Time*, December 10, 1973, p. 30.
162. HAH 4H 566.
163. CE 2303.
164. CE 2332
165. Lepera, *Memoirs of a Scam Man*, pp. 80-81.
166. CE 2303 (587-7674); CE 2328.
167. CE 2328.
168. *Ibid.*
169. CE 1748.
170. CE 1692-93; 14H 445.
171. 14H 445.
172. HAH 9H 432.
173. CD 1144.

Chapter 19
The AGVA Alibi: Mob Perjury

1. Teresa, *My Life in the Mafia*, p. 345.
2. Sondern, *The Brotherhood of Evil*, p. 35.
3. *Ibid.*, p. 37.
4. *Ibid.*
5. *Ibid.*, pp. 37–38.
6. John McClellan, "Weak Link in Our War on the Mafia," *Reader's Digest*, April 6, 1970, reprinted in *U.S.-House, OC Control*, p. 113.
7. Cressey, *Theft of the Nation*, p. 212.
8. *Ibid.*
9. *Ibid.*
10. *Ibid.*, pp. 212–13.
11. 5H 200.
12. *Ibid.*; see "Ruby's AGVA Problem" below.
13. See "Mob Conspiracy" below.
14. See text below.
15. *U.S.-Senate, AGVA Hearings.*
16. *Ibid.*, pp. 629–30.
17. *Ibid.*, p. 94.
18. *Ibid.*, p. 213.
19. See Appendix 2, section 18.
20. *U.S.-Senate, AGVA Hearings*, p. 101.
21. *Ibid.*, pp. 209–10.
22. *Ibid.*, p. 630.
23. *Ibid.*, pp. 587–88.
24. *Ibid.*, p. 214.
25. *Ibid.*, pp. 92–93.
26. *Ibid.*, pp. 19–20.
27. Sheridan, *The Fall and Rise of Jimmy Hoffa*, pp. 210, 258; see also Kennedy, *The Enemy Within*, pp. 44–51.
28. *U.S.-Senate, AGVA Hearings*, pp. 3–4, 22–24.
29. HAH 9H 200.
30. HAH 9H 419, 1147.
31. HAH 9H 419.
32. HAH 9H 418–21.
33. HAH 9H 422–23.
34. HAH 9H 420.
35. HAH 9H 421.
36. HAH 9H 418.
37. HAH 9H 425.
38. HAH 9H 419.
39. HAH 9H 419–20.
40. *Ibid.*
41. HAH 9H 425, 428–29.
42. CE 1475.
43. HAH 9H 420–21.
44. HAH 9H 422.

45. CE 2303, 2308; CE 1543; CE 1322, p. 728.
46. CE 1543, p. 1.
47. CD 84, p. 229; 15H 29.
48. CD 84, p. 229.
49. CE 2309; JFK microfilm, vol. 5, p. T12; CD 84, p. 229.
50. 15H 28–29; 14H 460.
51. CE 2302; JFK microfilm, vol. 5, p. T17; CE 1322, p. 727; CE 2323.
52. CE 2323; 15H 217.
53. CE 2323.
54. 15H 217.
55. *Ibid.*
56. CE 2308, 2309; JFK microfilm, vol. 5, pp. T13, T16.
57. HAH 5H 171.
58. CE 2302, 2303; CE 1562.
59. 5H 200.
60. CE 1582.
61. See chapter 18, "August: The West Coast and New York."
62. *Ibid.*; CE 1244.
63. CE 1765.
64. CE 1543.
65. CE 1562.
66. See chapter 18, "August: The West Coast and New York."
67. WR 797; 15H 248, 212.
68. 15H 248, 415.
69. 15H 211–12.
70. 14H 459; 15H 211–12, 415; 5H 200.
71. CE 1543; 5H 200; 15H 212, 248–49.
72. CE 1543.
73. 15H 415; 5H 200; CE 1507; CE 1543; 15H 212–13; CE 1562; HAH 9H 463, 1048.
74. 15H 212–13, 415; 5H 200; CE 1543.
75. CE 1562; 5H 200; HAH 5H 172; HAH 9H 297–98, 465; CE 1507.
76. CE 1562; CE 1543; 15H 211–12; 5H 200.
77. 5H 200.
78. 14H 605; 15H 415; 15H 248.
79. HAH 9H 245, 348, 351, 405; 13H 322–23; 15H 192–93, 212, 220, 249, 415–16.
80. See note 73.
81. HAH 9H 245; 13H 322–23; 15H 249.
82. CE 1543; 15H 212.
83. 15H 248.
84. 15H 249, 415.
85. 15H 248.
86. See chapter 8.
87. CE 1322, p. 726.
88. See chapter 10.
89. See chapter 18, "Fall: Intensive Nationwide Contacts."
90. Crafard Exhibit 5226; 13H 502; 15H 416; see beginning of chapter 20.
91. 15H 416.
92. HAH 9H 206.

93. HAH 9H 244-47.
94. HAH 9H 242, 247-48.
95. See chapter 8, "Prostitution and Other Criminal Activities."
96. 15H 208; CE 1648; CE 1505; 15H 199.
97. HAH 9H 230-31.
98. 15H 211, 208.
99. CE 1517; CE 1543; 15H 210; CD 4, p. 533; 14H 343; HAH 9H 424.
100. *U.S.-Senate, AGVA Hearings*, pp. 629-30, 160.
101. 15H 208.
102. 15H 213.
103. 15H 208.
104. HAR 156; HAH 9H 426; 14H 601-2.
105. HAH 9H 424, 426.
106. CD 4, p. 533.
107. 15H 410.
108. 14H 605.
109. 14H 607.
110. 14H 605-7.
111. 14H 602.
112. 14H 605.
113. 14H 606.
114. 14H 605-8.
115. HAH 9H 1075.
116. CE 1521, 1523, 1526, CE 1561; CD 84, p. 219; CD 4, p. 666.
117. As cited in the prior note. Jada was employed at the Sho-Bar at the time of
     Ruby's early June visit, according to Sho-Bar managers Nick Graffagnini
     (CE 1526) and Henry Morici (CD 84, p. 219) and other witnesses (CE
     1521, 1522, 1524, 1525); Morici reported that Jada's engagement there ran
     from April 5 to June 12, 1963 (CD 4, p. 663). But Paul Cascio, who
     worked just across from the Sho-Bar, told the FBI that at the time of Ru-
     by's visit Jada was "a dancing girl at the 500 Club" (CE 1523). And Jada,
     who described Ruby's early June visit in some detail (CE 1561), stated only
     that she had been associated with her husband, Joseph Conforto, "in the
     operation of a strip tease club known as Madame Francine's," which
     closed in June 1963 (CE 1561).
118. CE 1561.
119. CE 1244.
120. 5H 200.
121. 14H 639.
122. 5H 200; C. Ray Hall Exhibit 3, p. 16; see chapter 16, "Dealings and Travels
     in 1959."
123. CD 84, pp. 131-32; CD 86, pp. 445, 486-89; CD 223, p. 136; JFK micro-
     film, vol. 5, pp. T9-18; CE 2303, 2308, 2309.
124. See chapter 6, "Racketeering in the Chicago Night Club District."
125. As cited in note 123.
126. CD 84, pp. 131-32.
127. CD 86, p. 486.
128. CD 86, p. 487; CD 84, p. 131.
129. JFK microfilm, vol. 5, p. T16.
130. CE 1561.

31. CD 223, p. 136.
32. JFK microfilm, vol. 5, p. T11; CE 2303, p. 242.
33. CD 84, pp. 131–132.
34. CE 1524; CE 1522.
35. CE 1526.
36. CD 4, p. 666.
37. HAH 9H 13–14, 38.
38. HAH 4H 565.
39. CD 84, p. 131.
40. CE 2331.
41. *Ibid*.
42. CE 2303.
43. HAH 9H 297–305.
44. HAH 9H 297, 298; HAH 9H 300–301, 304–5.
45. HAH 9H 298.
46. CE 2284.
47. CE 2243.
48. CE 1544.
49. *Ibid*.
50. CD 84, p. 229.
51. HAH 9H 1043.
52. Moldea, *The Hoffa Wars*, p. 155.
53. HAH 9H 1043.
54. *Ibid.*; HAH 9H 1047.
55. HAH 9H 1048.
56. HAR 155; HAH 9H 1049, 1075, 1077.
57. HAR 155.
58. CE 1697.
59. See chapter 9, "Lewis J. McWillie."
60. CD 360, p. 149.
61. See chapter 9, "Murray W. 'Dusty' Miller."
62. CE 2328.
63. *Ibid*.
64. CE 1765.
65. See chapter 9, "Joseph Glaser."
66. HAH 5H 171–72.
67. CE 1543, 1562, 2323; see also 15H 213.
68. CE 2323.
69. CE 1543.
70. CE 1562.
71. HAR 156n.

Chapter 20
The Mafia Killed
President Kennedy

1. *Newsweek*, July 30, 1979, p. 38.
2. 15H 406.
3. 15H 416.

4. Crafard Exhibit 5226; C. Ray Hall Exhibit 3, p. 3; 25H 318.
5. Crafard Exhibit 5226.
6. *Ibid.*
7. 13H 502.
8. 13H 424.
9. CE 1184; see CE 1300.
10. As cited in the prior note.
11. CE 1300.
12. See chapter 9, "Paul Roland Jones."
13. *Ibid.*
14. CD 1144.
15. CD 722, p. 8.
16. HAH 9H 486.
17. Kantor, *Who Was Jack Ruby?*, p. 22.
18. HAH 9H 485.
19. CE 2284; see also CE 2243; HAH 9H 454, 461.
20. CE 2284.
21. HAH 9H 458.
22. HAH 9H 458–59.
23. HAH 9H 459.
24. *Ibid.*
25. 5H 185.
26. HAH 9H 462.
27. *Ibid.*
28. 5H 185.
29. CE 2284.
30. CE 2243.
31. CE 2284.
32. CE 2243; CE 2284.
33. As cited in the prior note.
34. CE 2303 (the number was 935–1082); 5H 185.
35. CE 2379; C. Ray Hall Exhibit 3, p. 2; Crafard Exhibit 5226, p. 356; see 13H 245.
36. CD 86, pp. 366–67.
37. CE 2397.
38. Tortoriello was co-owner of the J. C. Adams Construction Company (CD 86, p. 256; see also 9H 349). J. C. Adams, in turn, had been a partner of Lester "Benny" Binion (CE 1692), the one-time rackets boss of Dallas (Reid and Demaris, *The Green Felt Jungle*, chapter 10; *U.S.–Senate, Kefauver Hearings*, part 2, p. 193; HAH 9H 530), in an enterprise which had employed Mobster Lewis McWillie (CE 1692). Adams was an associate of both Ruby (HAH 9H 349; CE 1322, p. 750) and Mafioso Joseph Campisi (HAH 9H 349).
39. HAH 9H 348–50, 353.
40. CD 86, pp. 256–57; Jada was the stage name of Janet Conforto.
41. CD 302, p. 20; CD 86, p. 366.
42. CE 2397; see Reid, *The Grim Reapers*, p. 292.
43. CD 302, p. 20.
44. CD 302, p. 41.
45. CD 302, p. 20.

46. *Ibid.*
47. *Ibid.*
48. CD 86, p. 367; CD 302, p. 20.
49. CE 2396.
50. CD 302, p. 41.
51. CD 86, p. 366.
52. CD 86, p. 367.
53. CE 2396; see CD 302, p. 41.
54. CE 2396.
55. Armstrong Exhibits 5300A-F. The subject is identified as Gloria Fillmon through the accounts of Larry Crafard (13H 493-94, 14H 70) and Gloria Fillmon (CE 2379).
56. Crafard Exhibit 5226, p. 356; CE 2379.
57. See note 35.
58. See chapter 19, "Other Alibis."
59. CD 86, pp. 256-57; HAH 9H 349.
60. CD 302, p. 20.
61. *Ibid.*
62. *Ibid.*
63. *Ibid.*
64. C. Ray Hall Exhibit 3, pp. 2-3.
65. CE 2270, 2888.
66. C. Ray Hall Exhibit 3, p. 3.
67. *Ibid.*
68. CE 2980; see CE 2400.
69. CE 2980, p. 13.
70. See chapter 16, "Ties to Extreme Right-Wing Elements."
71. Joachim Joesten, *The Case Against Lyndon Johnson in the Assassination of President Kennedy* (Munich: Dreischstr. 5, Selbstverlag, 1967), p. 9.
72. WR 296; see chapter 15, "Wanted for Treason."
73. CE 2002, p. 90.
74. *Ibid.*
75. *Ibid.*
76. CE 2245; CD 86, p. 495.
77. As cited in the prior note.
78. Noyes, *Legacy of Doubt*, p. 71.
79. *Ibid.*, pp. 58-59.
80. *Ibid.*, pp. 28-29, 39, 40, 58.
81. *Ibid.*, pp. 71-72.
82. *Ibid.*, p. 72.
83. *Ibid.*, pp. 65-66, 72-73, 75.
84. *Ibid.*, p. 75.
85. *Ibid.*
86. CE 2399.
87. *Ibid.*
88. CE 2270. Ruby subsequently specified that he attended to his downtown business in the late morning (C. Ray Hall Exhibit 3, pp. 2-3), and other witnesses saw him in that area between 11 a.m. and noon (CE 2265; CE 2002, p. 160).

89. CE 2399.
90. *Ibid*.
91. CE 2322.
92. *Ibid*.
93. CE 2399.
94. CE 2303. Telephone records for Ruby's home phone show one call that day at 6:40 p.m. to the Bull-Pen restaurant in nearby Arlington, Texas (CE 2302). That establishment, called frequently from Ruby's phones during the fall of 1963 (CE 2302, 2303), was operated by Ralph Paul (CE 2302), a night club partner of Ruby (WR 795) and an acquaintance of Ruby's roommate, George Senator (14H 284). Although Senator did not recall calling Paul from his home phone, he testified that he did place calls to Paul at the Bull-Pen and did occasionally use his home phone for local calls (14H 298, 284); thus Senator may have placed that 6:40 p.m. call. Note that Ruby said he was in the Carousel Club on November 21 from the afternoon until about 9:30 p.m. (C. Ray Hall Exhibit 3, p. 3). Thus, attributing that call to Ruby would fit his alibi no better than it would fit the reports of the Houston witnesses described in the text below.
95. CE 2384; CD 86, p. 496.
96. CE 2303 (the number was 729–0891).
97. CE 2302, 2303.
98. CE 2399.
99. *Ibid*.
100. *Ibid*.
101. *Ibid*.
102. *Ibid*.
103. *Ibid*.
104. *Ibid*.
105. *Ibid*.
106. CD 86, p. 496; see also CE 2384.
107. CE 1518.
108. CE 2399.
109. *Ibid*.
110. *Ibid*.
111. Secret Service Agent Elmer Moore reported simply, "Ruby has no noticeable facial scars" (CE2399). In light of the poor quality of his investigation of Ruby's activities of November 21 (*ibid*., see above), and his questionable role in assisting Ruby's presentation of his alibi (see chapter 14, "A Canned Alibi"), this simple assertion does not preclude a faint scar observable in the background of a heavy beard growth.
112. From the transcript of Jack Ruby's trial, March 10, 1964, reprinted in *Trauma*, vol. 6, no. 4 (1964), p. 67.
113. *Ibid*.
114. *Ibid*.
115. JFK microfilm, vol. 5, p. D17.
116. *Ibid*.
117. JFK microfilm, vol. 5, p. G5.
118. CE 2399.
119. *Ibid*.
120. *Ibid*.

121. *Ibid.*
122. *Ibid.*
123. *Ibid.*; C. Ray Hall Exhibit 2.
124. CE 2399.
125. *Ibid.*
126. *Ibid.*
127. See chapter 13, "The Carlins."
128. 13H 498–99; 13H 333–34.
129. 15H 642–43.
130. CD 722, p. 7.
131. Karen Carlin Exhibit 5318.
132. 15H 643–44.
133. See chapter 13, "The Carlins."
134. C. Ray Hall Exhibit 3, p. 3; 5H 183; CE 2259; CE 2274; CE 2344; CD 360, p. 130.
135. *Houston Post*, April 20, 1975, p. 2A.
136. CE 2259, 2274; HAH 9H 335.
137. See chapter 9, "Joseph Campisi."
138. HAH 9H 363–64, 374.
139. CE 2259.
140. *Dallas Morning News*, March 18, 1973, p. 53.
141. CE 2266–68; CD 86, p. 496.
142. CE 2266–68; HAH 9H 807.
143. CD 86, p. 531; CE 2267.
144. Decker Exhibit 5323, pp. 469, 527.
145. CE 2267; 15H 620–39; HAH 9H 805–941.
146. CE 2267.
147. CE 2266.
148. CD 86, pp. 527–28.
149. *Ibid.*; 15H 624–25; HAH 9H 806; see chapter 8, "Prostitution and Other Criminal Activities."
150. CD 86, p. 527.
151. CE 2267; 15H 622–23.
152. See chapter 19.
153. 15H 667.
154. 15H 339–40.
155. HAH 9H 806–7, 899–905; CE 2267; 15H 631–36.
156. Friday: 15H 630; HAH 9H 879. Sunday: Meyers testified that he heard about the Oswald shooting while driving to McKinney, Texas "early Sunday morning" before a 10 a.m. golf date in Sherman, at least 30 miles farther (HAH 9H 878, 914–16). But Ruby shot Oswald at 11:21 a.m. (WR 219). See also HAH 9H 807; CE 2267.
157. CD 223, p. 366.
158. *Ibid.*
159. *Ibid.*, p. 366–67.
160. *Ibid.*
161. *Ibid.*, p. 366.
162. WR 614.
163. CD 223, p. 367; cf. WR 614.
164. JFK microfilm, vol. 5, p. L1.

165. *Ibid.*
166. On November 24, 1963, Bill DeMar, who performed a mind reading act at the Carousel Club, told the Associated Press and the FBI that Oswald had been a patron at the Carousel Club nine days prior and had been one of the audience members to participate in his act (*Dallas Morning News*, November 25, 1963, p. 6; Crowe Exhibit 1). DeMar's burst of activity after Ruby shot Oswald, placing several calls to the Dallas Police Homicide Division and media contacts indicates how seriously he took this observation (CD 1193, p. 205, 209; CE 2995, pp. 500–505). DeMar then went into hiding upon advice from news media contacts that he was "in a dangerous position if, in fact, there was a compact between Oswald and Ruby and other members of the underworld"(CE 2995, p. 503) and that the people possibly interested in killing him were "friends of Jack's"(15H 110). Specific reports of meetings between Ruby and Oswald at the Carousel Club on October 4 and in early November, respectively, were furnished to authorities by Dallas attorney Carroll Jarnagin (CE 2821) and Wilbur Waldon Litchfield (CE 3149, 14H 107–8, see 13H 214–15). Also interesting is the positive testimony of Marguerite Oswald, Lee's mother, that she was shown a picture of Jack Ruby among several others by an FBI agent the day *before* Ruby shot Oswald.(1H 152–53,237–38; WR 364)
167. CE 2821.
168. Ruby volunteered that he and Oswald had private boxes "close together in the post office" (14H 542, 557, 567) and requested that the polygraph examiner ask him "Did you ever meet [Oswald] at the post office or at the club?" and "How many times did he come up to the club?" (14H 557) The latter question would have been strange for Ruby to have posed had he not known that they had met there.
169. Ruby told the FBI and the Warren Commission that he went directly home and to bed after closing the Carousel Club at about 2:00 a.m., Friday November 22 (C. Ray Hall Exhibit 3, p. 3; 5H 183). But his Carousel employee Larry Crafard provided the story that he accompanied Ruby for breakfast at the B&B Restaurant early that morning (Crafard Exhibit 5226). There is no possibility that Crafard could have been mistaken for Oswald since Crafard had "no front teeth," was "creepy," looked "like a bum" and had "sandy hair," as witnesses described him (CE 2403; Karen Carlin Exhibit 5318), whereas Oswald was good looking, had all of his front teeth, and had brown hair (WR 126; CE 3002).
170. CD 86, p. 526; JFK microfilm, vol. 5, p. L1.
171. CE 1019, p. 668.
172. CE 1020, pp. 679, 682–90; 2H 68, 143; see WR 43–45.
173. CE 1020, pp. 682–90.
174. *Ibid.*, p. 679.
175. *Ibid.*, p. 694.
176. *Ibid.*
177. *Ibid.*, pp. 671, 694–95, 702.
178. *Dallas Morning News*, September 5, 1982, p. 7F.
179. CD 86, p. 271.
180. 15H 660.
181. HAH 5H 46–49, 58, see pp. 20–21; CE 1693; Jim Marrs, "Oswald in San Antonio—the Kirkwood Connection," *Coverups*, November 1982, p. 1.

182. 15H 422; see 430.
183. 15H 422.
184. Hansen Exhibit 1. Hansen was not sure whether the incident occurred on November 22 or the day before, but believed it occurred on November 22 (15H 449); this is the date reported in National Archives, entry 45, Ruby-Oswald chronology, p. 840.
185. Hansen Exhibit 1; 15H 442.
186. Hansen Exhibit 1.
187. HAH 5H 168, 170; see chapter 17, "Mob Subversion."
188. C. Ray Hall Exhibit 3, p. 4; 5H 183; HAH 5H 170.
189. HAH 5H 170.
190. 5H 183; C. Ray Hall Exhibit 3, p. 4.
191. See chapter 17, "Mob Subversion."
192. HAH 5H 170.
193. C. Ray Hall Exhibit 3, p. 4.
194. 5H 183.
195. C. Ray Hall Exhibit 3, p. 4; 5H 183–84. Note that President Kennedy was shot at 12:30 (WR 48).
196. C. Ray Hall Exhibit 3, p. 4; 5H 183–84.
197. WR 32, 34; the Dallas Morning News Building is at Houston and Young streets.
198. C. Ray Hall Exhibit 2, p. 14.
199. CE 1322, p. 754.
200. 14H 564.
201. National Archives, entry 45, Ruby-Oswald chronology, p. 841.
202. 14H 564.
203. Thompson, *Six Seconds in Dallas*, chapter 3; Epstein, *Inquest*, chapter 3.
204. WR 52.
205. WR 50–52.
206. See "Three Assassination-Eve Contacts," this chapter.
207. See chapter 2.
208. See chapter 4, "Eugene Hale Brading."
209. *Ibid*.
210. *Ibid*.
211. *Ibid*.
212. HAH 9H 413.
213. HAH 9H 363–64, 374; CE 2259.
214. CE 2259; CD 86, pp. 138–39.
215. See chapter 12, "At Parkland Hospital."
216. CE 1763, 2430.
217. WR 6–7.
218. See chapter 12, "An Encounter with Dallas Policeman Harry Olsen."
219. See chapter 12, "At the Dallas Police Building."
220. See chapter 13.
221. See chapter 3.
222. 14H 567.
223. 15H 619–20.
224. 15H 620.
225. 15H 660.
226. *Ibid*.

227. Sybil Leek and Bert Sager, *The Assassination Chain* (New York: Corwin, 1976), p. 206. See also JFK microfilm, vol. 5, pp. B15–16; in light of other events, Carlin's period of absence may not be so easily explainable.

228. See chapter 5.

229. Malone, "The Secret Life of Jack Ruby," *New Times*, January 23, 1978, p. 51.; Jack Anderson, *Albuquerque Journal*, September 8, 1976; Jack Anderson, *Washington Post*, January 3, 1979, p. B15.

230. See chapter 14.

231. See chapter 14, "The Commission's Conduct of Ruby's Hearing."

232. 5H 198; see chapter 12, "Not Grieving."

233. 5H 206; see chapter 14, "Ruby's Disclosures."

234. 14H 543, 548, 565–66.

235. 14H 542, 557, 567.

236. 14H 543, 548.

237. 14H 566.

238. Buchanan, *Who Killed Kennedy?* (Secker and Warburg), pp. 130, 137–39.

Part VI:
Echoes of November 22

1. Navasky, *Kennedy Justice*, p. 49n; see also HAH 9H 21.

2. See chapter 17, "Base Alliances in the White House."

3. Navasky, p. 49n; Salerno and Tompkins, *The Crime Confederation*, pp. 271–73; Mollenhoff, *Strike Force*, pp. 5–6.

4. *Business Week*, November 23, 1963, p. 41; Scott, "The Death of Kennedy and the Vietnam War," in Blumenthal and Yazijian, eds., *Government by Gunplay: Assassination Conspiracy Theories from Dallas to Today*, p. 159.

5. Scott, "The Death of Kennedy and the Vietnam War," in Blumenthal and Yazijian, p. 159.

6. *Ibid.*, pp. 167–68.

7. Tad Szulc, *Compulsive Spy* (New York: Viking, 1974), pp. 96–98.

8. Anson, *"They've Killed the President!"* p. 325.

9. Scott, "The Death of Kennedy and the Vietnam War," in Blumenthal and Yazijian, p. 168.

10. *Ibid.*; Anson, p. 325.

11. "The Mob," part 2, *Life*, September 8, 1967, p. 101.

12. *Ibid.*

13. *Ibid.*

14. Tom Wicker, *JFK and LBJ: The Influence of Personality on Politics* (New York: William Morrow, 1968), pp. 183–85; Alfred Steinberg, *Sam Johnson's Boy* (New York: Macmillan, 1968), pp. 760–61.

15. See excerpts reprinted in Scott in Blumenthal and Yazijian, pp. 170–81.

16. *Ibid.*, pp. 156–57; see pp. 152–87 and reprints from and references to the Pentagon Papers in this source.

17. *Ibid.*, p. 157.

18. Anson, p. iv.

19. *Ibid.*, p. 325.

20. *Ibid.*, pp. 293–94; see also McCoy, *The Politics of Heroin in Southeast*

Asia, chapters 3–7; and Viorst, "The Mafia, the CIA, and the Kennedy Assassination," *Washingtonian*, November 1975, p. 114.

21. Anson, pp. 293–94; McCoy, p. 248.
22. Anson, p. 294; McCoy, p. 211.
23. Anson, p. 294.
24. Jeremiah O'Leary, "Haig Probe: Did Nixon Get Cash From Asia?" *Washington Star*, December 5, 1976, p. A11.
25. *Ibid.*
26. McCoy, pp. 186–87.
27. *Ibid.*; O'Leary, in *Washington Star*, December 5, 1976, p. A11.
28. O'Leary, in *Washington Star*, December 5, 1976, p. A11.
29. *Ibid.*
30. McCoy, pp. 186–87.
31. *Ibid.*; also see pp. 171–72, 218–219.
32. *Ibid.*, p. 213.
33. *Ibid.*
34. *Ibid.*, pp. 215–16.
35. *Ibid.*, p. 216; see Moldea, *The Hoffa Wars*, p. 352.

Chapter 21
More Assassinations

1. Gaia Servadio, *Mafioso* (New York: Stein and Day, 1976), p. 279.
2. Notes to *Sicily in Music and Song* (London: Argo Record Company, 1965), No. ZFB 71; Pantaleone, *The Mafia and Politics*, pp. 205–6.
3. Pantaleone, pp. 205–6.
4. *New York Times,* reprinted in Gage, *The Mafia Is Not an Equal Opportunity Employer*, p. 150; Eugene Methvin, "How the Mafia Preys on the Poor," *Reader's Digest*, September 1970, p. 55; Harry Kelly, Hearst newspapers, March 1970, reprinted in *U.S.–House, OC Control*, p. 423.
5. As cited in the prior note.
6. *New York Times,* reprinted in Gage, *The Mafia Is Not an Equal Opportunity Employer*, p. 150.
7. Cressey, *Theft of the Nation*, p. 196.
8. *U.S.–House, Criminal Justice Hearings*, p. 163.
9. *Ibid.*
10. Methvin, in *Reader's Digest*, p. 50.
11. *Ibid.*, p. 54; *U.S.–House, Criminal Justice Hearings*, p. 163; Salerno and Tompkins, *The Crime Confederation*, p. 360.
12. *U.S.–House, Criminal Justice Hearings*, p. 150.
13. Malcolm X, *The Autobiography of Malcolm X*, p. 84.
14. *Ibid.*, pp. 84–85.
15. *Ibid.*, p. 216.
16. *Ibid.*, p. 221.
17. Peter Goldman, *The Death and Life of Malcolm X*, p. 82.
18. Malcolm X, *The Autobiography of Malcolm X*, p. 221.
19. From a speech by Malcolm X at the founding rally of the Organization of Afro-American Unity, transcribed in Malcolm X, *By Any Means Necessary*, pp. 50–51.

20. Goldman, pp. 273–74; epilogue by Alex Haley in Malcolm X, *The Autobiography of Malcolm X*, pp. 434–35.
21. As cited in the prior note.
22. Goldman, pp. 274–76; epilogue by Alex Haley in Malcolm X, *The Autobiography of Malcolm X*, pp. 436–37.
23. As cited in the prior note.
24. Goldman, pp. 289–92.
25. Epilogue by Alex Haley in Malcolm X, *The Autobiography of Malcolm X*, p. 441; Goldman, pp. 291–92.
26. Goldman, p. 293; epilogue by Alex Haley in Malcolm X, *The Autobiography of Malcolm X*, p. 448.
27. Goldman, pp. 358–59.
28. *Ibid.*, p. 349.
29. *Ibid.*, p. 288; *New York Times*, February 23, 1965, p. 20.
30. Goldman, pp. 288, 335, 370.
31. *Ibid.*, p. 310.
32. *Ibid.*, p. 329.
33. *Ibid.*
34. *Ibid.*, pp. 304, 310–11, 321.
35. *Ibid.*, pp. 304, 321–22.
36. *Ibid.*, p. 304.
37. *Ibid.*
38. *Ibid.*, pp. 304–5, 323.
39. *Ibid.*, p. 324.
40. *Ibid.*, pp. 331, 333.
41. *Ibid.*, p. 311.
42. *Ibid.*, p. 331.
43. *Ibid.*
44. *Ibid.*, p. 329.
45. *Ibid.*
46. *Ibid.*
47. *Ibid.*, pp. 313–14.
48. *Ibid.*, p. 313.
49. *Ibid.*, pp. 315–17.
50. *Ibid.*, p. 315.
51. *Ibid.*, p. 316.
52. *Ibid.*
53. *Ibid.*, p. 317.
54. *Ibid.*
55. *Ibid.*
56. *Ibid.*
57. *Ibid.*, p. 349.
58. *Ibid.*
59. *Ibid.*, pp. 350–53.
60. Teresa, *My Life in the Mafia*, p. 178; Brill, *The Teamsters*, pp. 131, 139–40, 69–70; see Appendix 2, entries 6.15, 6.17, 21.23, 22.6, 22.12, and initial segment of chapter 19.
61. Allan Morrison, *Ebony*, October 1965, pp. 138–39; see James Farmer, *Freedom When?* (New York: Random House, 1965), p. 100.
62. Goldman, p. 367n, 373–74.

63. Mollenhoff, *Strike Force*, p. 113.
64. Demaris, *Captive City*, p. 14.
65. Mollenhoff, *Strike Force*, p. 113.
66. *Ibid.*, pp. 112–13.
67. Demaris, pp. 64, 324.
68. *Life*, May 30, 1969, p. 45.
69. Frank Hercules, "To Live in Harlem," *National Geographic*, February 1977, p. 201.
70. *Ibid.*
71. From a speech of Martin Luther King on August 28, 1963 in Washington, D.C., in Houston Peterson, ed., *A Treasury of the World's Great Speeches*, p. 839.
72. Martin Luther King, Jr., "Beyond the Los Angeles Riots. Next Stop: The North," *Saturday Review*, November 13, 1965, p. 34.
73. Louis Lomax, *To Kill a Black Man*, p. 165.
74. *Ibid.*
75. Mark Lane and Dick Gregory, *Code Name Zorro* (New York: Pocket Books, 1977), chapter 18.
76. *New York Times*, March 11, 1969, pp. 1, 16.
77. *Ibid.*
78. *Ibid.*
79. *Ibid.*
80. *Ibid.*
81. *Ibid.*
82. *Ibid.*
83. *New York Times*, March 14, 1969, p. 10.
84. *New York Times*, March 13, 1969, p. 22.
85. *New York Times*, March 17, 1969, p. 23.
86. *New York Times*, March 13, 1969, p. 22.
87. *New York Times*, June 11 and 13, 1978.
88. *Washington Post*, December 31, 1978, p. A1.
89. "The Politics of Conspiracy," conference at Boston University, general session, Morse Auditorium, February 1, 1975, tape-recorded by author.
90. *Ibid.*
91. *The Two Kennedys*, shown at Orson Welles Theater, Cambridge, Mass., March 14, 1976.
92. *Ibid.*
93. HAH-MLK 13H 267–68.
94. See chapters 4 and 18.
95. HAR 334.
96. HAH-MLK 13H 268, 274, 275, 278.
97. HAH-MLK 13H 275, 278.
98. *Ibid.*; HAR 353.
99. HAH-MLK 13H 278; HAR 353.
100. HAR 352, 305–6; see HAH-MLK 13H 272.
101. HAR 332.
102. HAH-MLK 13H 268.
103. HAH-MLK 13H 269–70.
104. HAH-MLK 13H 270.
105. HAH-MLK 13H 280–81.

106. *U.S.-House, OC Control*, pp. 416–17.
107. HAH-MLK 13H 280.
108. HAH-MLK 13H 268, 273.
109. HAR 387–88; names spelled as determined correct by the House Assassinations Committee.
110. HAR 387–88.
111. *Ibid.*; see HAH-MLK 13H 276–77.
112. HAR 387.
113. HAR 388.
114. *Ibid.*
115. *Ibid.*
116. *Ibid.*
117. *Ibid.*
118. HAR 385–86.
119. HAR 386.
120. *Ibid.*
121. *Ibid.*
122. *Ibid.*
123. Kaiser, *"RFK Must Die!"* pp. 15–27; *New York Times*, June 5, 1968, p. 1.
124. Turner and Christian, *The Assassination of Robert F. Kennedy*, pp. xiii-xiv.
125. *Ibid.*, p. 178.
126. Kaiser, p. 29; Turner and Christian, p. xiv. The photo of Kennedy with the necktie near his right hand was widely published, for example, in the *Los Angeles Herald Examiner*, "extra," June 6, 1968, p. 1; and Turner and Christian, photo section, p. 3.
127. Kaiser, pp. 26–30, Appendix A.
128. Aurelius, *The Meditations of Marcus Aurelius*, I.16.
129. See chapter 5, "Assassination Plots by Jimmy Hoffa," and Moldea, *The Hoffa Wars*, p. 150.
130. See chapter 5.
131. Sheridan, *The Fall and Rise of Jimmy Hoffa*, p. 300.
132. See chapter 9, "Frank Chavez."
133. Sheridan, p. 407.
134. *Ibid.*, pp. 406–8.
135. *Ibid.*
136. Turner and Christian, p. 54.
137. *New York Times*, June 5, 1968, p. 1.
138. Turner and Christian, p. xiii.
139. *Ibid.*, p. 26.
140. *Ibid.*
141. Stated by Braden on a radio show with Pat Buchanan and the author on WRC, Washington, D.C., November 24, 1983.
142. Turner and Christian, p. 27.
143. See chapter 4, "Jim Garrison."
144. Noyes, *Legacy of Doubt*, pp. 232–35; Turner and Christian, p. 27.
145. Turner and Christian, p. 320.
146. Kaiser, p. 469.
147. Moldea, *The Hoffa Wars*, pp. 187, 256–58, 262; Teresa, pp. 4, 301, 307–9.
148. Teresa, pp. 4, 299.

149. Moldea, *The Hoffa Wars*, p. 187.
150. Kaiser, p. 276.
151. *Ibid.*
152. *Ibid.*
153. Houghton, *Special Unit Senator*, pp. 5–7, 89.
154. *Ibid.*, p. 89.
155. Kaiser, pp. 209, 216–17; Turner and Christian, pp. 108–9.
156. WR 786–87.
157. Kaiser, pp. 205, 209; Godfrey Janson, *Why Robert Kennedy Was Killed* (New York: Third Press, 1970), p. 126; Turner and Christian, p. 216.
158. *U.S.–Senate, Kefauver Hearings*, part 5, pp. 391, 399–400.
159. Houghton, p. 191.
160. Jack Anderson's column, *San Francisco Chronicle*, December 31, 1970, p. 25.
161. Kaiser, p. 537; Turner and Christian, p. 220.
162. Turner and Christian, p. 220.
163. *Ibid.*
164. Kaiser, pp. 206, 322; Turner and Christian, p. 220.
165. Kaiser, p. 537.
166. Turner and Christian, p. 220.
167. Peter Dale Scott, Paul L. Hoch, and Russell Stetler, eds., *The Assassinations: Dallas and Beyond* (New York: Vintage Books, 1976), p. 334.
168. Betsy Langman and Alexander Cockburn, "Sirhan's Gun," *Harper's*, January 1975, p. 18; Turner and Christian, pp. 162, 376, 379; Lowenstein, "The Murder of Robert Kennedy," *Saturday Review*, February 19, 1977, pp. 6–17; Dan Moldea, "Who Really Killed Bobby Kennedy?" *Regardie's*, June 1987, p. 63.
169. Langman and Cockburn, in *Harper's*, p. 18; Turner and Christian, p. 376.
170. A Los Angeles Police report dated July 8, 1968, reproduced in Turner and Christian, p. 376.
171. Langman and Cockburn, in *Harper's*, p. 18.
172. *Ibid.*; Turner and Christian, p. 162.
173. A Los Angeles Police report dated July 8, 1968, reproduced in Turner and Christian, p. 376.
174. Lowenstein, in *Saturday Review*, pp. 6–7; Langman and Cockburn, in *Harper's*, pp. 18–20; Turner and Christian, p. 162.
175. Langman and Cockburn, in *Harper's*, pp. 18–20; Turner and Christian, p. 162; Moldea, in *Regardie's*, pp. 62, 64.
176. Turner and Christian, p. 162.
177. Langman and Cockburn, in *Harper's*, p. 18; Turner and Christian, p. 162; Lowenstein, in *Saturday Review*, p. 6; William Harper affidavit, December 28, 1970, reproduced in Turner and Christian, pp. 378–81.
178. Lowenstein, in *Saturday Review*, p. 8.
179. Filmed and tape recorded interview of Uecker by Theodore Charach in the film *The Second Gun*, shown at Boston University on February 1, 1975; Lowenstein, in *Saturday Review*, p. 8.
180. As cited in the prior note.
181. William Harper affidavit, December 28, 1970, reproduced in Turner and Christian, pp. 378–81.
182. Turner and Christian, p. 158.

183. William Harper affidavit, December 28, 1970, reproduced in Turner and Christian, pp. 378–81.

184. *Ibid.*

185. *Ibid.*

186. Langman and Cockburn, in *Harper's*, p. 26.

187. Turner and Christian, pp. 171–73.

188. *Ibid.*, pp. 174–77.

189. *Ibid.*

190. *Ibid.*, p. 178; Lowenstein, in *Saturday Review*, pp. 7–8.

191. As cited in the prior note.

192. Turner and Christian, pp. 177–91.

193. Lowenstein, in *Saturday Review*, pp. 8–9.

194. *Ibid.*, p. 9

195. Turner and Christian, p. 172.

196. *Ibid.*, p. 178.

197. Lowenstein, in *Saturday Review*, p. 10.

198. "Charts and photographs showing layout of Ambassador Hotel area where shooting occurred," series E, reproduced in Turner and Christian, photo section, p. 12; see Turner and Christian, p. 186.

199. As cited in the prior note.

200. As reproduced in Turner and Christian, photo section, p. 11; see Turner and Christian, Exhibit 2, p. 347.

201. As cited in note 198.

202. Moldea, in *Regardie's*, p. 69.

203. Turner and Christian, Exhibit 4, pp. 350–51.

204. *Ibid.*, Exhibit 3, pp. 348–49.

205. As cited in note 198; also Turner and Christian, pp. 178–81, 345–46, photo section p. 10.

206. Turner and Christian, pp. 187–88.

207. *Ibid.*, pp. 9–10, 175–77, 241–44; Lowenstein, in *Saturday Review*, p. 9.

208. Turner and Christian, p. 191.

209. William Harper affidavit, December 28, 1970, reproduced in Turner and Christian, pp. 378–81; Langman and Cockburn, in *Harper's*, p. 18; Turner and Christian, p. 162; Lowenstein, in *Saturday Review*, p. 6.

210. Filmed and tape-recorded interview of Cesar by Charach in the movie *The Second Gun*, shown at Boston University on February 1, 1975; Turner and Christian, pp. 165–68; Kaiser, p. 26.

211. Moldea, in *Regardie's*, pp. 76–78.

212. Cesar interview, in *The Second Gun*.

213. William Harper affidavit, December 28, 1970, reproduced in Turner and Christian, pp. 378–81.

214. Cesar interview, in *The Second Gun*.

215. Turner and Christian, p. 161.

216. *Ibid.*, pp. 161–62.

217. KNXT newscast, June 5, 1968, played in *The Second Gun*.

218. *France Soir*, June 6, 1968, p. 8 ("Un garde du corps de Kennedy, dégaine à son tour, fait feu de la hanche, comme dans un western").

219. Recorded in *The Second Gun*.

220. Turner and Christian, p. 165.

221. *Ibid.*, pp. 165–66; *The Second Gun*.

222. As cited in the prior note.
223. Turner and Christian, p. 166.
224. *Ibid.*; *The Second Gun*.
225. Turner and Christian, pp. 166–67.
226. *Los Angeles Herald Examiner*, "extra," June 6, 1968, p. 1, reproduced in Turner and Christian, photo section, p. 3.
227. Turner and Christian, photo section, p. 2.
228. Turner and Christian, p. 167.
229. *Ibid.*, pp. 157–58.
230. Statement of Charach at "The Politics of Conspiracy," conference at Boston University, workshop on the RFK assassination, George Sherman Student Center, February 2, 1975, tape-recorded by author.
231. *Ibid.*
232. *Ibid.*
233. *Ibid.*
234. *Ibid.*
235. Reid, *Mickey Cohen: Mobster*, pp. 185–86.
236. Turner and Christian, p. 165.
237. Conversation between Alex Bottus, Theodore Charach and the author, "The Politics of Conspiracy," conference, Sherman Center Conference Auditorium, Boston University, February 2, 1975, tape-recording in author's possession.
238. *Ibid.*
239. *Ibid.*
240. *Ibid.*
241. Moldea, in *Regardie's*, p. 74.
242. Conversation with Bottus, February 2, 1975.
243. *Ibid.*
244. Walsh, *New York Times*, September 10, 1973, p. 28; see chapter 22, "Bebe Rebozo, C. Arnholt Smith and Murray Chotiner."
245. Conversation with Bottus, February 2, 1975.
246. *Ibid.*
247. See chapter 1, "The Assassination of Chicago Mayor Anton Cermak."
248. *Ibid.*
249. *Ibid.*
250. Demaris, p. 120; see chapter 1, "The Assassination of Chicago Mayor Anton Cermak."
251. Lyle, *The Dry and Lawless Years*, p. 267; Demaris, p. 120.
252. Allsop, *The Bootleggers*, pp. 169–70.
253. *Ibid.*, p. 170.
254. Turner and Christian, pp. 163–64; also as reported by Charach in *The Second Gun*.
255. Cooper declared, "We will stipulate that these fragments did come from Senator Kennedy. We will further stipulate they came from the gun." As reported by Theodore Charach in *The Second Gun*.
256. A few moments after Cooper's stipulation, Wolfer testified, "Because of the damage, I cannot say positively that it was fired from that gun, that is Sirhan's gun." As reported by Charach in *The Second Gun*.
257. Reid, *The Grim Reapers*, pp. 187, 189–91; *New York Times*, January 7, 1969, p. 25; Kaiser, p. 229.

258. As cited in the prior note.
259. *New York Times*, September 24, 1969, p. 41, August 26, 1969, p. 20, January 7, 1969, p. 25.
260. As cited in the prior note.
261. Dorman, *Payoff*, pp. 47–49.
262. *Time*, November 21, 1977, p. 39.
263. Kaiser, pp. 229, 244–45.
264. Noyes, p. 238; Kaiser, p. 245.
265. Noyes, p. 238; Kaiser, p. 241.
266. Kaiser, p. 241.
267. Noyes, p. 238.
268. *Ibid.*
269. Turner and Christian, pp. 109, 114–18.
270. *Ibid.*, p. 116.
271. *Washington Monthly*, February 29, 1979, p. 7.
272. Turner and Christian, pp. 115–18, 152, 314–15.
273. See the displayed footnote earlier in this section.
274. *Washington Star*, July 12, 1979, p. 1.
275. *Ibid.*
276. See chapter 17, "Mob Subversion."
277. *Ibid.*
278. Reid, *The Grim Reapers*, pp. 203–4; see Appendix 2, entry 24.6. Nani is identified as a Mafia member in *U.S.–Senate, OC and Narcotics Hearings*, p. 308, chart D.
279. *Albuquerque Journal*, March 9, 1977, p. 1.
280. *Ibid.*
281. Moldea, *The Hoffa Wars*, p. 104.
282. Sheridan, p. 508; see chapter 22, "Bebe Rebozo, C. Arnholt Smith and Murray Chotiner."

Chapter 22
Richard Nixon and the Mob

1. Dorman, *Payoff*, p. 13.
2. Gage, *The Mafia Is Not an Equal Opportunity Employer*, pp. 98–116; *Newsweek*, July 31, 1972, pp. 21–22; *Newsweek*, January 19, 1970, p. 23; *U.S.–House, OC in Sports*, p. 752.
3. Gerth, in Blumenthal and Yazijian, *Government By Gunplay: Assassination Conspiracy Theories from Dallas to Today*, p. 151.
4. The close Nixon-Rebozo relationship is well known; i.e., see Gerth, in Blumenthal and Yazijian, pp. 139–40.
5. Scott, "From Dallas to Watergate," in Blumenthal and Yazijian, p. 128; Gerth, in Blumenthal and Yazijian, p. 142; Moldea, *The Hoffa Wars*, p. 105; *U.S.–Senate, OC and Narcotics Hearings*, p. 1049.
6. *Ibid.*
7. Scott, "From Dallas to Watergate," in Blumenthal and Yazijian, p. 114; HAH KH 7–8.
8. Moldea, *The Hoffa Wars*, p. 105.
9. Gerth, in Blumenthal and Yazijian, pp. 137–39, 141–47; Scott, "From

Dallas to Watergate," in Blumenthal and Yazijian, pp. 128–29; Moldea, *The Hoffa Wars*, pp. 104–6.

10. Scott, "From Dallas to Watergate," in Blumenthal and Yazijian, pp. 128–29.

11. *Ibid.*

12. *Ibid.*

13. *New York Times*, January 21, 1974, p. 18.

14. Messick, *Lansky*, p. 192; Waller, *The Swiss Bank Connection*, pp. 145–46.

15. Reid, *The Grim Reapers*, pp. 119–23, 139–40; Waller, pp. 123–35; Hank Messick and Burt Goldblatt, *The Mobs and the Mafia*, pp. 195–96; Gerth, in Blumenthal and Yazijian, pp. 137–39.

16. Gerth, in Blumenthal and Yazijian, p. 140.

17. *New York Times*, January 21, 1974, p. 1.

18. Gerth, in Blumenthal and Yazijian, p. 139; Waller, pp. 132–33.

19. *Life*, February 3, 1967, pp. 68–69.

20. Waller, p. 133; Gerth, in Blumenthal and Yazijian, p. 138.

21. *New York Times*, January 21, 1974, p. 18.

22. *New York Times*, September 10, 1973, pp. 1, 28.

23. *Ibid.*, p. 28.

24. Jeff Gerth, statement at "The Politics of Conspiracy," conference at Boston University, workshop on organized crime, George Sherman Student Center, February 1, 1975, tape-recorded by author.

25. *New York Times*, September 10, 1973, p. 28.

26. *Ibid.*, pp. 1, 28.

27. *Washington Post*, October 11, 1984, p. A18.

28. *New York Times*, September 10, 1973, pp. 1, 28.

29. *Ibid.*, p. 28.

30. *Ibid.*

31. *Ibid.*

32. *Ibid.*

33. See chapter 21.

34. Gerth, in Blumenthal and Yazijian, p. 149.

35. Sheridan, *The Fall and Rise of Jimmy Hoffa*, p. 465; Waller, p. 126; Gerth, in Blumenthal and Yazijian, p. 135; Moldea, *The Hoffa Wars*, pp. 103–5.

36. Waller, p. 126; Moldea, *The Hoffa Wars*, p. 104; Gerth, in Blumenthal and Yazijian, p. 135.

37. Sheridan, p. 508.

38. Waller, p. 127; Moldea, *The Hoffa Wars*, p. 104.

39. Bernard Fensterwald, Jr., *Coincidence or Conspiracy* (New York: Zebra Books, 1977), p. 128.

40. Moldea, *The Hoffa Wars*, p. 104.

41. Waller, p. 126.

42. Moldea, *The Hoffa Wars*, pp. 104–5, 260–61.

43. Sheridan, pp. 465, 493, 504.

44. *Ibid.*, pp. 408, 492.

45. Noyes, *Legacy of Doubt*, p. 142.

46. Sheridan, pp. 408–11, 430, 465, 492–94, 496, 498–504, 508, 511, 513–14, 520, 525, 526, 535.

47. Sheridan, *passim*.

48. "The Mob," part 1, *Life*, September 1, 1967, p. 22.
49. Sheridan, pp. 408–11, 430, 465, 492–94, 496, 498–504, 508, 511, 513–14, 520, 525, 526, 535.
50. Sheridan, pp. 8–9, 521.
51. Moldea, *The Hoffa Wars*, p. 261.
52. Sheridan, p. 9.
53. *Ibid.*, p. 7.
54. *New York Times*, December 24, 1971, p. 24.
55. *Los Angeles Times*, June 1, 1973, section II, p. 6.
56. Noyes, p. 34.
57. Moldea, *The Hoffa Wars*, pp. 316–17; Brill, *The Teamsters*, pp. 102–4.
58. As cited in the prior note; see Reid, *The Grim Reapers*, p. 287 for identification of Accardo.
59. Moldea, *The Hoffa Wars*, p. 317; Brill, p. 103.
60. As cited in the prior note.
61. As cited in the prior note.
62. Moldea, *The Hoffa Wars*, p. 317.
63. *Ibid.*; Brill, pp. 103–4.
64. Moldea, *The Hoffa Wars*, p. 317.
65. *Ibid.*; see also Noyes, p. 244 concerning Chotiner's presence there on another occasion.
66. Moldea, *The Hoffa Wars*, p. 318.
67. *Ibid.*; Brill, p. 104.
68. As cited in the prior note.
69. *New York Times*, April 30, 1973, p. 30.
70. *Ibid.*
71. *Chicago Tribune*, April 29, 1973, p. 6.
72. Gerth, in Blumenthal and Yazijian, p. 150; Dorman, *Payoff*, pp. 205–11.
73. Clark Mollenhoff, *Game Plan for Disaster* (New York: Norton, 1976), pp. 192–93, 329–30; Brill, p. 104; *Arizona Republic*, March 21, 1977, p. A7.
74. Brill, p. 104; *Arizona Republic*, March 21, 1977, p. A7; *Washington Post*, April 16, 1981, pp. A1, A13.
75. *Washington Post*, April 15, 1981, p. A10, April 16, 1981, pp. A1, A13; *Arizona Republic*, March 21, 1977, p. A7.
76. *Time*, August 8, 1977, p. 28; see also Moldea, *The Hoffa Wars*, p. 320; Brill, pp. 64, 105.
77. *Time*, August 8, 1977, p. 28.
78. Moldea, *The Hoffa Wars*, pp. 112, 417; Brill, p. 131; NBC Evening News, "Segment 3," June 14, 1978; *New York Times*, May 30, 1980, p. B2.
79. *Time*, August 8, 1977, p. 28.
80. *Ibid.*; Moldea, *The Hoffa Wars*, p. 7; Brill, chapter 6.
81. *Washington Post*, January 21, 1983, p. 1.
82. Moldea, *The Hoffa Wars*, p. 7.
83. *Time*, August 8, 1977, p. 28.
84. *Ibid.*
85. *Ibid.*
86. *Ibid.* Indeed, as *Time* noted, hotel records showed that Provenzano's courier was in Las Vegas on January 6, while Colson's calendar showed that Colson spoke to Fitzsimmons on January 8.
87. Moldea, *The Hoffa Wars*, p. 320.

88. Quoted in Gerth, in Blumenthal and Yazijian, pp. 131–32.
89. *Time*, August 8, 1977, p. 28.
90. *Ibid.*
91. White House Transcripts, March 21, 1973, 10:12–11:15 a.m., cited in Moldea, *The Hoffa Wars*, pp. 318–19, 432; also quoted in *Time*, August 8, 1977, p. 28 (there are minor discrepancies between the two sources).
92. *Ibid.*
93. *Ibid.*
94. Moldea, *The Hoffa Wars*, p. 319.
95. *Ibid.*
96. *New York Times*, September 24, 1981, p. D26.
97. *Ibid.*
98. Dick Russell, "Charles Colson," *Argosy*, March 1976, p. 57.
99. *Washington Post*, December 2, 1973, p. A6.
100. Mickey Cohen, *Mickey Cohen: In My Own Words* (Englewood Cliffs, N.J.: Prentice-Hall, 1975), p. 223.
101. *Ibid.*
102. Moldea, *The Hoffa Wars*, pp. 108, 260.
103. *Ibid.*
104. HAR 176; Moldea, *The Hoffa Wars*, pp. 142–43; Sheridan, pp. 224–25, 247–51, 257.
105. HAR 176; Moldea, *The Hoffa Wars*, pp. 172–73; Sheridan, p. 217.
106. Jeremiah O'Leary, "Haig Probe: Did Nixon Get Cash From Asia?" *Washington Star*, December 5, 1976, p. A11; see Moldea, *The Hoffa Wars*, pp. 351–52.
107. Moldea, *The Hoffa Wars*, p. 352.
108. As cited in Gerth, in Blumenthal and Yazijian, p. 130.
109. *Ibid.*
110. *Newsweek*, December 29, 1980, p. 19; *Albuquerque Journal*, March 19, 1980, p. B3; Ovid Demaris, *The Last Mafioso* (New York: Times Books, 1981), p. 363.
111. Gerth, in Blumenthal and Yazijian, p. 130; for Provenzano's background, see Moldea, *The Hoffa Wars*, pp. 112, 417; Brill, p. 131; NBC Evening News, "Segment 3," June 14, 1978; *New York Times*, May 30, 1980, p. B2.
112. Mollenhoff, *Strike Force*, pp. 29–30.
113. *Ibid.*, p. 32.
114. *Ibid.*
115. *Ibid.*
116. *Ibid.*, pp. 32–33.
117. *Ibid.*, p. 29.
118. *Ibid.*, p. 30.
119. *Ibid.*
120. *Ibid.*
121. *New York Times*, July 6, 1973, p. 20.
122. *Ibid.*
123. Mollenhoff, *Strike Force*, pp. 30, 33.
124. *Ibid.*, chapter 2.
125. *Newsweek*, June 23, 1969, pp. 37–38.
126. *Ibid.*
127. Mollenhoff, *Strike Force*, pp. 29–34, 144.

128. *New York Times*, July 6, 1973, p. 20; July 20, 1973, p. 13.
129. *New York Times*, July 6, 1973, p. 1, July 20, 1973, p. 13.
130. *Newsweek*, July 16, 1973, p. 19.
131. *New York Times*, July 20, 1973, p. 13.
132. *Ibid*.
133. *Ibid*.
134. *New York Times*, July 6, 1973, p. 1.
135. *New York Times*, August 9, 1973, p. 75, July 6, 1973, p. 20.
136. *Washington Post*, July 6, 1973, p. A4.
137. *U.S.-Senate, OC and Stolen Securities, 1973*, pp. 80–84.
138. *Ibid*., p. 284.
139. *Ibid*., p. 85.
140. *Ibid*., pp. 85, 87.
141. *Ibid*., p. 86.
142. *Ibid*., p. 122.
143. *Newsweek*, November 28, 1977, p. 66.
144. *Ibid*. Almost 20 Mob informants were killed in 1976 and 1977, as reported on NBC Evening News, "Segment 3," December 16, 1977; see also *Time*, November 21, 1977, p. 39.
145. *Newsweek*, November 28, 1977, p. 66.
146. *Ibid*.
147. Oglesby, in Blumenthal and Yazijian, p. 194.

Chapter 23
The Reagan Administration

1. *U.S.-Task Force Report*, p. 24.
2. See Appendix 2, section 19.
3. Grutzner, "How to Lock Out the Mafia," *Harvard Business Review*, March-April 1970, p. 49.
4. See Appendix 2, sections 13, 17c.
5. Between 1944 and 1964, only a few federally insured banks failed each year. But seven collapsed in the boom year of 1964 and four more collapsed in the first months of 1965. As Fred Cook wrote in *The Secret Rulers*, "Federal officials on every level hold that gangland mobs, entering the banking field, are mainly responsible." This view was expressed by Congressman Wright Patman, former chairman of the House Banking Committee, who charged "hoodlum connections with some of the biggest banks in the country." All information from Cook, *The Secret Rulers*, p. 367.
6. The banks that failed were San Diego's U.S. National Bank and New York's Franklin National and Security National Banks, as reported by Jeff Gerth, now a *New York Times* reporter, at "The Politics of Conspiracy," conference at Boston University, workshop on organized crime, George Sherman Student Center, February 1, 1975, tape-recorded by author.
7. See Appendix 2, entry 13.1 and section 13a.
8. *U.S.-House, OC and Worthless Securities*, p. 242.
9. See below.
10. *Wall Street Journal*, June 20, 1983, p. 1.

11. Robert I. Friedman, "Senator Paul Laxalt, The Man Who Runs The Reagan Campaign," *Mother Jones*, August-September, 1984, p. 34.
12. George Condon, Jr., "The Power Gamble: Paul Laxalt and the Nevada Gang," *Washington Dossier*, September 1983, p. 38.
13. Murray Waas, "The Senator and the Mob," *City Paper* (Washington, D.C.), May 25, 1984, p. 14.
14. Friedman, in *Mother Jones*, p. 34.
15. Pete Hamill, "With Friends Like These," *Village Voice*, August 21, 1984, p. 13.
16. Moldea, *The Hoffa Wars*, p. 7; *Time*, August 8, 1977, p. 28; Brill, *The Teamsters*, chapter 6; *Washington Post*, January 21, 1983, p. 1.
17. Moldea, *Dark Victory: Ronald Reagan, MCA, and the Mob*, p. 260.
18. Denny Walsh, "Agents Say Casino 'Skimmed' During Sen. Laxalt's Ownership," *Sacramento Bee*, November 1, 1983, p. A9.
19. Moldea, *Dark Victory*, p. 260.
20. *Washington Post*, January 21, 1983, p. 1.
21. *Ibid.*; see chapter 9, Irwin Weiner.
22. Moldea, *Dark Victory*, p. 24.
23. *Wall Street Journal*, June 20, 1983, p. 1; Friedman, in *Mother Jones*, p. 36; Dan Moldea, "Nevada's Senior Senator: Didn't See Anything Wrong With Moe Dalitz's Contributions," *Crime Control Digest*, June 11, 1984, p. 2.
24. Friedman, in *Mother Jones*, p. 36.
25. *Wall Street Journal*, June 20, 1983, p. 1.
26. *Ibid.*, p. 18.
27. Hamill, in *Village Voice*, p. 10.
28. *Ibid.*
29. Friedman, in *Mother Jones*, p. 36
30. Denny Walsh, "Laxalt Donors Included Gaming Figures With Mob Ties," *Sacramento Bee*, November 1, 1983, p. A8.
31. *Ibid.*
32. *Ibid.*
33. *Ibid.*
34. *Ibid.*
35. *Ibid.*
36. *Ibid.*
37. *Ibid.*
38. *Ibid.*; see, for example, CE 1692.
39. Denny Walsh, "Agents Say Casino 'Skimmed' During Sen. Laxalt's Ownership," *Sacramento Bee*, November 1, 1983, p. A8.
40. *Ibid.*, pp. A1, A9.
41. Walsh, in *Sacramento Bee*, November 1, 1983, pp. 1ff.
42. *Washington Post*, June 5, 1987, pp. 1ff.
43. *Ibid.*
44. *Ibid.*
45. Moldea, *Dark Victory*, p. 319; Waas, in *City Paper*, p.1.
46. Friedman, in *Mother Jones*, p. 34.
47. Dan Moldea, "Nevada's Senior Senator: Little Attention Has Been Focused on his 'Connections,' " *Crime Control Digest*, May 28, 1984, p. 2.
48. Friedman, in *Mother Jones*, p. 39.

49. *Ibid.*
50. Moldea, in *Crime Control Digest*, May 28, 1984, p. 3; *Washington Post*, December 12, 1985, p. A19.
51. Dan Moldea, "Reagan Administration Officials Closely Linked With OC," *Organized Crime Digest*, February 1982, p. 6.
52. *Washington Post*, September 29, 1984, p. A2.
53. Robert I. Friedman and Dan Moldea, "Networks Knuckle Under to Laxalt," *Village Voice*, March 5, 1985, p. 10.
54. *Ibid.*; Friedman, in *Mother Jones*, pp. 32, 34.
55. Friedman, in *Mother Jones*, p. 36.
56. Friedman and Moldea, in *Village Voice*, p. 10.
57. *Ibid.*
58. Mary McGrory column, *Washington Post*, March 6, 1986, p. A2.
59. Dan Moldea, "More Than Just Good Friends," *The Nation*, June 11, 1983, p. 732.
60. Jack Anderson, *Washington Post*, January 6, 1981, p. B13.
61. Brill, pp. 328–30.
62. Anderson, in *Washington Post*, January 6, 1981, p. B13.
63. *U.S.-President's Commission on OC, The Edge*, pp. 106–113.
64. *Albuquerque Journal*, March 19, 1980, p. B3.
65. *Ibid.*
66. Moldea, in *The Nation*, p. 732.
67. *U.S.-President's Commission on OC, The Edge*, p. 138.
68. Moldea, *Dark Victory*, p. 299.
69. Friedman, in *Mother Jones*, p. 38.
70. Moldea, *Dark Victory*, p. 343; *Washington Post*, September 17, 1987, p. A17.
71. *Washington Post*, November 14, 1985, p. A5.
72. *New York Times*, August 18, 1983, p. A21; Moldea, *Dark Victory*, p. 346–47.
73. Moldea, in *The Nation*, pp. 732–33.
74. *Ibid.*, p. 734.
75. *USA Today*, June 14, 1983, p. 8A.
76. *Washington Post*, June 10, 1987, pp. A1ff.
77. *Ibid.*
78. Moldea, in *The Nation*, p. 732.
79. *Ibid.*, p. 734.
80. *Ibid.*, p. 732.
81. Moldea, in *Organized Crime Digest*, February 1982, p. 7.
82. *Washington Post*, August 17, 1983, p. A4.
83. Hutchinson, *Imperfect Union*, p. 297.
84. *U.S.-President's Commission on OC, The Edge*, p. 47.
85. *Ibid.*, p. 33.
86. NBC Evening News, "Segment 3," September 6,7, 1977.
87. *Washington Post*, August 17, 1983, p. A4.
88. *Ibid.*
89. Hutchinson, *The Imperfect Union*, p.107.
90. *Washington Post*, August 17, 1983, p. A4.
91. *Ibid.*
92. *Ibid.*

93. Moldea, in *The Nation*, p. 733.
94. *Washington Post*, December 17, 1980, p A2.
95. Moldea, in *Organized Crime Digest*, p. 9.
96. *Washington Post*, January 28, 1981, p. A3.
97. *Washington Post*, February 18, 1981, p. A2.
98. *Washington Post*, May 30, 1985, p. A3.
99. *Ibid*.
100. *Ibid*.
101. *Washington Post*, February 8, 1981, p. A1.
102. Moldea, in *Organized Crime Digest*, pp. 8–9.
103. *Time*, September 13, 1982, p. 18.
104. Moldea, in *Organized Crime Digest*, p. 8.
105. *Time*, September 13, 1982, p. 17.
106. *Washington Post*, November 24, 1983, p. A6.
107. *Time*, September 13, 1982, pp. 17–18; Moldea, *Dark Victory*, p. 323.
108. *Time*, September 13, 1982, pp. 17–18.
109. *Ibid*., p. 17.
110. *New York Times*, October 6, 1983, p. B7; *Washington Post*, October 6, 1983, p. D2; *Washington Post*, May 26, 1987, p. A7.
111. *New York Times*, October 6, 1983, p. B7; *Washington Post*, October 6, 1983, p. D2.
112. *Washington Post*, September 20, 1983, p. A2.
113. *Ibid*. Silverman reopened his probe after receiving new information from the FBI indicating Donovan "had met in Miami with Willie Masselli and Albert Facchiano, a convicted loan shark and former captain in the Genovese Family, to set up no-show jobs for Mobsters on Schiavone construction sites" (*Time*, September 13, 1982, p. 17). Silverman again found "insufficient evidence" to prosecute Donovan, but called the lingering allegations about him "disturbing" (Moldea, *Dark Victory*, p. 324).
114. *Washington Post*, October 2, 1984, pp. 1ff.
115. *Washington Post*, April 4, 1986, p. A11.
116. *Washington Post*, April 4, 1986, p. A11. *Ibid*.
117. Moldea, in *Organized Crime Digest*, February 1982, p. 8; *Time*, October 15, 1984, p. 29.
118. *Washington Post*, May 26, 1987, pp. A1ff.
119. *Washington Post*, May 27, 1987, p. A7.
120. *New York Times*, April 4, 1986, p. B3.
121. *Ibid*.
122. *Ibid*.
123. *Washington Post*, May 26, 1987, p. A7.
124. *Washington Post*, May 16, 1987, p. A2.
125. Malcolm Johnson, "Into Hollywood," in Tyler, *Organized Crime in America*, pp. 199–205; see also Hutchinson, pp. 134–37.
126. *New York Times* reporter Jeff Gerth noted that "the movie industry since the 1930s has been controlled by organized crime." Stated at "The Politics of Conspiracy," conference at Boston University, workshop on organized crime, George Sherman Student Center, February 1, 1975, tape-recorded by author.
127. *Newsweek*, July 21, 1980, p. 31; Moldea, *Dark Victory*, p. 61.
128. Charles "Cherry Nose" Gioe was the Capone gang's "ambassador to Iowa"

in the 1930s, as noted by Clark Mollenhoff in *Strike Force: Organized Crime and the Government*, p. 37. Gioe was one of several Mobsters convicted in the 1940s of a massive extortion scheme against the Hollywood movie studios, as related by Johnson, in Tyler, p. 204. He is also noteworthy for introducing underworld IATSE official Willie Bioff, one of the leaders of this scheme, to Mobster Sidney Korshak, as noted by Ovid Demaris in *Captive City*, p. 202. Clark Mollenhoff, a journalist for the *Des Moines Register* during the early 1940s, writes that Gioe's successor, Luigi Fratto (Lew Farrell), and other Des Moines Mobsters had "a special interest in college athletes and sportswriters. Lew even offered to pick up the tab for me for a weekend 'you won't forget' in St. Louis or Chicago" (which Mollenhoff declined), as described by Mollenhoff (cited above), p. 39.

129. James Crawford, "Mr. Blacklist Goes to Washington," *Mother Jones*, June 1984, p. 10.
130. *Ibid*.
131. *Ibid*.
132. *Ibid*.
133. *Ibid*.
134. *Ibid*.
135. *Ibid*.
136. Moldea, in *Organized Crime Digest*, p. 7.
137. *Washington Post*, October 7, 1987, p. A19.
138. Moldea, in *Organized Crime Digest*, p. 7.
139. Blakey and Billings, *The Plot to Kill the President*, p. 381.
140. Gage, *The Mafia Is Not an Equal Opportunity Employer,* pp. 103, 110.
141. Moldea, in *Organized Crime Digest*, p. 10.
142. *Ibid*., pp. 10–11.
143. *Ibid*., p. 11.
144. *Ibid*.
145. *Washington Post*, July 27, 1984, p. A3.
146. *Ibid*.
147. *Ibid*.
148. *Ibid*.
149. *Ibid*.
150. *Time*, September 29, 1986, p. 19.
151. *New York Times*, November 7, 1983, pp. A1, D18; *Time*, September 29, 1986, pp. 14–22.
152. *New York Times*, January 14, 1987, pp. A1, B5; see Appendix 2, entry 18.19.
153. *Time*, September 29, 1986, p. 19.
154. *New York Times*, January 14, 1987, pp. A1, B5.
155. *Newsday*, August 27, 1987, p. 3.
156. See Appendix 2, section 18a.
157. *Washington Post*, June 10, 1987, p. A1ff.
158. See Appendix 2, section 18.
159. *Newsday*, September 10, 1986, pp. 27, 29.
160. See Appendix 2, part III.
161. See Appendix 2, entries 2.8, 2.9, 15.25.
162. *New York Times*, November 7, 1983, p. A1.

163. *Ibid.*
164. *Ibid.*, p. D18.
165. *Ibid.*
166. *Ibid.*
167. *Ibid.*
168. Moldea, *Dark Victory*, p. 318.
169. Moldea, in *The Nation*, p. 732.
170. *Washington Post*, July 27, 1983, p. A2.
171. *Ibid.*
172. Moldea, in *The Nation*, p. 734.
173. *Newsday*, January 15, 1986, p. 2.
174. *Ibid.*
175. *U.S.–President's Commission on OC, The Impact*, pp. 177, 209, 211.
176. *Ibid.*, p. 205.
177. Malachi Martin, *The Final Conclave* (New York: Pocket Books, 1978) pp. 32–34; *Washington Post*, March 25, 1979, pp. H1, H4.
178. DiFonzo, *St. Peter's Banker*, p. 74.
179. *Miami Herald*, March 5, 1980, p. 22A.
180. *Washington Post*, March 25, 1979, p. H1.
181. See, for example, Lernoux, *In Banks We Trust*, p. 185.
182. DiFonzo, p. 152.
183. *Ibid.*
184. *Ibid.*, p. 159. The offer was refused because candidates are prohibited from accepting anonymous political contributions.
185. Lernoux, p. 188.
186. DiFonzo, p. 93.
187. DiFonzo, pp. 85–86.
188. *Ibid.*, p. 225.
189. *New York Times*, December 27, 1982, p. D10.
190. Martin, p. 35.
191. *Washington Post*, March 25, 1979, p. H1.
192. Seymour M. Hersh, with Jeff Gerth, "SEC Presses Wide Investigation of Gulf and Western Conglomerate," *New York Times*, July 24, 1977, p. 34.
193. *Ibid.*
194. DiFonzo, pp. 87–88.
195. The Securities and Exchange Commission alleged that Gulf & Western and the Mob-linked Resorts International corporation inflated the value of a real estate property in the Bahamas by a factor of 12. (Information on Resorts International from Reid, *The Grim Reapers*, pp. 119–23, 139–40; Waller, *The Swiss Bank Connection*, pp. 123–35; Hank Messick and Burt Goldblatt, *The Mobs and the Mafia*, pp. 195–96; Gerth, in Blumenthal and Yazijian, eds., *Government By Gunplay*, pp. 137–39. Information on the Bahamian deal from *Washington Post*, November 27, 1979, p. A12.) These suspicious dealings fit the pattern of overvaluation of holdings, irregular financial reporting and stock price manipulation that have characterized the conglomerate's operations (Hersh, *New York Times*, July 24, 1977, pp. 1, 34; *Washington Post*, November 27, 1979, pp. A1, A12). According to government sources, as the *New York Times* put it, "many of these complex transactions had one thing in common: inflated appraisals of real estate and stocks that were used by Gulf & Western to hide its losses

and also to help acquire assets from other companies whose value was subsequently overstated" (Hersh, *New York Times*, July 24, 1977, p. 34).

196. Gulf & Western links to organized crime are suggested by the purchase of a Mexican Mafia hideaway by its real estate subsidiary, a questionable transaction between that subsidiary and the Teamsters pension fund, alleged fraud in Gulf & Western's own pension fund and Mobster Sidney Korshak's close involvement with the firm and its chairman, Charles Bludhorn (Seymour M. Hersh, with Jeff Gerth, "Major Corporations Seek Korshak's Labor Advice," *New York Times*, June 29, 1976, pp. 1, 16; *Washington Post*, November 27, 1979, p. A12).

197. DiFonzo, p. 258; *New York Times*, December 27, 1982, pp. 1ff.

198. DiFonzo, p. 259. Sindona and 75 members of the Gambino, Inzerillo and Spatola Mafia families were indicted in Sicily on charges of operating a $600 million-per-year heroin trade between their Italian island base and the United States. Simultaneously, Sindona was also accused of complicity, illegal possession of arms, fraud, using a false passport, and violating currency regulations (*ibid.*).

199. *Washington Post*, March 19, 1986, p. A22.

200. *New York Times*, March 23, 1986, p. 44.

201. Lernoux, pp. 179, 211, passim.

202. *Manchester Guardian*, March 8, 1986, p. 7. Further evidence of such Mafia-P2 collusion is Licio Gelli's role in securing Sindona a hiding place in the Palermo home of two well-known Sicilian Mobsters after he escaped from a New York detention center (Lernoux, p. 179).

203. *Manchester Guardian*, October 4, 1986, p. 19.

204. *New York Times*, December 27, 1982, p. D10.

205. Lernoux, p. 179.

206. DiFonzo, p. 67.

207. Lernoux, p. 179; *Wall Street Journal*, September 20, 1982, p. 35.

208. DiFonzo, pp. 69–71.

209. Sylvia Poggioli, National Public Radio report, January 19, 1987.

210. DiFonzo, pp. 102–05, 236.

211. Lernoux, pp. 176–78, 206–08.

212. *Ibid.*, p. 189.

213. *Ibid.*, p. 203.

214. Such continuing cooperation is suggested by incidents in the 1970s reported in chapter 15, "The CIA and the Mafia."

215. Martin, pp. 28–29, 33.

216. *Ibid.* pp. 29–33.

217. *Ibid.* pp. 28–29, 33.

218. *Ibid.*, pp. 35, 71.

219. *Ibid.*, pp. 35–36.

220. *Times* (London), February 13, 1983, pp. 33–34; Yallop, *In God's Name*, p. 128.

221. *New York Times*, December 27, 1982, p. D10.

222. *Newsweek*, August 16, 1982, p. 48.

223. *Ibid.*, pp. 48–49.

224. *Ibid.*; *Washington Post*, July 10, 1982, pp. B6, B7.

225. *Time*, September 13, 1982, p. 28.

226. Yallop, p. 177.

227. DiFonzo, p. 8.
228. Lernoux, p. 182; Yallop, p. 128.
229. *Washington Post*, July 10, 1984, p. A1.
230. *Ibid.*, pp. A1, A5.
231. *Ibid.*
232. *Washington Post*, February 28, 1987, p. A18.
233. *Newsweek*, March 9, 1987, p. 48.
234. *Washington Post*, July 18, 1987, p. A17.
235. *Washington Post*, July 10, 1982, p. B6; *Newsweek*, September 13, 1982, pp. 62, 65.
236. *Washington Post*, July 10, 1982, p. B6.
237. Yallop, pp. 2–6.
238. *Ibid.*, p. 208–214, 220; see also pp. 190–91, 177.
239. *Ibid.*, pp. 220–24.
240. *Ibid.*, pp. 248–49.
241. *Ibid.*, p. 319.
242. Frank Brodhead and Edward S. Herman, "The Press, the K.G.B. and the Pope," *The Nation*, July 2, 1983, p. 14.
243. *Washington Post*, October 28, 1984, p. A21.
244. *Time*, July 18, 1983, p. 37.
245. *Washington Post*, December 19, 1985, p. A31; *New York Times*, December 13, 1985, p. A3.
246. *Washington Post*, December 19, 1985, p. A31.
247. *Washington Post*, June 19, 1985, p. A23ff.
248. *New York Times*, March 25, 1985, p. D4; Diana Johnstone, "The Ledeen Connections," *In These Times,* September 8, 1982; Lernoux, p. 217.
249. *Wall Street Journal*, August 8, 1985, p. 12.
250. *Ibid.*; *Washington Post*, February 16, 1987, p. D4.
251. *Washington Post*, February 16, 1987, p. D4.
252. Telephone interview with Loren Jenkins, *Washington Post* Rome correspondent, October 8, 1987; *New York Times*, March 25, 1985, p. D4.
253. *Washington Post*, June 19, 1985, pp. A23ff. In his trial one of the accused Bulgarians, airline worker Sergei Antonov, produced witnesses to swear he was at work on the two days preceding the attack on the Pope, and at the Balkan Air office when the Pope was shot. This undermined Agca's claims that Antonov was helping him plan the attack the two days before and travelled with him to St. Peter's Square the day of the shooting (*Washington Post*, January 5, 1983, p. A16). Agca also admitted lying in identifying another Bulgarian, Todor S. Aivazov, as an accomplice; the Turk said a man photographed running from St. Peter's Square after the shooting was actually a Turkish friend of Agca, who was also charged (*Washington Post*, June 19, 1985, pp. A23ff).
254. *New York Times*, December 13, 1985, p. A3; *Wall Street Journal*, August 8, 1985, p. 12.
255. *Washington Post*, December 19, 1985, p. A31.
256. *Washington Post*, March 30, 1986, pp. 1ff.
257. George Black, "Delle Chiaie: From Bologna to Bolivia," *The Nation*, April 25, 1987, p. 540.
258. Jonathan Kwitny, "Why an Italian Spy Got Closely Involved In the Billygate Affair," *Wall Street Journal*, August 8, 1985, p. 1.

259. *Ibid.*

260. *Ibid.*; *New York Times*, March 25, 1985, p. D4.

261. *Washington Post*, February 16, 1987, p. D4.

262. Lernoux, p. 217. Despite ample evidence of his collaboration with Pazienza, Ledeen says he barely knew the Italian. Questioned about the relationship, Ledeen told the *Wall Street Journal*, "I wish you wouldn't ask" about it. "It's a waste of everyone's time" (*Wall Street Journal*, August 8, 1985, p. 12).

263. Telephone interview with Loren Jenkins, *Washington Post* Rome correspondent, October 8, 1987.

264. *Washington Inquirer*, June 29, 1984, p. 1.

265. *New York Times*, March 25, 1985, p. D4.

266. As cited in *Wall Street Journal*, August 8, 1985, p. 12.

267. *Washington Post*, February 16, 1987, p. D4.

268. *Ibid.*; *Wall Street Journal*, August 8, 1985, p. 12.

269. *Wall Street Journal*, August 8, 1985, p. 12.

270. *Washington Post*, February 16, 1987, p. D4.

271. *Wall Street Journal*, August 8, 1985, p. 12.

272. *Ibid.*; *Washington Post*, February 16, 1987, p. D4.

273. *Wall Street Journal*, August 8, 1985, p. 12.

274. *Washington Post*, February 16, 1987, p. D4.

275. *Ibid.*

276. Sylvia Poggioli, National Public Radio report, January 19, 1987.

277. *Ibid.*

278. *Ibid.*

279. *Ibid.*; *Manchester Guardian*, January 19, 1987, p. 5.

280. Sylvia Poggioli, National Public Radio report, January 19, 1987.

281. *Ibid.*

282. *Ibid.*

283. *Ibid.*

284. DiFonzo, p. 259; Yallop, p. 315; Lernoux, p. 217.

285. As cited above.

286. Yallop, p. 315.

287. Lernoux, p. 201.

288. *Ibid.*

289. *Ibid.* Guarino had also come to Sindona's aid in 1976, when the Italian and American governments were investigating charges that the financier had bought his Franklin National Bank shares with money illegally removed from Italy. Guarino gave the Justice Department a declaration and Gelli sent an affidavit arguing that the charges amounted to nothing more than a Communist plot to destroy Sindona (DiFonzo, pp. 228–29).

290. Lernoux, p. 201.

291. DiFonzo, p. 259.

292. Yallop, p. 315. According to *Commonweal*, Gelli is also "very well-acquainted with Vice-President Bush" and was "in a position to predict that Alexander Haig would become Secretary of State well before" the 1980 election (Eric R. Terzuolo, "Cracks in the Masonry," *Commonweal*, September 11, 1981, p. 498).

293. Peter G. Peterson, "The Morning After," *The Atlantic*, pp. 44, 47, 49.

294. *Ibid.*, pp. 43–69.

295. *U.S.-Senate, OC and Stolen Securities, 1971*, p. 672.

296. *The Washington Spectator*, June 1, 1987, p. 2. Ronald Reagan's fiscal 1988 budget proposed $312 billion for national defense, 73 percent more than the Carter Administration spent in fiscal 1981 (statistics from the Center for Defense Information, telephone interview, October 21, 1987).

Recommendations

1. The recent transfer of the RFK files from Los Angeles Police custody to the California State Archives was only brought about after years of pressure from public interest groups, politicians and private researchers. Spearheading this effort was Greg Stone, who has established the Foundation for Truth and Accountability to monitor the disclosure process. The Foundation's address is P.O. Box 85065, Los Angeles, California, 90072-065. Supervising this process is John Burns, California State Archivist, 1020 O Street, Room 130, Sacramento, California, 95814 (916 445-4293).

2. In 1882, an infestation of outlaw gangs was holding Arizona in a "condition of terrorism" [H.R. Exec. Doc. No. 188, 47th Cong., 1st Sess., serial set 2030 (1882), pp. 1–3; H.R. Exec. Doc. No. 58, 47th Cong., 1st Sess., serial set 2027 (1882), pp. 2–3; H.R. Exec. Doc. No. 1, 47th Cong., 1st Sess., serial set 2018 (1881), pp. 917, 921; H.R. Exec. Doc. No. 1, 48th Cong., 1st Sess., serial set 2191 (1883), p. 514; 17 Op. Atty. Gen. 334 (1882)]. With civil forces powerless to subdue them, Acting Governor John J. Gosper appealed to the federal government for military assistance [H.R. Exec. Doc. No. 1 (1881), p. 921]. In response, U.S. Attorney General Benjamin Harris Brewster affirmed that the president was "expressedly authorized to employ the military forces of the United States" against the Arizona gangs [17 Op. Atty. Gen. 335 (1882)]. Brewster cited R.S. 5298, which was amended in 1956 to become 10 U.S.C. 332 [17 Op. Atty. Gen. 334 (1882)]. President Chester A. Arthur issued a proclamation calling upon the Arizona gangs to disperse as a prerequisite to the use of troops under this statute, after which local authorities brought the outlaws under control [17 Op. Atty. Gen. 335 (1882); H.R. Exec. Doc. No. 1 (1883), p. 514]. President Arthur's intervention was grounded in Constitutional principle and precedent. The federal government is empowered to use troops "to execute the laws of the union" and is enjoined to protect the states against domestic violence under article I, section 8, and article IV, section 4, of the U.S. Constitution. These principles were reinforced by Supreme Court rulings in 1879 and 1895 [*Ex parte Siebold*, 100 U.S. 371, 395 (1879); *In re Debs*, 158 U.S. 564, 582 (1895)]. Since 1794, military force has been used to aid civil authorities on more than 100 occasions, including twice in the early 1960s when John F. Kennedy dispatched troops to quell racial violence in the South [*Dictionary of American History* (New York: Charles Scribner's Sons, 1976), vol. 4, p. 341; Theodore C. Sorensen, *Kennedy* (New York: Harper & Row, 1965), pp. 483–86, 491; Schlesinger, *Robert Kennedy and His Times*, pp. 341–47]. President Kennedy acted in these two cases under title 10, sections 332 and 333 of the U.S. Code [Proc. No. 3497, September 30, 1962, 27 Fed. Reg. 9681; Exec.

Order No. 11053, September 30, 1962, 27 Fed. Reg. 9693; *Alabama v. United States*, 373 U.S. 545 (1963)]. Similar to section 332 mentioned above, section 333 permits the president to employ military force to suppress "any insurrection, domestic violence, unlawful combination, or conspiracy" when civil authorities cannot or will not stop it from depriving citizens of their Constitutional rights or from obstructing justice [10 U.S.C. 333 (1956)].

Appendix 1
Additional Information on Jack Ruby

1. HAH 9H 385, 419; *Dallas Morning News*, March 28, 1974, p. 1A.
2. See text below.
3. *Dallas Morning News*, March 28, 1974.
4. *Ibid.*
5. CD 104, p. 64. Joseph Campisi also reported that Chapman was acquainted with Ruby (CE 1748).
6. CE 1322, p. 742.
7. HAH 9H 419.
8. HAH 9H 418–21.
9. HAH 9H 422–24.
10. HAH 9H 418, 425.
11. CE 1475.
12. 14H 601–2; HAR 156; HAH 9H 423.
13. CE 1475.
14. CD 1102c; CE 1504.
15. CD 1102c; CE 1504; WR 794.
16. As cited in the prior note.
17. C. Ray Hall Exhibit 1; CE 1227; 14H 112; CE 1228, 1504, 1764; WR 794.
18. CE 1693.
19. HAH 9H 527–28.
20. *Ibid.*
21. CD 1102d; CE 1692, 1754.
22. *Dallas Morning News*, March 29, 1974.
23. CE 1755.
24. CE 1755; CE 1322, p. 734. (Dave L. Miller Exhibit 1 and 15H 454 establish that Isadore and Dave L. Miller are brothers).
25. See Appendix 2, section 9a.
26. HAH 5H 115.
27. *Ibid.*
28. *Ibid.*
29. HAH 5H 161.
30. Wallace Turner, *Gambler's Money*, p. 127.
31. CD 84, p. 106.
32. HAH 5H 114.
33. CD 84, p. 106.
34. HAH 5H 115.
35. HAH 5H 223.

36. *Ibid.*; HAR 152.
37. CD 84, p. 106.
38. CE 1752.
39. CD 105, p. 135.
40. HAH 9H 382-83, 419; CE 1748; Alice Nichols Exhibit 5355; CD 4, p. 289; 14H 123.
41. HAH 9H 419.
42. CD 105, p. 135.
43. HAH 9H 359; see CE 1748 and CE 1752.
44. CD 105, p. 135.
45. CD 84, p. 229.
46. *Ibid.*
47. 14H 445.
48. *U.S.-Senate, AGVA Hearings,* summarized in pp. 629-31.
49. JFK microfilm, vol. 5, p. T12; CD 84, p. 229.
50. 15H 28-29.
51. 14H 445.
52. WR 801.
53. CE 1353.
54. *Ibid.*
55. CE 1628.
56. CE 1322, pp. 735-36. The FBI report describing these cards states that each bore the signature of the name listed (CE 1322, p. 736), and Alexander's name was listed (CE 1322, p. 735). A microfilm of the actual cards reveals a signed card for each name listed, except that Alexander's card is curiously missing (JFK microfilm, vol. 5, pp. R13-28).
57. WR 334.
58. CE 1628.
59. *Ibid.*
60. CD 1102c.
61. CE 1180.
62. WR 794-95, 801.
63. C. Ray Hall Exhibit 1.
64. CE 1227.
65. 14H 112; CE 1228; CE 1504; CE 1764.
66. 5H 103; CE 1760.
67. CE 1760.
68. 5H 103.
69. Several exclusive night clubs and restaurants are owned and operated by the Mafia; examples are reported in *U.S.-Senate, OC and Stolen Securities, 1971,* p. 816; Teresa, *My Life in the Mafia,* pp. 119-20; Davidson, "The Mafia: How It Bleeds New England," *Saturday Evening Post,* November 18, 1967, p. 29.
70. CE 1265; WR 793.
71. JFK microfilm, vol. 5, p. D20.
72. CE 2822; see chapter 8, "Prostitution and Other Criminal Activities."
73. 14H 445.
74. 5H 205.
75. CE 1693.
76. CE 1475.

77. See "Additional Underworld Contacts of Jack Ruby," this appendix.
78. HAH 9H 355.
79. See chapter 9, "Joseph Campisi."
80. CE 1184; CE 1300.
81. See chapter 9, "Paul Roland Jones."
82. CE 3061; 14H 354.
83. CE 2302, p. 237; C. Ray Hall Exhibit 1.
84. CE 2303, p. 241; C. Ray Hall Exhibit 1.
85. C. Ray Hall Exhibit 1; WR 795.
86. 13H 454–55.
87. CE 2305.
88. WR 794.
89. CE 2305; CE 2309, p. 255.
90. CE 2302, 2303, 2308, 2309; JFK microfilm, vol. 5, pp. T9–18.
91. CE 1322, pp. 746, 758–59, 764–66.
92. 14H 543.
93. See chapter 18.
94. WR 344.
95. WR 333.
96. 14H 298, 13H 500.
97. One party called from Ruby's home telephone on July 21, 1963 is identified as a friend of George Senator (JFK microfilm, vol. 5, p. T16), Ruby's roommate. Senator did not move into Ruby's apartment, however, until November 1, 1963 (CD 722, p. 2).
98. CE 2302, 2303, 2308, 2309; JFK microfilm, vol. 5, pp. T9–18.
99. See chapter 18, "August: The West Coast and New York."
100. CE 1521–26; CD 4, p. 663; see chapter 18, "May Through July: Focus in New Orleans."
101. CD 86, p. 486.

Appendix 2
Sources on the Mafia

1. *Time*, May 16, 1977, p. 32; Reid, *The Grim Reapers*, p. 6.
2. Sondern, *Brotherhood of Evil*, pp. 58–62; Reid, *The Grim Reapers*, pp. 146–50.
3. Salerno and Tompkins, *The Crime Confederation*, p. 280.
4. *New York Times*, May 25, 1959, p. 1.
5. *U.S.-President's Commission on OC, Appendix to The Edge*, p. 274.
6. Lawson, "Carnival of Crime," *Wall Street Journal*, January 12, 1970, p. 1; *U.S.-Senate, Gambling and OC*, p. 509.
7. *Dallas Morning News*, March 28, 29, 31, 1973, p. A1.
8. "The Mob," part 2, *Life*, September 8, 1967, p. 94; *Life*, September 29, 1967, p. 35; Chandler, "The 'Little Man' is Bigger Than Ever," *Life*, April 10, 1970, p. 33. Also Reid and Demaris, *The Green Felt Jungle*, pp. 85, 88, 91.
9. Meskil, *Don Carlo*, p. 137.
10. Dorman, *Payoff*, p. 100.

11. *U.S.-Senate, Kefauver Report, Third Interim*, pp. 82–83.
12. Reid, *The Grim Reapers*, pp. 158–59, 329.
13. Chandler, in *Life*, p. 34.
14. *Ibid.*, p. 33.
15. Noyes, *Legacy of Doubt*, p. 142.
16. Reid, *The Grim Reapers*, p. 160.
17. Noyes, p. 143; *U.S.-House, OC Control*, p. 412.
18. *U.S.-President's Commission on OC, The Impact*, p. 215.
19. *Life*, September 1, 1967, p. 44; Mollenhoff, *Strike Force*, p. 119.
20. *U.S.-Senate, OC and Narcotics Hearings*, p. 652, chart C; Kennedy, *The Enemy Within*, pp. 229–30.
21. *U.S.-Senate, OC and Stolen Securities, 1971*, pp. 637, 772–73, 841.
22. *Ibid.*, pp. 326, 267, 315, 317, 569.
23. *U.S.-Senate, OC and Narcotics Hearings*, p. 652, chart F.
24. *Ibid.*, p. 551; Teresa, *My Life in the Mafia*, p. 254.
25. *Washington Post*, November 8, 1985, p. A1.
26. *U.S.-Senate, OC and Stolen Securities, 1971*, p. 814.
27. *U.S.-Senate, OC and Narcotics Hearings*, p. 652, chart B.
28. *U.S.-Senate, OC and Stolen Securities, 1971*, p. 72.
29. *Ibid.*
30. *Ibid.*, p. 8.
31. *Ibid.*, pp. 1248–49.
32. *Ibid.*, pp. 326, 267, 315, 317, 569.
33. *Ibid.*, p. 271.
34. *Ibid.*, pp. 225–26, 281–82, 285–86.
35. *Ibid.*, pp. 284–85.
36. Demaris, *Captive City*, p. 81.
37. *U.S.-Senate, OC and Narcotics Hearings*, p. 550, Exhibit no. 53.
38. Dorman, *Payoff*, pp. 252–54.
39. *U.S.-Senate, OC and Stolen Securities, 1971*, pp. 647, 662–63.
40. *U.S.-Senate, OC and Narcotics Hearings*, p. 248, chart A.
41. Meskil, *Don Carlo*, pp. 163–64.
42. *Washington Post*, November 16, 1979, p. A16; *Newsweek*, November 26, 1979, p. 94.
43. "The Politics of Conspiracy," conference at Boston University, workshop on organized crime, George Sherman Student Center, February 1, 1975, tape-recorded by author.
44. *Ibid.*, chart C.
45. *Ibid.*, p. 274, chart B.
46. *U.S.-President's Commission on OC, The Impact*, p. 423.
47. Grutzner, "How to Lock Out the Mafia," *Harvard Business Review*, March-April 1970, p. 49.
48. Salerno and Tompkins, *The Crime Confederation*, p. 225.
49. As reprinted in Gage, *Mafia, U.S.A.*, p. 336.
50. *U.S.-House, OC Control*, p. 449.
51. *Time*, May 16, 1977, p. 33.
52. "The New Mafia," *Newsweek*, January 5, 1981, p. 40.
53. Bill Davidson, "New Orleans: Cosa Nostra's Wall Street," *Saturday Evening Post*, February 29, 1964, pp. 15ff.
54. *Time*, May 16, 1977, p. 33.

55. *U.S.-Senate, Gambling and OC*, p. 84.
56. See this appendix, section 14.
57. See this appendix, section 13.
58. See this appendix, section 17e.
59. See this appendix, section 6a.
60. *U.S.-Senate, Gambling and OC*, p. 84; Rufus King, *Gambling and Organized Crime*, pp. 33–34; *U.S.-Senate, Kefauver Report, Third Interim*, p. 95; Cook, *The Secret Rulers*, pp. 23–24; Allsop, *The Bootleggers*, p. xv; Ted Poston, "The Numbers Racket," *New York Post*, February 29–March 10, 1960, reprinted in Tyler, ed., *Organized Crime in America*, p. 264; Hutchinson, *The Imperfect Union*, p. 113; *U.S.-Senate, Kefauver Hearings*, part 5, pp. 1179–80; Dorman, *Payoff*, p. 154.
61. In 1960, Milton Wessel, former head of the U.S. attorney general's special committee on organized crime, estimated annual graft from nationwide illegal gambling at $4.5 billion (Cook, *A Two-Dollar Bet Means Murder*, pp. 9–11), or $19.3 billion in 1987 dollars.
62. Mollenhoff, *Strike Force*, p. 231.
63. *U.S.-Senate, OC and Narcotics Hearings*, p. 550, Exhibit no. 53.
64. Mollenhoff, *Strike Force*, pp. 7, 29.
65. Reid, *The Grim Reapers*, pp. 75–78.
66. *U.S.-Senate, OC and Narcotics Hearings*, p. 508, Exhibit no. 39.
67. *Ibid*.
68. *New York Times*, June 27–30, 1976, pp. 1ff.
69. Demaris, pp. 348–49.
70. Thomas Hage, "New Jersey—The Friendly State," in Gage, *Mafia, U.S.A.*, p. 307.
71. Waller, *The Swiss Bank Connection*, p. 126.
72. *U.S.-Senate, McClellan Labor Hearings*, pp. 12521, 12524.
73. *U.S.-Senate, OC and Narcotics Hearings*, p. 308, chart D.
74. Denny Walsh, "Banker Friend of Nixon is Target of U.S. Inquiry," *New York Times*, September 10, 1973, p. 28.
75. "The Mafia v. America," *Time*, August 22, 1969, p. 19; *Congressional Directory*, 1972, pp. 109, 292.
76. On November 15, 1979, Scotto was convicted of racketeering in a $300,000 shakedown of waterfront businessmen (*Washington Post*, November 16, 1979, p. A16; *Newsweek*, November 26, 1979, p. 94).
77. *U.S.-Senate, OC and Narcotics Hearings*, p. 508, Exhibit no. 40.
78. *Ibid.*, Exhibit no. 39.
79. Demaris, pp. 62–63, 139–42, 151–65, 185, 251–52, 296; "The Mob," part 1, *Life*, September 1, 1967, pp. 42B–43.
80. Noyes, pp. 34, 240–44.
81. *U.S.-Senate, OC and Stolen Securities, 1971*, pp. 647, 669.
82. *U.S.-Senate, OC and Narcotics Hearings*, p. 274, chart B.
83. NBC Evening News, "Segment 3," June 1, 1978.
84. "The Mob," part 1, *Life*, September 1, 1967, pp. 18–21; Reid, *The Grim Reapers*, pp. 37–39.
85. *Time* (1971), in Gage, *Mafia, U.S.A.*, pp. 179–80; see this appendix, entry 6.13.

Principal Sources

Following is a list of the most important references cited. U.S. Government documents are grouped separately after books and articles, alphabetically ordered by abbreviations designated for convenient cross-reference.

Allsop, Kenneth. *The Bootleggers: The Story of Chicago's Prohibition Era.* New Rochelle, N.Y.: Arlington House, 1968.

Anslinger, Harry J., and Oursler, Will. *The Murderers: The Story of the Narcotics Gangs.* New York: Farrar, Straus, and Cudahy, 1961.

——, with Gregory, J. Dennis. *The Protectors: The Heroic Story of the Narcotics Agents, Citizens, and Officials in Their Unending, Unsung Battles Against Organized Crime in America and Abroad.* New York: Farrar, Straus, 1964.

Anson, Robert Sam. *"They've Killed the President!": The Search for the Murderers of John F. Kennedy.* New York: Bantam, 1975.

Blakey, G. Robert, and Billings, Richard N. *The Plot to Kill the President.* New York: Times Books, 1981.

Blumenthal, Sid, and Yazijian, Harvey, eds. *Government By Gunplay: Assassination Conspiracy Theories From Dallas to Today.* New York: New American Library, Signet, 1976.

Brashler, William. *The Don: The Life and Death of Sam Giancana.* New York: Harper & Row, 1977.

Brill, Steven. *The Teamsters.* New York: Simon and Schuster, 1978.

Buchanan, Thomas G. *Who Killed Kennedy?* London: Secker & Warburg, 1964.

——. *Who Killed Kennedy?* New York: Putnam, 1964 (substantially different from the Secker & Warburg edition).

Chandler, David. "The 'Little Man' is Bigger Than Ever." *Life*, April 10, 1970, pp. 31–36.

Cook, Fred J. *The Secret Rulers: Criminal Syndicates and How They Control the U.S. Underworld.* New York: Duell, Sloan and Pearce, 1966.

——. *A Two-Dollar Bet Means Murder.* New York: Dial, 1961.

——. *Walter Reuther: Building the House of Labor.* Chicago: Encyclopaedia Britannica Press, 1963.

Cormier, Frank, and Eaton, William J. *Reuther.* Englewood Cliffs, N.J.: Prentice-Hall, 1970.

Cressey, Donald R. *Theft of the Nation: The Structure and Operations of Organized Crime in America.* New York: Harper & Row, Harper Colophon Books, 1969.

Crile, George, III. "The Mafia, the CIA, and Castro." *Washington Post*, May 16, 1976, pp. C1, C4.

Davidson, Bill. "How the Mob Controls Chicago." *Saturday Evening Post*, November 9, 1963, pp. 17–27.

——. "The Mafia: How It Bleeds New England." *Saturday Evening Post*, November 18, 1967, pp. 27–31.

——. "New Orleans: Cosa Nostra's Wall Street." *Saturday Evening Post*, February 29, 1964, pp. 15–21.

Davis, John H. *The Kennedys: Dynasty and Disaster 1848–1984*. New York: McGraw-Hill, 1984.

Demaris, Ovid. *Captive City*. New York: Lyle Stuart, 1969.

Denison, George. "Smut: The Mafia's Newest Racket." *Reader's Digest*, December 1971, pp. 157–60.

DiFonzo, Luigi. *St. Peter's Banker*. New York: Franklin Watts, 1983.

Dorman, Michael. "LBJ and the Racketeers." *Ramparts*, May 1968, pp. 26–35.

——. *Payoff*. New York: Berkley, 1972.

Ehrmann, Herbert B. *The Case That Will Not Die: Commonwealth vs. Sacco and Vanzetti*. Boston: Little, Brown, 1969.

——. *The Untried Case: The Sacco-Vanzetti Case and the Morelli Gang*. 2d ed. New York: Vanguard, 1960.

Epstein, Edward Jay. *Counterplot*. New York: Viking, 1969.

——. *Inquest: The Warren Commission and the Establishment of Truth*. New York: Viking, Bantam, 1966.

Feuerlicht, Roberta S. *Justice Crucified: The Story of Sacco and Vanzetti*. New York: McGraw-Hill, 1977.

Files of Evidence Connected With the Investigation of the Assassination of President John F. Kennedy (official documents from the Texas attorney general's investigation of the JFK assassination), 1963–64. In the Library of Congress rare book collection. Also on microfilm, Washington, D.C.: Microcard Editions, 1967.

Gage, Nicholas. "How Organized Crime Invades the Home." *Good Housekeeping*, August 1971, pp. 68ff.

——. *The Mafia Is Not an Equal Opportunity Employer*. New York: Dell, 1971.

——, ed. *Mafia, U.S.A.* Chicago: Playboy Press, 1972.

Gartner, Michael, comp. *Crime and Business: What You Should Know About the Infiltration of Crime into Business—and of Business into Crime* (selections from the *Wall Street Journal*, 1968–70). Princeton: Dow Jones Books, 1971.

Gerth, Jeff. "Richard M. Nixon and Organized Crime." In *Government By Gunplay*, edited by Sid Blumenthal and Harvey Yazijian, pp. 130–51. New York: New American Library, Signet, 1976.

Goldman, Peter. *The Death and Life of Malcolm X*. New York: Harper & Row, 1973.

Gottfried, Alex. *Boss Cermak of Chicago: A Study of Political Leadership*. Seattle: University of Washington Press, 1962.

Gould, Jean, and Hickok, Lorena. *Walter Reuther: Labor's Rugged Individualist*. New York: Dodd, Mead, 1972.

Grutzner, Charles. "How to Lock Out the Mafia." *Harvard Business Review*, March–April 1970, pp. 45–58.

Hersh, Seymour M., with Gerth, Jeff. "The Contrasting Lives of Sidney R. Korshak." Four-part series. *New York Times*, June 27–30, 1976.

Hilsman, Roger. *To Move a Nation: The Politics of Foreign Policy in the Administration of John F. Kennedy.* Garden City, N.Y.: Doubleday, 1967.

Houghton, Robert A., with Taylor, Theodore. *Special Unit Senator: The Investigation of the Assassination of Senator Robert F. Kennedy.* New York: Random House, 1970.

Hurt, Henry. *Reasonable Doubt: An Investigation into the Assassination of John F. Kennedy.* New York: Holt, Rinehart & Winston, 1985.

Hutchinson, John. *The Imperfect Union: A History of Corruption in American Trade Unions.* New York: Dutton, 1970.

Investigative Reporters and Editors Inc., Phoenix Project. Report on organized crime in Arizona. *Albuquerque Journal,* March 13–April 2, 1977.

Joesten, Joachim. *Oswald: Assassin or Fall Guy?* New York: Marzani & Munsell, 1964.

Jones, Penn, Jr. *Forgive My Grief: A Critical Review of the Warren Commission Report on the Assassination of President John F. Kennedy,* vols. I and II. Midlothian, Texas: *Midlothian Mirror,* 1966–67.

Kaiser, Robert Blair. *"R.F.K. Must Die!": A History of the Robert Kennedy Assassination and its Aftermath.* New York: Dutton, 1970.

Kantor, Seth. *Who was Jack Ruby?* New York: Everest House, 1978.

Kefauver, Estes. *Crime in America.* Garden City, N.Y.: Doubleday, 1951.

Kennedy, Robert F. *The Enemy Within.* New York: Popular Library, 1960.

——. "Robert Kennedy Defines the Menace." *New York Times Magazine,* October 13, 1963, pp. 15ff.

King, Martin Luther, Jr. "Beyond the Los Angeles Riots. Next Stop: The North." *Saturday Review,* November 13, 1965, pp. 33ff.

King, Rufus. *Gambling and Organized Crime.* Washington, D.C.: Public Affairs Press, 1969.

Kobler, John. *Capone: The Life and World of Al Capone.* New York: Putnam, 1971.

Khrushchev, Nikita S. *Khrushchev Remembers.* Translated and edited by Strobe Talbott. New York: Little, Brown; Bantam, 1971.

Lambert, William. "A Deeper Debt of Gratitude to the Mob." *Life,* November 10, 1967, pp. 38–38B.

——. "Strange Help-Hoffa Campaign of the U.S. Senator from Missouri." *Life,* May 26, 1967, pp. 26ff.

Landesco, John. *Organized Crime in Chicago.* Chicago: University of Chicago Press, 1968.

Lane, Mark. *Rush to Judgment: A Critique of the Warren Commission's Inquiry into the Murders of President John F. Kennedy, Officer J. D. Tippit and Lee Harvey Oswald.* New York: Holt, Rinehart & Winston, 1966.

Langman, Betsy, and Cockburn, Alexander. "Sirhan's Gun: Further Inquiries into the Assassination of Robert F. Kennedy." *Harper's,* January 1975, pp. 16–27.

Lawson, Herbert G. "Carnival of Crime." *Wall Street Journal,* January 12, 1970, p. 1.

Lernoux, Penny. *In Banks We Trust*. Garden City, N.Y.: Anchor Press/Doubleday, 1984.

Lepera, Pasty A., and Goodman, Walter. *Memoirs of a Scam Man: The Life and Deals of Patsy Anthony Lepera*. New York: Farrar, Straus, and Giroux, 1974.

Lewis, Norman. *The Honored Society: A Searching Look at the Mafia*. New York: Putnam, 1964.

Lomax, Louis E. *To Kill a Black Man*. Los Angeles: Holloway House, 1968.

Lowenstein, Allard K. "The Murder of Robert Kennedy." *Saturday Review,* February 19, 1977, pp. 6–17.

Lyle, John H. *The Dry and Lawless Years*. Englewood Cliffs, N.J.: Prentice-Hall, 1960.

McClellan, John L. *Crime Without Punishment*. New York: Duell, Sloan and Pearce, 1962.

McCoy, Alfred W., with Read, Cathleen B., and Adams, Leonard P., II. *The Politics of Heroin in Southeast Asia*. New York: Harper & Row, 1972.

Maas, Peter. *Serpico*. New York: Bantam, 1974.

——. *The Valachi Papers*. New York: Bantam, 1969.

"The Mafia: Big, Bad and Booming." *Time*, May 16, 1977, pp. 32–42.

"The Mafia v. America." *Time*, August 22, 1969, pp. 17–27.

Malone, William Scott. "The Secret Life of Jack Ruby." *New Times*, January 23, 1978, pp. 46–51.

Manchester, William R. *The Death of a President: November 20–November 25, 1963*. New York: Harper & Row, 1967.

Marchetti, Victor, and Marks, John D. *The CIA and the Cult of Intelligence*. New York: Dell, 1974.

Meagher, Sylvia. *Accessories After the Fact: The Warren Commission, the Authorities, and the Report*. Indianapolis: Bobbs-Merrill, 1967.

Meskil, Paul S. *Don Carlo: Boss of Bosses*. New York: Popular Library, 1973.

——. *The Luparelli Tapes: The True Story of the Mafia Hitman Who Contracted to Kill Both Joey Gallo and His Own Wife*. Chicago: Playboy Press, 1976.

Messick, Hank. *Lansky*. 2d rev. ed. New York: Berkley, Berkley Medallion, 1973.

——. *Secret File*. New York: Putnam, 1969.

——. *Syndicate Abroad*. New York: Macmillan, 1969.

Methvin, Eugene H. "How Organized Crime Corrupts Our Law Enforcers." *Reader's Digest*, January 1972, pp. 85–89.

——. "How the Mafia Preys on the Poor." *Reader's Digest*, September 1970, pp. 49–55.

——. "Mafia War on the A&P." *Reader's Digest*, July 1970, pp. 71–76.

"The Mob." *Life*, part 1, September 1, 1967, pp. 15–21; part 2, September 8, 1967, pp. 91–104.

Model, F. Peter, and Groden, Robert J. F. *JFK: The Case for Conspiracy*. New York: Manor Books, 1976.

Moldea, Dan E. *The Hoffa Wars: Teamsters, Rebels, Politicians and the Mob*. New York: Paddington, 1978.

——. *Dark Victory: Ronald Reagan, MCA, and the Mob.* New York: Viking, 1986.

——. "Who Really Killed Bobby Kennedy?" *Regardie's,* June 1987, pp. 57–84.

Mollenhoff, Clark R. *Strike Force: Organized Crime and the Government.* Englewood Cliffs, NJ.: Prentice-Hall, 1972.

——. *Tentacles of Power: The Story of Jimmy Hoffa.* Cleveland: World Publishing, 1965.

Navasky, Victor S. *Kennedy Justice.* New York: Atheneum, 1971.

Noyes, Peter. *Legacy of Doubt.* New York: Pinnacle, 1973.

O'Donnell, Kenneth P., and Powers, David F. *"Johnny, We Hardly Knew Ye": Memories of John Fitzgerald Kennedy.* Boston: Little, Brown, 1972.

Oglesby, Carl, and Goldberg, Jeff. "Did the Mob Kill Kennedy?" *Washington Post,* February 25, 1979, pp. B1, B4.

Pantaleone, Michele. *The Mafia and Politics.* New York: Coward-McCann, 1966.

Peterson, Houston, ed. *A Treasury of the World's Great Speeches.* Rev. and enl. ed. New York: Simon and Schuster, 1965.

Ransom, Harry H. "Containing Central Intelligence." *New Republic,* December 11, 1965, pp. 12–15.

Reid, Ed. *The Grim Reapers: The Anatomy of Organized Crime in America.* New York: Henry Regnery, Bantam, 1970.

——. *Mickey Cohen: Mobster.* New York: Pinnacle, 1973.

——, and Demaris, Ovid. *The Green Felt Jungle.* New York: Trident, 1963.

Rogers, Warren. "The Persecution of Clay Shaw: How One Man Ruined Another and Subverted Our Legal System." *Look,* August 26, 1969, pp. 53–60.

Sackett, Russell; Smith, Sandy; and Lambert, William. "The Congressman and the Hoodlum." *Life,* August 9, 1968, pp. 20–27.

Salerno, Ralph, and Tompkins, John S. *The Crime Confederation: Cosa Nostra and Allied Operations in Organized Crime.* Garden City, N.Y.: Doubleday, 1969. Salinger, Pierre. *With Kennedy.* Garden City, N.Y.: Doubleday, 1966.

Schlesinger, Arthur M., Jr. *A Thousand Days: John F. Kennedy in the White House.* Boston: Houghton Mifflin, 1965.

——. *Robert Kennedy and His Times.* New York: Ballantine, 1979.

Schulz, William. "The Mob's Grip on New Jersey." *Reader's Digest,* February 1971, pp. 111–15.

Scott, Peter Dale. *Crime and Cover-Up: The CIA, the Mafia and the Dallas-Watergate Connection.* Berkeley: Westworks, 1977.

——. "The Death of Kennedy and the Vietnam War." In Blumenthal, Sid, and Yazijian, Harvey, eds. *Government By Gunplay,* pp. 152–87. New York: New American Library, Signet, 1976.

——. "From Dallas to Watergate." In Blumenthal, Sid, and Yazijian, Harvey, eds. *Government By Gunplay,* pp. 113–29. New York: New American Library, Signet, 1976.

Sheridan, Walter. *The Fall and Rise of Jimmy Hoffa.* New York: Saturday Review Press, 1972.

Siciliano, Vincent. *Unless They Kill Me First*. New York: Hawthorn, 1970.

Smith, Sandy. "Corruption Behind the Swinging Clubs." *Life*, December 6, 1968, pp. 35–43.

Sondern, Frederic J. *Brotherhood of Evil: The Mafia*. New York: Farrar, Straus, and Cudahy, 1959.

Stevenson, Charles. "The Tyranny of Terrorism in the Building Trades, Special Report, Installment no. 1." *Reader's Digest*, June 1973, pp. 89–94.

Teresa, Vincent, with Renner, Thomas C. *My Life in the Mafia*. Garden City, N.Y.: Doubleday, 1973.

Thompson, Josiah. *Six Seconds in Dallas: A Micro-Study of the Kennedy Assassination*. New York: B. Geis Assoc., dist. by Random House, 1967.

Turner, Wallace. *Gambler's Money: The New Force in American Life*. Boston: Houghton Mifflin, 1965.

Turner, William W. "Crime Is Too Big for the FBI." *The Nation,* November 8, 1965, pp. 322–28.

———. *Hoover's FBI: The Men and the Myth*. Los Angeles: Sherbourne, 1970.

———, and Christian, Jonn G. *The Assassination of Robert F. Kennedy: The Conspiracy and the Cover-up, 1968–1978*. New York: Random House, 1978.

Tyler, Gus, ed. *Organized Crime in America: A Book of Readings*. Ann Arbor: University of Michigan Press, Ann Arbor Paperbacks, 1967.

Viorst, Milton. "The Mafia, the CIA, and the Kennedy Assassination." *Washingtonian*, November 1975, pp. 113–18.

Waldman, Steven. "The Best and the Worst of American Unions." *Washington Monthly*, July-August, 1987, pp. 28–38.

Waller, Leslie. *The Swiss Bank Connection*. New York: New American Library, Signet, 1972.

Walsh, Denny. "The Governor and the Mobster." *Life*, May 2, 1969, pp. 28–32A.

———. "The Mob: It Racks Up Overtime on a Government Payroll." *Life*, February 14, 1969, pp. 52–56.

———. "The Mayor, the Mob and the Lawyer." *Life*, May 29, 1970, pp. 24–31.

Wennblom, Ralph D. "How the Mafia Drives Up Meat Prices." *Farm Journal*, August 1972, pp. 18–19.

———. "How the Mafia Gets Its Cut." *Farm Journal*, September 1972, pp. 24–26.

Winter-Berger, Robert N. *The Washington Payoff: An Insider's View of Corruption in Government*. New York: Dell, 1972.

Wise, David, and Ross, Thomas B. *The Invisible Government*. New York: Random House, Vintage Books, 1974.

X, Malcolm, with Haley, Alex. *The Autobiography of Malcolm X*. New York: Grove, 1966.

X, Malcolm. *By Any Means Necessary: Speeches, Interviews and a Letter by Malcolm X*. Edited by George Breitman. New York: Pathfinder, 1970.

Yallop, David. *In God's Name*. New York: Bantam Books, 1984.

U.S. GOVERNMENT DOCUMENTS

listed by abbreviations used in citations

U.S.–Cargo Theft and OC: U.S. Department of Justice. Law Enforcement Assistance Administration. *Cargo Theft and Organized Crime: Desk-Book for Management and Law Enforcement.* DOT P 5200.6. Washington, D.C., 1972. TD1.8:C19/3.

U.S.–House, Assassination Appendix, JFK: U.S. Congress. House. Select Committee on Assassinations. *Investigation of the Assassination of President John F. Kennedy: Appendix to Hearings Before the Select Committee on Assassinations.* Hearings pursuant to H.R. 222 and H.R. 433, 95th Congress, and H.R. 49, 96th Congress. March 1979. 95th Congress, 2d Session. (Vols. 6–12.)

U.S.–House, Assassination Appendix, MLK: U.S. Congress. House. Select Committee on Assassinations. *Investigation of the Assassination of Martin Luther King, Jr.: Appendix to Hearings Before the Select Committee on Assassinations.* Hearings pursuant to H.R. 222 and H.R. 433, 95th Congress, and H.R. 49, 96th Congress. March 1979. 95th Congress, 2d Session. (Vol. 13.)

U.S.–House, Assassination Hearings, JFK: U.S. Congress. House. Select Committee on Assassinations. *Investigation of the Assassination of President John F. Kennedy.* Hearings pursuant to H.R. 222 and H.R. 433, 95th Congress, and H.R. 49, 96th Congress. September 6–December 29, 1978. 95th Congress, 2d Session. (Vols. 1–5.)

U.S.–House, Assassination Report: U.S. Congress. House. Select Committee on Assassinations. *Report of the Select Committee on Assassinations: Findings and Recommendations.* Report pursuant to H.R. 222 and H.R. 433, 95th Congress, and H.R. 49, 96th Congress. March 29, 1979. 95th Congress, 2d Session. H. Rpt. 95–1828, part 2.

U.S.–House, Crime in America: U.S. Congress. House. Select Committee on Crime. *Crime in America: Aspects of Organized Crime, Court Delay, and Juvenile Justice.* Hearings pursuant to H.R. 17. December 4–8, 1969. 91st Congress, 1st Session. Y4.C86/3:C86/6.

U.S.–House, Criminal Justice Hearings: U.S. Congress. House. Select Committee on Crime. *The Improvement and Reform of Law Enforcement and Criminal Justice in the United States.* Hearings pursuant to H.R. 17. July 28–September 18, 1969. 91st Congress, 1st Session. Y4.C86/3:L41.

U.S.–House, Federal Effort Against OC: U.S. Congress. House. Committee on Government Operations. *The Federal Effort Against Organized Crime: Hearings Before a Subcommittee of the Committee on Government Operations.* June 13, 20, and 27, 1967. 90th Congress, 1st Session. Y4.G74/7:C86/2/pt. 2.

U.S.–House, OC and Worthless Securities: U.S. Congress. House. Select Committee on Crime. *Organized Crime: Techniques for Converting Worthless Securities into Cash.* Hearings. December 7–9, 1971. 1972. 92d Congress, 1st Session. Y4.C86/3:C86/8.

U.S.–House, OC Control: U.S. Congress. House. Committee on the Judiciary. Subcommittee Number Five. *Organized Crime Control.* Hearings pursuant to S. 30 and related proposals. May 20–August 5, 1970. 91st Congress, 2d Session. Y4.J89/1:91–27.

U.S.-House, OC in Sports: U.S. Congress. House. Select Committee on Crime. *Organized Crime in Sports (racing).* Hearings. May 9–July 27, 1972. 1973. 92d Congress, 2d Session. Y4.C86/3:C86/15/pts. 1–4.

U.S.-President's Commission on OC, The Edge: U.S. President's Commission on Organized Crime. *Report to the President and the Attorney General, The Edge: Organized Crime, Business, and Labor Unions.* Washington, D.C., 1986. Pr40.8:C86/Ed3.

U.S.-President's Commission on OC, America's Habit: U.S. President's Commission on Organized Crime. *Report to the President and the Attorney General, America's Habit: Drug Abuse, Drug Trafficking, and Organized Crime.* Washington, D.C., 1986. Pr40.8: C86/D84.

U.S.-President's Commission on OC, The Impact: U.S. President's Commission on Organized Crime. *Report to the President and the Attorney General, The Impact: Organized Crime Today.* Washington, D.C., 1986. Pr40.8: C86/Im7.

U.S.-President's Commission on OC, Appendix to The Edge: U.S. President's Commission on Organized Crime. *Report to the President and the Attorney General, The Edge: Organized Crime, Business, and Labor Unions Appendix.* Washington, D.C., 1985. Pr40.8:C86/ Ed 3/ app.

U.S.-President's Commission on OC, OC and Gambling: U.S. President's Commission on Organized Crime. *Record of Hearing VII, June 24–26, 1985, New York, New York, Organized Crime and Gambling.* Washington, D.C., 1985. Pr40.8:C86/G14.

U.S.-President's Commission on OC, OC and Labor-Management Racketeering: U.S. President's Commission on Organized Crime. *Record of Hearing VI, April 22–24, 1985, Chicago, Illinois, Organized Crime and Labor-Management Racketeering in the United States.* Washington, D.C., 1985. Pr40.8: C86/L11.

U.S.-President's Commission on OC, OC and Money Laundering: U.S. President's Commission on Organized Crime. *Record of Hearing II, March 14, 1984, New York, New York, Organized Crime and Money Laundering.* Washington, D.C., 1984. Pr40.8:C86/M74.

U.S.-OC Control Act of 1970: Organized Crime Control Act of 1970. Pursuant to S. 30. October 15, 1970. 91st Congress, 2d Session. Public Law No. 91–452.

U.S.-Senate, AGVA Hearings: U.S. Congress. Senate. Committee on Government Operations. Permanent Subcommittee on Investigations. *American Guild of Variety Artists.* Hearings pursuant to S. 250. June 20–26, 1962. 87th Congress, 2d Session. Y4.G74/6:Am3/pt. 2.

U.S.-Senate, Bobby Baker Hearings: U.S. Congress. Senate. Committee on Rules and Administration. *Financial or Business Interests of Officers or Employees of the Senate.* Hearings pursuant to S. 212 and S. 221. February 19–26, 1964. 88th Congress, 1st and 2d Sessions. Y4.R86/2:F49/pt. 14.

U.S.-Senate, Gambling and OC: U.S. Congress. Senate. Committee on Government Operations. Permanent Subcommittee on Investigations. *Gambling and Organized Crime.* Hearings pursuant to S. 69. August 22–25, 1961. 87th Congress, 1st Session. Y4.G74/6:G14/pt. 1.

U.S.-Senate, Intelligence Report, Foreign Assassinations: U.S. Congress.

Senate. Select Committee to Study Governmental Operations with Respect to Intelligence Activities. *Alleged Assassination Plots Involving Foreign Leaders: Interim Report.* November 20, 1975. 94th Congress, 1st Session. S. Rpt. 94–465.

U.S.–Senate, Intelligence Report, JFK Assassination: U.S. Congress. Senate. Select Committee to Study Governmental Operations with Respect to Intelligence Activities. *Final Report, Book Five, The Investigation of the Assassination of President John F. Kennedy: Performance of the Intelligence Agencies.* 1976. 94th Congress, 2d Session. S. Rpt. 94–755.

U.S.–Senate, Kefauver Hearings: U.S. Congress. Senate. Special Committee to Investigate Organized Crime in Interstate Commerce. *Investigation of Organized Crime in Interstate Commerce.* Hearings pursuant to S. 202 and S. 129. May 26, 1950–August 7, 1951. 81st Congress, 2d Session, and 82d Congress, 1st Session. Y4.C86/2:C86/ pts. 1–19.

U.S.–Senate, Kefauver Report, Second Interim: U.S. Congress. Senate. Special Committee to Investigate Organized Crime in Interstate Commerce. *Second Interim Report.* Pursuant to S. 202. February 28, 1951. 82d Congress, 1st Session. S. Rpt. 82–141. *U.S.–Senate, Kefauver Report, Third Interim*: U.S. Congress. Senate. Special Committee to Investigate Organized Crime in Interstate Commerce. *Third Interim Report.* Pursuant to S. 202. May 1, 1951. 82d Congress, 1st Session. S. Rpt. 82–307.

U.S.–Senate, McClellan Labor Hearings: U.S. Congress. Senate. Select Committee on Improper Activities in the Labor or Management Field. *Investigation of Improper Activities in the Labor or Management Field.* Hearings pursuant to S. 74 and S. 221, 85th Congress, and S. 44, 86th Congress. February 26, 1957–September 9, 1959. 85th Congress, 1st and 2d Sessions, and 86th Congress, 1st Session. Y4.Im:7:L11/ pts. 1–58.

U.S.–Senate, OC and Narcotics Hearings: U.S. Congress. Senate. Committee on Government Operations. Permanent Subcommittee on Investigations. *Organized Crime and Illicit Traffic in Narcotics.* Hearings pursuant to S. 17 and S. 278. September 25, 1963–July 30, 1964. 88th Congress, 1st and 2d Sessions. Y4.G74/6:C86/pts. 1–4.

U.S.–Senate, OC and Narcotics Report: U.S. Congress. Senate. Committee on Government Operations. Permanent Subcommittee on Investigations. *Organized Crime and Illicit Traffic in Narcotics.* March 4, 1965. 89th Congress, 1st Session. S. Rpt. 89–72.

U.S.–Senate, OC and Stolen Securities, 1971: U.S. Congress. Senate. Committee on Government Operations. Permanent Subcommittee on Investigations. *Organized Crime, Stolen Securities.* Hearings pursuant to sec. 4 of S. 31. April 27–August 4, 1971. 92d Congress, 1st Session. Y4.G74/6:C86/2/pts. 1–4.

U.S.–Senate, OC and Stolen Securities, 1973: U.S. Congress. Senate. Committee on Government Operations. Permanent Subcommittee on Investigations. *Organized Crime, Securities Thefts and Frauds* (Second Series). Hearings pursuant to sec. 4 of S. 46. June 29 and July 13, 1973. 93rd Congress, 1st Session. Y4.G74/6:C86/2/973/pt. 1.

U.S.–Task Force Report: U.S. President's Commission on Law Enforcement and Administration of Justice. Task Force on Organized Crime. *Task Force Report: Organized Crime.* Washington, D.C., 1967. Pr36.8:L41/Or3.

U.S.–Warren Commission Hearings and Exhibits: U.S. President's Commission on the Assassination of President John F. Kennedy. *Investigation of the Assassination of President John F. Kennedy.* Hearings pursuant to Executive Order 11130 and S.J. Res. 137, 88th Congress. Washington, D.C., 1964. Pr36.8:K38/ H35/v. 1–26.

U.S.–Warren Commission Report: U.S. President's Commission on the Assassination of President John F. Kennedy. *Report of the President's Commission on the Assassination of President John F. Kennedy.* Washington, D.C., 1964. Pr36.8:K38/R29.

Index

Aase, Jean, 293
Abadie, William, 115, 116, 118, 119, 147, 149
Abati, Scappatora, 470
Accardo, Tony, 33, 337, 359, 473
Ace Guard Service, 328
Acoustical Society of America, 45
Acropolis, John, 433
Adams, Joey, 274, 275
Adams Oil Co., 130
Adamy, Clarence, 388
Addonizio, Hugh, 50, 465
Adduci, James, 465
Adelstein, Bernard, 433
AFL, 27, 33, 34, 102, 356, 435
AFL-CIO, 101, 352, 438
Agca, Ali, 365, 366, 593
Agnew, Spiro, 333, 342
Agro, Salvatore, 459
Aguirre, Felix, 335
Ahern, Frank, 470
Air Traffic Controllers Union, 351
Aiuppa, Joseph, 399, 412
Aivazov, Todor S., 593
Akros Dynamics, 211
Alamotel, 62
Albert, Carl, 476
Alderisio, Felix (Milwaukee Phil), 134, 251, 314, 434, 452
Aleman, José, Jr., 84, 85, 86
Alessio, John, 328, 332, 335, 470
Alex, Gus, 465, 472
Alexander, William, 142, 199, 289, 383, 597
Ali, Muhammad, 268
Alinsky, Saul, 25, 329
Alkana, Irving, 113
Allegra, Melchiorre, 397, 398
Allegretti, James, 105, 106, 273
Allen, Charles, 436
Allen, O.K., 80
Allen, Rosemary, 142
Allsop, Kenneth, 25, 330
Alo, Vincent (Jimmy Blue Eyes), 152
Alongi, Dominick, 400
Alvarez, Louis, 46
Ambassador Hotel (Los Angeles), 318–320, 323, 324, 328
American Academy of Forensic Sciences, 38, 323
American Guild of Variety Artists (AGVA), 173, 270–279, 281, 282, 283, 290, 294, 381, 382
American Weekly, 480
AMLASH, 216, 234
Ammirati, George, 457
Anastasia, Albert, 400, 403, 445
Ancona, Sam, 437
Anderson, Jack, 58, 133, 212, 245, 266, 478
Andretta, Stephen, 438
Angiulo, Gennaro, 270, 397, 404, 423, 454, 463
Annenberg, Moe, 150
Annunzio, Frank, 473–474

Anslinger, Harry, 34, 76
Anson, Robert Sam, 75, 78, 207, 306
Antonov, Sergei, 593
Anzelmo, Salvatore, 432
Apalachin Mafia convention, 83, 112, 122, 127, 209, 244, 270, 385, 399, 435
Aponte, Hector, 126
Argent Corporation, 411–412
Armstrong, Andrew, 175, 176, 177, 277, 290
Armstrong, Louis, 263
Arnold, Gordon, 41
Arthur, Chester A., 595
Arthur's Farm, 421
Arvey, Jake, 466
Aschkenasy, Ernest, 45–47
Associated Booking Corporation, 129, 263
Aston, Cheryl, 561
Aston, Dewey, 562
Auction City (Somerville, Massachusetts), 434
Audubon Ballroom (New York), 311–313
Aurelio, Thomas, 460
Aurelius, Marcus, 319
Ayo, Anthony, 222, 549
Ayotte, Eugene, 398

Bachelor's III, 421
Badalamente, Salvatore, 430–431
Badalamenti, Gaetano, 414
Badger State Cheese Co. (Wisconsin), 484
Baer, Maish, 100, 104
Bailey, John, 142
Bailey, William, 324
Baioni, Larry, 414, 469
Baker, Robert B. (Barney), 121, 122, 137, 151, 268, 281, 282, 467
Baker, Robert G. (Bobby), 203, 244, 249–250, 314, 430, 483
Bakery and Confectionery Workers Union, 466
Baletto, George, 457
Balistrieri, Frank, 412
Ball, Joe, 188
Banca Privata Italiana, 361
Banco Ambrosiano, 363, 364, 365
Banister, Guy, 61, 64
Bankers Trust Co., 432
Baptist Foundation of America, 431
Barbara, Joseph, 270, 399
Barboza, Joseph, 399, 400, 403–404, 411, 415, 420, 421, 451
Barger, James, 44–47
Barrett, James, 419
Barrigan, James, 144
Barrow, Clyde, 247
Bartels, John, 458
Bas, Marvin, 137
Batchelor, Charles, 383
Batista, Fulgencio, 136, 211, 212, 215, 221
Battaglia, Sam, 134, 452
Battle, W. Preston, 316

Bauer, Bruno, 436
Baum. William, 483
Bauman, Roger, 69, 289
Bay of Pigs Invasion, 61, 66, 207, 218, 234, 334
Beauboeuf, Alvin, 61, 62
Becker, Edward, 81-83, 225, 242, 243, 251, 257
Bella Napoli Café (Providence), 457
Belli, Melvin, 188
Bello, Manuel, 475
Bellotti, Francis, 469
Beneen, Senator, 410
Bennett, Harry, 28
Berkshire Downs Race Track(Massachusetts), 468
Bertram, Lane, 290-293
Bevilacqua, Joseph, 459
Bickers, Benny, 131, 146, 225
Billings, Richard, 88, 89, 251
Binion, Lester (Benny), 131, 140, 347-348, 535, 568
Bintliff, Russell, 307, 340
Bioff, Willie, 446, 590
Bischoff, Willie, 131, 223
Bishop, Joey, 241
Bishop, Melvin, 30
Bissell, Richard, 215
Blackstone, Milton, Advertising Agency, 262
Blackwell, Charles, 312
Blakey, G. Robert, 50, 88, 89, 133, 184, 218, 224, 227, 251, 255, 284, 358, 450
Blanco-Fernandez, Juan Francisco, 218
Blankenship, D.L. 145
Blassingame, Walter 262
Bliss, George, 442
Block, William, 136
Blodgett, Julian, 83
Bludhorn, Charles, 592
Bob Wills Ranch (Dallas), 113
Boccia, Ferdinand, 403
Boffa, Eugene, 437
Bogard, Albert, 56, 57
Boggs, Hale, 234, 476
Boiardo, Anthony, 50
Bolles, Don, 480
Bologna (Italy) railroad bombing, 362-363
Bolt, Beranek and Newman, Inc., 44
Bommarito, Joe, 401
Bonanno, Joseph, Jr., 239-240
Bonanno, Joseph, Mafia family, 359, 396, 462
Bonanno, Joseph, Sr., 358, 460, 461, 481
Bonds, Joe. See Locurto, Joseph
Bosch, Juan, 305
Boston Celtics, 421
Boston Patriots, 421
Bottus, Alex, 328, 329
Bowen, Ann, 239, 460
Bowers, Dr., 54
Bowers, Lee, 42, 54
Boyd, Jerry, 240, 461
Braden, Jim. See Brading, Eugene Hale
Braden, Tom, 320
Brading, Eugene Hale, 67-69, 73, 255, 289, 293, 298-299, 317, 381
Bradley, Edgar Eugene, 73

Bradley, Marshall, 291
Bradley, Tom, 329
Branch, Johnny, 150, 160
Breen, James, 118
Brennan, Peter, 333, 353
Brennan, William, 468
Brent, Jeff, 326
Brescia, Matty, 240
Brewer, Roy, 355, 356, 360
Brewster, Benjamin Harris, 595
Brewster, Daniel, 248
Briggs Manufacturing Co., 30
Bright, Al, 528
Brilab sting operation, 392
Brill, Steven, 88
Brocato, James, 125
Brocato, Robert, 125
Broccoli, Stephen, 441
Brooke, Edward, 468
Browder, Edward, 220
Brown, Edmund, Jr. (Jerry), 242, 331, 332
Brown, Edmund, Sr. (Pat), 331, 332, 333, 470
Brown, Morgan, 69, 289
Brown, Neil, 394, 398, 457
Brown, Oran, 57
Brown, Tom, 167
Browne, George, 446
Bruneau, Emile, 64
Bruner, Terry, 422
Brunker, Albert, 465
Bruno, Angelo, 429
Bryant, Ann, 287, 288
Buccieri, Fiore, 401
Buchanan, Thomas, 18, 19, 157
Buckley, Gerald, 401
Buckley, William F., 38
Budge, Hamer, 476
Bufalino, Russell, 209, 428, 436, 474, 483
Bufalino, William, 479
Buffa, Thomas, 402
Bugliosi, Vincent, 324
Building and Trades Council, New York City, 333
Bull-Pen Restaurant (Arlington, Texas), 169, 570
Bund, 100
Bunker, Jerry, 173
Buono, Philip, 354
Buscetta, Tommaso, 399, 409
Buscetta, Tommaso, Mafia family, 409
Bush, George, 594
Butler, George, 109-112, 136, 140
Butler, Norman 3X, 312
Buttitta, Ignazio, 309
Byrd, Glen, 142
Byrne, Bobby, 420
Byron, David, 103

Cabana Hotel (Dallas), 293, 294
Cady, Dick, 480
Cahill, Thomas, 470
Cahn, William, 420
Cain, Richard, 465-466
Cairns, John, 104

Cal Neva Lodge (Lake Tahoe), 131
Calamia, Leonard, 470
Calgrove, Paul, 144
Califano, Marshall, 134
Calvi, Roberto, 363, 364
Campagna, Louis, 24
Campbell, Judith, 89
Campisi, Joseph, 80, 107 122–124, 130, 140, 151, 192, 240–241, 264, 287, 293, 294, 299, 382, 571
Campisi, Sam, 123
Cangiano, Gus, 417
Cannon, Howard, 438
Cantalupo Realty Co., 402
Cantazaro, Robert, 443
Capezio, Tony, 100
Capone, Al, 23, 99, 100, 107, 133, 148, 150, 262, 286, 330, 385, 399, 404, 465, 473, 482
Capone gang, 25, 356, 435, 589
Capone, John, 106
Capone, Matty, 100
Capone, Ralph, 100
Capri Hotel (Cuba), 131, 135, 382
Capucci, Anthony, 426
Caracci, Frank, 124–125, 151, 260, 261, 263, 266–267, 280, 281, 300
Carillo, Anthony, 400
Carlin, Bruce, 155, 171–177, 178–179, 293
Carlin, Karen, 149, 155, 156, 167, 171–182, 184, 192, 293, 296, 299
Carlson, E.E., 143, 145, 383
Carnivali, Turiddu, 309
Carno, Nick, 267
Caro, Robert, 246, 248
Carona, Vic, 72
Carousel Club (Dallas), 113, 114, 118, 119, 131, 135, 142–144, 147, 149, 157, 159, 160, 164, 165, 168, 175, 176, 178, 179, 198, 226, 258, 259, 276–279, 284, 285, 289, 290, 293–295, 382, 383, 384, 560, 570, 572
Carr, Mrs. Billy Chester, 290, 291
Carr, Wagoner, 251
Carramusa, Carl, 401
Carroll, Roger, 68, 69, 289
Carter, Billy, 366
Carter, Cliff, 248
Carter, Jimmy, 359, 366, 595
Carter, John, 52
Cartier, Raymond, 17, 18, 19
Cascio, Paul, 566
Casey, William, 357
Castellammarese War, 410
Castro, Fidel, 61, 64, 84, 131, 135, 204, 207, 208, 210–212, 215–218, 219–225, 229, 234–235, 548
  Mob-CIA plots against, 58, 61, 63–64, 66, 71, 84, 133, 203, 207, 210–211, 215–218, 224, 227, 234, 251, 264, 305, 306, 334, 345, 360, 363
Castucci, Richard, 420
Catalano, Salvatore, 414
Catalanotte, Joe, 401
Cavagnaro, Joseph, 141
Cavallaro, Charles, 483

Cavallaro, Charles, Jr., 483
Cavallaro, Thomas, 483
Cecere, Daniel, 341
Cellar Door night club (Fort Worth), 295, 296, 298, 299
Cellini, Dino, 131, 413
Cement and Concrete Workers Union, 440, 441
Central Intelligence Agency, 66, 71, 203, 207, 208, 210–216, 233, 234, 241, 251, 306–307, 340, 345, 357, 361, 365, 366
Cermak, Anton, 23–26, 34, 150, 329, 330
Cerone, John, 401, 412, 462
Certified Concrete Co., 440
Cervantes, A.J., 464
Cervone, Bobbie, 440–441
Cesar, Thane Eugene, 325–332, 335
Chamber of Commerce (U.S.), 429
Chankalian, Armand, 459
Chapman, Bobby Joe, 381–382
Charach, Theodore, 325–326
Chavez, Cesar, 320
Chavez, Frank, 125–126, 151, 319
Cheramie, Rose, 54, 191
Cherry, Dave, 225, 226
Chicago Crime Commission, 473
Chicago Metropolitan SanitaryDistrict, 442
Chicago Tribune, 242, 478
Chinnici, Rocco, 409
Chotiner, Murray, 332, 336, 340
Christian Democratic Party (Italy), 408, 471
Christian, John, 320
Chrysler Office Building (Detroit), 428
Chrysler Office Building (New York), 447
Churchill Farms Estate (Louisiana), 62, 81, 83, 84
Cianflona, John, 484
Cimino, Dominic, 452
CIO, 16, 30, 32, 34
Cipango's (Dallas), 131
Cirello, Joseph. *See* Civello, Joseph
Civella, Nick, 401, 412, 436
Civello, Joseph, 19, 80, 112, 118, 121, 122, 127, 128, 149, 151, 184
Clark, Ramsey, 316
Clark, Robert, 239, 460
Clemente, Michelino, 78
Clemons, Acquilla, 56
Coffey, Melvin, 61
Cohen, Mickey, 88, 129, 152, 188, 286, 328, 331, 340
Cole, Jack, 278
Coleman, Delbert, 477
Colombo, Anthony, 479
Colombo, Joseph, 400–403, 423, 479
Colombo, Joseph, Mafia family, 405, 422, 435, 436, 458
Colonial Inn (Florida), 122, 219
Colony Sportsmen's Club (London), 413
Colson, Charles, 338–340, 584
Colvin, Hershey, 105
Conduit Workers Union, 447
Conference of Studio Unions, 356
Conforto, Janet (Jada), 144, 162, 279, 280, 281,

287, 288, 566
Conforto, Joseph, 566
Congress on Racial Equality (CORE), 310
Conley, Gene, 421
Connally, John, 37, 157, 174, 236, 237, 260, 295, 554
Connally, Nelly, 37, 39
Connell, Thomas, 137
Considine, Bob, 52
Continental Press, 136
Cook, Fred, 109
Cooke, Leon, 102, 103
Cooper, Grant, 330, 581
Corallo, Anthony, 395, 436, 447, 466
Cormier, Frank, 29
Corollo, Anthony, 400
Corona Breeding Farm, 322
Cosa Nostra. See Mafia
Costa, Gaetano, 408
Costello, Frank, 125, 150, 245, 250, 314, 391, 392, 399, 446, 460, 475
Cotrini, Giuseppe, 131, 223
Cotter, William, 417
Covelli, Gerald, 462
Crafard, Larry, 149, 165, 168, 175, 184, 192, 384, 285, 284, 572
Craig, Roger, 57-58, 191
Craig, Walter, 239, 240, 460, 461
Craven, Robert, 141
Cressey, Donald, 270, 390, 394
Crimaldi, Charles, 406
Crosby, James, 334
Cuban Revolutionary Council, 61, 64
Cudak, Robert, 398, 402, 426
Curry, Eileen, 118-119
Curry, Jesse, 41, 48, 141, 167
Curtis, Carl, 80
Cushing, Richard Cardinal, 38
Cy's Wee Wash It (Hialeah, Florida), 173

D'Amato, Paul (Skinny), 89
D'Arco, John, 473
Daily American (Rome), 361
Dal-Tex Building (Dallas), 67, 298
Dale, Joy, 119
Daley, Richard, 88, 465, 466
Dalitz, Moe, 152, 347, 350, 474
dalla Chiesa, Carlo, 409
Dallas City Hall, 180, 289
Dallas County Jail, 171, 186, 192, 198, 199
Dallas Cowboys, 381
Dallas Criminal Courts Building, 67
Dallas Federal Parole Building, 68
Dallas Morning News Building, 157, 297, 298
Dallas Police Building, 155, 158, 159, 179, 182, 186, 295, 299
Dallas Records Building, 67
Dallas Times Herald Building, 163
Datacomp Corporation, 431
Davis, George, 85
Davis, Sammy, Jr., 241
de Borchgrave, Arnaud, 366
Dean, John, 337, 339, 342

Dean, Patrick, 184
Deauville Gambling Casino (Cuba), 135
DeCarlo, Angelo (Ray), 257, 341, 342, 343, 422, 459
DeCavalcante, Sam, 423, 439
DeCavalcante tapes, 342, 396, 401, 439
Decker, Bill, 41, 140, 141, 183, 188-192
DeGalindez, Jesus, 305
DeGrandis, Joseph, 26
DeJohn, Nick, 112, 469
Del Charro Motel (California), 244, 245
Del Mar Race Track (California), 245, 321
Dellacroce, Aniello, 400, 430
Delmore, Nick, 439
DeLoach, Cartha, 243
DeLorean, John, 46
DeLucia, Paul, 473
DeLuna, Carl, 412
DeMar, Bill, 572
Demaris, Ovid, 102, 128
Democratic Party, 345
DeMohrenschilt, George, 58
Denet, Leo, 105
Department of Defense, 412, 428, 474
Department of Justice, 34, 46, 76, 77, 80, 88, 133, 232, 251, 261, 305, 343, 348, 358, 360, 393, 452, 472, 479
Department of State, 221
Department of Transportation, 393
DePaula, Frank, 421
DeRoss, John, 435
DeSapio, Carmine, 466
Desser, Arthur, 334
DeStefano, Sam, 406, 462
Detroit, Michigan Stove Works, 30
Detroit Times, 480
Deutsch, Sidney, 466
Dickey, O.C., 213
DiLeo, Lucas, 318
DiLorenzo, Matteo, 484
DiMase, Carmine, 458
Dio, Johnny. See Dioguardi, Johnny
Dio, Tommy. See Dioguardi, Tommy
Dioguardi, Johnny, 27, 33, 403, 447
Dioguardi, Tommy, 447
DiPiazza, Salvatore, 318
DiPierro, Angelo, 324
Ditta, Nick, 397
DiVarco, Joseph, 462
Dodd, Richard, 40, 42
Dolan, James Henry, 273, 278, 381, 382
Donneroummas, Frank, 322, 329
Donovan, Raymond, 352-355, 359, 360, 589
Donovan, William, 212
Doonesbury cartoon strip, 242, 331
Dorfman, Allen, 135, 337-341, 346, 347, 350, 438
Dorfman, Paul, 102, 126, 135, 151
Dorman, Michael, 50, 110, 333, 557
Doto, Joe (Adonis), 28
Douglas, Helen Gahagan, 340
Dowe, Kenneth, 119, 167-168
Downtown Lincoln-Mercury dealership

(Dallas), 56
Doyle, Everett, 433
Dozier, Gilbert, 357
Dragna, Jack, 136, 226
Dranow, Benjamin, 261
Dream Way Bar (Cicero, Illinois), 274, 382
Drury, William, 137
Dryer, Betty, 327
Duffy, William, 394, 400, 452, 456
Dukakis, Michael, 231
Dulles, Allen, 215, 233–234, 251
Dumont Corporation, 431
Duncan, Glen, 160, 533
DuPont, Henry, 415
Dupont Plaza Hotel (Puerto Rico), 126
Durso, Thomas, 456
Dyson, W.F., 289

E.F. Hutton, 459
Eastland, James, 316
Eaton, William, 29
Ebb Tide Restaurant (Massachusetts), 420
Eberhardt, August, 158
Eboli, Thomas, 400
Echevarria, Homer, 218
Eden Roc Hotel (Miami), 132, 268
Edwards, George, 33, 390, 395, 401, 453
Edwards, Sheffield, 215
Egyptian Lounge (Dallas), 123, 241, 293
Ehrlichman, John, 337, 339
Eisenhower, 207, 334
Elko, Stephen, 474
Ellington, Duke, 263
Ellis, Ben, 289
Ellis Park Race Track, 137
Elrod, Arthur, 466
Emerson, Wald, 327
Empire Room (Dallas), 150, 160
Environmental Protection Agency, 389
Epstein, Ben, 103
Epstein, Edward J., 71
Ervay Theater (Dallas), 113
Ervin, Sam, 80
Esposito, Frank, 401
Euzzino, Andrew, 437

Facchiano, Albert, 589
Fair Play for Cuba Committee, 63
Falcone, Pasquale, 422
Farmer, James, 314
Farrell, Lew. See Fratto, Luigi
Fascell, Dante, 447
Fast, Ernest, 273, 274
Faye, Bobby, 274, 275, 283
Federal Bureau of Investigation, 34, 38, 46, 54,
55, 61, 78, 80, 81, 85, 87, 89, 95, 105, 106,
115, 116, 122, 123, 132, 133, 134, 135, 148,
149, 165, 166, 167, 179, 180, 185, 186, 192,
197, 215, 216, 221, 222, 232, 233–236, 238,
242–246, 249, 251, 261, 262, 322, 324, 337,
338, 342, 348, 349, 353–355, 359, 392,
396–397, 404, 405, 412, 422, 434, 436, 456,
463, 472–473, 479, 554

Federal Bureau of Narcotics, 414
Federici, Joseph Frank, 287–288
Federici, Sandy, 287
Ferrie, David, 60–63, 66, 67, 69, 71, 73, 83, 218,
255, 317
Fillmon, Gloria, 288
Finck, Pierre, 554
Fiorini, Frank. See Sturgis, Frank
Fithian, Floyd, 279
Fitzsimmons, Frank, 337, 338, 341, 350, 584
500 Club (New Orleans), 260, 267, 281, 566
Flamingo Hotel (Las Vegas), 476
Flood, Daniel, 474
Flowers, Mr., 68
Floyd, Pretty Boy, 247
Flynn, Charles, 227
Flynt, Larry, 46
Food Handlers Union, 447
Ford Motor Co., 28, 389
Ford, Gerald, 185, 186, 190, 197, 235, 475
Ford, Henry, 28
Foreman, Percy, 316
Forlani, Arnaldo, 363
Forsythe, Norman, 431
Fortas, Abe, 250, 251
Fosco, Angelo, 358, 441
Foundation for Truth and Accountability, 595
Four Seasons (singing group), 422
Franklin National Bank, 361, 362, 586, 594
Franko, Frank, 483–484
Fratianno, James, 68, 273, 350, 381, 399
Fratto, Luigi, 467, 478, 590
Frederici, Joseph. See Federici, Joseph Frank
Fremont Casino (Las Vegas), 411
French Connection, 408, 456
Friar's Club (Beverly Hills), 330
Fritz, Will, 143, 158, 183
Frizzi, Guy, 404
Fry, John, 30
Fullerton Metals Co., 434
Furci, Frank Carmen, 307
Furino, Fred, 354
Fusco, Stephen, 459

Gage, Nicholas, 394
Gagliano, Frank, 400
Gaity Club (Chicago), 104
Galba, Emperor, 230
Galente, Carmine, 321
Galiano, Dominic, 420
Galiber, Joseph, 355
Gallagher, Cornelius, 471
Gallina, Gino, 393, 404, 472
Gallinaro, William, 402
Gallinghouse, G., 72
Gallo, Joseph, 26, 400
Gallo, Larry, 26
Gambino, Carlo, 397, 400, 426, 446, 484
Gambino, Carlo, Mafia family, 352, 409,
417–420, 428, 434, 444, 472, 484, 592
Garafalo, Bartholomew, 460
Garafola, Anthony, 417
Gardiner, John, 464

Gardner, Mr., of Ambassador Hotel, 327
Gardner, Richard, 366
Gargano, Michael, 456
Garner, Darrell, 55
Garrison, Jim, 53, 57, 60, 70–73, 320
Gas Value service stations, 423
Gelli, Licio, 362, 365, 367, 592, 594
Genovese, Vito, 150, 192, 213, 227, 270, 287, 403, 526
Genovese, Vito, Mafia family, 352, 419, 444, 472, 484
Gentile, Nicola, 398, 410
Geoghegan, William, 76
Gershwin, George, 208
Gerth, Jeff, 333–334, 446
Gervais, Pershing, 71
Giancana, Sam, 86, 89, 131–134, 136, 216, 250–251, 264, 266, 267, 314, 465, 466, 469, 473, 474, 477
Giardano, Anthony, 439, 464
Gibbons, Harold, 88
Gibson, Kenneth, 465
Gilbain Building Co., 441
Giliberti, Anthony, 436
Gill, G. Wray, 61, 62, 69, 73
Gioe, Charles (Cherry Nose), 589
Giuliani, Rudolph, 358
Glaser, Joseph, 128–129, 263, 274, 283, 300
Gleason, Thomas, 352
Glick, Allen, 347, 411
Glimco, Joseph, 437, 463
Glitta, Mike, 453
Golden, William, 484
Goldman, Peter, 312
Goldstein, Frank, 101, 268, 283, 532
Gordon, Waxey, 150
Gorman, Richard, 461–462
Gosper, John J., 595
Gotti, John, 437
Gould, Jean, 31
Graffagnini, Nick, 125, 260, 281, 566
Grande Cheese Co. (Wisconsin), 484
Granello, Salvatore, 475
Grant, Eva, 51, 102, 113, 123, 128, 175, 177, 178, 259, 263, 268, 294, 382, 384
Greco, Michele, 362, 409
Greco, Salvatore, 409
Green, Milton, 27
Green, Shirley, 458
Greene, Bob, 480
Gregory, Dick, 316
Gremillion, Jack, 432
Griffin, Burt, 193, 222, 228, 233, 289
Gross, Murray, 416
Groussard, Serge, 17, 18, 19, 489
Gruber, Al, 129, 268, 282, 285, 286
Gruber, Sammy, 286
Grutzner, Charles, 394
Guarino, Philip, 367, 594
Guglielmo, John, 131, 223
Gulf & Western Corporation, 362, 591, 592
Gurney, Edward, 402, 417
Guthrie, Steve, 109–112, 118, 136, 140

Guzik, Jake, 136
Gym Club, 100

H&H Restaurant, 100
Haig, Alexander, 366, 594
Haldeman, H.R., 337, 339
Haley, Alex, 311
Halfen, Jack, 247, 248, 478
Hall, Harry, 117–119, 147, 149, 160–161, 517, 518
Hall, Travis, 142
Hallmark, Garrett, 168
Hand, Peter, 393
Hanes, Arthur, 316
Hanley, Edward T., 438
Hannan, Eddie, 457
Hansen, T.M., 296
Hardee, Jack, 116, 118, 119, 147, 517
Hargis, Bobby, 48
Harper, Carl, 53
Harper, William, 323, 325, 327
Harvard University, 230, 361
Hatch, Orrin, 359
Hatcher, Richard, 464–465
Hawkins, Ray, 142
Hayer, Talmadge, 311–314
Hayes, Floyd, 457
Hazel Park Race Track (Detroit), 428
Helen Bar (Detroit), 32
Helmick, Wanda, 169
Hemming, Gerry, 225
Heng, Huu Tim, 307
Hennessey, David, 394, 410
Henrici's Restaurant (Chicago), 263, 561–562
Hercules, Frank, 314
Herion, Donald, 411
Hernando's Hideaway (Dallas), 113
Herring, Charles, 247
Hersh, Seymour, 214
Hickok, Lorena, 31
Hill, Thomas, 228, 534
Hilton Hotel (New York), 150, 262, 263, 275
Hoffa, James, Jr., 529
Hoffa, James Riddle, 27, 30, 73, 75, 78, 85–91, 95, 102, 121, 122, 125, 126, 128, 129, 135–136, 211, 216, 240, 248, 250, 255, 258, 267, 273, 286, 300, 314, 319, 321, 334–338, 340, 347, 438, 467, 470, 472, 477, 478, 529, 557
Holiday Inn (Las Vegas), 132
Holland, S.M., 39, 40, 42, 43, 44, 47, 496
Hoover, J. Edgar, 38, 76, 89, 197, 232–235, 244–246, 249, 251, 316, 359, 383, 469, 476
Horner, Henry, 101
Horseshoe Club (Las Vegas), 130
Hotel and Restaurant Employees Union, 27, 435–438, 464
Houghton, Robert, 68, 321
House Assassinations Committee. See House Select Committee on Assassinations
House Banking Committee, 474
House Committee on Government Operations, 447
House Judiciary Committee, 270, 473

616

House Select Committee on Assassinations, 17,
20, 27, 38–40, 44–47, 50, 54, 58, 63–67, 78,
84, 87, 91, 111, 122, 124, 132–136, 158, 160,
166, 198, 215–218, 223, 241, 243, 255, 266,
268, 273, 281, 283, 284, 316–318, 396–397,
549, 556
House Select Committee on Crime, 345
Howard Johnson's Restaurant (Arlington, Texas),
260
Howard, Tom, 51, 160, 166, 182, 183
Hubert, Leon, 193, 222, 228, 289
Huddleston, Walter, 435
Hudson, Charles, 462
Hudson, John Wilson, 224
Hugel, Max, 357
Hughes Commission, 390
Hughes, Howard, 340
Hughes, John, 310
Humes, James, 235
Humphreys, Murray, 100, 473
Hundley, William, 245
Hunt, E. Howard, 208, 339
Hunt, H.L., 117, 193, 210, 228, 229, 288, 289
Hunt, Lamar, 69, 228, 288, 289
Hunt, Nelson Bunker, 69, 210, 228, 289
Hunt Oil Co., 69, 228, 289
Hunt, Sam, 100
Hunter, Bill, 51, 168
Husman, Governor, 130

Ice Pick Barney, 400
Igoe, Michael, 437, 462
Illinois Crime Commission, 104
Immigration and Naturalization Service 124, 223
Inciso, Angelo, 33
Internal Revenue Service, 150, 335, 343
International Alliance of Theatre Stage Employ-
ees, 315–316, 375, 376
International Brotherhood of Teamsters, 27, 76,
86, 87, 102, 121, 122, 125, 126, 129, 131, 135,
193, 211, 240, 244, 249, 261, 264, 267, 268,
273, 336–341, 346, 350, 351, 352, 358, 360,
411, 412, 419, 430, 433–438, 443, 445, 447,
457, 462, 477, 478, 479, 480, 592
Central States Pension Fund, 86, 135, 351, 438,
443
Local 27, 433
Local 266, 26
Local 295, 418
Local 320, 136
Local 456, 433
Local 560, 437
Local 707, 436
Local 730, 122
Local 814, 396, 436
Local 901, 125, 319
Local 945, 389
International Longshoremen's Association, 27,
352, 444, 445, 472
International Union of Operating Engineers, 442
Investigative Reporters and Editors Group, 480
Inzerillo, Salvatore, 409
Inzerillo, Salvatore, Mafia family, 409, 592

Isaacs, Godfrey, 327
Italian-American Civil Rights League, 479
Ivey, J.T., 142

J.C. Adams Construction Co., 568
J&J Cartage Co., 482
Jace, Mike, 427
Jackson, George, 472
Jackson, Henry, 139, 342
Jackson, William, 401
Jacobs, Clarence, 31
Jada. See Conforto, Janet
Jarnagin, Carroll, 295, 572
Jaworski, Leon, 186
Joesten, Joachim, 52, 210
John Birch Society, 190, 194, 210, 228, 534
John Paul I, Pope, 364, 365
John Paul II, Pope, 365, 593
Johnson, Blaney Mack, 219, 222
Johnson, Clemon, 40
Johnson, Lyndon B., 37, 38, 204, 210, 234,
244–251, 260, 298, 305, 306, 396, 471
Johnson, Thomas 15X, 312, 313
Johnston, Frank, 159
Jones, Clifford, 482
Jones, Janice, 143
Jones, Paul Roland, 101, 103, 110–113, 117, 121,
130, 136, 140, 144, 151, 161, 185, 285, 383
Jones, Penn, 52
Jopel Construction Co., 355
Joseph, Ellis, 137
Joseph's Department Store (Boston), 434

Kahoe, E. Michael, 394
Kaiser, Robert Blair, 321
Kaminsky, Eileen, 186
Kantor, Seth, 129, 157, 158, 260, 286
Kattar, George, 468
Katzenbach, Nicholas, 38, 232, 233, 246, 553
Kavner, Richard, 126
Kay, Kathy, 163–165, 184, 192
Kefauver Committee. See Senate Special Com-
mittee to Investigate Organized Crime in
Interstate Commerce
Kefauver, Estes, 28, 80, 247
Kehoe, John, 481
Kelley, Clarence, 359
Kelly, Herbert, 143, 146
Kelly, Jack, 104, 161
Kenmore Hospital (Boston), 423
Kennedy, Caroline, 160, 187, 198
Kennedy, Edward, 438
Kennedy, Jacqueline, 39, 160, 198
Kenney, John F., passim
Kennedy, John F., Airport, 418, 485
Kennedy, Joseph, 88
Kennedy, Regis, 61
Kennedy, Robert F., passim
Kennedy, John, 459
Kent State University, 45
Kenyatta, Charles, 314
Kerner, Otto, 391
Key Biscayne Bank, 334

Keyes Realty Co. (Florida), 334
KGB (USSR), 365
Khrushchev, Nikita, 208–209, 217
Kilgallen, Dorothy, 52
Killam, Hank, 53
Killam, Wanda Joyce, 52
Kilpatrick, John, 33, 34
King, Martin Luther, Jr., 21, 38, 208, 245, 308, 309, 315–318, 390
King, Rufus, 139
Kirk, Travis, 183
Kirkwood, Pat, 295, 296, 298, 299
Kirkwood, W.C., 296
Kistle, Oscar, 226
Kleindienst, Richard, 337, 338
KLIF radio station (Dallas), 160, 162–164, 167–168, 193, 240, 532, 533–534
Knapp Commission, 451
Knight, Russ, 160, 533
Koethe, Jim, 51, 167
Kohn, Aaron, 79, 115, 125, 133, 392, 394, 421, 457
Kolod, Ruby, 347
Korshak, Marshall, 465
Korshak, Sidney, 128, 225, 241–243, 251, 263, 275, 283, 331, 465, 476–478, 590, 592
Kreig, Margaret, 388
Ku Klux Klan, 317
Kutner, Louis, 112
Ky, Nguyen Cao, 307

La Charda, Salvadore, 318
La Costa Country Club (California), 337, 338, 341, 350, 474
La Fitte, Pierre, 482
La Louisiane Restaurant (NewOrleans), 72–73
La Stella Restaurant (New York), 83, 391, 399
Laborers International Union, 27, 358, 435, 438–443, 446
Labriola, Paul, 110, 112
Labro, Phillippe, 159
Lacey, Frederick, 405, 448
LaMonte, Frank, 127
Landie, Sol, 401
Lansky, Jake, 122, 131, 132, 223
Lansky, Meyer, 131, 132, 150, 152, 212, 223, 334–335, 382, 404, 413, 423, 432, 469, 476
LaPlaca, Peter, 398
Lardino, Danny, 110
Lardner, George, Jr., 60
LaTempa, Peter, 192, 213
Laundry Workers Union, 461, 462
Lawford, Peter, 89, 241
Lawrence, Mary, 294
Laxalt, Paul, 308, 346–349, 359–360
Laxalt, Peter, 348
Leavell, Joan, 144
Ledeen, Michael, 366, 594
Lee, H.L. See Oswald, Lee Harvey
Lee, Tony, 401
Lemoine, Peter, 400
Lepera, Patsy, 121, 268, 405, 417, 429
Lewis, Ben, 466

Lewis, Clint, 142
Lewisberg (Pennsylvania) Federal Penitentiary, 321
Liberto, Frank, 318
Liberto, Liberto and Latch Produce Store (Memphis), 318
Liberto, Salvatore, 318
Liberty Broadcasting Network, 240
Libonati, Roland, 473, 474
Licavoli, James, 350
Licavoli, Peter, 401, 424, 461
Licavoli, Thomas, 470
Liddy, G. Gordon, 339
Liebler, Wesley, 237
Light, Martin, 428
Lightnin' magazine, 25
Lindsay, John, 466
Lippmann, Walter, 38
Lipsky, Marcus, 110, 112
Lipton, Lewis, 355
Liston, Sonny, 268
Litchfield, Wilbur Waldon, 572
Little Lynn, See Carlin, Karen
LoCicero, Richard, 402
Locurto, Joseph, 113, 119, 143, 381, 383
Loeb, William, 477
Loesch, Frank, 25, 435
Lomax, Louis, 315–316
Lombardo, Joseph, 412, 438
Lombardo, Peter, 31
Lombardozzi, Carmine, 398, 447
Lombardozzi, John, 463
Lonardo, Angelo, 399
Long, Earl, 393
Long, Huey, 125, 391
Long, Russell, 73, 125
Louisiana Civil Air Patrol, 66
Louisiana Loan and Thrift Co., 432
Louisiana State Hospital, 53
Loverde, Frank, 105, 106
Lowell, Abbott Lawrence, 230
Lucas B&B Restaurant, 294, 572
Lucchese, Thomas, 419, 459
Lucchese, Thomas, Mafia family, 419
Luciano, Charles (Lucky), 212, 213, 399
Luparelli, Joseph, 397, 403, 425, 458
Lurie, Alfred, 262
Lyle, John, 23, 25

McCann, William, 357
McCarthy, Joseph, 244, 356
McClellan Committee. *See* Senate Permanent Subcommittee onInvestigations or Senate Select Committee on Improper Activities in the Labor or Management Field
McClellan, John, 76, 102, 272, 402, 424, 480
McClory, Robert, 447
McCormack, Edward, 483
McCormack, John, 249, 475, 476
McCoy, Alfred, 307
McCurley, A.D., 42
McDade, Joseph, 310, 390, 391, 424
MacDonnell, Herbert, 323

Maceo, Sam, 131, 166
McGee, H.L., 182
McGovern's Bar (Chicago), 104, 105
McGrath Service, Inc., 444
McKeown, Robert, 222, 225, 549
McKinney, Stewart, 148, 238
McKissick, Floyd, 310, 390
McLendon, Gordon, 162, 240, 533
McNamara, Robert, 209, 305
McSwiggin, William, 410
McWillie, Lewis, 121, 128, 131–132, 136, 141, 149, 151, 223–225, 228, 241, 259, 260, 261–263, 268, 283, 296, 382, 383, 552, 554, 555, 567
Madame Francine's (Dallas), 566
Mafia, passim
Magaddino, Stefano, 78, 397, 406
Maggio, Peter, 428
Maheu, Robert, 216
Malatesta, Peter, 342
Malcolm X, 308, 310–315, 390, 412, 425, 451
Malone, Carlos, 137
Malone, William Scott, 219
Maloney, William, 442
Manchester Union Leader (New Hampshire), 477
Mancuso, Thomas, 421
Manno, Pat, 110
Manson, Charles, 324
Maranzano, Salvatore, 77, 410
Marcello, Carlos, 20, 60–65, 70–74, 79–91, 95, 121–125, 127, 133, 136, 150, 193, 211, 218, 242, 243, 247, 255, 257–262, 266, 267, 274, 281, 293, 300, 317–321, 331, 336, 340, 350, 359, 379, 383, 391, 392, 400, 559
Marcello, Carlos, Mafia family, 123, 444, 472
Marcello, Joseph, Jr., 73, 400
Marcello, Pete, 259, 260
Marcello, Sammy, 73
Marchesi, Vincent (Piggy Mack), 263
Marcinkus, Paul, 363, 364
Marcus, Greil, 331
Marcus, Jack, 119
Marcus, James, 466
Marcy, Pat, 461, 465, 473
Marie's Lounge (New Orleans), 317
Marino, Mario, 72
Marquette Building (Dallas), 69
Martens, Layton, 62
Martin, Dean, 241, 330
Martin, Jim, 51, 166
Martin, John, 102
Martinez, Eugenio, 334
Martinez, Paulino Sierra, 215, 218
Mason Tenders Union, 441
Massachusetts Crime Commission, 139
Massachusetts Institute of Technology, 361
Masselli, Nat, 353
Masselli, William, 353–355, 589
Mastriana, Louis, 413, 435
Matta, Giovanni, 471
Matthews, Elizabeth, 131, 264
Matthews, J. Neal, 247
Matthews, Michael, 464

Matthews, Russell D. 130–131, 136, 140, 225, 228, 241, 264, 268, 381
Matula, Frank, 129, 286
Maynard, Carl, 119
Mayor, Georgia, 298
Mazzei, Irwin, 107, 273–275, 283
Meagher, Sylvia, 199
Meany, George, 32
Medico Industries, 209, 428, 474
Medico, Phillip, 428
Medico, William, 209, 428
Medina, Ben, 442
Meese, Edwin, 350
Meli, Vincent, 482
Melli, Frank, 425
Meltzer, Harold (Happy), 68
Menditto, Alexander, 460
Menolia, Guy, Jr., 466
Merindaceli, Duke of, 407
Methvin, Eugene, 27
Meyers, Larry, 119, 294
Miami Heart Institute, 423
Michael's Dairies, Inc. (Philadelphia), 428
Michaels, Jimmy, 464
Miller, Arthur, 356
Miller, Austin, 40
Miller, Dave, 100, 382
Miller, Giles, 112
Miller, Isadore Max, 139, 382
Miller, Murray (Dusty), 132, 268, 283
Miller, William, 261, 282
Minutemen, 61, 71, 207, 208, 320
Miranda, Michael, 400
Mitchell, John, 479
Modica, Joe, 403, 468
Moldea, Dan, 126, 136, 328, 338, 348
Molinas, Jack, 422
Mollenhoff, Clark, 75, 336, 467, 476, 478
Montana, John, 406
Montgomery, L.D., 155
Mooney, Nancy Jane, 55
Moore, Bobby Gene, 127, 128
Moore, Edwin, 467
Moore, Elmer, 186–189, 290, 570
Moore, Richard, 337
Moran, Jim. See Brocato, James
Morelli, Frank (Butsey), 231
Morgenthau, Robert, 406
Morici, Henry, 566
Morris, Edward, Jr., 104
Morris, Joseph, 410
Moschiano, Anthony, 456
Motel Drug Service, 173, 293
Motto, Daniel, 466
Moynihan, Daniel Patrick, 320
Mullen, Francis, Jr. (Bud), 353
Mundt, Karl, 80, 272
Murchison, Clint, Jr., 244–245, 250
Murder, Incorporated, 18, 19, 90, 400, 403
Murphy, Thomas, 40
Murray Packing Co., 434
Murret, Charles (Dutz), 64, 65, 257
Murret, Lillian, 64

Muskie, Edmund, 339
Mussolini, Benito, 213, 214, 362-363, 409
Mynier, Elaine, 224

Nadjari, Maurice, 456
Namath, Joe, 421
Nani, Sebastiano, 332, 470
Naples, Joey, 484
National Academy of Sciences, 46, 47
National Advisory Commission on Civil Disorders, 391
National Association for Air Freight, 418
National Association of Food Chains, 388
Nautical Cafe, 404
Navasky, Victor, 76
Nazarian, Jackie, 403, 457
Nazi Party, 71
Nelson, Gary, 461
Nemerov, Bernard, 348
Nevada Gaming Commission, 357
New Mexico State RacingCommission, 332
New Orleans Metropolitan Crime Commission, 133, 261
New Orleans Saints, 421
New York City Transit Authority, 354
New York *Daily Mirror,* 480
New York Jets, 421
New York Joint Legislative Committee on Crime, 459
New York State Crime Commission, 445
New York State Joint Legislative Committee on Crime, 310, 390
New York Times, 480
Newberry, Ted, 23, 24
Newman, Morton William, 51
Newman, Paul, 160
Newman, William, 41
Nichols Garage (Dallas), 167, 175, 176, 177-178
Nichols, Roger, 431
Nicoletti, Charles, 452
Nitti, Frank, 24, 100, 399
Nixon, Richard M., 204, 207, 214, 234, 308, 333-347, 350-352, 357, 360, 361, 367, 472
Noguchi, Thomas, 322, 324
Noonan, Connie, 352
Notaro, Tony, 397
Nowlin, Duane, 69, 289
Noyes, Peter, 58, 60, 68

O'Brien, Carlton, 411
O'Brien, Gerald, 31
O'Brien, Thomas, 473
O'Donnell, Kenneth, 209, 233
O'Halloran, Dorothy, 431
O'Neill, Thomas P., Jr., (Tip), 233
O'Sullivan, Frederick, 266-267
Ochs, Martin, 110
Odierno, Salvatore, 354
Odio, Annie, 66
Odio, Sylvia, 65-66
Ogilvie, Richard, 442
Old French Opera House (NewOrleans), 260, 261, 263, 280, 281

Olsen, Harry, 163-165, 184, 299
Ormsby House (Carson City), 348
Osticco, James, 428
Oswald, Lee Harvey, 17, 37, 38, 49, 52, 53, 55-58, 63-67, 69, 73, 82, 126, 154, 155, 157, 158, 160, 171, 180, 181, 182, 183, 184, 216-217, 218, 232, 234, 237, 251, 255, 257, 266, 294, 295, 299, 300, 317, 571, 572
Oswald, Marguerite, 65, 572
Oswald, Marina, 63, 64, 65, 237
Oswald, Russell, 475
Oxford, J.L., 42

Painters and Decorators Union, 447
Palmer, Tom, 165, 173, 274, 278
Palmieri, Ernest, 389
Pandico, Giovanni, 365
Panitz, Meyer, 382
Panzarella, Edward, 459
Pappas, Ike, 163, 533
Paradise Island Casino (Bahamas), 335
Parilli, Babe, 421
Parisi, Joe, 433
Parker, Bonnie, 247
Parkland Hospital (Dallas), 37, 40, 157, 158, 162, 186, 236, 299
Parsons, Russell, 331
Partin, Edward, 73, 86, 87, 88, 534
Parvin, Albert, 476-477
Parvin, Albert, Foundation, 476
Parvin-Dohrman Corporation, 476-477
Pasley, Max, 481
Patman, Wright, 431, 586
Patriarca, Raymond, 359, 396, 398, 400, 403, 412, 415, 421, 434, 441, 450, 454, 457, 468, 469, 475
Patriarca, Raymond, Mafia Family, 399, 420
Patrick, Lenny, 102, 107, 128, 132-133, 135, 136, 151, 185, 267-268, 466
Patrono, Johnny Ross, 382
Patrusky, Martin, 324
Patton, George, 214
Paul VI, Pope, 363
Paul, Ralph, 114, 168, 177, 294, 570
Pazienza, Francesco, 365-367, 594
Pecora, Nofio, 64, 133, 151, 262, 268, 273, 381
Pellicano, Anthony, 46
Pelligrino, Peter, 127
Pelou, François, 159
Penn, Stanley, 447
Pentagon Papers, 306
Pepper, Claude, 345, 416, 431, 464
Peppino, Don, 150
Pepsi-Cola Co., 307
Percy, Charles, 402, 425-426, 432
Percy, Valerie, 426
Perrin, Robert, 226
Perrone, Gaspar, 30
Perrone, Santo, 30, 31, 415
Persico, Carmine, 395-396, 421, 436, 458
Peterson, Henry, 445
Peterson, Virgil, 481

Petrosino, Joseph, 410
Pettit, Tom, 182–183
Piersante, Vince, 415, 453
Pietra, Angelo, 412
Pike, Roy. *See* Ryan, Mickey
Pilotto, Al, 441
Pipefitters Union, 443
Pisciotta, Gaspare, 192
Pitts, Elnora, 181, 184
Pittsburgh Sun-Telegraph, 480
Plopi, Walter, 463
Poff, Richard, 424
Polito, Joseph, 434
Polizzi, Al, 334
Polley, Stanley, 432, 455, 475
Pollock, Seymour, 430
Polverino, Joseph, 341
Pope, Ralph, 33
Posner, Herman, 446
Powell, Adam Clayton, 454, 476
Powell, Nancy, 146, 173, 175–177, 284, 296
Powell, Paul, 469
Powell, Robert, 441
Powers, Dave, 233
President's Commission on theAssassination of
    President John F.Kennedy. *See* Warren
    Commission
President's Commission on Organized Crime, 27,
    345, 350, 359–360, 393, 435, 437–438
President's Task Force on Organized Crime
    (Commission on LawEnforcement and
    Administration of Justice), 393, 450
Presser, Jackie, 341, 350–351, 360, 437, 438
Presser, William, 350, 351
Price, J.C., 42
Prio, Ross, 484
Progressive Drug. Co., 430
Propaganda Due (P2) lodge, 362–368, 592
Provenzano, Tony, 126, 338, 341, 350, 437, 438,
    584
Provincial Motel (New Orleans), 317, 318
Psychological Stress Evaluator, 196
Puzzangara, Joe, 403

Quinn, Paul, 452
Psychological Stress Evaluator, 196
Racketeer Influenced and Corrupt Organizations
    (RICO) Act, 358, 359, 360, 379, 387, 395, 437,
    438
Raft, George, 413
Ragen, James, 136, 185
Ramistella, Henry. *See*Donneroummas, Frank
Ramos Ducos, Leopoldo, 126, 191
Rankin, J. Lee, 196, 234
Rare Earth (singing group), 421
Rastelli, Philip, 436, 462
Ratteni, Nick, 433
Ratterman, George, 449
Ray, James Earl, 316–318
Raymond, Michael, 50, 398, 400, 416, 430, 432,
    448, 455, 475
Ray's Hardware Store (Dallas), 132
Reagan, Ronald, 204, 308, 345, 346, 348–352,

355–360, 364, 366–368, 595
Rebozo, Bebe, 334–335, 340
Rector, Milton, 424
Redlich, Norman, 237
Red-O-Lier, 475
Reece, Gloria, 292
Reeves, Huey, 175–178
Reid, Ed, 81, 83, 242, 243
Reles, Abe, 192
Renda, Carl, 30
Rennell, Lord, 214
Reprise Record Co., 261
Republican Party, 85, 345
Requena, Andres, 305
Resorts International, 334, 591
Reuther, Victor, 29, 31, 34
Reuther, Walter, 23, 27–34
Revill, Jack, 181, 539
Rex Carting Co. (New York), 433
Reynolds, Warren, 54–56
Richey, Warren, 180, 538
Ricca, Paul. *See* DeLucia, Paul
Ricchiuti, William, 403, 417, 426
Rice Hotel (Dallas), 291
Rich, Nancy Perrin, 138, 142, 144, 146, 225–227
Riesel, Victor, 27, 403, 443
Rinaldi, Dominic, 459
Ritchie, Donald Joseph, 31, 32
Riverside Hotel (Reno), 131, 261
Riviera Hotel (Las Vegas), 128, 478
Rizzo, Vincent, 417, 484–485
Roberts, Dennis, 389
Roberts, Donald, 180
Robertson, Vic, Jr., 158, 160
Rockefeller, Nelson, 210
Rockman, Milton, 412
Rogers, Warren, 91
Rogovin, Charles, 414
Rollins, Ed, 350
Roofers Union, 443
Rooney, John, 475–476
Roosevelt, Franklin Delano, 24
Roosevelt, James, 476
Roosevelt Raceway (New York), 420
Roppolo, Carl, 81, 83
Roschek, Urban, 106
Roselli, Johnny, 58, 89, 133–134, 136, 156, 216,
    225, 264, 266, 300, 330
Rosenthal, Frank, 347, 412
Ross, Barney, 99, 262, 275, 286, 300
Ross Trucking Co., 432
Rothermal, Paul, 69, 289
Rothman, Norman, 131, 211–212, 223
Roulette Records, 422
Rourke, Alexander, 215
Rowley, James, 43
Royal Coach Inn (Houston), 124
Rozelle, Pete, 421
RSO Records, 422
Rubenstein, Fanny, 99
Rubenstein, Harry, 105, 280

Rubenstein, Hyman, 101, 103, 104, 117, 267
Rubenstein, Jack. *See* Ruby, Jack
Rubenstein, Joseph, 99
Ruby, Jack, *passim*
Ruddy, Al, 479
Rushing, Ray, 181, 539
Russell, Dick (*Village Voice*), 340
Russell, Richard, 234
Russo, Anthony, 483
Russo, Joseph (Fatty), 403, 458
Rutledge, John, 158
Ryan, Dennis, 441–442
Ryan, Mickey, 107, 146, 290, 528

S.G.S. Associates, 447
Sacco, Nicola, 230, 231
Sacramento Bee, 348
Saia, Frank (Tickie), 124
Saia, Sam, 65
Salas, Luis, 248
Salerno, Anthony, 395, 436
Salerno, Ralph, 23, 96–98, 244, 310, 390, 425, 447
Salvatore, Rocco, 452
Samish, Adrian, 469
Sands Hotel (Las Vegas), 72
Santa Anita Race Track (Los Angeles), 100, 134, 321
Santaniello, Leo, 469
Saperstein, Louis, 341
Saporito, Michael, 462
Saporito, Robert, 462
Sartor, William, 317, 318
Saxbe, William, 484
SCA Services, Inc., 389
Scalise, Joseph, 439
Scarborough Downs (Massachusetts), 421
Scarfo, Nicodemo, 464
Scarne, John, 212
Scarpa, Gregory, 402
Schaeffer, James, 398, 417, 426
Schenck, Nicholas, 446
Schiavone Construction Co., 352–355, 589
Schiavone, Ronald, 353, 354
Schlesinger, Arthur, Jr., 38, 245
Schulberg, Budd, 472, 479–480
Schulman, Donald, 326
Schulman, Solly, 101
Schwartz, Louis, 458
Schweiker, Richard, 230
Scialo, Dominick, 460
Scopo, Ralph, 435, 440
Scott Byron Motel, 84
Scott, Peter Dale, 85
Scotto, Anthony, 444, 472, 600
Scranton, Paul, 85
Scrap Iron and Junk Handlers Union, 101, 103
Screen Actors Guild, 356
Secret Service, 43, 295, 296
Securities and Exchange Commission, 362, 475, 476, 591
Securities Validation Corporation, 415
Security National Bank, 586

Seidband, Sidney, 115
Senate Appropriations Committee, 348
Senate Government OperationsCommittee, 415–416
Senate Intelligence Committee. *See* Senate Select Committee to Study Government Operations withRespect to Intelligence Activities
Senate Labor Committee, 353
Senate Permanent Subcommittee on Investiga-tions, 214, 272, 342, 343, 402
Senate Rackets Committee. *See* Senate Perma-nent Subcommittee on Investigations
Senate Select Committee on Improper Activities in the Labor orManagement Field (McClellan Committee), 26, 76, 77, 78, 109, 112, 393, 442, 479, 492
Senate Select Committee to Study Government Operations withRespect to Intelligence Activities (Senate Intelligence Committee), 37, 58, 216, 232, 233, 243, 266
Senate Special Committee toInvestigate Orga-nized Crime in Interstate Commerce (Kefauver Committee), 28, 29, 30, 101, 109, 112, 125, 137, 140, 247, 393, 401–402, 411, 427, 469
Senator, George, 51, 123, 165, 166, 179, 184, 191, 384, 538, 570, 598
Serpico, John, 443
Serritella, Vince, 453
Severeign, Joe, 532
Sharpe, Alton, 274, 283
Shaw, Clay, 70, 71
Shaw, Robert, 237
Sheeran, Frank, 437
Shenker, Morris, 347, 463
Shepard, Charles, 458
Sheraton Lincoln Hotel (Houston), 150
Sheridan, Walter, 70, 319, 336
Sherman Hotel, 100
Shippers, David, 463
Sho-Bar (New Orleans), 259, 260, 280, 281, 566
Shore Club (Chicago), 453
Shore, Michael, 189, 261–263
Shorman, Robert Lee, 104, 142
Shoulders, Lou, 438
Sica, Joe, 68
Siciliano, Vincent, 441
Siefert, David, 135
Siegel, Bugsy, 122, 152, 347
Silver Spur Club (Dallas), 113, 149, 383
Silverman, Leon, 354, 355, 589
Simmons, James, 40, 42
Simon's Garage, 163, 184
Simpson, Johnny, 163, 164
Sinatra, Frank, 89, 131, 241, 330, 333, 342, 357
Sindona, Michele, 361–363, 367, 592, 594
Singleton, Penny, 273, 274
Singleton, Ray, 143
Siragusa, Charles, 136
Sirhan, Sirhan, 49, 319, 321–327, 329–331
Sirica, John, 45, 398
"Sixty Minutes" (CBS), 349, 355
Slater and Morill Shoe Co., 231
Slatin, Joe, 113

Smaldone, Clyde, 68
Smaldone, Eugene, 68
Small Business Administration, 124, 133, 393
Smith, C. Arnholt, 335
Smith, D'Alton, 336, 534
Smith, Hugh, 143
Smith, Joe, 40, 43
Smith, John, 180, 538
Smith, L.C., 42
Smith, Mrs. Earl, 52
Smith, William French, 348, 349, 364
Smitherman, William, 481
Società Generale Immobiliare, 362
Solomon, E.R., 517
Sol's Bar and Restaurant (Dallas), 517
Sol's Turf Bar (Dallas), 517
Sorrentino, Pasqual, 461
Southland Hotel (Dallas), 131, 165, 166, 535
Sovereign Club (Dallas), 113, 142, 143, 146
Spadolini, Giovanni, 409
Spatola, Rosario, Mafia family, 592
Spinelli, Salvatore, 481
Standifer, Roy, 158
Stardust Hotel (Las Vegas), 411, 477
Staten Island Advance, 479
Stavola, Michael, 483
Stein, Charles, 317, 318
Stella, Pasquale, 382
Sterling, Claire, 365, 366
Stevenson, Adlai, 473
Stone, Greg, 595
Stone, Walter, 411, 429, 441
Streisand, Barbra, 263
Strell, Bayard, 467
Sturgis, Frank, 212, 215
Sullivan, Jack, 248
Sullivan, William, 232, 243, 245–246
Surprise, Joey, 433
Surrey, Robert, 210
Swanton, John, 410
Sweig, Martin, 475, 476
Szulc, Tad, 305

Tabet, Louis. See La Fitte, Pierre
Tacitus, 230, 251
Taglianetti airtels, 396, 405, 468, 469
Taglianetti, Louis, 396, 405
Tameleo, Henry, 400, 403–404, 415, 420, 426, 434, 450, 468
Tamello, Henry. See Tameleo, Henry
Tammi True. See Powell, Nancy
Tanglewood Apartments (Dallas), 287, 288
Tannenbaum, Harold, 280–281
Tanner, Hans, 215
Taylor, Maxwell, 209
Teamsters Union. See International Brotherhood of Teamsters
Telvi, Abraham, 27, 403
Teresa, Vincent, 90–91, 231, 270, 398, 400, 403, 412, 413, 415, 418, 423, 426, 427, 434, 450, 454
Terminal Annex Building (Dallas), 43
Termine, Sam, 65

Terranova, Cesare, 408
Texas Adams Oil Co., 130
Texas Bar Association, 183
Texas School Book DepositoryBuilding (Dallas), 37, 39, 43, 44, 45, 235, 297, 298
The Enemy Within, 26, 480
Thomas, Cary, 312
Thompson, Dolores, 220
Thompson, Josiah, 43, 44
Thompson, Mary, 220
Three Dog Night (singing group), 421–422
Thunderbird Hotel (Las Vegas), 131, 132, 259–263, 382
Tice, Wilma, 158
Timphony, Frank, 71
Tippit, J.D., 37, 54–56, 237, 299, 300
Tisci, Anthony, 474
Tolson, Clyde, 245
Tonahill, Joe, 160, 187
Toohill, James, 354
Top of the Hill Club (Dallas), 131, 552
Torch Club (Chicago), 104
Torrio, Johnny, 150
Tortoriello, Frank, 287–288, 568
Touhy, Roger, 23, 25, 435
Tourine, Charlie, 413
Towler, Martin, 291
Town and Country Motel (New Orleans), 62, 318
Toy and Novelty Workers Union, 447
Trafficante, Santos, Jr., 75, 83–86, 88–91, 95, 121, 131, 134–136, 211, 216, 223–225, 228, 255, 258, 264, 266, 267, 273, 283, 300, 307, 319, 321, 359, 381, 400
Trafficante, Santos, Sr., 398
Trammel, Connie, 288, 290, 532
Tramunti, Carmine, 421
Transit-Mix Concrete Corporation, 440
Tresca, Carlos, 213
Trescornia detention camp, 224
Tropical Tourist Court, 261, 262, 268
Tropicana Hotel (Cuba), 119, 131, 223, 241
Trujillo, Rafael, 305
Trupiano, Matthew, 441
Trupiano, Mike, 439
Turner, Smokey, 532
Turner, William, 320
Turnman, Reagan, 141
Twentieth Century Industries, 430

U.S. National Bank, 328, 335, 586
Uecker, Karl, 323
Ullo, Joe, 421, 422
Union Gastronomica, 125
United Auto Workers union, 27–34
United Farm Workers union, 320
United Textile Workers union, 447
University of Chicago, 361

Valachi, Joseph, 77, 90, 149, 217, 240, 395–398, 401, 406, 447
Vanzetti, Bartolomeo, 231
Vario, Leonard, 405
Vario, Paul, 405, 459

Vastola, Gaetano, 439, 483
Vatican, 360, 363–365
Vegas Club (Dallas), 113, 127, 178, 198, 276, 382, 384
Vertigo Key Club (Chicago), 106
Veterans Administration, 424
Veteran's Cabin, 286
Vic Construction Co., 405
Vietnam War, 17, 84, 203, 209, 217, 305–307, 333
Viorst, Milton, 112
Visconti, Robert, 412
Vizzini, Cologero, 214
Vogue Credit Jewelers, 434
Voloshen, Nathan, 250, 432, 475, 476
Volpe, Angelo, 452

Wade, Henry, 145, 158, 159
Waggenheim, Phil, 414
Wald, Jerry, 479
Waldo, Thayer, 159
Walker, Edwin, 190, 210
Walker, Ira, 179
Wall, Breck, 141, 278
Wall, Charles, 398
Walsh, Denny, 348
Walthers, Buddy, 142
Ward, Baxter, 324
Warehousemen's Union, 439
Warner, Roger, 171, 172
Warren Commission, 19, 20, 38, 39, 40, 49, 52, 55, 65, 66, 70, 99, 100, 102–103, 106, 107, 111, 116, 117, 128, 129, 144, 145, 148, 166, 192–197, 203, 215, 225, 230–240, 243, 246, 251, 255, 320, 383, 538, 554
Warren, Earl, 38, 164, 165, 166, 186–197, 228, 234, 300, 331
Wasserman, Jack, 62
Watergate, 17, 45, 203, 212, 235, 334, 337, 339
Wavetronics, 475
Webb, Del, 244
Webster, William, 349, 359
Weinberg, James, 110
Weiner, Irwin, 134–136, 151, 189, 261, 267, 273, 279, 282–283, 347, 381
Weinstein, Abe, 276
Weinstein, Barney, 276
Weisberg, Willie, 78
Weiss, George, 457
Weiss, Mark, 45–47, 54
Weiss, Victor, 53
Weitzman, Seymour, 42
Wertheimer, Mert, 122
Wessel, Milton, 600

Westchester Carting Co. (New York), 433
Western Union office (Dallas), 155, 182, 299
Westgate-California conglomerate, 335
Whaley, William, 57
White. George. See Raymond, Michael
White Russians, 71
Wiener, Louie, 482
Williams, Bill, 291
Williams, Edward Bennett, 216, 245, 250, 314
Williams, Elmer, 25
Williams, Paul, 403
Williams, Robert, 457
Williams, Roy L., 351, 435–436
Willis, Phillip, 48
Wilner, Jack, 111–112
Wilson, John, Jr., 144
Wilson, O.W., 404
Wilson, William, 364
Winborn, Walter, 40
Winter, Howie, 404
Winter-Berger, Robert, 249–250, 432, 475, 476
Wolfer, DeWayne, 322, 330, 581
Wood, Leonard, 178
Woodard, James, 220
Woodward, Mary Elizabeth, 41
"World News Tonight" (ABC), 349
Wuenche, Edward, 417, 430
Wyman, Sidney, 347

Yablonsky, Joseph, 349
Yackovelli, Joseph, 397, 403, 458
Yallop, David, 364, 365
Yanover, Jack, 274, 382
Yaras, Dave, 128, 135–137, 185, 401
Yarborough, Ralph, 40
Young, Whitney, 310, 390
Youngblood, Rufus, 298
Younger, Evelle, 324, 331

Zagri, Sid, 248
Zangara, Giuseppe, 24, 25–26, 329, 330
Zapas, Gus, 263, 562
Zapruder, Abraham, 48
Zelmanowitz, Gerald, 257, 342–343, 406, 422, 459
Zerelli, Joseph, 125
Zerelli, Joseph, Mafia family, 125
Zerilla, Anthony, 397
Zicarelli, Joseph, 305, 421, 471
Ziegler, Dennis, 442
Zito, Joseph, 483
Zoppi, Tony, 240, 241, 251, 283, 296–297, 555
Zuckerman, Nate, 105
Zuta, Jack, 142

624